♻ Na

PLAYFAIR
CRICKET ANNUAL
1997
50th edition

EDITED BY BILL FRINDALL

All statistics by the Editor unless otherwise credited

Playfair Competition	2
Sponsor's Message	5
Editorial Preface	6
Playfair's Origins by Peter West	8
The 1997 Season	
England v Australia – Register and Records	9
County Register, Records and 1996 Championship Averages	15
University Cricket	108
Umpires – TCCB First-Class and ICC International Panels	114
The 1996 Season	
Statistical Highlights	117
Young Cricketers of the Year	122
First-Class Averages 1996	123
Britannic Assurance County Championship	139
NatWest Trophy	141
Benson and Hedges Cup	147
Sunday League	150
County Caps Awarded	152
Minor Counties Championship and Averages	152
Second XI Championship	156
Current Career Records	
First-Class Cricket	157
Leading Current Players	175
Test Matches	176
Limited-Overs Internationals	185
Cricket Records	
First-Class Cricket	196
Limited-Overs Internationals	205
Test Matches	212
Test Match Scores and Averages	222
Fixtures	
Second XI Fixtures	271
Minor Counties Fixtures	275
Principal Fixtures	278
ICC Tours Programme and Women's Cricket	286
Fielding Chart	287

PLAYFAIR CRICKET COMPETITION 1997

TEST CRICKET QUIZ

£1500 TO BE WON

PLUS NATWEST FINAL TICKETS AND HOSPITALITY
PLUS 25 CONSOLATION PRIZES

First Prize   £500 + overnight accommodation (B and B) at the Regents Park Hilton Hotel (opposite Lord's) on 5 and 6 September + TWO tickets to the 1997 NatWest Trophy Final + NatWest hospitality

Second Prize £400 + TWO tickets to the 1997 NatWest Trophy Final

Third Prize   £300 + TWO tickets to the 1997 NatWest Trophy Final

Fourth Prize £200

Fifth Prize   £100

Consolation prizes

Senders of the next 25 correct entries will each receive a copy of

A LOT OF HARD YAKKA
Triumph and torment: a county cricketer's life

by Simon Hughes, published by Headline at £16.99

'You won't read a better inside story of cricket and the men who play it for a living. Vigorous, funny and full of insight from a gifted observer. It was a book waiting to be written and Simon Hughes has done it.' – **Michael Parkinson.**

Closing date for entries
12.00 noon on 22 July 1997

Winning entries will be drawn by the Man of the Match Adjudicator
at one of the NatWest semi-finals on 12/13 August.

PLAYFAIR CRICKET COMPETITION 1997
CRICKET QUIZ
ENTRY FORM

Please PRINT your answers in the spaces provided and answer every question.

The answers to all ten questions can be found within this Annual

1 After whom is this Annual named? ....
2 Who is the only English batsman to score 2000 Test match runs in Australia? ....
3 In which city could you watch international cricket at the R. Premadasa Stadium? ....
4 Who has been elevated to the first-class list of umpires this season? ....
5 Which currently registered county cricketer was born in Yokohama? ....
6 Who was the last bowler to take a hat-trick in an Ashes Test match? ....
7 Which country is sending an 'A' touring team to England this season? ....
8 Who is alone in scoring a century and taking four wickets with successive balls in a first-class match? ....
9 Which bowler returned an analysis for six for 18 in a Lord's final? ....
10 Who, in 1973, became the first holders of the Lord's Taverners' Trophy? ....

Your name and address:

....

....

....

Your daytime telephone number: ....

Post to: PLAYFAIR CRICKET COMPETITION, Special Events, The Gibson Hall, Bishopsgate, London EC2M 4BQ.

Entries must be received before noon on 22 July 1997. All-correct entries will go into the prize-winning draw on 12 August and an announcement detailing all prize-winners will appear in the October edition of *The Cricketer* magazine. A list of winners is available on request by writing to Barry Franks at the above address and enclosing a stamped addressed envelope.

Rules: All entries must be on this official form. Proof of posting is not proof of entry. The decision of the editor regarding the answers to this quiz shall be final and binding; no correspondence may be entered into.

1996 PLAYFAIR CRICKET COMPETITION

CRICKET QUIZ ANSWERS

1 Which team was first admitted to the County Championship in 1905? **NORTHAMPTONSHIRE**

2 On which ground did Andrew Symonds break the world six-hitting records? **ABERGAVENNY**

3 Which bowler last season achieved a hat-trick in which all three victims were lbw? **M.C. (Mark) ILOTT**

4 Who is the only batsman to score 400 in a first-class innings on more than one occasion? **W.H. (Bill) PONSFORD**

5 In which town could you have watched a Test match at the Arbab Niaz Stadium in 1995? **PESHAWAR**

6 Who is the only batsman to score 8000 runs in Limited-Overs Internationals? **D.L. (Desmond) HAYNES**

7 Which team will stage a home first-class match at Boghall Cricket Club this season? **SCOTLAND**

8 Who was the last bowler to take 100 first-class wickets in a season? **Anil KUMBLE**

9 Who was the last bowler to take 200 first-class wickets in a season? **G.A.R. (Tony) LOCK**

10 Which substitute fielder achieved two stumpings during a first-class match last season? **M.J. (Malcolm) BIRKS**

There were 975 sets of correct answers from a record total of 1382 entries. The winners were drawn by John Lever MBE (Essex and England) at the 1996 semi-final between Lancashire and Yorkshire at Old Trafford on 13 August.

First Prize:	£500 + two nights' accommodation + two tickets to include hospitality at the 1996 NatWest Trophy Final	R.A. PARRISH (Slough)
Second Prize:	£400 + two tickets to the 1996 NatWest Trophy Final	M. KIDD (Bromsgrove)
Third Prize:	£300 + two tickets to the 1996 NatWest Trophy Final	C.J.S. GALE (Hull)
Fourth Prize:	£200	A.J. BLAKE (Birmingham)
Fifth Prize:	£100	T.J.W. SAUNDERS (Manchester)

25 Runners-up: each winning a signed copy of *ONE-MAN COMMITTEE* by Ray Illingworth and Jack Bannister:

N.Adey	(Derby)	H.B.Friedlaender	(Enfield)
P.Astbury	(Macclesfield)	N.Gee	(Bletchley)
S.Barnes	(Oldham)	I.Gold	(West Ealing)
D.Batters	(York)	L.E.Hanks	(Poole)
S.R.R.Bourne	(Sevenoaks)	D.Harris	(Poplar)
S.Brodkin	(Edgware)	E.L.Hopkinson	(King's Lynn)
G.E.Carter	(Brighton)	S.Miller	(Edinburgh)
R.G.Davies	(Tredegar)	G.Paterson	(Sevenoaks)
A.Debenham	(Purley)	B.W.Ragg	(Rotherham)
M.Debenham	(Purley)	L.Rathbone	(Cardiff)
G.Farrington	(Reading)	G.Springett	(Wimbledon)
P.Fearn	(Coventry)	D.Thompson	(Bolton)
B.Forbes	(Hitchin)		

SPONSOR'S MESSAGE FROM

♻ NatWest

This year NatWest enters into its seventeenth year of sponsorship of the NatWest Trophy competition. Since the sponsorship started in 1981 NatWest has become more and more committed to the game.

In 1996 we added to our sponsorship the NatWest Development of Excellence Programme under the expert eye of Micky Stewart. We are delighted with its progress and must offer our congratulations to the NatWest England Under-19 team for winning their winter series in Pakistan. We firmly believe that by investing in NatWest Development of Excellence, which culminates in the NatWest England Under-19 team, we are securing a brighter future for English cricket.

Our support for cricket extends beyond the outfield and we are pleased to continue our sponsorship of the *NatWest Playfair Cricket Annual*, which is held by many as the cricketers' 'bible'.

In addition to the *NatWest Playfair Cricket Annual*, NatWest announced at the time of the 1996 Final that we had entered into a new partnership with the MCC to build a new Media Centre at Lord's between the Compton and Edrich Stands. The NatWest Media Centre will be completed in 1998 in readiness for the 1999 World Cup.

The year 1997 is one of celebration. Firstly, we congratulate the arrival of the ECB, *NatWest Playfair* on its 50th anniversary and *Test Match Special* on its 40th anniversary. Perhaps there will be a page in the 1998 Annual featuring statistics relating to celebrations; let us hope that the Ashes will be regained, thus giving us another cause for congratulations.

EDITORIAL PREFACE

Fiftieth birthdays are rather special and it is an honour to be at the helm as *Playfair* celebrates its golden jubilee. Few cricket publications have survived to reach this mark. Apart from John Wisden's famous Almanack, now well past its hundred, and Sir Pelham Warner's magazine, now in its 77th year, only a few county and overseas annuals have reached that elusive half century.

Thoughts inevitably turn to *Playfair*'s founding editor, Peter West, and to Roy Webber, his industrious statistician. When they conceived this publication during the post-war austerity of 1947, did either of them have the slightest inkling that their brainchild would become the world's biggest-selling annual cricket publication? I was delighted that Peter accepted an invitation to pen some notes on the Annual's conception, including the fascinating story behind its title. Peter's comings and goings are heavily associated with Ashes series. Although *Playfair*'s launch coincided with the arrival of Bradman's invincible 1948 side, the final edition under his editorship heralded the retrieval of the urn in 1953, while his last overseas tour was as the *Daily Telegraph*'s correspondent on Mike Gatting's victorious 1986-87 expedition. Hopefully his contribution in another Ashes year will complete an unusual hat-trick of England wins.

For 32 of its issues the Annual was under the editorship of Gordon Ross, who, in association with Roy Webber, also produced that boon for collectors of overseas statistics, *Playfair Cricket Monthly*. It was Webber's sudden death in 1962 that led to a change of publishers (from Playfair Books to Dickens Press) and the Annual's reduction in format from its original near-octavo size to the 'pocket' dimensions which Frank Thorogood's *Daily News* annuals had popularised in the Twenties and Thirties. Gordon was closely associated with the introduction of limited-overs county cricket in the form of the Gillette Cup and it was he who conceived 'Man of the Match' awards. In 1975 he persuaded Gillette Industries to become the Annual's first sponsors and no doubt influenced NatWest's succession when they took over the 60-over knockout competition in 1981.

It is indeed a bonus that publication of both the inaugural issue and this fiftieth edition should coincide with an Australian summer. No Test series creates the special aura of one between England and the 'Old Enemy'. Despite their much-improved performances during this winter, Michael Atherton's team will have to play consistently and at their very peak if they are to have any chance of terminating our visitors' 14-year tenure of The Ashes. Australia's annihilation of South Africa, despite employing just three specialist bowlers on a flat pitch at The Wanderers, graphically illustrates the magnitude of England's task. Let's hope for fine weather and some high-quality and closely contested cricket. For the first time our cover features two players: Graham Thorpe and Shane Warne. Their duels this summer are eagerly awaited. No doubt English devotees of the *Playfair* hex will hope that it affects only the left-hand half of our montage, as opposed to the left-handed half.

By another intriguing coincidence, the current *Who's Who* includes a notable 'Playfair', Sir Edward of that ilk, who is a former director of our sponsors. This is the sixteenth edition under their patronage and the second to include the name of NatWest in its title. May the association endure throughout our second half-century. A special word of thanks to Barbara Quinn, now Brand Communication Manager, and to NatWest's Special Events team for administering our competition, a task which through their own fault involved twice the normal workload. Last year they asked me to boost the number of entrants by restricting the questions to material in the Annual itself. The success of this ploy can be measured by the number of entries more than doubling from 631 in 1995 to a record 1382. One letter from an irate reader in Crookhill, County Durham, complained that the quiz 'was far, far too easy'. Although his criticism was fair, it would have borne more weight had his entry not contained two incorrect answers. I have tried to make this year's quiz a tad harder but ALL the answers can again be found within these pages.

Your correspondence is vital in helping us to include data that interests you and to bring the book in line with the ever-changing face of domestic and international cricket. A suggestion that we should indicate the indentity of each county's overseas player, not readily apparent if several members of the same staff have their origins abroad, has been implemented, as have one or two other ideas. Not so the request from a colonel in Sutton for the county register to include the identity of each player's legal representative and each county's tally of sponsored cars!

Thanks are again due to our publishers, Headline, who are themselves celebrating a birthday, their tenth, and in particular to Ian Marshall, their sports publisher, who has diligently overseen the last eight editions. A special word too for Chris Leggett and his typesetting team at Letterpart for again coping with delayed deadlines so that we could update the Test and Limited-Overs career records, as well as the County Register, to include England's performances in New Zealand.

Once again, I have been generously assisted by many kind providers of information, particularly by the county clubs' administrations, scorers and statisticians; by Kate Jenkins and Tony Brown at the ECB; by Clive Hitchcock of the ICC; and by David Armstrong of the MCCA. Philip Bailey has again meticulously compiled the first-class career records and solved many riddles. Special thanks are due to my wife, Debbie, for proof-checking and for her unenviable task of keying-in the scorecards of this winter's limited-overs internationals (75 to date, an absurd number), and to my computer guru, Peter Thirlby, for miraculously reviving his brainchild when it crashed yesterday on the threshold of compiling the career records.

BILL FRINDALL
Urchfont
18 March 1997

PLAYFAIR'S ORIGINS

The *Playfair Cricket Annual*, with the England and seventeen county crests adorning its cover in full colour, made its bow in 1948 at about the time when Don Bradman on his last tour was reaching three figures against Worcestershire: a modest effort compared with the three double hundreds he had made against them in the corresponding fixture before the Second World War. He told me years later that he was carrying a niggling injury at the time and thus was anxious not to overtax himself.

Why Playfair? When ideas for a title were being tossed around I recalled the name of Sir Nigel Playfair, actor/manager between the wars. In due course, it received the endorsement of C.B.Fry, who declared in his foreword to the first issue that it was a very proper title for a book about the noble game.

I had first met him in the press box at Taunton, and felt I was sitting at God's right hand. Over 30,000 runs for Sussex, Hampshire, Oxford and England, football for Corinthians, Southampton and England, world long jump record holder, a rugby Blue missed only because of injury. Outshining, at Wadham College, Oxford, two men later to sit in the British Cabinet. Reputedly offered the throne of Albania. Can there have been a greater all-rounder, academic and sporting, in the twentieth century?

It was a pleasure in the first issue, which cost three shillings and sixpence, to range over that blissful summer of 1947 when Denis Compton and Bill Edrich averaged 90 and 80 respectively, scoring thirty hundreds and 7,355 runs between them. Less so to recall that the M.C.C. touring side in the West Indies, admittedly without such luminaries as the two Middlesex heroes as well as Len Hutton and Alec Bedser, returned home without a single win to its name. Three batsmen whose names began with a 'W' had arrived in the Caribbean but, not quite yet, messrs. Ramadhin and Valentine.

Facts and figures in the introductory Playfair were provided by Roy Webber, then secretary of the Cricket Book Society, who before very long was to be appointed scorer for B.B.C. television. He was to become in his time almost as well known to a wider cricketing audience as the present editor is today.

Playfair's print and presentation may have been less pragmatic in its early days but its modern counterpart, with its worldwide coverage, packs a quite remarkable punch for its poundage and is a yet more essential *vade mecum* for the game's disciples. Going into a second half century it could not be in better hands.

PETER WEST

AUSTRALIA REGISTER

Australia's touring team had not been selected at the time of going to press. Career statistics are up to the start of their tour of South Africa (13 February). See page 15 for key to abbreviations, and pages 176-84 and 185-94 for full Test Match and Limited-Overs International records respectively.

BEVAN, Michael Gwyl – *see YORKSHIRE*.

BICHEL, Andrew John, b Laidley 27 Aug 1970. RHB, RFM. Queensland 1992-93 to date. **Tests**: 2 (1996-97); HS 18 v WI (Perth) 1996-97; BB 1-31. **LOI**: 4 (1996-97); HS 16*; BB 3-17. **F-c**: HS 61*; BB 6-79.

BLEWETT, Gregory Scott, b North Adelaide 29 Oct 1971. Son of R.K. (S Australia 1975-76 to 1978-79). RHB, RMF. S Australia 1991-92 to date. **Tests**: 13 (1994-95 to 1996-97); HS 115 v E (Perth) 1994-95; BB 2-25 v P (Hobart) 1995-96. Scored 102* v E (Adelaide) on debut. **LOI**: 16 (1994-95 to 1996-97; HS 57*; BB 2-34). **F-c**: HS 268; BB 4-39.

ELLIOTT, Matthew Thomas Gray, b Chelsea 28 Sep 1971. LHB, LM. Victoria 1992-93 to date. **Tests**: 2 (1996-97); HS 78* v WI (Sydney) 1996-97. **F-c**: HS 203; BB 1-23.

GILCHRIST, Adam Craig, b Bellingen, NSW 14 Nov 1971. LHB, WK. NSW 1992-93 to 1993-94. WA 1994-95 to date. **LOI**: 2 (1996-97; HS 18). **F-c**: HS 189*.

GILLESPIE, Jason Neil, b Darlinghurst, NSW 19 Apr 1975. RHB, RFM. S Australia 1994-95 to date. **Tests**: 2 (1996-97); HS 16* and BB 2-62 v WI (Sydney) 1996-97. **LOI**: 5 (1996-97; HS 6; BB 2-39). **F-c**: HS 39; BB 6-68.

HAYDEN, Matthew Lawrence (Marist C, Ashgrove; Queensland U of Tech), b Kingaroy 29 Oct 1971. 6'2". LHB, RM. Queensland 1991-92 to date. **Tests**: 4 (1993-94 to 1996-97); HS 125 v WI (Adelaide) 1996-97. **LOI**: 13 (1993 to 1993-94; HS 67). **F-c**: HS 234; BB 1-24.

HEALY, Ian Andrew (Brisbane State HS), b Spring Hill, Brisbane 30 Apr 1964. 5'9". RHB, WK. Queensland 1986-87 to date. *Wisden* 1993. **Tests**: 85 (1988-89 to 1996-97); HS 161* v WI (Brisbane) 1996-97. **LOI**: 161 (1988-89 to 1996-97, 4 as captain; HS 56). **F-c**: HS 161*.

HOGG, George Bradley, b Narrogin 6 Feb 1971. LHB, SLC. W Australia 1993-94 to date. **Tests**: 1 (1996-97); HS 4 and BB 1-69 v I (Delhi) 1996-97. **LOI**: 7 (1996-97; HS 11*; BB 1-23). **F-c**: HS 111*; BB 5-59.

JULIAN, Brendon Paul – *see SURREY*.

KASPROWICZ, Michael Scott (Brisbane State HS), b South Brisbane 10 Feb 1972. 6'4". RHB, RF. Queensland 1989-90 to date. Essex 1994; cap 1994. **Tests**: 2 (1996-97); HS 21 v WI (Sydney) 1996-97; BB –. **LOI**: 2 (1995-96; HS –; BB 1-32). **F-c**: HS 49; BB 7-64.

LANGER, Justin Lee (Aquinas C; U of WA), b Perth 21 Nov 1970. 5'8". LHB, RM. W Australia 1991-92 to date. **Tests**: 8 (1992-93 to 1996-97); HS 69 v P (Lahore) 1994-95. **LOI**: 7 (1993-94 to 1994-95; HS 36). **F-c**: HS 241*.

LAW, Stuart Grant – *see ESSEX*.

LEE, Shane – *see SOMERSET*.

McGRATH, Glenn Donald (Narromine HS), b Dubbo, NSW 9 Feb 1970. 6'6". RHB, RF. NSW 1992-93 to date. **Tests**: 25 (1993-94 to 1996-97); HS 24 v WI (Sydney) 1996-97. BB 6-47 v WI (Port-of-Spain) 1994-95. **LOI**: 66 (1993-94 to 1996-97; HS 10; BB 5-52). **F-c**: HS 24; BB 6-47.

MOODY, Thomas Masson – *see WORCESTERSHIRE*.

PONTING, Ricky Thomas (Brooks HS), b Launceston 19 Dec 1974. 5'10". RHB, OB. Tasmania 1992-93 to date. **Tests**: 6 (1995-96 to 1996-97); HS 96 v SL (Perth) 1995-96 (on debut); BB 1-0. **LOI**: 33 (1994-95 to 1996-97; HS 123). **F-c**: HS 211; BB 1-0.

REIFFEL, Paul Ronald (Jordanville TS), b Box Hill, Victoria 19 Apr 1966. 6'2". RHB, RFM. Victoria 1987-88 to date. **Tests**: 25 (1991-92 to 1996-97); HS 56 v SL (Adelaide) 1995-96. BB 6-71 v E (Birmingham) 1993. **LOI**: 71 (1991-92 to 1996-97); HS 58; BB 4-13). **F-c**: HS 86; BB 6-57.

SLATER, Michael Jonathon – *see YORKSHIRE*.

STUART, Anthony Mark, b Newcastle, NSW 2 Jan 1970. RHB, RFM. NSW 1994-95 to date. **LOI**: 3 (1996-97); HS 1; BB 5-26 inc hat-trick v P (Melbourne) 1996-97). **F-c**: HS 14*; BB 4-22.

TAYLOR, Mark Anthony (Mt Austin HS, Wagga Wagga; Chatswood HS, Stoney; U of NSW), b Leeton, NSW 27 Oct 1964. 5'10". LHB, RM. NSW 1985-86 to date. *Wisden* 1989. **Tests**: 78 (1988-89 to 1996-97, 24 as captain); HS 219 v E (Nottingham) 1989. BB 1-11. **LOI**: 109 (1989-90 to 1996-97, 63 as captain; HS 105). **F-c**: HS 219; BB 1-4.

WARNE, Shane Keith (Hampton HS; Mentone GS), b Ferntree Gully, Melbourne 13 Sep 1969. 6'0". RHB, LBG. Victoria 1990-91 to date. *Wisden* 1993. **Tests**: 49 (1991-92 to 1996-97); HS 74* v NZ (Brisbane) 1993-94; BB 8-71 v E (Brisbane) 1994-95; hat-trick v E (Melbourne) 1994-95. **LOI**: 67 (1992-93 to 1996-97); HS 55; BB 5-33). **F-c**: HS 74*; BB 8-71.

WAUGH, Mark Edward (East Hills HS), b Canterbury, Sydney 2 Jun 1965. Younger twin of Steve. 6'1". RHB, RMF/OB. NSW 1985-86 to date. Essex 1988-90, 1992 and 1995; cap 1989. *Wisden* 1990. **Tests**: 60 (1990-91 to 1996-97); HS 140 v E (Brisbane) 1994-95; BB 5-40 v E (Adelaide) 1994-95. **LOI**: 128 (1988-89 to 1996-97; HS 130; BB 5-24). **F-c**: HS 229*; BB 5-37.

WAUGH, Stephen Rodger (East Hills HS), b Canterbury, Sydney 2 Jun 1965. Elder twin of Mark. 5'11". RHB, RMF. NSW 1984-85 to date. Somerset 1987-88. **Tests**: 86 (1985-86 to 1996-97); HS 200 v WI (Kingston) 1994-95; BB 5-28 v SA (Cape Town) 1993-94. **LOI**: 211 (1985-86 to 1996-97; HS 102*; BB 4-33). **F-c**: HS 216*; BB 6-51.

YOUNG, Shaun – *see GLOUCESTERSHIRE*.

ENGLAND v AUSTRALIA
1876-77 to 1994-95

Captains

Season	England	Australia	T	E	A	D
1876-77	James Lillywhite	D.W.Gregory	2	1	1	–
1878-79	Lord Harris	D.W.Gregory	1	–	1	–
1880	Lord Harris	W.L.Murdoch	1	1	–	–
1881-82	A.Shaw	W.L.Murdoch	4	–	2	2
1882	A.N.Hornby	W.L.Murdoch	1	–	1	–
1882-83	Hon. Ivo Bligh	W.L.Murdoch	4	2	2	–
1884	Lord Harris[1]	W.L.Murdoch	3	1	–	2
1884-85	A.Shrewsbury	T.Horan[2]	5	3	2	–
1886	A.G.Steel	H.J.H.Scott	3	3	–	–
1886-87	A.Shrewsbury	P.S.McDonnell	2	2	–	–
1887-88	W.W.Read	P.S.McDonnell	1	1	–	–
1888	W.G.Grace[3]	P.S.McDonnell	3	2	1	–
1890	W.G.Grace	W.I.Murdoch	2	2	–	–

10

Season	England	Australia	T	E	A	D
1891-92	W.G.Grace	J.McC.Blackham	3	1	2	–
1893	W.G.Grace[4]	J.McC.Blackham	3	1	–	2
1894-95	A.E.Stoddart	G.Giffen[5]	5	3	2	–
1896	W.G.Grace	G.H.S.Trott	3	2	1	–
1897-98	A.E.Stoddart[6]	G.H.S.Trott	5	1	4	–
1899	A.C.MacLaren[7]	J.Darling	5	–	1	4
1901-02	A.C.MacLaren	J.Darling[8]	5	1	4	–
1902	A.C.MacLaren	J. Darling	5	1	2	2
1903-04	P.F.Warner	M.A.Boble	5	3	2	–
1905	Hon F.S.Jackson	J.Darling	5	2	–	3
1907-08	A.O.Jones[9]	M.A.Noble	5	1	4	–
1909	A.C.MacLaren	M.A.Noble	5	1	2	2
1911-12	J.W.H.T.Douglas	C.Hill	5	4	1	–
1912	C.B.Fry	S.E.Gregory	3	1	–	2
1920-21	J.W.H.T.Douglas	W.W.Armstrong	5	–	5	–
1921	Hon L.H.Tennyson[10]	W.W.Armstrong	5	–	3	2
1924-25	A.E.R.Gilligan	H.L.Collins	5	1	4	–
1926	A.W.Carr[11]	H.L.Collins[12]	5	1	–	4
1928-29	A.P.F.Chapman[13]	J.Ryder	5	4	1	–
1930	A.P.F.Chapman[14]	W.M.Woodfull	5	1	2	2
1932-33	D.R.Jardine	W.M.Woodfull	5	4	1	–
1934	R.E.S.Wyatt[15]	W.M.Woodfull	5	1	2	2
1936-37	G.O.B.Allen	D.G.Bradman	5	2	3	–
1938	W.R.Hammond	D.G.Bradman	4	1	1	2
1946-47	W.R.Hammond[16]	D.G.Bradman	5	–	3	2
1948	N.W.D.Yardley	D.G.Bradman	5	–	4	1
1950-51	F.R.Brown	A.L.Hassett	5	1	4	–
1953	L.Hutton	A.L.Hassett	5	1	–	4
1954-55	L.Hutton	I.W.Johnson[17]	5	3	1	1
1956	P.B.H.May	I.W.Johnson	5	2	1	2
1958-59	P.B.H.May	R.Benaud	5	–	4	1
1961	P.B.H.May[18]	R.Benaud[19]	5	1	2	2
1962-63	E.R.Dexter	R.Benaud	5	1	1	3
1964	E.R.Dexter	R.B.Simpson	5	–	1	4
1965-66	M.J.K.Smith	R.B.Simpson[20]	5	1	1	3
1968	M.C.Cowdry[21]	W.M.Lawry[22]	5	1	1	3
1970-71	R.Illingworth	W.M.Lawry[23]	6	2	–	4
1972	R.Illingworth	I.M.Chappell	5	2	2	1
1974-75	M.H.Denness[24]	I.M.Chappell	6	1	4	1
1975	A.W.Greig[25]	I.M.Chappell	4	–	1	3
1976-77	A.W.Greig	G.S.Chappell	1	–	1	–
1977	J.M.Brearley	G.S.Chappell	5	3	–	2
1978-79	J.M.Brearley	G.N.Yallop	6	5	1	–
1979-80	J.M.Brearley	G.S.Chappell	3	–	3	–
1980	I.T.Botham	G.S.Chappell	1	–	–	1
1981	J.M.Brearley[26]	K.J.Hughes	6	3	1	2
1982-83	R.G.D.Willis	G.S.Chappell	5	1	2	2
1985	D.I.Gower	A.R.Border	6	3	1	2
1986-87	M.W.Gatting	A.R.Border	5	2	1	2
1987-88	M.W.Gatting	A.R.Border	1	–	–	1
1989	D.I.Gower	A.R.Border	6	–	4	2
1990-91	G.A.Gooch[27]	A.R.Border	5	–	3	2
1993	G.A.Gooch[28]	A.R.Border	6	1	4	1
1994-95	M.A.Atherton	M.A.Taylor	5	1	3	1

	T	E	A	D
The Oval	31	14	5	12
Manchester	26	7	6	13
Lord's	30	5	12	13
Nottingham	17	3	5	9
Leeds	21	6	7	8
Birmingham	9	3	2	4
Sheffield	1	–	1	–
Melbourne	50	18	25	7
Sydney	50	20	23	7
Adelaide	26	8	13	5
Brisbane	16	5	8	3
Perth	8	1	4	3
In England	135	38	38	59
In Australia	150	52	73	25
Totals	285	90	111	84

The following deputised for the official captain or were appointed for only a minor proportion of the series:
[1]A.N.Hornby (1st). [2]W.L.Murdoch (1st), H.H.Massie (3rd), J.M.Blackham (4th). [3]A.G.Steel (1st). [4]A.E.Stoddart (1st). [5]J.M.Blackham (1st). [6]A.C.MacLaren (1st, 2nd, 5th). [7]W.G.Grace (1st). [8]H.Trumble (4th, 5th). [9]F.L.Fane (1st, 2nd, 3rd). [10]J.W.H.T.Douglas (1st, 2nd). [11]A.P.F.Chapman (5th). [12]W.Bardsley (3rd, 4th). [13]J.C.White (5th). [14]R.E.S.Wyatt (5th). [15]C.F.Walters (1st). [16]N.W.D.Yardley (5th). [17]A.R.Morris (2nd). [18]M.C.Cowdrey (1st, 2nd). [19]R.N.Harvey (2nd). [20]B.C.Booth (1st, 3rd). [21]T.W.Graveney (4th). [22]B.N.Jarman (4th). [23]I.M.Chappell (7th). [24]J.H.Edrich (4th). [25]M.H.Denness (1st). [26]I.T.Botham (1st, 2nd). [27]A.J.Lamb (1st). [28]M.A.Atherton (5th, 6th).

HIGHEST INNINGS TOTALS

England	in England	903-7d	The Oval	1938
	in Australia	636	Sydney	1928-29
Australia	in England	729-6d	Lord's	1930
	in Austalia	659-8d	Sydney	1946-47

LOWEST INNINGS TOTALS

England	in England	52	The Oval	1948
	in Australia	45	Sydney	1886-87
Australia	in England	36	Birmingham	1902
	in Australia	42	Sydney	1887-88

HIGHEST INDIVIDUAL INNINGS

England	in England	364	L.Hutton	The Oval	1938
	in Australia	287	R.E.Foster	Sydney	1903-04
Austalia	in England	334	D.G.Bradman	Leeds	1930
	in Australia	307	R.M.Cowper	Melbourne	1965-66

HIGHEST AGGREGATE OF RUNS IN A SERIES

England	in England	732 (av 81.33)	D.I.Gower	1985
	in Australia	905 (av 113.12)	W.R.Hammond	1928-29
Australia	in England	974 (av 139.14)	D.G.Bradman	1930
	in Australia	810 (av 90.00)	D.G.Bradman	1936-37

RECORD WICKET PARTNERSHIPS – ENGLAND

1st	323	J.B.Hobbs (178), W.Rhodes (179)	Melbourne	1911-12
2nd	382	L.Hutton (364), M.Leyland (187)	The Oval	1938
3rd	262	W.R.Hammond (177), D.R.Jardine (98)	Adelaide	1928-29
4th	222	W.R.Hammond (240), E.Paynter (99)	Lord's	1938
5th	206	E.Paynter (216*), D.C.S.Compton (102)	Nottingham	1938
6th {	215	L.Hutton (364), J.Hardstaff, jr (169*)	The Oval	1938
	215	G.Boycott (107), A.P.E.Knott (135)	Nottingham	1977
7th	143	F.E.Woolley (133*), J.Vine (36)	Sydney	1911-12
8th	124	E.H.Hendren (169), H.Larwood (70)	Brisbane	1928-29
9th	151	W.H.Scotton (90), W.W.Read (117)	The Oval	1884
10th	130	R.E.Foster (287), W.Rhodes (40*)	Sydney	1903-04

RECORD WICKET PARTNERSHIPS – AUSTRALIA

1st	329	G.R.Marsh (138), M.A.Taylor (219)	Nottingham	1989
2nd	451	W.H.Ponsford (266), D.G.Bradman (244)	The Oval	1934
3rd	276	D.G.Bradman (187), A.L.Hassett (128)	Brisbane	1946-47
4th	388	W.H.Ponsford (181), D.G.Bradman (304)	Leeds	1934
5th	405	S.G.Barnes (234), D.G.Bradman (234)	Sydney	1946-47
6th	346	J.H.Fingleton (136), D.G.Bradman (270)	Melbourne	1936-37
7th	165	C.Hill (188), H.Trumble (46)	Melbourne	1897-98
8th	243	R.J.Hartigan (113), C.Hill (160)	Adelaide	1907-08
9th	154	S.E.Gregory (201), J.M.Blackham (74)	Sydney	1894-95
10th	127	J.M.Taylor (108), A.A.Mailey (46*)	Sydney	1924-25

BEST INNINGS BOWLING ANALYSIS

England	in England	10- 53	J.C.Laker	Manchester	1956
	in Australia	8- 35	G.A.Lohmann	Sydney	1886-87
Australia	in England	8- 31	F.Laver	Manchester	1909
	in Australia	9-121	A.A.Mailey	Melbourne	1920-21

BEST MATCH BOWLING ANALYSIS

England	in England	19- 90	J.C.Laker	Manchester	1956
	in Austalia	15-124	W.Rhodes	Melbourne	1903-04
Australia	in England	16-137	R.A.L.Massie	Lord's	1972
	in Australia	13- 77	M.A.Noble	Melbourne	1901-02

HAT-TRICKS

England	W.Bates	Melbourne	1882-83
	J.Briggs	Sydney	1891-92
	J.T.Hearne	Leeds	1899
Australia	F.R.Spofforth	Melbourne	1878-79
	H.Trumble	Melbourne	1901-02
	H.Trumble	Melbourne	1903-04
	S.K.Warne	Melbourne	1994-95

HIGHEST AGGREGATE OF WICKETS IN A SERIES

England	in England	46 (av 9.60)	J.C.Laker	1956
	in Australia	38 (av 23.18)	M.W.Tate	1924-25
Austalia	in England	42 (av 21.26)	T.M.Alderman	1981
	in Australia	41 (av 12.85)	R.M.Hogg	1978-79

2000 RUNS

	Test	I	NO	HS	Runs	Avge
D.G.Bradman (A)	37	63	7	334	5028	89.78
J.B.Hobbs (E)	41	71	4	187	3636	54.26
A.R.Border (A)	47	82	19	200*	3548	56.31
D.I.Gower (E)	42	77	4	215	3269	44.78
G.Boycott (E)	38	71	9	191	2945	47.50
W.R.Hammond (E)	33	58	3	251	2852	51.85
H.Sutcliffe (E)	27	46	5	194	2741	66.85
C.Hill (A)	41	76	1	188	2660	35.46
J.H.Edrich (E)	32	57	3	175	2644	48.96
G.A.Gooch (E)	42	79	0	196	2632	33.31
G.S.Chappell (A)	35	65	8	144	2619	45.94
M.C.Cowdrey (E)	43	75	4	113	2433	34.26
L.Hutton (E)	27	49	6	364	2428	56.46
R.N.Harvey (A)	37	68	5	167	2416	38.34
V.T.Trumper (A)	40	74	5	185*	2263	32.79
D.C.Boon (A)	31	57	8	184*	2237	45.65
W.M.Lawry (A)	29	51	5	166	2233	48.54
S.E.Gregory (A)	52	92	7	201	2193	25.80
W.W.Armstrong (A)	42	71	9	158	2172	35.03
I.M.Chappell (A)	30	56	4	192	2138	41.11
K.F.Barrington (E)	23	39	6	256	2111	63.96
A.R.Morris (A)	24	43	2	206	2080	50.73

D.G.Bradman holds the unique record of scoring 2000 runs in both countries in this series (2674 runs in England and 2354 in Australia). J.B.Hobbs is the only other batsman to score 2000 runs in either country (2493 runs in Australia).

100 WICKETS

	Tests	Balls	Runs	Wkts	BB	5wI	Avge
D.K.Lillee (A)	29	8516	3507	167	7- 89	11	21.00
I.T.Botham (E)	36	8479	4093	148	6- 78	9	27.65
H.Trumble (A)	31	7895	2945	141	8- 65	9	20.88
R.G.D.Willis (E)	35	7294	3346	128	8- 43	7	26.14
M.A.Noble (A)	39	6845	2860	115	7- 17	9	24.68
R.R.Lindwall (A)	29	6728	2559	114	7- 63	6	22.44
W.Rhodes (E)	41	5791	2616	109	8- 68	6	24.00
S.F.Barnes (E)	20	5749	2288	106	7- 60	12	21.58
C.V.Grimmett (A)	22	9224	3439	106	6- 37	11	32.44
D.L.Underwood (E)	29	8000	2770	105	7- 50	4	26.38
A.V.Bedser (E)	21	7065	2859	104	7- 44	7	27.49
G.Giffen (A)	31	6457	2791	103	7-117	7	27.09
W.J.O'Reilly (A)	19	7864	2587	102	7- 54	8	25.36
R.Peel (E)	20	5216	1715	101	7- 31	5	16.98
C.T.B.Turner (A)	17	5195	1670	101	7- 43	11	16.53
T.M.Alderman (A)	17	4717	2117	100	6- 47	11	21.17
J.R.Thomson (A)	21	4951	2418	100	6- 46	5	24.18

75 WICKET-KEEPING DISMISSALS

	Tests	Ct	St	Total
R.W.Marsh (A)	42	141	7	148
A.P.E.Knott (E)	34	97	8	105
W.A.S.Oldfield (A)	38	59	31	90
I.A.Healy (A)	22	82	7	89
A.F.A.Lilley (E)	32	65	19	84
A.T.W.Grout (A)	22	69	7	76
T.G.Evans (E)	31	63	12	75

THE FIRST-CLASS COUNTIES REGISTER, RECORDS AND 1996 AVERAGES

Career statistics: Test and L-O Internationals to 4 March 1997
(exc South Africa v Australia 1st Test); first-class to end of 1996 season.

ABBREVIATIONS
General

*	not out/unbroken partnership	f-c	first-class
b	born	HS	Highest Score
BB	Best innings bowling analysis	LOI	Limited-Overs Internationals
Cap	Awarded 1st XI County Cap	Tests	Official Test Matches
Tours	Overseas tours involving first-class appearances		

Awards

BHC	Benson and Hedges Cup 'Gold' Award
NWT	NatWest Trophy/Gillette Cup 'Man of the Match' Award
Wisden 1996	One of *Wisden Cricketers' Almanack*'s Five Cricketers of 1996
YC 1996	Cricket Writers' Club Young Cricketer of 1996

Competitions

BHC	Benson and Hedges Cup
GC	Gillette Cup
NWT	NatWest Trophy
SL	Sunday League

Playing Categories

LB	Bowls right-arm leg-breaks
LBG	Bowls right-arm leg-breaks and googlies
LF	Bowls left-arm fast
LFM	Bowls left-arm fast-medium
LHB	Bats left-handed
LM	Bowls left-arm medium pace
LMF	Bowls left-arm medium fast
OB	Bowls right-arm off-breaks
RF	Bowls right-arm fast
RFM	Bowls right-arm fast-medium
RHB	Bats right-handed
RM	Bowls right-arm medium pace
RMF	Bowls right-arm medium-fast
RSM	Bowls right-arm slow-medium
SLA	Bowls left-arm leg-breaks
SLC	Bowls left-arm 'Chinaman'
WK	Wicket-keeper

Education

BHS	Boys' High School
BS	Boys' School
C	College
CE	College of Education
CFE	College of Further Education
CHE	College of Higher Education
CS	Comprehensive School
GS	Grammar School
HS	High School
IHE	Institute of Higher Education
LSE	London School of Economics
RGS	Royal Grammar School
S	School
SFC	Sixth Form College
SM	Secondary Modern School
SS	Secondary School
TC	Technical College
T(H)S	Technical (High) School
U	University
UMIST	University of Manchester Institute of Science and Technology

Teams (see also p 123)

Cav	Cavaliers	NT	Northern Transvaal
CD	Central Districts	OFS	(Orange) Free State
DHR	D.H.Robins' XI	PIA	Pakistan International Airlines
Eng Co	English Counties XI	Q	Queensland
EP	Eastern Province	RW	Rest of the World XI
GW	Griqualand West	SAB	South African Breweries XI
Int XI	International XI	SAU	South African Universities
IW	International Wanderers	WA	Western Australia
ND	Northern Districts	WP	Western Province
NSW	New South Wales	Z	Zimbabwe (Rhodesia)

DERBYSHIRE

Formation of Present Club: 4 November 1870
Colours: Chocolate, Amber and Pale Blue
Badge: Rose and Crown
Championships: (1) 1936
NatWest Trophy/Gillette Cup Winners: (1) 1981
Benson and Hedges Cup Winners: (1) 1993
Sunday League Champions: (1) 1990
Match Awards: NWT 37; BHC 63

Secretary/General Manager: S.Edwards.
   County Cricket Ground, Nottingham Road, Derby DE2 6DA (Tel 01332 383211)
Captain/Overseas Player: D.M.Jones. **Vice-Captain:** P.A.J.DeFreitas.
1997 Beneficiary: D.E.Malcolm. **Scorer:** S.W.Tacey.

ADAMS, Christopher John (Repton S), b Whitwell 6 May 1970. 6'0". RHB, OB. Debut 1988; cap 1992. 1000 runs (3); most – 1742 (1996). BB 4-29 v Lancs (Derby) 1991. Awards: NWT 1; BHC 3. **NWT:** HS 109* v Sussex (Hove) 1995. BB 1-15 v Berks (Derby) 1992. **BHC:** HS 100* v Durham (Chesterfield) 1996. **SL:** HS 141* v Kent (Chesterfield) 1992. BB 2-15 v Essex (Chelmsford) 1993.

ALDRED, Paul (Lady Manner's S, Bakewell), b Chellaston 4 Feb 1969. RHB, RM. Debut 1995. Cheshire 1994. HS 33 v Warwks (Birmingham) 1995. BB 3-47 v Young A (Chesterfield) 1995. BAC BB 3-89 v Surrey (Derby) 1995. **BHC:** HS 7 and BB 2-35 v Warwks (Birmingham) 1996. **SL:** HS 11* v Northants (Derby) 1995. BB 4-41 v Leics (Derby) 1996. Hockey for Derbyshire.

BARNETT, Kim John (Leek HS), b Stoke-on-Trent, Staffs 17 Jul 1960. 6'1". RHB, LB. Debut 1979; cap 1982; captain 1983-95; benefit 1992. Boland 1982-83 to 1987-88. Staffordshire 1976. *Wisden* 1988. **Tests:** 4 (1988 to 1989); HS 80 v A (Leeds) 1989. **LOI:** 1 (1988; HS 84). Tours: SA 1989-90 (Eng XI); NZ 1979-80 (DHR); SL 1985-86 (Eng B). 1000 runs (13); most – 1734 (1984). HS 239* v Leics (Leicester) 1988. BB 6-28 v Glam (Chesterfield) 1991. Awards: NWT 3; BHC 10. **NWT:** HS 113* v Glos (Bristol) 1994. BB 6-24 v Cumberland (Kendal) 1984. **BHC:** 115 v Glos (Derby) 1987. BB 1-1. **SL:** HS 131* v Essex (Derby) 1984. BB 3-26 v Worcs (Chesterfield) 1996.

CASSAR, Matthew Edward (Sir Joseph Banks HS, Sydney), b Sydney, Australia 16 Oct 1972. 6'0". RHB, RFM. Debut 1994. Qualified for England 1997. HS 66 v NZ (Derby) 1994. BB 4-54 v OU (Oxford) 1995.

CORK, Dominic Gerald (St Joseph's C, Stoke-on-Trent), b Newcastle-under-Lyme, Staffs 7 Aug 1971. 6'2". RHB, RFM. Debut 1990; cap 1993. *Wisden* 1995. Staffordshire 1989-90. **Tests:** 19 (1995 to 1996-97); HS 59 v NZ (Auckland) 1996-97; BB 7-43 v WI (Lord's) 1995 – on debut (record England analysis by Test match debutant); hat-trick v WI (Manchester) 1995 – the first in Test history to occur in the opening over of a day's play. **LOI:** 25 (1992 to 1996-97; HS 31*; BB 3-27). Tours: A 1992-93 (Eng A); SA 1993-94 (Eng A), 1995-96; WI 1991-92 (Eng A); NZ 1996-97; I 1994-95 (Eng A). HS 104 v Glos (Cheltenham) 1993. 50 wkts (3); most – 90 (1995). BB 9-43 (13-93 match) v Northants (Derby) 1995. Took 8-53 before lunch on his 20th birthday v Essex (Derby) 1991. 2 hat-tricks: 1994 and 1995 (*see Tests*). Awards: NWT 2; BHC 3. **NWT:** HS 62 v Kent (Derby) 1994. BB 5-18 v Berks (Derby) 1992. **BHC:** HS 92* v Lancs (Lord's) 1993. BB 5-49 v Lancs (Chesterfield) 1996. **SL:** HS 66 v Sussex (Eastbourne) 1994. BB 4-44 v Warwks (Chesterfield) 1994.

DEAN, Kevin James (Leek HS; Leek C), b Derby 16 Oct 1975. 6'5". LHB, LMF. Debut 1996. HS 12 v Worcs (Chesterfield) 1996. BB 3-47 v Notts (Derby) 1996. **NWT:** HS 0*. BB 3-52 v Staffs (Stone) 1996. **SL:** HS 8*. BB 5-32 v Glos (Derby) 1996.

DeFREITAS, Phillip Anthony Jason (Willesden HS, London), b Scotts Head, Dominica 18 Feb 1966. 6'0". RHB, RFM. UK resident since 1976. Leicestershire 1985-88; cap 1986. Lancashire 1989-93; cap 1989. Boland 1993-94 and 1995-96. Derbyshire debut/cap 1994. *Wisden* 1991. MCC YC. **Tests:** 44 (1986-87 to 1995-96); HS 88 v A (Adelaide) 1994-95; BB 7-70 v SL (Lord's) 1991. **LOI:** 101 (1986-87 to 1995-96; HS 67; BB 4-35). Tours: A 1986-87, 1990-91, 1994-95; WI 1989-90; NZ 1987-88, 1991-92; P 1987-88; I 1992-93; Z 1988-89 (La). HS 113 Le v Notts (Worksop) 1988. De HS 108 v Leics (Derby) 1994. 50 wkts (9); most – 94 (1986). BB 7-21 La v Middx (Lord's) 1989. De BB 7-101 v Warwks (Derby) 1996. Hat-trick (Derby) 1996. Awards: NWT 5; BHC 4. **NWT:** HS 69 Le v Lancs (Leicester) 1986. BB 5-13 La v Cumberland (Kendal) 1989. **BHC:** HS 75* La v Hants (Manchester) 1990. BB 5-16 La v Essex (Chelmsford) 1992. **SL:** HS 72* v Kent (Derby) 1996. BB 5-26 La v Hants (Southampton) 1993.

GRIFFITHS, Steven Paul (Beechen Cliff S, Bath; Brunel C of Art & Technology, Bristol), b Hereford 31 May 1973. RHB, WK. 5'11". Debut 1995. HS 20 v Surrey (Derby) 1995.

HARRIS, Andrew James (Hadfield CS; Glossopdale Community C), b Ashton-under-Lyne, Lancs 26 Jun 1973. 6'1". RHB, RM. Debut 1994; cap 1996. Tour: A 1996-97 (Eng A). HS 17 v Glam (Cardiff) 1996. BB 6-40 (12-83 match) v Middx (Derby) 1996. 50 wkts (1): 72 (1996). **NWT:** HS 11* and BB 3-58 v Kent (Derby) 1996. **BHC:** HS 5. BB 1-34. **SL:** HS 2. BB 3-15 v Durham (Chester-le-St) 1995.

JONES, Dean Mervyn (Mount Waverley HS), b Coburg, Victoria, Australia 24 Mar 1961. 6'1". RHB, OB. Victoria 1981-82 to date; captain 1993-94 to 1995-96. Durham 1992; cap 1992. Derbyshire debut/cap 1996; captain 1996 to date. *Wisden* 1989. **Tests** (A): 52 (1983-84 to 1992-93); HS 216 v WI (Adelaide) 1988-89; BB 1-5. **LOI** (A): 164 (1983-84 to 1993-94; HS 145; BB 2-34). Tours (A): E 1987 (RW), 1989, 1991 (Vic); WI 1983-84, 1990-91; NZ 1989-90; I 1986-87; P 1988-89; Z 1985-86 (Young A). 1000 runs (3+5); most – 1510 (1989). HS 324* Victoria v S Australia (Melbourne) 1994-95. De/BAC HS 214* v Yorks (Sheffield) 1996. BB 5-112 v Hants (Southampton) 1996. Award: BHC 1. **NWT:** HS 100* v Lancs (Manchester) 1996. BB 2-0 v Staffs (Stone) 1996. **BHC:** HS 142 v Minor C (Derby) 1996. BB 2-34 Du v Comb Us (Cambridge) 1992. **SL:** HS 118 v Middx (Derby) 1996. BB 2-15 v Northants (Northampton) 1996.

KHAN, Gul Abbass (Valentine S, Ilford; Ipswich S; Swansea U; Keble C, Oxford), b Gujrat, Pakistan 31 Dec 1973. 5'8". RHB, LBG. Essex staff 1993-95. Debut (Oxford U) 1996, scoring 94 v Leics (Oxford); blue 1996. Derbyshire debut 1996. HS 101* OU v Kent (Canterbury) 1996. De HS 15 v SA A (Chesterfield) 1996. BAC HS 4. BB 2-48 OU v Hants (Oxford) 1996. **NWT:** HS 15 v Lancs (Manchester) 1996. **BHC** (Brit Us): HS 147 v Glam (Cambridge) 1996. **SL:** HS 27 v Glos (Derby) 1996.

KRIKKEN, Karl Matthew (Rivington & Blackrod HS & SFC), b Bolton, Lancs 9 Apr 1969. Son of B.E. (Lancs and Worcs 1966-69). 5'9". RHB, WK. GW 1988-89. Derbyshire debut 1989; cap 1992. HS 104 v Lancs (Manchester) 1996. **NWT:** HS 55 v Kent (Derby) 1996. **BHC:** HS 37* v Worcs (Worcester) 1992 and v Lancs (Lord's) 1993. **SL:** HS 44* v Essex (Chelmsford) 1991.

LACEY, Simon James (Aldercar CS; Ripley Mill Hill SFC), b Nottingham 9 Mar 1975. 5'11". RHB, OB. Staff 1996 – awaiting f-c debut.

MALCOLM, Devon Eugene (St Elizabeth THS; Richmond C, Sheffield; Derby CHE), b Kingston, Jamaica 22 Feb 1963. Qualified for England 1987. 6'2". RHB, RF. Debut 1984; cap 1989; benefit 1997. *Wisden* 1994. **Tests:** 36 (1989 to 1995-96); HS 29 v A (Sydney) 1994-95; BB 9-57 v SA (Oval) 1994 – sixth best analysis in Test cricket. **LOI:** 10 (1990 to 1993-94; HS 4; BB 3-40). Tours: A 1990-91, 1994-95; SA 1995-96; WI 1989-90, 1991-92 (Eng A), 1993-94; I 1992-93. HS 51 v Surrey (Derby) 1989. 50 wkts (5); most – 82 (1996). BB 9-57 (*see Tests*). De BB 6-52 v Glam (Cardiff) 1996. Award: BHC 1. **NWT:** HS 10* v Leics (Derby) 1992. BB 3-29 v Devon (Exmouth) 1993. **BHC:** HS 15 v Comb Us (Oxford) 1991. BB 5-27 v Middx (Derby) 1988. **SL:** HS 42 v Surrey (Oval) 1996. BB 4-21 v Surrey (Derby) 1989 and v Leics (Knypersley) 1990.

MAY, Michael Robert (The Bolsover S; NE Derbyshire CFE), b Chesterfield 22 Jul 1971. 5'9". RHB, OB. Debut 1996. HS 63* v SA A (Chesterfield) 1996.

OWEN, John Edward Houghton (Spondon S, Derby), b Derby 7 Aug 1971. 5'10". RHB, occ OB. Debut 1995. HS 105 v Glam (Cardiff) 1996. **NWT:** HS 7. **BHC:** HS 49 v Warwks (Birmingham) 1996. **SL:** HS 45 v Surrey (Derby) 1995.

ROBERTS, Glenn Martin (King James's HS and Greenhead C, Huddersfield; Leeds Met U), b Huddersfield, Yorks 4 Nov 1973. 5'11". LHB, SLA. Debut 1996. HS 52 and BB 1-55 v Somerset (Taunton) 1996 (on debut). **SL:** HS 6*. BB 2-28 v Worcs (Chesterfield) 1996.

ROLLINS, Adrian Stewart (Little Ilford CS), b Barking, Essex 8 Feb 1972. Brother of R.J. (*see ESSEX*). 6'5". RHB, WK, occ RM. Debut 1993; cap 1995. 1000 runs (2); most – 1101 (1996). HS 200* v Glos (Bristol) 1995. BB 1-19. **NWT:** HS 56 v Sussex (Hove) 1995. **BHC:** HS 70 v Lancs (Derby) 1994. **SL:** HS 126* v Surrey (Derby) 1995.

SPENDLOVE, Benjamin Lee (Trent C), b Belper 4 Nov 1978. 6'1". RHB, OB. Staff 1996 – awaiting f-c debut.

TWEATS, Timothy Andrew (Endon HS; Stoke-on-Trent SFC), b Stoke-on-Trent, Staffs 18 Apr 1974. 6'3". RHB, RM. Debut 1992. HS 89* v CU (Cambridge) 1996. BAC HS 78* v Worcs (Kidderminster) 1995. BB 1-23. **NWT:** HS 16 v Warwks (Derby) 1995. **BHC:** HS 10 v Lancs (Chesterfield) 1996. **SL:** HS 19 v Glam (Derby) 1995.

VANDRAU, Matthew James (St Stithian's C, Johannesburg; St John's C, Jo'burg; Witwatersrand U), b Epsom, Surrey 22 Jul 1969. Son of B.M. (Transvaal B 1963). 6'3½". RHB, OB. Transvaal/Transvaal B 1990-91 to date. Derbyshire debut 1991. HS 66 v Kent (Derby) 1994. BB 6-34 v Hants (Southampton) 1996. **NWT:** HS 27 v Kent (Derby) 1994. BB 2-36 v Durham (Darlington) 1994. **BHC:** HS 12* v Lancs (Chesterfield) 1996. BB 1-46. **SL:** HS 32* v Kent (Canterbury) 1993. BB 3-25 v Leics (Derby) 1994.

WOMBLE, David Robert (St Thomas More S, Longton; City of Stoke-on-Trent SFC; Leeds Met U), b Stoke-on-Trent, Staffs 23 Feb 1977. 5'11". RHB, RM. Staffordshire 1996. Summer contract – awaiting f-c debut. **SL:** HS – .

NEWCOMERS

BLACKWELL, Ian David (Brookfield Community S), b Chesterfield 10 Jun 1978. LHB, SLA.

CLARKE, Vincent Paul (Sacred Heart C, Perth, Australia; Perth C), b Liverpool, Lancs 11 Nov 1971. 6'3". RHB, RM/LB. Somerset 1994. Leicestershire 1995-96. HS 43 Le v P (Leicester) 1996. BAC HS 38 Sm v Glos (Bristol) 1994 – on debut. BB 3-72 Le v Worcs (Worcester) 1995. **BHC:** HS 22 Sm v Surrey (Oval) 1994. **SL:** HS 26 Sm v Leics (Leicester) 1994. BB 1-15 (twice).

HAYHURST, Andrew Neil (Worsley Wardley HS; Eccles SFC; Leeds Poly), b Davy-hulme, Manchester 23 Nov 1962. 5'11". RHB, RM. Lancashire 1985-89. Somerset 1990-96; cap 1990; captain 1994-96. Tours: WI 1986-87 (La); Z 1988-89 (La). 1000 runs (3); most – 1559 (1990). HS 172* Sm v Glos (Bath) 1991. BB 4-27 La v Middx (Manchester) 1987. Awards: NWT 2; BHC 2. **NWT:** HS 91* and BB 5-60 Sm v Warwks (Birmingham) 1991. **BHC:** HS 95 Sm v Notts (Nottingham) 1992. BB 4-50 La v Worcs (Worcester) 1987. **SL:** HS 84 La v Leics (Manchester) 1988. BB 4-37 La v Glam (Pontypridd) 1988 and Sm v Sussex (Hove) 1990.

SMITH, Trevor (Broxtowe C), b Derby 18 Jan 1977. LHB, RM.

DEPARTURES (who made first-class appearances in 1996)

BASE, Simon John (Fish Hoek HS, Cape Town), b Maidstone, Kent 2 Jan 1960. 6'2". RHB, RMF. W Province 1981-82 to 1983-84. Glamorgan 1986-87. Boland 1987-88 to 1988-89. Border 1989-90 to date. Derbyshire 1988-96; cap 1990. HS 58 v Yorks (Chesterfield) 1990. 50 wkts (1): 60 (1989). BB 7-60 v Yorks (Chesterfield) 1989. **NWT:** HS 4. BB 2-49 Gm v Sussex (Hove) 1986. **BHC:** HS 15* v Somerset (Taunton) 1990. BB 3-33 v Minor C (Wellington) 1990. **SL:** HS 31 v Kent (Canterbury) 1993. BB 4-14 v Northants (Derby) 1991 and v Glos (Cheltenham) 1993.

continued on p 106

DERBYSHIRE 1996

RESULTS SUMMARY

	Place	Won	Lost	Tied	Drew	No Result
Britannic Assurance Championship	2nd	9	3	–	5	–
All First-Class Matches		10	3	–	7	–
NatWest Trophy	Quarter-Finalist					
Benson and Hedges Cup	4th in Group A					
Sunday League	11th	7	7	1	–	2

BRITANNIC ASSURANCE CHAMPIONSHIP AVERAGES

BATTING AND FIELDING

Cap		M	I	NO	HS	Runs	Avge	100	50	Ct/St
1992	C.J.Adams	17	32	2	239	1590	53.00	6	6	30
1996	D.M.Jones	17	32	5	214*	1338	49.55	4	5	13
1982	K.J.Barnett	17	33	2	200*	1436	46.32	3	9	4
1993	D.G.Cork	11	19	4	97	583	38.86	–	5	7
1992	K.M.Krikken	17	27	7	104	776	38.80	1	2	60/3
–	J.E.H.Owen	7	12	–	105	434	36.16	2	2	3
1995	C.M.Wells	10	17	2	165	512	34.13	1	2	4
1995	A.S.Rollins	16	31	4	131	905	33.51	2	4	9
1992	T.J.G.O'Gorman	10	18	2	109*	515	32.18	1	4	7
1994	P.A.J.DeFreitas	13	21	–	60	356	16.95	–	1	8
–	P.Aldred	4	5	2	33	50	16.66	–	–	2
–	M.J.Vandrau	8	15	5	29	141	14.10	–	–	4
1996	A.J.Harris	11	15	3	17	102	8.50	–	–	3
–	T.A.Tweats	2	4	–	26	33	8.25	–	–	4
1989	D.E.Malcolm	16	21	5	21	98	6.12	–	–	1
–	K.J.Dean	6	7	1	12	29	4.83	–	–	1
–	G.A.Khan	2	4	–	4	10	2.50	–	–	4

Also batted (1 match each): S.J.Base (cap 1990) 1; M.R.May 16; G.M.Roberts 52 (1 ct).

BOWLING

	O	M	R	W	Avge	Best	5wI	10wM
K.J.Dean	85.1	23	264	11	24.00	3- 47	–	–
P.A.J.DeFreitas	522.2	103	1610	62	25.96	7-101	4	–
A.J.Harris	351.1	69	1282	48	26.70	6- 40	2	1
D.G.Cork	323.2	70	1039	35	29.68	4- 53	–	–
D.E.Malcolm	586.1	86	2407	73	32.97	6- 52	6	2
K.J.Barnett	126.2	11	458	10	45.80	3- 26	–	–
M.J.Vandrau	162	23	546	10	54.60	6- 34	1	–

Also bowled: C.J.Adams 10-1-32-0; P.Aldred 97.5-17-388-6; S.J.Base 23.2-4-105-1; D.M.Jones 76.4-11-313-9; G.M.Roberts 36-18-73-1; A.S.Rollins 2-0-25-0; C.M.Wells 154-37-411-9.

The First-Class Averages (pp 123-38) give the records of Derbyshire players in all first-class county matches (their other opponents being the Indians, South Africa A and Cambridge University), with the exception of:
   D.G.Cork 12-20-5-101*-684-45.60-1-5-7ct. 337.2-72-1088-35-31.08-4/53.
   G.A.Khan 3-6-0-15-35-5.83-0-0-4ct. 2-0-20-0.

DERBYSHIRE RECORDS

FIRST-CLASS CRICKET

Highest Total	For 645		v	Hampshire	Derby	1898
	V 662		by	Yorkshire	Chesterfield	1898
Lowest Total	For 16		v	Notts	Nottingham	1879
	V 23		by	Hampshire	Burton upon T	1958
Highest Innings	For 274	G.A.Davidson	v	Lancashire	Manchester	1896
	V 343*	P.A.Perrin	for	Essex	Chesterfield	1904

Highest Partnership for each Wicket

1st	322	H.Storer/J.Bowden	v	Essex	Derby	1929
2nd	349	C.S.Elliott/J.D.Eggar	v	Notts	Nottingham	1947
3rd	291	P.N.Kirsten/D.S.Steele	v	Somerset	Taunton	1981
4th	328	P.Vaulkhard/D.Smith	v	Notts	Nottingham	1946
5th	302*†	J.E.Morris/D.G.Cork	v	Glos	Cheltenham	1993
6th	212	G.M.Lee/T.S.Worthington	v	Essex	Chesterfield	1932
7th	241*	G.H.Pope/A.E.G.Rhodes	v	Hampshire	Portsmouth	1948
8th	198	K.M.Krikken/D.G.Cork	v	Lancashire	Manchester	1996
9th	283	A.Warren/J.Chapman	v	Warwicks	Blackwell	1910
10th	132	A.Hill/M.Jean-Jacques	v	Yorkshire	Sheffield	1986

† 346 runs were added for this wicket in two separate partnerships.

Best Bowling	For 10- 40	W.Bestwick	v	Glamorgan	Cardiff	1921
(Innings)	V 10- 45	R.L.Johnson	for	Middlesex	Derby	1994
Best Bowling	For 17-103	W.Mycroft	v	Hampshire	Southampton	1876
(Match)	V 16-101	G.Giffen	for	Australians	Derby	1886

Most Runs – Season	2165	D.B.Carr	(av 48.11)	1959
Most Runs – Career	21570	K.J.Barnett	(av 40.46)	1979-96
Most 100s – Season	8	P.N.Kirsten		1982
Most 100s – Career	49	K.J.Barnett		1979-96
Most Wkts – Season	168	T.B.Mitchell	(av 19.55)	1935
Most Wkts – Career	1670	H.L.Jackson	(av 17.11)	1947-63

LIMITED-OVERS CRICKET

Highest Total	NWT	365-3		v	Cornwall	Derby	1986
	BHC	366-4		v	Comb Us	Oxford	1991
	SL	292-9		v	Worcs	Knypersley	1985
Lowest Total	NWT	79		v	Surrey	The Oval	1967
	BHC	98		v	Worcs	Derby	1994
	SL	61		v	Hampshire	Portsmouth	1990
Highest Innings	NWT	153	A.Hill	v	Cornwall	Derby	1986
	BHC	142	D.M.Jones	v	Minor C	Derby	1996
	SL	141*	C.J.Adams	v	Kent	Chesterfield	1992
Best Bowling	NWT	8-21	M.A.Holding	v	Sussex	Hove	1988
	BHC	6-33	E.J.Barlow	v	Glos	Bristol	1978
	SL	6- 7	M.Hendrick	v	Notts	Nottingham	1972

DURHAM

Formation of Present Club: 10 May 1882
Colours: Navy blue, yellow and maroon
Badge: Coat of Arms of the County of Durham
Championships: (0) 16th 1994
NatWest Trophy/Gillette Cup Winners: (0) Quarter-Finalist 1992
Benson and Hedges Cup Winners: (0) Second Round 1994
Sunday League Champions: (0) Seventh 1993
Match Awards: NWT 19; BHC 8.

Chief Executive: M.Candlish
County Ground, Riverside, Chester-le-Street, Co Durham DH3 3QR.
(Tel 0191 387 1717)
Captain/Overseas Player: D.C.Boon. **1997 Beneficiary:** None. **Scorer:** B.Hunt

BETTS, Melvyn Morris (Fyndoune CS, Sacriston), b Sacriston 26 Mar 1975. 5'10". RHB, RMF. Debut 1993; cap 1994. HS 57* v Sussex (Hove) 1996. BB 5-68 v Glos (Chester-le-St) 1996. **NWT:** HS 11 v Essex (Chelmsford) 1996. BB 3-33 v Scot (Chester-le-St) 1996. **BHC:** HS – . BB 2-36 v Minor C (Chester-le-St) 1996. **SL:** HS 14* v Lancs (Manchester) and v Derbys (Chester-le-St) 1996. BB 3-26 v Yorks (Chester-le-St) 1996.

BLENKIRON, Darren Andrew (Bishop Barrington CS, Bishop Auckland), b Solihull, Warwks 4 Feb 1974. Son of W. (Warwks 1964-74, Durham 1975-76). 5'10". LHB, RM. Staff/cap 1992; debut 1994. HS 45 v Glam (Swansea) 1995. BB 4-43 v Glam (Chester-le-St) 1996. **NWT:** HS 56 v Glam (Darlington) 1991. **SL:** HS 56 v Somerset (Chester-le-St) 1995. BB 1-25.

BOILING, James (Rutlish S, Merton; Durham U), b New Delhi, India 8 Apr 1968. 6'4". RHB, OB. Surrey 1988-94. Durham debut/cap 1995. Tour: A 1992-93 (Eng A). HS 69 v WI (Chester-le-St) 1995. BAC HS 34* Sy v Durham (Darlington) 1994. BB 6-84 (10-203 match) Sy v Glos (Bristol) 1992. Du BB 5-73 v Notts (Chester-le-St) 1995. Award: BHC 1. **NWT:** HS 46* v Essex (Chelmsford) 1996. BB 4-22 v Herefords (Chester-le-St) 1996. **BHC:** HS 15 v Derbys (Chesterfield) 1996. BB 3-9 Comb Us v Surrey (Cambridge) 1989. **SL:** HS 27 v Warwks (Birmingham) 1996. BB 5-24 Sy v Hants (Basingstoke) 1992.

BROWN, Simon John Emmerson (Boldon CS), b Cleadon 29 Jun 1969, 6'3". RHB, LFM. Northamptonshire 1987-90. Durham debut/cap 1992; captain 1996 (part). **Tests:** 1 (1996); HS 10* and BB 1-60 v P (Lord's) 1996. HS 69 v Leics (Durham) 1994. 50 wkts (4); most – 79 (1996). BB 7-70 v A (Durham) 1993. BAC BB 7-105 v Kent (Canterbury) 1992. Award: NWT 1. **NWT:** HS 7*. BB 5-22 v Cheshire (Bowdon) 1994. **BHC:** HS 12 v Warwks (Birmingham) 1996. BB 3-39 v Notts (Stockton) 1995. **SL:** HS 18 v Derbys (Derby) 1996. BB 4-20 v Yorks (Leeds) 1995.

CAMPBELL, Colin Lockey (Blaydon CS & SFC), b Newcastle-upon-Tyne, Northumb 11 Aug 1977. 6'6". RHB, RFM. Debut/cap 1996. HS 1. BB 1-29. **SL:** HS 0. BB 2-45 v Glos (Chester-le-St) 1996.

COLLINGWOOD, Paul David (Blackfyne CS; Derwentside C), b Shotley Bridge 26 May 1976. 5'11". RHB, RMF. Debut 1996 v Northants (Chester-le-St) taking wicket of D.J.Capel with his first ball before scoring 91 and 16. Cap 1996. HS 91 and BB 1-13 v Northants (Chester-le-St) 1996 (on debut). **NWT:** HS 28 v Essex (Chelmsford) 1996. **BHC:** HS 17 v Lancs (Manchester) 1996. BB 3-38 v Minor C (Chester-le-St) 1996. **SL:** HS 61* v Kent (Maidstone) 1996. BB 1-37.

COX, David Mathew (Greenford HS), b Southall, Middx 2 Mar 1972. 5'10". LHB, SLA. Staff/cap 1993; debut 1994. Hertfordshire 1992. MCC YC. HS 95* v Somerset (Weston-s-M) 1996. BB 5-97 (10-236 match) v Warwks (Birmingham) 1995. **SL:** HS 7. BB 2-34 v Essex (Hartlepool) 1996.

DALEY, James Arthur (Hetton CS), b Sunderland 24 Sep 1973. 5'10". RHB, RM. Debut/cap 1992. MCC YC. HS 159* v Hants (Portsmouth) 1994. **BHC:** HS 33 v Lancs (Manchester) 1996. **SL:** HS 98* v Kent (Canterbury) 1994.

FOSTER, Michael James (New C, Pontefract), b Leeds, Yorks 17 Sep 1972. 6'1". RHB, RFM. Yorkshire 1993-94. Northamptonshire staff 1995. Durham debut/cap 1996. HS 63* Y v OU (Oxford) 1994. BAC HS 49 Y v Durham (Durham) 1994. Du HS 25 v Yorks (Chester-le-St) 1996. BB 4-21 v Middx (Lord's) 1996. **BHC:** HS 52 v Lancs (Manchester) 1996. BB 2-52 v Derbys (Chesterfield) 1996. **SL:** HS 118 Y v Leics (Leicester) 1993. BB 2-30 Nh v Durham (Northampton) 1995.

HARMISON, Stephen James (Ashington HS), b Ashington, Northumb 23 Oct 1978. 6'3". RHB, RFM. Debut 1996; uncapped (not on staff). Northumberland 1996. HS 6.

HUTTON, Stewart (De Brus S, Skelton; Cleveland TC), b Stockton-on-Tees 30 Nov 1969. 6'0". LHB, RSM. Debut/cap 1992. HS 172* v OU (Oxford) 1996. BAC HS 101 v Northants (Hartlepool) 1994. Award: NWT 1. **NWT:** HS 125 v Herefords (Chester-le-St) 1995. **BHC:** HS 36 v Derbys (Chesterfield) 1996. **SL:** HS 81 v Leics (Chester-le-St) 1996.

KILLEEN, Neil (Greencroft CS; Derwentside C; Teesside U), b Shotley Bridge 17 Oct 1975. 6'2". RHB, RFM. Debut/cap 1995. HS 48 v Somerset (Chester-le-St) 1995. BB 5-118 v Sussex (Hartlepool) 1995. **NWT:** HS – . BB 1-46. **BHC:** HS 8 and BB 2-43 Comb Us v H (Oxford) 1995. HS 32 v Middx (Lord's) 1996. BB 5-26 v Northants (Northampton) 1995.

LIGERTWOOD, David George Coutts (St Peter's C, Adelaide; Adelaide U), b Oxford 16 May 1969. 5'8". RHB, WK. Surrey 1992. Durham debut/cap 1995. Hertfordshire 1990-91. HS 56 v Surrey (Stockton) 1996. **NWT:** HS 30 v Scot (Chester-le-St) 1996. **BHC:** HS – . **SL:** HS 54 v Leics (Chester-le-St) 1996.

LUGSDEN, Steven (St Edmund Campion S, Low Fell), b Gateshead 10 Jul 1976. 6'2". RHB, RFM. Debut 1993 aged 17yr 27d (youngest Durham f-c player); cap 1994. HS 9. BB 3-45 v Lancs (Chester-le-St) 1996. **SL:** BB 1-55.

MORRIS, John Edward (Shavington CS; Dane Bank CFE), b Crewe, Cheshire 1 Apr 1964. 5'10". RHB, RM. Derbyshire 1982-93; cap 1986. GW 1988-89 and 1993-94. Durham debut/cap 1994. **Tests:** 3 (1990); HS 32 v I (Oval) 1990. **LOI:** 8 (1990-91; HS 63*). Tour: A 1990-91. 1000 runs (10); most – 1739 (1986). HS 229 De v Glos (Cheltenham) 1993. Du HS 204 v Warwks (Birmingham) 1994. BB 1-6. Du BB 1-37. Awards: NWT 2; BHC 2. **NWT:** HS 109 v Scot (Chester-le-St) 1996. **BHC:** HS 145 v Leics (Leicester) 1996. **SL:** HS 134 De v Somerset (Taunton) 1990.

PRATT, Andrew (Willington Parkside CS; Durham New C), Helmington Row, Crook 4 Mar 1975. 6'0". LHB, WK. Staff/cap 1996 – awaiting f-c debut. MCC YC.

ROSEBERRY, Michael Anthony (Durham S), b Sunderland 28 Nov 1966. Elder brother of A. (Leics and Glam 1992-94). 6'1". RHB, RM. Middlesex 1986-94; cap 1990. Durham debut/cap 1995; captain 1995-96. Tour: A 1992-93 (Eng A). 1000 runs (4) inc 2000 (1): 2044 (1992). HS 185 M v Leics (Lord's) 1993. Du HS 145* v OU (Oxford) 1996. BB 1-1. Awards: NWT 1; BHC 1. **NWT:** HS 121 v Herefords (Chester-le-St) 1995. BB 1-22. **BHC:** HS 84 M v Minor C (Lord's) 1992. **SL:** HS 119* M v Surrey (Oval) 1994.

SAGGERS, Martin John (Springwood HS, King's Lynn; Huddersfield U), b King's Lynn, Norfolk 23 May 1972. 6'2". RHB, RMF. Debut/cap 1996. Norfolk 1995-96. HS 18 v Somerset (Weston-s-M) 1996. BB 6-65 v Glam (Chester-le-St) 1996. Award: BHC 1. **BHC:** (Minor C) HS 34* v Leics (Jesmond) 1996. BB 2-49 v Durham (Chester-le-St) 1996. **SL:** HS 13 and BB 2-24 v Warwks (Birmingham) 1996.

SEARLE, Jason Paul (John Bentley S, Calne; Swindon C), b Bath, Somerset 16 May 1976. 5'9". RHB, OB. Staff/cap 1993; debut 1994. HS 5*. BB 2-126 v Surrey (Oval) 1995. **BHC:** HS – . **SL:** HS – .

WALKER, Alan (Shelley HS), b Emley, Yorks 7 Jul 1962. 5'11". LHB, RFM. Northamptonshire 1983-93; cap 1987. Durham debut/cap 1994. Tour: SA 1991-92 (Nh). HS 41* Nh v Warwks (Birmingham) 1987. Du HS 29 v WI (Chester-le-St) 1995. 50 wkts (1): 54 (1988). BB 8-118 (14-177 match) v Essex (Chelmsford) 1995. Award: NWT 1. **NWT:** HS 13 v Derbys (Darlington) 1994. BB 4-7 Nh v Ire (Northampton) 1987. **BHC:** HS 15* Nh v Notts (Nottingham) 1987. BB 4-42 v Minor C (Jesmond) 1995. **SL:** HS 30 Nh v Durham (Northampton) 1993. BB 4-21 Nh v Worcs (Worcester) 1985.

WESTON, Robin Michael Swann (Durham S; Loughborough U), b Durham 7 Jun 1975. Brother of W.P.C. (*see WORCESTERSHIRE*). 5'10". RHB, LB. Staff/cap 1994; debut 1995. Minor C debut 1991 when aged 15yr 355d (Durham record). HS 15 v P (Chester-le-St) 1996. BAC HS 9. BB 1-41. **SL:** HS 13 v Warwks (Birmingham) 1996.

WOOD, John (Crofton HS; Wakefield District C; Leeds Poly), b Crofton, Yorks 22 Jul 1970. 6'3". RHB, RFM. GW in Nissan Shield 1990-91. Debut/cap 1992. HS 63* v Notts (Chester-le-St) 1993. BB 6-110 v Essex (Stockton) 1994. **NWT:** HS 1. BB 2-22 v Ireland (Dublin) 1992. **BHC:** HS 27 v Leics (Stockton) 1995. BB 3-50 v Warwicks (Birmingham) 1995. **SL:** HS 28 and BB 2-26 v Worcs (Worcester) 1994.

NEWCOMERS

BOON, David Clarence (Launceston GS), b Launceston, Australia 29 Dec 1960. 5'7½". RHB, OB. Tasmania 1978-79 to date; captain 1992-93 to date. Joins Durham 1997 as captain. MBE. **Tests** (A): 107, inc 60 in succession (1984-85 to 1995-96); HS 200 v NZ (Perth) 1989-90. **LOI** (A): 181 (1983-84 to 1994-95; HS 122). Tours: E 1985, 1989, 1993; SA 1993-94; WI 1990-91, 1994-95; NZ 1985-86, 1989-90, 1992-93; I 1986-87; P 1988-89, 1994-95; SL 1992-93; Z 1995-96 (Tas – captain). 1000 runs (2+7); most – 1437 (1993). HS 227 Tasmania v Victoria (Melbourne) 1983-84. BB 1-0.

LEWIS, Jonathan James Benjamin (King Edward VI S, Chelmsford; Roehampton IHE), b Isleworth, Middx 21 May 1970. 5'9½". RHB, RSM. Essex 1990-96; cap 1994; scored 116* on debut v Surrey (Oval). HS 136* Ex v Notts (Nottingham) 1993. **NWT:** HS 24* Ex v Sussex (Hove) 1994. **BHC:** HS 19 Ex v Glos (Chelmsford) 1995. **SL:** HS 53* Ex v Leics (Leicester) 1996.

SPEAK, Nicholas Jason (Parrs Wood HS, Manchester), b Manchester 21 Nov 1966. 6'0". RHB, RM/OB. Lancashire 1986-87 to 1996; cap 1992. Tours (La): WI 1986-87, 1995-96. 1000 runs (3); most – 1892 (1992). HS 232 La v Leics (Leicester) 1992. BB 1-0. Award: BHC 1. **NWT:** HS 83 La v Oxon (Aston Rowant) 1996. **BHC:** HS 82 La v Hants (Manchester) 1992. **SL:** HS 102* La v Leics (Leicester) 1992.

SPEIGHT, Martin Peter (Hurstpierpoint C; Durham U), b Walsall, Staffs 24 Oct 1967. 5'9". RHB, WK. Sussex 1986-96; cap 1991. Wellington 1989-90 to 1992-93. 1000 runs (3); most – 1375 (1990). HS 184 Sx v Notts (Eastbourne) 1993. BB 1-2. Awards: BHC 2. **NWT:** HS 50 Sx v Warwks (Lord's) 1993. **BHC:** HS 83 Comb Us v Glos (Bristol) 1988. **SL:** HS 126 Sx v Somerset (Taunton) 1993.

DEPARTURES (who made first-class appearances in 1996)

BAINBRIDGE, Philip (Hanley HS; Stoke-on-Trent SFC; Borough Road CE), b Sneyd Green, Stoke-on-Trent, Staffs 16 Apr 1958. 5'10". RHB, RM. Gloucestershire 1977-90; cap 1981; benefit 1989. Durham 1992-96; cap 1992; captain 1994; testimonial 1996. *Wisden* 1985. Tours: SL 1986-87 (Gs); Z 1984-85 (EC). 1000 runs (9); most – 1644 (1985). HS 169 Gs v Yorks (Cheltenham) 1988. Du HS 150* v Essex (Chelmsford) 1993. BB 8-53 Gs v Somerset (Bristol) 1986. Du BB 5-53 v Yorks (Leeds) 1993. Awards: NWT 1; BHC 3. **NWT:** HS 89 Gs v Leics (Leicester) 1988. BB 3-49 Gs v Scot (Bristol) 1983. **BHC:** HS 96 Gs v Hants (Southampton) 1989. BB 4-38 v Worcs (Worcester) 1992. **SL:** HS 106* Gs v Somerset (Bristol) 1986. BB 3-49 Gs v Middx (Lord's) 1987.

BIRBECK, Shaun David (Hetton CS), b Easington Lane 26 Jul 1972. Brother of A. (Durham 1983-90). 5'11". LHB, RM. Durham 1994-96; cap 1994. HS 75* v Derbys (Chester-le-St) 1996. BB 3-88 v Sussex (Hove) 1996. **NWT:** HS – . BB 2-27 v Herefords (Chester-le-St) 1995. **BHC:** HS 5. BB 3-64 v Minor C (Jesmond) 1995. **SL:** HS 24 v Notts (Nottingham) 1996. BB 1-14.

continued on p 106

DURHAM 1996

RESULTS SUMMARY

	Place	Won	Lost	Drew	No Result
Britannic Assurance Championship	18th	–	12	5	–
All First-Class Matches		–	13	6	–
NatWest Trophy	2nd Round				
Benson and Hedges Cup	5th in Group A				
Sunday League	18th	1	15	–	1

BRITANNIC ASSURANCE CHAMPIONSHIP AVERAGES
BATTING AND FIELDING

Cap		M	I	NO	HS	Runs	Avge	100	50	Ct/St
1993	D.M.Cox	7	13	4	95*	434	48.22	–	4	2
1996	S.L.Campbell	15	27	–	118	1019	37.74	1	7	15
1992	P.Bainbridge	11	19	1	83	617	34.27	–	5	10
1992	S.Hutton	12	23	1	143*	599	27.22	1	1	5
1992	J.A.Daley	9	17	2	36	357	23.80	–	–	6
1992	D.A.Blenkiron	9	16	2	130	328	23.42	1	–	4
1996	P.D.Collingwood	11	20	–	91	464	23.20	–	2	6
1992	C.W.Scott	6	10	1	59	208	23.11	–	2	19
1995	D.G.C.Ligertwood	11	21	5	56	324	20.25	–	1	26/5
1994	M.M.Betts	13	21	3	57*	308	17.11	–	1	4
1995	M.A.Roseberry	15	27	–	60	458	16.96	–	2	6
1992	S.J.E.Brown	16	27	4	60	389	16.91	–	1	3
1994	J.E.Morris	15	28	–	83	410	14.64	–	3	6
1996	M.J.Saggers	4	7	1	18	69	11.50	–	–	–
1995	J.Boiling	7	11	4	31*	79	11.28	–	–	8
1996	M.J.Foster	3	6	–	25	67	11.16	–	–	–
1994	A.Walker	3	6	3	20	25	8.33	–	–	–
1992	J.Wood	8	14	2	35*	76	6.33	–	–	4
1994	S.Lugsden	3	5	1	9	19	4.75	–	–	1
1995	N.Killeen	3	6	2	3	4	4.60	–	–	1

Also batted (1 match each): S.D.Birbeck (cap 1994) 0, 8; C.L.Campbell (cap 1996) 7; S.J.Harmison 6, 4; J.I.Longley (cap 1994) 2, 4; (2 matches – cap 1994) R.M.S.Weston 3, 9, 2 (1 ct). *Note: Durham award caps on signature of contract and not on merit.*

BOWLING

	O	M	R	W	Avge	Best	5wI	10wM
S.Lugsden	70.3	9	262	11	23.81	3-45	–	–
S.J.E.Brown	567.1	98	1859	69	26.94	6-77	4	–
N.Killeen	83.2	18	293	10	29.30	4-57	–	–
D.M.Cox	306	87	883	26	33.96	5-97	2	1
M.J.Saggers	87.5	9	232	10	37.20	6-65	1	–
M.M.Betts	375.5	48	1708	44	38.81	5-68	2	–
J.Wood	263.3	41	1112	24	46.33	4-60	–	–

Also bowled: P.Bainbridge 123.3-23-382-7; S.D.Birbeck 31-9-88-3; D.A.Blenkiron 37.5-9-123-5; J.Boiling 237.1-77-532-8; C.L.Campbell 15.2-3-44-1; S.L.Campbell 16.4-3-60-1; P.D.Collingwood 55.2-7-181-3; M.J.Foster 93.3-15-311-8; S.J.Harmison 9-1-77-0; J.E.Morris 1-0-10-0; A.Walker 80-13-277-2; R.M.S.Weston 1-1-0-0.

The First-Class Averages (pp 123-38) give the records of Durham players in all first-class county matches (their other opponents being the Pakistanis and Oxford University), with the exception of:

S.J.E.Brown 18-29-4-60-393-15.72-0-1-4ct. 609.1-105-1992-77-25.87-6/77-5-0.
J.A.Daley 11-20-3-36-401-23.58-0-0-7ct. Did not bowl.

DURHAM RECORDS

FIRST-CLASS CRICKET

Highest Total	For	625-6d		v	Derbyshire	Chesterfield	1994
	V	810-4d		by	Warwicks	Birmingham	1994
Lowest Total	For	67		v	Middlesex	Lord's	1996
	V	73		by	Oxford U	Oxford	1994
Highest Innings	For	204	J.E.Morris	v	Warwicks	Birmingham	1994
	V	501*	B.C.Lara	for	Warwicks	Birmingham	1994

Highest Partnership for each Wicket

1st	334*	S.Hutton/M.A.Roseberry	v	Oxford U	Oxford	1996
2nd	206	W.Larkins/D.M.Jones	v	Glamorgan	Cardiff	1992
3rd	205	G.Fowler/S.Hutton	v	Yorkshire	Leeds	1993
4th	201	W.Larkins/J.A.Daley	v	Somerset	Taunton	1992
5th	185	P.W.G.Parker/J.A.Daley	v	Warwicks	Darlington	1993
6th	152	I.T.Botham/A.C.Cummins	v	Worcs	Stockton	1993
7th	106	I.Smith/D.A.Graveney	v	Somerset	Taunton	1992
8th	134	A.C.Cummins/D.A.Graveney	v	Warwicks	Birmingham	1994
9th	127	D.G.C.Ligertwood/S.J.E.Brown	v	Surrey	Stockton	1996
10th	103	M.M.Betts/D.M.Cox	v	Sussex	Hove	1996

Best Bowling	For	8-118	A.Walker	v	Essex	Chelmsford	1995
(Innings)	V	8- 22	D.Follet	for	Middlesex	Lord's	1996
Best Bowling	For	14-177	A.Walker	v	Essex	Chelmsford	1995
(Match)	V	12- 68	J.N.B.Bovill	for	Hampshire	Stockton	1995

Most Runs – Season	1536	W.Larkins	(av 37.46)	1992
Most Runs – Career	4278	W.Larkins	(av 37.52)	1992-95
Most 100s – Season	4	D.M.Jones		1992
	4	W.Larkins		1992
	4	J.E.Morris		1994
Most 100s – Career	10	W.Larkins		1992-95
Most Wkts – Season	77	S.J.E.Brown	(av 25.87)	1996
Most Wkts – Career	313	S.J.E.Brown	(av 31.37)	1992-96

LIMITED-OVERS CRICKET

Highest Total	NWT	326-4		v	Herefords	Chester-le-St[2]	1995
	BHC	271-6		v	Comb Us	Cambridge	1992
	SL	281-2		v	Derbyshire	Durham	1993
Lowest Total	NWT	82		v	Worcs	Chester-le-St[1]	1968
	BHC	162		v	Derbyshire	Chesterfield	1996
	SL	99		v	Warwicks	Birmingham	1994
Highest Innings	NWT	125	S.Hutton	v	Herefords	Chester-le-St[2]	1995
	BHC	145	J.E.Morris	v	Leics	Leicester	1996
	SL	131*	W.Larkins	v	Hampshire	Portsmouth	1994
Best Bowling	NWT	7-32	S.P.Davis	v	Lancashire	Chester-le-St[1]	1983
	BHC	4-38	P.Bainbridge	v	Worcs	Worcester	1992
	SL	5-26	N.Killeen	v	Northants	Northampton	1995

[1] Chester-le-Street CC (Ropery Lane)   [2] Riverside Ground

ESSEX

Formation of Present Club: 14 January 1876
Colours: Blue, Gold and Red
Badge: Three Seaxes above Scroll bearing 'Essex'
Championships: (6) 1979, 1983, 1984, 1986, 1991, 1992
NatWest Trophy/Gillette Cup Winners: (1) 1985
Benson and Hedges Cup Winners: (1) 1979
Sunday League Champions: (3) 1981, 1984, 1985
Match Awards: NWT 41; BHC 76

Secretary/General Manager: P.J.Edwards
County Ground, New Writtle Street, Chelmsford CM2 0PG (Tel 01245 252420)
Captain: P.J.Prichard. **Vice-Captain:** N.Hussain. **Overseas Player:** S.G.Law (*tbc*).
Beneficiary: A.W.Lilley. **Scorer:** C.F.Driver.

ANDREW, Stephen Jon Walter (Milton Abbey S; Portchester SS), b London 27 Jan 1966. 6'3". RHB, RMF. Hampshire 1984-89. Essex debut 1990. HS 35 v Northants (Chelmsford) 1990. BB 7-47 v Lancs (Manchester) 1993. Awards: BHC 2. **NWT:** HS 1*. BB 2-34 v Scot (Chelmsford) 1990. **BHC:** HS 4*. BB 5-24 H v Essex (Chelmsford) 1987. **SL:** HS 32 v Yorks (Leeds) 1996. BB 4-50 H v Middx (Southampton) 1988.

COUSINS, Darren Mark (Netherhall CS; Impington Village C), b Cambridge 24 Sep 1971. 6'2". RHB, RMF. Debut 1993. Cambridgeshire 1990. HS 18* v Durham (Chelmsford) 1995. BB 6-35 v CU (Cambridge) 1994. BAC BB 3-73 v Leics (Chelmsford) 1995. **NWT:** HS 1*. BB 1-33. **BHC:** HS 12* v Glam (Chelmsford) 1995. BB 1-33. **SL:** HS 6. BB 3-18 v Warwks (Birmingham) 1994.

COWAN, Ashley Preston (Framlingham C), b Hitchin, Herts 7 May 1975. 6'4". RHB, RFM. Debut 1995. Cambridgeshire 1993. HS 34 v Sussex (Chelmsford) 1996. BB 5-68 (inc hat-trick) v Glos (Colchester) 1996. Hat-trick 1996. **NWT:** HS 11 v Lancs (Lord's) 1996. BB 1-44. **BHC:** HS 1. BB 1-38. **SL:** HS 22* v Warwks (Birmingham) 1996. BB 2-17 v Hants (Southampton) 1996.

GOOCH, Graham Alan (Norlington Jr HS), b Leytonstone 23 Jul 1953. 6'0". RHB, RM. Debut 1973; cap 1975; captain 1986-87 and 1989-94; benefit 1985; testimonial 1995. W Province 1982-83 to 1983-84. *Wisden* 1979. OBE 1991. **Tests:** 118 (1975 to 1994-95, 34 as captain); HS 333 and record match aggregate of 456 v I (Lord's) 1990; BB 3-39 v P (Manchester) 1992. **LOI:** 125 (1976 to 1994-95, 50 as captain; HS 142; BB 3-19). Tours (C=captain): A 1978-79, 1979-80, 1990-91C, 1994-95; SA 1981-82 (SAB); WI 1980-81, 1985-86, 1989-90C; NZ 1991-92C; I 1979-80, 1981-82, 1992-93C; P 1987-88; SL 1981-82. 1000 runs (20+1) inc 2000 (5); most − 2746 (1990). HS 333 (*Tests*). Ex HS 275 v Kent (Chelmsford) 1988. BB 7-14 v Worcs (Ilford) 1982. Awards: NWT 9 (record); BHC 22 (record). **NWT:** HS 144 v Hants (Chelmsford) 1990. BB 5-8 v Cheshire (Chester) 1996. **BHC:** HS 198* v Sussex (Hove) 1982. BB 3-24 v Sussex (Hove) 1982. **SL:** HS 176 v Glam (Chelmsford) 1983. BB 4-33 v Worcs (Southend) 1984.

GOODWIN, Giles Jeremy Anthony (Felsted S; UMIST), b Isle of Sheppey, Kent 16 Sep 1976. 6'3". RHB, SLA. Staff 1996 – awaiting f-c debut.

GRAYSON, Adrian Paul (Bedale CS), b Ripon, Yorks 31 Mar 1971. 6'1". RHB, SLA. Yorkshire 1990-95. Essex debut/cap 1996. Tour: SA 1991-92 (Y). 1000 runs (1): 1046 (1994). HS 140 v Middx (Lord's) 1996. BB 4-82 v Hants (Southampton) 1996. **NWT:** HS 29 Y v Deven (Exmouth) 1994. BB 3-24 v Lancs (Lord's) 1996. **BHC:** HS 22* Y v Hants (Southampton) 1994. BB 3-30 v Kent (Chelmsford) 1996. **SL:** HS 55 Y v Kent (Maidstone) 1994. BB 4-25 Y v Glam (Cardiff) 1994.

GROVE, Jamie Oliver, b Bury St Edmunds, Suffolk 3 Jul 1979. 6'1". RHB, RFM. Staff 1996 – awaiting f-c debut.

HIBBERT, Andrew James Edward (St Edward's CS and SFC, Romford), b Harold Wood 17 Dec 1974. 5'11½. RHB, RM. Debut 1995. Awaiting BAC debut. HS 85 v CU (Cambridge) 1996. **SL:** HS 25 v Glos (Colchester) 1996.

HODGSON, Timothy Philip (Wellington C; Durham U), b Guildford, Surrey 27 Mar 1975. Brother of J.S. (Cambridge U 1994); great-nephew of N.A.Knox (Surrey and England 1904-10). 5'10". LHB, RM. Staff 1996 – awaiting f-c debut. **SL:** HS 21 v Glos (Colchester) 1996.

HUSSAIN, Nasser (Forest S, Snaresbrook; Durham U), b Madras, India 28 Mar 1968. Son of J. (Madras 1966-67); brother of M. (Worcs 1985). 5'11". RHB, LB. Debut 1987; cap 1989. YC 1989. **Tests:** 17 (1989-90 to 1996-97); HS 128 v I (Birmingham) 1996. **LOI:** 12 (1989-90 to 1996-97, 1 as captain; HS 49*). Tours: WI 1989-90, 1991-92 (Eng A), 1993-94; NZ 1996-97; P 1990-91 (Eng A), 1995-96 (Eng A – captain); SL 1990-91 (Eng A); Z 1996-97. 1000 runs (4); most – 1854 (1995). HS 197 v Surrey (Oval) 1990. BB 1-38. Awards: NWT 2; BHC 2. **NWT:** HS 108 v Cumberland (Chelmsford) 1992. **BHC:** HS 118 Comb Us v Somerset (Taunton) 1989. **SL:** HS 83 v Kent (Canterbury) 1995.

HYAM, Barry James (Havering SFC), b Romford 9 Sep 1975. RHB, WK. Debut 1993. MCC YC. HS 49 v P (Chelmsford) 1996. BAC HS 1. **SL:** HS 0.

ILOTT, Mark Christopher (Francis Combe S, Garston), b Watford, Herts 27 Aug 1970. 6'0½". LHB, LFM. Debut 1988; cap 1993. Hertfordshire 1987-88 (at 16, the youngest to represent that county). **Tests:** 5 (1993 to 1995-96); HS 15 v A (Oval) 1993; BB 3-48 v SA (Durban) 1995-96. Tours: A 1992-93 (Eng A); SA 1993-94 (Eng A), 1995-96; I 1994-95 (Eng A – captain); SL 1990-91 (Eng A). HS 60 Eng A v Warwks (Birmingham) 1995. Ex HS 58 v Worcs (Worcester) 1996. 50 wkts (5); most – 78 (1995). BB 9-19 (14-105 match; inc hat-trick – all lbw) v Northants (Luton) 1995. Hat-trick 1995. Award: BHC 1. **NWT:** HS 54* v Cheshire (Chester) 1995. BB 2-23 v Cumberland (Chelmsford) 1992. **BHC:** HS 21 v Glam (Chelmsford) 1995. BB 5-21 v Scot (Forfar) 1993. **SL:** HS 56* v Sussex (Hove) 1995. BB 4-15 v Derbys (Derby) 1992.

IRANI, Ronald Charles (Smithills CS, Bolton), b Leigh, Lancs 26 Oct 1971. 6'3". RHB, RMF. Lancashire 1990-93. Essex debut/cap 1994. **Tests:** 2 (1996); HS 41 v I (Lord's) 1996; BB 1-22. **LOI:** 10 (1996 to 1996-97; HS 45*; BB 1-23). Tours: NZ 1996-97; P 1995-96 (Eng A); Z 1996-97. 1000 runs (2); most – 1165 (1995). HS 119 v Worcs (Worcester) 1994. BB 5-19 Eng A v Comb XI (Karachi) 1995-96. Ex BB 5-27 v Notts (Chelmsford) 1996. Award: NWT 1; BHC 1. **NWT:** HS 124 v Durham (Chelmsford) 1996. BB 4-49 v Sussex (Hove) 1996. **BHC:** HS 62* and BB 4-30 v Brit Us (Chelmsford) 1996. **SL:** HS 101* v Glos (Cheltenham) 1995. BB 3-22 v Worcs (Worcester) 1994.

LAW, Stuart Grant (Craigslea State HS), b Herston, Brisbane, Australia 18 Oct 1968. 6'2". RHB, RM/LB. Queensland 1988-89 to date; captain 1994-95 to date. Essex debut/cap 1996. **Tests** (A): 1 (1995-96); HS 54* v SL (Perth) 1995-96. **LOI** (A): 37 (1994-95 to 1996-97; HS 110; BB 2-22). Tour (Young A): E 1995. 1000 runs (2); most – 1545 (1996). HS 179 Q v Tasmania (Brisbane) 1988-89. Ex HS 172 v Durham (Hartlepool) 1996. BB 5-39 Q v Tasmania (Brisbane) 1995-96. Ex BB 3-100 v Notts (Chelmsford) 1996. Awards: NWT 2; BHC 1. **NWT:** HS 107 v Hants (Southampton) 1996. BB 2-36 v Devon (Chelmsford) 1996. **BHC:** HS 116 v Somerset (Taunton) 1996. BB 2-57 v Somerset (Taunton) 1996. **SL:** HS 120 v Sussex (Chelmsford) 1996. BB 4-40 v Middx (Lord's) 1996.

PETERS, Stephen David (Coopers Coborn & Co S), b Harold Wood 10 Dec 1978. 5'9". RHB. Debut 1996 scoring 110 and 12* v CU (Cambridge). HS 110 (as above). BAC HS 11 v Yorks (Leeds) 1996. **SL:** HS 1.

POWELL, Jonathan Christopher (Chelmsford C), b Harold Wood 13 Jun 1979. 5'10". RHB, OB. Staff 1996 – awaiting f-c debut. **SL:** HS – and BB 2-62 v Sussex (Chelmsford) 1996.

PRICHARD, Paul John (Brentwood HS), b Billericay 7 Jan 1965. 5'10". RHB, RSM. Debut 1984; cap 1986; captain 1995 to date; benefit 1996. Tour: A 1992-93 (Eng A). 1000 runs (7); most – 1485 (1992). HS 245 v Leics (Chelmsford) 1990. BB 1-28. Awards: NWT 1; BHC 2. **NWT:** HS 94 v Oxon (Chelmsford) 1985. **BHC:** HS 107 v Scot (Glasgow) 1990. **SL:** HS 107 v Notts (Nottingham) 1993.

ROBINSON, Darren David John (Tabor HS, Braintree; Chelmsford CFE), b Braintree 2 Mar 1973. 5'10½". RHB, RMF. Debut 1993. HS 123 v Glos (Cheltenham) 1995. **NWT:** HS 55 v Yorks (Chelmsford) 1995. **BHC:** HS 36 v Glam (Cardiff) 1996. **SL:** HS 80 v Surrey (Southend) 1996.

ROLLINS, Robert John (Little Ilford CS), b Plaistow 30 Jan 1974. 5'9". RHB, RM, WK. Brother of A.S. (see DERBYSHIRE). Debut 1992; cap 1995. HS 133* v Glam (Swansea) 1995. **NWT:** HS 54* v Durham (Chelmsford) 1996. **BHC:** HS 3. **SL:** HS 32 v Leics (Leicester) 1996 and v Notts (Chelmsford) 1996.

SUCH, Peter Mark (Harry Carlton CS, Ex Leake, Notts), b Helensburgh, Dunbartonshire 12 Jun 1964. 5'11". RHB, OB. Nottinghamshire 1982-86. Leicestershire 1987-89. Essex debut 1990; cap 1991. **Tests:** 8 (1993 to 1994); HS 14* and BB 6-67 v A (Manchester) 1993 – on debut. Tours (Eng A): A 1992-93; SA 1993-94. HS 54 v Worcs (Chelmsford) 1993. 50 wkts (4); most – 82 (1996). BB 8-93 (11-160 match) v Hants (Colchester) 1995. **NWT:** HS 8*. BB 3-56 v Durham (Chelmsford) 1996. **BHC:** HS 10* v Glam (Cardiff) 1996. BB 4-43 v Northants (Northampton) 1994. **SL:** HS 19* v Notts (Ilford) 1994. BB 5-32 v Yorks (Chelmsford) 1993.

WILLIAMS, Neil FitzGerald (Acland Burghley CS), b Hope Well, St Vincent 2 Jul 1962. 5'11". RHB, RFM. Middlesex 1982-94; cap 1984; benefit 1994. Essex debut 1995; cap 1996. Windward Is 1982-83 and 1989-90 to 1991-92. Tasmania 1983-84. MCC YC. **Tests:** 1 (1990); HS 38 and BB 2-148 v I (Oval) 1990. Tour: Z 1984-85 (EC). HS 77 M v Warwks (Birmingham) 1991. Ex HS 39 v Worcs (Worcester) 1996. 50 wkts (3); most – 63 (1983). BB 8-75 (12-139 match) M v Glos (Lord's) 1992. Ex BB 5-43 v Glos (Colchester) 1996. Award: BHC 1. **NWT:** HS 11* v Lancs (Lord's) 1996. BB 4-36 M v Derbys (Derby) 1983. **BHC:** HS 29* M v Surrey (Lord's) 1985. BB 3-16 M v Comb Us (Cambridge) 1982. **SL:** HS 43 M v Somerset (Lord's) 1988. BB 4-39 M v Surrey (Oval) 1988.

WILSON, Daniel Graeme (St Mary's S, Bishop's Stortford; Cheltenham & Gloucester U), b Paddington, London 18 Feb 1977. 6'2". RHB, RM. Summer contract – awaiting f-c debut. Scored 52* and took 2-40 v SA A (limited-overs match) 1996. **SL:** HS 7. BB 3-40 v Sussex (Chelmsford) 1996.

NEWCOMERS

FLANAGAN, Ian Nicholas, b Colchester 5 Jun 1980. LHB, OB.

LAW, Danny Richard (Steyning GS), b Lambeth, London 15 Jul 1975. 6'5". RHB, RFM. Sussex 1993-96; cap 1996. HS 115 Sx v Young A (Hove) 1995. BAC HS 97 Sx v Glos (Bristol) 1996. BB 5-33 Sx v Durham (Hove) 1996. **NWT:** HS 18 and BB 1-2 Sx v Ire (Belfast) 1996. **BHC:** HS 8. BB 1-44. **SL:** HS 79* Sx v Kent (Tunbridge W) 1996. BB 3-34 Sx v Worcs (Worcester) 1996.

DEPARTURES (who made first-class appearances in 1996)

CHILDS, John Henry (Audley Park SM, Torquay), b Plymouth, Devon 15 Aug 1951. 6'0". LHB, SLA. Gloucestershire 1975-84; cap 1977. Essex 1985-96; cap 1986; benefit 1994. Devon 1973-74. Wisden 1986. **Tests:** 2 (1988); HS 2*; BB 1-13. HS 43 v Hants (Chelmsford) 1992. 50 wkts (9); most – 89 (1986). BB 9-56 Gs v Somerset (Bristol) 1981. Ex BB 8-58 v Glos (Colchester) 1988. Award: BHC 1. **NWT:** HS 14* Gs v Hants (Bristol) 1983. BB 2-15 Gs v Ire (Dublin) 1981. **BHC:** HS 10 Gs v Somerset (Bristol) 1979. BB 3-36 Gs v Glam (Bristol) 1982. **SL:** HS 16* Gs v Warwks (Bristol) 1981. BB 4-15 Gs v Northants (Northampton) 1976.

DERBYSHIRE, Nicholas Alexander (Ampleforth C; Goldsmith's C, London U), b Ramsbottom, Lancs 11 Sep 1970. 5'11½". RHB, RFM. Lancashire 1994. Essex 1995-96. HS 17 v Durham (Chelmsford) 1995. BB 1-18. BAC BB 1-20. **BHC:** HS –.

LEWIS, J.J. – see DURHAM.

28

ESSEX 1996

RESULTS SUMMARY

	Place	Won	Lost	Drew	No Result
Britannic Assurance Championship	**5th**	8	5	4	–
All First-Class Matches		9	6	5	–
NatWest Trophy	Finalist				
Benson and Hedges Cup	3rd in Group C				
Sunday League	**17th**	4	12	–	1

BRITANNIC ASSURANCE CHAMPIONSHIP AVERAGES

BATTING AND FIELDING

Cap		M	I	NO	HS	Runs	Avge	100	50	Ct/St
1975	G.A.Gooch	17	30	1	201	1944	67.03	8	6	18
1996	S.G.Law	14	24	1	172	1379	59.95	5	5	24
1989	N.Hussain	11	19	–	158	811	42.68	1	5	12
1994	R.C.Irani	14	23	3	110*	816	40.80	1	7	6
1994	J.J.B.Lewis	4	7	2	69	181	36.20	–	2	10
1996	A.P.Grayson	16	28	2	140	936	36.00	2	3	19
–	D.D.J.Robinson	9	17	2	75	515	34.33	–	5	3
1986	P.J.Prichard	17	28	–	108	877	31.32	1	5	11
1995	R.J.Rollins	17	28	3	74*	541	21.64	–	2	47/5
1993	M.C.Ilott	15	22	2	58	343	17.15	–	1	3
1996	N.F.Williams	12	16	3	39	221	17.00	–	–	2
1991	P.M.Such	16	20	10	54	168	16.80	–	1	8
–	A.P.Cowan	13	18	5	34	155	11.92	–	–	6
–	S.J.W.Andrew	7	11	5	13	53	8.83	–	–	2

Also batted: J.H.Childs (3 matches – cap 1986) 1*, 0*, 0; S.D.Peters (2 matches) 4, 0, 11 (2 ct).

BOWLING

	O	M	R	W	Avge	Best	5wI	10wM
P.M.Such	680	168	1914	70	27.34	8-118	5	1
N.F.Williams	331.4	59	1160	35	33.14	5- 43	2	–
R.C.Irani	308.2	57	1029	31	33.19	5- 27	1	–
M.C.Ilott	505.2	105	1526	45	33.91	5- 53	2	–
A.P.Cowan	348.2	56	1262	37	34.10	5- 68	1	–
S.J.W.Andrew	132.4	33	398	10	39.80	3- 67	–	–
A.P.Grayson	260.3	58	726	18	40.33	4- 82	–	–
S.G.Law	199.4	44	734	13	56.46	3-100	–	–

Also bowled: J.H.Childs 122.4-33-357-8; G.A.Gooch 21-7-57-2.

The First-Class Averages (pp 123-38) give the records of Essex players in all first-class county matches (their other opponents being the Indians, the Pakistanis and Cambridge University), with the exception of:

A.P.Cowan 14-19-6-34-177-13.61-0-0-6ct. 379.2-63-1364-37-36.86-5/68-1-0.
N.Hussain 12-21-0-158-903-43.00-1-6-12ct. Did not bowl.
R.C.Irani 16-27-4-110*-923-40.13-1-7-8ct. 348.1-62-1169-40-29.22-5/27-1-0.
R.J.Rollins 19-32-4-74*-688-24.57-0-3-50ct-6st. Did not bowl.

29

ESSEX RECORDS

FIRST-CLASS CRICKET

Highest Total	For	761-6d		v	Leics	Chelmsford	1990
	V	803-4d		by	Kent	Brentwood	1934
Lowest Total	For	30		v	Yorkshire	Leyton	1901
	V	14		by	Surrey	Chelmsford	1983
Highest Innings	For	343*	P.A.Perrin	v	Derbyshire	Chesterfield	1904
	V	332	W.H.Ashdown	for	Kent	Brentwood	1934

Highest Partnership for each Wicket

1st	316	G.A.Gooch/P.J.Prichard	v	Kent	Chelmsford	1994
2nd	403	G.A.Gooch/P.J.Prichard	v	Leics	Chelmsford	1990
3rd	347*	M.E.Waugh/N.Hussain	v	Lancashire	Ilford	1992
4th	314	Salim Malik/N.Hussain	v	Surrey	The Oval	1991
5th	316	N.Hussain/M.A.Garnham	v	Leics	Leicester	1991
6th	206	J.W.H.T.Douglas/J.O'Connor	v	Glos	Cheltenham	1923
	206	B.R.Knight/R.A.G.Luckin	v	Middlesex	Brentwood	1962
7th	261	J.W.H.T.Douglas/J.Freeman	v	Lancashire	Leyton	1914
8th	263	D.R.Wilcox/R.M.Taylor	v	Warwicks	Southend	1946
9th	251	J.W.H.T.Douglas/S.N.Hare	v	Derbyshire	Leyton	1921
10th	218	F.H.Vigar/T.P.B.Smith	v	Derbyshire	Chesterfield	1947

Best Bowling	For	10- 32	H.Pickett	v	Leics	Leyton	1895
(Innings)	V	10- 40	E.G.Dennett	for	Glos	Bristol	1906
Best Bowling	For	17-119	W.Mead	v	Hampshire	Southampton	1895
(Match)	V	17- 56	C.W.L.Parker	for	Glos	Gloucester	1925

Most Runs – Season	2559	G.A.Gooch	(av 67.34)	1984
Most Runs – Career	30332	G.A.Gooch	(av 52.56)	1973-96
Most 100s – Season	9	J.O'Connor		1934
	9	D.J.Insole		1955
Most 100s – Career	94	G.A.Gooch		1973-96
Most Wkts – Season	172	T.P.B Smith	(av 27.13)	1947
Most Wkts – Career	1610	T.P.B.Smith	(av 26.68)	1929-51

LIMITED-OVERS CRICKET

Highest Total	NWT	386-5		v	Wiltshire	Chelmsford	1988
	BHC	388-7		v	Scotland	Chelmsford	1992
	SL	310-5		v	Glamorgan	Southend	1983
Lowest Total	NWT	57		v	Lancashire	Lord's	1996
	BHC	61		v	Lancashire	Chelmsford	1992
	SL	69		v	Derbyshire	Chesterfield	1974
Highest Innings	NWT	144	G.A.Gooch	v	Hampshire	Chelmsford	1990
	BHC	198*	G.A.Gooch	v	Sussex	Hove	1982
	SL	176	G.A.Gooch	v	Glamorgan	Southend	1983
Best Bowling	NWT	5- 8	J.K.Lever	v	Middlesex	Westcliff	1972
		5- 8	G.A.Gooch	v	Cheshire	Chester	1995
	BHC	5-13	J.K.Lever	v	Middlesex	Lord's	1985
	SL	8-26	K.D.Boyce	v	Lancashire	Manchester	1971

GLAMORGAN

Formation of Present Club: 6 July 1888
Colours: Blue and Gold
Badge: Gold Daffodil
Championships: (2) 1948, 1969
NatWest Trophy/Gillette Cup Winners: (0) Finalists 1977
Benson and Hedges Cup Winners: (0) Semi-Finalists 1988
Sunday League Champions: (1) 1993
Match Awards: NWT 36; BHC 49

Secretary: G.R.Stone. **Cricket Secretary:** M.J.Fatkin
  Sophia Gardens, Cardiff, CF1 9XR (Tel 01222 343478)
Captain: M.P.Maynard. **Vice-Captain:** P.A.Cottey (*tbc*).
Overseas Player: Waqar Younis. **1997 Beneficiary:** C.P.Metson. **Scorer:** B.T.Denning

BUTCHER, Gary Paul (Trinity S; Riddlesdown S; Heath Clark C), b Clapham, London 11 Mar 1975. Son of A.R. (Surrey, Glam and England 1972-92); brother of M.A. (*see SURREY*). 5'9". RHB, RM. Debut 1994. Tours (Gm): SA 1995-96; Z 1994-95. HS 89 v Northants (Northampton) 1996. BB 7-77 v Glos (Bristol) 1996. **NWT:** HS 48 and BB 1-50 v Worcs (Cardiff) 1996. **BHC:** HS 3*. BB 2-21 v Warwks (Cardiff) 1996. **SL:** HS 20* v Sussex (Hove) 1996. BB 4-32 v Glos (Bristol) 1996.

COSKER, Dean Andrew (Millfield S), b Weymouth, Dorset 7 Jan 1978. 5'11". RHB, SLA. Debut 1996. HS 24 and 4-60 v Lancs (Cardiff) 1996 (on debut). **SL:** HS 4 and BB 2-38 v Leics (Swansea) 1996.

COTTEY, Phillip Anthony (Bishopston CS, Swansea), b Swansea 2 Jun 1966. 5'4". RHB, OB. Debut 1986; cap 1992. E Transvaal 1991-92. Tours (Gm): SA 1995-96; Z 1990-91, 1994-95. 1000 runs (6); most – 1543 (1996). HS 203 and BB 4-49 v Leics (Swansea) 1996. **NWT:** HS 61* v Leics (Leicester) 1995. BB 1-11. **BHC:** HS 68 v Hants (Southampton) 1989. BB 1-49. **SL:** HS 92* v Hants (Ebbw Vale) 1991. BB 4-56 v Essex (Chelmsford) 1996.

CROFT, Robert Damien Bale (St John Lloyd Catholic CS; W Glam IHE), b Morriston 25 May 1970. 5'10½". RHB, OB. Debut 1989; cap 1992. **Tests:** 5 (1996 to 1996-97); HS 31 and BB 5-95 v NZ (Christchurch) 1996-97. **LOI:** 11 (1996 to 1996-97; HS 30*; BB 2-26). Tours: SA 1993-94 (Eng A), 1995-96 (Gm); WI 1991-92 (Eng A); NZ 1996-97; Z 1990-91 (Gm), 1994-95 (Gm), 1996-97. HS 143 v Somerset (Taunton) 1995. 50 wkts (4); most – 76 (1996). BB 8-66 (14-169 match) v Warwks (Swansea) 1992. **NWT:** HS 50 v Essex (Cardiff) 1994. BB 3-30 v Lincs (Swansea) 1994. **BHC:** HS 50 v Middx (Lord's) 1995. BB 4-30 v Essex (Cardiff) 1996. **SL:** HS 68 v Northants (Northampton) 1996. BB 6-20 v Worcs (Cardiff) 1994.

DALE, Adrian (Chepstow CS; Swansea U), b Germiston, SA 24 Oct 1968 (to UK at 6 mths). 5'11½". RHB, RM. Debut 1989; cap 1992. Tours (Gm): SA 1993-94 (Eng A), 1995-96; Z 1990-91, 1994-95. 1000 runs (2); most – 1472 (1993). HS 214* v Middx (Cardiff) 1993. BB 6-18 v Warwks (Cardiff) 1993. Awards: NWT 1; BHC 1. **NWT:** HS 110 v Lincs (Swansea) 1994. BB 3-54 v Worcs (Swansea) 1993. **BHC:** HS 53 v Comb Us (Cardiff) 1992. BB 5-41 v Middx (Lord's) 1996. **SL:** HS 67* v Derbys (Heanor) 1989. BB 6-22 v Durham (Colwyn Bay) 1993.

DAVIES, Andrew Philip (Dwr-y-Felin CS; Christ C, Brecon), b Neath 7 Nov 1976. 5'11". RHB, RMF. Debut 1995. Wales (MC). HS 11* v P (Pontypridd) 1996. BAC HS – . BB 1-25.

EDWARDS, Gareth John Maldwyn (Brynhyfryd S, Ruthin; University C, London), b St Asaph 13 Nov 1976. 6'2". RHB, OB. Staff 1996 – awaiting f-c debut.

EVANS, Alun Wyn (Fishguard SS; Neath Tertiary C), b Glanamman, Dyfed 20 Aug 1975. 5'8". RHB, RM. Debut 1996 v OU (Oxford), scoring 66* and 71*. MCC YC. HS 71* (as above). BAC HS 48* v Notts (Worksop) 1996. **SL:** HS 50* v Glos (Bristol) 1996.

JAMES, Stephen Peter (Monmouth S; Swansea U; Hughes Hall, Cambridge), b Lydney, Glos 7 Sep 1967. 6'0". RHB. Debut 1985; cap 1992. Cambridge U 1989-90; blue 1989-90. Mashonaland 1993-94 to date. Tours (Gm): SA 1995-96; Z 1990-91. 1000 runs (4); most – 1766 (1996). HS 235 v Notts (Worksop) 1996. Awards: NWT 1; BHC 2. **NWT:** HS 123 v Lincs (Swansea) 1994. **BHC:** HS 135 v Comb Us (Cardiff) 1992. **SL:** HS 107 v Sussex (Llanelli) 1993.

MAYNARD, Matthew Peter (David Hughes S, Anglesey), b Oldham, Lancs 21 Mar 1966. 5'10½". RHB, RM. Debut 1985 v Yorks (Swansea), scoring 102 out of 117 in 87 min, reaching 100 with 3 sixes off successive balls; cap 1987; captain 1996 to date; benefit 1996. N Districts 1990-91/1991-92. Otago 1996-97. YC 1988. **Tests:** 4 (1988 to 1993-94); HS 35 v WI (Kingston) 1993-94. **LOI:** 10 (1993-94 to 1996; HS 41). Tours: SA 1989-90 (Eng XI), 1995-96 (Gm – captain); WI 1993-94; Z 1994-95 (Gm). 1000 runs (10); most – 1803 (1991). HS 243 v Hants (Southampton) 1991. BB 3-21 v OU (Oxford) 1987. BAC BB 1-3. Awards: NWT 4; BHC 7. **NWT:** HS 151* v Durham (Darlington) 1991. **BHC:** HS 151* v Middx (Lord's) 1996. **SL:** HS 122* v Leics (Swansea) 1992.

METSON, Colin Peter (Enfield GS; Stanborough S, Welwyn Garden City; Durham U), b Goffs Oak, Herts 2 Jul 1963. 5'5½". RHB, WK. Middlesex 1981-86. Glamorgan debut/cap 1987; benefit 1997. Tour: SA 1995-96 (Gm). HS 96 M v Glos (Uxbridge) 1984. Gm HS 84 v Kent (Maidstone) 1991. Award: NWT 1. **NWT:** HS 21 v Notts (Nottingham) 1992. **BHC:** HS 23 v Kent (Swansea) 1990. **SL:** HS 30* v Hants (Bournemouth) 1990.

MORRIS, Hugh (Blundell's S), b Cardiff 5 Oct 1963. 5'8". LHB, RM. Debut 1981; cap 1986; captain 1986-89 and 1993-95; benefit 1994. **Tests:** 3 (1991); HS 44 v WI (Oval) 1991. Tours (Eng A)(C=captain): SA 1993-94C, 1995-96 (Gm); WI 1991-92C; SL 1990-91C; Z 1994-95C (Gm). 1000 runs (9) inc 2000 (1): 2276 – inc 10 hundreds – both Gm records (1990). HS 202* v Yorks (Cardiff) 1996. BB 1-6. BAC BB 1-45. Awards: NWT 2; BHC 3. **NWT:** HS 154* v Staffs (Cardiff) 1989. **BHC:** HS 143* v Hants (Southampton) 1989. BB 1-14. **SL:** HS 127* v Surrey (Swansea) 1994.

PARKIN, Owen Thomas (Bournemouth GS, Bath U), b Coventry, Warwks 24 Sep 1972. 6'2". RHB, RFM. Dorset 1992. Debut 1994. HS 14 v Warwks (Birmingham) 1996. BB 3-22 v Durham (Chester-le-St) 1996. **NWT:** HS 1* and BB 3-23 v Worcs (Cardiff) 1996. **SL:** HS – . BB 5-28 v Sussex (Hove) 1996.

SHAW, Adrian David (Neath Tertiary C), b Neath 17 Feb 1972. 5'11". RHB, WK. Wales (MC) 1990-92. Debut 1994. HS 74 v Surrey (Cardiff) 1996. **SL:** HS 36* v Glos (Bristol) 1996.

THOMAS, Stuart Darren (Graig CS, Llanelli; Neath Tertiary C), b Morriston 25 Jan 1975. 6'0". LHB, RFM. Debut v Derbys (Chesterfield) 1992, taking 5-80 when aged 17yr 217d. Tours (Gm): SA 1995-96; Z 1994-95. HS 78* v Glos (Abergavenny) 1995. BB 5-76 v Worcs (Worcester) 1993. Award: BHC 1. **NWT:** HS – . **BHC:** HS 27* v Essex (Cardiff) 1996. BB 6-20 v Comb Us (Cardiff) 1995. **SL:** HS 20* v Northants (Northampton) 1996. BB 3-44 v Ex (Pontypridd) 1995.

WATKIN, Steven Llewellyn (Cymer Afan CS; S Glamorgan CHE), b Maesteg 15 Sep 1964. 6'0". RHB, RMF. Debut 1986; cap 1989. *Wisden* 1993. **Tests:** 3 (1991 to 1993); HS 13 and BB 4-65 v A (Oval) 1993. **LOI:** 4 (1993-94; HS 4; BB 4-49). Tours: SA 1995-96 (Gm); WI 1991-92 (Eng A), 1993-94; P 1990-91 (Eng A); Z 1989-90 (Eng A), 1990-91 (Gm), 1994-95 (Gm). HS 41 v Worcs (Worcester) 1992. 50 wkts (8); most – 94 (1989). BB 8-59 v Warwks (Birmingham) 1988. Awards: NWT 1; BHC 1. **NWT:** HS 13 v Worcs (Cardiff) 1996. BB 4-26 v Middx (Cardiff) 1995. **BHC:** HS 15 v Hants (Southampton) 1991. BB 4-31 v Kent (Canterbury) 1996. **SL:** HS 31* v Derbys (Checkley) 1991. BB 5-23 v Warwks (Birmingham) 1990.

NEWCOMERS

JONES, Simon Philip, b Swansea 25 Dec 1978. Son of I.J. (Glamorgan and England 1960-68). RHB, RFM.

WAQAR YOUNIS (Government C, Vehari), b Vehari, Pakistan 16 Nov 1969. 6'0". RHB, RF. Multan 1987-88 to 1990-91. United Bank 1988-89 to date. Surrey 1990-91 and 1993; cap 1990. *Wisden* 1991. **Tests** (P): 44 (1989-90 to 1996-97, 1 as captain); HS 34 v NZ (Christchurch) 1995-96; BB 7-76 v NZ (Faisalabad) 1990-91. **LOI** (P): 150 (1989-90 to 1996-97; HS 37; BB 6-26). Tours (P): E 1992, 1996; A 1989-90, 1995-96; WI 1992-93; NZ 1992-93, 1993-94, 1995-96; SL 1994-95. HS 55 P v Natal (Durban) 1994-95. BAC HS 31 Sy v Yorks (Guildford) 1991. 50 wkts (3+3) inc 100 (1): 113 (1991). BB 7-64 United Bank v ADBP (Lahore) 1990-91. BAC BB 7-73 Sy v Warwks (Oval) 1990. Awards: NWT 2. **NWT:** HS 26 Sy v Essex (Oval) 1991. BB 5-40 Sy v Northants (Oval) 1991. **BHC:** HS 5*. BB 3-29 Sy v Somerset (Taunton) 1991. **SL:** HS 39 Sy v Hants (Oval) 1993. BB 5-26 Sy v Kent (Oval) 1990.

DEPARTURES (who made first-class appearances in 1996)

BARWICK, Stephen Royston (Cwrt Sart CS; Dwr-y-Felin CS), b Neath 6 Sep 1960. 6'2". RHB, RM/OB. Glamorgan 1981-96; cap 1987; benefit 1995. Tour: Z 1994-95 (Gm). HS 30 v Hants (Bournemouth) 1988. 50 wkts (2); most – 64 (1989). BB 8-42 v Worcs (Worcester) 1983. Award: BHC 1. **NWT:** HS 6. BB 5-26 v Surrey (Swansea) 1992. **BHC:** HS 18 v Kent (Canterbury) 1984. BB 4-11 Minor C (Swansea) 1985. **SL:** HS 48* v Worcs (Worcester) 1989. BB 6-28 v Derbys (Derby) 1993.

DALTON, Alistair John (Millfield S), b Bridgend 27 Apr 1973. 5'7". RHB, RM. Wales (MC) 1992-94. Glamorgan 1994-96. HS 51* v SA (Pontypridd) 1994. BAC HS 46 v Derbys (Derby) 1995. **SL:** HS 19 v Hants (Southampton) 1994.

GIBSON, Ottis Delroy (Ellerslie SS), b Sion Hill, Bridgetown, Barbados 16 Mar 1969. 6'2". RHB, RF. Barbados 1990-91 to date. Border 1992-93 to date. Glamorgan 1994-96; cap 1994. **Tests** (WI): 1 (1995); HS 29 and BB 2-81 v E (Lord's) 1995. **LOI** (WI): 13 (1995 to 1995-96; HS 52; BB 5-40). Tours (WI): E 1995; A 1995-96. HS 101* WI v Somerset (Taunton) 1995. Gm HS 97 v Leics (Swansea) 1996. 50 wkts (1): 60 (1994). BB 7-55 Border v Natal (Durban) 1994-95. Gm BB 6-64 v Worcs (Cardiff) 1994. Award: NWT 1. **NWT:** HS 44 and BB 3-34 v Essex (Cardiff) 1994. **BHC:** HS 68 v Warwks (Cardiff) 1996. BB 2-50 v Surrey (Oval) 1994. **SL:** HS 47* v Northants (Northampton) 1996. BB 2-18 v Kent (Cardiff) 1996.

HEMP, D.L. – *see WARWICKSHIRE.*

KENDRICK, Neil Michael (Wilson's GS), b Bromley, Kent 11 Nov 1967. 5'11". RHB, SLA. Surrey 1988-94. Glamorgan 1994-95 to 1996. Tour: Z 1994-95 (Gm). HS 59 v Surrey (Oval) 1995. 50 wkts (1): 51 (1992). BB 7-115 Sy v Notts (Oval) 1993. Gm BB 4-70 v Kent (Tunbridge Wells) 1995. **NWT:** HS – . BB 1-51. **BHC:** HS 24 and BB 2-47 Sy v Kent (Canterbury) 1992. **SL:** HS 13* and BB 2-48 Sy v Warwks (Guildford) 1994.

GLAMORGAN 1996

RESULTS SUMMARY

	Place	Won	Lost	Drew	No Result
Britannic Assurance Championship	10th	6	5	6	–
All First-Class Matches		6	6	9	–
NatWest Trophy	1st Round				
Benson and Hedges Cup	Quarter-Finalists				
Sunday League	13th	7	8	–	2

BRITANNIC ASSURANCE CHAMPIONSHIP AVERAGES

BATTING AND FIELDING

Cap		M	I	NO	HS	Runs	Avge	100	50	Ct/St
1992	P.A.Cottey	17	31	6	203	1476	59.04	4	9	14
1987	M.P.Maynard	15	28	3	214	1470	58.80	5	6	20
1986	H.Morris	16	30	1	202*	1530	52.75	5	9	14
1992	S.P.James	17	32	–	235	1532	47.87	6	5	14
–	O.D.Gibson	8	13	3	97	408	40.80	–	3	6
1994	D.L.Hemp	5	9	1	95	267	33.37	–	1	5
–	G.P.Butcher	12	21	3	89	547	30.38	–	4	8
1992	A.Dale	12	21	1	120	585	29.25	1	3	4
1992	R.D.B.Croft	15	24	4	78	543	27.15	–	4	12
–	A.W.Evans	4	7	1	48*	148	24.66	–	–	3
–	O.T.Parkin	7	9	6	14	60	20.00	–	–	3
–	A.D.Shaw	10	13	1	74	234	19.50	–	2	24/4
–	S.D.Thomas	8	13	2	48	175	15.90	–	–	2
1989	S.L.Watkin	16	18	5	34	124	9.53	–	–	7
–	D.A.Cosker	5	6	1	24	45	9.00	–	–	3
1987	S.R.Barwick	5	5	1	20*	32	8.00	–	–	2
1987	C.P.Metson	7	11	4	18*	53	7.57	–	–	12/2
–	N.M.Kendrick	8	8	4	16*	19	4.75	–	–	4

BOWLING

	O	M	R	W	Avge	Best	5wI	10wM
S.L.Watkin	580.4	149	1692	63	26.85	4- 28	–	–
R.D.B.Croft	807.5	205	2050	67	30.59	6- 78	4	–
G.P.Butcher	180.1	27	716	20	35.80	7- 77	1	–
A.Dale	137.1	35	466	12	38.83	4- 52	–	–
D.A.Cosker	155.4	38	622	16	38.87	4- 60	–	–
N.M.Kendrick	188	63	516	13	39.69	4- 89	–	–
O.T.Parkin	174.4	41	553	13	42.53	3- 22	–	–
O.D.Gibson	243	41	991	20	49.55	3- 43	–	–
S.D.Thomas	228	25	924	16	57.75	5-121	1	–

Also bowled: S.R.Barwick 114.3-39-286-2; P.A.Cottey 34-3-107-4; D.L.Hemp 9-0-60-0; M.P.Maynard 7.3-4-7-0.

The First-Class Averages (pp 123-38) give the records of Glamorgan players in all first-class county matches (their other opponents being the Pakistanis, South Africa A, Cambridge University and Oxford University), with the exception of:
  R.D.B.Croft 18-27-5-78-634-28.81-0-5-13ct. 892-225-2315-72-32.15-6/78-4-0.
  H.Morris 17-31-2-202*-1656-57.10-6-9-14ct. Did not bowl.

GLAMORGAN RECORDS

FIRST-CLASS CRICKET

Highest Total	For 587-8d		v	Derbyshire	Cardiff	1951
	V 657-7d		by	Warwicks	Birmingham	1994
Lowest Total	For 22		v	Lancashire	Liverpool	1924
	V 33		by	Leics	Ebbw Vale	1965
Highest Innings	For 287*	D.E.Davies	v	Glos	Newport	1939
	V 313*	S.J.Cook	for	Somerset	Cardiff	1990

Highest Partnership for each Wicket

1st	330	A.Jones/R.C.Fredericks	v	Northants	Swansea	1972
2nd	249	S.P.James/H.Morris	v	Oxford U	Oxford	1987
3rd	313	D.E.Davies/W.E.Jones	v	Essex	Brentwood	1948
4th	425*	A.Dale/I.V.A.Richards	v	Middlesex	Cardiff	1993
5th	264	M.Robinson/S.W.Montgomery	v	Hampshire	Bournemouth	1949
6th	230	W.E.Jones/B.L.Muncer	v	Worcs	Worcester	1953
7th	211	P.A.Cottey/O.D.Gibson	v	Leics	Swansea	1996
8th	202	D.Davies/J.J.Hills	v	Sussex	Eastbourne	1928
9th	203*	J.J.Hills/J.C.Clay	v	Worcs	Swansea	1929
10th	143	T.Davies/S.A.B.Daniels	v	Glos	Swansea	1982

Best Bowling	For 10- 51	J.Mercer	v	Worcs	Worcester	1936
(Innings)	V 10- 18	G.Geary	for	Leics	Pontypridd	1929
Best Bowling	For 17-212	J.C.Clay	v	Worcs	Swansea	1937
(Match)	V 16- 96	G.Geary	for	Leics	Pontypridd	1929

Most Runs – Season	2276 H.Morris	(av 55.51)		1990
Most Runs – Career	34056 A.Jones	(av 33.03)		1957-83
Most 100s – Season	10 H.Morris			1990
Most 100s – Career	52 A.Jones			1957-83
Most Wkts – Season	176 J.C.Clay	(av 17.34)		1937
Most Wkts – Career	2174 D.J.Shepherd	(av 20.95)		1950-72

LIMITED-OVERS CRICKET

Highest Total	NWT	345-2		v	Durham	Darlington	1991
	BHC	318-3		v	Comb Us	Cardiff	1995
	SL	287-8		v	Middlesex	Cardiff	1993
Lowest Total	NWT	76		v	Northants	Northampton	1968
	BHC	68		v	Lancashire	Manchester	1973
	SL	42		v	Derbyshire	Swansea	1979
Highest Innings	NWT	162*	I.V.A.Richards	v	Oxfordshire	Swansea	1993
	BHC	151*	M.P.Maynard	v	Middlesex	Lord's	1996
	SL	130*	J.A.Hopkins	v	Somerset	Bath	1983
Best Bowling	NWT	5-13	R.J.Shastri	v	Scotland	Edinburgh	1988
	BHC	6-20	S.D.Thomas	v	Comb Us	Cardiff	1995
	SL	6-20	R.D.B.Croft	v	Worcs	Cardiff	1994

GLOUCESTERSHIRE

Formation of Present Club: 1871
Colours: Blue, Gold, Brown, Silver, Green and Red
Badge: Coat of Arms of the City and County of Bristol
Championships (since 1890): (0) Second 1930, 1931, 1947, 1959, 1969, 1986
NatWest Trophy/Gillette Cup Winners: (1) 1973
Benson and Hedges Cup Winners: (1) 1977
Sunday League Champions: (0) Second 1988
Match Awards: NWT 41; BHC 51

Chief Executive: C.Sextone. **Cricket Secretary:** P.G.M.August
County Ground, Nevil Road, Bristol BS7 9EJ (Tel 0117 924 5216)
Captain: *tba*. **Vice-Captain:** M.W.Alleyne (*tbc*). **Overseas Player:** S.Young (*tbc*).
1997 Beneficiary: Gloucestershire CCC. **Scorer:** H.T.Gerrish

ALLEYNE, Mark Wayne (Harrison C, Barbados; Cardinal Pole S, London E9; Haringey Cricket C), b Tottenham, London 23 May 1968. 5'10". RHB, RM. Debut 1986; cap 1990. Tours (Gs): SL 1986-87, 1992-93. 1000 runs (4); most – 1121 (1991). HS 256 v Northants (Northampton) 1990. 50 wkts (1): 54 (1996). BB 5-32 v Sussex (Bristol) 1996. Awards: NWT 1; BHC 1. **NWT:** HS 73 v Herts (Bristol) 1993. BB 5-30 v Lincs (Gloucester) 1990. **BHC:** HS 75 v Hants (Bristol) 1996. BB 5-27 v Comb Us (Bristol) 1988. **SL:** HS 134* v Leics (Bristol) 1992. BB 5-28 v Glam (Ebbw Vale) 1995.

AVERIS, James Maxwell Michael (Bristol Cathedral S; Portsmouth U), b Bristol 28 May 1974. 5'11". RHB, RFM. Summer contract – awaiting f-c debut. **SL:** HS 2*. BB 2-35 v Essex (Colchester) 1996. Rugby for Bristol.

BALL, Martyn Charles John (King Edmund SS; Bath CFE), b Bristol 26 Apr 1970. 5'8". RHB, OB. Debut 1988; cap 1996. Tour (Gs): SL 1992-93. HS 71 v Notts (Bristol) 1993. BB 8-46 (14-169 match) v Somerset (Taunton) 1993. **NWT:** HS 31 v Lincs (Sleaford) 1996. BB 3-42 v Lancs (Gloucester) 1989. **BHC:** HS 25 v Lancs (Manchester) 1996. BB 3-26 v Comb Us (Bristol) 1995. **SL:** HS 28* v Worcs (Worcester) 1994. BB 3-24 v Somerset (Taunton) 1993.

CAWDRON, Michael John (Cheltenham C), b Luton, Beds 7 Oct 1974. 6'2". LHB, RM. Staff 1994 – awaiting f-c debut. **BHC:** HS – and BB 2-48 v Surrey (Oval) 1996. **SL:** HS 50 v Essex (Cheltenham) 1995. BB 1-23.

CUNLIFFE, Robert John (Banbury S; Banbury TC), b Oxford 8 Nov 1973. 5'10". RHB, RM. Debut 1994. Oxfordshire 1991-94. HS 190* v OU (Bristol) 1995. BAC HS 92* v Lancs (Cheltenham) 1995. Award: BHC 1. **NWT:** HS 40 v Durham (Chester-le-St) 1996. **BHC:** HS 137* v Surrey (Oval) 1996. **SL:** HS 52 v Middx (Lord's) 1996.

DAVIS, Richard Peter (King Ethelbert's S, Birchington; Thanet TC), b Westbrook, Margate, Kent 18 Mar 1966. 6'3". RHB, SLA. Kent 1986-93; cap 1990. Warwickshire 1993-94 to 1995; cap 1994. Gloucestershire debut 1996. Tours: SA 1994-95 (Wa); Z 1992-93 (K), 1993-94 (Wa). HS 67 K v Hants (Southampton) 1989. Gs HS 43 v Northants (Bristol) 1996. 50 wkts (2); most – 74 (1992). BB 7-64 K v Durham (Gateshead) 1992. Gs BB 4-93 v Lancs (Manchester) 1996. Award: BHC 1. **NWT:** HS 22 K v Warwks (Birmingham) 1992. BB 3-19 K v Bucks (Canterbury) 1988. **BHC:** HS 18* K v Glam (Canterbury) 1993. BB 2-25 v Sussex (Bristol) 1996. **SL:** HS 40* K v Northants (Canterbury) 1991. BB 5-52 K v Somerset (Bath) 1989.

DAWSON, Robert Ian (Millfield S; Newcastle Poly), b Exmouth, Devon 29 Mar 1970. 5'11". RHB, RM. Debut 1992. Devon 1988-91. 1000 runs (1): 1112 (1996). HS 127* v CU (Bristol) 1996. BAC HS 101 v Worcs (Gloucester) 1995. BB 2-38 v Derbys (Chesterfield) 1994. **NWT:** HS 60 v Devon (Bristol) 1994. BB 1-37. **BHC:** HS 38 v Middx (Bristol) and v Somerset (Bristol) 1995. **SL:** HS 85 v Worcs (Worcester) 1996.

HANCOCK, Timothy Harold Coulter (St Edward's S, Oxford; Henley C), b Reading, Berks 20 Apr 1972. 5'10". RHB, RM. Debut 1991. Oxfordshire 1990. Tour: SL 1992-93 (Gs). HS 123 v Essex (Chelmsford) 1994. BB 3-10 v Glam (Abergavenny) 1993. **NWT:** HS 45 and BB 2-7 v Herts (Bristol) 1993. **BHC:** HS 71* v Sussex (Bristol) 1996. BB 3-13 v Hants (Bristol) 1996. **SL:** HS 46 v Sussex (Hove) 1993. BB 2-6 v Notts (Nottingham) 1996.

HEWSON, Dominic Robert (Cheltenham C), b Cheltenham 3 Oct 1974. 5'8". RHB, occ RM. Debut 1996. HS 87 v Hants (Southampton) 1996 (on BAC debut). **SL:** HS 3.

LAWRENCE, David Valentine ('Syd') (Linden S), b Gloucester 28 Jan 1964. 6'2". RHB, RF. Gloucestershire 1981-91; cap 1985; benefit 1993. Returns to county cricket after absence of five seasons (fractured kneecap). YC 1985. **Tests:** 5 (1988 to 1991-92); HS 34 v WI (Nottingham) 1991; BB 5-106 v WI (Oval) 1991. **LOI:** 1 (1991; HS – ; BB 4-67). Tours: Guyana 1990-91; SL 1985-86 (Eng B); 1986-87 (Gs). HS 66 v Glam (Abergavenny) 1991. 50 wkts (5); most – 85 (1985). BB 7-47 v Surrey (Cheltenham) 1988. Hat-trick 1990. Awards: NWT 2; BHC 4. **NWT:** HS 5*. BB 5-17 v Norfolk (Bristol) 1991. **BHC:** HS 23 and BB 6-20 v Comb Us (Bristol) 1991. **SL:** HS 38* v Yorks (Scarborough) 1991. BB 5-18 v Somerset (Bristol) 1990.

LEWIS, Jonathan (Churchfields S, Swindon; Swindon C), b Aylesbury, Bucks 26 Aug 1975. 6'2". RHB, RMF. Debut 1995. Wiltshire 1993. Northamptonshire staff 1994. HS 22* v I (Bristol) 1996. BAC HS 20 v Somerset (Bristol) 1996. BB 4-34 (8-121 match) v Durham (Bristol) 1995. **NWT:** HS 6*. BB 3-27 v Somerset (Taunton) 1996. **BHC:** HS – . BB 3-31 v Ireland (Dublin) 1996. **SL:** HS 9*. BB 3-27 v Warwks (Birmingham) 1995.

LYNCH, Monte Alan (Ryden's S, Walton-on-Thames), b Georgetown, British Guiana 21 May 1958. 5'8". RHB, OB. Surrey 1977-94; cap 1982; benefit 1991. Gloucestershire debut/cap 1995. Guyana 1982-83. **LOI:** 3 (1988; HS 6). Tours: SA 1983-84 (WI XI); P 1981-82 (Int). 1000 runs (9); most – 1714 (1985). HS 172* Sy v Kent (Oval) 1989. Gs HS 114 v Kent (Canterbury) 1995. BB 3-6 Sy v Glam (Swansea) 1981. Gs BB – . Awards: NWT 1; BHC 4. **NWT:** HS 129 Sy v Durham (Oval) 1992. BB 2-28 Sy v Glam (Swansea) 1992. **BHC:** HS 112* Sy v Kent (Oval) 1987. **SL:** HS 136 Sy v Yorks (Bradford) 1985. BB 2-2 Sy v Northants (Guildford) 1987 and Sy v Essex (Hove) 1990.

RUSSELL, Robert Charles (**'Jack'**) (Archway CS), b Stroud 15 Aug 1963. 5'8½". LHB, WK, occ OB. Debut 1981 – youngest Glos wicket-keeper (17yr 307d), setting record for most match dismissals on f-c debut – 8 v SL (Bristol); cap 1985; benefit 1994; captain 1995. *Wisden* 1989. MBE 1996. **Tests:** 49 (1988 to 1996); HS 128* v A (Manchester) 1989; 11 ct v SA (Jo'burg) 1995-96 (Test record); 27 dis 1995-96 series v SA (Eng record). **LOI:** 38 (1987-88 to 1996-97; HS 50). Tours: A 1990-91, 1992-93 (Eng A); SA 1995-96; WI 1989-90, 1993-94; NZ 1991-92, 1996-97; P 1987-88; SL 1986-87 (Gs); Z 1996-97. HS 129* Eng XI v Boland (Paarl) 1995-96. Gs HS 124 v Notts (Nottingham) 1996. BB 1-4. Awards: BHC 2. **NWT:** HS 59* v Suffolk (Bristol) 1995. **BHC:** HS 51 v Worcs (Worcester) 1991. **SL:** HS 108 v Worcs (Hereford) 1986.

SHEERAZ, Kamran Pasha (Licensed Victuallers' S, Ascot; E Berkshire C, Langley), b Wellington, Shropshire 28 Dec 1973. 6'0". RHB, RMF. Debut 1994. Bedfordshire 1992. HS 3*. BAC HS 3. BB 6-67 v WI (Bristol) 1995. BAC BB 3-89 v Derbys (Bristol) 1995. **SL:** HS 14* v Surrey (Oval) 1995. BB 2-20 v Middx (Bristol) 1995.

SMITH, Andrew Michael (Queen Elizabeth BS, Wakefield; Exeter U), b Dewsbury, Yorks 1 Oct 1967. 5'9". RHB, LMF. Debut 1991; cap 1995. Tour: P 1995-96 (Eng A – part). HS 55* v Notts (Nottingham) 1996. 50 wkts (2); most – 60 (1996). BB 8-73 (10-118 match) v Middx (Lord's) 1996. Award: BHC 1. **NWT:** HS 13 v Somerset (Taunton) 1996. BB 3-21 v Lincs (Sleaford) 1996. **BHC:** HS 15* Comb Us v Surrey (Oxford) 1990. BB 6-39 v Hants (Southampton) 1995. **SL:** HS 26* v Kent (Moreton-in-M) 1996. BB 4-38 v Leics (Bristol) 1992.

TRAINOR, Nicholas James (St Edmund Campion S, Low Fell), b Gateshead, Co Durham 29 Jun 1975. 6'1". RHB, OB. Debut 1996. Northumberland 1995. HS 67 v Surrey (Gloucester) 1996 (on debut). **NWT:** HS 14 v Lincs (Sleaford) 1996. **BHC:** HS 25 v Lancs (Manchester) 1996. **SL:** HS 20 v Notts (Nottingham) 1996.

WILLIAMS, Richard Charles James (**'Reggie'**) (Millfield S), b Southmead, Bristol 8 Aug 1969. 5'8". LHB, WK. Debut 1990; cap 1996. Tour: SL 1992-93 (Gs). HS 90 v OU (Bristol) 1995. BAC HS 55* v Derbys (Gloucester) 1991. **SL:** HS 19 v Essex (Cheltenham) 1995.

WINDOWS, Matthew Guy Newman (Clifton C; Durham U), b Bristol 5 Apr 1973. Son of A.R. (Glos and CU 1960-68). 5'7". RHB, RSM. Debut 1992. Combined Us 1995. HS 184 v Warwks (Cheltenham) 1996. BB 1-6 (Comb Us). **NWT:** HS 33 v Devon (Bristol) 1994. **BHC:** HS 16* Comb Us v Lancs (Oxford) 1994. **SL:** HS 72 v Somerset (Bristol) 1994.

WRIGHT, Anthony John (Alleyn's GS) b Stevenage, Herts 27 Jun 1962. 6'0". RHB, RM. Gloucestershire debut 1982; cap 1987; captain 1990-93; benefit 1996. Tours (Gs): SL 1986-87, 1992-93 (captain). 1000 runs (6); most – 1596 (1991). HS 193 v Notts (Bristol) 1995. BB 1-16. Awards: NWT 3; BHC 2. **NWT:** HS 142* v Suffolk (Bristol) 1995. **BHC:** HS 123 v Ireland (Dublin) 1996. **SL:** HS 96 v Sussex (Bristol) 1996.

NEWCOMERS

READ, Christopher Mark Wells (Torquay GS), b Paignton, Devon 10 Aug 1978. RHB, WK.

YOUNG, Shaun, b Burnie, Australia 13 Jun 1970. LHB, RFM. Tasmania 1991-92 to date. Tour: E 1995 (Young A); Z 1995-96 (Tas). HS 175* Tasmania v Queensland (Brisbane) 1995-96. BB 5-36 (10-124 match) Tasmania v Victoria (Melbourne) 1994-95.

DEPARTURES (who made first-class appearances in 1996)

BODEN, David Jonathan Peter (Alleynes HS, Stone; Stafford CFE), b Eccleshall, Staffs 26 Nov 1970. 6'3". RHB, RMF. Middlesex 1989. Essex 1992-93. Gloucestershire debut 1995. HS 5. Gs HS 2. BB 4-11 M v OU (Oxford) 1989 – on debut. Gs BB 3-38 v OU (Bristol) 1995. BAC BB 2-73 v Hants (Bristol) 1995. **NWT:** HS – . BB 6-26 v Suffolk (Bristol) 1995. **SL:** HS 5. BB 3-34 v Hants (Bristol) 1995.

COOPER, Kevin Edwin (Hucknall National SS), b Hucknall, Notts 27 Dec 1957. 6'1". LHB, RFM. Nottinghamshire 1976-92; cap 1980; benefit 1990. Gloucestershire 1992-93 to 1996; cap 1995. Tour: SL 1992-93 (Gs). HS 52 v Lancs (Cheltenham) 1993. 50 wkts (8) inc 100 (1): 101 (1988). BB 8-44 Nt v Middx (Lord's) 1984. Gs BB 5-83 v Yorks (Sheffield) 1993. Awards: NWT 1; BHC 2. **NWT:** HS 11 Nt v Glos (Nottingham) 1982. BB 4-49 Nt v Warwks (Nottingham) 1985. **BHC:** HS 25* Nt v Lancs (Manchester) 1983. BB 4-9 Nt v Yorks (Nottingham) 1989. **SL:** HS 31 Nt v Glos (Nottingham) 1984. BB 4-25 Nt v Hants (Nottingham) 1976.

SYMONDS, Andrew (All Saints Anglican School, Mudgeeraba, Queensland), b Birmingham 9 Jun 1975. 6'1½". RHB, OB. Emigrated to Australia when 18 months old. Queensland 1994-95 to date. Australian CA. Gloucestershire 1995-96; cap 1996. YC 1995. Surrendered England qualification by appearing for Australia A v WI 1996-97. 1000 runs (2); most – 1438 (1995). HS 254* v Glam (Abergavenny) 1995 (including record 16 sixes); hit record 20 sixes in match. BB 3-77 Q v NSW (Sydney) 1994-95. Gs BB 2-21 v Northants (Bristol) 1996. Awards: NWT 1; BHC 2. **NWT:** HS 87 and BB 1-18 v Lincs (Sleaford) 1996. **BHC:** HS 95 v Comb Us (Bristol) 1995. **SL:** HS 76 v Notts (Nottingham) 1996. BB 3-34 v Essex (Colchester) 1996.

WALSH, Courtney Andrew (Excelsior HS), b Kingston, Jamaica 30 Oct 1962. 6'5½". RHB, RF. Jamaica 1981-82 to date (captain 1990-91 to date). Gloucestershire 1984-96; cap 1985; captain 1993-94 and 1996; benefit 1992. *Wisden* 1986. **Tests** (WI): 87 (1984-85 to 1996-97, 13 as captain); HS 30* v A (Melbourne) 1988-89; BB 7-37 (13-55 match) v NZ (Wellington) 1994-95. **LOI** (WI): 171 (1984-85 to 1996-97, 31 as captain). HS 30; BB 5-1). Tours (WI)(C=captain): E 1984, 1988, 1991, 1995; A 1984-85, 1986-87, 1988-89, 1992-93, 1995-96; NZ 1986-87, 1994-95C; I 1987-88, 1994-95C; P 1986-87, 1990-91; SL 1993; Z 1983-84 (Young WI). HS 66 v Kent (Cheltenham) 1994. 50 wkts (9+2) inc 100 (1): 118 (1986). BB 9-72 v Somerset (Bristol) 1986. Hat-trick 1988-89 (WI). Awards: NWT 2. **NWT:** HS 37 v Herts (Bristol) 1993. BB 6-21 v Kent (Bristol) 1990 and v Cheshire (Bristol) 1992. **BHC:** HS 28 v Comb Us (Bristol) 1989. BB 2-19 v Scot 1985. **SL:** HS 38 v Derbys (Derby) 1996. BB 4-19 v Kent (Cheltenham) 1987. Unavailable 1997.

GLOUCESTERSHIRE 1996

RESULTS SUMMARY

	Place	Won	Lost	Drew	No Result
Britannic Assurance Championship	13th	5	7	5	–
All First-Class Matches		5	7	6	–
NatWest Trophy	2nd Round				
Benson and Hedges Cup	Quarter-Finalist				
Sunday League	16th	4	10	–	3

BRITANNIC ASSURANCE CHAMPIONSHIP AVERAGES

BATTING AND FIELDING

Cap		M	I	NO	HS	Runs	Avge	100	50	Ct/St
1985	R.C.Russell	13	21	4	75	634	37.29	–	7	31/2
1995	M.A.Lynch	10	17	1	72	548	34.25	–	5	9
1996	A.Symonds	17	28	–	127	949	33.89	2	4	8
1990	M.W.Alleyne	17	28	2	149	831	31.96	1	3	14
–	T.H.C.Hancock	14	25	3	116	672	30.54	1	4	10
–	M.G.N.Windows	9	17	2	184	443	29.53	1	1	4
1987	A.J.Wright	9	17	–	106	415	24.41	1	3	11
–	R.J.Cunliffe	6	11	–	82	252	22.90	–	2	1
–	D.R.Hewson	5	10	1	87	206	22.88	–	2	1
–	N.J.Trainor	8	14	1	67	261	20.07	–	2	5
1996	R.C.J.Williams	4	7	–	44	124	17.71	–	–	12
1995	A.M.Smith	16	25	3	55*	364	16.54	–	1	2
–	R.P.Davis	14	21	2	43	292	15.36	–	–	15
1985	C.A.Walsh	15	24	13	25	154	14.00	–	–	7
1996	M.C.J.Ball	13	21	4	46	236	13.88	–	–	15
–	R.I.Dawson	6	11	1	21	123	12.30	–	–	–
–	J.Lewis	9	15	1	20	97	6.92	–	–	3

Also batted (1 match each): D.J.P.Boden 1 (1 ct); K.E.Cooper (cap 1995) 5.

BOWLING

	O	M	R	W	Avge	Best	5wI	10wM
C.A.Walsh	526.3	144	1432	85	16.84	6-22	7	1
M.W.Alleyne	422	115	1209	47	25.72	5-32	1	–
A.M.Smith	487.3	114	1615	60	26.91	8-73	3	1
A.Symonds	118.3	25	374	12	31.16	2-21	–	–
J.Lewis	234	53	743	16	46.43	3-74	–	–
R.P.Davis	280.2	68	905	19	47.63	4-93	–	–
M.C.J.Ball	225	61	639	13	49.15	3-40	–	–

Also bowled: D.J.P.Boden 31-5-121-1; K.E.Cooper 39-12-82-5; R.I.Dawson 0.2-0-4-0;
T.H.C.Hancock 13-4-46-0; N.J.Trainor 1-0-4-0.

The First-Class Averages (pp 123-38) give the records of Gloucestershire players in all first-class county matches (their other opponents being the Indians), with the exception of R.C.Russell whose full county figures are as above.

GLOUCESTERSHIRE RECORDS

FIRST-CLASS CRICKET

Highest Total	For	653-6d		v Glamorgan	Bristol	1928
	V	774-7d		by Australians	Bristol	1948
Lowest Total	For	17		v Australians	Cheltenham	1896
	V	12		by Northants	Gloucester	1907
Highest Innings	For	318*	W.G.Grace	v Yorkshire	Cheltenham	1876
	V	296	A.O.Jones	for Notts	Nottingham	1903

Highest Partnership for each Wicket

1st	395	D.M.Young/R.B.Nicholls	v	Oxford U	Oxford	1962
2nd	256	C.T.M.Pugh/T.W.Graveney	v	Derbyshire	Chesterfield	1960
3rd	336	W.R.Hammond/B.H.Lyon	v	Leics	Leicester	1933
4th	321	W.R.Hammond/W.L.Neale	v	Leics	Gloucester	1937
5th	261	W.G.Grace/W.O.Moberley	v	Yorkshire	Cheltenham	1876
6th	320	G.L.Jessop/J.H.Board	v	Sussex	Hove	1903
7th	248	W.G.Grace/E.L.Thomas	v	Sussex	Hove	1896
8th	239	W.R.Hammond/A.E.Wilson	v	Lancashire	Bristol	1938
9th	193	W.G.Grace/S.A.P.Kitcat	v	Sussex	Bristol	1896
10th	131	W.R.Gouldsworthy/J.G.Bessant	v	Somerset	Bristol	1923

Best Bowling	For	10-40	E.G.Dennett	v Essex	Bristol	1906
(Innings)	V	10-66	A.A.Mailey	for Australians	Cheltenham	1921
		10-66	K.Smales	for Notts	Stroud	1956
Best Bowling	For	17-56	C.W.L.Parker	v Essex	Gloucester	1925
(Match)	V	15-87	A.J.Conway	for Worcs	Moreton-in-M	1914

Most Runs – Season	2860	W.R.Hammond	(av 69.75)	1933
Most Runs – Career	33664	W.R.Hammond	(av 57.05)	1920-51
Most 100s – Season	13	W.R.Hammond		1938
Most 100s – Career	113	W.R.Hammond		1920-51
Most Wkts – Season	222	T.W.J.Goddard	(av 16.80)	1937
	222	T.W.J.Goddard	(av 16.37)	1947
Most Wkts – Career	3170	C.W.L.Parker	(av 19.43)	1903-35

LIMITED-OVERS CRICKET

Highest Total	NWT	327-7		v Berkshire	Reading	1966
	BHC	308-3		v Ireland	Dublin	1996
	SL	284-4		v Leics	Cheltenham	1996
Lowest Total	NWT	82		v Notts	Bristol	1987
	BHC	62		v Hampshire	Bristol	1975
	SL	49		v Middlesex	Bristol	1978
Highest Innings	NWT	158	Zaheer Abbas	v Leics	Leicester	1983
	BHC	154*	M.J.Procter	v Somerset	Taunton	1972
	SL	134*	M.W.Alleyne	v Leics	Bristol	1992
Best Bowling	NWT	6-21	C.A.Walsh	v Kent	Bristol	1990
		6-21	C.A.Walsh	v Cheshire	Bristol	1992
	BHC	6-13	M.J.Procter	v Hampshire	Southampton	1977
	SL	6-52	J.N.Shepherd	v Kent	Bristol	1983

HAMPSHIRE

Formation of Present Club: 12 August 1863
Colours: Blue, Gold and White
Badge: Tudor Rose and Crown
Championships: (2) 1961, 1973
NatWest Trophy/Gillette Cup Winners: (1) 1991
Benson and Hedges Cup Winners: (2) 1988, 1992
Sunday League Champions: (3) 1975, 1978, 1986
Match Awards: NWT 53; BHC 62

Chief Executive: A.F.Baker
County Cricket Ground, Northlands Road, Southampton SO15 2UE
(Tel 01703 333788)
Captain: J.P.Stephenson. **Vice-Captain:** R.A.Smith. **Overseas Player:** *tba.*
1997 Beneficiary: C.A.Connor. **Scorer:** V.H Isaacs

AYMES, Adrian Nigel (Bellemoor SM, Southampton), b Southampton 4 Jun 1964. 6'0". RHB, WK. Debut 1987; cap 1991. HS 113 v Essex (Southampton) 1996. BB 1-75. **NWT:** HS 34 v Kent (Southampton) 1994. **BHC:** HS 38 v Surrey (Oval) 1996. **SL:** HS 54 v Durham (Portsmouth) 1994.

BOVILL, James Noel Bruce (Charterhouse; Durham U), b High Wycombe, Bucks 2 Jun 1971. Son of M.E. (Dorset 1957-60). 6'1". RHB, RFM. Debut 1993. Combined Us 1994. Buckinghamshire 1990-92. HS 31 v Worcs (Southampton) 1995. BB 6-29 (12-68 match) v Durham (Stockton) 1995. **BHC:** HS 14* Comb Us v Glam (Cardiff) 1992. BB 2-21 Comb Us v Lancs (Oxford) 1994. **SL:** HS 7*. BB 3-40 v Surrey (Oval) 1993.

CONNOR, Cardigan Adolphus (The Valley SS, Anguilla; Langley C, Berkshire), b The Valley, Anguilla 24 Mar 1961. 5'9". RHB, RFM. Debut 1984; cap 1988; benefit 1997. Buckinghamshire 1979-83. HS 59 v Surrey (Oval) 1993. 50 wkts (5); most – 72 (1994). BB 9-38 v Glos (Southampton) 1996. Award: NWT 1. **NWT:** HS 13 v Yorks (Southampton) 1990. BB 4-11 v Cambs (March) 1994. **BHC:** HS 11 v Glos (Southampton) 1995. BB 4-19 v Sussex (Hove) 1989. **SL:** HS 25 v Middx (Lord's) 1993. BB 5-25 v Northants (Basingstoke) 1996.

DIBDEN, Richard Rockley (Mountbatten S, Romsey; Barton Peveril C, Eastleigh; Loughborough U), b Southampton 29 Jan 1975. 6'0". RHB, OB. Debut 1995. British Us 1996. HS 1. H HS 0*. BB 2-36 v Yorks (Southampton) 1995.

FRANCIS, Simon Richard George (Yardley Court, Tonbridge; King Edward VI S, Southampton), b Bromley, Kent 15 Aug 1978. 6'2". RHB, RMF. Staff 1996 – awaiting f-c debut.

GARAWAY, Mark (Sandown HS, IoW), b Swindon, Wilts 20 Jul 1973. 5'8". RHB, WK. Debut 1996. MCC YC. Awaiting BAC debut. HS 44 v CU (Cambridge) 1996.

JAMES, Kevan David (Edmonton County HS), b Lambeth, London 18 Mar 1961. 6'0". LHB, LMF. Middlesex 1980-84. Wellington 1982-83. Hampshire debut 1985; cap 1989. 1000 runs (2); most – 1274 (1991). HS 162 v Glam (Cardiff) 1989. BB 6-22 v A (Southampton) 1985. BAC BB 6-38 v Derbys (Derby) 1995. Achieved unique double of 4 wkts in 4 balls and a hundred (103) v I (Southampton) 1996. **NWT:** HS 42 v Glam (Cardiff) 1989. BB 4-42 v Worcs (Worcester) 1996. **BHC:** HS 56 v Glos (Bristol) 1996. BB 3-31 v Middx 1987 and v Glam 1988. **SL:** HS 66 v Glos (Trowbridge) 1989. BB 6-35 v Notts (Southampton) 1996.

KEECH, Matthew (Northumberland Park S), b Hampstead 21 Oct 1970. 6'0". RHB, RM. Middlesex 1991-93. Hampshire debut 1994. MCC YC. HS 104 v Sussex (Arundel) 1996. BB 2-28 M v Glos (Bristol) 1993. H HB 1-43. Scored 251 (256 balls) v Glam II (Usk) – Hants II record. **NWT:** HS 3. **BHC:** HS 47 M v Warwks (Lord's) 1991. BB 1-37. **SL:** HS 98 v Worcs (Southampton) 1995. BB 2-22 M v Northants (Lord's) 1993.

KENDALL, William Salwey (Bradfield C; Keble C, Oxford), b Wimbledon, Surrey 18 Dec 1973. 5'10". RHB, RM. Oxford U 1994-96; blue 1995-96. Hampshire debut 1996. 1000 runs (1): 1045 (1996). HS 145* OU v CU (Lord's) 1996. H HS 103* and BB 2-46 v Notts (Southampton) 1996. BB 3-37 OU v Derbys (Oxford) 1995. **BHC:** HS 23 Comb Us v Hants (Oxford) 1995. **SL:** HS 38* v Leics (Leicester) 1996.

LANEY, Jason Scott (Pewsey Vale SS; St John's SFC, Marlborough; Leeds U), b Winchester 27 Apr 1973. 5'10". RHB, OB. Debut 1995; cap 1996. Matabeleland 1995-96. 1000 runs (1): 1163 (1996). HS 112 v OU (Oxford) 1996. BAC HS 105 v Kent (Canterbury) 1996. Award: NWT 1. **NWT:** HS 153 v Norfolk (Southampton) 1996. **BHC:** HS 41 v Surrey (Oval) 1996. **SL:** HS 57 v Kent (Canterbury) 1996.

MARU, Rajesh Jamandass (Rook's Heath HS, Harrow; Pinner SFC), b Nairobi, Kenya 28 Oct 1962. 5'6". RHB, SLA. Middlesex 1980-82. Hampshire debut 1984; cap 1986. Tour: Z 1980-81 (Mx). HS 74 v Glos (Gloucester) 1988. 50 wkts (4); most – 73 (1985). BB 8-41 v Kent (Southampton) 1989. **NWT:** HS 22 v Yorks (Southampton) 1990. BB 3-46 v Leics (Leicester) 1990. **BHC:** HS 9. BB 3-46 v Comb Us (Southampton) 1990. **SL:** HS 33* v Glam (Ebbw Vale) 1991. BB 3-30 v Leics (Leicester) 1988.

MASCARENHAS, Adrian Dimitri (Trinity C, Perth, Australia), b Hammersmith, London 30 Oct 1977. Parents born in Ceylon. Resident in Perth 1979-96. RHB, RMF. Debut 1996, taking 6-88 v Glamorgan (Southampton); took 14 wickets in first two BAC matches. Dorset 1996. HS 14 v Kent (Canterbury) 1996. BB 6-88 (as above). **SL:** HS 7*. BB 2-34 v Kent (Canterbury) 1996.

MILBURN, Stuart Mark (Upper Nidderdale HS), b Harrogate, Yorks 29 Sep 1972. 6'1". RHB, RMF. Yorkshire 1992-95. Hampshire debut 1996. HS 54* v I (Southampton) 1996. BAC HS 25 v Yorks (Harrogate) 1996. BB 4-68 Y v Northants (Sheffield) 1995. H BB 3-47 v Warwks (Birmingham) 1996. **NWT:** HS 27 v Essex (Southampton) 1996. **BHC:** HS 2. BB 2-7 v Ire (Southampton) 1996. **SL:** HS 13* Y v Surrey (Oval) 1995. BB 2-18 v Sussex (Arundel) 1996.

RENSHAW, Simon John (Birkenhead S; Leeds U), b Bebington, Cheshire 6 Mar 1974. 6'3". RHB, RMF. Combined U 1995. Hampshire debut 1996. Cheshire 1994-95. HS 9*. BB 4-56 v Leics (Leicester) 1996. **BHC:** HS 0*. BB 2-34 Comb Us v Hants (Oxford) 1995. **SL:** HS 6*. BB 2-18 v Leics (Leicester) 1996.

SAVIDENT, Lee (Guernsey GS; Guernsey CFE), b Guernsey 22 Oct 1976. 6'5". RHB, RM. Staff 1996 – awaiting f-c debut.

SMITH, Robin Arnold (Northlands BHS), b Durban, SA 13 Sep 1963. Brother of C.L. (Natal, Glam, Hants and England 1977-78 to 1992) and grandson of Dr V.L.Shearer (Natal). 5'11". RHB, LB. Natal 1980-81 to 1984-85. Hampshire debut 1982; cap 1985; benefit 1996. *Wisden* 1989. **Tests:** 62 (1988 to 1995-96); HS 175 v WI (St John's) 1993-94. **LOI:** 71 (1988 to 1995-96; HS 167* – Eng record). Tours: A 1990-91; SA 1995-96; WI 1989-90, 1993-94; NZ 1991-92; I/SL 1992-93. 1000 runs (10); most – 1577 (1989). HS 209* v Essex (Southend) 1987. BB 2-11 v Surrey (Southampton) 1985. Awards: NWT 7; BHC 5. **NWT:** HS 158 v Worcs (Worcester) 1996. BB 2-13 v Berks (Southampton) 1985. **BHC:** HS 155* v Glam (Southampton) 1989. **SL:** HS 131 v Notts (Nottingham) 1989. BB 1-0.

STEPHENSON, John Patrick (Felsted S; Durham U), b Stebbing, Essex 14 Mar 1965. 6'1". RHB, RM. Essex 1985-94 (cap 1989). Hampshire debut/cap 1995; captain 1996 to date. Boland 1988-89. **Tests:** 1 (1989); HS 25 v A (Oval) 1989. Tours: WI 1991-92 (Eng A); Z 1989-90 (Eng A). 1000 runs (5); most – 1887 (1990). HS 202* Ex v Somerset (Bath) 1990. H HS 127 v Lancs (Portsmouth) 1995. BB 7-51 v Middx (Lord's) 1995. Awards: BHC 5. **NWT:** HS 107 v Norfolk (Southampton) 1996. BB 3-78 Ex v Lancs (Chelmsford) 1992. **BHC:** HS 142 Ex v Warwks (Birmingham) 1991. BB 3-22 Ex v Northants (Northampton) 1990. **SL:** HS 110* v Essex (Southampton) 1996. BB 5-58 Ex v Glos (Chelmsford) 1992.

TREAGUS, Glyn Robert (King Edward VI S, Southampton; Brighton U), b Rustington, Sussex 10 Dec 1974. 5'10". RHB, OB. Staff 1996 – awaiting f-c debut. Hockey for Hampshire 1990-91.

UDAL, Shaun David (Cove CS), b Cove, Farnborough 18 Mar 1969. Grandson of G.F.U. (Middx 1932 and Leics 1946); great-great-grandson of J.S. (MCC 1871-75). 6'2". RHB, OB. Debut 1989; cap 1992. **LOI:** 10 (1994 to 1995; HS 11*; BB 2-37). Tours: A 1994-95; P 1995-96 (Eng A). HS 94 v Glam (Southampton) 1994. 50 wkts (4); most – 74 (1993). BB 8-50 v Sussex (Southampton) 1992. Awards: NWT 1; BHC 1. **NWT:** HS 18 v Essex (Southampton) 1996. BB 3-39 v Kent (Southampton) 1992. **BHC:** HS 32 v Glos (Bristol) 1996. BB 4-40 v Middx (Southampton) 1992. **SL:** HS 54 v Middx (Portsmouth) 1996. BB 4-51 v Northants (Bournemouth) 1992.

WHITAKER, Paul Robert (Whitcliffe Mount S), b Keighley, Yorks 28 Jun 1973. 5'9". LHB, OB. Debut 1994. Derbyshire staff 1992-93. HS 119 v Worcs (Southampton) 1995. BB 3-36 v OU (Oxford) 1996. BAC BB 2-64 v Lancs (Manchester) 1996. Award: BHC 1. **NWT:** HS 13 v Leics (Leicester) 1995. BB 3-48 v Essex (Southampton) 1996. **BHC:** HS 53 v Sussex (Southampton) 1996. BB 2-33 v Surrey (Oval) 1996. **SL:** HS 97 v Worcs (Southampton) 1995. BB 3-44 v Surrey (Southampton) 1996.

WHITE, Giles William (Millfield S; Loughborough U), b Barnstaple, Devon 23 Mar 1972. 6'0". RHB, LB. Somerset 1991 (one match). Combined Us 1994. Hampshire debut 1994. Devon 1988-94. HS 104 Comb Us v NZ (Cambridge) 1994. H HS 73* v Durham (Portsmouth) 1994. BB 1-30. **NWT:** HS 11 and BB 1-45 Devon v Kent (Canterbury) 1992. **BHC:** HS 37* v Glam (Southampton) 1995. **SL:** HS 59 v Middx (Lord's) 1995.

NEWCOMERS

KENWAY, Derek Anthony (St George's S, Southampton; Barton Peveril C, Eastleigh), b Fareham 12 Jun 1978. RHB, WK.

SWARBRICK, Matthew (Bournemouth C), b Stockport, Cheshire 8 Aug 1977. RHB.

DEPARTURES (who made first-class appearances in 1996)

BENJAMIN, Winston Keithroy Matthew (All Saints S, Antigua), b St John's, Antigua 31 Dec 1964. 6'3". RHB, RFM. Debut (Rest of World XI) 1985. Leeward Is 1985-86 to date. Leicestershire 1986-90 and 1992; cap 1989. Hampshire 1994-96. Cheshire 1985. **Tests** (WI): 21 (1987-88 to 1994-95); HS 85 v NZ (Christchurch) 1994-95; BB 4-46 v SL (Moratuwa) 1993-94. **LOI** (WI): 85 (1986-87 to 1995; HS 31; BB 5-22). Tours (WI): E 1985 (RW), 1988, 1995 (part); A 1986-87, 1988-89; NZ 1994-95; I 1987-88; P 1986-87; SL 1993-94. HS 117 v Essex (Southampton) 1996. 50 wkts (1): 69 (1989). BB 7-54 (inc hat-trick) Le v A (Leicester) 1989. BAC BB 7-83 Le v Lancs (Leicester) 1993. H BB 6-46 v Worcs (Worcester) 1994. Hat-trick 1989. Awards: BHC 2. **NWT:** HS 41 v Essex (Southampton) 1996. BB 5-32 Le v Derbys (Derby) 1992. **BHC:** HS 58* v Ire (Southampton) 1996. BB 5-17 Le v Minor C (Leicester) 1986. **SL:** HS 104* v Northants (Basingstoke) 1996. BB 4-19 Le v Lancs (Leicester) 1986.

BOTHAM, Liam James (Rossall S), b Doncaster, Yorks 26 Aug 1977. Son of I.T. (Somerset, Worcs, Durham, Queensland and England 1974-93). 6'0". RHB, RMF. Hampshire 1996. HS 30 and BB 5-67 v Middx (Portsmouth) 1996 (on debut). **SL:** HS 1. Rugby for West Hartlepool.

MORRIS, Robert Sean Millner (Stowe S; Durham U), b Great Horwood, Bucks 10 Sep 1968. RHB, OB. 6'0". Hampshire 1992-96. HS 174 v Notts (Basingstoke) 1994. **NWT:** HS 39 v Glos (Bristol) 1996. **BHC:** HS – . **SL:** HS 87 v Glos (Basingstoke) 1995.

TERRY, Vivian Paul (Millfield S), b Osnabruck, W Germany 14 Jan 1959. 6'0". RHB, RM. Hampshire 1978-96; cap 1983; benefit 1994. **Tests:** 2 (1984); HS 8. Tour: Z 1984-85 (EC). 1000 runs (11); most – 1469 (1993). HS 190 v SL (Southampton) 1988. BAC HS 180 v Derbys (Derby) 1990. Awards: NWT 4; BHC 4. **NWT:** HS 165* v Berks (Southampton) 1985. **BHC:** HS 134 v Comb Us (Southampton) 1990. **SL:** HS 142 v Leics (Southampton) 1986.

THURSFIELD, M.J. – *see SUSSEX.*

43

HAMPSHIRE 1996

RESULTS SUMMARY

	Place	Won	Lost	Drew	No Result
Britannic Assurance Championship	14th	3	7	7	–
All First-Class Matches		4	7	9	–
NatWest Trophy	Quarter-Finalist				
Benson and Hedges Cup	3rd in Group D				
Sunday League	15th	4	10	–	3

BRITANNIC ASSURANCE CHAMPIONSHIP AVERAGES

BATTING AND FIELDING

Cap		M	I	NO	HS	Runs	Avge	100	50	Ct/St
1985	R.A.Smith	16	29	2	179	1348	49.92	3	8	1
–	W.S.Kendall	8	16	2	103*	601	42.92	1	4	11
1991	A.N.Aymes	17	30	12	113	770	42.77	2	2	39/1
–	M.Keech	10	18	2	104	644	40.25	1	6	8
1983	V.P.Terry	5	9	1	87*	301	37.62	–	3	10
1996	J.S.Laney	14	26	–	105	932	35.84	2	5	8
–	W.K.M.Benjamin	2	4	–	117	140	35.00	1	–	3
–	G.W.White	11	21	2	73	579	30.47	–	6	12
1989	K.D.James	12	22	1	118*	635	30.23	1	3	6
1995	J.P.Stephenson	13	23	2	85	550	26.19	–	5	6
1986	R.J.Maru	11	17	5	55*	303	25.25	–	1	17
–	P.R.Whitaker	9	17	1	67*	385	24.06	–	3	4
1992	S.D.Udal	14	21	3	50*	374	20.77	–	1	11
1988	C.A.Connor	9	12	3	42	140	15.55	–	–	–
–	S.M.Milburn	8	10	–	25	109	10.90	–	–	–
–	J.N.B.Bovill	12	18	2	29	123	7.68	–	–	–
–	R.S.M.Morris	3	6	–	11	44	7.33	–	–	2
–	S.J.Renshaw	6	7	5	9*	10	5.00	–	–	3

Also batted: L.J.Botham (3 matches) 30, 1, 0 (2 ct); A.D.Mascarenhas (2 matches) 10, 14, 0; M.J.Thursfield (2 matches) 4, 18.

BOWLING

	O	M	R	W	Avge	Best	5wI	10wM
A.D.Mascarenhas	92	21	297	16	18.56	6-88	1	–
C.A.Connor	342.4	91	1033	48	21.52	9-38	2	–
J.P.Stephenson	314.4	68	1035	36	28.75	6-48	3	–
K.D.James	276.1	53	808	25	32.32	3-17	–	–
J.N.B.Bovill	288	52	1047	31	33.77	5-58	1	–
R.J.Maru	306.2	101	734	18	40.77	3-50	–	–
S.M.Milburn	215.4	39	791	17	46.52	3-47	–	–
S.J.Renshaw	192.5	48	689	14	49.21	4-56	–	–
S.D.Udal	416.5	135	1333	26	51.26	5-82	1	–

Also bowled: W.K.M.Benjamin 69.2-13-201-6; L.J.Botham 55-9-268-8; M.Keech 18-3-46-0; W.S.Kendall 14-1-47-2; J.S.Laney 14-2-61-0; M.J.Thursfield 40-5-158-0; P.R.Whitaker 81-14-311-3; G.W.White 17-2-75-0.

The First-Class Averages (pp 123-38) give the records of Hampshire players in all first-class county matches (their other opponents being the Indians, Cambridge University and Oxford University), with the exception of W.S.Kendall whose full county figures are as above.

HAMPSHIRE RECORDS

FIRST-CLASS CRICKET

Highest Total	For	672-7d		v	Somerset	Taunton	1899
	V	742		by	Surrey	The Oval	1909
Lowest Total	For	15		v	Warwicks	Birmingham	1922
	V	23		by	Yorkshire	Middlesbrough	1965
Highest Innings	For	316	R.H.Moore	v	Warwicks	Bournemouth	1937
	V	302*	P.Holmes	for	Yorkshire	Portsmouth	1920

Highest Partnership for each Wicket

1st	347	V.P.Terry/C.L.Smith	v	Warwicks	Birmingham	1987
2nd	321	G.Brown/E.I.M.Barrett	v	Glos	Southampton	1920
3rd	344	C.P.Mead/G.Brown	v	Yorkshire	Portsmouth	1927
4th	263	R.E.Marshall/D.A.Livingstone	v	Middlesex	Lord's	1970
5th	235	G.Hill/D.F.Walker	v	Sussex	Portsmouth	1937
6th	411	R.M.Poore/E.G.Wynyard	v	Somerset	Taunton	1899
7th	325	G.Brown/C.H.Abercrombie	v	Essex	Leyton	1913
8th	227	K.D.James/T.M.Tremlett	v	Somerset	Taunton	1985
9th	230	D.A.Livingstone/A.T.Castell	v	Surrey	Southampton	1962
10th	192	H.A.W.Bowell/W.H.Livsey	v	Worcs	Bournemouth	1921

Best Bowling	For	9- 25	R.M.H.Cottam	v	Lancashire	Manchester	1965
(Innings)	V	10- 46	W.Hickton	for	Lancashire	Manchester	1870
Best Bowling	For	16- 88	J.A.Newman	v	Somerset	Weston-s-Mare	1927
(Match)	V	17-119	W.Mead	for	Essex	Southampton	1895

Most Runs – Season	2854	C.P.Mead	(av 79.27)	1928
Most Runs – Career	48892	C.P.Mead	(av 48.84)	1905-36
Most 100s – Season	12	C.P.Mead		1928
Most 100s – Career	138	C.P.Mead		1905-36
Most Wkts – Season	190	A.S.Kennedy	(av 15.61)	1922
Most Wkts – Career	2669	D.Shackleton	(av 18.23)	1948-69

LIMITED-OVERS CRICKET

Highest Total	NWT	371-4		v	Glamorgan	Southampton	1975
	BHC	321-1		v	Minor C (S)	Amersham	1973
	SL	313-2		v	Sussex	Portsmouth	1993
Lowest Total	NWT	98		v	Lancashire	Manchester	1975
	BHC	50		v	Yorkshire	Leeds	1991
	SL	43		v	Essex	Basingstoke	1972
Highest Innings	NWT	177	C.G.Greenidge	v	Glamorgan	Southampton	1975
	BHC	173*	C.G.Greenidge	v	Minor C (S)	Amersham	1973
	SL	172	C.G.Greenidge	v	Surrey	Southampton	1987
Best Bowling	NWT	7-30	P.J.Sainsbury	v	Norfolk	Southampton	1965
	BHC	5-13	S.T.Jefferies	v	Derbyshire	Lord's	1988
	SL	6-20	T.E.Jesty	v	Glamorgan	Cardiff	1975

KENT

Formation of Present Club: 1 March 1859
Substantial Reorganisation: 6 December 1870
Colours: Maroon and White
Badge: White Horse on a Red Ground
Championships: (6) 1906, 1909, 1910, 1913, 1970, 1978
Joint Championship: (1) 1977
NatWest Trophy/Gillette Cup Winners: (2) 1967, 1974
Benson and Hedges Cup Winners: (3) 1973, 1976, 1978
Sunday League Champions: (4) 1972, 1973, 1976, 1995
Match Awards: NWT 47; BHC 81

Secretary: S.T.W.Anderson OBE, MC
    St Lawrence Ground, Canterbury, CT1 3NZ (Tel 01227 456886)
Captain: S.A.Marsh. **Overseas Player:** P.A.Strang. **1997 Beneficiary:** G.R.Cowdrey.
Scorer: J.C.Foley

COWDREY, Graham Robert (Tonbridge S; Durham U), b Farnborough 27 Jun 1964.
Brother of C.S. (Kent, Glam and England 1977-92), son of M.C. (Kent and England
1950-76), grandson of E.A. (Europeans). 5'11". RHB, RM. Debut 1984; cap 1988; benefit
1997. 1000 runs (1): most – 1576 (1990). HS 147 v Glos (Bristol) 1992. BB 1-5. Award:
BHC 1. **NWT:** HS 41 v Derbys (Derby) 1996. BB 2-4 v Devon (Canterbury) 1993. **BHC:**
HS 70* v Leics (Canterbury) 1991. BB 1-6. **SL:** HS 105* v Hants (Southampton) 1995.
BB 4-15 v Essex (Ilford) 1987.

EALHAM, Mark Alan (Stour Valley SS, Chartham), b Willesborough, Ashford 27 Aug
1969. Son of A.G.E. (Kent 1966-82). 5'9". RHB, RMF. Debut 1989; cap 1992. **Tests:** 2
(1996); HS 51 and BB 4-21 v I (Nottingham) 1996. **LOI:** 2 (1996; HS 40). Tours: A
1996-97 (Eng A); Z 1992-93 (K). HS 121 v Notts (Nottingham) 1995. BB 8-36 (10-74
match) v Warwks (Birmingham) 1996. Awards: NWT 2; BHC 4. **NWT:** HS 58* v
Warwks (Birmingham) 1993. BB 4-10 v Derbys (Derby) 1994. **BHC:** HS 75 v Brit Us
(Oxford) 1996. BB 4-29 v Somerset (Canterbury) 1992. **SL:** HS 112 v Derbys
(Maidstone) 1995 (off 44 balls – SL record). BB 6-53 v Hants (Basingstoke) 1993.

FLEMING, Matthew Valentine (St Aubyns S, Rottingdean; Eton C), b Macclesfield,
Cheshire 12 Dec 1964. 5'11½". RHB, RM. Debut 1989; cap 1990. Tour: Z 1992-93 (K).
HS 116 v WI (Canterbury) 1991 and v Derbys (Derby) 1996. BB 4-31 v Glos (Tunbridge
W) 1993. Awards: NWT 1; BHC 4. **NWT:** HS 53 v Devon (Canterbury) 1992. BB 3-34 v
Hants (Southampton) 1992. **BHC:** HS 72 v Brit Us (Oxford) 1996. BB 3-18 v Ire
(Comber) 1995. **SL:** HS 112 v Essex (Ilford) 1996. BB 4-13 v Yorks (Canterbury) 1996.

FORD, James Antony (Tonbridge S; Durham U), b Pembury 30 Mar 1976. 5'8". RHB,
SLA. Debut 1996. Awaiting BAC debut. HS – . Hockey for Northern Us and Durham.

FULTON, David Paul (The Judd S; Kent U), b Lewisham 15 Nov 1971. 6'2". RHB, SLA.
Debut 1992. HS 134* and BB 1-37 v OU (Canterbury) 1996. **NWT:** HS 88 v Leics
(Leicester) 1996. **NWT:** HS 19 v Staffs (Stone) 1995. **BHC:** HS 25 v Lancs (Lord's)
1995. **SL:** HS 29 v Lancs (Manchester) 1993.

HEADLEY, Dean Warren (Oldswinford Hospital S; Worcester RGS), b Norton, Stourbridge, Worcs 27 Jan 1970. Son of R.G.A. (Worcs, Jamaica and WI 1958-74); grandson of
G.A. (Jamaica and WI 1927-28 to 1953-54). 6'4". RHB, RFM. Middlesex 1991-92; took 5-46
on BAC debut, including wicket of A.A.Metcalfe with his first ball. Kent debut 1992-93; cap
1993. **LOI:** 2 (1996; HS 3*). Tours (Eng A): A 1996-97; P 1995-96; Z 1992-93 (K). HS 91 M
v Leics (Leicester) 1992. K HS 63* v Somerset (Canterbury) 1996. 50 wkts (1): 51 (1996).
BB 8-98 (inc hat-trick; 11-165 match) v Derbys (Derby) 1996. 3 hat-tricks (v Derbys, Worcs
and Hants) 1996. Award: BHC 1. **NWT:** HS 24* v Warwks (Birmingham) 1995. BB 5-20 M v
Salop (Telford) 1992. **BHC:** HS 26 M v Surrey (Lord's) 1991. BB 4-19 M v Sussex (Hove)
1992. **SL:** HS 29* v Glos (Moreton-in-M) 1996. BB 6-42 v Surrey (Canterbury) 1995.

HOUSE, William John (Sevenoaks S; Gonville & Caius C, Cambridge), b Sheffield, Yorks 16 Mar 1976. 5'11". LHB, RM. Debut (Cambridge U) 1996, scoring 136 v Derbys in his second innings; blue 1996. Awaiting Kent debut. HS 136 (as above). BB 1-44. **BHC:** (Brit Us) HS 22 v Middx (Cambridge) 1996. **SL:** HS 19* v Derbys (Derby) 1996.

IGGLESDEN, Alan Paul (Churchill S, Westerham), b Farnborough 8 Oct 1964. 6'6". RHB, RFM. Debut 1986; cap 1989; testimonial 1998. W Province 1987-88. Boland 1992-93. **Tests:** 3 (1989 to 1993-94); HS 3*; BB 2-91 v A (Oval) 1989. **LOI:** 4 (1993-94; HS 18; BB 2-12). Tours: WI 1993-94; Z 1989-90 (Eng A), 1992-93 (K). HS 41 v Surrey (Canterbury) 1988. 50 wkts (4); most – 56 (1989). BB 7-28 (12-66 match) Boland v GW (Kimberley) 1992-93. K BB 6-34 v Surrey (Canterbury) 1988. **NWT:** HS 12* v Oxon (Oxford) 1990. BB 4-29 v Cambs (Canterbury) 1991. **BHC:** HS 26* v Worcs (Worcester) 1991. BB 3-24 v Scot (Glasgow) 1991 and v Notts (Nottingham) 1992. **SL:** HS 13* (twice). BB 5-13 v Sussex (Hove) 1989.

LLONG, Nigel James (Ashford North S), b Ashford 11 Feb 1969. 6'0". LHB, OB. Debut 1990; cap 1993. Tour: Z 1992-93 (K). HS 130 v Hants (Canterbury) 1996. BB 5-21 v Middx (Canterbury) 1996. Award: NWT 1. **NWT:** HS 115* and BB 3-36 v Cambs (March) 1996. **BHC:** HS 31 v Glam (Canterbury) 1996. BB 2-38 v Brit Us (Oxford) 1996. **SL:** HS 70 v Sussex (Tunbridge W) 1996. BB 4-24 v Sussex (Hove) 1993.

McCAGUE, Martin John (Hedland Sr HS; Carine Tafe C), b Larne, N Ireland 24 May 1969. 6'5". RHB, RF. W Australia 1990-91 to 1991-92. Kent debut 1991; cap 1992. **Tests:** 3 (1993 to 1994-95); HS 11 v A (Leeds) 1993; BB 4-121 v A (Nottingham) 1993. Tours: A 1994-95 (part); SA 1993-94 (Eng A). HS 63* v Surrey (Oval) 1996. 50 wkts (4); most – 76 (1996). BB 9-86 (15-147 match) v Derbys (Derby) 1994. Hat-trick 1996. Award: NWT 1. **NWT:** HS 31* v Staffs (Stone) 1995. BB 5-26 v Middx (Canterbury) 1993. **BHC:** HS 30 v Derbys (Canterbury) 1992. BB 5-43 v Somerset (Canterbury) 1992. **SL:** HS 22* v Glam (Swansea) 1992. BB 5-40 v Essex (Canterbury) 1995.

MARSH, Steven Andrew (Walderslade SS; Mid-Kent CFE), b Westminster, London 27 Jan 1961. 5'10". RHB, WK. Debut 1982; cap 1986; benefit 1995; captain 1996 to date. Tour: Z 1992-93 (K – captain). HS 127 v Essex (Ilford) 1996. BB 2-20 v Warwks (Birmingham) 1990. Set world f-c record by holding eight catches in an innings AND scoring a hundred (v Middx at Lord's) 1991. **NWT:** HS 55 v Warwks (Birmingham) 1995. BB 1-3. **BHC:** HS 71 v Lancs (Manchester) 1991. **SL:** HS 59 v Leics (Canterbury) 1991.

PATEL, Minal Mahesh (Dartford GS; Erith TC), b Bombay, India 7 Jul 1970. 5'9". RHB, SLA. Debut 1989; cap 1994. **Tests:** 2 (1996); HS 27 and BB 1-101 v I (Nottingham) 1996. Tour: I 1994-95 (Eng A). HS 56 v Leics (Canterbury) 1995. 50 wkts (2); most – 90 (1994). BB 8-96 v Lancs (Canterbury) 1994. **NWT:** HS 5*. BB 2-29 v Oxon (Oxford) 1990. **BHC:** HS 18* v Glam (Canterbury) 1996. BB 2-29 v Somerset (Canterbury) 1995. **SL:** HS 5. BB 3-50 v Northants (Northampton) 1994.

PHILLIPS, Ben James (Langley Park S and SFC, Beckenham), b Lewisham 30 Sep 1974. 6'6". RHB, RFM. Debut 1996. HS 2 (twice). BB 3-34 v Sussex (Tunbridge W) 1996 (on debut). **SL:** HS 29 v Glam (Cardiff) 1996. BB 2-42 v Somerset (Canterbury) 1996.

PRESTON, Nicholas William (Meopham SS; Gravesend GS; Exeter U), b Dartford 22 Jan 1972. 6'1". RHB, RFM. Debut 1996. HS 17* v Derbys (Derby) 1996. BB 4-68 v Yorks (Canterbury) 1996. **NWT:** HS – . **SL:** HS 7*.

SMITH, Edward Thomas (Tonbridge S; Peterhouse C, Cambridge), b Pembury 19 Jul 1977. 6'2". RHB, RM. Debut (Cambridge U) 1996, scoring 101 v Glam (Cambridge); blue 1996. Kent debut 1996. HS 101 (as above). K HS 31 v Derbys (Derby) 1996 (on debut).

STANFORD, Edward John (The Downs Ss, Dartford), b Dartford 21 Jan 1971. 5'10". LHB, SLA. Debut 1995. HS 10* v Durham (Maidstone) 1996. BB 3-84 v Leics (Leicester) 1996.

THOMPSON, Dr Julian Barton deCourcy (The Judd S, Tonbridge; Guy's Hospital Medical S, London U), b Cape Town, SA 28 Oct 1968. 6'4". RHB, RFM. Debut 1994. HS 40* v CU (Folkestone) 1995. BAC HS 37 v Essex (Ilford) 1996. BB 5-72 v Surrey (Oval) 1996. Awards: BHC 2. **BHC:** HS 12* v Glam (Canterbury) 1996. BB 3-29 v Middx (Canterbury) 1996. **SL:** HS 30 v Glam (Cardiff) 1996. BB 3-26 v Sussex (Tunbridge W) 1996.

WALKER, Matthew Jonathan (King's S, Rochester), b Gravesend 2 Jan 1974. Grandson of Jack (Kent 1949). 5'8". LHB, RM. Debut 1992-93 (Z tour). UK debut 1994. Tour: Z 1992-93 (K). HS 275* v Somerset (Canterbury) 1996. Award: BHC 1. **NWT:** HS 51 v Derbys (Derby) 1996. **BHC:** HS 69* v Sussex (Hove) 1995. **SL:** HS 69* v Derbys (Derby) 1994.

WALSH, Christopher David (Tonbridge S; Exeter U), b Pembury 6 Nov 1975. Son of D.R. (Oxford U 1966-69). 6'1". RHB, LB. Debut 1996. Awaiting BAC debut. HS 56* v OU (Canterbury) 1996 (on debut).

WARD, Trevor Robert (Hextable CS, nr Swanley), b Farningham 18 Jan 1968. 5'11". RHB, OB. Debut 1986; cap 1989. Tour: Z 1992-93 (K). 1000 runs (5); most – 1648 (1992). HS 235* v Middx (Canterbury) 1991. BB 2-10 v Yorks (Canterbury) 1996. Awards: NWT 1; BHC 2. **NWT:** HS 120 v Berks (Finchampstead) 1994. BB 1-28. **BHC:** HS 125 v Surrey (Canterbury) 1995. **SL:** HS 131 v Notts (Nottingham) 1993. BB 3-20 v Glam (Canterbury) 1989.

WILLIS, Simon Charles (Wilmington GS), b Greenwich, London 19 Mar 1974. 5'8". RHB, OB, WK. Debut 1993. HS 82 v CU (Folkestone) 1995. BAC HS 78 v Northants (Northampton) 1996. **NWT:** HS 19* v Staffs (Stone) 1995. **SL:** HS 31* v Worcs (Canterbury) 1996.

WREN, Timothy Neil (Harvey GS, Folkestone), b Folkestone 26 Mar 1970. 6'3". RHB, LM. Debut 1990. Tour: Z 1992-93 (K). HS 23 v Sussex (Hove) 1995. BB 6-48 v Somerset (Canterbury) 1994. Award: BHC 1. **NWT:** HS 1*. BB 1-51. **BHC:** HS 7. BB 6-41 v Somerset (Canterbury) 1995. **SL:** HS 7*. BB 3-20 v Yorks (Leeds) 1995.

NEWCOMERS

KEY, Robert W.T. (Colfe's S), b East Dulwich, London 12 May 1979. RHB, OB. His mother played for Kent Ladies.

STRANG, Paul Andrew (Falcon C; Cape Town U), b Bulawayo, Rhodesia 28 Jul 1970. Elder brother of B.C. (Mashonaland and Zimbabwe 1994-95 to date). RHB, LBG. Debut (Zimbabwe B) 1992-93. Mashonaland Country Dists 1993-94 to 1995-96. Mashonaland 1996-97. **Tests** (Z): 13 (1994-95 to 1996-97); HS 106* v P (Sheikhupura) 1996-97; BB 5-106 v SL (Colombo) 1996-97. **LOI** (Z): 33 (1994-95 to 1996-97); HS 47; BB 5-21). Tours (Z): E 1996 (MCC); A 1994-95; SA 1993-94 (Z Board), 1994-95 (Z Board), 1995-96 (Z A); NZ 1995-96; P 1996-97; SL 1996-97. HS 106* (*Tests*). BB 7-75 Mashonaland CD v Mashonaland U-24 (Harare South) 1994-95.

WELLS, Alan Peter (Tideway CS, Newhaven), b Newhaven, Sussex 2 Oct 1961. Younger brother of C.M. (Sussex, Derbyshire, Border and WP 1979-96). 6'0". RHB, RM. Sussex 1981; cap 1986; captain 1992-96; benefit 1996. Border 1981-82. **Tests:** 1 (1995); HS 3*. **LOI:** 1 (1995; HS 15). Tours (Eng A): SA 1989-90 (Eng XI), 1993-94; I 1994-95 (captain). 1000 runs (10); most – 1784 (1991). HS 253* Sx v Yorks (Middlesbrough) 1991. BB 3-67 Sx v Worcs (Worcester) 1987. Awards: NWT 3. **NWT:** HS 119 Sx v Bucks (Beaconsfield) 1992. **BHC:** HS 74 Sx v Middx (Hove) 1990. BB 1-17. **SL:** HS 127 Sx v Hants (Portsmouth) 1993. BB 1-0.

DEPARTURE (who made first-class appearances in 1996)

HOOPER, Carl Llewellyn (Christchurch SS, Georgetown), b Georgetown, Guyana 15 Dec 1966. 6'1". RHB, OB. Demerara 1983-84. Guyana 1984-85 to date. Kent 1992-94, 1996; cap 1992. **Tests** (WI): 57 (1987-88 to 1996-97); HS 178* v P (St John's) 1992-93; BB 5-40 v P (P-o-S) 1992-93. **LOI** (WI): 150 (1986-87 to 1996-97; HS 113*; BB 4-34). Tours (WI): E 1988, 1991, 1995; A 1988-89, 1991-92, 1992-93, 1995-96; NZ 1986-87; I 1987-88, 1994-95; P 1990-91; SL 1993-94; Z 1986-87 (Young WI), 1989-90 (Young WI). 1000 runs (6); most – 1579 (1994). HS 236* v Glam (Canterbury) 1993. BB 5-33 WI v Queensland (Brisbane) 1988-89. K BB 5-52 v Durham (Canterbury) 1994. Awards: NWT 1; BHC 1. **NWT:** HS 136* v Berks (Finchampstead) 1994. BB 2-12 v Middx (Canterbury) 1993. **BHC:** HS 98 v Somerset (Maidstone) 1996. BB 3-28 v Yorks (Leeds) 1992. **SL:** HS 145 v Leics (Leicester) 1996. BB 5-41 v Essex (Maidstone) 1993. Unavailable 1997.

KENT 1996

RESULTS SUMMARY

	Place	Won	Lost	Tied	Drew
Britannic Assurance Championship	4th	9	2	–	6
All First-Class Matches		9	3	–	7
NatWest Trophy	2nd Round				
Benson and Hedges Cup	Quarter-Finalist				
Sunday League	10th	8	8	1	–

BRITANNIC ASSURANCE CHAMPIONSHIP AVERAGES

BATTING AND FIELDING

Cap		M	I	NO	HS	Runs	Avge	100	50	Ct/St
–	M.J.Walker	7	13	3	275*	606	60.60	1	2	2
1992	C.L.Hooper	17	29	2	155	1287	47.66	3	9	33
–	S.C.Willis	3	4	1	78	129	43.00	–	1	6
1989	T.R.Ward	17	29	1	161	1191	42.53	2	8	10
1993	N.J.Llong	12	20	2	130	719	39.94	2	5	12
1988	G.R.Cowdrey	10	15	–	111	506	33.73	1	3	4
1992	M.A.Ealham	11	18	4	74	452	32.28	–	3	5
1990	M.V.Fleming	17	28	2	116	814	31.30	2	3	7
–	D.P.Fulton	15	27	2	88	643	25.72	–	4	24
1986	S.A.Marsh	14	22	1	127	449	21.38	1	2	28/6
1993	D.W.Headley	10	14	3	63*	226	20.54	–	1	3
1992	M.J.McCague	17	24	7	63*	347	20.41	–	1	10
–	J.B.D.Thompson	4	5	–	37	89	17.80	–	–	–
1994	M.M.Patel	14	19	3	33	224	14.00	–	–	6
–	N.W.Preston	7	11	4	17*	63	9.00	–	–	3
–	T.N.Wren	6	5	2	8	15	5.00	–	–	2

Also batted: B.J.Phillips (3 matches) 2, 1, 2 (1 ct); E.T.Smith (1 match) 31, 26; E.J.Stanford (2 matches) 0*, 10*, 2* (1 ct).

BOWLING

	O	M	R	W	Avge	Best	5wI	10wM
M.A.Ealham	295.4	101	726	36	20.16	8-36	3	1
M.J.McCague	564	114	1815	75	24.20	6-51	3	–
D.W.Headley	364	59	1235	45	27.44	8-98	2	1
M.V.Fleming	163	31	472	17	27.76	3- 6	–	–
C.L.Hooper	321.3	83	789	26	30.34	4- 7	–	–
N.W.Preston	119.5	25	326	10	32.60	4-68	–	–
M.M.Patel	469	142	1186	29	40.89	6-97	2	1

Also bowled: G.R.Cowdrey 8-3-23-0; D.P.Fulton 4-1-28-0; N.J.Llong 52.5-17-135-9; S.A.Marsh 6-4-5-0; B.J.Phillips 40-12-109-4; E.J.Stanford 67.3-22-158-5; J.B.D.Thompson 75.2-14-268-7; M.J.Walker 1-0-19-0; T.R.Ward 9-3-29-2; T.N.Wren 92-17-347-8.

The First-Class Averages (pp 123-38) give the records of Kent players in all first-class county matches (their other opponents being the Pakistanis and Oxford University), with the exception of E.T.Smith whose full county figures are as above, and:

M.A.Ealham 12-20-4-74-537-33.56-0-4-6ct. 321.4-108-803-40-20.07-8/36-3-1.
M.M.Patel 16-21-5-33-233-14.56-0-0-7ct. 540-168-1374-32-42.93-6/97-2-1.

KENT RECORDS

FIRST-CLASS CRICKET

Highest Total	For	803-4d		v	Essex	Brentwood	1934
	V	676		by	Australians	Canterbury	1921
Lowest Total	For	18		v	Sussex	Gravesend	1867
	V	16		by	Warwicks	Tonbridge	1913
Highest Innings	For	332	W.H.Ashdown	v	Essex	Brentwood	1934
	V	344	W.G.Grace	for	MCC	Canterbury	1876

Highest Partnership for each Wicket

1st	300	N.R.Taylor/M.R.Benson	v	Derbyshire	Canterbury	1991
2nd	366	S.G.Hinks/N.R.Taylor	v	Middlesex	Canterbury	1990
3rd	321*	A.Hearne/J.R.Mason	v	Notts	Nottingham	1899
4th	368	P.A.de Silva/G.R.Cowdrey	v	Derbyshire	Maidstone	1995
5th	277	F.E.Woolley/L.E.G.Ames	v	New Zealand	Canterbury	1931
6th	315	P.A.de Silva/M.A.Ealham	v	Notts	Nottingham	1995
7th	248	A.P.Day/E.Humphreys	v	Somerset	Taunton	1908
8th	157	A.L.Hilder/A.C.Wright	v	Essex	Gravesend	1924
9th	161	B.R.Edrich/F.Ridgway	v	Sussex	Tunbridge W	1949
10th	235	F.E.Woolley/A.Fielder	v	Worcs	Stourbridge	1909

Best Bowling	For	10- 30	C.Blythe	v	Northants	Northampton	1907
(Innings)	V	10- 48	C.H.G.Bland	for	Sussex	Tonbridge	1899
Best Bowling	For	17- 48	C.Blythe	v	Northants	Northampton	1907
(Match)	V	17-106	T.W.J.Goddard	for	Glos	Bristol	1939

Most Runs – Season	2894	F.E.Woolley	(av 59.06)	1928
Most Runs – Career	47868	F.E.Woolley	(av 41.77)	1906-38
Most 100s – Season	10	F.E.Woolley		1928
	10	F.E.Woolley		1934
Most 100s – Career	122	F.E.Woolley		1906-38
Most Wkts – Season	262	A.P.Freeman	(av 14.74)	1933
Most Wkts – Career	3340	A.P.Freeman	(av 17.64)	1914-36

LIMITED-OVERS CRICKET

Highest Total	NWT	384-6		v	Berkshire	Finchampstead	1994
	BHC	338-6		v	Somerset	Maidstone	1996
	SL	327-6		v	Leics	Canterbury	1993
Lowest Total	NWT	60		v	Somerset	Taunton	1979
	BHC	73		v	Middlesex	Canterbury	1979
	SL	83		v	Middlesex	Lord's	1984
Highest Innings	NWT	136*	C.L.Hooper	v	Berkshire	Finchampstead	1994
	BHC	143	C.J.Tavaré	v	Somerset	Taunton	1985
	SL	145	C.L.Hooper	v	Leics	Leicester	1996
Best Bowling	NWT	8-31	D.L.Underwood	v	Scotland	Edinburgh	1987
	BHC	6-41	T.N.Wren	v	Somerset	Canterbury	1995
	SL	6- 9	R.A.Woolmer	v	Derbyshire	Chesterfield	1979

LANCASHIRE

Formation of Present Club: 12 January 1864
Colours: Red, Green and Blue
Badge: Red Rose
Championships (since 1890): (7) 1897, 1904, 1926, 1927, 1928, 1930, 1934
Joint Championship: (1) 1950
NatWest Trophy/Gillette Cup Winners: (6) 1970, 1971, 1972, 1975, 1990, 1996
Benson and Hedges Cup Winners: (4) 1984, 1990, 1995, 1996
Sunday League Champions: (3) 1969, 1970, 1989
Match Awards: NWT 62; BHC 71

Chief Executive: J.M.Bower. **Cricket Secretary:** D.M.R.Edmundson Old Trafford, Manchester M16 0PX (Tel 0161 282 4021/4014/4148)
Captain: M.Watkinson. **Vice-Captain/Overseas Player:** Wasim Akram.
1997 Beneficiary: M.A.Atherton. **Scorer:** W.Davies

ATHERTON, Michael Andrew (Manchester GS; Downing C, Cambridge), b Failsworth, Manchester 23 Mar 1968. 5'11". RHB, LB. Cambridge U 1987-89; blue 1987-88-89; captain 1988-89. Lancashire debut 1987; cap 1989; benefit 1997. YC 1990. *Wisden* 1990. **Tests:** 67 (1989 to 1996-97, 40 as captain); HS 185* v SA (Jo'burg) 1995-96; BB 1-20. **LOI:** 50 (1990 to 1996-97, 40 as captain); HS 127. Tours (C=captain): A 1990-91, 1994-95C; SA 1995-96C; WI 1993-94C, 1995-96 (La); NZ 1996-97C; I/SL 1992-93; Z 1989-90 (Eng A), 1996-97C. 1000 runs (6); most – 1924 (1990). Scored 1193 in season of f-c debut. HS 199 v Durham (Gateshead) 1992. BB 6-78 v Notts (Nottingham) 1990. Awards: NWT 3; BHC 2. **NWT:** HS 115 v Derbys (Manchester) 1996. BB 2-15 v Glos (Manchester) 1990. **BHC:** HS 121* v Durham (Manchester) 1996. BB 4-42 Comb Us v Somerset (Taunton) 1989. **SL:** HS 111 v Essex (Colchester) 1990. BB 3-33 v Notts (Nottingham) 1990.

AUSTIN, Ian David (Haslingden HS), b Haslingden 30 May 1966. 5'10". LHB, RM. Debut 1987; cap 1990. Tours (La): WI 1995-96; Z 1988-89. HS 115* v Derbys (Blackpool) 1992. BB 5-23 (10-60 match) v Middx (Manchester) 1994. Awards: NWT 1; BHC 2. **NWT:** HS 57 v Surrey (Oval) 1994. BB 3-32 v Yorks (Leeds) 1995. **BHC:** HS 80 v Worcs (Worcester) 1987. BB 4-8 v Minor C (Leek) 1995. **SL:** HS 48 v Middx (Lord's) 1991. BB 5-56 v Derbys (Derby) 1991.

BROWN, Christopher (Failsworth HS; Tameside TC), b Oldham 16 Aug 1974. 6'2". RHB, OB. Staff 1994 – awaiting f-c debut.

CHAPPLE, Glen (West Craven HS; Nelson & Colne C), b Skipton, Yorks 23 Jan 1974. 6'1". RHB, RFM. Debut 1992; cap 1994. Tours (Eng A): A 1996-97; WI 1995-96 (La); I 1994-95. HS 109* v Glam (Manchester) 1993 (100 off 27 balls in contrived circumstances). HS (authentic) 58 v Durham (Manchester) 1995. 50 wkts (2); most – 55 (1994). BB 6-48 v Durham (Stockton) 1994. Award: NWT 1. **NWT:** HS 4. BB 6-18 v Essex (Lord's) 1996. **BHC:** HS 8. BB 3-31 v Minor C (Manchester) 1996. **SL:** HS 43 v Worcs (Manchester) 1996. BB 3-29 v Hants (Manchester) 1994 and v Surrey (Manchester) 1996.

CHILTON, Mark James (Manchester GS; Durham U), b Sheffield, Yorks 2 Oct 1976. 6'3". RHB, RM. Staff 1996 – awaiting f-c debut.

CRAWLEY, John Paul (Manchester GS; Trinity C, Cambridge), b Maldon, Essex 21 Sep 1971. Brother of M.A. (Oxford U, Lancs and Notts 1987-94) and P.M. (Cambridge U 1992). 6'1". RHB, RM. Debut 1990; cap 1994. Cambridge U 1991-93; blue 1991-92-93; captain 1992-93. YC 1994. **Tests:** 17 (1994 to 1996-97); HS 112 v Z (Bulawayo) 1996-97. **LOI:** 9 (1994-95 to 1996-97); HS 73). Tours: A 1994-95; SA 1993-94 (Eng A), 1995-96; WI 1995-96 (La); NZ 1996-97; Z 1996-97. 1000 runs (5); most – 1570 (1994). HS 286 England A v E Province (Port Elizabeth) 1993-94. La HS 281* v Somerset (Southport) 1994. BB 1-90. Award: BHC 1. **NWT:** HS 66 v Essex (Lord's) 1996. **BHC:** HS 114 v Notts (Manchester) 1995. **SL:** HS 91 v Kent (Canterbury) 1994.

FAIRBROTHER, Neil Harvey (Lymm GS), b Warrington 9 Sep 1963. 5'8". LHB, LM. Debut 1982; cap 1985; captain 1992-93; benefit 1995. Transvaal 1994-95. **Tests:** 10 (1987 to 1992-93); HS 83 v I (Madras) 1992-93. **LOI:** 56 (1986-87 to 1995-96 (HS 113). Tours: NZ 1987-88, 1991-92; I/SL 1992-93; P 1987-88, 1990-91 (Eng A); SL 1990-91 (Eng A). 1000 runs (5); most – 1740 (1990). HS 366 v Surrey (Oval) 1990 (ground record), including 311 in a day and 100 or more in each session. BB 2-91 v Notts (Manchester) 1987. Awards: NWT 5; BHC 8. **NWT:** HS 93* v Leics (Leicester) 1986. BB 1-28. **BHC:** HS 116* v Scot (Manchester) 1988. BB 1-17. **SL:** HS 116* v Notts (Nottingham) 1988. BB 1-33.

FLINTOFF, Andrew (Ribbleton Hall HS), b Preston 6 Dec 1977. 6'4". RHB, RM. Debut 1995. HS 7. **BHC:** HS – . BB 1-10. **SL:** HS 22 v Hants (Portsmouth) 1995.

GALLIAN, Jason Edward Riche (Pittwater House S, Sydney; Keble C, Oxford), b Manly, Sydney, Australia 25 Jun 1971. Qualified for England 1994. 6'0". RHB, RM. Debut 1990, taking wicket of D.A.Hagan (OU) with his first ball; cap 1994. Oxford U 1992-93; blue 1992-93; captain 1993. Captained Australia YC v England YC 1989-90, scoring 158* in 1st 'Test'. **Tests:** 3 (1995 to 1995-96); HS 28 v SA (Pt Elizabeth) 1995-96. Tours: A 1996-97 (Eng A); I 1995-96 (La); SA 1995-96 (part); I 1994-95 (Eng A); P 1995-96 (Eng A). 1000 runs (2); most – 1156 (1996). HS 312 v Derbys (Manchester) 1996 (record score at Old Trafford). BB 6-115 v Surrey (Southport) 1996. Awards: NWT 1; BHC 1. **NWT:** HS 101* v Norfolk (Manchester) 1995. BB 1-11. **BHC:** HS 134 v Notts (Manchester) 1995. BB 5-15 v Minor C (Leek) 1995. **SL:** HS 85 v Kent (Canterbury) 1996. BB 2-10 v Somerset (Manchester) 1994.

GREEN, Richard James (Bridgewater HS, Cheshire; Mid-Cheshire C), b Warrington 13 Mar 1976. 6'1". RHB, RM. Debut 1995. HS 25* v Northants (Northampton) 1996. BB 6-41 v Yorks (Manchester) 1996 (non-BAC match). BAC BB 4-78 v Northants (Northampton) 1996. **SL:** HS 0*. BB 3-38 v Durham (Manchester) 1995.

HARVEY, Mark Edward (Habergham HS; Loughborough U), b Burnley 26 Jun 1974. 5'9". RHB, RM/LB. Debut 1994. Combined Us 1995. HS 23 v Notts (Nottingham) 1994 and Comb Us v WI (Oxford) 1995. **BHC:** (Brit Us) HS 5.

HAYNES, Jamie Jonathan (St Edmunds C, Canberra; Canberra U), b Bristol 5 Jul 1974. 5'11". RHB, WK. Debut 1996. Represented Australian Capital Territory at cricket and Australian Rules football. HS 16 v Middx (Manchester) 1966 (on debut). **SL:** HS – .

HEGG, Warren Kevin (Unsworth HS, Bury; Stand C, Whitefield), b Whitefield 23 Feb 1968. 5'8". RHB, WK. Debut 1986; cap 1989. Tours: A 1996-97 (Eng A); WI 1986-87 (La), 1995-96 (La); SL 1990-91 (Eng A); Z 1988-89 (La). HS 134 v Leics (Manchester) 1996. Held 11 catches (equalling world f-c match record) v Derbys (Chesterfield) 1989. Award: BHC 1. **NWT:** HS 35 v Yorks (Manchester) 1996. **BHC:** HS 81 v Yorks (Manchester) 1996. **SL:** HS 52 v Glam (Colwyn Bay) 1994.

KEEDY, Gary (Garforth CS), b Wakefield, Yorks 27 Nov 1974. 6'0". LHB, SLA. Yorkshire 1994 (one match). Lancashire debut 1995. Tour: WI 1995-96 (La). HS 26 v Essex (Chelmsford) 1996. BB 4-35 v Somerset (Taunton) 1995. **SL:** HS – . BB 1-40.

LLOYD, Graham David (Hollins County HS), b Accrington 1 Jul HS 1969. Son of D. (Lancs and England 1965-83). 5'9". RHB, RM. Debut 1988; cap 1992. **LOI:** 2 (1996; HS 15). Tours: A 1992-93 (Eng A); WI 1995-96 (La). 1000 runs (3); most – 1389 (1992). HS 241 v Essex (Chelmsford) 1996. BB 1-4. Awards: BHC 2. **NWT:** HS 81 v Yorks (Manchester) 1996. BB 1-23. **BHC:** HS 81* v Leics (Manchester) 1995. **SL:** HS 116 v Glam (Swansea) 1996.

McKEOWN, Patrick Christopher (Merchant Taylors S; Rossall S), b Liverpool 1 Jun 1976. 6'3". RHB, OB. Debut 1996. HS 64 v Warwks (Birmingham) 1996. **SL:** HS 69 v Northants (Northampton) 1996.

MARTIN, Peter James (Danum S, Doncaster), b Accrington 15 Nov 1968. 6'4". RHB, RFM. Debut 1989; cap 1994. **Tests:** 7 (1995 to 1996); HS 29 v WI (Lord's) 1995; BB 4-60 v SA (Durban) 1995-96. **LOI:** 16 (1995 to 1996; HS 6; BB 4-44). Tour: SA 1995-96.

Martin, P.J. – continued:
HS 133 v Durham (Gateshead) 1992. 50 wkts (1): 54 (1994). BB 7-50 v Notts (Nottingham) 1996. Award: NWT 1. **NWT:** HS 16 v Surrey (Oval) 1994. BB 4-36 v Northants (Manchester) 1996. **BHC:** HS 10* v Surrey (Oval) 1993. BB 3-43 v Leics (Leicester) 1996 **SL:** HS 35* v Worcs (Manchester) 1996. BB 5-32 v Durham (Stockton) 1994.

RIDGWAY, Paul Mathew (Settle HS), b Airedale, Yorks 13 Feb 1977. 6'4". RHB, RFM. Staff 1996 – awaiting f-c debut.

SHADFORD, Darren James (Breeze Hill HS; Oldham TC), b Oldham 4 Mar 1975. 6'3". RHB, RMF. Debut 1995. HS 1. BB 2-40 v Surrey (Oval) 1995. **SL:** HS – .

TITCHARD, Stephen Paul (Lymm County HS; Priestley C), b Warrington 17 Dec 1967. 6'3". RHB, RM. Debut 1990; cap 1995. HS 163 v Essex (Chelmsford) 1996. BB 1-51. Award: NWT 1. **NWT:** HS 92 v Worcs (Manchester) 1995. **BHC:** HS 82 v Surrey (Oval) 1992. **SL:** HS 96 v Essex (Chelmsford) 1994.

WASIM AKRAM (Islamia C), b Lahore, Pakistan 3 Jun 1966. 6'3". LHB, LF. PACO 1984-85/1985-86. Lahore 1985-86 to 1986-87. PIA 1987-88 to date. Lancashire debut 1988; cap 1989; benefit 1998. *Wisden* 1992. **Tests** (P): 72 (1984-85 to 1996-97, 14 as captain); HS 257* v Z (Sheikhupura) 1996-97; BB 7-119 v NZ (Wellington) 1993-94. **LOI** (P): 227 (1984-85 to 1996-97, 61 as captain): HS 86; BB 5-15). Tours (P) (C=captain): E 1987, 1992; Can: A 1988-89, 1989-90, 1991-92, 1992-93, 1995-96C; WI 1987-88, 1992-93C; NZ 1984-85, 1992-93, 1993-94, 1995-96C; I 1986-87; SL 1984-85 (P U-23), 1985-86, 1994-95. HS 257* (*Tests*). La HS 122 v Hants (Basingstoke) 1991. 50 wkts (5+1); most – 82 (1992). BB 8-30 (13-147 match) v Somerset (Southport) 1994. Hat-trick 1988. Awards: BHC 2. **NWT:** HS 50 v Surrey (Oval) 1994. BB 4-27 v Lincs (Manchester) 1988. **BHC:** HS 64 v Worcs (Worcester) 1995. BB 5-10 v Leics (Leicester) 1993. **SL:** HS 51* v Yorks (Manchester) 1993. BB 5-41 v Northants (Northampton) 1994.

WATKINSON, Michael (Rivington and Blackrod HS, Horwich), b Westhoughton 1 Aug 1961. 6'1". RHB, RMF/OB. Debut 1982; cap 1987; captain 1994 to date; benefit 1996. Cheshire 1982. **Tests:** 4 (1995 to 1995-96); HS 82* v WI (Nottingham) 1995; BB 3-64 v WI (Manchester) 1995 – on debut. **LOI:** 1 (1995-96; HS –). Tours: SA 1995-96; WI 1995-96 (La – captain). 1000 runs (1): 1016 (1993). HS 161 v Essex (Manchester) 1995. 50 wkts (7); most – 66 (1992). BB 8-30 (11-87 match) v Hants (Manchester) 1994 – completing match 'double' with 128 runs. Hat-trick 1992. Awards: NWT 2; BHC 3. **NWT:** HS 90 and BB 3-14 v Glos (Manchester) 1990. **BHC:** HS 76 v Northants (Northampton) 1992. BB 5-44 v Derbys (Chesterfield) 1996. **SL:** HS 121 v Notts (Nottingham) 1996. BB 5-46 v Warwks (Manchester) 1996.

WOOD, Nathan Theodore (Wm Hulme's GS), b Thornhill Edge, Yorks 4 Oct 1974. Son of B. (Yorks, Lancs, Derbys and England 1964-83). 5'8". LHB, OB. Debut 1996. HS 1.

YATES, Gary (Manchester GS), b Ashton-under-Lyne 20 Sep 1967. 6'0". RHB, OB. Debut 1990; cap 1994. HS 134* v Northants (Manchester) 1993. BB 5-34 v Hants (Manchester) 1994. **NWT:** HS 9 (twice). BB 2-42 v Derbys (Manchester) 1996. **BHC:** HS 26 v Yorks (Manchester) 1996. BB 3-42 v Warwks (Birmingham) 1995. **SL:** HS 38 v Essex (Chelmsford) 1996. BB 4-34 v Warwks (Birmingham) 1994.

DEPARTURES (who made first-class appearances in 1996)

ELWORTHY, Steven (Chaplin HS, Gwelo; Shannon HS, Jo'burg; Witwatersrand U), b Bulawayo, Rhodesia 23 Feb 1965. 6'4". RHB, RFM. Transvaal B 1987-88. N Transvaal 1988-89 to date. Lancashire 1995-96 to 1996. Tours: WI 1995-96 (La); Z 1994-95 (SA A). HS 88 v Worcs (Manchester) 1996 (non-BAC match). BAC HS 45 v Worcs (Manchester) 1996. BB 7-65 NT v Natal (Durban) 1994-95. La BB 4-80 v Glos (Manchester) 1996. **NWT:** HS 8 and BB 4-40 v Northants (Manchester) 1996. **BHC:** HS 13 v Durham (Manchester) 1996. BB 4-14 v Glos (Manchester) 1996. **SL:** HS 15 v Glos and v Surrey (Manchester) 1996. BB 2-33 v Sussex (Hove) 1996.

SPEAK, N.J. – *see DURHAM.*

LANCASHIRE 1996

RESULTS SUMMARY

	Place	Won	Lost	Drew
Britannic Assurance Championship	15th	2	6	9
All First-Class Matches		2	6	10
NatWest Trophy	Winners			
Benson and Hedges Cup	Winners			
Sunday League	9th	9	8	–

BRITANNIC ASSURANCE CHAMPIONSHIP AVERAGES

BATTING AND FIELDING

Cap		M	I	NO	HS	Runs	Avge	100	50	Ct/St
1990	I.D.Austin	9	11	3	95*	433	54.12	–	3	4
1985	N.H.Fairbrother	12	20	–	204	1068	53.40	2	8	10
1994	J.P.Crawley	12	20	3	112*	904	53.17	2	7	3
1992	G.D.Lloyd	14	24	1	241	1161	50.47	3	4	6
1994	J.E.R.Gallian	14	27	3	312	1136	47.33	3	3	10
1995	S.P.Titchard	12	22	2	163	935	46.75	2	5	11
1989	W.K.Hegg	16	24	6	134	686	38.11	1	3	45/5
1989	M.A.Atherton	8	14	–	98	519	37.07	–	5	3
1992	N.J.Speak	11	19	3	138*	559	34.93	1	3	10
1987	M.Watkinson	16	26	1	64	610	24.40	–	2	11
1994	P.J.Martin	12	16	4	42	251	20.91	–	–	1
1994	G.Chapple	15	21	6	37*	313	20.86	–	–	1
–	S.Elworthy	11	15	2	45	200	15.38	–	–	5
–	R.J.Green	3	3	1	25*	77	12.83	–	–	2
–	G.Keedy	13	13	7	26	65	10.83	–	–	7

Also batted: J.J.Haynes (1 match) 16, 10 (1 st); P.C.McKeown (2 matches) 9, 64 (1 ct); N.T.Wood (1 match) 1; G.Yates (2 matches - cap 1994) 16, 0, 0 (1 ct).

BOWLING

	O	M	R	W	Avge	Best	5wI	10wM
P.J.Martin	393.4	96	1091	43	25.37	7- 50	1	–
I.D.Austin	200.4	51	602	21	28.66	5-116	1	–
J.E.R.Gallian	143.4	28	552	16	34.50	6-115	1	–
R.J.Green	170.5	32	558	16	34.87	4- 78	–	–
G.Chapple	448.1	90	1572	45	34.93	5- 64	1	–
M.Watkinson	428	75	1489	37	40.24	5- 15	1	–
S.Elworthy	284.1	40	1076	26	41.38	4- 80	–	–
G.Keedy	457.1	123	1183	23	51.43	3- 45	–	–

Also bowled: M.A.Atherton 5-1-15-0; G.D.Lloyd 2-0-4-1; N.J.Speak 6-0-27-0; S.P.Titchard 35-7-110-1; G.Yates 83.2-16-313-5.

The First-Class Averages (pp 123-38) give the records of Lancashire players in all first-class county matches (their other opponents being Yorkshire in a non-Championship match), with the exception of G.Chapple, J.P.Crawley, J.E.R.Gallian, P.J.Martin and M.Watkinson whose full county figures are as above, and:
  M.A.Atherton 9-16-0-98-538-33.62-0-5-3ct. 5-1-15-0.

LANCASHIRE RECORDS

FIRST-CLASS CRICKET

Highest Total	For	863	v	Surrey	The Oval	1990
	V	707-9d	by	Surrey	The Oval	1990
Lowest Total	For	25	v	Derbyshire	Manchester	1871
	V	22	by	Glamorgan	Liverpool	1924
Highest Innings	For	424	A.C.MacLaren	v	Somerset	Taunton	1895
	V	315*	T.W.Hayward	for	Surrey	The Oval	1898

Highest Partnership for each Wicket

1st	368	A.C.MacLaren/R.H.Spooner	v	Glos	Liverpool	1903
2nd	371	F.B.Watson/G.E.Tyldesley	v	Surrey	Manchester	1928
3rd	364	M.A.Atherton/N.H.Fairbrother	v	Surrey	The Oval	1990
4th	358	S.P.Titchard/G.D.Lloyd	v	Essex	Chelmsford	1996
5th	249	B.Wood/A.Kennedy	v	Warwicks	Birmingham	1975
6th	278	J.Iddon/H.R.W.Butterworth	v	Sussex	Manchester	1932
7th	245	A.H.Hornby/J.Sharp	v	Leics	Manchester	1912
8th	158	J.Lyon/R.M.Ratcliffe	v	Warwicks	Manchester	1979
9th	142	L.O.S.Poidevin/A.Kermode	v	Sussex	Eastbourne	1907
10th	173	J.Briggs/R.Pilling	v	Surrey	Liverpool	1885

Best Bowling	For	10-46	W.Hickton	v	Hampshire	Manchester	1870
(Innings)	V	10-40	G.O.B.Allen	for	Middlesex	Lord's	1929
Best Bowling	For	17-91	H.Dean	v	Yorkshire	Liverpool	1913
(Match)	V	16-65	G.Giffen	for	Australians	Manchester	1886

Most Runs – Season	2633	J.T.Tyldesley	(av 56.02)		1901
Most Runs – Career	34222	G.E.Tyldesley	(av 45.20)		1909-36
Most 100s – Season	11	C.Hallows			1928
Most 100s – Career	90	G.E.Tyldesley			1909-36
Most Wkts – Season	198	E.A.McDonald	(av 18.55)		1925
Most Wkts – Career	1816	J.B.Statham	(av 15.12)		1950-68

LIMITED-OVERS CRICKET

Highest Total	NWT	372-5		v	Glos	Manchester	1990
	BHC	353-7		v	Notts	Manchester	1995
	SL	300-7		v	Leics	Leicester	1993
Lowest Total	NWT	59		v	Worcs	Worcester	1963
	BHC	82		v	Yorkshire	Bradford	1972
	SL	71		v	Essex	Chelmsford	1987
Highest Innings	NWT	131	A.Kennedy	v	Middlesex	Manchester	1978
	BHC	136	G.Fowler	v	Sussex	Manchester	1991
	SL	134*	C.H.Lloyd	v	Somerset	Manchester	1970
Best Bowling	NWT	6-18	G.Chapple	v	Essex	Lord's	1996
	BHC	6-10	C.E.H.Croft	v	Scotland	Manchester	1982
	SL	6-29	D.P.Hughes	v	Somerset	Manchester	1977

LEICESTERSHIRE

Formation of Present Club: 25 March 1879
Colours: Dark Green and Scarlet
Badge: Gold Running Fox on Green Ground
Championships: (2) 1975, 1996
NatWest Trophy/Gillette Cup Winners: (0) Finalist 1992
Benson and Hedges Cup Winners: (3) 1972, 1975, 1985
Sunday League Champions: (2) 1974, 1977
Match Awards: NWT 37; BHC 62

Chief Executive: A.O.Norman. **Administrative Secretary:** K.P.Hill
County Ground, Grace Road, Leicester LE2 8AD (Tel 0116 283 2128)
Captain: J.J.Whitaker. **Overseas Player:** P.V.Simmons.
1997 Joint Beneficiaries: R.A.Cobb and P.Whitticase. **Scorer:** G.A.York.

BRIMSON, Matthew Thomas (Chislehurst & Sidcup GS; Durham U), b Plumstead,
London 1 Dec 1970. 6'0". RHB, SLA. Kent staff 1991. Debut 1993. HS 25 v Surrey
(Leicester) 1995. BB 5-12 v Sussex (Leicester) 1996. **NWT:** HS 9 and BB 3-34 v Sussex
(Leicester) 1996. **BHC:** HS – . BB 1-56. **SL:** HS 4*. BB 3-23 v Glam (Swansea) 1996.

CROWE, Carl Daniel (Lutterworth GS), b Leicester 25 Nov 1975. 6'0". RHB, OB.
Debut 1995. HS 9. **SL:** HS – .

DAKIN, Jonathan Michael (King Edward VII S, Johannesburg) b Hitchin, Herts 28 Feb
1973. 6'4". LHB, RM. Debut 1993. HS 101* and BAC BB 2-20 v Notts (Leicester) 1995.
BB 4-45 v CU (Cambridge) 1993 (on debut). Award: BHC 1. **NWT:** HS 26 v Hants
(Leicester) 1995 and v Berks (Leicester) 1996. **BHC:** HS 108* v Durham
(Leicester) 1996. **SL:** HS 45 v Notts (Leicester) 1995. BB 3-23 v Somerset (W-s-M) 1995.

HABIB, Aftab (Millfield S; Taunton S), b Reading, Berkshire 7 Feb 1972. 5'11". Cousin
of Zahid Sadiq (Surrey and Derbys 1988-90). RHB, RMF. Middlesex 1992 (one match).
Leicestershire debut 1995. HS 215 v Worcs (Leicester) 1996. **NWT:** HS 35 v Berks
(Leicester) 1996. **SL:** HS 99* v Glos (Cheltenham) 1996.

MACMILLAN, Gregor Innes (Guildford County S; Charterhouse; Southampton U;
Keble C, Oxford), b Guildford, Surrey 7 Aug 1969. 6'5". RHB, OB. Oxford U 1993-95;
blue 1993-94-95; captain 1995. Leicestershire debut 1995, scoring 103 v Sussex (Hove).
HS 122 v Surrey (Leicester) 1995. BB 3-13 OU v CU (Lord's) 1993. Le BB 2-44 v Glam
(Swansea) 1996. **NWT:** HS 9. BB 1-13. **BHC:** HS 77 Comb Us v Hants (Oxford) 1995.
BB 1-18. **SL:** HS 58 v Glos (Cheltenham) 1996. BB 2-37 v Glam (Swansea) 1996.

MADDY, Darren Lee (Wreake Valley C), b Leicester 23 May 1974. 5'9". RHB, RM/OB.
Debut 1994; cap 1996. HS 131 v OU (Oxford) 1996. BAC HS 101* v Northants
(Leicester) 1996. BB 2-21 v Lancs (Manchester) 1996. **NWT:** HS 34 and BB 2-38 v
Hants (Leicester) 1995. **BHC:** HS 61 v Durham (Leicester) 1996. BB 3-32 v Leics
(Leicester) 1996. **SL:** HS 106* v Durham (Chester-le-St) 1996. BB 3-29 v Surrey
(Leicester) 1995.

MASON, Timothy James (Denstone C), b Leicester 12 Apr 1975. 5'8". RHB, OB. Debut
1994. HS 3. BB 1-22. **NWT:** HS 5. **BHC:** HS 19 v Warwks (Birmingham) 1996. BB 2-35
v Minor C (Jesmond) 1996. **SL:** HS 17* v Somerset (Weston-s-M) 1995. BB 2-41 v
Warwks (Leicester) 1995.

MILLNS, David James (Garibaldi CS), b Clipstone, Notts 27 Feb 1965. 6'3". LHB, RF.
Nottinghamshire 1988-89. Leicestershire debut 1990; cap 1991. Tour: A 1992-93 (Eng A).
HS 103 v Essex (Leicester) 1996. 50 wkts (4); most – 76 (1994). BB 9-37 (12-91 match)
v Derbys (Derby) 1991. Award: NWT 1. **NWT:** HS 29* v Derbys (Derby) 1992. BB 3-22
v Norfolk (Leicester) 1992. **BHC:** HS 39* v Warwks (Birmingham) 1996. BB 4-26 v
Durham (Stockton) 1992. **SL:** HS 20* v Notts (Leicester) 1991. BB 2-11 v Somerset
(Leicester) 1994.

MULLALLY, Alan David (Cannington HS, Perth, Australia; Wembley TC), b Southend-on-Sea, Essex 12 Jul 1969. 6'5". RHB, LFM. W Australia 1987-88 to 1989-90. Victoria 1990-91. Hampshire (1 match) 1988. Leicestershire debut 1990; cap 1993. **Tests:** 9 (1996 to 1996-97); HS 24 v P (Oval) 1996; BB 3-44 v P (Lord's) 1996. **LOI:** 8 (1996 to 1996-97; HS 20; BB 3-29). Tours: NZ 1996-97; Z 1996-97. HS 75 v Middx (Leicester) 1996. 50 wkts (3); most – 70 (1996). BB 7-72 (10-170 match) v Glos (Leicester) 1993. **NWT:** HS 19* v Bucks (Marlow) 1993. BB 2-22 v Derbys (Derby) and v Northants (Lord's) 1992. **BHC:** HS 11 v Surrey (Leicester) 1992. BB 3-39 v Minor C (Leicester) 1995. **SL:** HS 38 v Kent (Leicester) 1994. BB 5-15 v Warwks (Birmingham) 1996.

NIXON, Paul Andrew (Ullswater HS, Penrith), b Carlisle, Cumberland 21 Oct 1970. 6'0". LHB, WK. Debut 1989; cap 1994. Cumberland 1987. MCC YC. Tour: I 1994-95 (Eng A). 1000 runs (1): 1046 (1994). HS 131 v Hants (Leicester) 1994. **NWT:** HS 39 v Sussex (Leicester) 1996. **BHC:** HS 27 v Worcs (Leicester) 1993. **SL:** HS 84 v Sussex (Hove) 1995.

ORMOND, James (St Thomas More S, Nuneaton), b Walsgrave, Coventry, Warwks 20 Aug 1977. 6'3". RHB, RMF. Debut 1995. Awaiting BAC debut. HS – . BB 2-65 v OU (Oxford) 1995. **SL:** HS 2*. BB 1-32.

PARSONS, Gordon James (Woodside County SS, Slough), b Slough, Bucks 17 Oct 1959. Brother-in-law of W.J.Cronje (OFS, Leics and South Africa). 6'1". LHB, RMF. Leicestershire 1978-85 and 1989 to date; cap 1984; joint benefit 1994. Warwickshire 1986-88; cap 1987. Boland 1983-84 to 1984-85. GW 1985-86 to 1986-87. OFS 1988-89 to date. Buckinghamshire 1977. Tours: NZ 1979-80 (DHR); Z 1980-81 (Le). HS 76 Boland v W Province B (Cape Town) 1984-85. Le HS 73 v Durham (Leicester) 1995. 50 wkts (3); most – 67 (1984). BB 9-72 Boland v Transvaal B (Johannesburg) 1984-85. Le BB 6-11 v OU (Oxford) 1985. BAC BB 6-70 v Surrey (Oval) 1984. Awards: BHC 2. **NWT:** HS 25* v Glam (Leicester) 1995. BB 2-11 v Wilts (Swindon) 1984. **BHC:** HS 63* and BB 4-12 v Scot (Leicester) 1989. **SL:** HS 38* v Lancs (Leicester) 1993. BB 4-19 v Essex (Harlow) 1984.

PIERSON, Adrian Roger Kirshaw (Kent C, Canterbury; Hatfield Poly), b Enfield, Middx 21 Jul 1963. 6'4". RHB, OB. Warwickshire 1985-91. Leicestershire debut 1993; cap 1995. Cambridgeshire 1992. MCC YC. HS 58 v Lancs (Leicester) 1993. 50 wkts (1): 69 (1995). BB 8-42 v Warwks (Birmingham) 1994. Awards: NWT 1; BHC 1. **NWT:** HS 20* v Hants (Leicester) 1995. BB 3-20 Wa v Wilts (Birmingham) 1989. **BHC:** HS 11 Wa v Minor C (Walsall) 1986. BB 3-34 Wa v Lancs (Birmingham) 1988. **SL:** HS 29* v Kent (Leicester) 1994. BB 5-36 v Derbys (Leicester) 1995.

ROBINSON, Phillip Edward (Greenhead GS, Keighley), b Keighley, Yorks 3 Aug 1963. 5'9". RHB, LM. Yorkshire 1984-91; cap 1988. Leicestershire debut 1992. Cumberland 1992. 1000 runs (3); most – 1402 (1990). HS 189 Y v Lancs (Scarborough) 1991. Le HS 86 v Glam (Cardiff) 1994. BB 1-10. Le BB 1-13. Awards: NWT 1; BHC 2. **NWT:** HS 73 v Norfolk (Leicester) 1992. **BHC:** HS 73* Y v Hants (Southampton) 1990. **SL:** HS 104 v Lancs (Manchester) 1992.

SIMMONS, Philip Verant (Holy Cross C, Arima), b Arima, Trinidad 18 Apr 1963. 6'3½". RHB, RM. Debut for N Trinidad 1982-83. Trinidad 1982-83 to date; captain 1988-89. Durham 1990-92 (NWT only). Leicestershire debut/cap 1994. **Tests** (WI): 25 (1987-88 to 1996-97); HS 110 and BB 2-34 v A (Melbourne) 1992-93. **LOI** (WI): 119 (1987-88 to 1996-97; HS 122; BB 4-3). Tours (WI): E 1988 (part), 1991, 1992 (RW), 1993 (RW), 1995; A 1992-93, 1995-96; I 1987-88, 1994-95; SL 1993-94; Z 1983-84 (Young WI), 1986-87 (Young WI). 1000 runs (2); most – 1244 (1996). HS 261 v Northants (Leicester) 1994 – on Le debut (county record). 50 wkts (1): 56 (1996). BB 6-14 v Durhan (Chester-le-St) 1996. Award: BHC 1. **NWT:** HS 82 v Berks (Leicester) 1996. BB 3-31 v Cumb (Netherfield) 1994. **BHC:** HS 64 and BB 1-29 v Ire (Leicester) 1994. **SL:** HS 140 v Middx (Leicester) 1994. BB 5-37 v Middx (Leicester) 1996.

SMITH, Benjamin Francis (Kibworth HS), b Corby, Northants 3 Apr 1972. 5'9". RHB, RM. Debut 1990; cap 1995. 1000 runs (1): 1243 (1996). HS 190 v Glam (Swansea) 1996. BB 1-5. Award: NWT 1. **NWT:** HS 63* v Cumb (Netherfield) 1994. **BHC:** HS 61 v Warwks (Birmingham) 1996. **SL:** HS 115 v Somerset (W-s-M) 1995.

STEVENS, Darren Ian (Hinkley C), b Leicester 30 Apr 1976. 5'11". RHB, RM. Staff 1996 – awaiting f-c debut.

SUTCLIFFE, Iain John (Leeds GS; Queen's C, Oxford U), b Leeds, Yorks 20 Dec 1974. 6'2". LHB, occ OB. Oxford U 1994-96; blue 1995-96. Leicestershire debut 1995. HS 163* OU v Hants (Oxford) 1995. Le HS 34 v Sussex (Hove) 1995. BB 2-21 OU v CU (Lord's) 1996. **NWT:** HS 68 v Glam (Leicester) 1995. **BHC:** HS 39 Comb Us v Essex (Cambridge) 1995. **SL:** HS 14 v Sussex (Hove) 1995. Boxing blue 1993-94.

WELLS, Vincent John (Sir William Nottidge S, Whitstable), b Dartford, Kent 6 Aug 1965. 6'0". RHB, RMF. Kent 1988-91. Leicestershire debut 1992; cap 1994. 1000 runs (1): 1331 (1996). HS 204 v Northants (Leicester) 1996. BB 5-43 K v Leics (Leicester) 1990. Le BB 5-50 (inc hat-trick) v Durham (Durham) 1994. Awards: NWT 2; BHC 1. **NWT:** 201 v Berks (Leicester) 1996. BB 3-38 v Durham (Leicester) 1992. **BHC:** HS 60 v Derbys (Leicester) 1996. BB 4-37 v Worcs (Leicester) 1993. **SL:** HS 101 v Middx (Leicester) 1994. BB 5-10 v Surrey (Oval) 1994.

WHITAKER, John James (Uppingham S), b Skipton, Yorks 5 May 1962. 5'10". RHB, OB. Debut 1983; cap 1986; benefit 1993; captain 1996 to date. *Wisden* 1986. YC 1986. **Tests:** 1 (1986-87); HS 11 v A (Adelaide) 1986-87. **LOI:** 2 (1986-87; HS 44*). Tours: A 1986-87; Z 1989-90 (Eng A). 1000 runs (10); most – 1767 (1990). HS 200* v Yorks (Bradford) 1996. BB 1-29. Awards: NWT 1; BHC 2. **NWT:** HS 155 v Wilts (Swindon) 1984. **BHC:** HS 100 v Kent (Canterbury) 1991. **SL:** HS 132 v Glam (Swansea) 1984.

WHITTICASE, Philip (Crestwood CS, Kingswinford), b Marston Green, Solihull 15 Mar 1965. 5'8". RHB, WK. Leicestershire 1984-92 and 1995; cap 1987; joint benefit 1997. HS 114* v Hants (Bournemouth) 1991. **NWT:** HS 32 v Lancs (Leicester) 1986. **BHC:** HS 45 v Notts (Nottingham) 1990. **SL:** HS 38 v Northants (Leicester) 1990.

WILLIAMSON, Dominic (St Leonard's CS, Durham; Durham SFC), b Durham 15 Nov 1975. 5'8". RHB, RM. Debut 1996. Awaiting BAC debut. MCC YC. HS – . BB 1-32. **BHC:** HS 6. BB 1-64. **SL:** HS 9. BB 3-29 v Yorks (Bradford) 1996.

NEWCOMERS

THOMAS, Anatole ('Tolly'), b London 26 Mar 1970. RHB, RFM.

DEPARTURES (who made first-class appearances in 1996)

CLARKE, V.P. – *see DERBYSHIRE*.

REMY, Carlos Charles (St Aloysus C; Haringey Cricket C), b Castries, St Lucia 24 Jul 1968. 5'9". RHB, RM. Sussex 1989-95. Leicestershire 1996. HS 60 Sx v Northants (Northampton) 1994. Le HS – . BB 4-63 Sx v CU (Hove) 1990. BAC BB 3-27 Sx v Lancs (Hove) 1992. **NWT:** HS 1. **BHC:** HS 7. **SL:** HS 19 Sx v Essex (Hove) 1993. BB 4-31 Sx v Lancs (Hove) 1992.

LEICESTERSHIRE 1996

RESULTS SUMMARY

	Place	Won	Lost	Drew	No Result
Britannic Assurance Championship	1st	10	1	6	–
All First-Class Matches		10	2	8	–
NatWest Trophy	2nd Round				
Benson and Hedges Cup	3rd in Group A				
Sunday League	12th	7	7	–	3

BRITANNIC ASSURANCE CHAMPIONSHIP AVERAGES

BATTING AND FIELDING

Cap		M	I	NO	HS	Runs	Avge	100	50	Ct/St
1986	J.J.Whitaker	15	21	3	218	1046	58.11	4	2	2
1994	P.V.Simmons	16	23	2	171	1186	56.47	4	6	33
1994	V.J.Wells	17	25	–	204	1172	46.88	4	1	19
1995	B.F.Smith	17	25	2	190	1068	46.43	2	4	3
1994	P.A.Nixon	17	23	3	106	729	36.45	2	4	50/4
–	A.Habib	14	21	2	215	652	34.31	1	1	10
1996	D.L.Maddy	17	25	1	101*	815	33.95	1	3	18
1993	A.D.Mullally	9	8	1	75	195	27.85	–	2	1
1991	D.J.Millns	16	18	1	103	389	22.88	1	1	5
1995	A.R.K.Pierson	17	21	10	44	248	22.54	–	–	11
–	G.I.Macmillan	6	10	1	41	176	19.55	–	–	–
1984	G.J.Parsons	16	20	4	53	266	16.62	–	2	20
–	M.T.Brimson	10	10	4	13*	37	6.16	–	–	2

BOWLING

	O	M	R	W	Avge	Best	5wI	10wM
P.V.Simmons	364.4	87	1021	56	18.23	6- 14	3	–
A.D.Mullally	316.4	86	987	47	21.00	6- 47	3	1
D.J.Millns	466.1	119	1437	67	21.44	6- 54	2	1
V.J.Wells	234.1	65	688	24	28.66	4- 44	–	–
M.T.Brimson	288.2	62	849	29	29.27	5- 12	2	–
A.R.K.Pierson	444.2	93	1333	42	31.73	6-158	2	–
G.J.Parsons	488	148	1352	40	33.80	4- 21	–	–

Also bowled: G.I.Macmillan 14-2-58-2; D.L.Maddy 25-9-60-2.

The First-Class Averages (pp 123-38) give the records of Leicestershire players in all first-class county matches (their other opponents being the Indians, the Pakistanis and Oxford University), with the exception of:
A.D.Mullally 11-8-1-75-195-27.85-0-2-1ct. 349.2-90-1099-48-22.89-6/47-3-1.

LEICESTERSHIRE RECORDS

FIRST-CLASS CRICKET

Highest Total	For	701-4d		v	Worcs	Worcester	1906
	V	761-6d		by	Essex	Chelmsford	1990
Lowest Total	For	25		v	Kent	Leicester	1912
	V	24		by	Glamorgan	Leicester	1971
		24		by	Oxford U	Oxford	1985
Highest Innings	For	261	P.V.Simmons	v	Northants	Leicester	1994
	V	341	G.H.Hirst	for	Yorkshire	Leicester	1905

Highest Partnership for each Wicket

1st	390	B.Dudleston/J.F.Steele	v	Derbyshire	Leicester	1979
2nd	289*	J.C.Balderstone/D.I.Gower	v	Essex	Leicester	1981
3rd	316*	W.Watson/A.Wharton	v	Somerset	Taunton	1961
4th	290*	P.Willey/T.J.Boon	v	Warwicks	Leicester	1984
5th	320	J.J.Whitaker/A.Habib	v	Worcs	Leicester	1996
6th	284	P.V.Simmons/P.A.Nixon	v	Durham	Chester-le-St	1996
7th	219*	J.D.R.Benson/P.Whitticase	v	Hampshire	Bournemouth	1991
8th	172	P.A.Nixon/D.J.Millns	v	Lancashire	Manchester	1996
9th	160	W.W.Odell/R.T.Crawford	v	Worcs	Leicester	1902
10th	228	R.Illingworth/K.Higgs	v	Northants	Leicester	1977

Best Bowling	For	10- 18	G.Geary	v	Glamorgan	Pontypridd	1929
(Innings)	V	10- 32	H.Pickett	for	Essex	Leyton	1895
Best Bowling	For	16- 96	G.Geary	v	Glamorgan	Pontypridd	1929
(Match)	V	16-102	C.Blythe	for	Kent	Leicester	1909

Most Runs – Season	2446	L.G.Berry	(av 52.04)		1937
Most Runs – Career	30143	L.G.Berry	(av 30.32)		1924-51
Most 100s – Season	7	L.G.Berry			1937
	7	W.Watson			1959
	7	B.F.Davison			1982
Most 100s – Career	45	L.G.Berry			1924-51
Most Wkts – Season	170	J.E.Walsh	(av 18.96)		1948
Most Wkts – Career	2130	W.E.Astill	(av 23.19)		1906-39

LIMITED-OVERS CRICKET

Highest Total	NWT	406-5		v	Berkshire	Leicester	1996
	BHC	327-4		v	Warwicks	Coventry	1972
	SL	344-4		v	Durham	Chester-le-St	1996
Lowest Total	NWT	56		v	Northants	Leicester	1964
	BHC	56		v	Minor C	Wellington	1982
	SL	36		v	Sussex	Leicester	1973
Highest Innings	NWT	201	V.J.Wells	v	Berkshire	Leicester	1996
	BHC	158*	B.F.Davison	v	Warwicks	Coventry	1972
	SL	152	B.Dudleston	v	Lancashire	Manchester	1975
Best Bowling	NWT	6-20	K.Higgs	v	Staffs	Longton	1975
	BHC	6-35	L.B.Taylor	v	Worcs	Worcester	1982
	SL	6-17	K.Higgs	v	Glamorgan	Leicester	1973

MIDDLESEX

Formation of Present Club: 2 February 1864
Colours: Blue
Badge: Three Seaxes
Championships (since 1890): (10) 1903, 1920, 1921, 1947, 1976, 1980, 1982, 1985, 1990, 1993
Joint Championships: (2) 1949, 1977
NatWest Trophy/Gillette Cup Winners: (4) 1977, 1980, 1984, 1988
Benson and Hedges Cup Winners: (2) 1983, 1986
Sunday League Champions: (1) 1992
Match Awards: NWT 52; BHC 57

Secretary: J.Hardstaff MBE
    Lord's Cricket Ground, London NW8 8QN (Tel 0171 289 1300/286 1310)
Captain: M.W.Gatting. **Overseas Player:** *tba.* **1997 Beneficiary:** A.R.C.Fraser.
Scorer: M.J.Smith

BLANCHETT, Ian Neale (Downham Market SFC; Luton U), b Melbourne, Australia 2 Oct 1975. 6'4". RHB, RFM. Norfolk 1993-94. Staff 1996 – awaiting f-c debut.

BROWN, Keith Robert (Chace S, Enfield), b Edmonton 18 Mar 1963. Brother of G.K. (Middx 1986 and Durham 1992). 5'11". RHB, WK, RSM. Debut 1984; cap 1990. MCC YC. 1000 runs (2); most – 1505 (1990). HS 200* v Notts (Lord's) 1990. BB 2-7 v Glos (Bristol) 1987. Awards: NWT 2; BHC 1. **NWT:** HS 103* v Surrey (Uxbridge) 1990. **BHC:** HS 75 v Comb Us (Lord's) 1995. **SL:** HS 102 v Somerset (Lord's) 1988.

DUTCH, Keith Philip (Nower Hill HS; Weald C), b Harrow 21 Mar 1973. 5'10". RHB, OB. Debut 1993. MCC YC. HS 27 v Notts (Nottingham) 1996. BB 3-25 v Somerset (Uxbridge) 1996. **BHC:** HS 13 v Glam (Lord's) 1996. **SL:** HS 21* v Sussex (Lord's) 1995. BB 3-10 v Durham (Lord's) 1996.

EVANS, Matthew Robert (Bedford S; Loughborough U), b Gravesend, Kent 27 Nov 1974. 6'4". RHB, RMF. Hertfordshire 1993 to date. Staff 1996 – awaiting f-c debut. **BHC:** (Brit Us) HS 16* v Middx (Cambridge) 1996. BB 3-64 v Kent (Oxford) 1996.

FAY, Richard Anthony (Brondesbury & Kilburn HS; Queens Park Community S; City of Westminster C), b Kilburn, London 14 May 1974. Great-nephew of M.W.Tate (Sussex and England 1912-37). 6'4". RHB, RMF. MCC YC. Debut 1995. HS 26 and BB 4-53 v Glam (Lord's) 1996. **NWT:** HS 0. BB 2-43 v Cumb (Carlisle) 1996. **BHC:** HS 1. BB 1-13. **SL:** HS 12* v Sussex (Lord's) 1995. BB 4-33 v Warwks (Lord's) 1996.

FRASER, Angus Robert Charles (Gayton HS, Harrow; Orange Sr HS, Edgware), b Billinge, Lancs 8 Aug 1965. Brother of A.G.J. (Middx and Essex 1986-92). 6'5". RHB, RMF. Debut 1984; cap 1988; benefit 1992. *Wisden* 1995. **Tests:** 32 (1989 to 1995-96); HS 29 v A (Nottingham) 1989; BB 8-75 v WI (Bridgetown) 1993-94 – record England analysis v WI. **LOI:** 33 (1989-90 to 1995); HS 38*; BB 4-22). Tours: A 1990-91, 1994-95 (part); SA 1995-96; WI 1989-90, 1993-94. HS 92 v Surrey (Oval) 1990. 50 wkts (6); most – 92 (1989). BB 8-75 (*Tests*). M BB 7-40 v Leics (Lord's) 1993. **NWT:** HS 19 v Durham (Darlington) 1989. BB 4-34 v Yorks (Leeds) 1988. **BHC:** HS 13* v Essex (Lord's) 1988. BB 4-49 v Kent (Canterbury) 1995. **SL:** HS 30* v Kent (Canterbury) 1988. BB 5-32 v Derbys (Lord's) 1995.

GATTING, Michael William (John Kelly HS), b Kingsbury 6 Jun 1957. 5'10". RHB, RM. Debut 1975; cap 1977; captain 1983 to date; benefit 1988; testimonial 1996. YC 1981. *Wisden* 1983. OBE 1987. **Tests:** 79 (1977-78 to 1994-95, 23 as captain); HS 207 v I (Madras) 1984-85; BB 1-14. **LOI:** 92 (1977-78 to 1992-93, 37 as captain; HS 115*; BB 3-32). Tours (C=captain): A 1986-87C, 1987-88C, 1994-95; SA 1989-90C (Eng XI); WI 1980-81, 1985-86; NZ 1977-78, 1983-84, 1987-88C; I/SL 1981-82, 1984-85, 1992-93; P 1977-78, 1983-84, 1987-88C; Z 1980-81 (Mx). 1000 runs (17+1) inc 2000 (3); most –

61

GATTING, M.W. – continued:
2257 (1984). HS 258 v Somerset (Bath) 1984. BB 5-34 v Glam (Swansea) 1982. Awards: NWT 7; BHC 11. **NWT:** HS 132* v Sussex (Lord's) 1989. BB 2-14 (twice). **BHC:** HS 143* v Sussex (Hove) 1985. BB 4-49 v Sussex (Lord's) 1984. **SL:** HS 124* v Leics (Leicester) 1990. BB 4-30 v Glos (Bristol) 1989.

GOODCHILD, David John (Whitmore HS; Weald C; N London U), b Harrow 17 Sep 1976. 6'2". RHB, RM. Debut 1996. HS 4.

HARRISON, Jason Christian (Great Marlow SM; Bucks CHE), b Amersham, Bucks 15 Jan 1972. 6'3". RHB, OB. Debut 1994. Buckinghamshire 1991-93. HS 46* v CU (Cambridge) 1995. BAC HS 40 v Kent (Canterbury) 1996. **BHC:** HS 24 v Glam (Lord's) 1996. **SL:** HS 13* v Warwks (Birmingham) 1995. BB 1-3.

HEWITT, James Peter (Teddington S; Richmond C; City of Westminster C), b Southwark, London 26 Feb 1976. 6'2½". LHB, RMF. Debut 1996. HS 72 v CU (Cambridge) 1996. BAC HS 45 and BB 3-27 v Northants (Northampton) 1996. Took wicket of R.I.Dawson (Glos) with first ball in f-c cricket. **SL:** HS 16* v Essex (Lord's) 1996. BB 3-26 v Hants (Portsmouth) 1996.

JOHNSON, Richard Leonard (Sunbury Manor S; S Pelthorne C), b Chertsey, Surrey 29 Dec 1974. 6'2". RHB, RMF. Debut 1992; cap 1995. Tour: I 1994-95 (Eng A – part). HS 50* v CU (Cambridge) 1994. BAC HS 47 v Hants (Southampton) 1994. BB 10-45 v Derbys (Derby) 1994 (second youngest to take all ten wickets in any f-c match). **NWT:** HS 33 and BB 3-33 v Glam (Cardiff) 1995. **BHC:** HS 9. BB 1-17. **SL:** HS 29 v Worcs (Lord's) 1996. BB 4-66 v Worcs (Worcester) 1993.

MOFFAT, Scott Park (Aldenham S, Elstree; Swansea U), b Germiston, SA 1 Feb 1973. 6'0". RHB, OB. Debut 1996. Awaiting BAC debut. Hertfordshire 1993 to date. HS 0.

NASH, David Charles (Sunbury Manor S; Malvern C), b Chertsey, Surrey 19 Jan 1978. 5'8". RHB, WK. Staff 1995 – awaiting f-c debut. **SL:** HS – .

POOLEY, Jason Calvin (Acton HS), b Hammersmith 8 Aug 1969. 6'0". LHB, occ OB. Debut 1989; cap 1995. Tour: P 1995-96 (Eng A). 1000 runs (1): 1335 (1995). HS 138* v CU (Cambridge) 1996. BAC HS 136 v Glos (Bristol) 1995. **NWT:** HS 36 v Cumb (Carlisle) 1996. **BHC:** HS 50 v Glam (Lord's) 1996. **SL:** HS 109 v Derbys (Lord's) 1991.

RAMPRAKASH, Mark Ravin (Gayton HS; Harrow Weald SFC), b Bushey, Herts 5 Sep 1969. 5'9". RHB, RM. Debut 1987; cap 1990. YC 1991. **Tests:** 19 (1991 to 1995-96); HS 72 v A (Perth) 1994-95. **LOI:** 10 (1991 to 1995-96; HS 32). Tours: A 1994-95 (part); SA 1995-96; WI 1991-92 (Eng A), 1993-94; NZ 1991-92; I 1994-95 (Eng A); P 1990-91 (Eng A); SL 1990-91 (Eng A). 1000 runs (3) inc 2000 (1): 2258 (1995). HS 235 v Yorks (Leeds) 1995. BB 3-91 v Somerset (Taunton) 1995. Awards: NWT 1; BHC 3. **NWT:** HS 104 v Surrey (Uxbridge) 1990. BB 2-15 v Ire (Dublin) 1991. **BHC:** HS 119* v Northants (Lord's) 1994. BB 3-35 v Brit Us (Cambridge) 1996. **SL:** HS 147* v Worcs (Lord's) 1990. BB 5-38 v Leics (Lord's) 1993.

RASHID, Umer Bin Abdul (Ealing Green HS; Ealing Tertiary C; Southbank U), b Southampton, Hants 6 Feb 1976. 6'3". LHB, SLA. Debut 1996. HS 9. **BHC:** (Brit Us) HS 29 v Middx (Cambridge) 1996. BB 2-57 v Essex (Chelmsford) 1996. **SL:** HS 8. BB 2-34 v Yorks (Leeds) 1995.

SHAH, Owais Alam (Isleworth & Syon S), b Karachi, Pakistan 22 Oct 1978. 6'0". RHB, OB. Debut 1996. Tour: A 1996-97 (Eng A). HS 75 and BB 1-24 v Somerset (Uxbridge) 1996. **NWT:** HS 11 v Yorks (Leeds) 1996. **BHC:** HS 42* v Kent (Canterbury) 1996. **SL:** HS 64 v Yorks (Leeds) 1995. BB 1-4.

TUFNELL, Philip Clive Roderick (Highgate S), b Barnet, Herts 29 Apr 1966. 6'0". RHB, SLA. Debut 1986; cap 1990. MCC YC. **Tests:** 27 (1990-91 to 1996-97); HS 22* v I (Madras) 1992-93; BB 7-47 (11-147 match) v NZ (Christchurch) 1991-92. **LOI:** 20 (1990-91 to 1996-97; HS 5*; BB 4-22). Tours: A 1990-91, 1994-95; WI 1993-94; NZ 1991-92, 1996-97; I/SL 1992-93, Z 1996-97. HS 67* v Worcs (Lord's) 1996. 50 wkts (6); most – 88 (1991). BB 8-29 v Glam (Cardiff) 1993. Award: NWT 1. **NWT:** HS 8. BB 3-29 v Herts (Lord's) 1988. **BHC:** HS 18 v Warwks (Lord's) 1991. BB 3-32 v Northants (Lord's) 1994. **SL:** HS 13* v Glam (Merthyr Tydfil) 1989. BB 5-28 v Leics (Lord's) 1993.

WEEKES, Paul Nicholas (Homerton House SS, Hackney), b Hackney, London 8 Jul 1969. 5'10". LHB, OB. Debut 1990; cap 1993. Tour: I 1994-95 (Eng A). MCC YC. 1000 runs (1): 1218 (1996). HS 171* v Somerset (Uxbridge) 1996. BB 8-39 v Glam (Lord's) 1996. Awards: NWT 2; BHC 3. **NWT:** HS 143* v Cornwall (St Austell) 1995. BB 3-35 v Cumb (Carlisle) 1996. **BHC:** HS 67* v Essex (Chelmsford) 1995. BB 3-32 v Warwks (Lord's) 1994. **SL:** HS 119 v Glam (Lord's) 1996. BB 4-29 v Glos and 4-29 v Essex (Lord's) 1996.

WELLINGS, Peter Edward (Smestow CS, Wolverhampton; Thames Valley U), b Wolverhampton, Staffs 5 Mar 1970. 6'1". RHB, RM. Debut 1996. HS 48 v Kent (Canterbury) 1996. **NWT:** HS 9*. BB 1-20. **BHC:** HS 14* v Glam (Lord's) 1996. BB 1-45. **SL:** HS 42 v Somerset (Uxbridge) 1996. BB 1-22.

NEWCOMERS

LARAMAN, Aaron William (Enfield GS), b Enfield 10 Jan 1979. RHB, RFM.

LYE, David Frank (Honiton Community C), b Exeter, Devon 11 Apr 1979. RHB, RM.

MARTIN, Neil Donald (Verulam S), b Enfield 19 Aug 1979. RHB, RFM.

STRAUSS, Andrew J., b Johannesburg, SA 2 Mar 1977. LHB.

DEPARTURES (who made first-class appearances in 1996)

CARR, John Donald (Repton S; Worcester C, Oxford), b St John's Wood 15 Jun 1963. Son of D.B. (Derbys, OU and England 1945-63). 5'11". RHB, RM. Oxford U 1983-85; blue 1983-84-85. Middlesex 1983-89 and 1992-96; cap 1987. Hertfordshire 1982-84 and 1991. 1000 runs (5); most – 1543 (1994). HS 261* v Glos (Lord's) 1994. BB 6-61 v Glos (Lord's) 1985. **NWT:** HS 83 v Hants (Southampton) 1989. BB 2-19 v Surrey (Oval) 1988. **BHC:** HS 70 v Leics (Leicester) 1992. BB 3-22 Comb Us v Glos (Bristol) 1984. **SL:** HS 106 v Glos (Lord's) 1996. BB 4-21 v Surrey (Lord's) 1989.

FELTHAM, Mark Andrew (Tiffin S), b St John's Wood 26 June 1963. 6'2½". RHB, RMF. Surrey 1983-92 (cap 1990). Middlesex 1993-96; cap 1995. MCC YC. HS 101 Sy v Middx (Oval) 1990. M HS 73 v Notts (Lord's) 1993. 50 wkts (1): 56 (1988). BB 6-41 v WI (Lord's) 1995. BAC BB 6-53 Sy v Leics (Oval) 1990. Awards: BHC 2. **NWT:** HS 37* v Glam (Cardiff) 1995. BB 2-23 v Wales MC (Northop Hall) 1994. **BHC:** HS 35 Sy v Kent (Canterbury) 1992. BB 5-28 Sy v Comb Us (Cambridge) 1989. **SL:** HS 75 v Leics (Leicester) 1994. BB 5-51 v Hants (Lord's) 1995.

FOLLETT, D. – see *NORTHAMPTONSHIRE*.

GOULD, Ian James (Westgate SS, Cippenham), b Taplow, Bucks 19 Aug 1957. 5'8". LHB, WK. Middlesex 1975 to 1980-81, 1996; cap 1977. Auckland 1979-80. Sussex 1981-90; cap 1981; captain 1987; benefit 1990. MCC YC. **LOI:** 18 (1982-83 to 1983; HS 42). Tours: A 1982-83; P 1980-81 (Int); Z 1980-81 (M). HS 128 v Worcs (Worcester) 1978. BB 3-10 Sx v Surrey (Oval) 1989. Awards: NWT 1; BHC 3. **NWT:** HS 88 Sx v Yorks (Leeds) 1986. **BHC:** HS 72 Sx v Kent (Hove) 1982. BB 1-0. **SL:** HS 84* Sx v Surrey (Oval) 1989. Middlesex coach 1991 to date. Reappeared in one match (v OU) 1996.

NASH, Dion Joseph (Dargaville HS; Auckland GS; Otago U), b Auckland, NZ 20 Nov 1971. 6'1". RHB, RFM. N Districts 1990-91 to 1991-92, 1995-96 to date. Otago 1992-93 to 1993-94. Middlesex 1995-96; cap 1995. **Tests** (NZ): 14 (1992-93 to 1995-96); HS 56 and BB 6-76 (11-169 match) v E (Lord's) 1994. **LOI** (NZ): 28 (1992-93 to 1995-96; HS 40*; BB 3-26). Tours (NZ): E 1994; SA 1994-95; WI 1995-96; I 1995-96; SL 1992-93; Z 1992-93. HS 67 v Essex (Chelmsford) 1995. 50 wkts (1): 52 (1995). BB 6-30 NZ Academy XI v ND (Rotorua) 1993-94. M BB 5-35 v Hants (Lord's) 1995. **NWT:** HS 4. BB 1-36. **BHC:** HS 54 v Comb Us (Lord's) 1995. BB 2-31 v Glos (Bristol) 1995. **SL:** HS 35 v Notts (Lord's) 1995. BB 3-34 v Glos (Bristol) 1995.

63

MIDDLESEX 1996

RESULTS SUMMARY

	Place	Won	Lost	Drew	No Result
Britannic Assurance Championship	9th	7	6	4	–
All First-Class Matches		7	6	6	–
NatWest Trophy	2nd Round				
Benson and Hedges Cup	5th in Group C				
Sunday League	7th	9	7	–	1

BRITANNIC ASSURANCE CHAMPIONSHIP AVERAGES

BATTING AND FIELDING

Cap		M	I	NO	HS	Runs	Avge	100	50	Ct/St
1990	M.R.Ramprakash	16	29	2	169	1406	52.07	4	8	7
1993	P.N.Weekes	17	32	2	171*	1191	39.70	4	4	10
1990	K.R.Brown	17	30	5	83	884	35.36	–	8	59/1
–	P.E.Wellings	4	8	1	48	237	33.85	–	–	1
1977	M.W.Gatting	14	23	–	171	761	33.08	1	6	9
1987	J.D.Carr	15	26	1	94	706	28.24	–	4	27
–	O.A.Shah	5	9	1	75	212	26.50	–	2	2
1995	J.C.Pooley	16	30	–	111	695	23.16	1	4	22
–	D.Follett	4	6	5	17	22	22.00	–	–	2
–	J.P.Hewitt	8	12	2	45	209	20.90	–	–	5
1990	P.C.R.Tufnell	16	26	10	67*	290	18.12	–	1	7
–	J.C.Harrison	5	10	1	40	151	16.77	–	–	7
1995	R.L.Johnson	11	20	1	37*	243	12.78	–	–	1
1988	A.R.C.Fraser	17	28	6	33	238	10.81	–	–	3
–	K.P.Dutch	3	4	–	27	39	9.75	–	–	2
–	R.A.Fay	14	24	2	26	163	7.40	–	–	3
1995	M.A.Feltham	2	4	–	1	1	0.25	–	–	–

Also batted (1 match each): D.J.Goodchild 4, 0; D.J.Nash (cap 1995) 1 (1 ct);
U.B.A.Rashid 9, 6.

BOWLING

	O	M	R	W	Avge	Best	5wI	10wM
D.Follett	115.2	21	458	23	19.91	8-22	3	1
P.C.R.Tufnell	780.4	259	1568	72	21.77	7-49	5	1
J.P.Hewitt	167.3	35	647	21	30.80	3-27	–	–
A.R.C.Fraser	592.4	138	1636	49	33.38	5-55	2	1
R.L.Johnson	242.5	36	878	25	35.12	5-29	1	–
R.A.Fay	350	82	1088	30	36.26	4-53	–	–
P.N.Weekes	322	63	948	25	37.92	8-39	1	–

Also bowled: K.P.Dutch 23-4-85-3; M.A.Feltham 57-14-185-4; M.W.Gatting 4-0-25-0;
D.J.Goodchild 4.5-0-26-0; D.J.Nash 10-1-44-1; J.C.Pooley 4-0-42-0; M.R.Ramprakash
31-4-121-3; U.B.A.Rashid 6-1-17-0; O.A.Shah 5-0-24-1.

The First-Class Averages (pp 123-38) give the records of Middlesex players in all
first-class county matches (their other opponents being Cambridge University and Oxford
University), with the exception of M.R.Ramprakash whose full county figures are as
above, and:
   J.C.Pooley 17-32-1-138*-843-27.19-2-4-22ct. 4-0-42-0.

MIDDLESEX RECORDS

FIRST-CLASS CRICKET

Highest Total	For	642-3d		v	Hampshire	Southampton	1923
	V	665		by	W Indies	Lord's	1939
Lowest Total	For	20		v	MCC	Lord's	1864
	V	31		by	Glos	Bristol	1924
Highest Innings	For	331*	J.D.B.Robertson	v	Worcs	Worcester	1949
	V	316*	J.B.Hobbs	for	Surrey	Lord's	1926

Highest Partnership for each Wicket

1st	367*	G.D.Barlow/W.N.Slack	v	Kent	Lord's	1981
2nd	380	F.A.Tarrant/J.W.Hearne	v	Lancashire	Lord's	1914
3rd	424*	W.J.Edrich/D.C.S.Compton	v	Somerset	Lord's	1948
4th	325	J.W.Hearne/E.H.Hendren	v	Hampshire	Lord's	1919
5th	338	R.S.Lucas/T.C.O'Brien	v	Sussex	Hove	1895
6th	270	J.D.Carr/P.N.Weekes	v	Glos	Lord's	1994
7th	271*	E.H.Hendren/F.T.Mann	v	Notts	Nottingham	1925
8th	182*	M.H.C.Doll/H.R.Murrell	v	Notts	Lord's	1913
9th	160*	E.H.Hendren/T.J.Durston	v	Essex	Leyton	1927
10th	230	R.W.Nicholls/W.Roche	v	Kent	Lord's	1899

Best Bowling	For	10- 40	G.O.B.Allen	v	Lancashire	Lord's	1929
(Innings)	V	9- 38	R.C.Glasgow†	for	Somerset	Lord's	1924
Best Bowling	For	16-114	G.Burton	v	Yorkshire	Sheffield	1888
(Match)		16-114	J.T.Hearne	v	Lancashire	Manchester	1898
	V	16-109	C.W.L.Parker	for	Glos	Cheltenham	1930

Most Runs – Season	2669	E.H.Hendren	(av 83.41)	1923
Most Runs – Career	40302	E.H.Hendren	(av 48.81)	1907-37
Most 100s – Season	13	D.C.S.Compton		1947
Most 100s – Career	119	E.H.Hendren		1907-37
Most Wkts – Season	158	F.J.Titmus	(av 14.63)	1955
Most Wkts – Career	2361	F.J.Titmus	(av 21.27)	1949-82

LIMITED-OVERS CRICKET

Highest Total	NWT	304-7		v	Surrey	The Oval	1995
		304-8		v	Cornwall	St Austell	1995
	BHC	325-5		v	Leics	Leicester	1992
	SL	290-6		v	Worcs	Lord's	1990
Lowest Total	NWT	41		v	Essex	Westcliff	1972
	BHC	73		v	Essex	Lord's	1985
	SL	23		v	Yorkshire	Leeds	1974
Highest Innings	NWT	158	G.D.Barlow	v	Lancashire	Lord's	1984
	BHC	143*	M.W.Gatting	v	Sussex	Hove	1985
	SL	147*	M.R.Ramprakash	v	Worcs	Lord's	1990
Best Bowling	NWT	6-15	W.W.Daniel	v	Sussex	Hove	1980
	BHC	7-12	W.W.Daniel	v	Minor C (E)	Ipswich	1978
	SL	6- 6	R.W.Hooker	v	Surrey	Lord's	1969

† R.C.Robertson-Glasgow

NORTHAMPTONSHIRE

Formation of Present Club: 31 July 1878
Colours: Maroon
Badge: Tudor Rose
Championships: (0) Second 1912, 1957, 1965, 1976
NatWest Trophy/Gillette Cup Winners: (2) 1976, 1992
Benson and Hedges Cup Winners: (1) 1980
Sunday League Champions: (0) Third 1991
Match Awards: NWT 49; BHC 50

Chief Executive: S.P.Coverdale
    County Ground, Wantage Road, Northampton, NN1 4TJ (Tel 01604 32917)
Captain: R.J.Bailey. **Overseas Player:** Mohammad Akram.
1997 Beneficiary: D.Ripley. **Scorer:** A.C.Kingston

BAILEY, Robert John (Biddulph HS), b Biddulph, Staffs 28 Oct 1963. 6'3". RHB, OB. Debut 1982; cap 1985; benefit 1993; captain 1996 to date. Staffordshire 1980. YC 1984. **Tests:** 4 (1988 to 1989-90); HS 43 v WI (Oval) 1988. **LOI:** 4 (1984-85 to 1989-90; HS 43*). Tours: SA 1991-92 (Nh); WI 1989-90; Z 1994-95 (Nh). 1000 runs (12); most – 1987 (1990). HS 224* v Glam (Swansea) 1986. BB 5-54 v Notts (Northampton) 1993. Awards: NWT 7; BHC 9. **NWT:** HS 145 v Staffs (Stone) 1991. BB 3-47 v Notts (Northampton) 1990. **BHC:** HS 134 v Glos (Northampton) 1987. BB 1-22. **SL:** HS 125* v Derbys (Derby) 1987. BB 3-23 v Leics (Leicester) 1987.

BAILEY, Tobin Michael Barnaby (Bedford S; Loughborough U), b Kettering 28 Aug 1976. 5'10". RHB, WK. Debut 1996. Bedfordshire 1994 to date. HS 31* v Lancs (Northampton) 1996.

BOSWELL, Scott Antony John (Pocklington S; Wolverhampton U), b Fulford, Yorks 11 Sep 1974. 6'5". RHB, RFM. Debut (British Us) 1996. Northamptonshire debut 1996. HS 2* (Nh – twice). BB 2-52 v P (Northampton) 1996. **BHC:** HS 14 Brit Us v Essex (Chelmsford) 1996. BB (Nh) 1-6. **SL:** HS 2. BB 1-20.

BROWN, Jason Fred (St Margaret Ward HS & SFC), b Newcastle-under-Lyme, Staffs 10 Oct 1974. 6'0". RHB, OB. Debut 1996. Staffordshire 1994 to date. HS 0*.

CAPEL, David John (Roade CS), b Northampton 6 Feb 1963. 5'11". RHB, RMF. Debut 1981; cap 1986; benefit 1994. E Province 1985-86 to 1986-87. **Tests:** 15 (1987 to 1989-90); HS 98 v P (Karachi) 1987-88; BB 3-88 v WI (Bridgetown) 1989-90. **LOI:** 23 (1986-87 to 1989-90; HS 50*; BB 3-38). Tours: A 1987-88, 1992-93 (Eng A); WI 1989-90; NZ 1987-88; P 1987-88. 1000 runs (3); most – 1311 (1989). HS 175 v Leics (Northampton) 1995. 50 wkts (4); most – 63 (1986). BB 7-44 v Warwks (Birmingham) 1995. Awards: NWT 3. **NWT:** HS 101 v Notts (Northampton) 1990. BB 3-21 v Glam (Swansea) 1992. **BHC:** HS 97 v Yorks (Lord's) 1987. BB 4-29 v Warwks (Birmingham) 1986. **SL:** HS 121 v Glam (Northampton) 1990. BB 4-30 v Yorks (Middlesbrough) 1982.

CURRAN, Kevin Malcolm (Marandellas HS), b Rusape, S Rhodesia 7 Sep 1959. Son of K.P. (Rhodesia 1947-48 to 1953-54). 6'1". RHB, RMF. Zimbabwe 1980-81 to 1987-88. Qualified for England 1994. Natal 1988-89. Gloucestershire 1985-90; cap 1985. Northamptonshire debut 1991; cap 1992. Boland 1994-95. **LOI** (Z): 11 (1983 to 1987-88; HS 73; BB 3-65). Tours (Z): E 1982; SL 1983-84. 1000 runs (6); most – 1353 (1986). HS 150 v Leics (Leicester) 1996. 50 wkts (5); most – 67 (1993). BB 7-47 Natal v Transvaal (Johannesburg) 1988-89 and v Yorks (Harrogate) 1993. Awards: NWT 2; BHC 2. **NWT:** HS 78* v Cambs (Northampton) 1992. BB 4-34 Gs v Northants (Bristol) 1985. **BHC:** HS 57 Gs v Derbys (Derby) 1987. BB 4-38 v Worcs (Northampton) 1995. **SL:** HS 119* v Kent (Canterbury) 1990. BB 5-15 Gs v Leics (Gloucester) 1988.

EMBUREY, John Ernest (Peckham Manor SS), b Peckham, London 20 Aug 1952. 6'2". RHB, OB. Middlesex 1973-95; cap 1977; benefit 1986; testimonial 1995. Northamptonshire debut 1996; coach 1996 to date. *Wisden* 1983. W Province 1982-83/1983-84. **Tests:** 64 (1978 to 1995, 2 as captain); HS 75 v NZ (Nottingham) 1986; BB 7-78 v A (Sydney) 1986-87. **LOI:** 61 (1979-80 to 1992-93, 4 as captain; HS 34; BB 4-37). Tours: A 1978-79, 1979-80, 1986-87, 1987-88; SA 1981-82 (SAB), 1989-90 (Eng XI); WI 1980-81, 1985-86; NZ 1987-88; I 1979-80, 1981-82, 1992-93; P 1987-88; SL 1977-78 (DHR), 1981-82, 1991-92; Z 1980-81 (Mx). HS 133 M v Essex (Chelmsford) 1983. Nh HS 67* v Notts (Nottingham) 1996. 50 wkts (17) inc 100 (1): 103 (1983). BB 8-40 (12-115 match) M v Hants (Lord's) 1993. Nh BB 4-48 v Essex (Chelmsford) 1996. Awards: NWT 2; BHC 7. **NWT:** HS 46 v Lancs (Manchester) 1996. BB 3-11 M v Sussex (Lord's) 1989. **BHC:** HS 50 M v Kent (Lord's) 1984. BB 5-37 M v Somerset (Taunton) 1991. **SL:** HS 50 M v Lancs (Blackpool) 1988. BB 5-23 M v Somerset (Taunton) 1991.

FORDHAM, Alan (Bedford Modern S; Durham U), b Bedford 9 Nov 1964. 6'1". RHB, RM. Debut 1986; cap 1990. Bedfordshire 1982-85. Tours (Nh): SA 1991-92; Z 1994-95. 1000 runs (5); most – 1840 (1991). HS 206* v Yorks (Leeds) 1990. BB 1-0. Awards: NWT 4; BHC 3. **NWT:** HS 132* v Leics (Northampton) 1991. BB 1-3. **BHC:** HS 108 v Scot (Northampton) 1995. **SL:** HS 111 v Durham (Hartlepool) 1994.

HUGHES, John Gareth (Sir Christopher Hatton SS, Wellingborough; Sheffield City Poly), b Wellingborough 3 May 1971. 6'1". RHB, RM. Debut 1990. Tours (Nh): SA 1991-92; Z 1994-95. HS 17 and BB 5-69 v Hants (Southampton) 1994. **BHC:** HS 9. BB 2-47 v Derbys (Derby) 1995. **SL:** HS 21 v Kent (Canterbury) 1993. BB 2-39 v Derbys (Northampton) 1995.

INNES, Kevin John (Weston Favell Upper S), b Wellingborough 24 Sep 1975. 5'10". RHB, RM. 2nd XI debut 1990 (aged 14yr 8m – Northamptonshire record). Debut 1994. HS 63 and BB 4-61 v Lancs (Northampton) 1996. **BHC:** HS 1. BB 1-25. **SL:** HS 5. BB 1-35.

LOYE, Malachy Bernhard (Moulton S), b Northampton 27 Sep 1972. 6'2". RHB, OB. Debut 1991; cap 1994. Tours: SA 1993-94 (Eng A); Z 1994-95 (Nh). 1000 runs (1): 1048 (1996). HS 205 v Yorks (Northampton) 1996. **NWT:** HS 65 v Essex (Chelmsford) 1993. **BHC:** HS 68* v Middx (Lord's) 1994. **SL:** HS 122 v Somerset (Luton) 1993.

MONTGOMERIE, Richard Robert (Rugby S; Worcester C, Oxford), b Rugby, Warwks 3 Jul 1971. 5'10½". RHB, OB. Oxford U 1991-94; blue 1991-92-93-94; captain 1994; half blues for rackets and real tennis. Northamptonshire debut 1991; cap 1995. Tour: Z 1994-95 (Nh). 1000 runs (2); most – 1178 (1996). HS 192 v Kent (Canterbury) 1995. **NWT:** HS 109 v Notts (Nottingham) 1995. **BHC:** HS 75 Comb Us v Worcs (Oxford) 1992. **SL:** HS 77 v Notts (Nottingham) 1996.

PENBERTHY, Anthony Leonard (Camborne CS), b Troon, Cornwall 1 Sep 1969. 6'1". LHB, RM. Debut 1989; cap 1994. Cornwall 1987-89. Tours (Nh): SA 1991-92; Z 1994-95. HS 101* v CU (Cambridge) 1990. BAC HS 88* v Somerset (Taunton) 1994. BB 5-37 v Glam (Swansea) 1993. Took wicket of M.A.Taylor (A) with his first ball in f-c cricket. **NWT:** HS 79 v Lancs (Manchester) 1996. BB 2-29 v Glam (Swansea) 1992. **BHC:** HS 41 v Warwks (Northampton) 1996. BB 3-38 v Notts (Northampton) 1996. **SL:** HS 80 v Lancs (Northampton) 1996. BB 5-36 v Glos (Northampton) 1993.

RIPLEY, David (Royds SS, Leeds), b Leeds, Yorks 13 Sep 1966. 5'9". RHB, WK. Debut 1984; cap 1987; benefit 1997. Tours (Nh): SA 1991-92; Z 1994-95. HS 134* v Yorks (Scarborough) 1986. BB 2-89 v Essex (Ilford) 1987. Award: BHC 1. **NWT:** HS 27* v Durham (Darlington) 1984. **BHC:** HS 36* v Glos (Bristol) 1991. **SL:** HS 52* v Surrey (Northampton) 1993.

ROBERTS, David James (Mullion CS), b Truro, Cornwall 29 Dec 1976. Cousin of C.K.Bullen (Surrey 1982-91). 5'11". RHB, RSM. Debut 1996. HS 73 v Essex (Chelmsford) 1996.

SALES, David John Grimwood (Caterham S; Cumnor House S), b Carshalton, Surrey 3 Dec 1977. 6'0". RHB, RM. Debut 1996 v Worcs (Kidderminster) scoring 0 and 210* – record Championship score on f-c debut; youngest (18yr 237d) to score 200 in a Championship match. HS 210* (as above). **SL:** HS 70* (off 56 balls) v Essex (Chelmsford) 1994, when 16yr 289d (youngest to score SL fifty). Soccer for Wimbledon and Crystal Palace.

SNAPE, Jeremy Nicholas (Denstone C; Durham U), b Stoke-on-Trent, Staffs 27 Apr 1973. 5'8½". RHB, OB. Debut 1992. Combined Us 1994. Tour: Z 1994-95 (Nh). HS 87 v Mashonaland Select XI (Harare) 1994-95. UK HS 64 v OU (Oxford) 1996. BAC HS 55 v Glam (Cardiff) 1995. BB 5-65 v Durham (Northampton) 1995. Award: BHC 1. **NWT:** HS 21 v Warwks (Lord's) 1995. BB 2-44 v Glos (Bristol) 1995. **BHC:** HS 52 Comb Us v Hants (Southampton) 1993. BB 3-35 Comb Us v Worcs (Oxford) 1992. **SL:** HS 31* v Leics (Leicester) 1994. BB 3-25 v Essex (Northampton) 1993.

STEELE, Mark Vincent (Wellingborough S; Kettering Tresham Inst), b Kettering 13 Nov 1976. Son of D.S. (Northants, Derbys and England 1963-81); nephew of J.F. (Leics, Natal and Glamorgan 1970-86). 6'0". LHB, RMF. Staff 1995 – awaiting f-c debut.

SWANN, Alec James (Risade S; Sponne S, Towcester), b Northampton 26 Oct 1976. Elder brother of G.P. (*below*). 6'1". RHB, OB/RM. Debut 1996. Bedfordshire 1994. HS 76* v OU (Oxford) 1996 (on debut). BAC HS 14 v Glos (Bristol) 1996.

TAYLOR, Jonathan Paul (Pingle S, Swadlincote), b Ashby-de-la-Zouch, Leics 8 Aug 1964. 6'2". LHB, LFM. Derbyshire 1984-86. Northamptonshire debut 1991; cap 1992. Staffordshire 1989-90. **Tests:** 2 (1992-93 to 1994); HS 17* v I (Calcutta) 1992-93. BB 1-18. **LOI:** 1 (1992-93; HS 1). Tours: SA 1993-94 (Eng A – part); I 1992-93; Z 1994-95 (Nh). HS 86 v Durham (Northampton) 1995. 50 wkts (4); most – 69 (1993). BB 7-23 v Hants (Bournemouth) 1992. Award: BHC 1. **NWT:** HS 9. BB 4-34 v Glos (Bristol) 1995. **BHC:** HS 7*. BB 5-45 v Notts (Northampton) 1996. **SL:** HS 24 v Worcs (Northampton) 1993. BB 3-14 De v Glos (Gloucester) 1986.

WALTON, Timothy Charles (Leeds GS; Newcastle upon Tyne Poly), b Low Head, Yorks 8 Nov 1972. 6'0½". RHB, RM. Debut 1994. HS 71 v Somerset (Northampton) 1995. BB 1-26. Award: BHC 1. **BHC:** HS 70 v Warwks (Northampton) 1996. BB 1-27. **SL:** HS 72 v Glos (Bristol) 1994. BB 2-27 v Leics (Leicester) 1992.

WARREN, Russell John (Kingsthorpe Upper S), b Northampton 10 Sep 1971. 6'1". RHB, OB. Debut 1992; cap 1995. HS 201* v Glam (Northampton) 1996. Award: NWT 1. **NWT:** HS 100* v Ire (Northampton) 1994. **BHC:** HS 23 v Derbys (Derby) 1995. **SL:** HS 71* v Leics (Northampton) 1993.

NEWCOMERS

DAVIES, Michael Kenton, b Ashby-de-la-Zouch, Leics 17 Jul 1976. RHB, SLA.

DOBSON, Andrew Michael, b Scunthorpe, Lincs 6 Apr 1980. LHB, RFM.

FOLLETT, David (Moorland Road HS, Burslem; Stoke-on-Trent TC), b Newcastle-under-Lyme, Staffs 14 Oct 1968. 6'2". RHB, RFM. Middlesex 1995-96. Staffordshire 1994. HS 17 M v Yorks (Lord's) 1996. BB 2-44 M v Durham (Lord's) 1996. **BHC:** HS 4. BB 2-44 M v Hants (Lord's) 1995. **SL:** HS – . BB 2-47 M v Y (Lord's) 1996.

LOGAN, Richard James, b Stone, Staffs 28 Jan 1980. RHB, RFM.

MOHAMMAD AKRAM, b Islamabad, Pakistan 10 Sep 1972. RHB, RFM. Rawalpindi 1992-93 to date. **Tests** (P): 6 (1995-96 to 1996-97); HS 5 and BB 3-39 v SL (Sialkot) 1995-96. **LOI** (P): 7 (1995-96; HS 7*; BB 2-36). Tours (P): E 1996; A 1995-96. HS 24 Rawalpindi v Karachi Blues (Rawalpindi) 1993-94. UK HS 4*. BB 7-51 P v Leics (Leicester) 1996.

SWANN, Graeme Peter (Sponne S, Towcester), b Northampton 24 Mar 1979. Younger brother of A.J. (*above*). RHB, OB.

DEPARTURES – see p 106

NORTHAMPTONSHIRE 1996

RESULTS SUMMARY

	Place	Won	Lost	Drew	No Result
Britannic Assurance Championship	16th	3	8	6	–
All First-Class Matches		3	8	8	–
NatWest Trophy	2nd Round				
Benson and Hedges Cup	Finalist				
Sunday League	6th	10	6	–	1

BRITANNIC ASSURANCE CHAMPIONSHIP AVERAGES

BATTING AND FIELDING

Cap		M	I	NO	HS	Runs	Avge	100	50	Ct/St
1992	K.M.Curran	15	28	5	150	1242	59.14	2	8	14
1987	D.Ripley	9	14	6	88*	412	51.50	–	3	22
1994	M.B.Loye	12	22	1	205	974	46.38	2	4	4
–	D.J.G.Sales	4	8	1	210*	280	40.00	1	–	4
1985	R.J.Bailey	11	20	2	163	686	38.11	1	3	7
–	D.J.Roberts	3	6	–	73	182	30.33	–	1	–
1995	R.J.Warren	10	17	1	201*	485	30.31	1	1	18/1
1995	R.R.Montgomerie	15	29	3	127	774	29.76	2	4	12
1986	D.J.Capel	15	28	1	103	803	29.74	1	4	12
–	T.C.Walton	5	9	–	58	247	27.44	–	3	2
1994	A.L.Penberthy	17	28	4	87	628	26.16	–	3	9
1990	A.Fordham	9	16	2	53	321	22.92	–	2	8
–	J.E.Emburey	11	13	4	67*	200	22.22	–	1	6
–	K.J.Innes	4	5	–	63	108	21.60	–	1	3
–	J.N.Snape	8	13	2	37	201	18.27	–	–	3
–	A.R.Roberts	5	8	–	39	141	17.62	–	–	1
1992	J.P.Taylor	17	23	9	57	242	17.28	–	1	3
1990	C.E.L.Ambrose	9	13	2	25*	116	10.54	–	–	11
–	A.J.Swann	2	4	–	14	24	6.00	–	–	–

Also batted: T.M.B.Bailey (2 matches) 31*, 2 (4 ct); (1 match each): S.A.J.Boswell 1, 2*; J.F.Brown 0* (1 ct); J.G.Hughes 8 (1 ct); N.A.Mallender (cap 1984) 13, 11 (1 ct).

BOWLING

	O	M	R	W	Avge	Best	5wI	10wM
C.E.L.Ambrose	284.4	80	717	43	16.67	6-26	5	1
J.P.Taylor	549.2	116	1766	64	27.59	7-88	3	1
A.L.Penberthy	352.2	68	1077	34	31.67	5-92	1	–
D.J.Capel	324	55	1087	30	36.23	3-31	–	–
J.E.Emburey	396.2	94	1042	27	38.59	4-48	–	–
J.N.Snape	257.1	50	841	19	44.26	4-42	–	–
K.M.Curran	180	34	641	11	58.27	3-75	–	–

Also bowled: R.J.Bailey 48.3-6-145-1; S.A.J.Boswell 23.4-4-67-1; J.F.Brown 22-6-64-0; J.G.Hughes 24-4-93-2; K.J.Innes 59.7-19-193-8; N.A.Mallender 24-5-90-0; A.R.Roberts 142.5-33-470-7; T.C.Walton 19-1-71-2.

The First-Class Averages (pp 123-38) give the records of Northamptonshire players in all first-class county matches (their other opponents being the Pakistanis and Oxford University), with the exception of:
S.A.J.Boswell 2-3-2-2*-5-5.00-0-0-0ct. 55.4-7-196-5-39.20-2/52.
R.R.Montgomerie 17-32-3-168-1111-38.31-4-4-15ct. Did not bowl.

NORTHAMPTONSHIRE RECORDS

FIRST-CLASS CRICKET

Highest Total	For	781-7d		v	Notts	Northampton	1995
	V	670-9d		by	Sussex	Hove	1921
Lowest Total	For	12		v	Glos	Gloucester	1907
	V	33		by	Lancashire	Northampton	1977
Highest Innings	For	300	R.Subba Row	v	Surrey	The Oval	1958
	V	333	K.S.Duleepsinhji	for	Sussex	Hove	1930

Highest Partnership for each Wicket

1st	372	R.R.Montgomerie/M.B.Loye	v	Yorkshire	Northampton	1996
2nd	344	G.Cook/R.J.Boyd-Moss	v	Lancashire	Northampton	1986
3rd	393	A.Fordham/A.J.Lamb	v	Yorkshire	Leeds	1990
4th	370	R.T.Virgin/P.Willey	v	Somerset	Northampton	1976
5th	347	D.Brookes/D.W.Barrick	v	Essex	Northampton	1952
6th	376	R.Subba Row/A.Lightfoot	v	Surrey	The Oval	1958
7th	229	W.W.Timms/F.A.Walden	v	Warwicks	Northampton	1926
8th	164	D.Ripley/N.G.B.Cook	v	Lancashire	Manchester	1987
9th	156	R.Subba Row/S.Starkie	v	Lancashire	Northampton	1955
10th	148	B.W.Bellamy/J.V.Murdin	v	Glamorgan	Northampton	1925

Best Bowling	For	10-127	V.W.C.Jupp	v	Kent	Tunbridge W	1932
(Innings)	V	10- 30	C.Blythe	for	Kent	Northampton	1907
Best Bowling	For	15- 31	G.E.Tribe	v	Yorkshire	Northampton	1958
(Match)	V	17- 48	C.Blythe	for	Kent	Northampton	1907

Most Runs – Season	2198	D.Brookes	(av 51.11)	1952
Most Runs – Career	28980	D.Brookes	(av 36.13)	1934-59
Most 100s – Season	8	R.A.Haywood		1921
Most 100s – Career	67	D.Brookes		1934-59
Most Wkts – Season	175	G.E.Tribe	(av 18.70)	1955
Most Wkts – Career	1097	E.W.Clark	(av 21.31)	1922-47

LIMITED-OVERS CRICKET

Highest Total	NWT	360-2		v	Staffs	Northampton	1990
	BHC	304-6		v	Scotland	Northampton	1995
	SL	306-2		v	Surrey	Guildford	1985
Lowest Total	NWT	62		v	Leics	Leicester	1974
	BHC	85		v	Sussex	Northampton	1978
	SL	41		v	Middlesex	Northampton	1972
Highest Innings	NWT	145	R.J.Bailey	v	Staffs	Stone	1991
	BHC	134	R.J.Bailey	v	Glos	Northampton	1987
	SL	172*	W.Larkins	v	Warwicks	Luton	1983
Best Bowling	NWT	7-37	N.A.Mallender	v	Worcs	Northampton	1984
	BHC	5-21	Sarfraz Nawaz	v	Middlesex	Lord's	1980
	SL	7-39	A.Hodgson	v	Somerset	Northampton	1976

NOTTINGHAMSHIRE

Formation of Present Club: March/April 1841
Substantial Reorganisation: 11 December 1866
Colours: Green and Gold
Badge: Badge of City of Nottingham
Championships (since 1890): (4) 1907, 1929, 1981, 1987
NatWest Trophy/Gillette Cup Winners: (1) 1987
Benson and Hedges Cup Winners: (1) 1989
Sunday League Champions: (1) 1991
Match Awards: NWT 37; BHC 63

Secretary/General Manager: B.Robson
   Trent Bridge, Nottingham NG2 6AG (Tel 0115 982 1525)
Captain: P.Johnson. **Overseas Player:** C.L.Cairns (*tbc*). **1997 Beneficiary:** None.
Scorer: G.Stringfellow

AFFORD, John Andrew (Spalding GS; Stamford CFE), b Crowland, Lincs 12 May 1964. 6'1½". RHB, SLA. Debut 1984; cap 1990. Tour: Z 1989-90 (Eng A). HS 22* v Leics (Nottingham) 1989. 50 wkts (5); most – 57 (1991, 1993). BB 6-51 v Lancs (Nottingham) 1996. Awards: BHC 2. **NWT:** HS 2*. BB 3-32 v Herts (Hitchin) 1989. **BHC:** HS 1*. BB 4-38 v Kent (Nottingham) 1989. **SL:** HS 1. BB 3-33 v Northants (Northampton) 1993.

AFZAAL, Usman (Manvers Pierrepont CS; S Notts C), b Rawalpindi, Pakistan 9 Jun 1977. 6'0". LHB, SLA. Debut 1995. HS 67* v Hants (Southampton) 1996. BB 2-41 v Yorks (Nottingham) 1995. **NWT:** HS 26* v Northants (Nottingham) 1995. **SL:** HS 2. BB 2-25 v Yorks (Cleethorpes) 1995.

ARCHER, Graeme Francis (Heron Brook Middle S; King Edward VI HS, Stafford), b Carlisle, Cumberland 26 Sep 1970. 6'1". RHB, OB. Debut 1992; cap 1995. Staffordshire 1990. 1000 runs (1): 1171 (1995). HS 168 v Glam (Worksop) 1994. BB 3-18 v Hants (Southampton) 1996. **NWT:** HS 39 v Cheshire (Warrington) 1993. **BHC:** HS 74 v Lancs (Manchester) 1995. **SL:** HS 53 v Hants (Nottingham) 1995. BB 2-16 v Surrey (Guildford) 1995.

BATES, Richard Terry (Bourne GS; Stamford CFE), b Stamford, Lincs 17 Jun 1972. 6'1". RHB, OB. Debut 1993. Lincolnshire 1990-91. HS 34 v Worcs (Worcester) 1996. BB 5-88 v Durham (Chester-le-St) 1995. Award: BHC 1. **NWT:** HS 1. **BHC:** HS 27 v Yorks (Leeds) 1996. BB 3-21 v Scot (Nottingham) 1996. **SL:** HS 16 v Worcs (Worcester) 1994 and v Hants (Southampton) 1996. BB 3-42 v Sussex (Nottingham) 1996.

BOWEN, Mark Nicholas (Sacred Heart, Redcar; St Mary's C; Tees Side Poly), b Redcar, Yorks 6 Dec 1967. 6'2". RHB, RM. Northamptonshire 1991-92/1994. Nottinghamshire debut 1995. Tour: SA 1991-92 (Nh). HS 23* Nh v Durham (Northampton) 1993. Nt HS 22 v Glos (Nottingham) and v Kent (Tunbridge W)1996. BB 5-53 v Derbys (Derby) 1996. **NWT:** HS 0*. **BHC:** HS 0. BB 1-39. **SL:** HS 27* Nh v Kent (Northampton) 1994. BB 3-28 v Essex (Chelmsford) 1996.

CAIRNS, Christopher Lance (Christchurch BHS), b Picton, NZ 13 Jun 1970. Son of B.L. (CD, Otago, ND and NZ 1971-86). 6'2". RHB, RFM. Nottinghamshire 1988-89, 1992-93 and 1995 to date; cap 1993. N Districts 1988-89. Canterbury 1990-91 to date. Tests (NZ): 21 (1989-90 to 1996-97); HS 120 v Z (Auckland) 1995-96; BB 6-52 v E (Auckland) 1991-92. LOI (NZ): 62 (1990-91 to 1996-97); HS 103; BB 4-55. Tours (NZ): A 1989-90, 1993-94; WI 1995-96 (part); I 1995-96. 1000 runs (1): 1171 (1995). HS 120 (*Tests*). Nt HS 115 v Middx (Lord's) 1995. 50 wkts (3); most – 56 (1992). BB 8-47 (15-83 match) v Sussex (Arundel) 1995. Awards: NWT 2; BHC 1. **NWT:** HS 77 v Glam (Nottingham) 1992. BB 4-18 v Cheshire (Warrington) 1993. **BHC:** HS 46 and BB 4-47 v Durham (Stockton) 1995. **SL:** HS 126* v Surrey (Oval) 1993. BB 6-52 v Kent (Nottingham) 1993.

DOWMAN, Mathew Peter (St Hugh's CS; Grantham C), b Grantham, Lincs 10 May 1974. 5'10". LHB, RMF. Debut 1994. Scored 267 for England YC v WI YC (Hove) 1993 – record score in youth 'Tests'. HS 107 v OU (Oxford) 1995 and v Surrey (Nottingham) 1996. BB 2-43 v Leics (Nottingham) 1996. BHC: HS 19* and BB 3-21 v Worcs (Nottingham) 1996. SL: HS 74* v Glam (Nottingham) 1996. BB 2-34 v Warwks (Birmingham) 1996.

EVANS, Kevin Paul (Colonel Frank Seely S) b Calverton 10 Sep 1963. Elder brother of R.J. (Notts 1987-90). RHB, RMF. Debut 1984; cap 1990. HS 104 v Surrey (Nottingham) 1992 and v Sussex (Nottingham) 1994. BB 6-67 v Yorks (Nottingham) 1993. Awards: BHC 2. NWT: HS 21 v Worcs (Worcester) 1994. BB 6-10 v Northumb (Jesmond) 1994. BHC: HS 47 v Lancs (Manchester) 1995. BB 4-19 v Minor C (Leek) 1995. SL: HS 30 v Kent (Canterbury) 1990 and v Hants (Southampton) 1992. BB 4-26 v Kent (Canterbury) 1994.

FRANKS, Paul John (Southwell Minster CS), b Mansfield 3 Feb 1979. 6'2". LHB, RMF. Debut 1996. HS – and BB 2-65 v Hants (Southampton) 1996 (on debut).

GIE, Noel Addison (Trent C), b Pretoria, SA 12 Apr 1977. UK resident since 1984. Son of C.A. (WP and SAU 1970-71 to 1980-81). 6'0". RHB, RM. Debut 1995. HS 34 v Glam (Cardiff) 1995.

HART, Jamie Paul (Millfield S), b Blackpool, Lancs 31 Dec 1975. Son of P. (Nottingham Forest footballer). 6'3". RHB, RM. Debut 1996. HS 18* v Yorks (Scarborough) 1996 (on debut). SL: HS – . BB 1-48.

HINDSON, James Edward (Toot Hill CS, Bingham), b Huddersfield, Yorks 13 Sep 1973. 6'1". RHB, SLA. Debut 1992. HS 53* v OU (Oxford) 1995. BAC HS 47 v Kent (Nottingham) 1995. 50 wkts (1): 65 (1995). BB 5-42 v CU (Nottingham) 1992. BAC BB 5-53 v Glam (Worksop) 1994. NWT: HS 16* and BB 2-57 v Northants (Nottingham) 1995. BHC: HS 41* and BB 1-69 v Lancs (Manchester) 1995. SL: HS 21 v Middx (Nottingham) 1994. BB 4-19 v Worcs (Worcester) 1994.

JOHNSON, Paul (Grove CS, Balderton), b Newark 24 Apr 1965. 5'7". RHB, RM. Debut 1982; cap 1986; benefit 1995; captain 1996 to date. Tour: WI 1991-92 (Eng A). 1000 runs (8); most – 1518 (1990). HS 187 v Lancs (Manchester) 1993. BB 1-9. BAC BB 1-14. Awards: NWT 2; BHC 3. NWT: HS 146 v Northumb (Jesmond) 1994. BHC: HS 104* v Essex (Chelmsford) 1990. SL: HS 167* v Kent (Nottingham) 1993.

METCALFE, Ashley Anthony (Bradford GS; University C, London), b Horsforth, Yorks 25 Dec 1963. 5'8". RHB, OB. Yorkshire 1983-95 (scoring 122 v Notts (Bradford) on debut; cap 1986; benefit 1995). Nottinghamshire debut 1996. YC 1986. OFS 1988-89. Tours (Y): SA 1991-92, 1992-93; WI 1986-87. 1000 runs (6) inc 2000 (1): 2047 (1990). HS 216* Y v Middx (Leeds) 1988. Nt HS 128 v Glam (Worksop) 1996. BB 2-18 Y v Warwks (Scarborough) 1987. Awards: NWT 2; BHC 5. NWT: HS 127* Y v Warwks (Leeds) 1990. BB 2-44 Y v Wilts (Trowbridge) 1987. BHC: HS 114 Y v Lancs (Manchester) 1991. SL: HS 116 Y v Middx (Lord's) 1991.

NEWELL, Michael (West Bridgford CS), b Blackburn, Lancs 25 Feb 1965. 5'8". RHB, LB. Debut 1984; cap 1987. 1000 runs (1): 1054 (1987). HS 203* v Derbys (Derby) 1987. BB 2-38 v SL (Nottingham) 1988. BAC BB 1-0. NWT: HS 60 v Derbys (Derby) 1987. BHC: HS 39 v Somerset (Taunton) 1989. SL: HS 109* v Essex (Southend) 1990.

NOON, Wayne Michael (Caistor S), b Grimsby, Lincs 5 Feb 1971. 5'9". RHB, WK. Northamptonshire 1989-93. Nottinghamshire debut 1994; cap 1995. Canterbury 1994-95. Worcs 2nd XI debut when aged 15yr 199d. Tour: SA 1991-92 (Nh). HS 75 v Northants (Nottingham) 1994. NWT: HS 34 v Worcs (Worcester) 1994. BHC: HS 23 v Warwks (Nottingham) 1995. SL: HS 38 v Durham (Chester-le-St) 1995.

PICK, Robert Andrew (Alderman Derbyshire CS; High Pavement SFC), b Nottingham 19 Nov 1963. 5'10". LHB, RFM. Debut 1983; cap 1987; benefit 1996. Wellington 1989-90. Tours: WI 1991-92 (Eng A); SL 1990-91 (Eng A). HS 65* v Northants (Nottingham) 1994. 50 wkts (5); most – 67 (1991). BB 7-128 v Leics (Leicester) 1990. Awards: NWT 2; BHC 1. NWT: HS 34* v Sussex (Hove) 1994. BB 5-22 v Glos (Bristol) 1987. BHC: HS 25* v Hants (Southampton) 1991. BB 4-42 v Northants (Nottingham) 1987. SL: HS 58* v Essex (Nottingham) 1995. BB 4-32 v Glos (Moreton-in-M) 1987.

POLLARD, Paul Raymond (Gedling CS), b Carlton, Nottingham 24 Sep 1968. 5'11". LHB, RM. Debut 1987; cap 1992. 1000 runs (3); most – 1463 (1993). HS 180 v Derbys (Nottingham) 1993. BB 2-79 v Glos (Bristol) 1994. **NWT:** HS 96 v Northants (Nottingham) 1995. **BHC:** HS 104 v Surrey (Nottingham) 1994. **SL:** HS 132* v Somerset (Nottingham) 1995.

RICHES, Ian (Ancaster HS, Lincoln; Luton U), b Lincoln 12 Sep 1975. 6'2". RHB, LFM. Summer contract – awaiting f-c debut. **SL:** HS – .

ROBINSON, Robert Timothy (Dunstable GS; High Pavement SFC; Sheffield U), b Sutton in Ashfield 21 Nov 1958. 6'0". RHB, RM. Debut 1978; cap 1983; captain 1988-95; benefit 1992. *Wisden* 1985. **Tests:** 29 (1984-85 to 1989); HS 175 v A (Leeds) 1985. **LOI:** 26 (1984-85 to 1988; HS 83). Tours: A 1987-88; SA 1989-90 (Eng XI); NZ 1987-88; WI 1985-86; I/SL 1984-85; P 1987-88. 1000 runs (14) inc 2000 (1): 2032 (1984). HS 220* v Yorks (Nottingham) 1990. BB 1-22. Awards: NWT 4; BHC 7. **NWT:** HS 139 v Worcs (Worcester) 1985. **BHC:** HS 120 v Scot (Glasgow) 1985. **SL:** HS 119* v Lancs (Nottingham) 1994.

TOLLEY, Christopher Mark (King Edward VI C, Stourbridge; Loughborough U), b Kidderminster, Worcs 30 Dec 1967. 5'9". RHB, LMF. Worcestershire 1989-95; cap 1993. Nottinghamshire debut 1996. Tours (Wo): Z 1990-91, 1993-94. HS 84 Wo v Derbys (Derby) 1994. BB 5-55 Wo v Kent (Worcester) 1993. Nt HS 67 and BB 4-68 v Kent (Tunbridge W) 1996. Award: BHC 1. **NWT:** HS 16 v Yorks (Leeds) 1996. BB 3-25 Wo v Derbys (Worcester) 1993. **BHC:** HS 77 Comb Us v Lancs (Cambridge) 1990. BB 1-12. **SL:** HS 30 Wo v Hants (Southampton) 1995. BB 5-16 v Hants (Southampton) 1996.

WALKER, Lyndsay Nicholas Paton (Cardiff HS, NSW), b Armidale, NSW, Australia 22 Jun 1974. 6'0". RHB, WK. Debut 1994. HS 36 v Northants (Nottingham) 1996. **NWT:** HS 1.

WELTON, Guy Edward (Healing CS; Grimsby C), b Grimsby, Lincs 4 May 1978. 6'1". RHB, OB. Staff 1996 – awaiting f-c debut. MCC YC. Soccer for Grimsby Town (reserves; sub in one 1st team match).

DEPARTURES (who made first-class appearances in 1996)

BROADHURST, Mark (Kingstone S, Barnsley), b Worsborough Common, Barnsley, Yorks 20 Jun 1974. 6'0". RHB, RFM. Yorkshire 1991-94. Tour: SA 1992-93 (Y). Nottinghamshire 1996; no BAC appearances. HS 6. Nt HS – . BB 3-61 Y v OU (Oxford) 1991. **SL:** HS – .

CHAPMAN, R.J. – *see WORCESTERSHIRE.*

MIKE, Gregory Wentworth (Claremont CS; Basford Hall C), b Nottingham 14 Jul 1966. 6'0". RHB, RMF. Nottinghamshire 1989-96. HS 66* v OU (Oxford) 1995. BAC HS 61* v Warwks (Birmingham) 1992. BB 5-44 v Yorks (Middlesbrough) 1994. **NWT:** HS 5*. BB 1-71. **BHC:** HS 29 v Kent (Nottingham) 1989. BB 4-44 v Somerset (Nottingham) 1993. **SL:** HS 51* v Middx (Lord's) 1993. BB 4-41 v Northants (Nottingham) 1994.

PENNETT, David Barrington (Benton Park GS, Rawdon), b Leeds, Yorks 26 Oct 1969. 6'0". RHB, RMF. Nottinghamshire 1992-96. HS 50 v Durham (Chester-le-St) 1995. BB 5-36 v Durham (Chester-le-St) 1993. **NWT:** HS – . BB 1-22. **BHC:** HS 4*. BB 2-57 v Yorks (Leeds) 1996. **SL:** HS 12* v Durham (Nottingham) 1992. BB 3-27 v Worcs (Nottingham) 1995.

WILEMAN, Jonathan Ritchie (Stancliffe Hall S, Darley Dale; Malvern C; Salford), b Sheffield, Yorks 19 Aug 1970. 6'1". RHB, RSM. Nottinghamshire debut 1992 and 1995-96; scored 109 v CU (Nottingham) in his first f-c innings for the County. Subsequently appeared for Comb U v A (Oxford) 1993 and Minor C v SA (Torquay) 1994. Lincolnshire 1993-94. HS 109 (*as above*). BAC HS 37 v Lancs (Liverpool) 1995. BB 2-33 v Hants (Nottingham) 1995. **NWT:** HS 12 v Northants (Nottingham) 1995. BB 1-9. **BHC:** HS 0. **SL:** HS 51* v Sussex (Arundel) 1995. BB 4-21 v Glos (Bristol) 1995.

NOTTINGHAMSHIRE 1996

RESULTS SUMMARY

	Place	Won	Lost	Drew	No Result
Britannic Assurance Championship	17th	1	9	7	–
All First-Class Matches		1	9	9	–
NatWest Trophy	1st Round				
Benson and Hedges Cup	3rd in Group B				
Sunday League	2nd	12	4	–	1

BRITANNIC ASSURANCE CHAMPIONSHIP AVERAGES

BATTING AND FIELDING

Cap		M	I	NO	HS	Runs	Avge	100	50	Ct/St
1983	R.T.Robinson	17	31	2	184	1302	44.89	3	6	8
1995	G.F.Archer	12	22	2	143	819	40.95	2	4	15
1993	C.L.Cairns	16	29	5	114	946	39.41	1	6	10
–	A.A.Metcalfe	12	22	–	128	771	35.04	1	3	4
1990	K.P.Evans	13	18	3	71	482	32.13	–	4	3
1986	P.Johnson	17	32	2	109	954	31.80	2	6	10
1992	P.R.Pollard	12	23	1	86	631	28.68	–	5	9
–	U.Afzaal	4	8	1	67*	191	27.28	–	2	1
–	M.P.Dowman	7	12	–	107	288	24.00	1	–	4
–	C.M.Tolley	8	12	1	67	263	23.90	–	1	2
–	L.N.P.Walker	4	6	1	36	93	18.60	–	–	14/2
1995	W.M.Noon	13	21	3	57	332	18.44	–	1	30/3
–	R.T.Bates	10	14	1	34	214	16.46	–	–	7
–	M.N.Bowen	12	18	2	22	173	10.81	–	–	3
1987	R.A.Pick	6	8	–	32	66	8.25	–	–	1
–	D.B.Pennett	3	4	–	10	27	6.75	–	–	1
1990	J.A.Afford	17	23	14	11*	34	3.77	–	–	7
–	G.W.Mike	2	4	–	7	12	3.00	–	–	1

Also played (1 match each): P.J.Franks did not bat; J.P.Hart 18*, 0*.

BOWLING

	O	M	R	W	Avge	Best	5wI	10wM
J.A.Afford	543.5	155	1382	47	29.40	6- 51	2	–
M.N.Bowen	356.2	60	1263	32	39.46	5- 53	2	–
C.L.Cairns	427.3	73	1461	37	39.48	6-110	1	–
K.P.Evans	404.1	99	1179	29	40.65	5- 30	2	–
R.T.Bates	255.2	41	895	19	47.10	3- 42	–	–
C.M.Tolley	193	42	709	13	54.53	4- 68	–	–

Also bowled: U.Afzaal 24-1-117-2; G.F.Archer 27-5-98-3; M.P.Dowman 32-9-108-2; P.J.Franks 41-14-102-3; J.P.Hart 18-7-51-0; P.Johnson 12-2-51-1; G.W.Mike 39-5-172-2; W.M.Noon 4-1-22-0; D.B.Pennett 9-1-55-376-7; R.A.Pick 155.1-31-483-7; R.T.Robinson 1-0-4-0.

The First-Class Averages (pp 123-38) give the records of Nottinghamshire players in all first-class county matches (their other opponents being South Africa A and Oxford University).

NOTTINGHAMSHIRE RECORDS

FIRST-CLASS CRICKET

Highest Total	For	739-7d		v	Leics	Nottingham	1903
	V	781-7d		by	Northants	Northampton	1995
Lowest Total	For	13		v	Yorkshire	Nottingham	1901
	V	16		by	Derbyshire	Nottingham	1879
		16		by	Surrey	The Oval	1880
Highest Innings	For	312*	W.W.Keeton	v	Middlesex	The Oval	1939
	V	345	C.G.Macartney	for	Australians	Nottingham	1921

Highest Partnership for each Wicket

1st	391	A.O.Jones/A.Shrewsbury	v	Glos	Bristol	1899
2nd	398	A.Shrewsbury/W.Gunn	v	Sussex	Nottingham	1890
3rd	369	W.Gunn/J.R.Gunn	v	Leics	Nottingham	1903
4th	361	A.O.Jones/J.R.Gunn	v	Essex	Leyton	1905
5th	266	A.Shrewsbury/W.Gunn	v	Sussex	Hove	1884
6th	303*	F.H.Winrow/P.F.Harvey	v	Derbyshire	Nottingham	1947
7th	301	C.C.Lewis/B.N.French	v	Durham	Chester-le-St	1993
8th	220	G.F.H.Heane/R.Winrow	v	Somerset	Nottingham	1935
9th	170	J.C.Adams/K.P.Evans	v	Somerset	Taunton	1994
10th	152	E.B.Alletson/W.Riley	v	Sussex	Hove	1911

Best Bowling	For	10-66	K.Smales	v	Glos	Stroud	1956
(Innings)	V	10-10	H.Verity	for	Yorkshire	Leeds	1932
Best Bowling	For	17-89	F.C.Matthews	v	Northants	Nottingham	1923
(Match)	V	17-89	W.G.Grace	for	Glos	Cheltenham	1877

Most Runs – Season	2620	W.W.Whysall	(av 53.46)	1929
Most Runs – Career	31592	G.Gunn	(av 35.69)	1902-32
Most 100s – Season	9	W.W.Whysall		1928
	9	M.J.Harris		1971
	9	B.C.Broad		1990
Most 100s – Career	65	J.Hardstaff, jr		1930-55
Most Wkts – Season	181	B.Dooland	(av 14.96)	1954
Most Wkts – Career	1653	T.G.Wass	(av 20.34)	1896-1920

LIMITED-OVERS CRICKET

Highest Total	NWT	344-6		v	Northumb	Jesmond	1994
	BHC	296-6		v	Kent	Nottingham	1989
	SL	329-6		v	Derbyshire	Nottingham	1993
Lowest Total	NWT	123		v	Yorkshire	Scarborough	1969
	BHC	74		v	Leics	Leicester	1987
	SL	66		v	Yorkshire	Bradford	1969
Highest Innings	NWT	149*	D.W.Randall	v	Devon	Torquay	1988
	BHC	130*	C.E.B.Rice	v	Scotland	Glasgow	1982
	SL	167*	P.Johnson	v	Kent	Nottingham	1993
Best Bowling	NWT	6-10	K.P.Evans	v	Northumb	Jesmond	1994
	BHC	6-22	M.K.Bore	v	Leics	Leicester	1980
		6-22	C.E.B.Rice	v	Northants	Northampton	1981
	SL	6-12	R.J.Hadlee	v	Lancashire	Nottingham	1980

SOMERSET

Formation of Present Club: 18 August 1875
Colours: Black, White and Maroon
Badge: Somerset Dragon
Championships: (0) Third 1892, 1958, 1963, 1966, 1981
NatWest Trophy/Gillette Cup Winners: (2) 1979, 1983
Benson and Hedges Cup Winners: (2) 1981, 1982
Sunday League Champions: (1) 1979
Match Awards: NWT 48; BHC 60

Chief Executive: P.W.Anderson
   The County Ground, Taunton TA1 1JT (Tel 01823 272946)
Captain: P.D.Bowler. **Overseas Player:** Mushtaq Ahmed. **1997 Beneficiary:** G.D.Rose.
Scorer: D.A.Oldam

BISHOP, Ian Emlyn (Castle S; Somerset C of Art & Tech), b Taunton 26 Aug 1977. 6'1".
RHB, RMF. Debut 1996. Awaiting BAC debut. HS 2.

BOWLER, Peter Duncan (Educated at Canberra, Australia), b Plymouth, Devon 30 Jul
1963. 6'1". RHB, OB, occ WK. Leicestershire 1986 – first to score hundred on f-c debut
for Leics (100* and 62 v Hants). Derbyshire 1988-94; cap 1989;
scored 155* v CU (Cambridge) on debut – only instance of hundreds on debut for two
counties. Somerset debut/cap 1995; captain 1997. 1000 runs (8) inc 2000 (1): 2044
(1992). HS 241* De v Hants (Portsmouth) 1992. Sm HS 207 v Surrey (Taunton) 1996.
BB 3-41 De v Leics (Leicester) 1991 and De v Yorks (Chesterfield) 1991. Sm BB 2-54 v
Derbys (Taunton) 1996. Awards: BHC 3. **NWT:** HS 111 De v Berks (Derby) 1992. **BHC:**
HS 109 De v Somerset (Taunton) 1990. BB 1-15. **SL:** HS 138* De v Somerset (Derby)
1993. BB 3-31 De v Glos (Cheltenham) 1991.

CADDICK, Andrew Richard (Papanui HS), b Christchurch, NZ 21 Nov 1968. Son of
English emigrants – qualified for England 1992. 6'5". RHB, RFM. Debut 1991; cap 1992.
Represented NZ in 1987-88 Youth World Cup. **Tests:** 11 (1993 to 1996-97); HS 29* v WI
(Kingston) 1993-94; BB 6-65 v WI (P-o-S) 1993-94. **LOI:** 9 (1993 to 1996-97; HS 20*;
BB 3-35). Tours: A 1992-93 (Eng A); WI 1993-94; NZ 1996-97; Z 1996-97. HS 92 v
Worcs (Worcester) 1995. 50 wkts (4); most – 73 (1996). BB 9-32 (12-120 match) v Lancs
(Taunton) 1993. Award: NWT 1. **NWT:** HS 8. BB 6-30 v Glos (Taunton) 1992. **BHC:** HS
28 v Kent (Canterbury) 1995. BB 5-51 v Brit Us (Taunton) 1996. **SL:** HS 39 v Hants
(Taunton) 1996. BB 4-18 v Lancs (Manchester) 1992.

COTTAM, Andrew Colin (Axminster SS), b Northampton 14 Jul 1973. Son of R.M.H.
(Hants, Northants and England 1963-76). 6'1". RHB, SLA. Somerset 1992-93 and 1996.
Derbyshire 1995. Devon 1993. Northamptonshire staff 1994. HS 36 and BB 2-5 De v OU
(Oxford) 1995. BAC HS 31 v Glos (Gloucester) 1992. BAC BB 2-127 v Middx
(Uxbridge) 1996. **NWT:** HS 2. BB 1-45. **SL:** HS – .

DIMOND, Matthew (Castle S; Richard Huish C), b Taunton 24 Sep 1975. 6'1". RHB,
RMF. Debut 1994. HS 26 v Derbys (Derby) 1995. BB 4-73 v Yorks (Bradford) 1994.
BHC: HS – . **SL:** HS – .

ECCLESTONE, Simon Charles (Bryanston S; Durham U; Keble C, Oxford), b Great
Dunmow, Essex 16 Jul 1971. 6'3". LHB, RM. Oxford U 1994; blue 1994. Somerset debut
1994. Cambridgeshire 1990-94. HS 94 v Kent (Canterbury) 1996. BB 4-66 OU v Surrey
(Oval) 1994. BAC BB 2-48 v Notts (Nottingham) 1995. Award: BHC 1. **NWT:** HS 52 v
Surrey (Oval) 1996. **BHC:** HS 112* v Middx (Lord's) 1996. BB 2-44 v Kent (Canter-
bury) 1995. **SL:** HS 130 v Surrey (Taunton) 1996. BB 4-31 v Essex (Weston-s-M) 1994.

HARDEN, Richard John (King's C, Taunton), b Bridgwater 16 Aug 1965. 5'11". RHB, SLA. Debut 1985; cap 1989; benefit 1996. C Districts 1987-88. 1000 runs (7); most – 1460 (1990). HS 187 v Notts (Taunton) 1992. BB 2-7 CD v Canterbury (Blenheim) 1987-88. Sm BB 2-24 v Hants (Taunton) 1986. Award: NWT 1. **NWT:** HS 108* v Scot (Taunton) 1992. **BHC:** HS 76 v Kent (Canterbury) 1992. **SL:** HS 100* v Durham (Chester-le-St) 1995.

HOLLOWAY, Piran Christopher Laity (Millfield S; Taunton S; Loughborough U), b Helston, Cornwall 1 Oct 1970. 5'8". LHB, WK. Warwickshire 1988-93. Somerset debut 1994. HS 168 v Middx (Uxbridge) 1996. **NWT:** HS 50 v Warwks (Birmingham) 1995. **BHC:** HS 27 Comb Us v Derbys (Oxford) 1991. **SL:** HS 66 v Leics (Weston-s-M) 1995.

KERR, Jason Ian Douglas (Withins HS; Bolton C), b Bolton, Lancs 7 Apr 1974. 6'2". RHB, RMF. Debut 1993. HS 80 and BB 5-82 v WI (Taunton) 1995. BAC HS 68* v Derbys (Taunton) 1996. BAC BB 4-68 v Sussex (Bath) 1995. **NWT:** HS 3. BB 2-74 v Warwks (Birmingham) 1995. **BHC:** HS – . BB 2-35 v Sussex (Taunton) 1995. **SL:** HS 17 v Northants (Luton) 1993. BB 3-27 v Essex (Taunton) 1996.

LATHWELL, Mark Nicholas (Braunton S, Devon), b Bletchley, Bucks 26 Dec 1971. 5'8". RHB, RM. Debut 1991; cap 1992. YC 1993. MCC YC. **Tests:** 2 (1993); HS 33 v A (Nottingham) 1993. Tours (Eng A): A 1992-93; SA 1993-94. 1000 runs (5); most – 1230 (1994). HS 206 v Surrey (Bath) 1994. BB 2-21 v Sussex (Hove) 1994. Awards: NWT 1; BHC 1. **NWT:** HS 103 and BB 1-23 v Salop (Telford) 1993. **BHC:** HS 121 v Middx (Lord's) 1996. **SL:** HS 117 v Notts (Taunton) 1994.

MUSHTAQ AHMED, b Sahiwal, Pakistan 28 Jun 1970. 5'5". RHB, LBG. Multan 1986-87 to 1990-91. United Bank 1986-87 to date. Somerset 1993-95; cap 1993. **Tests** (P): 26 (1989-90 to 1996-97); HS 42 v NZ (Rawalpindi) 1996-97; BB 7-56 (10-171 match) v NZ (Christchurch) 1995-96. **LOI** (P): 119 (1988-89 to 1996-97; HS 26; BB 5-36). Tours (P): E 1992, 1996; A 1989-90, 1991-92, 1992-93, 1995-96; WI 1992-93; NZ 1992-93, 1993-94, 1995-96; SL 1994-95. HS 90 and Sm BB 7-91 (12-175 match) v Sussex (Taunton) 1993. 50 wkts (3+1); most – 95 (1995). BB 9-93 Multan v Peshawar (Sahiwal) 1990-91. Awards: NWT 1; BHC 1. **NWT:** HS 35 v Surrey (Taunton) 1993. BB 3-26 v Oxon (Aston Rowant) 1994. **BHC:** HS 21 v Surrey (Taunton) 1995. BB 4-29 v Sussex (Taunton) 1995. **SL:** HS 32 v Middx (Bath) 1993. BB 3-17 v Glos (Taunton) 1993.

PARSONS, Keith Alan (The Castle S, Taunton; Richard Huish SFC), b Taunton 2 May 1973. Identical twin brother of K.J. (Somerset staff 1992-94). 6'1". RHB, RM. Debut 1992. HS 105 v Young A (Taunton) 1995. BAC HS 83* v Middx (Uxbridge) 1996. BB 2-11 v Derbys (Derby) 1995. **NWT:** HS 51 and BB 2-46 v Suffolk (Taunton) 1996. **BHC:** HS 33* v Brit Us (Taunton) 1996. BB 2-60 v Kent (Maidstone) 1996. **SL:** HS 56 v Sussex (Hove) 1996. BB 3-36 v Leics (Leics) 1996.

ROSE, Graham David (Northumberland Park S, Tottenham), b Tottenham, London 12 Apr 1964. 6'4". RHB, RM. Middlesex 1985-86. Somerset debut 1987; cap 1988; benefit 1997. 1000 runs (1): 1000 (1990). HS 138 v Sussex (Taunton) 1993. 50 wkts (3); most – 57 (1988). BB 7-47 (13-88 match) v Notts (Taunton) 1996. Awards: BHC 3. **NWT:** HS 110 v Devon (Torquay) 1990. BB 3-11 v Salop (Telford) 1993. **BHC:** HS 79 v Surrey (Taunton) 1995. BB 4-21 v Ire (Erlington) 1995. **SL:** HS 148 v Glam (Neath) 1990. BB 4-26 v Kent (Taunton) 1993.

SHINE, Kevin James (Maiden Erlegh CS), b Bracknell, Berks 22 Feb 1969. 6'2½". RHB, RFM. Hampshire 1989-93. Middlesex 1994-95. Somerset debut 1996. Berkshire 1986. HS 40 and Sm BB 6-95 v Surrey (Taunton) 1996 (on Sm debut). BB 8-47 (8 wkts in 38 balls inc hat-trick and 4 in 5; 13-105 match) H v Lancs (Manchester) 1992. **NWT:** HS – . BB 3-31 M v Wales MC (Northop Hall) 1994. **BHC:** HS 38* v Kent (Maidstone) 1996. BB 4-68 H v Surrey (Oval) 1990. **SL:** HS 2*. BB 4-31 v Northants (Taunton) 1996.

TRESCOTHICK, Marcus Edward (Sir Bernard Lovell S), b Keynsham 25 Dec 1975. 6'2". LHB, RM. Debut 1993. HS 178 v Hants (Taunton) 1996. BB 4-36 (inc hat-trick) v Young A (Taunton) 1995. Award: NWT 1. **NWT:** HS 116 v Oxon (Aston Rowant) 1994. **BHC:** HS 122 v Ire (Erlington) 1995. **SL:** HS 74 v Yorks (Leeds) 1994. BB 1-13.

TRUMP, Harvey Russell John (Millfield S), b Taunton 11 Oct 1968. 6'0". RHB, OB. Debut 1988; cap 1994. HS 48 v Notts (Taunton) 1988 – on debut. 50 wkts (1): 51 (1991). BB 7-52 (inc hat-trick; 14-104 match) v Glos (Gloucester) 1992. Award: NWT 1. **NWT:** HS 10* v Warwks (Birmingham) 1995. BB 3-15 v Glos (Taunton) 1996. **BHC:** HS 11 v Kent (Canterbury). BB 3-17 v Ire (Erlington) 1995. **SL:** HS 19 v Kent (Taunton) 1991. BB 3-19 v Essex (Weston-s-M) 1994.

TURNER, Robert Julian (Millfield S; Magdalene C, Cambridge), b Malvern, Worcs 25 Nov 1967. 6'1½". RHB, WK. Brother of S.J. (Somerset 1984-85). Cambridge U 1988-91; blue 1988-89-90-91; captain 1991. Somerset debut 1991; cap 1994. HS 106* v Derbys (Derby) 1995. Award: BHC 1. **NWT:** HS 40 v Suffolk (Taunton) 1996. **BHC:** HS 70 v Glam (Cardiff) 1996. **SL:** HS 39 v Northants (Taunton) 1996.

Van TROOST, Adrianus Petrus (**'Andre'**) (Spieringshoek C, Schiedam), b Schiedam, Holland Oct 1972. 6'7". RHB, RF. Debut 1991. Qualified for England 1998. Holland 1990 (inc ICC Trophy final v Zimbabwe). HS 35 v Lancs (Taunton) 1993. BB 6-48 v Essex (Taunton) 1992. **NWT:** HS 17* v Surrey (Taunton) 1993. BB 5-22 v Oxon (Aston Rowant) 1994. **BHC:** HS 9* and BB 2-38 v Notts (Nottingham) 1993. **SL:** HS 9*. BB 4-23 v Notts (Taunton) 1994.

NEWCOMERS

BURNS, Michael (Walney CS), b Barrow-in-Furness, Lancs 6 Jun 1969. 6'0". RHB, WK, occ RM. Cumberland 1988-90. Warwickshire 1992-96. HS 81 Wa v Notts (Birmingham) 1996. **NWT:** HS 37* Wa v Cornwall (St Austell) 1996. **BHC:** HS 22 Wa v Leics (Leicester) 1993. **SL:** HS 37 Wa v Derbys (Birmingham) 1994 and Wa v Notts (Birmingham) 1996.

MORGAN, Haydn John (Westland S, Torquay), b Torquay, Devon 5 Jul 1973. RHB, OB.

SUTTON, Luke David (Millfield S), b Keynsham 4 Oct 1976. RHB, WK.

TREGO, Samuel Marc, b Weston-super-Mare 7 Jun 1977. RHB, OB.

DEPARTURES (who made first-class appearances in 1996)

BATTY, Jeremy David (Bingley GS; Horsforth C), b Bradford, Yorks 15 May 1971. Brother of G.J. (*see YORKSHIRE*). 6'1". RHB, OB. Yorkshire 1989-94. Somerset 1995-96. Tours (Y): SA 1991-92, 1992-93. HS 51 Y v SL (Leeds) 1991. BAC HS 50 Y v Notts (Nottingham) 1993. Sm HS 45* v WI (Taunton) 1995. BB 6-48 Y v Notts (Worksop) 1991. Sm BB 5-85 v Hants (Taunton) 1996. Award: BHC 1. **NWT:** HS 4. BB 1-17. **BHC:** HS 19* v Surrey (Taunton) 1995. BB 2-13 v Glos (Bristol) 1995. **SL:** HS 13* and BB 4-33 Y v Kent (Scarborough) 1991.

HAYHURST, A.N. – *see DERBYSHIRE.*

LEE, Shane (Oak Flats HS; Wollongong U), b Wollongong, NSW, Australia 8 Aug 1973. 6'2". RHB, RFM. NSW 1992-93 to date. Somerset 1996; cap 1996. Australian CA. **LOI** (A): 8 (1995-96). HS 39; BB 1-20). Tour (NSW): E 1995. 1000 runs (1): 1300 (1996). HS 167* v Worcs (Bath) 1996. BB 4-20 NSW v Tasmania (Sydney) 1995-96. Sm BB 4-52 v Sussex (Hove) 1996. Award: NWT 1. **NWT:** HS 104 v Suffolk (Taunton) 1996. **BHC:** HS 23 and BB 3-60 v Brit Us (Taunton) 1996. **SL:** HS 71* v Glam (Swansea) 1996. BB 4-40 v Sussex (Hove) 1996.

SOMERSET 1996

RESULTS SUMMARY

	Place	Won	Lost	Drew	No Result
Britannic Assurance Championship	11th	5	6	6	–
All First-Class Matches		5	7	7	–
NatWest Trophy	Quarter-Finalist				
Benson and Hedges Cup	4th in Group C				
Sunday League	**5th**	10	6	–	1

BRITANNIC ASSURANCE CHAMPIONSHIP AVERAGES

BATTING AND FIELDING

Cap		M	I	NO	HS	Runs	Avge	100	50	Ct/St
1996	S.Lee	16	23	3	167*	1300	65.00	5	5	14
1992	M.N.Lathwell	16	28	4	109	1059	44.12	1	7	10
1995	P.D.Bowler	17	30	4	207	1075	41.34	2	5	5
–	P.C.L.Holloway	9	14	1	168	482	37.07	1	3	6
1989	R.J.Harden	12	20	1	136	676	35.57	1	5	11
1994	R.J.Turner	17	25	6	100*	645	33.94	1	3	61/3
–	K.A.Parsons	6	11	1	83*	332	33.20	–	3	2
–	S.C.Ecclestone	6	9	1	94	237	29.62	–	2	2
–	J.I.D.Kerr	5	7	3	68*	116	29.00	–	1	–
–	M.E.Trescothick	13	22	–	178	628	28.54	1	1	11
1988	G.D.Rose	14	19	4	93*	338	22.53	–	1	8
1990	A.N.Hayhurst	9	13	1	96	224	18.66	–	2	2
–	J.D.Batty	14	20	4	44	276	17.25	–	–	4
1992	A.R.Caddick	13	17	4	38	187	14.38	–	–	7
–	K.J.Shine	10	12	2	40	91	9.10	–	–	4
–	A.P.van Troost	5	6	1	11	22	4.40	–	–	–

Also batted: A.C.Cottam (2 matches) 3, 12; H.R.J.Trump (3 matches – cap 1994) 0*, 0 (3 ct).

BOWLING

	O	M	R	W	Avge	Best	5wI	10wM
G.D.Rose	382.2	96	1171	50	23.42	7- 47	3	1
A.R.Caddick	524.5	120	1743	65	26.81	7- 83	6	3
K.J.Shine	238.3	43	1007	32	31.46	6- 95	2	–
J.D.Batty	411.5	88	1298	29	44.75	5- 85	1	–
S.Lee	397.3	62	1705	36	47.36	4- 52	–	–
J.I.D.Kerr	116	14	512	10	51.20	3-108	–	–

Also bowled: P.D.Bowler 31.3-2-177-3; A.C.Cottam 89-22-248-3; R.J.Harden 8-0-42-1; A.N.Hayhurst 25-5-91-1; P.C.L.Holloway 4.4-1-34-0; K.A.Parsons 29-7-102-1; M.E.Trescothick 23-1-97-0; H.R.J.Trump 43-10-179-4; R.J.Turner 1-0-3-0; A.P.van Troost 92.3-12-409-9.

The First-Class Averages (pp 123-38) give the records of Somerset players in all first-class county matches (their other opponents being the Pakistanis and South Africa A), with the exception of:
    A.R.Caddick 14-19-5-38-195-13.92-0-0-7ct. 546.5-121-1864-67-27.82-7/83-6-3.

SOMERSET RECORDS

FIRST-CLASS CRICKET

Highest Total	For	675-9d		v	Hampshire	Bath	1924
	V	811		by	Surrey	The Oval	1899
Lowest Total	For	25		v	Glos	Bristol	1947
	V	22		by	Glos	Bristol	1920
Highest Innings	For	322	I.V.A.Richards	v	Warwicks	Taunton	1985
	V	424	A.C.MacLaren	for	Lancashire	Taunton	1895

Highest Partnership for each Wicket

1st	346	H.T.Hewett/L.C.H.Palairet	v	Yorkshire	Taunton	1892
2nd	290	J.C.W.MacBryan/M.D.Lyon	v	Derbyshire	Buxton	1924
3rd	319	P.M.Roebuck/M.D.Crowe	v	Leics	Taunton	1984
4th	310	P.W.Denning/I.T.Botham	v	Glos	Taunton	1980
5th	235	J.C.White/C.C.C.Case	v	Glos	Taunton	1927
6th	265	W.E.Alley/K.E.Palmer	v	Northants	Northampton	1961
7th	278*	S.Lee/R.J.Turner	v	Worcs	Bath	1996
8th	172	I.V.A.Richards/I.T.Botham	v	Leics	Leicester	1983
9th	183	C.H.M.Greetham/H.W.Stephenson	v	Leics	Weston-s-Mare	1963
	183	C.J.Tavaré/N.A.Mallender	v	Sussex	Hove	1990
10th	143	J.J.Bridges/A.H.D.Gibbs	v	Essex	Weston-s-Mare	1919

Best Bowling	For	10- 49	E.J.Tyler	v	Surrey	Taunton	1895
(Innings)	V	10- 35	A.Drake	for	Yorkshire	Weston-s-Mare	1914
Best Bowling	For	16- 83	J.C.White	v	Worcs	Bath	1919
(Match)	V	17-137	W.Brearley	for	Lancashire	Manchester	1905

Most Runs – Season	2761	W.E.Alley	(av 58.74)	1961
Most Runs – Career	21142	H.Gimblett	(av 36.96)	1935-54
Most 100s – Season	11	S.J.Cook		1991
Most 100s – Career	49	H.Gimblett		1935-54
Most Wkts – Season	169	A.W.Wellard	(av 19.24)	1938
Most Wkts – Career	2166	J.C.White	(av 18.02)	1909-37

LIMITED-OVERS CRICKET

Highest Total	NWT	413-4		v	Devon	Torquay	1990
	BHC	322-4		v	Middlesex	Lord's	1996
	SL	360-3		v	Glamorgan	Neath	1990
Lowest Total	NWT	59		v	Middlesex	Lord's	1977
	BHC	98		v	Middlesex	Lord's	1982
	SL	58		v	Essex	Chelmsford	1977
Highest Innings	NWT	162*	C.J.Tavaré	v	Devon	Torquay	1990
	BHC	177	S.J.Cook	v	Sussex	Hove	1990
	SL	175*	I.T.Botham	v	Northants	Wellingborough	1986
Best Bowling	NWT	7-15	R.P.Lefebvre	v	Devon	Torquay	1990
	BHC	5-14	J.Garner	v	Surrey	Lord's	1981
	SL	6-24	I.V.A.Richards	v	Lancashire	Manchester	1983

SURREY

Formation of Present Club: 22 August 1845
Colours: Chocolate
Badge: Prince of Wales' Feathers
Championships (since 1890): (15) 1890, 1891, 1892, 1894, 1895, 1899, 1914, 1952, 1953, 1954, 1955, 1956, 1957, 1958, 1971. Joint: (1) 1950
NatWest Trophy/Gillette Cup Winners: (1) 1982
Benson and Hedges Cup Winners: (1) 1974
Sunday League Champions: (1) 1996
Match Awards: NWT 44; BHC 58

Chief Executive: P.C.J.Sheldon
Kennington Oval, London, SE11 5SS (Tel 0171 582 6660)
Captain: A.J.Stewart. **Vice-Captain:** A.J.Hollioake. **Overseas Player:** B.P.Julian.
1997 Beneficiary: M.P.Bicknell. **Scorer:** K.R.Booth.

BENJAMIN, Joseph Emmanuel (Cayon HS, St Kitts; Mount Pleasant S, Highgate, Birmingham), b Christ Church, St Kitts 2 Feb 1961. 6'2". RHB, RMF. Warwickshire 1988-91. Surrey debut 1992; cap 1993. Staffordshire 1986-88. **Tests:** 1 (1994); HS 0 and BB 4-42 v SA (Oval) 1994. **LOI:** 2 (1994-95; HS 0; BB 1-22). Tour: A 1994-95. HS 49 v Essex (Oval) 1995. 50 wkts (3); most – 80 (1994). BB 6-19 v Notts (Oval) 1993. Awards: NWT 2; BHC 1. **NWT:** HS 25 v Worcs (Oval) 1994. BB 4-20 v Berks (Oval) 1995. **BHC:** HS 20 Wa v Worcs (Birmingham) 1990. BB 4-27 v Somerset (Taunton) 1995. **SL:** HS 24 Wa v Lancs (Manchester) 1990. BB 4-44 v Middx (Oval) 1992.

BICKNELL, Darren John (Robert Haining SS; Guildford TC), b Guildford 24 Jun 1967. Elder brother of M.P. 6'4". LHB, SLA. Debut 1987; cap 1990. Tours (Eng A): WI 1991-92; P 1990-91; SL 1990-91; Z 1989-90. 1000 runs (6); most – 1888 (1991). HS 235* v Notts (Nottingham) 1994. BB 3-7 v Sussex (Guildford) 1996. Awards: NWT 1; BHC 3. **NWT:** HS 135* v Yorks (Oval) 1989. **BHC:** HS 119 v Hants (Oval) 1990. **SL:** HS 125 v Durham (Durham) 1992. BB 1-11.

BICKNELL, Martin Paul (Robert Haining SS), b Guildford 14 Jan 1969. Younger brother of D.J. 6'3". RHB, RFM. Debut 1986; cap 1989; benefit 1997. **Tests:** 2 (1993); HS 14 and BB 3-99 v A (Birmingham) 1993. **LOI:** 7 (1990-91; HS 31*; BB 3-55). Tours: A 1990-91; SA 1993-94 (Eng A); Z 1989-90 (Eng A). HS 88 v Hants (Southampton) 1992. 50 wkts (6); most – 71 (1992). BB 9-45 v CU (Oval) 1988. BAC BB 7-52 v Sussex (Oval) 1991. Award: BHC 1. **NWT:** HS 66* v Northants (Oval) 1991. BB 4-35 v Somerset (Taunton) 1993. **BHC:** HS 43 v Kent (Canterbury) 1995. BB 4-49 v Somerset (Oval) 1994. **SL:** HS 25 v Glam (Oval) 1995. BB 5-12 v Northants (Oval) 1994.

BROWN, Alistair Duncan (Caterham S), b Beckenham, Kent 11 Feb 1970. 5'10". RHB, occ LB. Debut 1992; cap 1994. **LOI:** 3 (1996; HS 118). 1000 runs (3); most – 1382 (1993). HS 187 v Glos (Oval) 1995. Award: BHC 1. **NWT:** HS 72 v Holland (Oval) 1996. **BHC:** HS 117* v Sussex (Hove) 1996. **SL:** HS 142* v Middx (Oval) 1994.

BUTCHER, Mark Alan (Trinity S; Archbishop Tenison's S, Croydon), b Croydon 23 Aug 1972. Son of A.R. (Surrey, Glamorgan and England 1972-92); brother of G.P. (see *GLAMORGAN*). 5'11". LHB, RM. Debut 1992; cap 1996. Tour: A 1996-97 (Eng A). 1000 runs (2); most – 1604 (1996). HS 167 v Durham (Oval) 1995. BB 4-31 v Worcs (Oval) 1994. Award: NWT 1. **NWT:** HS 91 v Somerset (Oval) 1996. BB 2-57 v Somerset (Taunton) 1993. **BHC:** HS 42* v Hants (Oval) 1996. BB 3-37 v Somerset (Oval) 1994. **SL:** HS 57 v Hants (Southampton) 1996. BB 3-23 v Sussex (Oval) 1992.

HOLLIOAKE, Adam John (St George's C, Weybridge), b Melbourne, Australia 5 Sep 1971. Brother of B.C. 5'11". RHB, RMF. Debut 1993, scoring 13 and 123 v Derbys (Ilkeston); cap 1995. Qualified for England 1992. **LOI:** 2 (1996; HS 15; BB 4-23). Tour: A 1996-97 (Eng A – captain). 1000 runs (2); most – 1522 (1996). HS 138 v Leics (Oval) 1994. BB 4-22 v Yorks (Oval) 1995. **NWT:** HS 60 v Worcs (Oval) 1994. BB 4-53 v Middx (Oval) 1995. **BHC:** HS 45 v Glos (Oval) 1996. BB 4-34 v Hants (Oval) 1996. **SL:** HS 93 v Kent (Canterbury) 1995. BB 5-44 v Sussex (Guildford) 1996.

HOLLIOAKE, Benjamin Caine (Millfield S), b Melbourne, Australia 11 Nov 1977. Brother of A.J. 6'2". RHB, RMF. Debut 1996. HS 46 v Warwks (Oval) 1996. BB 4-74 v Yorks (Middlesbrough) 1996 (on debut). **NWT:** HS – . **BHC:** HS – . BB 1-25. **SL:** HS 22* v Lancs (Manchester) 1996. BB 5-10 v Derbys (Oval) 1996. Rugby for Somerset. Hockey for West of England.

JULIAN, Brendon Paul (Guildford GS, WA), b Hamilton, NZ 10 Aug 1970. 6'5". RHB, LFM. W Australia 1989-90 to date. Surrey debut/cap 1996. **Tests** (A): 7 (1993 to 1995-96); HS 56* v E (Nottingham) 1993; BB 4-36 v WI (Bridgetown) 1994-95. **LOI** (A): 2 (1993 to 1994-95; HS 11; BB 3-50). Tours (A): E 1993; WI 1994-95. HS 119 v Lancs (Southport) 1996. 50 wkts (1): 61 (1996). BB 6-37 v Northants (Oval) 1996. **NWT:** HS 23 v Holland (Oval) 1996. BB 4-46 v Somerset (Oval) 1996. **BHC:** HS 27 v Glos (Oval) 1996. BB 3-28 v Sussex (Hove) 1996. **SL:** HS 41 v Derbys (Oval) 1996. BB 3-5 v Glos (Gloucester) 1996.

KENNIS, Gregor John (Tiffin S), b Yokohama, Japan 9 Mar 1974. 6'1". RHB, OB. MCC YC. Debut 1994. HS 29 v Kent (Canterbury) 1995. Scored 258 (395 balls, 41 fours) v Leics II (Kibworth) 1995 – Surrey II record. **SL:** HS 5.

KNOTT, James Alan (City of Westminster C), b Canterbury, Kent 14 Jun 1975. Son of A.P.E. (Kent, Tasmania and England 1964-85). 5'6". RHB, WK. Debut 1995. Awaiting BAC debut. MCC YC. HS 49* v SA A (Oval) 1996.

LEWIS, Clairmonte Christopher (Willesden HS, London), b Georgetown, Guyana 14 Feb 1968. 6'2½". RHB, RFM. Leicestershire 1987-91; cap 1990. Nottinghamshire 1992-94; cap 1994. Surrey debut 1996. **Tests:** 32 (1990 to 1996); HS 117 v I (Madras) 1992-93; BB 6-111 v WI (Birmingham) 1991. **LOI:** 51 (1989-90 to 1996; HS 33; BB 4-30). Tours: A 1990-91 (part), 1994-95 (part); WI 1989-90 (part), 1993-94; NZ 1991-92; I/SL 1992-93. HS 247 Nt v Durham (Chester-le-St) 1993. Sy HS 94 v Warwks (Oval) 1996. 50 wkts (2); most – 56 (1990). BB 6-22 Le v OU (Oxford) 1988. BAC BB 6-55 Le v Glam (Cardiff) 1990. Sy BB 5-25 v Leics (Oval) 1996. Award: NWT 1. **NWT:** HS 89 Nt v Northumb (Jesmond) 1994. BB 3-24 Nt v Somerset (Nottingham) 1993. **BHC:** HS 48* Nt v Minor C (Nottingham) 1994. BB 5-46 Nt v Kent (Nottingham) 1992. **SL:** HS 93* v Essex (Leicester) 1990. BB 4-13 Le v Essex (Leicester) 1988.

NOWELL, Richard William (Trinity S, Croydon), b Croydon 29 Dec 1975. 6'1". LHB, SLA. Debut 1995. HS 28* v SA A (Oval) 1996. BAC HS 27 v Warwks (Birmingham) 1995. BB 4-43 v Notts (Guildford) 1995. **NWT:** HS 2*. **BHC:** HS 15* and BB 1-35 v Sussex (Oval) 1995. **SL:** HS 0.

PATTERSON, Mark William (Belfast Royal Academy; Ulster U), b Belfast, N Ireland 2 Feb 1974. Elder brother of A.D. (Ireland 1996). 6'1". RHB, RFM. Debut 1996, taking 6-80 v SA A (Oval) 1996. Awaiting BAC debut. Soccer (goalkeeper) for N Ireland, Irish Us and Coleraine. HS 4 and BB 6-80 (as above).

PEARSON, Richard Michael (Batley GS; St John's, Cambridge), b Batley, Yorks 27 Jan 1972. 6'3". RHB, OB. Cambridge U 1991-92; blue 1991-92. Northamptonshire 1992. Essex 1994-95. Surrey debut 1996. HS 37 v Sussex (Guildford) 1996. BB 5-108 CU v Warwks (Cambridge) 1992. Sy/BAC BB 5-142 v Essex (Southend) 1996. **NWT:** HS 11 v Holland (Oval) 1996. BB 1-39. **BHC:** HS 12* v Yorks (Oval) 1996. BB 3-46 Ex v Glos (Chelmsford) 1995. **SL:** HS 9*. BB 3-33 Ex v Leics (Leicester) 1994 and v Warwks (Oval) 1996.

RATCLIFFE, Jason David (Sharman's Cross SS; Solihull SFC), b Solihull, Warwks 19 Jun 1969. Son of D.P. (Warwks 1957-68). 6'4". RHB, RM. Warwickshire 1988-94. Surrey debut 1995. Tours (Wa): SA 1991-92, 1992-93; Z 1993-94. HS 127* Wa v CU (Cambridge) 1989. BAC HS 101 Wa v Sussex (Birmingham) 1993. Sy HS 75 v Glam (Oval) 1995. BB 2-26 v Yorks (Middlesbrough) 1996. Awards: NWT 2. **NWT:** HS 105 Wa v Yorks (Leeds) 1993. **BHC:** HS 29 Wa v Surrey (Oval) 1991. **SL:** HS 42 v Durham (Stockport) 1996. BB 2-11 Wa v Glam (Neath) 1993.

SHAHID, Nadeem (Ipswich S), b Karachi, Pakistan 23 Apr 1969. 6'0". RHB, LB. Essex 1989-94. Surrey debut 1995. Suffolk 1988. 1000 runs (1): 1003 (1990). HS 139 v Yorks (Oval) 1995. BB 3-91 Ex v Surrey (Oval) 1990. Sy BB 3-93 v SA A (Oval) 1996. **NWT:** HS 85* Ex v Glam (Cardiff) 1994. BB 1-0. **BHC:** HS 65* and BB 1-59 v Kent (Canterbury) 1995. **SL:** HS 101 v Derbys (Derby) 1995.

STEWART, Alec James (Tiffin S), b Merton 8 Apr 1963. Son of M.J. (Surrey and England 1954-72). 5'11". RHB, WK. Debut 1981; cap 1985; captain 1992 to date; benefit 1994. *Wisden* 1992. **Tests:** 63 (1989-90 to 1996-97, 2 as captain); HS 190 v P (Birmingham) 1992. **LOI:** 87 (1989-90 to 1996-97, 7 as captain; HS 103). Tours: A 1990-91, 1994-95; SA 1995-96; WI 1989-90, 1993-94; NZ 1991-92, 1996-97; I 1992-93; SL 1992-93 (captain); Z 1996-97. 1000 runs (8); most – 1665 (1986). HS 206* v Essex (Oval) 1989. BB 1-7. Held 11 catches (equalling world f-c match record) v Leics (Leicester) 1989. Awards: NWT 3; BHC 5. **NWT:** HS 125* v Essex (Oval) 1996. **BHC:** HS 167* v Somerset (Oval) 1994. **SL:** HS 125 v Lancs (Oval) 1990.

THORPE, Graham Paul (Weydon CS; Farnham SFC), b Farnham 1 Aug 1969. 5'11". LHB, RM. Debut 1988; cap 1991. **Tests:** 37 (1993 to 1996-97); HS 123 v A (Perth) 1994-95; scored 114* v A (Nottingham) 1993 on debut. **LOI:** 36 (1993 to 1996-97; HS 89 – twice; BB 2-15). Tours: A 1992-93 (Eng A), 1994-95; SA 1995-96; WI 1991-92 (Eng A), 1993-94; NZ 1996-97; P 1990-91 (Eng A); SL 1990-91 (Eng A); Z 1989-90 (Eng A), 1996-97. 1000 runs (7); most – 1895 (1992). HS 216 v Somerset (Oval) 1992. BB 4-40 v A (Oval) 1993. BAC BB 2-14 v Derbys (Oval) 1996. Awards: NWT 2. **NWT:** HS 145* v Lancs (Oval) 1994. **BHC:** HS 103 v Lancs (Oval) 1993. BB 3-35 v Middx (Lord's) 1989. **SL:** HS 115* v Lancs (Manchester) 1991. BB 3-21 v Somerset (Oval) 1991.

TUDOR, Alex Jeremy (St Mark's S, Hammersmith; City of Westminster C), b West Brompton, London 23 Oct 1977. 6'5". RHB, RF. Debut 1995. HS 56 v Leics (Leicester) 1995. BB 5-32 v Derbys (Derby) 1995. **NWT:** HS – . BB 1-27. **SL:** HS 29* v Essex (Oval) 1995. BB 1-19.

WARD, Ian James (Millfield S), b Plymouth, Devon 30 Sep 1972. 5'8½". LHB, RM. Surrey 1992 and 1996. HS 15 v SA A (Oval) 1996. **NWT:** HS 14 v Holland (Oval) 1996. **SL:** HS 1*.

NEWCOMERS

BATTY, Jonathan Neil (Wheatley Park S, Oxon; Repton S; Durham U; Keble C, Oxford), b Chesterfield, Derbys 18 Apr 1974. 5'10". RHB, WK. Durham U 1995; captain. Comb U 1995. Oxford U 1996; blue 1996. Oxfordshire 1993 to date. HS 56 OU v Northants (Oxford) 1996. **NWT:** (Oxon) HS 1. **BHC:** (Minor C) HS 26* v Warwks (Jesmond) 1996.

SALISBURY, Ian David Kenneth (Moulton CS), b Northampton 21 Jan 1970. 5'11". RHB, LBG. Sussex 1989-96; cap 1991. MCC YC. YC 1992. *Wisden* 1992. **Tests:** 9 (1992 to 1996); HS 50 v P (Manchester) 1992. BB 4-163 v WI (Georgetown) 1993-94. **LOI:** 4 (1992-93 to 1993-94; HS 5; BB 3-41). Tours: WI 1991-92 (Eng A), 1993-94; I 1992-93; 1994-95 (Eng A); P 1990-91 (Eng A), 1995-96 (Eng A); SL 1990-91 (Eng A). HS 86 Eng A v Pak A (Rawalpindi) 1995-96. BAC HS 83 Sx v Glam (Hove) 1996. 50 wkts (4); most – 87 (1992). BB 8-75 (11-169 match) Sx v Essex (Chelmsford) 1996. Awards: NWT 1; BHC 1. **NWT:** HS 33 Sx v Ire (Belfast) 1996. BB 3-28 Sx v Bucks (Beaconsfield) 1992. **BHC:** HS 19 Sx v Hants (Southampton) 1996. BB 3-40 Sx v Kent (Canterbury) 1991. **SL:** HS 48* Sx v Glam (Swansea) 1995. BB 5-30 Sx v Leics (Leicester) 1992.

DEPARTURES – see p 107

SURREY 1996

RESULTS SUMMARY

	Place	Won	Lost	Drew	No Result
Britannic Assurance Championship	3rd	8	2	7	–
All First-Class Matches		8	3	7	–
NatWest Trophy	Semi-Finalist				
Benson and Hedges Cup	Quarter-Finalist				
Sunday League	1st	12	4	–	1

BRITANNIC ASSURANCE CHAMPIONSHIP AVERAGES

BATTING AND FIELDING

Cap		M	I	NO	HS	Runs	Avge	100	50	Ct/St
1991	G.P.Thorpe	9	17	2	185	1044	69.60	5	4	10
1995	A.J.Hollioake	16	28	6	129	1521	69.13	5	8	18
1996	M.A.Butcher	17	32	3	160	1540	53.10	3	13	21
–	C.C.Lewis	8	13	1	94	442	36.83	–	3	13
1996	B.P.Julian	16	23	2	119	759	36.14	2	3	9
1990	D.J.Bicknell	17	31	3	129*	969	34.60	2	3	9
–	N.Shahid	10	17	3	101	448	32.00	1	3	5
–	J.D.Ratcliffe	8	14	1	68*	403	31.00	–	3	5
1985	A.J.Stewart	9	16	1	80	434	28.93	–	3	10
–	R.M.Pearson	14	14	9	37	142	28.40	–	–	3
1990	D.M.Ward	2	4	1	64*	81	27.00	–	1	2
1989	M.P.Bicknell	16	18	5	59*	333	25.61	–	1	2
1996	G.J.Kersey	15	20	4	68*	402	25.12	–	3	45/1
1994	A.D.Brown	14	22	2	57	361	18.05	–	3	14
1993	J.E.Benjamin	13	14	6	38*	141	17.62	–	–	1
–	B.C.Hollioake	3	4	–	46	63	15.75	–	–	3

BOWLING

	O	M	R	W	Avge	Best	5wI	10wM
D.J.Bicknell	124.2	21	368	16	23.00	3- 7	–	–
M.P.Bicknell	568.1	146	1633	66	24.74	5- 17	3	–
B.C.Hollioake	65	12	252	10	25.20	4- 74	–	–
B.P.Julian	447.4	86	1762	61	28.88	6- 37	3	–
J.E.Benjamin	375.3	83	1217	39	31.20	4- 17	–	–
C.C.Lewis	260.4	50	889	27	32.92	5- 25	1	–
R.M.Pearson	475	101	1509	31	48.67	5-142	1	–
A.J.Hollioake	226	44	764	12	63.66	3- 80	–	–

Also bowled: A.D.Brown 6-2-8-0; M.A.Butcher 52-7-233-7; J.D.Ratcliffe 19-3-75-3;
N.Shahid 52-11-170-3; A.J.Stewart 2-0-24-0; G.P.Thorpe 23-8-64-2.

The First-Class Averages (pp 123-38) give the records of Surrey players in all first-class
county matches (their other opponents being South Africa A), with the exception of
M.A.Butcher, A.J.Hollioake, A.J.Stewart and G.P.Thorpe whose full county figures are as
above, and:
    A.D.Brown 15-24-2-69-462-21.00-0-4-18ct. 6-2-8-0.
    C.C.Lewis 9-15-1-94-543-38.78-0-4-13ct. 285.4-55-977-29-33.68-5/25-1-0.

SURREY RECORDS

FIRST-CLASS CRICKET

Highest Total	For 811		v	Somerset	The Oval	1899
	V 863		by	Lancashire	The Oval	1990
Lowest Total	For 14		v	Essex	Chelmsford	1983
	V 16		by	MCC	Lord's	1872
Highest Innings	For 357*	R.Abel	v	Somerset	The Oval	1899
	V 366	N.H.Fairbrother	for	Lancashire	The Oval	1990

Highest Partnership for each Wicket

1st	428	J.B.Hobbs/A.Sandham	v	Oxford U	The Oval	1926
2nd	371	J.B.Hobbs/E.G.Hayes	v	Hampshire	The Oval	1909
3rd	413	D.J.Bicknell/D.M.Ward	v	Kent	Canterbury	1990
4th	448	R.Abel/T.W.Hayward	v	Yorkshire	The Oval	1899
5th	308	J.N.Crawford/F.C.Holland	v	Somerset	The Oval	1908
6th	298	A.Sandham/H.S.Harrison	v	Sussex	The Oval	1913
7th	262	C.J.Richards/K.T.Medlycott	v	Kent	The Oval	1987
8th	205	I.A.Greig/M.P.Bicknell	v	Lancashire	The Oval	1990
9th	168	E.R.T.Holmes/E.W.J.Brooks	v	Hampshire	The Oval	1936
10th	173	A.Ducat/A.Sandham	v	Essex	Leyton	1921

Best Bowling	For 10-43	T.Rushby	v	Somerset	Taunton	1921
(Innings)	V 10-28	W.P.Howell	for	Australians	The Oval	1899
Best Bowling	For 16-83	G.A.R.Lock	v	Kent	Blackheath	1956
(Match)	V 15-57	W.P.Howell	for	Australians	The Oval	1899

Most Runs – Season	3246 T.W.Hayward	(av 72.13)	1906
Most Runs – Career	43554 J.B.Hobbs	(av 49.72)	1905-34
Most 100s – Season	13 T.W.Hayward		1906
	13 J.B.Hobbs		1925
Most 100s – Career	144 J.B.Hobbs		1905-34
Most Wkts – Season	252 T.Richardson	(av 13.94)	1895
Most Wkts – Career	1775 T.Richardson	(av 17.87)	1892-1904

LIMITED-OVERS CRICKET

Highest Total	NWT	350		v	Worcs	The Oval	1994
	BHC	333-6		v	Hampshire	The Oval	1996
	SL	375-4		v	Yorkshire	Scarborough	1994
Lowest Total	NWT	74		v	Kent	The Oval	1967
	BHC	89		v	Notts	Nottingham	1984
	SL	64		v	Worcs	Worcester	1978
Highest Innings	NWT	146	G.S.Clinton	v	Kent	Canterbury	1985
	BHC	167*	A.J.Stewart	v	Somerset	The Oval	1994
	SL	142*	A.D.Brown	v	Middlesex	The Oval	1994
Best Bowling	NWT	7-33	R.D.Jackman	v	Yorkshire	Harrogate	1970
	BHC	5-15	S.G.Kenlock	v	Ireland	The Oval	1995
	SL	6-25	Intikhab Alam	v	Derbyshire	The Oval	1974

SUSSEX

Formation of Present Club: 1 March 1839
Substantial Reorganisation: August 1857
Colours: Dark Blue, Light Blue and Gold
Badge: County Arms of Six Martlets
Championships: (0) Second 1902, 1903, 1932, 1933, 1934, 1953, 1981
NatWest Trophy/Gillette Cup Winners: (4) 1963, 1964, 1978, 1986
Benson and Hedges Cup Winners: (0) Semi-Finalists 1982
Sunday League Champions: (1) 1982
Match Awards: NWT 52; BHC 51

Secretary: N.Bett
   County Ground, Eaton Road, Hove BN3 3AN (Tel 01273 732161)
Captain: P.Moores. **Overseas Player:** V.C.Drakes. **1997 Beneficiary:** None.
Scorer: L.V.Chandler

ATHEY, Charles **William** Jeffrey (Stainsby SS; Acklam Hall HS), b Middlesbrough, Yorks 27 Sep 1957. 5'9½". RHB, RM. Yorkshire 1976-83; cap 1980. Gloucestershire 1984-92; cap 1985; captain 1989; benefit 1990. Sussex debut/cap 1993. **Tests:** 23 (1980 to 1988); HS 123 v P (Lord's) 1987. **LOI:** 31 (1980 to 1987-88; HS 142*). Tours: A 1986-87, 1987-88; SA 1989-90 (Eng A); WI 1980-81; NZ 1979-80 (DHR), 1987-88; P 1987-88; SL 1985-86 (Eng B). 1000 runs (13); most – 1812 (1984). HS 184 Eng B v Sri Lanka (Galle) 1985-86. BAC HS 181 Gs v Sussex (Cheltenham) 1992. Sx HS 169* v Kent (Tunbridge W) 1994. BB 3-3 Gs v Hants (Bristol) 1985. Sx BB 2-40 v Notts (Eastbourne) 1993. Awards: NWT 4; BHC 6. **NWT:** HS 115 Y v Kent (Leeds) 1980. BB 1-18. **BHC:** HS 118 v Kent (Hove) 1995. BB 4-48 Gs v Comb Us (Bristol) 1984. **SL:** HS 121* Gs v Worcs (Moreton-in-M) 1985. BB 5-35 Y v Derbys (Chesterfield) 1981.

BATES, Justin Jonathan (Hurstpierpoint C), b Farnborough, Hants 9 Apr 1976. 5'11". RHB, OB. Sussex staff 1995 – awaiting f-c debut. **SL:** HS 8.

DRAKES, Vasbert Conniel (St Lucy SS), b St James, Barbados 5 Aug 1969. 6'2". RHB, RFM. Barbados 1991-92 to date. Sussex debut/cap 1996. **LOI** (WI): 5 (1994-95; HS 16; BB 1-36). Tour (WI): E 1995. HS 180* Barbados v Leeward Is (Anguilla) 1994-95. Sx HS 145* v Essex (Chelmsford) 1996. 50 wkts (1): 50 (1996). BB 7-47 Barbados v Guyana (Bridgetown) 1994-95. UK BB 5-20 WI v Kent (Canterbury) 1995. Sx BB 5-47 v Derbys (Hove) 1996. **NWT:** HS 35 v Yorks (Hove) 1996. BB 2-19 v Ire (Belfast) 1996. **BHC:** HS 26 v Surrey (Hove) 1996. BB 5-19 v Ire (Hove) 1996. **SL:** HS 37 v Hants (Arundel) 1996. BB 4-50 v Surrey (Guildford) 1996.

EDWARDS, Alexander David (Imberhorne CS, E Grinstead; Loughborough U), b Cuckfield 2 Aug 1975. 6'0". RHB, RFM. Combined Us 1995. Sussex debut 1995. Awaiting BAC debut. HS 22 and BB 3-83 v Young A (Hove) 1995. **BHC:** HS 7*. BB 2-51 Comb Us v Middx (Lord's) 1995. **SL:** HS – .

GREENFIELD, Keith (Falmer HS), b Brighton 6 Dec 1968. 6'0". RHB, RM. Debut 1987; cap 1996. HS 154* v Glam (Hove) 1996. BB 2-40 v Essex (Hove) 1993. Award: NWT 1. **NWT:** HS 96* v Wales (Hove) 1993. BB 2-35 v Glam (Hove) 1993. **BHC:** HS 62 v Leics (Leicester) 1992. BB 1-35. **SL:** HS 102 v Notts (Arundel) 1995. BB 3-34 v Northants (Hove) 1992.

HAYWOOD, Giles Ronald (Lancing C), b Chichester 8 Sep 1979. 6'1". LHB, RM. Summer contract – final year at Lancing – awaiting f-c debut. **SL:** HS 4.

HUMPHRIES, Shaun (The Weald, Billingshurst; Kingston C, London), b Horsham 11 Jan 1973. 5'9". RHB, WK. Debut 1993. HS – . Awaiting BAC debut.

JARVIS, Paul William (Bydales CS, Marske), b Redcar, Yorks 29 Jun 1965. 5'10". RHB, RFM. Yorkshire 1981-93; cap 1986; youngest Yorkshire debutant at 16yr 75d. Sussex debut 1994. **Tests:** 9 (1987-88 to 1992-93); HS 29* and BB 4-107 v WI (Lord's) 1988. **LOI:** 16 (1987-88 to 1993; HS 16*; BB 5-35). Tours: SA 1989-90 (Eng XI); WI 1986-87 (Y); NZ 1987-88; I/SL 1992-93; P 1987-88. HS 80 Y v Northants (Scarborough) 1992. Sx HS 70* v SA (Hove) 1994. 50 wkts (4); most – 81 (1987). BB 7-55 Y v Surrey (Leeds) 1986. Sx BB 7-58 v Somerset (Hove) 1994. Hat-trick 1985 (Y). **NWT:** HS 34* v Yorks (Hove) 1996. BB 4-41 Y v Leics (Leeds) 1987. **BHC:** HS 42 Y v Lancs (Leeds) 1990. BB 4-34 Y v Warwks (Birmingham) 1992. **SL:** HS 43 v Surrey (Guildford) 1996. BB 6-27 Y v Somerset (Taunton) 1989.

KIRTLEY, Robert James (Clifton C), b Eastbourne 10 Jan 1975. 6'0". RHB, RFM. Debut 1995. Mashonaland 1996-97. HS 7* and BB 5-51 TCCB XI v SA A (Chester-le-St) 1996. Sx HS 7. Sx BB 4-94 v Essex (Chelmsford) 1996. Took 5-53 (7-88 match) for Mashonaland v Eng XI (Harare) 1996-97. **SL:** HS 2. BB 1-19.

LENHAM, Neil John (Brighton C), b Worthing 17 Dec 1965. Son of L.J. (Sussex 1956-70). 5'11". RHB, RM. Debut 1984; cap 1990. 1000 runs (3); most – 1663 (1990). HS 222* v Kent (Hove) 1992. BB 4-13 v Durham (Durham) 1993. Awards: NWT 2; BHC 1. **NWT:** HS 129* v Devon (Hove) 1995. BB 2-12 v Ire (Downpatrick) 1990. **BHC:** HS 82 v Somerset (Hove) 1986. BB 1-3. **SL:** HS 86 v Kent (Hove) 1991. BB 5-28 v Durham (Durham) 1993.

LEWRY, Jason David (Durrington HS, Worthing), b Worthing 2 Apr 1971. 6'2". LHB, LMF. Debut 1994; cap 1996. HS 34 v Kent (Hove) 1995. BB 6-43 v Worcs (Eastbourne) 1995. **NWT:** HS 5*. BB 3-45 v Leics (Leicester) 1996. **BHC:** HS 14* v Ire (Hove) 1995. **SL:** HS 7*. BB 4-29 v Somerset (Bath) 1995.

MARTIN-JENKINS, Robin Simon Christopher (Radley C; Durham U), b Guildford, Surrey 28 Oct 1975. Son of C.M.J. (*Daily Telegraph* Cricket Correspondent). 6'5". RHB, RFM. Debut 1995. British Us 1996. HS 50 v Northants (Hove) 1995. BB 1-26. BAC BB – . **BHC** (Brit Us): HS 12 v Glam (Cambridge) 1996. BB 3-46 v Kent (Oxford) 1996. **SL:** HS 10 v Northants (Hove) 1995. BB 2-41 v Middx (Lord's) 1995.

MOORES, Peter (King Edward VI S, Macclesfield), b Macclesfield, Cheshire 18 Dec 1962. 6'0". RHB, WK. Worcestershire 1983-84. Sussex debut 1985; cap 1989; captain 1997. OFS 1988-89. HS 185 v CU (Hove) 1996. BAC HS 119* v Surrey (Guildford) 1996. **NWT:** HS 26 v Scot (Edinburgh) 1991. **BHC:** HS 76 v Middx (Hove) 1990. **SL:** HS 89* v Leics (Hove) 1995.

NEWELL, Keith (Ifield Community C), b Crawley 25 Mar 1972. Brother of M. 6'0". RHB, RM. Debut 1996. Matabeleland 1995-96. HS 135 v WI (Hove) 1995. BAC HS 63 v Glam (Swansea) 1995 – on debut. BB 1-38. BAC BB – . **NWT:** HS 52 v Derbys (Hove) 1995. **BHC:** HS 46 v Glos (Bristol) 1996. BB 1-25. **SL:** HS 76* v Kent (Hove) 1995. BB 1-12.

NEWELL, Mark (Hazelwick SS; City of Westminster C), b Crawley 19 Mar 1973. Brother of K. 6'1½". RHB, OB. Debut 1996. MCC YC. HS 0. **SL:** HS 69 v Northants (Northampton) 1996.

PEIRCE, Michael Toby Edward (Ardingly C; Durham U), b Maidenhead, Berks 14 Jun 1973. 5'10". LHB, SLA. Combined Us 1994. Sussex 1995. HS 60 v Worcs (Eastbourne) 1995. **BHC:** HS 44 Comb Us v Middx (Lord's) 1995. **SL:** HS 7.

PHILLIPS, Nicholas Charles (Wm Parker S, Hastings), b Pembury, Kent 10 May 1974. 5'10½". RHB, OB. Debut 1993. HS 53 v Young A (Hove) 1995. BB 3-39 v CU (Hove) 1993. BAC HS 52 and BB 3-78 v Lancs (Lytham) 1995. **BHC:** HS 10 v Surrey (Hove) 1996. **SL:** HS 38* v Essex (Chelmsford) 1996. BB 2-19 v Somerset (Hove) 1994.

RADFORD, Toby Alexander (St Bartholomew's S, Newbury; Loughborough U), b Caerphilly, Glam 3 Dec 1971. 5'10". RHB, OB. Middlesex 1994-95. Sussex debut 1996. HS 69 M v Essex (Chelmsford) 1995 – on BAC debut. Sx HS 53 v CU (Hove) 1996. BB (M) 1-0. **NWT:** HS 82 M v Surrey (Oval) 1995. **SL:** HS 38 M v Worcs (Worcester) 1993.

RAO, Rajesh Krishnakant (Alperton HS; Brighton U), b Park Royal, Middlesex 9 Dec 1974. 5'10". RHB, LBG. Debut 1996. MCC YC. HS 38 v Somerset (Hove) 1996. **SL:** HS 91 v Glos (Bristol) 1996. BB 3-31 v Worcs (Worcester) 1996.

STRONG, Michael Richard (Brighton C; Brunel U), b Cuckfield 28 Jun 1974. 6'1". LHB, RMF. Summer contract – awaiting f-c debut. **SL:** HS 2*.

NEWCOMERS

KHAN, Amer Ali (Muslim Modle HS, Lahore; MAO C, Lahore), b Lahore, Pakistan 5 Nov 1969. 5'9½". RHB, LB. Rawalpindi 1987-88 (one match as AAMER ALI). Middlesex 1995. HS – . BB 4-51 M v CU (Cambridge) 1995.

PYEMONT, James Patrick (Tonbridge S), b Eastbourne 10 Apr 1978. Son of C.P. (Cambridge U 1967; cricket and hockey blue). RHB, OB.

ROBINSON, Mark Andrew (Hull GS), b Hull, Yorks 23 Nov 1966. 6'3". RHB, RFM. Northamptonshire 1987-90; cap 1990. Canterbury 1988-89. Yorkshire 1991-95; cap 1992. Tours (Y): SA 1991-92, 1992-93. Failed to score in 12 successive f-c innings 1990 – world record. HS 23 Y v Glos (Middlesbrough) 1995. 50 wkts (1): 50 (1992). BB 9-37 (12-124 match) Y v Northants (Harrogate) 1993. Award: BHC 1. **NWT:** HS 3*. BB 4-32 Nh v Somerset (Taunton) 1989. **BHC:** HS 3*. BB 3-20 Nh v Scot (Glasgow) 1989. **SL:** HS 7. BB 4-23 Y v Northants (Leeds) 1993.

TAYLOR, Neil Royston (Cray Valley THS), b Orpington, Kent 21 Jul 1959. 6'1". RHB, OB. Kent 1979-95, scoring 110 and 11 on debut v SL (Canterbury); cap 1982; benefit 1992. 1000 runs (10); most – 1979 (1990). HS 204 K v Surrey (Canterbury) 1990. BB 2-20 K v Somerset (Canterbury) 1985. Awards: BHC 8. **NWT:** HS 86 K v Staffs (Stone) 1995. BB 3-29 K v Dorset (Canterbury) 1989. **BHC:** HS 137 K v Surrey (Oval) 1988. **SL:** HS 95 K v Hants (Canterbury) 1990.

THURSFIELD, Martin John (Boldon CS), b South Shields, Co Durham 14 Dec 1971. 6'3". RHB, RM. Middlesex 1990. Hampshire 1992-96. MCC YC. HS 47 H v Glam (Southampton) 1994. BB 6-130 H v Middx (Southampton) 1994. **NWT:** HS – . BB 1-34. **BHC:** HS 19 H v Surrey (Oval) 1996. BB 2-33 H v Sussex (Southampton) 1996. **SL:** HS 9. BB 3-31 H v Leics (Leicester) 1994.

WILTON, Nicholas J, b Pembury, Kent 23 Sep 1978. RHB, WK.

DEPARTURES (who made first-class appearances in 1996)

GIDDINS, Edward Simon Hunter (Eastbourne C), b Eastbourne 20 Jul 1971. 6'4½". RHB, RMF. Sussex 1991-96; cap 1994. MCC YC. Tour: P 1995-96 (Eng A). HS 34 v Essex (Hove) 1995. 50 wkts (2); most – 68 (1995). BB 6-47 v Yorks (Eastbourne) 1996. **NWT:** HS 13 v Essex (Hove) 1994. BB 3-24 v Ire (Belfast) 1996. **BHC:** HS 0*. BB 3-28 v Surrey (Oval) 1995. **SL:** HS 9*. BB 4-23 v Kent (Tunbridge W) 1994. Banned from county cricket by TCCB until April 1998, when he will join Warwickshire.

HALL, James William (Chichester HS), b Chichester 30 Mar 1968. 6'3". RHB, OB. Sussex 1990-96; cap 1992. 1000 runs (2); most – 1140 (1990 – debut season). HS 140* v Lancs (Hove) 1992. Award: BHC 1. **NWT:** HS 70 v Derbys (Hove) 1995. **BHC:** HS 81 v Surrey (Hove) 1992. **SL:** HS 77 v Notts (Nottingham) 1992.

LAW, D.R. – see ESSEX.

SALISBURY, I.D.K. – see SURREY.

SPEIGHT, M.P. – see DURHAM.

WELLS, A.P. – see KENT.

SUSSEX 1996

RESULTS SUMMARY

	Place	Won	Lost	Drew	No Result
Britannic Assurance Championship	12th	6	9	2	–
All First-Class Matches		6	9	4	–
NatWest Trophy	Quarter-Finalist				
Benson and Hedges Cup	4th in Group D				
Sunday League	14th	6	9		2

BRITANNIC ASSURANCE CHAMPIONSHIP AVERAGES

BATTING AND FIELDING

Cap		M	I	NO	HS	Runs	Avge	100	50	Ct/St
–	N.C.Phillips	6	12	7	45	223	44.60	–	–	4
1990	N.J.Lenham	15	27	2	145	895	35.80	2	5	3
1986	A.P.Wells	17	31	–	122	1072	34.58	2	5	12
1996	K.Greenfield	13	24	3	154*	710	33.80	2	2	8
1993	C.W.J.Athey	17	31	–	111	980	31.61	3	4	15
1996	V.C.Drakes	15	27	3	145*	649	27.04	2	4	1
–	P.W.Jarvis	7	11	4	35	164	23.42	–	–	3
1996	D.R.Law	15	27	–	97	609	22.55	–	3	6
1989	P.Moores	17	31	4	119*	597	22.11	1	1	49/1
1991	M.P.Speight	9	17	1	122*	349	21.81	1	1	7
1991	I.D.K.Salisbury	14	24	2	83	473	21.50	–	3	7
1992	J.W.Hall	6	11	–	57	208	18.90	–	2	5
–	K.Newell	4	8	–	31	129	16.12	–	–	1
1996	J.D.Lewry	8	13	3	28*	138	13.80	–	–	–
–	T.A.Radford	4	6	–	14	30	5.00	–	–	1
1994	E.S.H.Giddins	12	15	5	11	46	4.60	–	–	–
–	R.J.Kirtley	6	11	3	7	15	1.87	–	–	4

Also batted (1 match each): M.Newell 0, 0 (1 ct); R.K.Rao 17, 38.

BOWLING

	O	M	R	W	Avge	Best	5wI	10wM
J.D.Lewry	264	46	816	36	22.66	6-44	4	1
E.S.H.Giddins	312.4	55	1012	40	25.30	6-47	2	–
I.D.K.Salisbury	391.2	93	1136	44	25.81	8-75	3	1
D.R.Law	281.4	42	1027	37	27.75	5-33	2	–
P.W.Jarvis	147	25	510	18	28.33	4-60	–	–
R.J.Kirtley	137.4	22	535	16	33.43	4-94	–	–
V.C.Drakes	454.3	79	1675	50	33.50	5-47	2	–
N.C.Phillips	182	35	626	10	62.60	2-54	–	–

Also bowled: K.Greenfield 23-6-52-0; N.J.Lenham 56.1-9-146-3; K.Newell 3-0-16-0.

The First-Class Averages (pp 123-38) give the records of Sussex players in all first-class county matches (their other opponents being the Indians and Cambridge University), with the exception of I.D.K.Salisbury whose full county figures are as above, and:

E.S.H.Giddins 13-15-5-11-46-4.60-0-0-0ct. 329.4-56-1092-41-26.63-6/47-2-0.
R.J.Kirtley 7-11-3-7-15-1.87-0-0-4ct. 162.4-26-657-19-34.57-4/94.
D.R.Law 16-27-0-97-609-22.55-0-3-6ct. 298.4-43-1099-38-28.92-5/33-2-0.
J.D.Lewry 9-13-3-28*-138-13.80-0-0-0ct. 276-49-864-38-22.73-6/44-4-1.
R.S.C.Martin-Jenkins 1 – did not bat – 0ct. 17-1-65-1-65.00-1/26.
A.P.Wells 18-33-1-122-1121-35.03-2-5-12ct. Did not bowl.

SUSSEX RECORDS

FIRST-CLASS CRICKET

Highest Total	For	705-8d		v	Surrey	Hastings	1902
	V	726		by	Notts	Nottingham	1895
Lowest Total	For	19		v	Surrey	Godalming	1830
		19		v	Notts	Hove	1873
	V	18		by	Kent	Gravesend	1867
Highest Innings	For	333	K.S.Duleepsinhji	v	Northants	Hove	1930
	V	322	E.Paynter	for	Lancashire	Hove	1937

Highest Partnership for each Wicket

1st	490	E.H.Bowley/J.G.Langridge	v	Middlesex	Hove	1933
2nd	385	E.H.Bowley/M.W.Tate	v	Northants	Hove	1921
3rd	298	K.S.Ranjitsinhji/E.H.Killick	v	Lancashire	Hove	1901
4th	326*	J.Langridge/G.Cox	v	Yorkshire	Leeds	1949
5th	297	J.H.Parks/H.W.Parks	v	Hampshire	Portsmouth	1937
6th	255	K.S.Duleepsinhji/M.W.Tate	v	Northants	Hove	1930
7th	344	K.S.Ranjitsinhji/W.Newham	v	Essex	Leyton	1902
8th	229*	C.L.A.Smith/G.Brann	v	Kent	Hove	1902
9th	178	H.W.Parks/A.F.Wensley	v	Derbyshire	Horsham	1930
10th	156	G.R.Cox/H.R.Butt	v	Cambridge U	Cambridge	1908

Best Bowling	For	10- 48	C.H.G.Bland	v	Kent	Tonbridge	1899
(Innings)	V	9- 11	A.P.Freeman	for	Kent	Hove	1922
Best Bowling	For	17-106	G.R.Cox	v	Warwicks	Horsham	1926
(Match)	V	17- 67	A.P.Freeman	for	Kent	Hove	1922

Most Runs – Season	2850	J.G.Langridge	(av 64.77)		1949
Most Runs – Career	34152	J.G.Langridge	(av 37.69)		1928-55
Most 100s – Season	12	J.G.Langridge			1949
Most 100s – Career	76	J.G.Langridge			1928-55
Most Wkts – Season	198	M.W.Tate	(av 13.47)		1925
Most Wkts – Career	2211	M.W.Tate	(av 17.41)		1912-37

LIMITED-OVERS CRICKET

Highest Total	NWT	384-9		v	Ireland	Belfast	1996
	BHC	305-6		v	Kent	Hove	1982
	SL	312-8		v	Hampshire	Portsmouth	1993
Lowest Total	NWT	49		v	Derbyshire	Chesterfield	1969
	BHC	61		v	Middlesex	Hove	1978
	SL	59		v	Glamorgan	Hove	1996
Highest Innings	NWT	141*	G.D.Mendis	v	Warwicks	Hove	1980
	BHC	118	C.W.J.Athey	v	Kent	Hove	1995
	SL	129	A.W.Greig	v	Yorkshire	Scarborough	1976
Best Bowling	NWT	6- 9	A.I.C.Dodemaide	v	Ireland	Downpatrick	1990
	BHC	5- 8	Imran Khan	v	Northants	Northampton	1978
	SL	7-41	A.N.Jones	v	Notts	Nottingham	1986

WARWICKSHIRE

Formation of Present Club: 8 April 1882
Substantial Reorganisation: 19 January 1884
Colours: Dark Blue, Gold and Silver
Badge: Bear and Ragged Staff
Championships: (5) 1911, 1951, 1972, 1994, 1995
NatWest Trophy/Gillette Cup Winners: (5) 1966, 1968, 1989, 1993, 1995
Benson and Hedges Cup Winners: (1) 1994
Sunday League Champions: (2) 1980, 1994
Match Awards: NWT 58; BHC 53

Chief Executive: D.L.Amiss MBE
  County Ground, Edgbaston, Birmingham, B5 7QU (Tel 0121 446 4422)
Captain: T.A.Munton. **Vice-Captain:** N.V.Knight. **Overseas Player:** A.A.Donald.
1997 Beneficiary: A.J.Moles. **Scorer:** A.E.Davis.

ALTREE, Darren Anthony (Ashlawn S, Rugby), b Rugby 30 Sep 1974. 5'10". RHB, LMF. Debut 1996. HS 0*. BB 3-41 v P (Birmingham) 1996. BAC BB 1-68.

BELL, Michael Anthony Vincent (Bishop Milner CS; Dudley TC), b Birmingham 19 Dec 1966. 6'2". RHB, LMF. Debut 1992. MCC YC. Tour (Wa): Z 1993-94. HS 22* and BB 7-48 v Glos (Birmingham) 1993. **NWT:** HS – . BB 2-41 v Northants (Lord's) 1995. **BHC:** HS – . BB 2-34 v Middx (Lord's) 1994. **SL:** HS 8*. BB 5-19 v Leics (Birmingham) 1994.

BROWN, Douglas Robert (Alloa Academy; W London IHE), b Stirling, Scotland 29 Oct 1969. 6'2". RHB, RFM. Scotland 1989. Warwickshire debut 1991-92 (SA tour); cap 1995. Wellington 1995-96. Tours (Wa): SA 1991-92, 1994-95. HS 85 v Essex (Ilford) 1995. BB 6-52 (11-120 match) v Kent (Birmingham) 1996. **NWT:** HS 67 v Cornwall (St Austell) 1996. BB 2-35 v Northants (Lord's) 1995. **BHC:** HS 44 v Glam (Cardiff) 1996. BB 3-43 v Leics (Leicester) 1995. **SL:** HS 78* v Notts (Nottingham) 1995. BB 4-47 v Hants (Birmingham) 1996.

DONALD, Allan Anthony (Grey College HS), b Bloemfontein, SA 20 Oct 1966. 6'2". RHB, RF. OFS 1985-86 to date. Warwickshire 1987-93 and 1995; cap 1989. *Wisden* 1991. Tests (SA): 30 (1991-92 to 1996-97); HS 33 and BB 8-71 (11-113 match) v Z (Harare) 1995-96. **LOI** (SA): 79 (1991-92 to 1996-97; HS 7*; BB 6-23). Tours (Wa): E 1994; A 1993-94; WI 1991-92; NZ 1994-95; SL 1993-94; Z 1995-96. HS 46* OFS v W Province (Cape Town) 1990-91. Wa HS 44 v Essex (Ilford) 1995. 50 wkts (4+1); most – 89 (1995). BB 8-37 OFS v Transvaal (Johannesburg) 1986-87. Wa BB 7-37 v Durham (Birmingham) 1992. Awards: NWT 3. **NWT:** HS 14* v Northants (Birmingham) 1992. BB 5-12 v Wilts (Birmingham) 1989. **BHC:** HS 23* v Leics (Leicester) 1989. BB 4-28 v Scot (Perth) 1987. **SL:** HS 18* v Middx (Lord's) 1988. BB 6-15 v Yorks (Birmingham) 1995.

EDMOND, Michael Denis (Airds HS, Cambelltown, NSW, Australia), b Barrow-in-Furness, Lancs 30 Jul 1969. 6'1". RHB, RMF. Debut 1996. Indoor Cricket for Australia. HS 8*. BB 1-6. **NWT:** HS 0. BB 1-24. **SL:** HS 5*. BB 1-26.

FROST, Tony (James Brinkley HS; Stoke-on-Trent C), b Stoke-on-Trent, Staffs 17 Nov 1975. 5'11". RHB, WK. Staff 1994 – awaiting f-c debut.

GILES, Ashley Fraser (George Abbot S, Guildford), b Chertsey, Surrey 19 Mar 1973. 6'3". RHB, SLA. Debut 1993; cap 1996. Tour: A 1996-97 (Eng A). HS 106* v Lancs (Birmingham) 1996. 50 wkts (1): 64 (1996). BB 6-45 v Durham (Birmingham) 1996. **NWT:** HS 21* v Derbys (Derby) 1995. BB 3-14 v Glam (Cardiff) 1995. **BHC:** HS 9. BB 1-49. **SL:** HS 36 v Derbys (Derby) 1996. BB 5-36 v Worcs (Birmingham) 1996.

KHAN, Wasim Gulzar (Small Heath CS; Josiah Mason SFC, Erdington), b Birmingham 26 Feb 1971. 6'1". LHB, LB. Debut 1995. HS 181 v Hants (Southampton) 1995. **BHC:** HS 0*. **SL:** HS 9.

KNIGHT, Nicholas Verity (Felsted S; Loughborough U), b Watford, Herts 28 Nov 1969. 6'0". LHB, occ RM. Essex 1991-94; cap 1994. Warwickshire debut 1994-95 (SA tour); cap 1995. **Tests:** 11 (1995 to 1996-97); HS 113 v P (Leeds) 1996. **LOI:** 10 (1996 to 1996-97; HS 125*). Tours: SA 1994-95 (Wa); NZ 1996-97; I 1994-95 (Eng A); P 1995-96 (Eng A); Z 1996-97. 1000 runs (1): 1196 (1996). HS 174 v Kent (Canterbury) 1995. BB 1-61. Awards: NWT 1; BHC 2. **NWT:** HS 151 v Somerset (Birmingham) 1995. **BHC:** HS 104 v Minor C (Jesmond) 1996. **SL:** HS 134 v Hants (Birmingham) 1996. BB 1-14.

McDONALD, Stephen (Bristnall Hall HS; Rowley Regis C), b Birmingham 2 Oct 1974. 5'10". RHB, OB. Staff 1996 – awaiting f-c debut. MCC YC.

MOLES, Andrew James (Finham Park CS; Butts CHE), b Solihull 12 Feb 1961. 5'10". RHB, RM. Debut 1986; cap 1987; benefit 1997. GW 1986-87 to 1988-89. Tours (Wa): SA 1991-92, 1992-93, 1994-95. 1000 runs (6); most – 1854 (1990). HS 230* GW v N Transvaal B (Verwoerdburg) 1988-89. Wa HS 224* v Glam (Swansea) 1990. BB 3-21 v OU (Oxford) 1987. BAC BB 3-50 v Essex (Chelmsford) 1987. Awards: NWT 2; BHC 2. **NWT:** HS 127 v Bucks (Birmingham) 1987. **BHC:** HS 89 v Lancs (Birmingham) 1995. BB 1-11. **SL:** HS 96* v Glam (Birmingham) 1992. BB 2-24 v Worcs (Worcester) 1987.

MUNTON, Timothy Alan (Sarson HS; King Edward VII Upper S), b Melton Mowbray, Leics 30 Jul 1965. 6'5". RHB, RMF. Debut 1985; cap 1987; captain 1997; benefit 1998. *Wisden* 1994. **Tests:** 2 (1992); HS 25* v P (Manchester) 1992; BB 2-22 v P (Leeds) 1992. Tours: SA 1992-93 (Wa); WI 1991-92 (Eng A); P 1990-91 (Eng A). 1995-96 (Eng A – part); SL 1990-91 (Eng A); Z 1993-94 (Wa). HS 54* v Worcs (Worcester) 1996. 50 wkts (5); most – 81 (1994). BB 8-89 (11-128 match) v Middx (Birmingham) 1991. Awards: NWT 2; BHC 1. **NWT:** HS 5. BB 3-36 v Kent (Canterbury) 1989. **BHC:** HS 13 v Leics (Leicester) 1989. BB 4-35 v Surrey (Oval) 1991. **SL:** HS 15* v Yorks (Scarborough) 1994. BB 5-23 v Glos (Moreton-in-Meh) 1996.

OSTLER, Dominic Piers (Princethorpe C; Solihull TC), b Solihull 15 Jul 1970. 6'3". RHB, occ RM. Debut 1990; cap 1991. Tours: SA 1992-93 (Wa); P 1995-96 (Eng A). 1000 runs (4); most – 1284 (1991). HS 208 v Surrey (Birmingham) 1995. Awards: NWT 2; BHC 1. **NWT:** HS 104 and BB 1-4 v Norfolk (Lakenham) 1993. **BHC:** HS 87 v Notts (Nottingham) 1995. **SL:** HS 91* v Sussex (Hove) 1996.

PENNEY, Trevor Lionel (Prince Edward S, Salisbury), b Salisbury, Rhodesia 12 Jun 1968. 6'0". RHB, RM. Qualified for England 1992. Boland 1991-92. Warwickshire debut 1991-92 (SA tour); UK debut v CU (Cambridge) 1992, scoring 102*; cap 1994. Mashonaland 1993-94. Tours (Wa): SA 1991-92, 1992-93, 1994-95; Z 1993-94. 1000 runs (2); most – 1295 (1996). HS 151 v Middx (Lord's) 1992. BB 3-18 Mashonaland v Mashonaland U-24 (Harare) 1993-94. Wa BB 1-40 (Z tour). BAC BB – . Award: NWT 1. **NWT:** HS 90 v Cornwall (St Austell) 1996. BB 1-8. **BHC:** HS 50* v Leics (Birmingham) 1996. **SL:** HS 83* v Kent (Canterbury) 1993.

PIPER, Keith John (Haringey Cricket C), b Leicester 18 Dec 1969. 5'6". RHB, WK. Debut 1989; cap 1992. Tours (Wa): SA 1991-92, 1992-93, 1994-95; I 1994-95 (Eng A); P 1995-96 (Eng A); Z 1993-94 (Wa). HS 116* v Durham (Birmingham) 1994. BB 1-57. **NWT:** HS 16* v Worcs (Lord's) 1994. **BHC:** HS 11* v Surrey (Oval) 1991. **SL:** HS 30 v Lancs (Manchester) 1990.

POWELL, Michael James (Lawrence Sheriff S, Rugby), b Bolton, Lancs 5 Apr 1975. 5'11". RHB, RM. Debut 1996. HS 39 v Glam (Birmingham) 1996. BB 1-18.

SINGH, Anurag (King Edward's, Birmingham; Gonville & Caius C, Cambridge), b Kanpur, India 9 Sep 1975. 5'11½". RHB, OB. Debut 1995. Cambridge U 1996; blue 1996. HS 157 CU v Sussex (Hove) 1996. Wa HS 23* v Worcs (Worcester) 1996. Award: BHC 1. **BHC:** (Brit Us) HS 123 v Somerset (Taunton) 1996. **SL:** HS 2.

SMALL, Gladstone Cleophas (Moseley S; Hall Green TC), b St George, Barbados 18 Oct 1961. 5'11". RHB, RFM. Debut 1979-80 (DHR XI in NZ). Warwickshire debut 1980; cap 1982; benefit 1992. S Australia 1985-86. **Tests:** 17 (1986 to 1990); HS 59 v A (Oval) 1989; BB 5-48 v A (Melbourne) 1986-87. **LOI:** 53 (1986-87 to 1992); HS 18*; BB 4-31. Tours: A 1986-87, 1990-91; SA 1992-93 (Wa), 1994-95 (Wa); WI 1989-90; NZ 1979-80 (DHR); P 1981-82 (Int); Z 1993-94 (Wa). HS 70 v Lancs (Manchester) 1988. 50 wkts (6);

SMALL, G.C. continued:
most – 80 (1988). BB 7-15 v Notts (Birmingham) 1988. Award: NWT 1. **NWT:** HS 33 v Surrey (Lord's) 1982. BB 3-22 v Glam (Cardiff) 1982. **BHC:** HS 22 v Kent (Canterbury) 1990. BB 4-22 v Glam (Birmingham) 1990. **SL:** HS 40* v Essex (Ilford) 1984. BB 5-29 v Surrey (Birmingham) 1980.

SMITH, Neil Michael Knight (Warwick S), b Birmingham 27 Jul 1967. Son of M.J.K. (Leics, Warwks and England 1951-75). 6'0". RHB, OB. Debut 1987; cap 1993. MCC YC. LOI: 7 (1995-96 and 1996; HS 31; BB 3-29). Tours (Wa): SA 1991-92, 1994-95; Z 1993-94. HS 161 v Yorks (Leeds) 1989. BB 7-42 v Lancs (Birmingham) 1994. Awards: NWT 1; BHC 2. **NWT:** HS 65 v Kent (Birmingham) 1995. BB 5-17 v Norfolk (Lakenham) 1993. **BHC:** HS 80 v Derbys (Birmingham) 1996. BB 3-29 v Middx (Lord's) 1994. **SL:** HS 111* v Sussex (Hove) 1996. BB 6-33 v Sussex (Birmingham) 1995.

VESTERGAARD, Soren (Fredericksberg C; Haslev Laerer Seminarium), b Copenhagen, Denmark 1 Mar 1972. 6'2". RHB, RFM. Represented Denmark in 1994 ICC Trophy. Awaiting f-c debut.

WAGH, Mark Anant (King Edward's S, Birmingham; Keble C, Oxford), b Birmingham 20 Oct 1976. 6'2". RHB, OB. Oxford U debut/blue 1996; captain 1997. Awaiting Warwickshire debut. HS 43 OU v Hants (Oxford) 1996. BB 3-82 OU v Glam (Oxford) 1996. **BHC:** (Brit Us) HS 23 v Middx (Cambridge) 1996. BB 1-39.

WELCH, Graeme (Hetton CS), b Durham 21 Mar 1972. 5'11½". RHB, RM. Debut 1994. Tour: SA 1994-95 (Wa). HS 84* v Notts (Birmingham) 1994. BB 4-50 v Sussex (Hove) 1996. **NWT:** HS 14 and BB 1-11 v Cornwall (St Austell) 1996. **BHC:** HS 27* v Lancs (Birmingham) 1996. BB 2-43 v Lancs (Manchester) 1996. **SL:** HS 54 v Northants (Northampton) 1996. BB 3-37 v Yorks (Leeds) 1996.

NEWCOMER

HEMP, David Lloyd (Olchfa CS; Millfield S; W Glamorgan C), b Bermuda 15 Nov 1970. UK resident since 1976. 6'0". LHB, RM. Glamorgan 1991-96; cap 1994. Wales (MC) 1992-94. Tours: SA 1995-96 (Gm); I 1994-95 (Eng A); Z 1994-95 (Gm). 1000 runs (1): 1452 (1994). HS 157 Gm v Glos (Abergavenny) 1995. BB 3-23 Gm v SA A (Cardiff) 1996. BAC BB 1-9. Awards: NWT 1; BHC 1. **NWT:** HS 78 Gm v Leics (Leicester) 1995. **BHC:** HS 121 Gm v Comb Us (Cardiff) 1995. **SL:** HS 74 Gm v Leics (Leicester) 1996. BB 1-14.

DEPARTURES (who made first-class appearances in 1996)

BURNS, M. – *see WARWICKSHIRE.*

POLLOCK, Shaun Maclean (Northwood HS; Durban U), b Port Elizabeth, SA 16 Jul 1973. Son of P.M. (EP and SA 1958-59 to 1971-72); nephew of R.G. (EP, Transvaal and SA 1960-61 to 1986-87). 6'3". RHB, RFM. Natal 1991-92 to date. Warwickshire 1996; cap 1996. Tests (SA): 8 (1995-96 to 1996-97); HS 79 v I (Jo'burg) 1996-97; BB 5-32 v E (Cape Town) 1995-96. LOI (SA): 25 (1995-96 to 1996-97; HS 75; BB 4-34). HS 150* v Glam (Birmingham) 1996. BB 7-33 Natal v Border (E London) 1995-96. Wa BB 6-56 v Middx (Lord's) 1996. Award: BHC 1. **NWT:** HS 23 and BB 4-37 v Surrey (Birmingham) 1996. **BHC:** HS 59* v Lancs (Manchester) 1996. BB 6-21 v Leics (Birmingham) 1996 – inc 4 wkts in 4 balls on Wa debut. **SL:** HS 57 v Kent (Birmingham) 1996. BB 3-27 v Worcs (Birmingham) 1996.

REEVE, Dermot Alexander (King George V S, Kowloon), b Kowloon, Hong Kong 2 Apr 1963. 6'0". RHB, RMF. Sussex 1983-87 (cap 1986). Warwickshire 1988-96; cap 1988; captain 1993-96; benefit 1996. *Wisden* 1995. OBE 1996. Hong Kong 1982 (ICC Trophy). MCC YC. Tests: 3 (1991-92); HS 59 v NZ (Christchurch) 1991-92 (on debut); BB 1-4. LOI: 29 (1991 to 1995-96; HS 35; BB 3-20). Tours (C=captain): SA 1992-93C (Wa), 1994-95C (Wa); NZ 1991-92; I 1992-93; Z 1993-94C (Wa). 1000 runs (2); most – 1412 (1990). HS 202* v Northants (Northampton) 1990. 50 wkts (2); most – 55 (1984). BB 7-37 Sx v Lancs (Lytham) 1987. Wa BB 6-73 v Kent (Tunbridge W) 1991. Awards: NWT 5; BHC 2. **NWT:** HS 81* v Sussex (Lord's) 1993. BB 4-20 Sx v Lancs (Lord's) 1986. **BHC:** HS 80 v Essex (Birmingham) 1991. BB 4-23 v Minor C (Jesmond) 1996. **SL:** HS 100 v Lancs (Birmingham) 1991. BB 5-23 v Essex (Birmingham) 1988. To Somerset as coach.

continued on p 107

WARWICKSHIRE 1996

RESULTS SUMMARY

	Pace	Won	Lost	Drew	No Result
Britannic Assurance Championship	8th	7	6	4	–
All First-Class Matches		9	6	4	–
NatWest Trophy	2nd Round				
Benson and Hedges Cup	Semi-Finalist				
Sunday League	4th	10	6	–	1

BRITANNIC ASSURANCE CHAMPIONSHIP AVERAGES

BATTING AND FIELDING

Cap		M	I	NO	HS	Runs	Avge	100	50	Ct/St
1989	D.A.Reeve	5	8	1	168*	351	50.14	1	–	7
1994	T.L.Penney	17	30	3	134	1221	45.22	3	7	13
1995	N.V.Knight	8	15	–	132	665	44.33	2	3	9
1987	A.J.Moles	13	25	–	176	903	36.12	2	4	7
1996	A.F.Giles	15	25	9	106*	555	34.68	1	4	11
1996	S.M.Pollock	13	21	1	150*	606	30.30	2	1	5
1993	N.M.K.Smith	14	25	4	74	583	27.76	–	3	10
1991	D.P.Ostler	15	27	1	90	712	27.38	–	7	28
–	M.Burns	7	13	1	81	305	25.41	–	3	12/1
1989	T.A.Munton	9	13	8	54*	118	23.60	–	1	2
–	W.G.Khan	14	26	1	130	579	23.16	2	1	7
–	M.J.Powell	4	8	–	39	182	22.75	–	–	2
1992	K.J.Piper	12	21	2	82	423	22.26	–	1	21/6
–	A.Singh	2	4	1	23*	66	22.00	–	–	3
1995	D.R.Brown	17	29	1	55	540	19.28	–	2	12
1982	G.C.Small	7	9	5	23*	55	13.75	–	–	2
–	G.Welch	11	15	1	45	166	11.85	–	–	6
–	D.A.Altree	2	4	2	0*	0	0.00	–	–	1

Also batted (1 match each): M.D.Edmond 8*; P.A.Smith (cap 1986) 21.

BOWLING

	O	M	R	W	Avge	Best	5wI	10wM
A.F.Giles	584.3	168	1530	55	27.81	6-45	3	–
S.M.Pollock	446.4	115	1183	42	28.16	6-56	1	–
G.C.Small	164	35	536	19	28.21	4-41	–	–
G.Welch	245.4	40	887	27	32.85	4-50	–	–
N.M.K.Smith	436.4	102	1268	36	35.22	5-76	3	–
T.A.Munton	315	84	897	25	35.88	3-29	–	–
D.R.Brown	365.2	71	1257	34	36.97	6-52	2	1

Also bowled: D.A.Altree 40-8-154-1; M.Burns 3-0-13-0; M.D.Edmond 16.5-1-79-1; W.G.Khan 2.1-1-2-0; M.J.Powell 4-0-18-1; D.A.Reeve 103-32-195-9; P.A.Smith 20-3-58-1.

The First-Class Averages (pp 123-38) give the records of Warwickshire players in all first-class county matches (their other opponents being the Pakistanis and Cambridge University), with the exception of:

N.V.Knight 10-19-2-132-929-54.64-3-4-10ct. Did not bowl.
T.A.Munton 11-14-9-54*-123-24.60-0-1-2ct. 362-103-997-28-35.60-3/29.
D.P.Ostler 17-31-3-90-850-30.35-0-8-35ct. Did not bowl.
A.Singh 3-6-1-23*-79-15.80-0-0-3ct. Did not bowl.

WARWICKSHIRE RECORDS

FIRST-CLASS CRICKET

Highest Total	For	810-4d		v	Durham	Birmingham	1994
	V	887		by	Yorkshire	Birmingham	1896
Lowest Total	For	16		v	Kent	Tonbridge	1913
	V	15		by	Hampshire	Birmingham	1922
Highest Innings	For	501*	B.C.Lara	v	Durham	Birmingham	1994
	V	322	I.V.A.Richards	for	Somerset	Taunton	1985

Highest Partnership for each Wicket

1st	377*	N.F.Horner/K.Ibadulla	v	Surrey	The Oval	1960
2nd	465*	J.A.Jameson/R.B.Kanhai	v	Glos	Birmingham	1974
3rd	327	S.P.Kinneir/W.G.Quaife	v	Lancashire	Birmingham	1901
4th	470	A.I.Kallicharran/G.W.Humpage	v	Lancashire	Southport	1982
5th	322*	B.C.Lara/K.J.Piper	v	Durham	Birmingham	1994
6th	220	H.E.Dollery/J.Buckingham	v	Derbyshire	Derby	1938
7th	250	H.E.Dollery/J.S.Ord	v	Kent	Maidstone	1953
8th	228	A.J.W.Croom/R.E.S.Wyatt	v	Worcs	Dudley	1925
9th	154	G.W.Stephens/A.J.W.Croom	v	Derbyshire	Birmingham	1925
10th	141	A.F.Giles/T.A.Munton	v	Worcs	Worcester	1996

Best Bowling	For	10-41	J.D.Bannister	v	Comb Servs	Birmingham	1959
(Innings)	V	10-36	H.Verity	for	Yorkshire	Leeds	1931
Best Bowling	For	15-76	S.Hargreave	v	Surrey	The Oval	1903
(Match)	V	17-92	A.P.Freeman	for	Kent	Folkestone	1932

Most Runs – Season	2417	M.J.K.Smith		(av 60.42)		1959
Most Runs – Career	35146	D.L.Amiss		(av 41.64)		1960-87
Most 100s – Season	9	A.I.Kallicharran				1984
	9	B.C.Lara				1994
Most 100s – Career	78	D.L.Amiss				1960-87
Most Wkts – Season	180	W.E.Hollies		(av 15.13)		1946
Most Wkts – Career	2201	W.E.Hollies		(av 20.45)		1932-57

LIMITED-OVERS CRICKET

Highest Total	NWT	392-5		v	Oxfordshire	Birmingham	1984
	BHC	369-8		v	Minor C	Jesmond	1996
	SL	301-6		v	Essex	Colchester	1982
Lowest Total	NWT	109		v	Kent	Canterbury	1971
	BHC	96		v	Leics	Leicester	1972
	SL	65		v	Kent	Maidstone	1979
Highest Innings	NWT	206	A.I.Kallicharran	v	Oxfordshire	Birmingham	1984
	BHC	137*	T.A.Lloyd	v	Lancashire	Birmingham	1985
	SL	134	N.V.Knight	v	Hampshire	Birmingham	1996
Best Bowling	NWT	6-32	K.Ibadulla	v	Hampshire	Birmingham	1965
		6-32	A.I.Kallicharran	v	Oxfordshire	Birmingham	1984
	BHC	7-32	R.G.D.Willis	v	Yorkshire	Birmingham	1981
	SL	6-15	A.A.Donald	v	Yorkshire	Birmingham	1995

WORCESTERSHIRE

Formation of Present Club: 11 March 1865
Colours: Dark Green and Black
Badge: Shield Argent a Fess between three Pears Sable
Championships: (5) 1964, 1965, 1974, 1988, 1989
NatWest Trophy/Gillette Cup Winners: (1) 1994
Benson and Hedges Cup Winners: (1) 1991
Sunday League Champions: (3) 1971, 1987, 1988
Match Awards: NWT 44; BHC 63

Secretary: Revd M.D.Vockins
  County Ground, New Road, Worcester, WR2 4QQ (Tel 01905 748474)
Captain/Overseas Player: T.M.Moody (*tbc*). **1997 Beneficiary:** R.K.Illingworth.
Scorer: J.W.Sewter

BRINKLEY, James Edward (Marist C, Canberra; Trinity C, Perth), b Helensburgh,
Scotland 13 Mar 1974. 6'3". RHB, RFM. Debut 1993-94 (Z tour). Matabeleland 1994-95
to date. Tour: Z 1993-94 (Wo). HS 29 Matabeleland v Mashonaland U-24 (Harare)
1994-95. BAC HS 5. BB 6-35 Matabeleland v Mashonaland CD (Harare South) 1994-95.
BAC BB 6-98 v Surrey (Oval) 1994 on UK debut. BHC: HS – . BB 2-44 v Northants
(Worcester) 1996. SL: HS 0. BB 2-26 v Hants (Worcester) 1996.

CURTIS, Timothy Stephen (Worcester RGS; Durham U; Magdalene C, Cambridge), b
Chislehurst, Kent 15 Jan 1960. 5'11". RHB, LB. Debut 1979; cap 1984; captain 1992-95;
benefit 1994. Cambridge U 1983; blue 1993. **Tests:** 5 (1988 to 1989); HS 41 v A
(Birmingham) 1989. Tours (Wo): Z 1990-91, 1993-94 (captain). 1000 runs (11); most –
1829 (1992). HS 248 v Somerset (Worcester) 1991. BB 2-17 v OU (Oxford) 1991. BAC
BB 2-72 v Warwks (Worcester) 1987 and v Derbys (Worcester) 1992. Awards: NWT 6;
BHC 2. **NWT:** HS 136* v Surrey (Oval) 1994. BB 1-6. **BHC:** HS 97 v Warwks
(Birmingham) 1994. **SL:** HS 124 v Somerset (Taunton) 1990.

DAWOOD, Ismail (Batley GS), b Dewsbury, Yorks 23 Jul 1976. 5'8". RHB, WK.
Northamptonshire 1994. Worcestershire debut 1996. HS 2*. **SL:** HS 2.

ELLIS, Scott William Kenneth (Shrewsbury S; Warwick U), b Newcastle-under-Lyme,
Staffs 3 Oct 1975. 6'3". RHB, RMF. Debut (Combined Us) v WI (Oxford) 1995 taking
5-59. Worcestershire debut 1996. HS 15 v Middx (Lord's) 1996. BB 5-59 (above). Wo BB
3-29 v Durham (Worcester) 1996. **NWT:** HS 0* and BB 2-34 v Glam (Cardiff) 1996.
BHC: (Brit U) HS 4. BB 1-50. **SL:** HS 1. BB 2-35 v Kent (Canterbury) 1996.

HAYNES, Gavin Richard (High Park S; King Edward VI S, Stourbridge), b Stourbridge
29 Sep 1969. 5'10". RHB, RM. Debut 1991; cap 1994. Tour: Z 1993-94 (Wo). 1000 runs
(1): 1021 (1994). HS 158 v Kent (Worcester) 1993. BB 4-33 v Kent (Worcester) 1995.
Awards: NWT 2; BHC 1. **NWT:** HS 116* v Cumberland (Worcester) 1995. BB 1-9.
BHC: HS 65 v Hants (Worcester) 1994. BB 3-17 v Derbys (Worcester) 1995. **SL:** HS 83
v Hants (Worcester) 1994. BB 4-21 v Surrey (Worcester) 1995.

HICK, Graeme Ashley (Prince Edward HS, Salisbury), b Salisbury, Rhodesia 23 May
1966. 6'3". RHB, OB. Zimbabwe 1983-84 to 1985-86. Worcestershire debut 1984; cap
1986. N Districts 1987-88 to 1988-89. Queensland 1990-91. *Wisden* 1986. **Tests:** 46
(1991 to 1996); HS 178 v I (Bombay) 1992-93; BB 4-126 v NZ (Wellington) 1991-92.
LOI: 62 (1991 to 1996; HS 105*; BB 3-41). Tours: E 1985 (Z); A 1994-95; SA 1995-96;
WI 1993-94; NZ 1991-92; I 1992-93; SL 1983-84 (Z), 1992-93; Z 1990-91 (Wo). 1000
runs (12+1) inc 2000 (3); most – 2713 (1988); youngest to score 2000 (1986). Scored
1019 runs before June 1988, including a record 410 runs in April. Fewest innings for
10,000 runs in county cricket (179). Youngest (24) to score 50 first-class hundreds. Scored
645 runs without being dismissed (UK record) in 1990. HS 405* (Worcs record and then
second highest in UK f-c matches) v Somerset (Taunton) 1988. BB 5-18 v Leics
(Worcester) 1995. Awards: NWT 4; BHC 11. **NWT:** HS 172* v Devon (Worcester) 1987.

HICK, G.A. continued:
BB 4-54 v Hants (Worcester) 1988 and v Surrey (Oval) 1994. **BHC:** HS 127* v Derbys (Worcester) 1995. BB 3-36 v Warwks (Birmingham) 1990. **SL:** HS 130 v Durham (Darlington) 1995. BB 4-21 v Somerset (Worcester) 1995.

ILLINGWORTH, Richard Keith (Salts GS), b Bradford, Yorks 23 Aug 1963. 5'11". RHB, SLA. Debut 1982; cap 1986; benefit 1997. Natal 1988-89. **Tests:** 9 (1991 to 1995-96); HS 28 v SA (Pt Elizabeth) 1995-96. 4-96 v WI (Nottingham) 1995. Took wicket of P.V.Simmons with his first ball in Tests – v WI (Nottingham) 1991. **LOI:** 25 (1991 to 1995-96); HS 14; BB 3-33). Tours: SA 1995-96; NZ 1991-92; P 1990-91 (Eng A); SL 1990-91 (Eng A); Z 1989-90 (Eng A), 1990-91 (Wo), 1993-94 (Wo). HS 120* v Warwks (Worcester) 1987 – as night-watchman. Scored 106 for England A v (Harare) 1989-90 – also as night-watchman. 50 wkts (5); most – 75 (1990). BB 7-50 v OU (Oxford) 1985. BAC BB 6-28 v Glos (Gloucester) 1993. **NWT:** HS 29* v Hants (Worcester) 1996. BB 4-20 v Devon (Worcester) 1987. **BHC:** HS 36* v Kent (Worcester) 1990. BB 4-36 v Yorks (Bradford) 1985. **SL:** HS 31 v Yorks (Worcester) 1994. BB 5-24 v Somerset (Worcester) 1983.

LAMPITT, Stuart Richard (Kingswinford S; Dudley TC), b Wolverhampton, Staffs 29 Jul 1966. 5'11". RHB, RMF. Debut 1985; cap 1989. Tours (Wo): Z 1990-91, 1993-94. HS 122 v Middx (Lord's) 1994. 50 wkts (5); most – 64 (1994). BB 5-32 v Kent (Worcester) 1989. Awards: NWT 1; BHC 4. **NWT:** HS 29 v Lancs (Manchester) 1995. BB 5-22 v Suffolk (Bury St E) 1990. **BHC:** HS 41 v Glam (Worcester) 1990. BB 6-26 v Derbys (Derby) 1994. **SL:** HS 41* v Leics (Worcester) 1993. BB 5-67 v Middx (Lord's) 1990.

LEATHERDALE, David Anthony (Pudsey Grangefield S), b Bradford, Yorks 26 Nov 1967. 5'10½". RHB, RM. Debut 1988; cap 1994. Tour: Z 1993-94 (Wo). HS 157 v Somerset (Worcester) 1991. BB 4-75 v SA A (Worcester) 1996. BAC BB 2-2 v Notts (Worcester) 1996. **NWT:** HS 43 v Hants (Worcester) 1988. BB 3-14 v Norfolk (Lakenham) 1994. **BHC:** HS 66 v Northants (Worcester) 1996. **SL:** HS 62* v Kent (Folkestone) 1988. BB 4-31 v Middx (Lord's) 1996.

MOODY, Thomas Masson (Guildford GS, WA), b Adelaide, Australia 2 Oct 1965. 6'6½". RHB, RM. W Australia 1985-86 to date; captain 1995-96 to date. Warwickshire 1990; cap 1990. Worcestershire debut/cap 1991. **Tests** (A): 8 (1989-90 to 1992-93); HS 106 v SL (Brisbane) 1989-90; BB 1-17. **LOI** (A): 40 (1987-88 to 1996-97; HS 89; BB 3-56). Tours (A): E 1989; I 1989-90 (WA); SL 1992-93. 1000 runs (5+1); most – 1887 (1991). HS 272 WA v Tasmania (Hobart) 1994-95. Wo/BAC HS 212 v Notts (Worcester) 1996. BB 7-38 WA v Tasmania (Hobart) 1995-96. Wo/BAC BB 7-92 (13-159 match) v Glos (Worcester) 1996. Awards: NWT 3; BHC 5. **NWT:** HS 180* v Surrey (Oval) 1994. BB 2-33 v Norfolk (Lakenham) 1994. **BHC:** HS 110* v Derbys (Worcester) 1991. BB 4-59 v Somerset (Worcester) 1992. **SL:** HS 160 v Kent (Worcester) 1991 (on Wo debut). BB 4-46 v Lancs (Manchester) 1996.

NEWPORT, Philip John (High Wycombe RGS; Portsmouth Poly), b High Wycombe, Bucks 11 Oct 1962. 6'3". RHB, RFM. Debut 1982; cap 1986. Boland 1987-88. N Transvaal 1992-93. Buckinghamshire 1981-82. **Tests:** 3 (1988 to 1990-91); HS 40* v A (Perth) 1990-91; BB 4-87 v SL (Lord's) 1988 (on debut). Tours: A 1990-91 (part); P 1990-91 (Eng A); SL 1990-91 (Eng A); Z 1993-94 (Wo). HS 98 v NZ (Worcester) 1990. BAC HS 96 v Essex (Worcester) 1990. 50 wkts (8); most – 93 (1988). BB 8-52 v Middx (Lord's) 1988. Award: BHC 1. **NWT:** HS 25 v Northants (Northampton) 1984. BB 4-30 v Northants (Worcester) 1994. **BHC:** HS 28 v Kent (Worcester) 1990. BB 5-22 v Warwks (Birmingham) 1987. **SL:** HS 26* v Leics (Leicester) 1987 and v Surrey (Worcester) 1993. BB 5-32 v Essex (Chelmsford) 1995.

PREECE, Benjamin Edward Ashley (Leasowes HS), b Birmingham 8 Nov 1976. 6'1". RHB, RFM. Debut 1996. HS 3* and BB 4-79 v SA A (Worcester) 1996. BAC HS 2. BAC BB 1-84. **SL:** HS 1*. BB 1-10.

RAWNSLEY, Matthew James (Shenley Court CS, Birmingham), b Birmingham 8 Jun 1976. 6'2". RHB, SLA. Debut 1996. HS 4*. BB 1-4. **SL:** HS 7.

RHODES, Steven John (Lapage Middle S; Carlton-Bolling S, Bradford), b Bradford, Yorks 17 Jun 1964. Son of W.E. (Notts 1961-64). 5'7". RHB, WK. Yorkshire 1981-84. Worcestershire debut 1985; cap 1986; benefit 1996. *Wisden* 1994. **Tests:** 11 (1994 to 1994-95); HS 65* v SA (Leeds) 1994. **LOI:** 9 (1989 to 1994-95); HS 56). Tours: A 1994-95; SA 1993-94 (Eng A); WI 1991-92 (Eng A); SL 1985-86 (Eng B), 1990-91 (Eng A); Z 1989-90 (Eng A), 1990-91 (Wo), 1993-94 (Wo). 1000 runs (1): 1018 (1995). HS 122* v Young A (Worcester) 1995. BAC HS 116* v Warwks (Worcester) 1992. Awards: NWT 1; BHC 1. **NWT:** HS 61 v Derbys (Worcester) 1989. **BHC:** HS 51* v Warwks (Birmingham) 1987. **SL:** HS 48* v Kent (Worcester) 1989.

SHERIYAR, Alamgir (George Dixon S; Joseph Chamberlain SFC; Oxford Poly), b Birmingham 15 Nov 1973. 6'1". RHB, LFM. Leicestershire 1994-95. Worcestershire debut 1996. HS 19 Le v WI (Leicester) 1995. BAC HS 18 Le v Northants (Northampton) 1995. Wo HS 13 v Derbys (Chesterfield) 1996. BB 6-30 Le v Young A (Leicester) 1995. Wo/BAC BB 6-99 v Sussex (Worcester) 1996. Hat-trick Le v Durham (Durham) 1994 (his second match). **NWT:** HS 10 v Hants (Worcester) 1996. BB 1*. BB 3-40 v Northants (Worcester) 1996. **SL:** HS 19 v Derbys (Chesterfield) 1996. BB 4-27 v Durham (Worcester) 1996.

SOLANKI, Vikram Singh (Regis S, Wolverhampton), b Udaipur, India 1 Apr 1976. 6'0". RHB, OB. Debut 1995. HS 90 v Surrey (Oval) 1996. BB 5-69 v Middx (Lord's) 1996. **NWT:** HS 50 v Glam (Cardiff) 1996. BB 1-48. **SL:** HS 55 v Yorks (Worcester) 1996. BB 1-19.

SPIRING, Karl Reuben (Monmouth S; Durham U), b Southport, Lancs 13 Nov 1974. 5'11". RHB, OB. Debut 1994. 1000 runs (1): 1084 (1996). HS 144 v Hants (Worcester) 1996. **NWT:** HS 25 v Hants (Worcester) 1996. **BHC:** HS 35 Comb Us v Essex (Cambridge) 1995. **SL:** HS 48 v Hants (Worcester) 1996.

THOMAS, Paul Anthony (Brodway S; Sutton C; Sandwell C), b Perry Barr, Birmingham 3 Jun 1971. 5'11". RHB, RFM. Debut 1995. Shropshire 1992-94. HS 25 v Warwks (Birmingham) 1995. BB 5-70 v WI (Worcester) 1995 – on debut. BAC BB 4-78 v Sussex (Eastbourne) 1995. **NWT:** HS – . BB 2-30 v Cumberland (Worcester) 1995. **BHC:** HS – . BB 1-34.

WESTON, William Philip Christopher (Durham S), b Durham 16 Jun 1973. Son of M.P. (Durham; England RFU; brother of R.M.S. (*see DURHAM*). 6'3". LHB, LM. Debut 1991; cap 1995. Tour: Z 1993-94 (Wo). 1000 runs (2); most – 1389 (1996). HS 171* v Lancs (Manchester) 1996. BB 2-39 v P (Worcester) 1992. BAC BB – . **NWT:** HS 31 v Scot (Edinburgh) 1993. **BHC:** HS 32* v Essex (Worcester) 1993. **SL:** HS 80* v Durham (Worcester) 1996.

NEWCOMERS

CHAPMAN, Robert James (Farnborough CS; S Notts CFE), b Nottingham 28 Jul 1972. Son of footballer R.O. ('Sammy') (Nottingham Forest, Notts County and Shrewsbury Town). 6'1". RHB, RFM. Nottinghamshire 1992-96. HS 25 Nt v Lancs (Nottingham) 1994. BB 4-109 Nt v SA A (Nottingham) 1996. BAC BB 3-119 Nt v Surrey (Guildford) 1995. **NWT:** HS – . **SL:** HS 4*. BB 2-36 Nt v Kent (Nottingham) 1995.

MIRZA, Maneer Mohammed, b Birmingham 1 Apr 1978. RHB, RFM. Summer contract.

PRICE, Stephen James (Hereford Cathedral S), b Shrewsbury, Shropshire 30 Mar 1979. RHB, OB. Summer contract.

SLADE, Neil D., b Worcester 16 Jul 1976. Son of D.N.F. (Worcs 1958-71). RHB, OB. Summer contract.

WILSON, Elliott J. (Felsted S), b London 3 Nov 1976. RHB. Summer contract.

DEPARTURES (who made first-class appearances in 1996)

AMJAD, Mohammed (Small Heath SS), b Marston Green, Birmingham 23 Mar 1971. 5'6". LHB, SLC. Worcestershire 1996. No BAC appearances. HS 7. Hafeez Muslim priest..

CHURCH, Matthew John (St George's C, Weybridge), b Guildford, Surrey 26 Jul 1972. 6'2". RHB, RM. Worcestershire 1994-96. MCC YC. HS 152 and BB 4-50 v OU (Oxford) 1996. BAC HS 38 v Yorks (Worcester) 1994. BAC BB 2-27 v Yorks (Worcester) 1996. **NWT:** HS 35 v Hants (Worcester) 1996. **BHC:** HS – . **SL:** HS 18 v Notts (Worcester) 1994.

RALPH, James Trevor (Harry Cheshire HS, Kidderminster), b Kidderminster 9 Oct 1975. 5'11". RHB, LB. Worcestershire 1996. No BAC appearances. HS 0.

WORCESTERSHIRE 1996

RESULTS SUMMARY

	Place	Won	Lost	Drew	No Result
Britannic Assurance Championship	7th	6	4	7	–
All First-Class Matches		6	5	9	–
NatWest Trophy	2nd Round				
Benson and Hedges Cup	4th in Group B				
Sunday League	8th	8	6	–	3

BRITANNIC ASSURANCE CHAMPIONSHIP AVERAGES

BATTING AND FIELDING

Cap		M	I	NO	HS	Runs	Avge	100	50	Ct/St
1991	T.M.Moody	17	30	2	212	1361	48.60	7	3	11
1986	G.A.Hick	12	22	1	150	987	47.00	4	3	16
	V.S.Solanki	12	20	3	90	734	43.17	–	6	8
	K.R.Spiring	15	27	5	144	912	41.45	3	6	4
1995	W.P.C.Weston	17	33	5	171*	1147	40.96	3	6	19
1986	S.J.Rhodes	17	26	5	110	835	39.76	1	6	33/8
1994	D.A.Leatherdale	9	15	2	122	436	33.53	1	3	5
1984	T.S.Curtis	16	30	2	118	933	33.32	2	5	8
1986	R.K.Illingworth	16	20	8	66*	388	32.33	–	1	10
1989	S.R.Lampitt	17	24	3	88	572	27.23	–	2	13
1986	P.J.Newport	5	6	–	68	142	23.66	–	1	1
–	M.J.Church	4	8	–	29	97	12.12	–	–	3
–	S.W.K.Ellis	8	8	4	15	46	11.50	–	–	6
–	P.A.Thomas	3	5	–	11	37	7.40	–	–	–
–	A.Sheriyar	15	15	9	13	38	6.33	–	–	4

Also batted: B.E.A.Preece (1 match) 0, 2 (1 ct); M.J.Rawnsley (3 matches) 4* (1 ct).

BOWLING

	O	M	R	W	Avge	Best	5wI	10wM
T.M.Moody	295.4	83	892	34	26.23	7- 92	3	1
V.S.Solanki	197.2	32	815	26	31.34	5- 69	3	1
P.J.Newport	170.3	39	643	19	33.84	6-100	1	–
S.R.Lampitt	485.5	92	1801	52	34.63	5- 58	2	–
R.K.Illingworth	636	195	1471	42	35.02	5- 40	2	–
A.Sheriyar	432	74	1576	34	46.35	6- 99	1	–
S.W.K.Ellis	159	26	630	13	48.46	3- 29	–	–

Also bowled: M.J.Church 24.1-3-98-4; T.S.Curtis 4.3-0-18-2; G.A.Hick 70-17-203-4;
D.A.Leatherdale 62.5-16-185-6; B.E.A.Preece 20-0-131-1; M.J.Rawnsley 41-12-132-3;
P.A.Thomas 52-4-296-4; W.P.C.Weston 1-0-1-0.

The First-Class Averages (pp 123-38) give the records of Worcestershire players in all
first-class county matches (their other opponents being the Indians, South Africa A and
Oxford University), with the exception of:
G.A.Hick 13-23-1-215-1202-54.63-5-3-16ct. 77-17-240-4-60.00-0/2/43.
R.K.Illingworth 18-21-9-66*-405-33.75-0-1-11ct. 702-204-1690-48-35.20-6/75-3-0.

WORCESTERSHIRE RECORDS

FIRST-CLASS CRICKET

Highest Total	For 670-7d		v Somerset	Worcester	1995
	V 701-4d		by Leics	Worcester	1906
Lowest Total	For 24		v Yorkshire	Huddersfield	1903
	V 30		by Hampshire	Worcester	1903
Highest Innings	For 405*	G.A.Hick	v Somerset	Taunton	1988
	V 331*	J.D.B.Robertson	for Middlesex	Worcester	1949

Highest Partnership for each Wicket

1st	309	F.L.Bowley/H.K.Foster	v Derbyshire	Derby	1901
2nd	300	W.P.C.Weston/G.A.Hick	v Indians	Worcester	1996
3rd	314	M.J.Horton/T.W.Graveney	v Somerset	Worcester	1962
4th	281	J.A.Ormrod/Younius Ahmed	v Notts	Nottingham	1979
5th	393	E.G.Arnold/W.B.Burns	v Warwicks	Birmingham	1909
6th	265	G.A.Hick/S.J.Rhodes	v Somerset	Taunton	1988
7th	205	G.A.Hick/P.J.Newport	v Yorkshire	Worcester	1988
8th	184	S.J.Rhodes/S.R.Lampitt	v Derbyshire	Kidderminster	1991
9th	181	J.A.Cuffe/R.D.Burrows	v Glos	Worcester	1907
10th	119	W.B.Burns/G.A.Wilson	v Somerset	Worcester	1906

Best Bowling	For 9- 23	C.F.Root	v Lancashire	Worcester	1931
(Innings)	V 10- 51	J.Mercer	for Glamorgan	Worcester	1936
Best Bowling	For 15- 87	A.J.Conway	v Glos	Moreton-in-M	1914
(Match)	V 17-212	J.C.Clay	for Glamorgan	Swansea	1937

Most Runs – Season	2654	H.H.I.Gibbons	(av 52.03)		1934
Most Runs – Career	34490	D.Kenyon	(av 34.18)		1946-67
Most 100s – Season	10	G.M.Turner			1970
	10	G.A.Hick			1988
Most 100s – Career	72†	G.M.Turner			1967-82
Most Wkts – Season	207	C.F.Root	(av 17.52)		1925
Most Wkts – Career	2143	R.T.D.Perks	(av 23.73)		1930-55

† G.A.Hick has scored 63 hundreds.

LIMITED-OVERS CRICKET

Highest Total	NWT	404-3		v Devon	Worcester	1987
	BHC	314-5		v Lancashire	Manchester	1980
	SL	307-4		v Derbyshire	Worcester	1975
Lowest Total	NWT	98		v Durham	Chester-le-St	1968
	BHC	81		v Leics	Worcester	1983
	SL	86		v Yorkshire	Leeds	1969
Highest Innings	NWT	180*	T.M.Moody	v Surrey	The Oval	1994
	BHC	143*	G.M.Turner	v Warwicks	Birmingham	1976
	SL	160	T.M.Moody	v Kent	Worcester	1991
Best Bowling	NWT	7-19	N.V.Radford	v Beds	Bedford	1991
	BHC	6- 8	N.Gifford	v Minor C (S)	High Wycombe	1979
	SL	6-26	A.P.Pridgeon	v Surrey	Worcester	1978

YORKSHIRE

Formation of Present Club: 8 January 1863
Substantial Reorganisation: 10 December 1891
Colours: Dark Blue, Light Blue and Gold
Badge: White Rose
Championships (since 1890): (29) 1893, 1896, 1898, 1900,
1901, 1902, 1905, 1908, 1912, 1919, 1922, 1923, 1924, 1925,
1931, 1932, 1933, 1935, 1937, 1938, 1939, 1946, 1959, 1960,
1962, 1963, 1966, 1967, 1968. Joint: (1) 1949
NatWest Trophy/Gillette Cup Winners: (2) 1965, 1969
Benson and Hedges Cup Winners: (1) 1987
Sunday League Champions: (1) 1983
Match Awards: NWT 31; BHC 62

Chief Executive: C.D.Hassell. **Secretary:** D.M.Ryder
 Headingley Cricket Ground, Leeds, LS6 3BU (Tel 0113 278 7394)
Captain: D.Byas **Overseas Player:** M.J.Slater *(tbc)*. **1997 beneficiary:** None.
Scorer: J.T.Potter

BATTY, Gareth Jon (Bingley GS), b Bradford 13 Oct 1977. Brother of J.D. (*see
SOMERSET*). 5'11". RHB, OB. Staff 1996 – awaiting f-c debut.

BLAKEY, Richard John (Rastrick GS), b Huddersfield 15 Jan 1967. 5'9". RHB, WK.
Debut 1985; cap 1987; benefit 1998. YC 1987. **Tests:** 2 (1992-93); HS 6. **LOI:** 3
(1992-93; HS 25). Tours: SA 1991-92 (Y); WI 1986-87 (Y); I 1992-93; P 1990-91 (Eng
A); SL 1990-91 (Eng A); Z 1989-90 (Eng A), 1995-96 (Y). 1000 runs (5); most – 1361
(1987). HS 221 Eng A v Z (Bulawayo) 1989-90. Y HS 204* v Glos (Leeds) 1987. BB
1-68. Awards: BHC 2. **NWT:** HS 75 v Warwks (Leeds) 1993. **BHC:** HS 80* v Lancs
(Manchester) 1996. **SL:** HS 130* v Kent (Scarborough) 1991.

BYAS, David (Scarborough C), b Kilham 26 Aug 1963. 6'4". LHB, RM. Debut 1986; cap
1991; captain 1996 to date. Tours (Y): SA 1991-92, 1992-93; Z 1995-96. 1000 runs (4);
most – 1913 (1995). HS 213 v Worcs (Scarborough) 1995. BB 3-55 v Derbys (Chesterfield) 1990. Award: BHC 1. **NWT:** HS 73* v Middx (Leeds) 1996. BB 1-23. **BHC:** HS
116* v Surrey (Oval) 1996. BB 2-38 v Somerset (Leeds) 1989. **SL:** HS 111* v Lancs
(Leeds) 1996. BB 3-19 v Notts (Leeds) 1989.

CHAPMAN, Colin Anthony (Beckfoot GS, Bingley; Bradford & Ilkley Art C), b
Bradford 8 Jun 1971. 5'8½". RHB, WK. Debut 1990. Tour: SA 1992-93 (Y). HS 20 v
Middx (Uxbridge) 1990. **NWT:** HS – . **SL:** HS 36* v Middx (Scarborough) 1990.

FISHER, Ian Douglas (Beckfoot GS, Bingley; Thomas Danby C, Leeds), b Bradford 31
Mar 1976. 5'10½". LHB, SLA. Debut 1996. UK debut 1996. Awaiting BAC
debut. Tour: Z 1995-96 (Y). HS 0*. BB 5-35 v Mashonaland Inv XI (Harare) 1995-96 (on
debut).

GOUGH, Darren (Priory CS, Lundwood), b Barnsley 18 Sep 1970. 5'11". RHB, RFM.
Debut 1989; cap 1993. **Tests:** 17 (1994 to 1996-97); HS 65 v NZ (Manchester) 1994 – on
debut; BB 6-49 v A (Sydney) 1994-95. **LOI:** 35 (1994 to 1996-97; HS 45; BB 5-44). Took
wickets with his sixth balls in both Tests and LOIs. Tours: A 1994-95; SA 1995-96 (Y),
1992-93 (Y), 1993-94 (Eng A), 1995-96; NZ 1996-97; Z 1996-97. HS 121 v Warwks
(Leeds) 1996. 50 wkts (4); most – 67 (1996). BB 7-28 (10-80 match) v Lancs (Leeds)
1995 (not BAC). BB 7-42 (10-96 match) v Somerset (Taunton) 1993. Hat-trick (and
4 wkts in 5 balls) v Kent (Leeds) 1995. Award: NWT 1. **NWT:** HS 42 v Lancs
(Manchester) 1996. BB 3-31 v Warwks (Leeds) 1993. **BHC:** HS 48* v Scot (Leeds) 1996.
BB 2-21 v Scot (Glasgow) 1995. **SL:** HS 72* v Leics (Leicester) 1991. BB 5-13 v Sussex
(Hove) 1994.

HAMILTON, Gavin Mark (Hurtsmere SS, Kent), b Broxburn, Scotland 16 Sep 1974. 6'1". RHB, RFM. Scotland 1993-94. Yorkshire debut 1994. Tour: Z 1995-96 (Y). HS 61 and BAC BB 3-65 v Essex (Leeds) 1996. BB 5-65 Scot v Ire (Eglinton) 1993. Y BB 3-41 v CU (Cambridge) 1995. **SL:** HS 16* v Kent (Maidstone) 1994. BB 4-27 v Warwks (Birmingham) 1995.

HARTLEY, Peter John (Greenhead GS; Bradford C), b Keighley 18 Apr 1960. 6'0". RHB, RMF. Warwickshire 1982. Yorkshire debut 1985; cap 1987; benefit 1996. Tours (Y): SA 1991-92; NZ 1986-87; Z 1995-96. HS 127* v Lancs (Manchester) 1988. 50 wkts (6); most – 81 (1995). BB 9-41 (inc hat-trick, 4 wkts in 5 balls and 5 in 9; 11-68 match) v Derbys (Chesterfield) 1995. Awards: NWT 1; BHC 2. **NWT:** HS 52 and BB 5-46 v Hants (Southampton) 1990. **BHC:** HS 29* v Notts (Nottingham) 1986. BB 5-43 v Scot (Leeds) 1986. **SL:** HS 52 v Glos (Bristol) 1996. BB 5-36 v Sussex (Scarborough) 1993.

HOGGARD, Matthew James (Grangefield S, Pudsey), b Leeds 31 Dec 1976. 6'2". RHB, RFM. Debut 1996. Awaiting BAC debut. HS 10 and BB 1-41 v SA A (Leeds) 1996.

HUTCHISON, Paul Michael (Crawshaw HS, Pudsey), b Leeds 9 Jun 1977. 6'3". LHB, LFM. Debut 1995-96 (Y tour). Rest 1996. Awaiting Yorks f-c debut in UK. Tour: Z 1995-96 (Y). HS 0. BB 4-23 v Mashonaland Inv XI (Harare) 1995-96 (on debut). UK BB 1-39 Rest v Eng A (Chelmsford) 1996.

KETTLEBOROUGH, Richard Allan (Worksop C), b Sheffield 15 Mar 1973. 6'0". LHB, RM. Debut 1994. Tour: Z 1995-96 (Y). HS 108 v Essex (Leeds) 1996. BB 2-26 v Notts (Scarborough) 1996. **SL:** HS 28 v Somerset (Leeds) 1994. BB 2-43 v Surrey (Oval) 1995.

McGRATH, Anthony (Yorkshire Martyrs Collegiate S), b Bradford 6 Oct 1975. 6'2". RHB, OB. Debut 1995. Tours (Eng A): A 1996-97; P 1995-96; Z 1995-96 (Y). HS 137 v Hants (Harrogate) 1996. **NWT:** HS 34 v Lancs (Manchester) 1996. **BHC:** HS 43 v Worcs (Worcester) 1996. BB 2-10 v Scot (Leeds) 1996. **SL:** HS 72 v Sussex (Scarborough) 1995.

MORRIS, Alexander Corfield (Holgate S; Barnsley C), b Barnsley 4 Oct 1976. 6'3". LHB, RMF. Debut 1995. Yorks 2nd XI debut when 16yr 332d. Tour: Z 1995-96 (Y). HS 60 v Lancs (Manchester) 1996 (not BAC). BAC HS 40 v Durham (Chester-le-St) 1996. BB 1-11. BAC BB 1-23. **NWT:** HS 1*. BB 1-43. **BHC:** – . **SL:** HS 48* and BB 2-19 v Durham (Chester-le-St) 1996.

MOXON, Martyn Douglas (Holgate GS, Barnsley), b Barnsley 4 May 1960. 6'0". RHB, RM. Debut 1981, scoring 5 and 116 v Essex (Leeds); cap 1984; captain 1990-95; benefit 1993. GW 1982-83 to 1983-84. *Wisden* 1992. **Tests:** 10 (1986 to 1989). HS 99 v NZ (Auckland) 1987-88. **LOI:** 8 (1984-85 to 1987-88; HS 70). Tours (C=captain): A 1987-88, 1992-93C (Eng A); SA 1992-93C (Y); WI 1986-87 (Y); NZ 1987-88; I 1984-85; SL 1984-85, 1985-86 (Eng B); Z 1995-96 (Y). 1000 runs (11); most – 1669 (1991). HS 274* v Worcs (Worcester) 1994. BB 3-24 v Hants (Southampton) 1989. Awards: NWT 5; BHC 7. **NWT:** HS 137 v Notts (Leeds) 1996. BB 2-19 v Norfolk (Leeds) 1990. **BHC:** HS 141* v Glam (Cardiff) 1991. BB 5-31 v Warwks (Leeds) 1991. **SL:** HS 129* v Surrey (Oval) 1991. BB 3-29 v Sussex (Hove) 1990.

PARKER, Bradley (Bingley GS), b Mirfield 23 Jun 1970. 5'11". RHB, RM. Debut 1992. Tour: Z 1995-96 (Y). HS 127 v Surrey (Scarborough) 1994. **NWT:** HS – . **SL:** HS 36 v Sussex (Hove) 1994.

SIDEBOTTOM, Ryan Jay (King James's GS, Almondbury), b Huddersfield 15 Jan 1978. Son of A. (Yorks, OFS and England 1973-91). 6'3". LHB, LFM. Staff 1996 – awaiting f-c debut.

SILVERWOOD, Christopher Eric Wilfred (Garforth CS), b Pontefract 5 Mar 1975. 6'1". RHB, RFM. Debut 1993; cap 1996. YC 1996. **Tests:** 1 (1996-97); HS 0 and BB 3-63 v Z (Bulawayo) 1996-97. **LOI:** 5 (1996-97; HS 12; BB 2-27). Tours: NZ 1996-97; Z 1995-96 (Y), 1996-97. HS 50 v Lancs (Manchester) 1995. BB 6-44 Eng XI v NZ A (Wanganui) 1996-97. Y BB 5-62 v Surrey (Oval) 1995. Award: BHC 1. **NWT:** HS 8*. BB 3-45 v Middx (Leeds) 1996. **BHC:** HS 2. BB 5-28 v Scot (Leeds) 1996. **SL:** HS 14* v Northants (Northampton) 1996. BB 4-26 v Durham (Chester-le-St) 1996.

STEMP, Richard David (Britannia HS, Rowley Regis), b Erdington, Birmingham 11 Dec 1967. 6'0". RHB, SLA. Worcestershire 1990-92. Yorkshire debut 1993; cap 1996. Tours (Eng A): SA 1992-93 (Y); I 1994-95; P 1995-96. HS 65 v Durham (Chester-le-St) 1996. BB 6-37 v Durham (Durham) 1994. **NWT:** HS 1*. BB 4-45 v Notts (Leeds) 1996. **BHC:** HS 1. BB 2-28 v Scot (Glasgow) 1995. **SL:** HS 23* v Warwks (Birmingham) 1993. BB 4-25 v Glos (Bristol) 1996.

VAUGHAN, Michael Paul (Silverdale CS, Sheffield), b Manchester, Lancs 29 Oct 1974. 6'2". RHB, OB. Debut 1993; cap 1995. Tours (Eng A): A 1996-97; I 1994-95; Z 1995-96 (Y). 1000 runs (3); most – 1244 (1995). HS 183 v Glam (Cardiff) 1996. BB 4-39 v OU (Oxford) 1994. BAC BB 4-62 v Surrey (Middlesbrough) 1996. **NWT:** HS 64 v Notts (Leeds) 1996. **BHC:** HS 60 v Worcs (Worcester) 1996. BB 1-22. **SL:** HS 71* v Sussex (Eastbourne) 1996.

WHARF, Alexander George (Buttershaw Upper S), b Bradford 4 Jun 1975. 6'5". RHB, RMF. Debut 1994. HS 62 v Glam (Cardiff) 1996. BB 4-29 v Lancs (Manchester) 1996 (not BAC). BAC BB 1-78. **BHC:** HS – . BB 4-29 v Notts (Leeds) 1996. **SL:** HS 2*. BB 3-39 v Warwks (Scarborough) 1994.

WHITE, Craig (Flora Hill HS, Bendigo, Australia; Bendigo HS), b Morley 16 Dec 1969. 6'0". RHB, RFM. Debut 1990; cap 1993. Victoria 1990-91 (2 matches). **Tests:** 8 (1994 to 1996-97); HS 51 v NZ (Lord's) 1994; BB 3-18 v NZ (Manchester) 1994. **LOI:** 15 (1994-95 to 1996-97); HS 38; BB 4-37. Tours: A 1994-95, 1996-97 (Eng A); SA 1991-92 (Y), 1992-93 (Y); NZ 1996-97; P 1995-96 (Eng A); Z 1996-97 (part). HS 181 v Lancs (Leeds) 1996. BB 5-40 v Essex (Leeds) 1994. Award: NWT 1. **NWT:** HS 113 and BB 3-38 v Ire (Leeds) 1995. **BHC:** HS 57* v Notts (Leeds) 1996. BB 2-30 v Northants (Leeds) 1993. **SL:** HS 63 v Surrey (Scarborough)'1992. BB 4-21 v Essex (Leeds) 1996.

WOOD, Matthew James (Shelley HS & SFC), b Huddersfield 6 Apr 1977. 5'9". RHB, OB. Staff 1996 – awaiting f-c debut.

NEWCOMERS

HOOD, James William (West Redcar S), b Middlesbrough 7 Sep 1976. LHB, RM.

ROBINSON, Ryan (Shelley HS), b Huddersfield 19 Oct 1976. RHB, RM.

SLATER, Michael Jonathon (Wagga Wagga HS), b Wagga Wagga, NSW, Australia 21 Feb 1970. 5'9". RHB, RM. NSW 1991-92 to date. **Tests:** 34 (1993 to 1996-97); HS 219 v SL (Perth) 1995-96; BB 1-4. **LOI:** 40 (1993-94 to 1996-97); HS 73). Tours (A): E 1993, 1995 (NSW); SA 1993-94; WI 1994-95; I 1996-97; P 1994-95; SL 1994-95. HS 219 (*Tests*). BB 1-4.

DEPARTURES (who made first-class appearances in 1996)

BEVAN, Michael Gwyl, b Belconnen, ACT, Australia 8 May 1970. LHB, SLC. S Australia 1989-90. NSW 1990-91 to date. Yorkshire 1995-96; cap 1995. **Tests** (A): 11 (1994-95 to 1996-97); HS 91 v P (Lahore) 1994-95; BB 6-82 (10-113 match) v WI (Adelaide) 1996-97. **LOI** (A): 49 (1993-94 to 1996-97); HS 79*; BB 3-36). Tours (A): P 1994-95; Z 1991-92 (Aus B). 1000 runs (2+1); most – 1598 (1995). HS 203* NSW v WA (Sydney) 1993-94. Y HS 160* v Surrey (Middlesbrough) 1996. BB 6-82 (*Tests*). Y BB 3-36 v Warwks (Leeds) 1996. Awards: NWT 2; BHC 3. **NWT:** HS 91* v Essex (Chelmsford) 1995. BB 2-47 v Lancs (Manchester) 1996. **BHC:** HS 95* v Lancs (Manchester) 1996. BB 1-25. **SL:** HS 103* v Glos (Middlesbrough) 1995. BB 5-29 v Sussex (Eastbourne) 1996.

SCHOFIELD, Christopher John (Kingstone S, Barnsley), b Barnsley 21 Mar 1976. 5'7". RHB. Yorkshire 1996. No BAC appearances. HS 25 v Lancs (Manchester) 1996 (not BAC).

YORKSHIRE 1996

RESULTS SUMMARY

	Place	Won	Lost	Drew
Britannic Assurance Championship	6th	8	5	4
All First-Class Matches		8	5	6
NatWest Trophy	Semi-Finalist			
Benson and Hedges Cup	Semi-Finalist			
Sunday League	3rd	11	6	–

BRITANNIC ASSURANCE CHAMPIONSHIP AVERAGES

BATTING AND FIELDING

Cap		M	I	NO	HS	Runs	Avge	100	50	Ct/St
1995	M.G.Bevan	12	22	3	160*	1225	64.47	3	8	6
1984	M.D.Moxon	13	23	3	213	961	48.05	2	5	5
1995	M.P.Vaughan	17	31	2	183	1156	39.86	3	6	4
1987	R.J.Blakey	17	28	6	109*	768	34.90	1	4	36/1
–	A.McGrath	17	29	1	137	909	32.46	2	4	10
1993	C.White	17	28	1	181	872	32.29	1	6	12
–	R.A.Kettleborough	5	7	–	108	222	31.71	1	–	6
1991	D.Byas	17	29	1	138	858	30.64	1	5	29
1993	D.Gough	15	24	3	121	494	23.52	1	2	5
1987	P.J.Hartley	16	24	3	89	476	22.66	–	3	6
1996	R.D.Stemp	17	22	8	65	230	16.42	–	2	8
–	A.C.Morris	4	7	–	40	96	13.71	–	–	4
1996	C.E.W.Silverwood	16	24	6	45*	198	11.00	–	–	6

Also batted (2 matches each): G.M.Hamilton 9*, 61, 0 (1 ct); A.G.Wharf 62, 41.

BOWLING

	O	M	R	W	Avge	Best	5wI	10wM
D.Gough	555.3	135	1498	66	22.69	6-36	2	–
C.White	282.2	47	1035	36	28.75	4-15	–	–
P.J.Hartley	459.2	96	1602	54	29.66	6-67	2	1
C.E.W.Silverwood	404.3	79	1442	47	30.68	5-72	2	–
R.D.Stemp	530.4	156	1442	37	38.97	5-38	1	–
M.P.Vaughan	186.3	28	726	16	45.37	4-62	–	–

Also bowled: M.G.Bevan 86.3-8-369-4; G.M.Hamilton 68.4-9-194-6; R.A.Kettleborough 12-1-40-2; A.McGrath 7-0-41-0; A.C.Morris 21-4-81-2; A.G.Wharf 31-5-166-1.

The First-Class Averages (pp 123-38) give the records of Yorkshire players in all first-class county matches (their other opponents being Lancashire in a non-Championship match and South Africa A), with the exception of M.D.Moxon whose full county figures are as above, and:

A.McGrath 18-31-2-137-962-33.17-2-5-10ct. 7-0-41-0.

R.D.Stemp 18-23-9-65-252-18.00-0-2-8ct. 556-163-1511-42-35.97-5/38-2-0.

Test Match and LOI statistics to 18 March 1996. See page 22 for key to abbreviations.

YORKSHIRE RECORDS

FIRST-CLASS CRICKET

Highest Total	For	887		v Warwicks	Birmingham	1896
	V	681-7d		by Leics	Bradford	1996
Lowest Total	For	23		v Hampshire	Middlesbrough	1965
	V	13		by Notts	Nottingham	1901
Highest Innings	For	341	G.H.Hirst	v Leics	Leicester	1905
	V	318*	W.G.Grace	for Glos	Cheltenham	1876

Highest Partnership for each Wicket

1st	555	P.Holmes/H.Sutcliffe	v Essex	Leyton	1932
2nd	346	W.Barber/M.Leyland	v Middlesex	Sheffield	1932
3rd	323*	H.Sutcliffe/M.Leyland	v Glamorgan	Huddersfield	1928
4th	312	D.Denton/G.H.Hirst	v Hampshire	Southampton	1914
5th	340	E.Wainwright/G.H.Hirst	v Surrey	The Oval	1899
6th	276	M.Leyland/E.Robinson	v Glamorgan	Swansea	1926
7th	254	W.Rhodes/D.C.F.Burton	v Hampshire	Dewsbury	1919
8th	292	R.Peel/Lord Hawke	v Warwicks	Birmingham	1896
9th	192	G.H.Hirst/S.Haigh	v Surrey	Bradford	1898
10th	149	G.Boycott/G.B.Stevenson	v Warwicks	Birmingham	1982

Best Bowling	For	10-10	H.Verity	v Notts	Leeds	1932
(Innings)	V	10-37	C.V.Grimmett	for Australians	Sheffield	1930
Best Bowling	For	17-91	H.Verity	v Essex	Leyton	1933
(Match)	V	17-91	H.Dean	for Lancashire	Liverpool	1913

Most Runs – Season	2883	H.Sutcliffe	(av 80.08)	1932
Most Runs – Career	38561	H.Sutcliffe	(av 50.20)	1919-45
Most 100s – Season	12	H.Sutcliffe		1932
Most 100s – Career	112	H.Sutcliffe		1919-45
Most Wkts – Season	240	W.Rhodes	(av 12.72)	1900
Most Wkts – Career	3608	W.Rhodes	(av 16.00)	1898-1930

LIMITED-OVERS CRICKET

Highest Total	NWT	345-5		v Notts	Leeds	1996
	BHC	317-5		v Scotland	Leeds	1986
	SL	318-7		v Leics	Leicester	1993
Lowest Total	NWT	76		v Surrey	Harrogate	1970
	BHC	88		v Worcs	Leeds	1995
	SL	56		v Warwicks	Birmingham	1995
Highest Innings	NWT	146	G.Boycott	v Surrey	Lord's	1965
	BHC	142	G.Boycott	v Worcs	Worcester	1980
	SL	130*	R.J.Blakey	v Kent	Scarborough	1991
Best Bowling	NWT	6-15	F.S.Trueman	v Somerset	Taunton	1965
	BHC	6-27	A.G.Nicholson	v Minor C (N)	Middlesbrough	1972
	SL	7-15	R.A.Hutton	v Worcs	Leeds	1969

GRIFFITH, Frank Alexander (Beaconsfield HS; Wm Morris HS; Haringey Cricket C), b Whipps Cross, Essex 15 Aug 1968. 6'0". RHB, RM. Derbyshire 1988-96. HS 81 v Glam (Chesterfield) 1992. BB 4-33 v Leics (Ilkeston) 1992. **NWT:** HS 8. BB 1-13. **BHC:** HS 24 v Leics (Leicester) 1996. BB 3-63 v Durham (Chesterfield) 1996. **SL:** HS 31 v Lancs (Manchester) 1994. BB 4-48 v Glam (Derby) 1993.

O'GORMAN, Timothy Joseph Gerard (St George's C, Weybridge; Durham U), b Woking, Surrey 15 May 1967. Grandson of J.G. (Surrey 1927). 6'2". RHB, OB. Derbyshire 1987-96; cap 1992. 1000 runs (2); most – 1116 (1991). HS 148 v Lancs (Manchester) 1991. BB 1-7. Award: NWT 1. **NWT:** HS 89 v Durham (Darlington) 1994. **BHC:** HS 49 v Northants (Derby) 1991 and v Lancs (Lord's) 1993. **SL:** HS 69 v Northants (Northampton) 1992.

WARNER, Allan Esmond (Tabernacle S, St Kitts), b Birmingham 12 May 1957. 5'7". RHB, RFM. Worcestershire 1982-84. Derbyshire 1985-96; cap 1987; benefit 1995. HS 95* v Kent (Canterbury) 1993. BB 6-21 v Lancs (Derby) 1995. Award: NWT 1. **NWT:** HS 32 v Kent (Canterbury) 1987. BB 4-39 v Salop (Chesterfield) 1990. **BHC:** HS 35* v Comb Us (Oxford) 1991. BB 4-36 v Notts (Nottingham) 1987. **SL:** HS 68 v Hants (Heanor) 1986. BB 5-39 v Worcs (Knapyer) 1985.

WELLS, Colin Mark (Tideway CS, Newhaven), b Newhaven, Sussex 3 Mar 1960. Elder brother of A.P. (*see KENT*). 5'11". RHB, RM. Sussex 1979-93 (cap 1982; benefit 1993). Derbyshire 1994-96; cap 1995. Border 1980-81. W Province 1984-85. **LOI:** 2 (1984-85; HS 17). 1000 runs (6); most – 1456 (1987). HS 203 Sx v Hants (Hove) 1984. De HS 165 v Glam (Cardiff) 1996. 50 wkts (2); most – 59 (1984). BB 7-42 Sx v Derbys (Derby) 1991. De BB 4-52 v Middx (Derby) 1994. Awards: BHC 3. **NWT:** HS 76 Sx v Ire (Hove) 1985. BB 3-16 Sx v Scot (Edinburgh) 1991. **BHC:** HS 117 Sx v Glam (Swansea) 1989. BB 4-21 Sx v Middx (Lord's) 1980. **SL:** HS 104* Sx v Warwks (Hove) 1983. BB 4-15 Sx v Worcs (Worcester) 1983. Joined Somerset as coach and 2nd XI captain 1997.

DURHAM – DEPARTURES (continued form p 23)

CAMPBELL, Sherwin Legay (Ellerslie SS), b Belle Plaine, St Andrew, Barbados 1 Nov 1970. 5'5". RHB, RM. Barbados 1990-91 to date. Durham 1996; cap 1996. **Tests** (WI): 16 (1994-95 to 1996-97); HS 208 v NZ (Bridgetown) 1995-96. **LOI** (WI): 36 (1994-95 to 1996-97; HS 86). Tours (WI): E 1995; A 1995-96; NZ 1994-95; I 1994-95. 1000 runs (2); most – 1225 (1995). HS 208 (*Tests*). Du HS 118 v Notts (Nottingham) 1996. BB 1-38. **NWT:** HS 39 v Essex (Chelmsford) 1996. **BHC:** HS 27 v Minor C (Chester-le-St) 1996. **SL:** HS 77 v Essex (Hartlepool) 1996.

LONGLEY, Jonathan Ian (Tonbridge S; Durham U), b New Brunswick, New Jersey, USA 12 Apr 1969. 5'7". RHB. Kent 1989-93. Durham 1994-96; cap 1994. Tour: Z 1992-93 (K). HS 110 K v CU (Cambridge) 1992. BAC/Du HS 100* v Derbys (Chesterfield) 1994 – on Du debut. Award: BHC 1. **NWT:** HS 9. **BHC:** HS 57 K v Somerset (Canterbury) 1992. **SL:** HS 92 v Somerset (Chester-le-St) 1995.

SCOTT, Christopher Wilmot (Robert Pattinson CS, N Hykeham), b Thorpe-on-the-Hill, Lincs 23 Jan 1964. 5'8". RHB, WK. Nottinghamshire 1981-91; cap 1988. Durham 1992-96; cap 1992. HS 108 v Surrey (Darlington) 1994. Held 10 catches for Notts in match v Derbys (Derby) 1988. **NWT:** HS 2. **BHC:** HS 27* v Derbys (Chesterfield) 1996. **SL:** HS 45 v Surrey (Darlington) 1994.

NORTHAMPTONSHIRE – DEPARTURES
(who made first-class appearances in 1996) continued from p 68

AMBROSE, Curtly Elconn Lynwall (All Saints Village SS), b Swetes Village, Antigua 21 Sep 1963. Cousin of R.M.Otto (Leeward Is 1979-80 to 1990-91). 6'7". LHB, RF. Leeward Is 1985-86 to date. Northamptonshire 1989-96; cap 1990. *Wisden* 1991. **Tests** (WI): 65 (1987-88 to 1996-97); HS 53 v A (P-of-S) 1990-91; BB 8-45 v E (Bridgetown) 1989-90. **LOI** (WI): 141 (1987-88 to 1996-97; HS 31*; BB 5-17). Tours (WI): E 1988, 1991, 1995; A 1988-89, 1992-93, 1995-96; NZ 1994-95; P 1990-91; SL 1993-94. HS 78

AMBROSE, C. continued:
v Somerset (Taunton) 1994. 50 wkts (5+1); most – 77 (1994). BB 8-45 (*Tests*). Nh BB 7-44 v Hants (Southampton) 1994. Award: NWT 1. **NWT:** HS 48 v Lancs (Lord's) 1990. BB 4-7 v Yorks (Northampton) 1992. **BHC:** HS 17* v Kent (Northampton) 1989. BB 4-31 v Essex (Northampton) 1992. **SL:** HS 37 v Notts (Nottingham) 1994. BB 4-20 v Lancs (Northampton) and v Kent (Northampton) 1994.

MALLENDER, Neil Alan (Beverley GS), b Kirk Sandall, Yorks 13 Aug 1961. 6'0". RHB, RFM. Northamptonshire 1980-86 and 1995-96; cap 1984. Somerset 1987-94; cap 1987; benefit 1994. Otago 1983-84 to 1992-93; captain 1990-91 to 1992-93. **Tests:** 2 (1992); HS 4; BB 5-50 v P (Leeds) 1992 – on debut. Tour: Z 1994-95 (Nh). HS 100* Otago v CD (Palmerston N) 1991-92. BAC HS 87* Sm v Sussex (Hove) 1990. Nh HS 71* v OU (Oxford) 1983. 50 wkts (6); most – 56 (1983). BB 7-27 Otago v Auckland (Auckland) 1984-85. UK BB 7-41 v Derbys (Northampton) 1982. Award: NWT 1. **NWT:** HS 11* (twice). BB 7-37 v Worcs (Northampton) 1984. **BHC:** HS 16* Sm v Hants (Taunton) 1988. BB 5-53 v Leics (Northampton) 1986. **SL:** HS 31* Sm v Durham (Hartlepool) 1993. BB 5-34 v Middx (Tring) 1981.

ROBERTS, Andrew Richard (Bishop Stopford CS, Kettering), b Kettering 16 Apr 1971. 5'6". RHB, LB. Northamptonshire 1989-96. Tour: SA 1991-92 (Nh). HS 62 v Notts (Nottingham) 1992. BB 6-72 v Lancs (Lytham) 1991. **NWT:** HS – . BB 1-23. **SL:** HS 20 v Essex (Chelmsford) 1994. BB 3-26 v Hants (Northampton) 1991.

WILD, Richard David (Crofton HS; Wakefield District C), b Barnsley, Yorks 23 May 1973. 6'4". RHB, RMF. Northamptonshire 1996. HS – . BB 1-62.

SURREY – DEPARTURES
(who made first-class appearances in 1996) continued from p 83

KENLOCK, Stratford Garfield (**'Mark'**) (Stockwell Manor S), b Portland, Jamaica 16 Apr 1965. 6'0". LHB, LFM. Surrey 1994-96. HS 12 v Northants (Northampton) 1995. BB 3-104 v Kent (Oval) 1994. Award: BHC 1. **BHC:** HS – . BB 5-15 v Ire (Oval) 1995. **SL:** HS 9. BB 4-30 v Yorks (Scarborough) 1994.

KERSEY, Graham James (Bexley & Erith Technical HS), b Plumstead, London 19 May 1971. Died Brisbane, Australia 31 Dec 1996 following injuries sustained in motor accident on Christmas Eve. 5'7". RHB, WK. Kent 1991-92. Surrey 1993-96; cap 1996. HS 83 v Yorks (Oval) 1995. **NWT:** HS 21 v Middx (Oval) 1995. **SL:** HS 50 v Durham (Oval) 1993.

SMITH, Andrew William (Sutton Manor HS), b Sutton 30 May 1969. Son of W.A. (Surrey 1961-70). 5'8". RHB, OB. Surrey 1993-96. HS 202* v OU (Oval) 1994. BAC HS 88 v Somerset (Oval) 1995. BB 5-103 v Somerset (Bath) 1994. Award: NWT 1. **NWT:** HS – . BB 3-25 v Leics (Leicester) 1993. **BHC:** HS 15* and BB 2-38 v Glam (Oval) 1994. **SL:** HS 58 v Derbys (Ilkeston) 1993. BB 3-56 v Glos (Oval) 1995.

WARD, David Mark (Haling Manor HS), b Croydon 10 Feb 1961. 6'1". RHB, OB, occ WK. Surrey 1985; cap 1990; benefit 1996. 1000 runs 2) inc 2000 (1): 2072 (1990). HS 294* v Derbys (Oval) 1994. BB 2-66 v Glos (Guildford) 1991. Awards: NWT 1; BHC 1. **NWT:** HS 101* v Glam (Swansea) 1992. **BHC:** HS 73 v Notts (Nottingham) 1994. **SL:** HS 112 v Kent (Oval) 1996.

WARWICKSHIRE – DEPARTURES (continued from p 93)

SMITH, Paul Andrew (Heaton GS), b Jesmond, Northumb 15 Apr 1964. Son of K.D. sr (Leics 1950-51) and brother of K.D. jr (Warwks 1973-85). 6'2". RHB, RFM. Warwickshire 1982-96; cap 1986; benefit 1995. MCC YC Tours (Wa): SA 1991-92, 1994-95. 1000 runs (2); most – 1508 (1986). HS 140 v Worcs (Worcester) 1989. BB 6-91 v Derbys (Birmingham) 1992. 2 hat-tricks: 1989, 1990. Awards: BHC 3. **NWT:** HS 79 v Durham (Birmingham) 1986. BB 4-37 v Yorks (Leeds) 1993. **BHC:** HS 74 v Northants (Birmingham) 1989. BB 3-28 v Middx (Lord's) 1991. **SL:** HS 93* v Middx (Birmingham) 1989. BB 5-36 v Worcs (Birmingham) 1993.

CAMBRIDGE v OXFORD 1996 – 151st UNIVERSITY MATCH

At Lord's, London on 2, 3, 4 July.
Toss: Cambridge University. Result: MATCH DRAWN.

OXFORD UNIVERSITY

*C.M.Gupte	run out	60		
I.J.Sutcliffe	c Churton b Whittall	55		
A.C.Ridley	c and b Haste	155		
G.A.Khan	c Whittall b Moffat	34		
W.S.Kendall	not out	145		
†J.N.Batty	b Whittall	27	(1) not out	30
H.S.Malik	lbw b Whittall	12	(2) not out	19
M.A.Wagh	not out	8		
R.B.Thomson				
S.P.du Preez				
A.W.Maclay				
Extras	(LB 11, W 6)	17	(B 7, LB 3, NB 4)	14
Total	(6 wickets declared)	**513**	(0 wickets declared)	**63**

CAMBRIDGE UNIVERSITY

*R.Q.Cake	c Kendall b Du Preez	23	run out	33
E.T.Smith	c Batty b Du Preez	40	lbw b Thomson	50
A.Singh	lbw b Maclay	36	c Malik b Thomson	45
R.O.Jones	not out	11	(6) lbw b Sutcliffe	8
W.J.House	not out	47	(4) c Khan b Sutcliffe	54
A.R.Whittall			(5) c Malik b Wagh	1
P.J.Deakin			not out	14
N.J.Haste			not out	51
†D.R.H.Churton				
G.R.Moffat				
R.W.Tennent				
Extras	(LB 3, NB 4)	7	(B 6, LB 4, W 5)	15
Total	(3 wickets declared)	**164**	(6 wickets)	**271**

CAMBRIDGE	O	M	R	W		O	M	R	W
Haste	31	4	141	1		5.5	0	35	0
Moffat	14	0	82	1					
Whittall	38	8	118	3		2	1	5	0
Tennent	15	3	64	0					
Deakin	5	1	15	0					
House	5	1	33	0					
Jones	16	3	49	0					
Singh					(2)	3	0	13	0
OXFORD									
Du Preez	13	2	78	2	(2)	10	3	33	0
Maclay	11	0	67	1	(1)	8	1	30	0
Wagh	2	0	12	0	(5)	13	0	37	1
Thomson	1	0	4	0		19	0	68	2
Malik					(3)	14	0	50	0
Sutcliffe						5	1	21	2
Khan						2	0	15	0
Ridley						1	0	3	0
Gupte						1	0	4	0

FALL OF WICKETS

Wkt	OU 1st	CU 1st	OU 2nd	CU 2nd
1st	107	34	–	86
2nd	140	79	–	87
3rd	230	111	–	172
4th	379	–	–	173
5th	478	–	–	198
6th	500	–	–	203
7th				
8th	–	–	–	–
9th	–	–	–	–
10th	–	–	–	–

Umpires: R.Julian and K.J.Lyons.

UNIVERSITY MATCH RESULTS

Played: 151. Wins: Cambridge 55; Oxford 48. Drawn: 48. Abandoned: 1.
This, the oldest surviving first-class fixture, dates from 1827 and, wartime interruptions apart, has been played annually since 1838. With the exception of five matches played in the area of Oxford (1829, 1843, 1846, 1848 and 1850), all the fixtures have been played at Lord's.

Year	Result	Year	Result	Year	Result	Year	Result
1827	Drawn	1873	Oxford	1911	Oxford	1959	Oxford
1829	Oxford	1874	Oxford	1912	Cambridge	1960	Drawn
1836	Oxford	1875	Oxford	1913	Cambridge	1961	Drawn
1838	Oxford	1876	Cambridge	1914	Oxford	1962	Drawn
1839	Cambridge	1877	Oxford	1919	Oxford	1963	Drawn
1840	Cambridge	1878	Cambridge	1920	Drawn	1964	Drawn
1841	Cambridge	1879	Cambridge	1921	Cambridge	1965	Drawn
1842	Cambridge	1880	Cambridge	1922	Cambridge	1966	Oxford
1843	Cambridge	1881	Oxford	1923	Oxford	1967	Drawn
1844	Drawn	1882	Cambridge	1924	Cambridge	1968	Drawn
1845	Cambridge	1883	Cambridge	1925	Drawn	1969	Drawn
1846	Oxford	1884	Oxford	1926	Cambridge	1970	Drawn
1847	Cambridge	1885	Cambridge	1927	Cambridge	1971	Drawn
1848	Oxford	1886	Oxford	1928	Drawn	1972	Cambridge
1849	Cambridge	1887	Oxford	1929	Drawn	1973	Drawn
1850	Oxford	1888	Drawn	1930	Cambridge	1974	Drawn
1851	Cambridge	1889	Cambridge	1931	Oxford	1975	Drawn
1852	Oxford	1890	Cambridge	1932	Drawn	1976	Oxford
1853	Oxford	1891	Cambridge	1933	Drawn	1977	Drawn
1854	Oxford	1892	Oxford	1934	Drawn	1978	Drawn
1855	Oxford	1893	Cambridge	1935	Cambridge	1979	Cambridge
1856	Cambridge	1894	Oxford	1936	Cambridge	1980	Drawn
1857	Oxford	1895	Cambridge	1937	Oxford	1981	Drawn
1858	Oxford	1896	Oxford	1938	Drawn	1982	Cambridge
1859	Cambridge	1897	Cambridge	1939	Oxford	1983	Drawn
1860	Cambridge	1898	Oxford	1946	Oxford	1984	Oxford
1861	Cambridge	1899	Drawn	1947	Drawn	1985	Drawn
1862	Cambridge	1900	Drawn	1948	Oxford	1986	Cambridge
1863	Oxford	1901	Drawn	1949	Cambridge	1987	Drawn
1864	Oxford	1902	Cambridge	1950	Drawn	1988	Abandoned
1865	Oxford	1903	Oxford	1951	Oxford	1989	Drawn
1866	Oxford	1904	Drawn	1952	Drawn	1990	Drawn
1867	Cambridge	1905	Cambridge	1953	Cambridge	1991	Drawn
1868	Cambridge	1906	Cambridge	1954	Drawn	1992	Cambridge
1869	Cambridge	1907	Cambridge	1955	Drawn	1993	Oxford
1870	Cambridge	1908	Oxford	1956	Drawn	1994	Drawn
1871	Oxford	1909	Drawn	1957	Cambridge	1995	Oxford
1872	Cambridge	1910	Oxford	1958	Cambridge	1996	Drawn

CAMBRIDGE UNIVERSITY

RESULTS SUMMARY

	Played	Won	Lost	Drew
All first-class matches	8	0	3	5

1996 FIRST-CLASS AVERAGES
† Blue 1996

BATTING AND FIELDING

	M	I	NO	HS	Runs	Avge	100	50	Ct/St
†W.J.House	8	15	5	136	526	52.60	2	2	2
†E.T.Smith	6	10	–	101	519	51.90	2	4	1
†A.Singh	8	15	1	157	590	42.14	2	1	2
†R.Q.Cake	8	15	3	102*	407	33.91	1	1	3
†A.R.Whittall	7	6	1	36	127	25.40	–	–	4
†N.J.Haste	6	6	2	51*	101	25.25	–	1	1
J.Ratledge	2	4	–	30	89	22.25	–	–	–
†P.J.Deakin	6	9	4	24*	100	20.00	–	–	–
†R.O.Jones	8	13	1	61	205	17.08	–	1	4
R.T.Ragnauth	6	11	1	29	121	12.10	–	–	1
†G.R.Moffat	8	8	3	27	45	9.00	–	–	4
†D.R.H.Churton	7	7	–	20	34	4.85	–	–	7/3

Also played: M.J.Birks (1 match) did not bat (1 ct); E.J.How (2 matches) 0*, 7*; A.N.Janisch (3 matches) 0, 25, 4*; †R.W.Tennent (2 matches) did not bat.

BOWLING

	O	M	R	W	Avge	Best	5wI	10wM
P.J.Deakin	71.1	9	249	9	27.66	2- 17	–	–
R.W.Tennent	38	5	136	4	34.00	2- 34	–	–
A.N.Janisch	70	12	263	4	65.75	2- 23	–	–
R.O.Jones	185.4	29	660	9	73.33	2- 45	–	–
N.J.Haste	165.5	16	673	8	84.12	3- 51	–	–
A.R.Whittall	274.3	56	932	10	93.20	3-103	–	–
G.R.Moffat	185	28	788	8	98.50	2- 50	–	–

Also bowled: W.J.House 89-8-412-2; E.J.How 27-5-161-0; A.Singh 3-0-13-0.

The following appeared in other first-class matches in 1996: R.Q.Cake and A.Singh for British Universities v Indians; A.Singh and E.T.Smith played first-class matches for Warwickshire and Kent respectively.

OXFORD UNIVERSITY

RESULTS SUMMARY

	Played	Won	Lost	Drew
All first-class matches	10	0	0	10

1996 FIRST-CLASS AVERAGES IN ALL MATCHES
† Blue 1996

BATTING AND FIELDING

	M	I	NO	HS	Runs	Avge	100	50	Ct/St
†W.S.Kendall	4	7	2	145*	444	88.80	2	2	3
†G.A.Khan	9	11	2	101*	517	57.44	1	3	3
†C.M.Gupte	10	13	1	132	606	50.50	2	3	1
†A.C.Ridley	7	9	–	155	417	46.33	2	1	1
†I.J.Sutcliffe	6	9	–	83	408	45.33	–	5	1
†R.B.Thomson	10	6	6	14*	34	–	–	–	1
†J.N.Batty	10	13	3	56	302	30.20	–	2	9/2
†H.S.Malik	10	13	3	61	240	24.00	–	1	7
M.E.D.Jarrett	7	6	2	50*	82	20.50	–	1	4
†M.A.Wagh	10	12	3	43	169	18.77	–	–	1
C.G.R.Lightfoot	4	4	1	9	15	5.00	–	–	–

Also played: J.J.Bull (2 matches) 4; †S.P.du Preez (10 matches) 1*, 9 (3 ct); †A.W.Maclay (2 matches) 1*; D.P.Mather (8 matches) 2, 0; G.J.Wright (1 match) did not bat.

BOWLING

	O	M	R	W	Avge	Best	5wI	10wM
M.A.Wagh	155.3	27	469	9	52.11	3- 82	–	–
R.B.Thomson	183.4	36	527	9	58.55	2- 24	–	–
D.P.Mather	137.4	19	536	9	59.55	3- 31	–	–
H.S.Malik	197	23	826	10	82.60	3-119	–	–
S.P.du Preez	168	24	634	5	126.80	2- 44	–	–

Also bowled: C.M.Gupte 2-0-10-0; M.E.D.Jarrett 2-0-5-0; W.S.Kendall 5-0-35-0; G.A.Khan 25-0-151-3; C.G.R.Lightfoot 27.5-5-129-2; A.W.Maclay 31-3-147-1; A.C.Ridley 5-1-19-0; I.J.Sutcliffe 12-1-47-2; G.J.Wright 9-0-33-0.

The following appeared in other first-class matches in 1996: C.M.Gupte, G.A.Khan, I.J.Sutcliffe and M.A.Wagh for British Universities v Indians; W.S.Kendall, G.A.Khan and I.J.Sutcliffe played first-class matches for Hampshire, Derbyshire and Leicestershire respectively.

CAMBRIDGE UNIVERSITY

BIRKS, Malcolm James (S Craven CS; Jesus C), b Keighley, Yorks 29 Jul 1975. 6'3½". RHB, WK. Debut 1995. HS 23* v Notts (Cambridge) 1995. Made 2 stumpings as a substitute v Yorks 1995.

CAKE, Russell Quentin (KCS, Wimbledon; St John's C), b Chertsey, Surrey 16 May 1973. 5'7". RHB. Debut 1993; blue 1993-94-95-96; captain 1996. HS 108 Comb Us v A (Oxford) 1993. CU HS 107 v Glam (Cambridge) 1994. Hockey blue. **BHC** (Br Us): HS 28 v Glam (Cambridge) 1996.

CHURTON, David Richard Harding (Wellington C; St Catharine's C); b Salisbury, Wilts 29 Mar 1975. 5'9". RHB, WK. Debut 1995; blue 1995-96. HS 39 v Warwks (Cambridge) 1995. Hockey blue.

DEAKIN, Peter James (Chorley St Michaels HS; Hughes Hall), b Liverpool, Lancs 9 Dec 1970. 5'11". RHB, OB. Debut/blue 1996. HS 24* v Middx (Cambridge) 1996. BB 2-17 v Sussex (Hove) 1996.

HASTE, Nicholas John (Wellingborough S; Pembroke C), b Northampton 13 Nov 1972. 6'0". RHB, RM. Debut 1993; blue 1993-94-95-96. HS 51* v OU (Lord's) 1996. BB 5-73 v OU (Lord's) 1995.

HOUSE, William John – *see KENT*.

HOW, Edward Joseph (Dr Challoner's GS, Amersham; Gonville & Caius C), b Amersham, Bucks 16 May 1974. 5'10". RHB, LMF. Debut/blue 1995. HS 1 v A. BB 1-24.

JANISCH, Adam Nicholas (Abingdon S; Trinity C), b Hammersmith Hospital, London 21 Oct 1975. 6'0". RHB, RM. Debut/blue 1995. HS 25 v Warwks (Cambridge) 1996. BB 3-38 v OU (Lord's) 1995.

JONES, Robin Owen (Malbank S; Millfield S; Durham U; Homerton C), b Crewe, Cheshire 4 Oct 1973. Brother of G.W. (Cambridge U 1991-94). 5'11". RHB, OB. Debut/blue 1996. Glamorgan staff 1993-94. HS 61 v Warwks (Cambridge) 1996. BB 2-45 v Hants (Cambridge) 1996. **NWT** (Wales MC): HS 23 v Sussex (Hove) 1993.

MOFFAT, Gavin Richard (RGS Lancaster; Durham U; Homerton C), b Morecambe, Lancs 9 Sep 1972. 6'2". RHB, RM. Debut/blue 1996. HS 27 and BB 2-50 v Warwks (Cambridge) 1996. Rugby for England U 21; blue 1995-96.

RAGNAUTH, Reimell Tagenath (The Perse S; Trinity Hall), b Cambridge 29 Mar 1975. 5'9". RHB. Debut/blue 1995. HS 82 v Kent (Folkestone) 1995. Hockey blue.

RATLEDGE, John (Bolton S; St John's C), b Preston, Lancs 8 Aug 1974. 5'8". RHB, RM. Debut 1994; blue 1994-95. HS 79 v Lancs (Cambridge) 1994. BB 1-16.

SINGH, Anurag – *see WARWICKSHIRE*.

SMITH, Edward Thomas – *see KENT*.

TENNENT, Robert Whitney (St Andrew's S, Bloemfontein; Natal U; St John's C), b Ficksburg, SA 30 Dec 1969. 6'0". RHB, RM. Debut/blue 1996. HS – . BB 2-34 v Sussex (Hove) 1996 taking wicket of T.A.Radford with his first ball in f-c cricket.

WHITTALL, Andrew Richard (Falcon C, Zimbabwe; Trinity C), b Umtali, Zimbabwe 28 Mar 1973. Cousin of G.J.Whittall (Zimbabwe). 6'3", RHB, OB. Debut 1993; blue 1993-94-95-96; captain 1994-95. **Tests** (Z): 3 (1996-97); HS 12 v SL (Colombo) 1996-97; BB 2-146 v P (Sheikhupura) 1996-97. **LOI** (Z): 4 (1996-97; HS 4*; BB 3-36). HS 91* v OU (Lord's) 1994. BB 6-46 (11-113 match) v Essex (Cambridge) 1995. **BHC** (Comb Us): HS 21 and BB 2-49 v Glos (Bristol) 1995.

OXFORD UNIVERSITY

BATTY, Jonathan Neil – *see SURREY.*

BULL, James Jonathan (Oakham S; Keble C), b Leicester 22 Dec 1976. 5'9". RHB, OB. Debut 1996. HS 4.

DU PREEZ, Stanley Pierre (Queens C; Diocesan C; Stellenbosch U; Keble C), b Port Elizabeth, SA 1 Jan 1969. 6'2". RHB, LMF. Debut/blue 1996. HS 9. BB 2-44 v Middx (Oxford) 1996. Rugby blue 1995.

GUPTE, Chinmay Madhukar (John Lyon S, Harrow; Pembroke C), b Poona, India 5 Jul 1972. Son of M.S. (Maharashtra). 5'7". RHB, SLA. Debut 1991; blue 1991-93-94-95-96; captain 1996. HS 132 v Worcs (Oxford) 1996. BB 2-41 v Notts (Oxford) 1991. **BHC** (Br Us): HS 54* v Essex (Chelmsford) 1996.

JARRETT, Michael Eugene Dominic (Harrow S; Girton C, Cambridge; St John's C, Oxford), b St Thomas' Hospital, London 18 Sep 1972. 5'9". RHB, RM. Cambridge U 1992-93; blue 1992-93. Oxford U debut 1995. HS 51 CU v Leics (Cambridge) 1993. OU HS 40 v Derbys (Oxford) 1995.

KENDALL, William Salwey – *see HAMPSHIRE.*

KHAN, Gul Abbass – *see DERBYSHIRE.*

LIGHTFOOT, Charles Gordon Rufus (Eton C; Keble C), b Amersham, Bucks 25 Feb 1976. 5'10". LHB, SLA. Debut 1996. HS 9. BB 2-65 v Glam (Oxford) 1996.

MACLAY, Alasdair Worsfold (Horris Hill S; Winchester C; St Edmund Hall), b Salisbury, Wilts 15 Oct 1973. 6'3". RHB, RMF. Debut 1993; blue 1994-96. HS 6*. BB 3-30 v CU (Lord's) 1994.

MALIK, Hasnain Siddiq (KCS, Wimbledon; Keble C), b Sargodha, Pakistan 21 Apr 1973. 5'11". LHB, OB. Debut 1992; blue 1994-95-96. HS 64* v Hants (Oxford) 1993. BB 3-10 v Hants (Oxford) 1994.

MATHER, David Peter (Wirral GS; St Hugh's C), b Bebington, Cheshire 20 Nov 1975. 5'11". LHB, LM. Debut/blue 1995. HS 8*. BB 4-65 v Durham (Oxford) 1995.

RIDLEY, Andrew Claude (St Aloysius C, Sydney; Sydney U; Exeter C), b Sydney, Australia 2 Aug 1968. 5'11". LHB, RM. Debut 1994; blue 1995-96. HS 155 v CU (Lord's) 1996. **BHC** (Br Us): HS 58 v Glam (Cambridge) 1996.

SUTCLIFFE, Iain John – *see LEICESTERSHIRE.*

THOMSON, Russell Bernard (St Stithians C; Cape Town U; Keble C), b Johannesburg, SA 16 Aug 1969. 6'3". RHB, RM. Debut/blue 1996. HS 14* and BB 2-24 v Worcs (Oxford) 1996.

WAGH, Mark Anant – *see WARWICKSHIRE.*

WRIGHT, Gavin James (Holmfirth HS; Greenhead C, Huddersfield; Balliol C), b Holmfirth, Yorks 15 Dec 1973. 6'3". RHB, RM. Debut 1996. HS – .

BRITISH UNIVERSITIES

The following represented British Universities v Indians at Cambridge and do not appear in the County or University registers:

BAHL, Jitin (Lampton S, Hounslow; Brighton U), b Hammersmith, London 16 Oct 1975. 5'9". RHB, WK. Debut (v Indians at Cambridge) 1996. MCC YC 1996. HS 0*. **BHC:** HS 1*.

MARC, Kervin (The London Oratory S; Central St Martin C of Art & Design), b Mon Repos, St Lucia 9 Jan 1975. 6'5". RHB, RFM. Middlesex 1994-95. MCC YC 1993. HS 9 M v Lancs (Manchester) 1994. BB 3-91 v I (Cambridge) 1996. **BHC:** HS 13 v Essex (Chelmsford) 1996. BB 2-30 v Middx (Cambridge) 1996.

FIRST-CLASS UMPIRES 1997

BALDERSTONE, John **Christopher** (Paddock Council S, Huddersfield), b Longwood, Huddersfield, Yorks 16 Nov 1940. RHB, SLA. Yorkshire 1961-69. Leicestershire 1971-86 (cap 1973; testimonial 1984). **Tests:** 2 (1976); HS 35 v WI (Leeds) 1976; BB 1-80. Tour: Z 1980-81 (Le). 1000 runs (11); most – 1482 (1982). HS 181* Le v Glos (Leicester) 1984. BB 6-25 Le v Hants (Southampton) 1978. Hat-trick 1976 (Le). F-c career: 390 matches; 19034 runs @ 34.11, 32 hundreds; 310 wickets @ 26.32; 210 ct. Soccer for Huddersfield Town, Carlisle United, Doncaster Rovers and Queen of the South. Appointed 1988. Umpired 1 LOI (1994).

BIRD, Harold Dennis (*'Dickie'*) (Raley SM, Barnsley), b Barnsley, Yorks 19 Apr 1933. RHB, RM. Yorkshire 1956-59. Leicestershire 1960-64 (cap 1960). MBE 1986. 1000 runs (1): 1028 (1960). HS 181* Y v Glam (Bradford) 1959. F-c career: 93 matches; 3314 runs @ 20.71, 2 hundreds. Appointed 1970. Umpired 66 Tests (world record – 1973 to 1996) and 68 LOI (1973 to 1995), including 1975, 1979, 1983 and 1987-88 World Cups (first 3 finals), 1985-86 Asia Cup and 7 Sharjah tournaments. International Panel 1994 to 1995-96.

BOND, John David (Bolton S), b Kearsley, Lancs 6 May 1932. RHB, LB. Lancashire 1955-72 (cap 1955; captain 1968-72; coach 1973; manager 1980-86; benefit 1970). Nottinghamshire 1974 (captain/coach 1974). 1000 runs (2); most – 2125 (1962). HS 157 La v Hants (Manchester) 1962. Test selector 1974. F-c career: 362 matches; 12125 runs @ 25.90, 14 hundreds; 222 ct. Appointed 1988.

BURGESS, Graham Iefvion (Millfield S), b Glastonbury, Somerset 5 May 1943. RHB, RM. Somerset 1966-79 (cap 1968; testimonial 1977). HS 129 v Glos (Taunton) 1973. BB 7-43 (13-75 match) v OU (Oxford) 1975. F-c career: 252 matches; 7129 runs @ 18.90, 2 hundreds; 474 wickets @ 28.57. Appointed 1991.

CLARKSON, Anthony (Harrogate GS), b Killinghall, Harrogate, Yorks 5 Sep 1939. RHB, OB. Yorkshire 1963. Somerset 1966-71 (cap 1968). Devon. 1000 runs (2); most – 1246 (1970). HS 131 Sm v Northants (Northampton) 1969. BB 3-51 Sm v Essex (Yeovil) 1967. F-c career: 110 matches; 4458 runs @ 25.18, 2 hundreds; 13 wickets @ 28.23. Appointed 1996.

CONSTANT, David John, b Bradford-on-Avon, Wilts 9 Nov 1941. LHB, SLA. Kent 1961-63. Leicestershire 1965-68. HS 80 Le v Glos (Bristol) 1966. F-c career: 61 matches; 1517 runs @ 19.20; 1 wicket @ 36.00. Appointed 1969. Umpired 36 Tests (1971 to 1988) and 30 LOI (1972 to 1996). Represented Gloucestershire at bowls 1984-86.

DUDLESTON, Barry (Stockport S), b Bebington, Cheshire 16 Jul 1945. RHB, SLA. Leicestershire 1966-80 (cap 1969; benefit 1980). Gloucestershire 1981-83. Rhodesia 1976-80. 1000 runs (8); most – 1374 (1970). HS 202 Le v Derbys (Leicester) 1979. BB 4-6 Le v Surrey (Leicester) 1972. F-c career: 295 matches; 14747 runs @ 32.48, 32 hundreds; 47 wickets @ 29.04. Appointed 1984. Umpired 2 Tests (1991 to 1992) and 1 LOI (1992).

HAMPSHIRE, John Harry (Oakwood THS, Rotherham), b Thurnscoe, Yorks 10 Feb 1941. RHB, LB. Son of J. (Yorks 1937); brother of A.W. (Yorks 1975). Yorkshire 1961-81 (cap 1963; benefit 1976; captain 1979-80). Derbyshire 1982-84 (cap 1982). Tasmania 1967-69, 1977-79. **Tests:** 8 (1969 to 1975); 403 runs @ 26.86, HS 107 v WI (Lord's) 1969 on debut (only England player to score hundred at Lord's on Test debut). Tours: A 1970-71; SA 1972-73 (DHR), 1974-75 (DHR); WI 1964-65 (Cav); NZ 1970-71; P 1967-68 (Cwlth XI); SL 1969-70; Z 1980-81 (Le XI). 1000 runs (15); most – 1596 (1978). HS 183* Y v Sussex (Hove) 1971. BB 7-52 Y v Glam (Cardiff) 1963. F-c career: 577 matches; 28059 runs @ 34.55, 43 hundreds; 30 wickets @ 54.56; 445 ct. Appointed 1985. Umpired 11 Tests (1989 to 1993) and 6 LOI (1989 to 1995).

HARRIS, John Henry, b Taunton, Somerset 13 Feb 1936. LHB, RFM. Somerset 1952-59. Suffolk 1960-62. Devon 1965. HS 41 v Worcs (Taunton) 1957. BB 3-29 v Worcs (Bristol) 1959. F-c career: 15 matches; 154 runs @ 11.00; 19 wickets @ 32.57. Appointed 1983.

HOLDER, John Wakefield (Combermere S, Barbados), b St George, Barbados 19 Mar 1945. RHB, RFM. Hampshire 1968-72. Hat-trick 1972. HS 33 v Sussex (Hove) 1971. BB 7-79 v Glos (Gloucester) 1972. F-c career: 47 matches; 374 runs @ 10.68; 139 wickets @ 24.56. Appointed 1983. Umpired 10 Tests (1988 to 1991) and 14 LOI (1988 to 1996) including 1989-90 Nehru Cup and one Sharjah tournament.

HOLDER, Vanburn Alonza (Richmond SM, Barbados), b Bridgetown, Barbados 8 Oct 1945. RHB, RFM. Barbados 1966-78. Worcestershire 1968-80 (cap 1970; benefit 1979). Shropshire 1981. **Tests** (WI): 40 (1969 to 1978-79); 682 runs @ 14.20, HS 42 v NZ (P-o-S) 1971-72; 109 wkts @ 33.27, BB 6-28 v A (P-o-S) 1977-78. **LOI** (WI): 12. Tours (WI): E 1969, 1973, 1976; A 1975-76; I 1974-75, 1978-79; P 1973-74 (RW), 1974-75; SL 1974-75, 1978-79. HS 122 Barbados v Trinidad (Bridgetown) 1973-74. BB 7-40 Wo v Glam (Cardiff) 1974. F-c career: 311 matches; 3559 runs @ 13.03, 1 hundred; 947 wickets @ 24.48. Appointed 1992.

JESTY, Trevor Edward (Privet County SS, Gosport), b Gosport, Hants 2 Jun 1948. RHB, RM. Hampshire 1966-84 (cap 1971; benefit 1982). Surrey 1985-87 (cap 1985; captain 1985). Lancashire 1988-91 (cap 1989). Border 1973-74. GW 1974-76, 1980-81. Canterbury 1979-80. *Wisden* 1983. **LOI**: 10. Tours: WI 1982-83 (Int); Z 1988-89 (La). 1000 runs (10); most – 1645 (1982). HS 248 H v CU (Cambridge) 1984. Scored 122* La v OU (Oxford) 1991 in his final f-c innings. 50 wkts (2); most – 52 (1981). BB 7-75 H v Worcs (Southampton) 1976. F-c career: 490 matches; 21916 runs @ 32.71, 35 hundreds; 585 wickets @ 27.47. Appointed 1994.

JONES, Allan Arthur (St John's C, Horsham), b Horley, Surrey 9 Dec 1947. RHB, RFM. Sussex 1966-69. Somerset 1970-75 (cap 1972). Northern Transvaal 1972-73. Middlesex 1976-79 (cap 1976). Orange Free State 1976-77. Glamorgan 1980-81. HS 33 M v Kent (Canterbury) 1978. BB 9-51 Sm v Sussex (Hove) 1972. F-c career: 214 matches; 799 runs @ 5.39; 549 wickets @ 28.07. Appointed 1985. Umpired 1 LOI (1996).

JULIAN, Raymond (Wigston SM), b Cosby, Leics 23 Aug 1936. RHB, WK. Leicestershire 1953-71 (cap 1961). HS 51 v Worcs (Worcester) 1962. F-c career: 192 matches; 2581 runs @ 9.73; 421 dismissals (382 ct, 39 st). Appointed 1972. Umpired 1 LOI (1996).

KITCHEN, Mervyn John (Backwell SM, Nailsea), b Nailsea, Somerset 1 Aug 1940. LHB, RM. Somerset 1960-79 (cap 1966; testimonial 1973). Tour: Rhodesia 1972-73 (Int W). 1000 runs (7); most – 1730 (1968). HS 189 v Pakistanis (Taunton) 1967. BB 1-4. F-c career: 354 matches; 15230 runs @ 26.25, 17 hundreds; 2 wickets @ 54.50. Appointed 1982. Umpired 12 Tests (1990 to 1996) and 19 LOI (1983 to 1996), including one Sharjah tournament. **Appointed to International Panel 1995.**

LEADBEATER, Barrie (Harehills SS), b Harehills, Leeds, Yorks 14 Aug 1943. RHB, RM. Yorkshire 1966-79 (cap 1969; joint benefit with G.A.Cope 1980). Tour: WI 1969-70 (DN). HS 140* v Hants (Portsmouth) 1976. F-c career: 147 matches; 5373 runs @ 25.34, 1 hundred; 1 wicket @ 5.00. Appointed 1981. Umpired 4 LOI (1983).

MEYER, Barrie John (Boscombe SS), b Bournemouth, Hants 21 Aug 1932. RHB, WK. Gloucestershire 1957-71 (cap 1958; benefit 1971). HS 63 v Indians (Cheltenham) 1959, v OU (Bristol) 1962, and v Sussex (Bristol) 1964. F-c career: 406 matches; 5367 runs @ 14.16; 826 dismissals (707 ct, 119 st). Soccer for Bristol Rovers, Plymouth Argyle, Newport County and Bristol City. Appointed 1973. Umpired 26 Tests (1978 to 1993) and 23 LOI (1977 to 1993), including 1979 and 1983 World Cup finals.

PALMER, Kenneth Ernest (Southbroom SM, Devizes), b Winchester, Hants 22 Apr 1937. RHB, RFM. Brother of R. (below) and father of G.V. (Somerset 1982-88). Somerset 1955-69 (cap 1958; testimonial 1968). Tours: WI 1963-64 (Cav); P 1963-64 (Cwlth XI). **Tests**: 1 (1964-65; while coaching in South Africa); 10 runs; 1 wicket. 1000 runs (1): 1036 (1961). 100 wickets (4); most – 139 (1961). HS 125* v Northants (Northampton) 1961. BB 9-57 v Notts (Nottingham) 1963. F-c career: 314 matches; 7761 runs @ 20.64, 2 hundreds; 866 wickets @ 21.34. Appointed 1972. Umpired 22 Tests (1978 to 1994) and 19 LOI (1977 to 1994). International Panel 1994.

PALMER, Roy (Southbroom SM, Devizes), b Devizes, Wilts 12 Jul 1942. RHB, RFM. Brother of K.E. (above). Somerset 1965-70. HS 84 v Leics (Taunton) 1967. BB 6-45 v

115

Middx (Lord's) 1967. F-c career: 74 matches; 1037 runs @ 13.29; 172 wickets @ 31.62. Appointed 1980. Umpired 2 Tests (1992 to 1993) and 8 LOI (1983 to 1995).

PLEWS, Nigel Trevor (Mundella GS, Nottingham), b Nottingham 5 Sep 1934. Former policeman (Fraud Squad). No first-class appearances. Appointed 1982. Umpired 11 Tests (1988 to 1995-96) and 16 LOI (1986 to 1996), including 2 Sharjah tournaments. International Panel 1994 to 1995-96.

SHARP, George (Elwick Road SS, Hartlepool), b West Hartlepool, Co Durham 12 Mar 1950. RHB, WK, occ LM. Northamptonshire 1968-85 (cap 1973; benefit 1982). HS 98 v Yorks (Northampton) 1983. BB 1-47. F-c career: 306 matches; 6254 runs @ 19.85; 1 wicket @ 70.00; 655 dismissals (565 ct, 90 st). Appointed 1992. Umpired 2 Tests (1996 to 1996-97) and 9 LOI (1995-96 to 1996-97), including tournaments in Sharjah (1) and Singapore (1). **Appointed to International Panel 1996.**

SHEPHERD, David Robert (Barnstaple GS; St Luke's C, Exeter), b Bideford, Devon 27 Dec 1940. RHB, RM. Gloucestershire 1965-79 (cap 1969; joint benefit with J.Davey 1978). Scored 108 on debut (v OU). Devon 1959-64. 1000 runs (2); most – 1079 (1970). HS 153 v Middx (Bristol) 1968. F-c career: 282 matches; 10672 runs @ 24.47, 12 hundreds; 2 wickets @ 53.00. Appointed 1981. Umpired 33 Tests (1985 to 1996-97) and 68 LOI (1983 to 1996), including 1987-88, 1991-92 and 1995-96 World Cups (1 final), 1985-86 Asia Cup and tournaments in Sharjah (5) and Canada (1). **Appointed to International Panel 1994.**

STEELE, John Frederick (Endon SS), b Brown Edge, Staffs 23 Jul 1946. RHB, SLA. Brother of D.S. (Northants, Derbys and England 1963-84). Leicestershire 1970-83 (cap 1971; benefit 1983). Natal 1973-74 to 1977-78. Glamorgan 1984-86 (cap 1984). Staffordshire 1965-69. Tour: SA 1974-75 (DHR). 1000 runs (6); most – 1347 (1972). HS 195 Le v Derbys (Leicester) 1971. BB 7-29 Natal B v GW (Umzinto) 1973-74, and Le v Glos (Leicester) 1980. F-c career: 379 matches; 15054 runs @ 28.95, 21 hundreds; 584 wickets @ 27.04; 413 ct. Appointed 1997.

WHITE, Robert Arthur (Chiswick GS), b Fulham, London 6 Oct 1936. LHB, OB. Middlesex 1958-65 (cap 1963). Nottinghamshire 1966-80 (cap 1966; benefit 1974). 1000 runs (1): 1355 (1963). HS 116* Nt v Surrey (Oval) 1963. BB 7-41 Nt v Derbys (Ilkeston) 1971. F-c career: 413 matches; 12452 runs @ 23.18, 5 hundreds; 693 wickets @ 30.50. Appointed 1983.

WHITEHEAD, Alan Geoffrey Thomas, b Butleigh, Somerset 28 Oct 1940. LHB, SLA. Somerset 1957-61. HS 15 v Hants (Southampton) 1959 and v Leics (Leicester) 1960. BB 6-74 v Sussex (Eastbourne) 1959. F-c career: 38 matches; 137 runs @ 5.70; 67 wickets @ 34.41. Appointed 1970. Umpired 5 Tests (1982 to 1987) and 13 LOI (1979 to 1996).

WILLEY, Peter (Seaham SS), b Sedgefield, Co Durham 6 Dec 1949. RHB, OB. Northamptonshire 1966-83 (cap 1971; benefit 1981). Leicestershire 1984-91 (cap 1984; captain 1987). E Province 1982-85. Northumberland 1992. **Tests:** 26 (1976 to 1986); 1184 runs @ 26.90, HS 102* v WI (St John's) 1980-81; 7 wkts @ 65.14, BB 2-73 v WI (Lord's) 1980-81. **LOI:** 26. Tours: A 1979-80; SA 1972-73 (DHR), 1981-82 (SAB); WI 1980-81, 1985-86; I 1979-80; SL 1977-78 (DHR). 1000 runs (10); most – 1783 (1982). HS 227 Nh v Somerset (Northampton) 1976. 50 wkts (3); most – 52 (1979). BB 7-37 Nh v OU (Oxford) 1975. F-c career: 559 matches; 24361 runs @ 30.56, 44 hundreds; 756 wickets @ 30.95. Appointed 1993. Umpired 5 Tests (1995-96 to 1996-97) and 2 LOI (1996). **Appointed to International Panel 1996.**

RESERVE FIRST-CLASS LIST: P.Adams, N.G.Cowley, M.J.Harris, J.W.Lloyds, K.J.Lyons, M.K.Reed.

INTERNATIONAL PANEL: M.J.Kitchen, G.Sharp, D.R.Shepherd, P.Willey (England); D.B.Hair, S.G.Randell (Australia); V.K.Ramaswamy, S.Venkataraghavan (India); D.B.Cowie, R.S.Dunne (New Zealand); Khizer Hayat, Mahboob Shah (Pakistan); C.J.Mitchley, D.L.Orchard (South Africa); B.C.Cooray, K.T.Francis (Sri Lanka); S.A.Bucknor, L.H.Barker (West Indies); I.D.Robinson, R.B.Tiffin (Zimbabwe).

TEXACO TROPHY PANEL: J.H.Hampshire, R.Julian, M.J.Kitchen, G.Sharp, D.R.Shepherd, P.Willey.

Test Match and LOI statistics to 27 February 1997. See page 15 for key to abbreviations.

THE 1996 FIRST-CLASS SEASON
STATISTICAL HIGHLIGHTS

HIGHEST INNINGS TOTALS († *Second innings*)

686	Lancashire v Essex	Chelmsford
681-7d*	Leicestershire v Yorkshire	Bradford
645-7d	Warwickshire v Sussex	Hove
638-8d	Leicestershire v Worcestershire	Leicester
616-7d	Kent v Somerset	Canterbury
601-9d	Northamptonshire v Nottinghamshire	Nottingham
597	Lancashire v Warwickshire	Birmingham
590	Kent v Essex	Ilford
587-9d	Lancashire v Derbyshire	Manchester
569	Gloucestershire v Warwickshire	Cheltenham
564	England v India (3rd Test)	Nottingham
561	Yorkshire v Derbyshire	Sheffield
558	Somerset v Surrey	Taunton
552-8d	Sussex v Durham	Hove
541	Somerset v Hampshire	Taunton
539	Hampshire v Essex	Southampton
536-8d	Yorkshire v Glamorgan	Cardiff
536	Leicestershire v Glamorgan	Swansea
532-8d	Essex v Gloucestershire	Colchester
531-4†	Northamptonshire v Yorkshire	Northampton
529-8d	Yorkshire v Lancashire	Leeds
524	Derbyshire v Somerset	Taunton
521-8d	Pakistan v England (3rd Test)	The Oval
521	India v England (3rd Test)	Nottingham
516-6d	Leicestershire v Durham	Chester-le-Street
513-4d	Hampshire v Nottinghamshire	Southampton
513-6d	Oxford University v Cambridge University	Lord's
512	Leicestershire v Middlesex	Leicester
509-3d	Glamorgan v Gloucestershire	Bristol
509-7d	South Africa A v Somerset	Taunton
509	Essex v Lancashire	Chelmsford
508	Yorkshire v Warwickshire	Leeds
505	Glamorgan v Lancashire	Cardiff
501	England v Pakistan (2nd Test)	Leeds

* *Highest total conceded by Yorkshire.*

HIGHEST FOURTH INNINGS TOTALS

449-9	Worcestershire (set 445) v Somerset	Bath

LOWEST INNINGS TOTALS († *One batsman retired hurt*)

67	Durham v Middlesex	Lord's
71	Gloucestershire v Leicestershire	Cheltenham
77	Worcestershire v South Africa A	Worcester
83	Somerset v Leicester	Leicester
85	Middlesex v Sussex	Horsham
89	Derbyshire v Leicestershire	Derby
97	Nottinghamshire v Essex	Chelmsford
98†	Nottinghamshire v Derbyshire	Derby
98	Derbyshire v Northamptonshire	Northampton

MATCH AGGREGATES OF 1500 RUNS
Runs-Wkts

1606-34	Somerset v Derbyshire	Taunton
1537-32	Surrey v Derbyshire	The Oval
1523-28	Lancashire v Derbyshire	Manchester
1523-36	Hampshire v Essex	Southampton
1512-27	Worcestershire v Northamptonshire	Kidderminster

FOUR HUNDREDS IN AN INNINGS
Glamorgan (509-3d) v Gloucestershire   Bristol
S.P.James 118, H.Morris 108, M.P.Maynard 145*, P.A.Cottey 101*

ELEVEN BOWLERS IN AN INNINGS
Kent v Yorkshire (223-4)   Canterbury

FIRST TO INDIVIDUAL TARGETS

1000 RUNS	M.G.Bevan	Yorkshire	June 24
2000 RUNS	No instance – most: 1944 runs G.A.Gooch (Essex)		
100 WICKETS	No instance – most: 85 wickets C.A.Walsh (Gloucestershire)		

DOUBLE HUNDREDS (24)

C.J.Adams	239	Derbyshire v Hampshire	Southampton
K.J.Barnett	200*	Derbyshire v Leicestershire	Derby
P.D.Bowler	207	Somerset v Surrey	Taunton
P.A.Cottey	203	Glamorgan v Leicestershire	Swansea
N.H.Fairbrother	204	Lancashire v Warwickshire	Birmingham
J.E.R.Gallian	312†	Lancashire v Derbyshire	Manchester
G.A.Gooch	201	Essex v Somerset	Taunton
A.Habib	215	Leicestershire v Worcestershire	Leicester
G.A.Hick	215	Worcestershire v Indians	Worcester
S.P.James	235	Glamorgan v Nottinghamshire	Worksop
D.M.Jones	214*	Derbyshire v Yorkshire	Sheffield
G.D.Lloyd	241	Lancashire v Essex	Chelmsford
M.B.Loye	205	Northamptonshire v Yorkshire	Northampton
M.P.Maynard	214	Glamorgan v Lancashire	Cardiff
T.M.Moody	212	Worcestershire v Nottinghamshire	Worcester
H.Morris	202*	Glamorgan v Yorkshire	Cardiff
M.D.Moxon	213	Yorkshire v Glamorgan	Cardiff
Saeed Anwar	219*	Pakistanis v Glamorgan	Pontypridd
D.J.G.Sales	210*	Northamptonshire v Worcestershire	Kidderminster
M.J.Walker	275*	Kent v Somerset	Canterbury
R.J.Warren	201*	Northamptonshire v Glamorgan	Northampton
V.J.Wells (2)	200	Leicestershire v Yorkshire	Bradford
	204	Leicestershire v Northamptonshire	Leicester
J.J.Whitaker	218	Leicestershire v Yorkshire	Bradford

     † *Record score at Old Trafford.*

HUNDRED IN EACH INNINGS OF A MATCH

C.J.Adams	125	136*	Derbyshire v Middlesex	Derby
A.J.Hollioake	128	117*	Surrey v Somerset	Taunton
T.M.Moody	106	169	Worcestershire v Northamptonshire	Kidderminster
P.N.Weekes	171*	160	Middlesex v Somerset	Uxbridge

FASTEST HUNDRED (SIR WALTER LAWRENCE TROPHY)

G.D.Lloyd	70 balls	Lancashire v Essex	Chelmsford

HUNDRED BEFORE LUNCH

Day

G.A.Gooch	62*-170*	2	Essex v Glamorgan	Chelmsford
W.J.House	0-117*	2	Cambridge University v Derbyshire	Cambridge
N.V.Knight	0-115*	1	Warwickshire v Sussex	Hove
S.G.Law (2)	0-104*	2	Essex v Indians	Chelmsford
	27*-161*	3	Essex v Durham	Hartlepool
G.D.Lloyd	42*-142	3	Lancashire v Glamorgan	Cardiff
M.P.Maynard	19*-128*	3	Glamorgan v Yorkshire	Cardiff
Saeed Anwar	0-111*	1	Pakistanis v Warwickshire	Birmingham
P.V.Simmons	28*-133*	2	Leicestershire v Durham	Chester-le-Street

HUNDRED ON FIRST-CLASS DEBUT

S.D.Peters	110	Essex v Cambridge University	Cambridge
D.J.G.Sales	210*†	Northamptonshire v Worcestershire	Kidderminster
E.T.Smith	101	Cambridge University v Glamorgan	Cambridge

† Record Championship score on first-class debut; youngest (18yr 237d) to score 200 in a Championship match.

HUNDRED ON FIRST-CLASS DEBUT IN BRITAIN

A.Jadeja	105*	Indians v Worcestershire	Worcester
V.Rathore	165	Indians v Worcestershire	Worcester
Saeed Anwar	219*	Pakistanis v Glamorgan	Pontypridd

CARRYING BAT THROUGH COMPLETED INNINGS

D.J.Bicknell	129*	Surrey (299) v Worcestershire	The Oval
A.S.Rollins	78*	Derbyshire (220) v Sussex	Hove
W.P.C.Weston	100*	Worcestershire (238) v Derbyshire	Chesterfield

AN HOUR BEFORE SCORING FIRST RUN

Min
64	G.J.Kersey (59*)	Surrey v Leicestershire	The Oval

AN HOUR WITHOUT ADDING TO SCORE

Min
70	A.R.K.Pierson (16)	Leicestershire v Gloucestershire	Cheltenham

NOTABLE PARTNERSHIPS († County record)

First Wicket

372†	R.R.Montgomerie/M.B.Loye	Northamptonshire v Yorkshire	Northampton
362	M.D.Moxon/M.P.Vaughan	Yorkshire v Glamorgan	Cardiff
334*†S.Hutton/M.A.Roseberry		Durham v Oxford University	Oxford
255*	R.R.Montgomerie/A.Fordham	Northamptonshire v Pakistanis	Northampton
255	W.P.C.Weston/M.J.Church	Worcestershire v Oxford University	Oxford

Second Wicket

300†	W.P.C.Weston/G.A.Hick	Worcestershire v Indians	Worcester
298	A.S.Rollins/C.J.Adams	Derbyshire v Hampshire	Southampton

Third Wicket

362*	Saeed Anwar/Inzamam-ul-Haq	Pakistanis v Glamorgan	Pontypridd
269	T.S.Curtis/T.M.Moody	Worcestershire v Northamptonshire	Kidderminster
255	S.C.Ganguly/S.R.Tendulkar	India v England (3rd Test)	Nottingham

Fourth Wicket

358†	S.P.Titchard/G.D.Lloyd	Lancashire v Essex	Chelmsford
278	D.M.Jones/J.E.Owen	Derbyshire v Yorkshire	Sheffield
272	D.Byas/A.McGrath	Yorkshire v Hampshire	Harrogate
251*	M.P.Maynard/P.A.Cottey	Glamorgan v Gloucestershire	Bristol

| 251 | N.J.Speak/G.D.Lloyd | Lancashire v Glamorgan | Cardiff |

Fifth Wicket

320†	J.J.Whitaker/A.Habib	Leicestershire v Worcestershire	Leicester
239	R.J.Warren/D.J.Capel	Northamptonshire v Glamorgan	Northampton
226	K.M.Curran/A.L.Penberthy	Northamptonshire v Leicestershire	Leicester

Sixth Wicket

| 284† | P.V.Simmons/P.A.Nixon | Leicestershire v Durham | Chester-le-Street |
| 252 | C.White/R.J.Blakey | Yorkshire v Lancashire | Leeds |

Seventh Wicket

| 278*†S.Lee/R.J.Turner | | Somerset v Worcestershire | Bath |
| 211† | P.A.Cottey/O.D.Gibson | Glamorgan v Leicestershire | Swansea |

Eighth Wicket

| 198† | K.M.Krikken/D.G.Cork | Derbyshire v Lancashire | Manchester |
| 172† | P.A.Nixon/D.J.Millns | Leicestershire v Lancashire | Manchester |

Ninth Wicket

| 127† | D.G.C.Ligertwood/S.J.E.Brown | Durham v Surrey | Stockton |

Tenth Wicket

141†	A.F.Giles/T.A.Munton	Warwickshire v Worcestershire	Worcester
113	P.J.Hartley/R.D.Stemp	Yorkshire v Middlesex	Lord's
112	P.V.Simmons/A.D.Mullally	Leicestershire v Middlesex	Leicester
110	C.E.W.Silverwood/R.D.Stemp	Yorkshire v Durham	Chester-le-Street
105	A.R.K.Pierson/A.D.Mullally	Leicestershire v Surrey	The Oval
103†	M.M.Betts/D.M.Cox	Durham v Sussex	Hove
101*	J.D.Carr/P.C.R.Tufnell	Middlesex v Worcestershire	Lord's

EIGHT OR MORE WICKETS IN AN INNINGS (9)

C.A.Connor	9- 38	Hampshire v Gloucestershire	Southampton
M.A.Ealham	8- 36	Kent v Warwickshire	Birmingham
D.Follett	8- 22	Middlesex v Durham	Lord's
G.M.Gilder	8- 22	South Africa A v Worcestershire	Worcester
D.W.Headley	8- 98	Kent v Derbyshire	Derby
I.D.K.Salisbury	8- 75	Sussex v Essex	Chelmsford
A.M.Smith	8- 73	Gloucestershire v Middlesex	Lord's
P.M.Such	8-118	Essex v Yorkshire	Leeds
P.N.Weekes	8- 39	Middlesex v Glamorgan	Lord's

TEN OR MORE WICKETS IN A MATCH (29)

C.E.L.Ambrose		11- 70	Northamptonshire v Derbyshire	Northampton
D.R.Brown		11-120	Warwickshire v Kent	Birmingham
A.R.Caddick	(3)	10-161	Somerset v Warwickshire	Taunton
		11-234	Somerset v Worcestershire	Bath
		10-180	Somerset v Sussex	Hove
D.M.Cox		10-236	Durham v Warwickshire	Birmingham
M.A.Ealham		10- 74	Kent v Warwickshire	Birmingham
D.Follett		10- 87	Middlesex v Durham	Lord's
A.R.C.Fraser		10-134	Middlesex v Hampshire	Portsmouth
G.M.Gilder		10- 65	South Africa A v Worcestershire	Worcester
A.J.Harris		12- 83	Derbyshire v Middlesex	Derby
P.J.Hartley		10-153	Yorkshire v Sussex	Eastbourne
D.W.Headley		11-165	Kent v Derbyshire	Derby
J.D.Lewry		11-147	Sussex v Leicestershire	Leicester
D.E.Malcolm	(2)	11-205	Derbyshire v Kent	Derby
		10-215	Derbyshire v Sussex	Hove
D.J.Millns		10-128	Leicestershire v Essex	Leicester
T.M.Moody		13-159	Worcestershire v Gloucestershire	Worcester
A.D.Mullally		11-130	Leicestershire v Derbyshire	Derby
Mushtaq Ahmed		10-108	Pakistanis v Somerset	Taunton

M.M.Patel	10-225	Kent v Essex	Ilford
G.D.Rose	13- 88	Somerset v Nottinghamshire	Taunton
I.D.K.Salisbury	11-169	Sussex v Essex	Chelmsford
A.M.Smith	10-118	Gloucestershire v Middlesex	Lord's
V.S.Solanki	10-256	Worcestershire v Lancashire	Manchester
P.M.Such	12-135	Essex v Somerset	Taunton
J.P.Taylor	11-104	Northamptonshire v Middlesex	Northampton
P.C.R.Tufnell	13-123	Middlesex v Lancashire	Manchester
C.A.Walsh	11-117	Gloucestershire v Warwickshire	Cheltenham

FOUR WICKETS WITH CONSECUTIVE BALLS

| K.D.James | Hampshire v Indians | Southampton |

HAT-TRICKS

A.P.Cowan	Essex v Gloucestershire	Colchester
D.W.Headley	Kent v Derbyshire	Derby
D.W.Headley	Kent v Worcestershire	Canterbury
D.W.Headley	Kent v Hampshire	Canterbury
K.D.James	Hampshire v Indians	Southampton
M.J.McCague	Kent v Hampshire	Canterbury

WICKET WITH FIRST BALL IN FIRST-CLASS CRICKET

P.D.Collingwood	Durham v Northamptonshire	Chester-le-Street
J.P.Hewitt	Middlesex v Gloucestershire	Lord's
R.W.Tennent	Cambridge University v Sussex	Hove

60 OVERS IN AN INNINGS

| A.F.Giles | 68.3-18-174-2 | Warwickshire v Yorkshire | Leeds |

100 AND FOUR WICKETS WITH CONSECUTIVE BALLS *(Unique instance)*

| K.D.James | 103, 5-74 | Hampshire v Indians | Southampton |

MATCH DOUBLE (100 RUNS AND 10 WICKETS)

| D.J.Millns | 103; 4-74, 6-54 | Leicestershire v Essex | Leicester |

SIX OR MORE WICKET-KEEPING DISMISSALS IN AN INNINGS

C.W.Scott	7 ct	Durham v Yorkshire	Chester-le-Street
W.K.Hegg	6 ct	Lancashire v Durham	Chester-le-Street
G.J.Kersey	6 ct	Surrey v Durham	Stockton
D.G.C.Ligertwood	5 ct, 1 st	Durham v Kent	Maidstone
L.N.P.Walker	4 ct, 2 st	Nottinghamshire v Gloucestershire	Nottingham

NINE OR MORE WICKET-KEEPING DISMISSALS IN A MATCH

C.W.Scott	10 ct	Durham v Yorkshire	Chester-le-Street
G.J.Kersey	9 ct	Surrey v Durham	Stockton
R.J.Turner	9 ct	Somerset v Yorkshire	Scarborough

NO BYES CONCEDED IN TOTAL OF 500 OR MORE

638-8d	S.J.Rhodes	Worcestershire v Leicestershire	Leicester
590	R.J.Rollins	Essex v Kent	Ilford
536-8d	C.P.Metson	Glamorgan v Yorkshire	Cardiff
516-6d	D.G.C.Ligertwood	Durham v Leicestershire	Chester-le-Street
513-4d	W.M.Noon	Nottinghamshire v Hampshire	Southampton
513-6d	D.R.H.Churton	Cambridge University v Oxford University	Lord's
509	W.K.Hegg	Lancashire v Essex	Chelmsford

UNUSUAL DISMISSALS
HANDLED THE BALL
K.M.Krikken (70)   Derbyshire v Indians   Derby

STUMPED BY A SUBSTITUTE
H.H.Gibbs (85) st sub (W.M.Noon) South Africa A v Nottinghamshire Nottingham

SIXTY EXTRAS IN AN INNINGS

	B	LB	W	NB		
79	5	16	4	54	Somerset (558) v Surrey	Taunton
72	3	25	3	41	Derbyshire (409) v Indians	Derby
67	34	15	2	16	Lancashire (597) v Warwickshire	Birmingham
60	1	22	3	34	Leicestershire (454-9d) v Essex	Leicester

Under TCCB regulations (Test matches excluded), two extras were scored for each no-ball, in addition to any runs scored off that ball. There were a further 11 instances of 50-59 extras in an innings.

YOUNG CRICKETER OF THE YEAR

This annual award, made by The Cricket Writers' Club (founded in 1946), is currently restricted to players qualified for England, Symonds meeting that requirement at the time of his award, and under the age of 23 on 1 May. In 1986 their ballot resulted in a dead heat. Only seven of their selections (marked †) have failed to win an England cap.

Year	Player	Year	Player
1950	R.Tattersall	1974	P.H.Edmonds
1951	P.B.H.May	1975	A.Kennedy†
1952	F.S.Trueman	1976	G.Miller
1953	M.C.Cowdrey	1977	I.T.Botham
1954	P.J.Loader	1978	D.I.Gower
1955	K.F.Barrington	1979	P.W.G.Parker
1956	B.Taylor†	1980	G.R.Dilley
1957	M.J.Stewart	1981	M.W.Gatting
1958	A.C.D.Ingleby-Mackenzie†	1982	N.G.Cowans
1959	G.Pullar	1983	N.A.Foster
1960	D.A.Allen	1984	R.J.Bailey
1961	P.H.Parfitt	1985	D.V.Lawrence
1962	P.J.Sharpe	1986	A.A.Metcalfe†
1963	G.Boycott		J.J.Whitaker
1964	J.M.Brearley	1987	R.J.Blakey
1965	A.P.E.Knott	1988	M.P.Maynard
1966	D.L.Underwood	1989	N.Hussain
1967	A.W.Greig	1990	M.A.Atherton
1968	R.M.H.Cottam	1991	M.R.Ramprakash
1969	A.Ward	1992	I.D.K.Salisbury
1970	C.M.Old	1993	M.N.Lathwell
1971	J.Whitehouse†	1994	J.P.Crawley
1972	D.R.Owen-Thomas†	1995	A.Symonds†
1973	M.Hendrick	1996	C.E.W.Silverwood

1996 FIRST-CLASS AVERAGES

These averages involve the 494 cricketers who played in the 204 first-class matches staged in the British Isles during the 1996 season.

'Cap' denotes the season in which the player was awarded a 1st XI cap by the county he represented in 1996. Durham award caps upon joining the playing staff and not on merit.

Team abbreviations: CU – Cambridge University; De – Derbyshire; Du – Durham; E – England; EA – England A; Ex – Essex; Gm – Glamorgan; Gs – Gloucestershire; H – Hampshire; Ind – India(ns); Ire – Ireland; K – Kent; La – Lancashire; Le – Leicestershire; M – Middlesex; MCC – Marylebone Cricket Club; Nh – Northamptonshire; Nt – Nottinghamshire; P – Pakistan(is); OU – Oxford University; R – The Rest; SAA – South Africa A; Sc – Scotland; Sm – Somerset; Sy – Surrey; Sx – Sussex; TCCB – Test & County Cricket Board XI; Us – British Universities; Wa – Warwickshire; Wo – Worcestershire; Y – Yorkshire.

† Left-handed batsman.

BATTING AND FIELDING

	Cap	M	I	NO	HS	Runs	Avge	100	50	Ct/St
†Aamir Sohail (P)	—	8	14	2	49	334	27.83	—	—	12
Ackerman, H.D.(SAA)	—	7	11	—	99	447	40.63	—	4	3
Adams, C.J.(De)	1992	20	36	3	239	1742	52.78	6	8	34
Adams, P.R.(SAA)	—	4	5	3	27	63	31.50	—	—	1
Afford, J.A.(Nt)	1990	18	24	14	11*	34	3.40	—	—	7
†Afzaal, U.(Nt)	—	6	10	1	67*	264	29.33	—	2	3
Aldred, P.(De)	—	5	5	2	33	50	16.66	—	—	2
Alleyne, M.W.(Gs)	1990	18	30	3	149	887	32.85	1	3	16
Allingham, M.J.D.(Sc)	—	1	2	2	50*	86	—	—	1	1
Altree, D.A.(Wa)	—	3	5	2	0*	0	0.00	—	—	1
†Ambrose, C.E.L.(Nh)	1990	9	13	2	25*	116	10.54	—	—	11
†Amjad, M.(Wo)	—	1	2	—	7	8	4.00	—	—	—
Andrew, S.J.W.(Ex)	—	10	14	6	13	61	7.62	—	—	2
Ankola, S.A.(Ind)	—	4	3	—	45	53	17.66	—	—	—
Archer, G.F.(Nt)	1995	13	24	3	143	918	43.71	2	5	17
†Arthurton, K.L.T.(MCC)	—	1	1	—	82	82	82.00	—	1	—
†Asif Mujtaba (P)	—	10	16	6	100*	445	44.50	1	2	8
Ata-ur-Rehman (P)	—	9	8	2	30	61	10.16	—	—	5
Atherton, M.A.(La/E)	1989	15	26	1	160	963	38.52	1	7	8
Athey, C.W.J.(Sx)	1993	18	33	—	111	1091	33.06	3	5	15
†Austin, I.D.(La)	1990	10	12	3	95*	437	48.55	—	3	4
Aymes, A.N.(H)	1991	19	32	12	113	801	40.05	2	2	42/3
Azharuddin, M.(Ind)	—	8	13	2	111*	439	39.90	1	3	3
Bahl, J.(Us)	—	1	1	1	0*	0	—	—	—	1
Bailey, R.J.(Nh)	1985	12	22	2	163	722	36.10	1	3	8
Bailey, T.M.B.(Nh)	—	2	2	1	31*	33	33.00	—	—	4
Bainbridge, P.(Du)	1992	11	19	1	83	617	34.27	—	5	10
Ball, M.C.J.(Gs)	1996	13	21	4	46	236	13.88	—	—	15
Barnett, K.J.(De)	1982	18	34	2	200*	1456	45.50	3	9	5
Barwick, S.R.(Gm)	1987	7	7	1	20*	34	5.66	—	—	1
Base, S.J.(De)	1990	1	1	—	1	1	1.00	—	—	—
Bates, R.T.(Nt)	—	11	15	1	34	229	16.35	—	—	8
Batty, J.D.(Sm)	—	16	24	4	44	321	16.05	—	—	4
Batty, J.N.(OU)	—	10	13	3	56	302	30.20	—	2	9/2
Benjamin, J.E.(Sy)	1993	13	14	6	38*	141	17.62	—	—	1
Benjamin, W.K.M.(H)	—	2	4	—	117	140	35.00	1	—	3
Betts, M.M.(Du)	1994	14	21	3	57*	308	17.11	—	1	4

123

	Cap	M	I	NO	HS	Runs	Avge	100	50	Ct/St
†Bevan, M.G.(Y)	1995	12	22	3	160*	1225	64.47	3	8	6
†Bicknell, D.J.(Sy)	1990	17	31	3	129*	969	34.60	2	3	9
Bicknell, M.P.(Sy)	1989	16	18	5	59*	333	25.61	–	1	2
†Birbeck, S.D.(Du)	1994	2	2	–	8	8	4.00	–	–	–
Birks, M.J.(CU)	–	1	–	–	–	–	–	–	–	1
Bishop, I.E.(Sm)	–	1	2	–	2	4	2.00	–	–	1
Blain, J.A.R.(Sc)	–	1	–	–	–	–	–	–	–	1
Blakey, R.J.(Y)	1987	19	30	6	109*	839	34.95	1	5	40/4
†Blenkiron, D.A.(Du)	1992	9	16	2	130	328	23.42	2	–	4
Boden, D.J.P.(Gs)	–	2	1	–	1	1	1.00	–	–	1
Boiling, J.(Du)	1995	8	11	4	31*	79	11.28	–	–	2
†Boje, N.(SAA)	–	7	9	2	89	289	41.28	–	3	5
Boswell, S.A.J.(Nh/Us)	–	3	4	2	2*	5	2.50	–	–	2
Botham, L.J.(H)	–	3	3	–	30	31	10.33	–	–	2
Bovill, J.N.B.(H)	–	14	19	2	29	131	7.70	–	–	5
Bowen, M.N.(Nt)	–	13	18	2	22	173	10.81	–	–	3
Bowler, P.D.(Sm)	1995	19	34	4	207	1228	40.93	2	7	5
Brimson, M.T.(Le)	–	12	12	6	13*	51	8.50	–	–	2
Broadhurst, M.(Nt)	–	1	–	–	–	–	–	–	–	1
Brown, A.D.(Sy/TCCB)	1994	16	26	3	79	555	24.13	–	5	21
Brown, D.R.(Wa)	1995	19	32	2	76	671	22.36	–	3	14
Brown, J.F.(Nh)	–	1	1	1	0*	0	–	–	–	1
Brown, K.R.(M)	1990	18	31	5	83	917	35.26	–	8	60/1
Brown, S.J.E.(Du/E)	1992	19	31	5	60	404	15.53	–	1	5
Browne, B.St A.(MCC)	–	1	–	–	–	–	–	–	–	–
Bull, J.J.(OU)	–	2	1	–	4	4	4.00	–	–	–
Burns, M.(Wa)	–	8	15	1	81	345	24.64	–	3	16/2
Butcher, G.P.(Gm)	–	14	24	4	89	679	33.95	–	5	8
†Butcher, M.A.(Sy/TCCB)	1996	18	34	3	160	1604	51.74	3	13	21
Butler, O.F.X.(Ire)	–	1	–	–	–	–	–	–	–	–
†Byas, D.(Y)	1991	19	32	2	138	933	31.10	1	5	32
Caddick, A.R.(Sm/E)	1992	15	20	5	38	199	13.26	–	–	7
Cairns, C.L.(Nt)	1993	16	29	5	114	946	39.41	1	6	10
Cake, R.Q.(CU/Us)	–	9	16	3	102*	425	32.69	1	1	3
Campbell, C.L.(Du)	1996	1	1	–	7	7	7.00	–	–	–
Campbell, S.L.(Du)	1996	16	29	–	118	1041	35.89	4	7	15
Capel, D.J.(Nh)	1986	16	30	2	103	814	29.07	1	4	13
Carr, J.D.(M)	1987	17	28	1	94	783	29.00	–	4	28
Chapman, R.J.(Nt)	–	2	1	–	0	0	0.00	–	–	1
Chapple, G.(La/R)	1994	16	23	6	37*	329	19.35	–	–	2
†Childs, J.H.(Ex)	1986	6	5	3	1*	1	0.50	–	–	1
Church, M.J.(Wo)	–	6	11	–	152	280	25.45	1	–	4
Churton, D.R.H.(CU)	–	7	7	–	20	34	4.85	–	–	7/3
Clarke, V.P.(Le)	–	1	2	–	43	43	21.50	–	–	1
Collingwood, P.D.(Du)	1996	11	20	–	91	464	23.20	–	2	6
Commins, J.B.(SAA)	–	9	15	3	114*	597	49.75	1	5	2
Connor, C.A.(H)	1988	10	12	3	42	140	15.55	–	–	4
†Cooper, K.E.(Gs)	1995	1	1	–	5	5	5.00	–	–	–
Cork, D.G.(De/E)	1993	18	29	6	101*	779	33.86	1	5	12
Cosker, D.A.(Gm)	–	5	6	1	24	45	9.00	–	–	3
Cottam, A.C.(Sm)	–	2	2	–	12	15	7.50	–	–	–
Cottey, P.A.(Gm)	1992	20	36	6	203	1543	51.43	4	9	16
Cowan, A.P.(Ex/TCCB)	–	15	20	6	34	188	13.42	–	–	6
Cowdrey, G.R.(K)	1988	11	17	–	111	529	31.11	1	3	5
†Cox, D.M.(Du)	1993	7	13	4	95*	434	48.22	–	4	2
Crawley, J.P.(La/R/E)	1994	15	25	3	112*	1102	50.09	3	8	6

124

	Cap	M	I	NO	HS	Runs	Avge	100	50	Ct/St
Croft, R.D.B.(Gm/MCC/E)	1992	20	30	6	78	647	26.95	–	5	15
Crookes, D.N.(SAA)	—	7	11	1	155*	566	56.60	2	3	8
Cunliffe, R.J.(Gs)	—	6	11	–	82	252	22.90	–	2	1
Curran, K.M.(Nh)	1992	15	28	7	150	1242	59.14	2	8	14
Curtis, T.S.(Wo)	1984	17	31	2	118	952	32.82	3	5	10
Dale, A.(Gm)	1992	15	25	1	120	690	28.75	1	4	5
Daley, J.A.(Du/TCCB)	1992	12	21	3	76	477	26.50	–	1	7
Dalton, A.J.(Gm)	—	2	3	–	17	37	12.33	–	–	–
Davies, A.G.(Sc)	—	1	2	1	24	29	29.00	–	–	3/2
†Davies, A.P.(Gm)	—	2	2	1	11*	19	19.00	–	–	–
Davis, R.P.(Gs)	—	15	22	2	43	308	15.40	–	–	18
Dawood, I.(Wo)	—	1	1	–	1	1	1.00	–	–	3
Dawson, R.I.(Gs)	—	7	13	1	21	141	11.75	–	–	–
Deakin, P.J.(CU)	—	6	9	4	24*	100	20.00	–	–	–
†Dean, K.J.(De)	—	8	8	1	12	33	4.71	–	–	1
DeFreitas, P.A.J.(De)	1994	14	22	–	60	394	17.90	–	1	12
Derbyshire, N.A.(Ex)	—	1	–	–	–	–	–	–	–	2
Dibden, R.R.(H/Us)	—	1	1	–	1	1	1.00	–	–	–
Dodemaide, A.I.C.(MCC)	—	1	1	1	62*	62	–	–	1	–
†Dowman, M.P.(Nt)	—	9	14	–	107	337	24.07	1	–	4
Drakes, V.C.(Sx)	1996	15	27	3	145*	649	27.04	2	4	1
Dravid, R.(Ind)	—	9	16	5	101*	553	50.27	1	4	6/1
Dunlop, A.R.(Ire)	—	1	2	–	57	58	29.00	–	1	1
Du Preez, S.P.(OU)	—	10	2	1	9	10	10.00	–	–	3
Dutch, K.P.(M)	—	3	4	–	27	39	9.75	–	–	2
Eagleson, R.L.(Ire)	—	1	2	2	50*	91	–	–	1	2
Ealham, M.A.(K/E)	1992	14	23	–	74	618	32.52	–	5	7
Ecclestone, S.C.(Sm)	—	8	13	1	94	334	27.83	–	3	2
Edmond, M.D.(Wa)	—	1	1	1	8*	8	–	–	–	–
Edwards, A.D.(Sx)	—	1	–	–	–	–	–	–	–	–
Ellis, S.W.K.(Wo)	—	9	10	4	15	63	10.50	–	–	6
Elworthy, S.(La)	—	12	16	2	88	288	20.57	–	1	5
Emburey, J.E.(Nh)	—	11	13	4	67*	200	22.22	–	1	6
Evans, A.W.(Gm)	—	7	13	3	71*	376	37.60	–	2	5
Evans, K.P.(Nt)	1990	14	18	3	71	482	32.13	–	4	3
†Fairbrother, N.H.(La)	1985	12	20	–	204	1068	53.40	2	8	10
Fay, R.A.(M)	—	15	24	2	26	163	7.40	–	–	5
Feltham, M.A.(M)	1995	3	5	1	13*	14	3.50	–	–	–
Fisher, I.D.(Y)	—	1	1	1	0*	0	–	–	–	–
Fleming, M.V.(K)	1990	18	30	2	116	855	30.53	2	3	9
Flintoff, A.(La)	—	1	1	–	2	2	2.00	–	–	1
†Flower, A.(MCC)	—	1	1	–	70	70	70.00	–	1	1
Flower, G.W.(MCC)	—	1	1	–	98	98	98.00	–	1	3
†Foley, G.I.(MCC)	—	1	1	–	14	14	14.00	–	–	–
Follett, D.(M)	—	6	6	5	17	22	22.00	–	–	2
Ford, J.A.(K)	—	1	–	–	–	–	–	–	–	1
Fordham, A.(Nh)	1990	10	18	3	144*	502	33.46	1	2	8
Foster, M.J.(Du)	1996	3	6	–	25	67	11.16	–	–	–
Francis, N.B.(MCC)	—	1	–	–	–	–	–	–	–	–
†Franks, P.J.(Nt)	—	1	–	–	–	–	–	–	–	–
Fraser, A.R.C.(M)	1988	18	28	6	33	238	10.81	–	–	3
Fulton, D.P.(K)	—	17	30	3	134*	852	31.55	1	5	25
Gallian, J.E.R.(La/R)	1994	15	29	3	312	1156	44.46	3	3	10
†Ganguly, S.C.(Ind)	—	9	14	6	136	762	95.25	3	4	1
Garaway, M.(H)	—	1	1	–	44	44	44.00	–	–	4/1
Gardner, G.E.(Sc)	—	1	1	1	2*	2	–	–	–	–

	Cap	M	I	NO	HS	Runs	Avge	100	50	Ct/St
Gatting, M.W.(M)	1977	16	25	–	171	901	36.04	1	8	10
Gibbs, H.H.(SAA)	–	8	14	1	183	867	66.69	2	5	9
Gibson, O.D.(Gm)	–	9	15	3	97	449	37.41	–	3	6
Giddins, E.S.H.(Sx/EA)	1994	14	16	6	11	55	5.50	–	–	–
Gie, N.A.(Nt)	–	1	–	–	–	–	–	–	–	–
Gilder, G.M.(SAA)	–	4	6	–	23	43	7.16	–	–	1
Giles, A.F.(Wa)	–	17	27	9	106*	600	33.33	1	4	11
Gillespie, P.G.(Ire)	–	1	2	–	53	53	26.50	–	1	–
Gooch, G.A.(Ex)	1975	17	30	1	201	1944	67.03	8	6	18
Goodchild, D.J.(M)	–	1	2	–	4	4	2.00	–	–	–
Gough, D.(Y)	1993	16	25	3	121	501	22.77	1	2	6
†Gould, I.J.(M)	1977	1	–	–	–	–	–	–	–	–
Govan, J.W.(Sc)	–	1	1	–	5	5	5.00	–	–	–
Grayson, A.P.(Ex)	1996	17	30	3	140	939	34.77	2	3	19
Green, R.J.(La)	–	7	10	3	25*	91	13.00	–	–	2
Greenfield, K.(Sx)	1996	14	26	4	154*	916	41.63	3	3	10
Griffith, F.A.(De)	–	1	–	–	–	–	–	–	–	–
Gupte, C.M.(OU/Us)	–	11	14	1	132	606	46.61	2	3	1
Habib, A.(Le)	–	16	24	2	215	792	36.00	1	2	10
Hall, J.W.(Sx)	1992	7	13	–	93	330	25.38	–	3	6
Hamilton, G.M.(Y)	–	4	5	1	61	71	17.75	–	1	2
Hancock, T.H.C.(Gs)	–	15	27	3	116	709	29.54	1	4	11
Harden, R.J.(Sm)	1989	12	20	1	136	676	35.57	1	5	11
Harmison, S.J.(Du)	–	1	2	–	6	10	5.00	–	–	–
Harris, A.J.(De)	1996	12	16	3	17	102	7.84	–	–	3
Harrison, G.D.(Ire)	–	1	2	–	46*	77	–	–	–	1
Harrison, J.C.(M)	–	7	13	2	40	199	18.09	–	–	10
Hart, J.P.(Nt)	–	1	2	–	18*	18	–	–	–	–
Hartley, P.J.(Y)	1987	16	24	3	89	476	22.66	–	3	6
Haste, N.J.(CU)	–	6	6	2	51*	101	25.25	–	1	1
Hayhurst, A.N.(Sm)	1990	9	13	1	96	224	18.66	–	2	2
Haynes, J.J.(La)	–	1	2	–	16	26	13.00	–	–	1
Headley, D.W.(K)	1993	12	16	3	63*	253	19.46	–	1	4
Hegg, W.K.(La)	1989	17	25	6	134	713	37.52	1	3	50/5
†Hemp, D.L.(Gm)	1994	8	13	2	103*	405	36.81	1	1	5
†Hewitt, J.P.(M)	–	10	15	4	72	312	28.36	–	1	5
Hewson, D.R.(Gs)	–	6	12	1	87	261	23.72	–	3	2
Hibbert, A.J.E.(Ex)	–	2	4	1	85	103	34.33	–	1	–
Hick, G.A.(Wo/E)	1986	17	29	1	215	1245	44.46	5	3	19
Hindson, J.E.(Nt)	–	1	–	–	–	–	–	–	–	–
Hirwani, N.D.(Ind)	–	5	–	–	–	–	–	–	–	1
Hoggard, M.J.(Y)	–	1	1	–	10	10	10.00	–	–	–
Hollioake, A.J.(Sy/TCCB)	1995	17	29	6	129	1522	66.17	5	8	18
Hollioake, B.C.(Sy)	–	3	4	–	46	63	15.75	–	–	3
†Holloway, P.C.L.(Sm)	–	10	16	1	168	535	35.66	1	3	7
Hooper, C.L.(K)	1992	17	29	2	155	1287	47.66	3	9	33
†House, W.J.(CU)	–	8	15	5	136	526	52.60	2	2	2
How, E.J.(CU)	–	2	2	2	7*	7	–	–	2	–
Hughes, J.G.(Nh)	–	2	3	–	8	22	7.33	–	–	1
Humphries, S.(Sx)	–	1	–	–	–	–	–	–	–	1
Hussain, N.(Ex/EA/E)	1989	18	31	1	158	1386	46.20	3	7	18
†Hutchison, P.M.(R)	–	1	2	–	0	0	0.00	–	–	1
†Hutton, S.(Du)	1992	14	26	2	172*	812	33.83	2	1	6
Hyam, B.J.(Ex)	–	2	4	–	49	73	18.25	–	–	3/1
Ijaz Ahmed (P)	–	9	16	2	141	664	47.42	2	4	2
Illingworth, R.K.(Wo/R)	1986	19	23	10	66*	420	32.30	–	1	11

126

	Cap	M	I	NO	HS	Runs	Avge	100	50	Ct/St
†Ilott, M.C.(Ex)	1993	17	24	2	58	343	15.59	–	1	4
Innes, K.J.(Nh)	–	4	5	–	63	108	21.60	–	1	3
Inzamam-ul-Haq (P)	–	9	14	2	169*	792	66.00	3	4	6
Irani, R.C.(Ex/EA/E)	1994	19	31	4	110*	1039	38.48	1	7	10
Jadeja, A.(Ind)	–	8	13	2	112*	489	44.45	2	2	6
†James, K.D.(H)	1989	13	23	1	118*	738	33.54	2	3	6
James, S.P.(Gm)	1992	20	38	1	235	1766	47.72	7	6	15
Janisch, A.N.(CU)	–	3	3	1	25	29	14.50	–	–	–
Jarrett, M.E.D.(OU)	–	7	6	2	50*	82	20.50	–	1	4
Jarvis, P.W.(Sx)	–	8	11	4	35	164	23.42	–	–	3
Johnson, P.(Nt)	1986	19	33	2	109	980	31.61	2	6	10
Johnson, R.L.(M)	1995	11	20	1	37*	243	12.78	–	–	1
Jones, D.M.(De)	1996	19	34	5	214*	1502	51.79	4	7	15
Jones, R.O.(CU)	–	8	13	1	61	205	17.08	–	1	4
†Joshi, S.B.(Ind)	–	5	7	1	22	67	11.16	–	–	–
Julian, B.P.(Sy)	1996	16	23	2	119	759	36.14	2	3	9
Kallis, J.H.(SAA)	–	4	4	–	92	128	32.00	–	1	1
Keech, M.(H)	–	12	21	3	104	793	44.05	1	7	9
†Keedy, G.(La)	–	14	14	8	26	73	12.16	–	–	7
Kendall, W.S.(H/OU)	–	12	23	4	145*	1045	55.00	3	6	13
Kendrick, N.M.(Gm)	–	10	11	6	16*	35	7.00	–	–	5
†Kenlock, S.G.(Sy)	–	1	1	–	5	5	2.50	–	–	–
Kennis, G.J.(Sy)	–	1	2	1	2*	3	3.00	–	–	1
Kerr, J.I.D.(Sm)	–	6	9	3	68*	176	29.33	–	2	–
Kersey, G.J.(Sy)	1996	15	20	4	68*	402	25.12	–	3	45/1
†Kettleborough, R.A.(Y)	–	7	9	–	108	307	34.11	1	1	6
Khan, G.A.(De/OU/Us)	–	13	18	2	101*	608	38.00	1	4	7
†Khan, W.G.(Wa)	–	15	28	1	130	738	27.33	3	2	11
Killeen, N.(Du)	1995	5	7	1	32	40	6.66	–	–	1
Kirtley, R.J.(Sx/TCCB)	–	8	12	4	7*	22	2.75	–	–	5
†Klusener, L.(SAA)	–	8	8	3	79	171	34.20	–	1	4
†Knight, N.V.(Wa/EA/E)	1995	15	28	3	132	1196	47.84	4	5	18
Knott, J.A.(Sy)	–	1	2	1	49*	52	52.00	–	–	2/1
†Koenig, S.G.(SAA)	–	7	11	–	46	221	20.09	–	–	3
Krikken, K.M.(De)	1992	19	29	7	104	882	40.09	1	3	64/3
Kumble, A.(Ind)	–	8	10	1	59*	112	12.44	–	1	1
Lampitt, S.R.(Wo)	1989	19	27	5	88	658	29.90	–	3	15
Laney, J.S.(H)	1996	17	30	–	112	1163	38.76	4	5	13
Lathwell, M.N.(Sm)	1992	18	32	4	109	1224	43.71	2	7	13
Law, D.R.(Sx/TCCB)	1996	17	28	–	97	619	22.10	–	3	7
Law, S.G.(Ex)	1996	15	26	1	172	1545	61.80	6	5	25
†Lawson, A.G.(MCC)	–	1	1	–	12	12	12.00	–	–	1
Leatherdale, D.A.(Wo)	1994	11	18	2	122	539	33.68	1	4	8
Lee, S.(Sm)	1996	17	25	4	167*	1300	61.90	5	5	14
Lenham, N.J.(Sx)	1990	16	28	3	145	903	36.12	2	5	3
Lewis, C.C.(Sy/E)	–	14	22	2	94	639	31.95	–	4	15
Lewis, D.A.(Ire)	–	1	2	–	71	99	49.50	–	1	3
Lewis, J.(Gs)	–	10	16	2	22*	119	8.50	–	–	4
Lewis, J.J.B.(Ex)	1994	6	11	2	69	238	26.44	–	2	11
†Lewry, J.D.(Sx/E)	1996	10	15	3	28*	138	11.50	–	–	–
Liebenberg, G.F.J.(SAA)	–	8	14	–	123	453	32.35	1	2	8
Ligertwood, D.G.C.(Du)	1995	12	23	5	56	367	20.38	–	1	31/5
†Lightfoot, C.G.R.(OU)	–	4	4	1	9	15	5.00	–	–	–
†Llong, N.J.(K)	1993	14	22	2	130	763	38.15	2	5	12
Lloyd, G.D.(La)	1992	15	25	1	241	1194	49.75	3	4	6
Lockhart, D.R.(Sc)	–	1	2	–	36	40	20.00	–	–	1

	Cap	M	I	NO	HS	Runs	Avge	100	50	Ct/St
Lockie, B.G.(Sc)	—	1	2	—	32	38	19.00	—	—	1
Longley, J.I.(Du)	1994	2	2	—	4	6	3.00	—	—	—
Loye, M.B.(Nh)	1994	14	25	2	205	1048	45.56	2	5	5
Lugsden, S.(Du)	1994	3	5	1	9	19	4.75	—	—	1
Lynch, M.A.(Gs)	1995	11	19	1	72	553	30.72	—	5	10
McCague, M.J.(K)	1992	18	26	7	63*	357	18.78	—	1	10
McCallan, W.K.(Ire)	—	1	2	—	51	62	31.00	—	1	—
McGrath, A.(Y/EA)	—	19	33	2	137	999	32.22	2	5	12
McKeown, P.C.(La)	—	2	2	—	64	73	36.50	—	1	1
Maclay, A.W.(OU)	—	2	1	1	1*	1	—	—	—	—
Macmillan, G.I.(Le)	—	7	12	1	41	201	18.27	—	—	—
Maddy, D.L.(Le)	1996	20	30	2	101*	958	34.21	1	4	18
Malcolm, D.E.(De)	1989	18	23	7	21	119	7.43	—	—	1
†Malik, H.S.(OU)	—	10	13	3	61	240	24.00	—	1	7
Mallender, N.A.(Nh)	1984	3	3	—	13	31	10.33	—	—	1
Manjrekar, S.V.(Ind)	—	9	15	2	101	540	41.53	1	4	4
Marc, K.(Us)	—	1	1	—	0	0	0.00	—	—	—
Marsh, S.A.(K)	1986	15	24	1	127	478	20.78	1	2	28/6
Martin, P.J.(La/E)	1994	13	18	4	42	278	19.85	—	—	1
Martin-Jenkins, R.S.C.(Sx/Us)	—	2	1	—	20	20	20.00	—	—	—
Maru, R.J.(H)	1986	11	17	5	55*	303	25.25	—	1	17
Mascarenhas, A.D.(H)	—	2	3	—	14	24	8.00	—	—	—
†Mather, D.P.(OU)	—	8	2	—	2	2	1.00	—	—	—
May, M.R.(De)	—	3	4	2	63*	160	80.00	—	1	1
Maynard, M.P.(Gm)	1987	17	30	4	214	1610	61.92	6	6	20
Metcalfe, A.A.(Nt)	—	12	22	—	128	771	35.04	1	3	4
Metson, C.P.(Gm)	1987	8	11	4	18*	53	7.57	—	—	14/2
Mhambrey, P.L.(Ind)	—	8	9	4	28	111	22.20	—	—	2
Mike, G.W.(Nt)	—	3	5	1	13*	25	6.25	—	—	2
Milburn, S.M.(H)	—	10	12	2	54*	180	18.00	—	1	—
†Millns, D.J.(Le)	1991	19	20	1	103	424	22.31	1	1	6
Moffat, G.R.(CU)	—	8	8	3	27	45	9.00	—	—	4
Moffat, S.P.(M)	—	1	1	—	0	0	0.00	—	—	—
Mohammad Akram (P)	—	6	5	5	4*	7	—	—	—	—
Moin Khan (P)	—	5	9	1	105	215	26.87	1	—	5/2
Moles, A.J.(Wa)	1987	13	25	—	176	903	36.12	2	4	7
Molins, G.L.(Ire)	—	1	—	—	—	—	—	—	—	—
Mongia, N.R.(Ind)	—	7	12	2	85	364	36.40	—	2	13/1
Montgomerie, R.R.(Nh/TCCB)	1995	18	34	3	168	1178	38.00	4	4	17
Moody, T.M.(Wo)	1991	19	31	3	212	1427	50.96	7	4	12
Moore, D.M.P.(Ire)	—	1	2	—	51	68	34.00	—	1	1
Moores, P.(Sx)	1989	19	32	4	185	782	27.92	2	1	50/2
†Morris, A.C.(Y)	—	6	9	—	60	189	21.00	—	1	6
†Morris, H.(Gm/MCC)	1986	18	32	2	202*	1666	55.53	6	9	14
Morris, J.E.(Du)	1994	17	31	1	83	429	14.30	—	3	9
Morris, R.S.M.(H)	—	5	9	—	112	195	21.66	1	—	5
Moxon, M.D.(Y/R)	1984	14	25	3	213	961	43.68	2	5	5
Mullally, A.D.(Le/E)	1993	17	17	5	75	249	20.75	—	2	1
Munton, T.A.(Wa/EA)	1989	12	15	9	54*	177	29.50	—	2	2
Mushtaq Ahmed (P)	—	7	9	1	38	118	14.75	—	—	4
Nash, D.J.(M)	1995	2	3	1	8*	15	7.50	—	—	1
Newell, K.(Sx)	—	5	9	1	105*	234	29.25	1	—	1
Newell, M.(Sx)	—	1	2	—	0	0	0.00	—	—	1
Newport, P.J.(Wo)	1986	6	6	—	68	142	23.66	—	1	1
†Nixon, P.A.(Le)	1994	20	27	5	106	880	40.00	3	4	56/6
Noon, W.M.(Nt)	1995	13	21	3	57	332	18.44	—	1	30/3

	Cap	M	I	NO	HS	Runs	Avge	100	50	Ct/St
†Nowell, R.W.(Sy)	—	1	2	1	28*	28	28.00	—	—	—
O'Gorman, T.J.G.(De)	1992	11	20	3	109*	636	37.41	1	6	7
Ostler, D.P.(Wa/EA)	1991	18	32	3	90	863	29.75	—	8	35
Owen, J.E.H(De)	—	9	15	—	105	499	33.26	2	2	3
Palframan, S.J.(SAA)	—	5	7	1	55	104	17.33	—	1	10/1
Parker, B.(Y)	—	1	1	—	59	59	59.00	—	1	—
Parkin, O.T.(Gm)	—	10	12	7	14	65	13.00	—	—	4
†Parsons, G.J.(Le)	1984	18	23	5	53	290	16.11	—	2	22
Parsons, K.A.(Sm)	—	8	15	1	83*	408	29.14	—	4	2
Patel, M.M.(K/E)	1994	18	23	5	33	278	15.44	—	—	9
Patterson, A.D.(Ire)	—	1	2	—	29	45	22.50	—	—	—
Patterson, M.W.(Sy)	—	1	2	—	4	6	3.00	—	—	—
Pearson, R.M.(Sy)	—	14	14	9	37	142	28.40	—	—	3
†Penberthy, A.L.(Nh)	1994	18	29	4	87	635	25.40	—	3	9
Pennett, D.B.(Nt)	—	3	4	—	10	27	6.75	—	—	1
Penney, T.L.(Wa)	1994	19	34	4	134	1295	43.16	3	8	14
Peters, S.D.(Ex)	—	4	7	1	110	142	23.66	1	—	5
Philip, I.L.(Sc)	—	1	2	—	110	112	56.00	1	—	1
Phillips, B.J.(K)	—	3	3	—	2	5	1.66	—	—	1
Phillips, N.C.(Sx)	—	8	12	7	45	223	44.60	—	—	5
†Pick, R.A.(Nt)	1987	6	8	—	32	66	8.25	—	—	1
Pierson, A.R.K.(Le)	1995	20	23	10	44	263	20.23	—	—	16
Piper, K.J.(Wa)	1992	13	22	2	82	429	21.45	—	1	21/6
†Pollard, P.R.(Nt)	1992	13	25	2	86	737	32.04	—	6	11
Pollock, S.M.(Wa)	1996	13	21	1	150*	606	30.30	2	1	5
†Pooley, J.C.(M/EA)	1995	18	34	2	138*	881	27.53	2	4	22
Pothas, N.(SAA)	—	6	9	2	90	309	44.14	—	3	15
Powell, M.J.(Wa)	—	4	8	—	39	182	22.75	—	—	2
Prasad, B.K.V.(Ind)	—	7	7	4	13	25	8.33	—	—	4
Preece, B.E.A.(Wo)	—	3	4	2	3*	5	2.50	—	—	1
Preston, N.W.(K)	—	8	11	4	17*	63	9.00	—	—	3
Prichard, P.J.(Ex)	1986	19	31	—	108	959	30.93	1	6	12
Pringle, M.W.(SAA)	—	4	6	—	105	170	28.33	1	1	—
Radford, T.A.(Sx)	—	5	8	—	53	97	12.12	—	1	2
Ragnauth, R.T.(CU)	—	6	11	1	29	121	12.10	—	—	1
Raju, S.L.V.(Ind)	—	8	6	3	31	33	11.00	—	—	—
Ralph, J.T.(Wo)	—	1	2	—	0	0	0.00	—	—	—
Ramprakash, M.R.(M/R)	1990	17	31	2	169	1441	49.68	4	8	7
Rao, R.K.(Sx)	—	2	3	1	38	87	43.50	—	—	—
Rashid Latif (P)	—	7	7	—	61	232	33.14	—	2	17/4
†Rashid, U.B.A.(M)	—	1	2	—	9	15	7.50	—	—	—
Ratcliffe, J.D.(Sy)	—	9	16	1	69	494	32.93	—	4	5
Rathore, V.(Ind)	—	10	17	—	165	805	47.35	1	7	9
Ratledge, J.(CU)	—	2	4	—	30	89	22.25	—	—	—
Rawnsley, M.J.(Wo)	—	4	1	—	4*	4	—	—	—	1
Reeve, D.A.(Wa)	1989	5	8	1	168*	351	50.14	1	—	7
Remy, C.C.(Le)	—	1	—	—	—	—	—	—	—	—
Renshaw, S.J.(H)	—	7	7	5	9*	10	5.00	—	—	3
Rhodes, S.J.(Wo)	1986	19	29	5	110	939	39.12	1	8	40/8
†Ridley, A.C.(OU)	—	7	9	—	155	417	46.33	2	1	1
Ripley, D.(Nh)	1987	11	16	7	88*	448	49.77	—	3	23
Roberts, A.R.(Nh)	—	6	8	—	39	141	17.62	—	—	1
Roberts, D.J.(Nh)	—	4	7	—	73	254	36.28	—	2	—
†Roberts, G.M.(De)	—	1	1	—	52	52	52.00	—	1	—
Robinson, D.D.J.(Ex)	—	12	23	2	97	738	35.14	—	8	6
Robinson, R.T.(Nt)	1983	17	31	2	184	1302	44.89	3	6	8

	Cap	M	I	NO	HS	Runs	Avge	100	50	Ct/St
Rollins, A.S.(De)	1995	19	36	5	131	1101	35.51	3	5	11
Rollins, R.J.(Ex/EA/TCCB)	1995	21	34	4	74*	719	23.96	–	3	56/6
Rose, G.D.(Sm)	1988	15	21	5	93*	408	25.50	–	2	8
Roseberry, M.A.(Du)	1995	17	30	2	145*	744	26.57	1	3	6
Russell, R.C.(Gs/R/E) †	1985	19	30	5	124	858	34.32	1	7	48/3
Rutherford, A.T.(Ire)	–	1					–	–	–	3
Saeed Anwar (P) †	–	10	19	1	219*	1224	68.00	5	4	6
Saggers, M.J.(Du)	1996	5	9	1	18	89	11.12	–	–	–
Sales, D.J.G.(Nh)	–	4	8	1	210*	280	40.00	1	–	4
Salim Malik (P)	–	9	14	4	104*	450	45.00	2	1	1
Salisbury, I.D.K.(Sx/TCCB/EA/E)	1991	18	30	3	83	562	20.81	–	3	8
Salmond, G.(Sc) †	–	1	2	–	181	181	90.50	1	–	–
Saqlain Mushtaq (P)	–	5	7	2	78	130	26.00	–	1	3
Schofield, C.J.(Y)	–	1	1	–	25	25	25.00	–	–	–
Schultz, B.N.(SAA) †	–	3	2	–	9	12	6.00	–	–	1
Scott, C.W.(Du)	1992	7	10	1	59	208	23.11	–	2	20
Shadab Kabir (P) †	–	7	12	1	99	390	35.45	–	3	6
Shah, O.A.(M)	–	5	9	1	75	212	26.50	–	2	2
Shahid Anwar (P)	–	3	6	1	89	166	33.20	–	1	–
Shahid Nazir (P)	–	3	3	1	13	21	10.50	–	–	–
Shahid, N.(Sy)	–	11	19	3	101	535	33.43	1	4	6
Shaw, A.D.(Gm)	–	13	18	1	74	281	16.52	–	2	28/5
Sheeraz, K.P.(Gs)	–	1	1	1	3*	3	–	–	–	–
Sheriyar, A.(Wo)	–	16	15	9	13	38	6.33	–	–	4
Shine, K.J.(Sm)	–	12	15	4	40	121	11.00	–	–	5
Sidhu, N.S.(Ind)	–	2	4	–	115	171	42.75	1	–	–
Silverwood, C.E.W.(Y)	1996	16	24	6	45*	198	11.00	–	–	6
Simmons, P.V.(Le)	1994	17	24	2	171	1244	56.54	4	7	35
Singh, A.(Wa/CU/Us)	–	12	22	2	157	718	35.90	2	1	6
Small, G.C.(Wa)	1982	7	9	5	23*	55	13.75	–	–	2
Smith, A.M.(Gs)	1995	16	25	3	55*	364	16.54	–	1	2
Smith, A.W.(Sy)	–	1	2	–	16	23	11.50	–	–	–
Smith, B.F.(Le)	1995	20	29	3	190	1243	47.80	3	4	5
Smith, E.T.(K/CU)	–	7	12	–	101	576	48.00	2	4	1
Smith, G.J.(SAA)	–	5	5	3	5	7	3.50	–	–	1
Smith, N.M.K.(Wa)	1993	16	27	4	74	626	27.21	–	3	11
Smith, P.A.(Wa)	1986	2	2	–	21	23	11.50	–	–	1
Smith, R.A.(H)	1985	17	31	2	179	1396	48.13	3	8	1
Snape, J.N.(Nh)	–	10	16	3	64	277	21.30	–	1	3
Solanki, V.S.(Wo)	–	14	24	3	90	828	39.42	–	6	9
Speak, N.J.(La)	1992	12	21	4	138*	579	34.05	1	3	10
Speight, M.P.(Sx)	1991	11	21	2	122*	514	27.05	1	3	9
Spiring, K.R.(Wo)	–	18	32	6	144	1084	41.69	3	7	9
Srinath, J.(Ind)	–	7	9	1	52	128	16.00	–	1	3
Stanford, E.J.(K) †	–	2	3	3	10*	12	–	–	–	1
Stemp, R.D.(Y/EA)	1996	19	24	9	65	260	17.33	–	2	8
Stephenson, J.P.(H)	1995	15	25	2	85	611	26.56	–	5	6
Stewart, A.J.(Sy/E)	1985	14	24	1	170	966	42.00	1	7	15/1
Strang, P.A.(MCC)	–	1	1	1	13*	13	–	–	–	1
Such, P.M.(Ex)	1991	19	22	11	54	176	16.00	–	1	12
Sutcliffe, I.J.(Le/OU/Us) †	–	8	12	–	83	443	36.91	–	5	1
Swann, A.J.(Nh)	–	3	5	1	76*	100	25.00	–	1	1
Symonds, A.(Gs)	1996	18	30	1	127	1097	37.82	3	4	9
Taylor, J.P.(Nh) †	1992	17	23	9	57	242	17.28	–	1	3
Telemachus, R.(SAA)	–	3	2	–	8	8	4.00	–	–	2
Tendulkar, S.R.(Ind)	–	7	11	–	177	707	64.27	2	5	5

130

	Cap	M	I	NO	HS	Runs	Avge	100	50	Ct/St
Tennant, A.M.(Sc)	—	1	—	—	—	—	—	—	—	—
Tennent, R.W.(CU)	—	2	—	—	—	—	—	—	—	—
Terry, V.P.(H)	1983	7	12	2	87*	379	37.90	—	3	12
Thomas, P.A.(Wo)	—	5	7	—	11	46	6.57	—	—	—
†Thomas, S.D.(Gm)	—	11	16	3	48	199	15.30	—	—	2
Thompson, J.B.D.(K)	—	5	5	—	37	89	17.80	—	—	—
Thomson, R.B.(OU)	—	10	6	6	14*	34	—	—	—	1
†Thorpe, G.P.(Sy/R/E)	1991	16	29	4	185	1569	62.76	6	7	18
Thursfield, M.J.(H)	—	5	5	2	37*	89	29.66	—	—	—
Titchard, S.P.(La)	1995	13	23	2	163	939	44.71	2	5	11
Tolley, C.M.(Nt)	—	9	14	2	67	306	25.50	—	1	2
Trainor, N.J.(Gs)	—	8	14	1	67	261	20.07	—	2	5
†Trescothick, M.E.(Sm)	—	15	26	—	178	720	27.69	1	2	11
Trump, H.R.J.(Sm)	1994	3	2	1	0*	0	0.00	—	—	3
Tufnell, P.C.R.(M)	1990	18	26	10	67*	290	18.12	—	1	7
Turner, R.J.(Sm)	1994	18	27	6	100*	668	31.80	1	3	64/3
Tweats, T.A.(De)	—	4	7	2	89*	130	26.00	—	1	4
Udal, S.D.(H)	1992	17	25	4	58	447	21.28	—	2	12
Vandrau, M.J.(De)	—	10	16	6	34*	175	17.50	—	—	4
Van Troost, A.P.(Sm)	—	6	8	2	11	27	4.50	—	—	—
Vaughan, M.P.(Y)	1995	18	32	2	183	1161	38.70	3	6	4
Wagh, M.A.(OU/Us)	—	11	13	3	43	198	19.80	—	—	4
†Walker, A.(Du)	1994	3	6	3	20	25	8.33	—	—	—
Walker, L.N.P.(Nt)	—	6	6	1	36	93	18.60	—	—	16/2
†Walker, M.J.(K)	—	8	13	3	275*	606	60.60	1	2	2
Walsh, C.A.(Gs)	1985	15	24	13	25	154	14.00	—	—	7
Walsh, C.D.(K)	—	1	1	1	56*	56	—	—	1	2
Walton, T.C.(Nh)	—	6	10	1	58	302	33.55	—	4	2
Waqar Younis (P)	—	7	7	2	8	19	3.80	—	—	2
Ward, D.M.(Sy)	1990	2	4	1	64*	81	27.00	—	1	2
†Ward, I.J.(Sy)	—	1	2	—	15	19	9.50	—	—	—
Ward, T.R.(K)	1989	18	31	1	161	1252	41.73	2	9	12
Warner, A.E.(De)	1987	1	—	—	—	—	—	—	—	—
Warren, R.J.(Nh)	1995	11	18	1	201*	486	28.58	1	1	19/1
†Wasim Akram (P)	—	7	9	1	68	211	26.37	—	1	4
Watkin, S.L.(Gm)	1989	18	20	6	34	153	10.92	—	—	9
Watkinson, M.(La/R)	1987	17	28	1	64	645	23.88	—	2	13
†Weekes, P.N.(M)	1993	19	35	2	171*	1218	36.90	4	4	11
Welch, G.(Wa)	—	13	17	1	45	210	13.12	—	—	9
Wellings, P.E.(M)	—	4	8	1	48	237	33.85	—	—	1
Wells, A.P.(Sx/TCCB)	1986	19	35	2	122	1206	36.54	2	6	13
Wells, C.M.(De)	1995	12	19	3	165	609	38.06	1	3	4
Wells, V.J.(Le)	1994	20	30	—	204	1331	44.36	4	3	20
Weston, R.M.S.(Du)	1994	3	5	—	15	29	5.80	—	—	1
†Weston, W.P.C.(Wo)	1995	20	37	5	171*	1389	43.40	4	7	20
Wharf, A.G.(Y)	—	4	4	1	62	121	40.33	—	1	1
Whitaker, J.J.(Le)	1986	16	23	3	218	1093	54.65	4	2	2
†Whitaker, P.R.(H)	—	12	22	3	67*	535	28.15	—	4	4
White, C.(Y)	1993	19	30	1	181	949	32.72	1	7	13
White, G.W.(H)	—	13	24	3	73	652	31.04	—	6	12
Whittall, A.R.(CU)	—	7	6	1	36	127	25.40	—	—	4
Wild, R.D.(Nh)	—	1	—	—	—	—	—	—	—	—
Wileman, J.R.(Nt)	—	1	—	—	—	—	—	—	—	—
Williams, N.F.(Ex)	1996	12	16	3	39	221	17.00	—	—	2
†Williams, R.C.J.(Gs)	1996	5	8	—	44	133	16.62	—	—	12/1
Williamson, D.(Le)	—	1	—	—	—	—	—	—	—	—

	Cap	M	I	NO	HS	Runs	Avge	100	50	Ct/St
Williamson, J.G.(Sc)	—	1	2	–	55	104	52.00	–	1	–
Willis, S.C.(K)	—	5	6	1	78	141	28.20	–	1	11
Windows, M.G.N.(Gs)	—	9	17	2	184	443	29.53	1	1	4
Wood, J.(Du)	1992	9	16	2	35*	97	6.92	–	–	4
†Wood, N.T.(La)	—	1	1	–	1	1	1.00	–	–	–
Wren, T.N.(K)	—	7	5	2	8	15	5.00	–	–	3
Wright, A.J.(Gs)	1987	9	17	–	106	415	24.41	1	3	11
Wright, G.J.(OU)	—	1	–	–	–	–	–	–	–	–
Yates, G.(La)	1994	3	5	1	16	21	5.25	–	–	2

BOWLING

See BATTING and FIELDING section for details of caps and teams.

	Cat	O	M	R	W	Avge	Best	5wI	10wM
Aamir Sohail	SLA	65.4	14	205	3	68.33	1- 4	–	–
Ackerman, H.D.	RM	5	1	10	0				
Adams, C.J.	OB	14	1	44	0				
Adams, P.R	SLC	108.4	19	390	10	39.00	4-116	–	–
Afford, J.A.	SLA	579.5	165	1471	51	28.84	6- 51	2	–
Afzaal, U.	SLA	44	3	199	3	66.33	1- 31	–	–
Aldred, P.	RM	139.5	21	537	8	67.12	2- 65	–	–
Alleyne, M.W.	RM	458.1	123	1316	54	24.37	5- 32	2	–
Allingham, M.J.D.	RM	22	4	98	4	24.50	3- 53	–	–
Altree, D.A.	LMF	67	9	267	6	44.50	3- 41	–	–
Ambrose, C.E.L.	RF	284.4	80	717	43	16.67	6- 26	5	1
Amjad, M.	SLC	4	0	25	0				
Andrew, S.J.W.	RMF	198.4	47	641	15	42.73	3- 67	–	–
Ankola, S.A.	RMF	76	9	285	8	35.62	4-120	–	–
Archer, G.F.	OB	27	5	98	3	32.66	3- 18	–	–
Asif Mujtaba	SLA	32	7	104	3	34.66	1- 8	–	–
Ata-ur-Rehman	RFM	184.4	24	710	17	41.76	4- 50	–	–
Atherton, M.A.	LB	12	2	35	1	35.00	1- 20	–	–
Austin, I.D.	RM	223.4	64	645	22	29.31	5-116	1	–
Bailey, R.J.	OB	55.2	9	161	2	80.50	1- 3	–	–
Bainbridge, P.	RM	123.3	23	382	7	54.57	2- 44	–	–
Ball, M.C.J.	OB	225	61	639	13	49.15	3- 40	–	–
Barnett, K.J.	LB	139.2	15	507	12	42.25	3- 26	–	–
Barwick, S.R.	RM/OB	163.1	54	391	5	78.20	2- 81	–	–
Base, S.J.	RMF	23.2	4	105	1	105.00	1-105	–	–
Bates, R.T.	OB	278.2	46	969	21	46.14	3- 42	–	–
Batty, J.D.	OB	486.4	99	1572	32	49.12	5- 85	1	–
Benjamin, J.E.	RMF	375.3	83	1217	39	31.20	4- 17	–	–
Benjamin, W.K.M.	RFM	69.2	13	201	6	33.50	4- 96	–	–
Betts, M.M.	RMF	389.5	48	1753	44	39.84	5- 68	2	–
Bevan, M.G.	SLC	86.3	8	369	4	92.25	3- 36	–	–
Bicknell, D.J.	SLA	124.2	21	368	16	23.00	3- 7	–	–
Bicknell, M.P.	RFM	568.1	146	1633	66	24.74	5- 17	3	–
Birbeck, S.D.	RM	42	9	144	4	36.00	3- 88	–	–
Bishop, I.E.	RMF	7	0	29	0				
Blain, J.A.R.	RFM	22	5	103	0				
Blenkiron, D.A.	RM	37.5	9	123	5	24.60	4- 43	–	–
Boden, D.J.P.	RMF	37	5	140	1	140.00	1- 50	–	–
Boiling, J.	OB	263.1	85	582	9	64.66	2- 69	–	–
Boje, N.	SLA	160.4	30	562	12	46.83	5- 58	1	–
Boswell, S.A.J.	RFM	73.4	9	243	7	34.71	2- 52	–	–
Botham, L.J.	RMF	55	9	268	8	33.50	5- 67	1	–

	Cat	O	M	R	W	Avge	Best	5wI	10wM
Bovill, J.N.B.	RFM	328	62	1199	34	35.26	5- 58	1	–
Bowen, M.N.	RM	366.2	64	1281	33	38.81	5- 53	2	–
Bowler, P.D.	OB	31.3	2	177	3	59.00	2- 54	–	–
Brimson, M.T.	SLA	360.2	76	1106	35	31.60	5- 12	2	–
Broadhurst, M.	RFM	7	0	60	0				
Brown, A.D.	LB	6	2	8	0				
Brown, D.R.	RFM	407.2	81	1410	40	35.25	6- 52	2	1
Brown, J.F.	OB	22	6	64	0				
Brown, S.J.E.	LFM	642.1	109	2130	79	26.96	6- 77	5	–
Browne, B.St A.	RF	29	7	111	1	111.00	1- 55	–	–
Burns, M.	RM	3	0	13	0				
Butcher, G.P.	RM	199.1	30	826	21	39.33	7- 77	1	–
Butcher, M.A.	RM	52	7	233	7	33.28	3- 23	–	–
Butler, O.F.X.	RF	9	0	31	0				
Caddick, A.R.	RFM	604.1	131	2029	73	27.79	7- 83	6	3
Cairns, C.L.	RFM	427.3	73	1461	37	39.48	6-110	1	–
Campbell, C.L.	RFM	15.2	3	44	1	44.00	1- 29	–	–
Campbell, S.L.	RM	16.4	3	60	1	60.00	1- 38	–	–
Capel, D.J.	RMF	348.1	57	1181	35	33.74	4- 60	–	–
Chapman, R.J.	RFM	40.5	4	183	6	30.50	4-109	–	–
Chapple, G.	RFM	477.1	94	1671	50	33.42	5- 64	2	–
Childs, J.H.	SLA	222.4	56	765	19	40.26	4- 99	–	–
Church, M.J.	RM	39.1	5	159	9	17.66	4- 50	–	–
Clarke, V.P.	RM/LB	11	1	52	1	52.00	1- 42	–	–
Collingwood, P.D.	RMF	55.2	7	181	3	60.33	1- 13	–	–
Connor, C.A.	RFM	362.4	99	1071	49	21.85	9- 38	2	–
Cooper, K.E.	RFM	39	12	82	5	16.40	4- 54	–	–
Cork, D.G.	RFM	589	121	1891	57	33.17	5-113	1	–
Cosker, D.A.	SLA	155.4	38	622	16	38.87	4- 60	–	–
Cottam, A.C.	SLA	89	22	248	3	82.66	2-127	–	–
Cottey, P.A.	OB	34	3	107	4	26.75	4- 49	–	–
Cowan, A.P.	RFM	409.2	67	1464	40	36.60	5- 68	1	–
Cowdrey, G.R.	RM	11.3	3	42	1	42.00	1- 19	–	–
Cox, D.M.	SLA	306	87	883	26	33.96	5- 97	2	1
Croft, R.D.B.	OB	955.4	237	2486	76	32.71	6- 78	4	–
Crookes, D.N.	OB	84	16	259	3	86.33	1- 7	–	–
Curran, K.M.	RMF	180	34	641	11	58.27	3- 75	–	–
Curtis, T.S.	LB	4.3	0	18	2	9.00	1- 1	–	–
Dale, A.	RM	141.1	36	470	12	39.16	4- 52	–	–
Davies, A.P.	RMF	26	5	118	1	118.00	1- 25	–	–
Davis, R.P.	SLA	314.2	70	1053	23	45.78	4- 93	–	–
Dawson, R.I.	RM	2.2	0	7	1	7.00	1- 3	–	–
Deakin, P.J.	OB	71.1	9	249	9	27.66	2- 17	–	–
Dean, K.J.	LMF	144.1	32	471	16	29.43	3- 47	–	–
DeFreitas, P.A.J.	RFM	545.2	105	1687	64	26.35	7-101	4	–
Derbyshire, N.A.	RFM	20	2	87	1	87.00	1- 67	–	–
Dibden, R.R.	OB	36	1	164	2	82.00	2-148	–	–
Dodemaide, A.I.C.	RFM	33	9	112	1	112.00	1- 92	–	–
Dowman, M.P.	RMF	36	10	122	2	61.00	2- 43	–	–
Drakes, V.C.	RFM	454.3	79	1675	50	33.50	5- 47	2	–
Du Preez, S.P.	LMF	168	24	634	5	126.80	2- 44	–	–
Dutch, K.P.	OB	23	4	85	3	28.33	3- 25	–	–
Eagleson, R.L.	RM	31.1	2	149	3	49.66	2- 50	–	–
Ealham, M.A.	RMF	401.4	130	995	47	21.17	8- 36	3	1
Edmond, M.D.	RMF	16.5	1	79	1	79.00	1- 6	–	–
Edwards, A.D.	RFM	13	2	64	0				

133

	Cat	O	M	R	W	Avge	Best	5wI	10wM
Ellis, S.W.K.	RMF	170	27	686	14	49.00	3- 29	–	–
Elworthy, S.	RFM	308.1	43	1165	28	41.60	4- 80	–	–
Emburey, J.E.	OB	396.2	94	1042	27	38.59	4- 48	–	–
Evans, K.P.	RMF	412.4	99	1217	30	40.56	5- 30	2	–
Fay, R.A.	RMF	360	84	1121	31	36.16	4- 53	–	–
Feltham, M.A.	RMF	57	14	185	4	46.25	3- 62	–	–
Fisher, I.D.	SLA	9	2	29	1	29.00	1- 29	–	–
Fleming, M.V.	RM	168.2	32	484	18	26.88	3- 6	–	–
Foley, G.I.	RM	37	5	140	2	70.00	1- 22	–	–
Follett, D.	RFM	147.2	26	589	23	25.60	8- 22	3	1
Ford, J.A.	SLA	11.2	1	54	0			–	–
Foster, M.J.	RFM	93.3	15	311	8	38.87	4- 21	–	–
Francis, N.B.	RF	37	13	101	5	20.20	4- 34	–	–
Franks, P.J.	RMF	41	14	102	3	34.00	2- 65	–	–
Fraser, A.R.C.	RMF	592.4	138	1636	49	33.38	5- 55	2	1
Fulton, D.P.	SLA	11	1	65	1	65.00	1- 37	–	–
Gallian, J.E.R.	RM	150.4	28	574	16	35.87	6-115	1	–
Ganguly, S.C.	RM	85.4	10	340	10	34.00	3- 71	–	–
Gardner, G.E.	RM	16	2	74	2	37.00	1- 36	–	–
Gatting, M.W.	RM	4	0	25	0			–	–
Gibbs, H.H.	RFM/LB	12	2	43	3	14.33	2- 14	–	–
Gibson, O.D.	RF	254	41	1040	20	52.00	3- 43	–	–
Giddins, E.S.H.	RMF	367.4	66	1204	48	25.08	6- 47	2	1
Gilder, G.M.	LFM	94.4	29	243	13	18.69	8- 22	1	1
Giles, A.F.	SLA	633.3	191	1615	64	25.23	6- 45	3	–
Gillespie, P.G.	RM	30	5	136	5	27.20	3- 93	–	–
Gooch, G.A.	RM	21	7	57	2	28.50	1- 20	–	–
Goodchild, D.J.	RM	4.5	0	26	0			–	–
Gough, D.	RFM	573.3	142	1535	67	22.91	6- 36	2	–
Govan, J.W.	OB	20	3	74	1	74.00	1- 65	–	–
Grayson, A.P.	SLA	264.3	58	759	18	42.16	4- 82	–	–
Green, R.J.	RM	187.5	36	599	22	27.22	6- 41	1	–
Greenfield, K.	RM	23	6	52	0			–	–
Griffith, F.A.	RM	27	1	137	1	137.00	1- 70	–	–
Gupte, C.M.	SLA	9	0	36	0			–	–
Hamilton, G.M.	RFM	101.4	12	304	8	38.00	3- 65	–	–
Hancock, T.H.C.	RM	18	4	60	0			–	–
Harden, R.J.	SLA	8	1	42	1	42.00	1- 39	–	–
Harmison, S.J.	RFM	9	1	77	0			–	–
Harris, A.J.	RM	379.1	76	1380	53	26.03	6- 40	2	1
Harrison, G.D.	OB	23	3	94	0			–	–
Hart, J.P.	RM	18	7	51	0			–	–
Hartley, P.J.	RMF	459.2	96	1602	54	29.66	6- 67	2	1
Haste, N.J.	RM	165.5	16	673	8	84.12	3- 51	–	–
Hayhurst, A.N.	RM	25	5	91	1	91.00	1- 8	–	–
Headley, D.W.	RFM	423	69	1387	51	27.19	8- 98	2	1
Hemp, D.L.	RM	21	2	113	4	28.25	3- 23	–	–
Hewitt, J.P.	RMF	179.3	38	681	24	28.37	3- 27	–	–
Hick, G.A.	OB	109	25	333	5	66.60	2- 43	–	–
Hindson, J.E	SLA	3	1	7	0				
Hirwani, N.D.	LBG	115.3	24	375	12	31.25	6- 60	1	–
Hoggard, M.J.	RFM	15	3	41	1	41.00	1- 41	–	–
Hollioake, A.J.	RMF	236	45	793	12	66.08	3- 80	–	–
Hollioake, B.C.	RMF	65	12	252	10	25.20	4- 74	–	–
Holloway, P.C.L.	(WK)	4.4	0	34	0				
Hooper, C.L.	OB	321.3	83	789	26	30.34	4- 7	–	–

134

	Cat	O	M	R	W	Avge	Best	5wI	10wM
House, W.J.	RM	89	8	412	2	206.00	1- 44	–	–
How, E.J.	LMF	27	5	161	0				
Hughes, J.G.	RM	53	11	221	3	73.66	2- 21	–	–
Hutchison, P.M.	LFM	22.1	1	123	1	123.00	1- 39	–	–
Ijaz Ahmed	LM	4.5	0	27	0				
Illingworth, R.K.	SLA	717.1	208	1721	51	33.74	6- 75	3	–
Ilott, M.C.	LFM	550.2	118	1666	50	33.32	5- 53	2	–
Innes, K.J.	RM	59	7	193	8	24.12	4- 61	–	–
Inzamam-ul-Haq	SLA	4	0	24	0				
Irani, R.C.	RMF	395	74	1320	47	28.08	5- 27	1	–
Jadeja, A.	RM	11	2	31	0				
James, K.D.	LMF	301.1	57	882	30	29.40	5- 74	1	–
Janisch, A.N.	RM	70	12	263	4	65.75	2- 23	–	–
Jarrett, M.E.D.	RM	2	0	5	0				
Jarvis, P.W.	RFM	168	27	592	19	31.15	4- 60	–	–
Johnson, P.	RM	12	2	51	1	51.00	1- 51	–	–
Johnson, R.L.	RMF	242.5	36	878	25	35.12	5- 29	1	–
Jones, D.M.	OB	77.4	11	321	9	35.66	5-112	1	–
Jones, R.O.	OB	185.4	29	660	9	73.33	2- 45	–	–
Joshi, S.B.	SLA	67.3	9	317	5	63.40	2- 41	–	–
Julian, B.P.	LFM	447.4	86	1762	61	28.88	6- 37	3	–
Kallis, J.H.	RM	56.3	19	145	6	24.16	4- 31	–	–
Keech, M.	RM	18	3	46	0				
Keedy, G.	SLA	475.1	131	1215	23	52.82	3- 45	–	–
Kendall, W.S.	RM	19	1	82	2	41.00	2- 46	–	–
Kendrick, N.M.	SLA	236	74	706	17	41.52	4- 89	–	–
Kenlock, S.G.	LFM	12	2	40	0				
Kerr, J.I.D.	RMF	131	16	586	11	53.27	3-108	–	–
Kettleborough, R.A.	RM	12	1	40	2	20.00	2- 26	–	–
Khan, G.A.	LBG	29	0	190	3	63.33	2- 48	–	–
Khan, W.G.	LB	2.1	1	2	0				
Killeen, N.	RFM	114.5	22	434	12	36.16	4- 57	–	–
Kirtley, R.J.	RFM	193.4	32	756	27	28.00	5- 51	1	–
Klusener, L.	RFM	232.3	44	783	31	25.25	5- 74	1	–
Koenig, S.G.	OB	3	2	5	0				
Kumble, A.	LBG	281	73	739	13	56.84	4-111	–	–
Lampitt, S.R.	RMF	520.5	102	1919	54	35.53	5- 58	2	–
Laney, J.S.	OB	14	2	61	0				
Lathwell, M.N.	RM	7.4	0	27	1	27.00	1- 14	–	–
Law, D.R.	RFM	320.4	45	1221	42	29.07	5- 33	2	–
Law, S.G.	RM/LB	208.4	46	760	14	54.28	3-100	–	–
Leatherdale, D.A.	RM	105.5	21	384	11	34.90	4- 75	–	–
Lee, S.	RFM	418.3	66	1770	40	44.25	4- 52	–	–
Lenham, N.J.	RM	56.1	9	146	3	48.66	1- 3	–	–
Lewis, C.C.	RFM	488.2	98	1597	45	35.48	5- 25	2	–
Lewis, J.	RMF	276	65	846	18	47.00	3- 74	–	–
Lewis, J.J.B.	RSM	4	0	16	0				
Lewry, J.D.	LMF	302	59	942	41	22.97	6- 44	4	1
Liebenberg, G.F.J.	RFM	3	2	1	0				
Lightfoot, C.G.R.	SLA	27.5	5	129	2	64.50	2- 65	–	–
Llong, N.J.	OB	80.5	23	249	11	22.63	5- 21	1	–
Lloyd, G.D.	RM	2	0	4	1	4.00	1- 4	–	–
Lugsden, S.	RFM	70.3	9	262	11	23.81	3- 45	–	–
McCague, M.J.	RF	590	117	1897	76	24.96	6- 51	3	–
McCallan, W.K.	OB	15	1	64	0				
McGrath, A.	OB	7	0	41	0				

135

	Cat	O	M	R	W	Avge	Best	5wI	10wM
Maclay, A.W.	RMF	31	3	147	1	147.00	1- 67	–	–
Macmillan, G.I.	OB	16	3	59	2	29.50	2- 44	–	–
Maddy, D.L.	RM/OB	36	11	104	4	26.00	2- 21	–	–
Malcolm, D.E.	RF	639.2	98	2597	82	31.67	6- 52	6	2
Malik, H.S.	OB	197	23	826	10	82.60	3-119	–	–
Mallender, N.A.	RFM	41	12	137	1	137.00	1- 27	–	–
Marc, K.	RFM	33	7	105	3	35.00	3- 91	–	–
Marsh, S.A.	(WK)	6	4	5	0				
Martin, P.J.	RMF	427.4	106	1161	44	26.38	7- 50	1	–
Martin-Jenkins, R.S.C.	RFM	58	13	158	1	158.00	1- 26	–	–
Maru, R.J.	SLA	306.2	101	734	18	40.77	3- 50	–	–
Mascarenhas, A.D.	RMF	92	21	297	16	18.56	6- 88	1	–
Mather, D.P.	LM	137.4	19	536	9	59.55	3- 31	–	–
May, M.R.	OB	3	0	19	0				
Maynard, M.P.	RM	7.3	4	7	0				
Mhambrey, P.L.	RMF	146	25	572	8	71.50	2- 23	–	–
Mike, G.W.	RMF	73.5	13	312	4	78.00	2- 34	–	–
Milburn, S.M.	RMF	257	44	939	17	55.23	3- 47	–	–
Millns, D.J.	RF	538.1	133	1659	72	23.04	6- 54	2	1
Moffat, G.R.	RM	185	28	788	8	98.50	2- 50	–	–
Mohammad Akram	RFM	128.2	21	473	14	33.78	7- 51	1	–
Moin Khan	(WK)	9	0	78	2	39.00	2- 78	–	–
Molins, G.L.	SLA	32.5	5	119	4	29.75	3- 62	–	–
Moody, T.M.	RM	319.5	86	956	37	25.83	7- 92	3	1
Moore, D.M.P.	RM	6	1	37	0				
Morris, A.C.	RMF	31	6	116	4	29.00	1- 11	–	–
Morris, J.E.	RM	1	0	10	0				
Mullally, A.D.	LFM	628.5	166	1774	70	25.34	6- 47	3	1
Munton, T.A.	RMF	404	116	1092	35	31.20	4- 41	–	–
Mushtaq Ahmed	LBG	325	85	861	41	21.00	7- 91	5	1
Nash, D.J.	RFM	10	1	44	1	44.00	1- 44	–	–
Newell, K.	RM	19	4	66	1	66.00	1- 38	–	–
Newport, P.J.	RFM	187.3	44	670	19	35.26	6-100	1	–
Noon, W.M.	(WK)	4	1	22	0				
Nowell, R.W.	SLA	31	5	133	2	66.50	2- 76	–	–
Parkin, O.T.	RFM	224.4	47	744	17	43.76	3- 22	–	–
Parsons, G.J.	RMF	555	170	1536	47	32.68	4- 21	–	–
Parsons, K.A.	RM	38	8	154	2	77.00	1- 24	–	–
Patel, M.M.	SLA	586	176	1554	33	47.09	6- 97	2	1
Patterson, M.W.	RFM	27.3	7	124	7	17.71	6- 80	1	–
Pearson, R.M.	OB	475	101	1509	31	48.67	5-142	1	–
Penberthy, A.L.	RM	352.2	68	1077	34	31.67	5- 92	1	–
Pennett, D.B.	RMF	91	15	376	7	53.71	4-116	–	–
Phillips, B.J.	RFM	40	12	109	4	27.25	3- 34	–	–
Phillips, N.C.	OB	224	50	778	13	59.84	2- 54	–	–
Pick, R.A.	RFM	155.1	31	483	7	69.00	3- 74	–	–
Pierson, A.R.K.	OB	544.2	108	1710	48	35.62	6-158	2	–
Pollock, S.M.	RFM	446.4	115	1183	42	28.16	6- 56	1	–
Pooley, J.C.	OB	4	0	42	0				
Pothas, N.	(WK)	1	0	5	0				
Powell, M.J.	RM	4	0	18	1	18.00	1- 18	–	–
Prasad, B.K.V.	RFM	252.3	59	734	25	29.36	5- 76	1	–
Preece, B.E.A.	RFM	76.2	3	388	8	48.50	4- 79	–	–
Preston, N.W.	RFM	130.5	27	352	11	32.00	4- 68	–	–
Pringle, M.W.	RFM	172.4	40	579	14	41.35	4- 90	–	–
Raju, S.L.V.	SLA	172	47	464	5	92.80	1- 10	–	–

	Cat	O	M	R	W	Avge	Best	5wI	10wM
Ramprakash, M.R.	RM	31	4	121	3	40.33	2- 26	–	–
Rao, R.K.	LBG	5	3	7	0			–	–
Rashid Latif	(WK)	5	1	26	0			–	–
Rashid, U.B.A.	SLA	6	1	17	0			–	–
Ratcliffe, J.D.	RM	42	7	166	5	33.20	2- 26	–	–
Rawnsley, M.J.	SLA	76	18	219	5	43.80	1- 4	–	–
Reeve, D.A.	RMF	103	32	195	9	21.66	5- 37	1	–
Renshaw, S.J.	RMF	206.5	51	743	15	49.53	4- 56	–	–
Ridley, A.C.	RM	5	1	19	0			–	–
Roberts, A.R.	LB	172.5	44	527	10	52.70	3- 57	–	–
Roberts, G.M.	SLA	36	18	73	1	73.00	1- 55	–	–
Robinson, D.D.J.	RMF	5	0	24	0			–	–
Robinson, R.T.	RM	1	0	4	0			–	–
Rollins, A.S.	RM	5	0	50	0			–	–
Rose, G.D.	RM	393.2	98	1218	50	24.36	7- 47	3	1
Saggers, M.J.	RMF	101	12	443	13	34.07	6- 65	1	–
Salim Malik	RM/LB	7	1	24	1	24.00	1- 9	–	–
Salisbury, I.D.K.	LBG	505	109	1506	52	28.96	8- 75	3	1
Saqlain Mushtaq	OB	166.5	43	456	29	15.72	6- 52	2	–
Schultz, B.N.	LF	67	6	297	6	49.50	2- 45	–	–
Shadab Kabir	OB	5	0	27	0			–	–
Shah, O.A.	OB	5	0	24	1	24.00	1- 24	–	–
Shahid Anwar	RMF	7.3	2	46	2	23.00	2- 46	–	–
Shahid Nazir	RFM	47	8	164	12	13.66	4- 43	–	–
Shahid, N.	LB	85.1	13	285	6	47.50	3- 93	–	–
Sheeraz, K.P.	RMF	39	6	142	1	142.00	1- 41	–	–
Sheriyar, A.	LFM	460	78	1661	37	44.89	6- 99	1	–
Shine, K.J.	RFM	276.3	44	1209	35	34.54	6- 95	2	–
Silverwood, C.E.W.	RFM	404.3	79	1442	47	30.68	5- 72	2	–
Simmons, P.V.	RM	364.4	87	1021	56	18.23	6- 14	3	–
Singh, A.	OB	4	0	14	0			–	–
Small, G.C.	RFM	164	35	536	19	28.21	4- 41	–	–
Smith, A.M.	LMF	487.3	114	1615	60	26.91	8- 73	3	1
Smith, A.W.	OB	7	0	61	0			–	–
Smith, G.J.	LFM	125.2	24	402	15	26.80	4- 70	–	–
Smith, N.M.K.	OB	486.4	115	1417	43	32.95	5- 76	3	–
Smith, P.A.	RFM	32.2	7	88	2	44.00	1- 12	–	–
Snape, J.N.	OB	313.3	62	1013	23	44.04	4- 42	–	–
Solanki, V.S.	OB	215.2	37	863	27	31.96	5- 69	3	1
Speak, N.J.	RM/OB	6	0	27	0			–	–
Srinath, J.	RFM	233.3	68	628	20	31.40	4-103	–	–
Stanford, E.J.	SLA	67.3	22	158	5	31.60	3- 84	–	–
Stemp, R.D.	SLA	566	165	1537	42	36.59	5- 38	2	–
Stephenson, J.P.	RM	336.4	73	1098	36	30.50	6- 48	3	–
Stewart, A.J.	RM	2	0	24	0			–	–
Strang, P.A.	LBG	46.3	10	134	2	67.00	1- 17	–	–
Such, P.M.	OB	771.4	190	2164	82	26.39	8-118	6	1
Sutcliffe, I.J.	OB	20	1	86	3	28.66	2- 21	–	–
Swann, A.J.	OB/RM	5	1	15	0			–	–
Symonds, A.	OB	118.3	25	374	12	31.16	2- 21	–	–
Taylor, J.P.	LFM	549.2	116	1766	64	27.59	7- 88	3	1
Telemachus, R.	RFM	40	5	188	7	26.85	4- 99	–	–
Tendulkar, S.R.	RM/OB	28	5	109	1	109.00	1- 28	–	–
Tennant, A.M.	SLA	32	13	122	3	40.66	3- 28	–	–
Tennent, R.W.	RM	38	5	136	4	34.00	4- 34	–	–
Thomas, P.A.	RFM	121	14	575	12	47.91	4- 33	–	–

137

	Cat	O	M	R	W	Avge	Best	5wI	10wM
Thomas, S.D.	RFM	295	33	1175	20	58.75	5-121	1	–
Thompson, J.B.D.	RFM	91.2	16	336	9	37.33	5- 72	1	–
Thomson, R.B.	RM	183.4	36	527	9	58.55	2- 24	–	–
Thorpe, G.P.	RM	38	12	87	2	43.50	2- 13	–	–
Thursfield, M.J.	RM	108.3	22	361	5	72.20	3- 45	–	–
Titchard, S.P.	RM	37	7	124	1	124.00	1- 51	–	–
Tolley, C.M.	LMF	216	37	804	14	57.42	4- 68	–	–
Trainor, N.J.	OB	1	0	4	0				
Trescothick, M.E.	RM	23	1	97	0				
Trump, H.R.J.	OB	43	10	179	4	44.75	3- 43	–	–
Tufnell, P.C.R.	SLA	839.1	273	1712	78	21.94	7- 49	6	1
Turner, R.J.	(WK)	1	0	3	0				
Tweats, T.A.	RM	3	0	14	0				
Udal, S.D.	OB	497.4	101	1582	34	46.52	5- 82	1	–
Vandrau, M.J.	OB	226	30	789	16	49.31	6- 34	1	–
Van Troost, A.P.	RF	107.4	12	485	9	53.88	4- 90	–	–
Vaughan, M.P.	OB	187.3	28	728	17	42.82	4- 62	–	–
Wagh, M.A.	OB	187.3	28	632	10	63.20	3- 82	–	–
Walker, A.	RFM	80	13	277	2	138.50	1- 50	–	–
Walker, M.J.	RM	1	0	19	0				
Walsh, C.A.	RF	526.3	144	1432	85	16.84	6- 22	7	1
Walsh, C.D.	LB	12	0	64	0				
Walton, T.C.	RM	29	2	113	2	56.50	1- 26	–	–
Waqar Younis	RF	195.1	42	654	30	21.80	5- 42	1	–
Ward, I.J.	RM	9	2	49	0				
Ward, T.R.	OB	9	3	29	2	14.50	2- 10	–	–
Warner, A.E.	RFM	8	0	41	1	41.00	1- 41	–	–
Wasim Akram	LF	271.5	67	787	32	24.59	5- 58	1	–
Watkin, S.L.	RMF	616.4	159	1797	67	26.82	4- 28	–	–
Watkinson, M.	RMF/OB	433	78	1501	37	40.56	5- 15	1	–
Weekes, P.N.	OB	371	75	1082	32	33.81	8- 39	2	–
Welch, G.	RM	275.5	42	1035	34	30.44	4- 50	–	–
Wells, C.M.	RM	164	40	440	9	48.88	2- 20	–	–
Wells, V.J.	RMF	255.1	69	765	26	29.42	4- 44	–	–
Weston, R.M.S.	LB	2	1	6	0				
Weston, W.P.C.	LM	7	0	36	0				
Wharf, A.G.	RMF	59.4	18	221	6	36.83	4- 29	–	–
Whitaker, P.R.	OB	118.2	26	423	10	42.30	3- 36	–	–
White, C.	RFM	299.2	51	1100	37	29.72	4- 15	–	–
White, G.W.	LB	17	2	75	0				
Whittall, A.R.	OB	274.3	56	932	10	93.20	3-103	–	–
Wild, R.D.	RMF	14	4	62	1	62.00	1- 62	–	–
Williams, N.F.	RFM	331.4	59	1160	35	33.14	5- 43	2	–
Williamson, D.	RM	29	8	95	1	95.00	1- 32	–	–
Williamson, J.G.	RM	33.2	9	123	2	61.50	2- 51	–	–
Wood, J.	RFM	291.3	46	1266	26	48.69	4- 60	–	–
Wren, T.N.	LM	112	22	409	9	45.44	5- 49	1	–
Wright, G.J.	RM	9	0	33	0				
Yates, G.	OB	93.2	20	325	5	65.00	3- 91	–	–

BRITANNIC ASSURANCE
COUNTY CHAMPIONSHIP 1996 FINAL TABLE

	P	W	L	D	Bonus Bat	Points Bowl	Total Points
1 LEICESTERSHIRE (7)	17	10	1	6	57	61	296
2 Derbyshire (14)	17	9	3	5	52	58	269
3 Surrey (12)	17	8	2	7	49	64	262
4 Kent (18)	17	9	2	6	47	52	261
5 Essex (5)	17	8	5	4	58	57	255
6 Yorkshire (8)	17	8	5	4	50	58	248
7 Worcestershire (10)	17	6	4	7	45	60	222
8 Warwickshire (1)	17	6	4	4	39	55	218
9 Middlesex (2)	17	7	6	4	30	59	213
10 Glamorgan (16)	17	6	5	6	50	43	207
11 Somerset (9)	17	5	6	6	38	61	197
12 Sussex (15)	17	6	9	2	36	58	196
13 Gloucestershire (6)	17	5	7	5	23	59	177
14 Hampshire (13)	17	3	7	7	41	56	166
15 Lancashire (4)	17	2	6	9	49	52	160
16 Northamptonshire (3)	17	3	8	6	36	57	159
17 Nottinghamshire (11)	17	1	9	7	42	52	131
18 Durham (17)	17	–	12	5	22	60	97

1995 final positions are shown in brackets.

SCORING OF POINTS 1996

(a) For a win, 16 points, plus any points scored in the first innings.

(b) In a tie, each side to score eight points, plus any points scored in the first innings.

(c) In a drawn match, each side to score three points, plus any points scored in the first innings (see also paragraph (f) below).

(d) If the scores are equal in a drawn match, the side batting in the fourth innings to score eight points plus any points scored in the first innings, and the opposing side to score three points plus any points scored in the first innings.

(e) **First Innings Points** (awarded only for the performances **in the first 120 overs** of each first innings and retained whatever the result of the match).

(i) A maximum of four batting points to be available as under:-	(ii) A maximum of four bowling points to be available as under:-
200 to 249 runs – 1 point	3 to 4 wickets taken – 1 point
250 to 299 runs – 2 points	5 to 6 wickets taken – 2 points
300 to 349 runs – 3 points	7 to 8 wickets taken – 3 points
350 runs or over – 4 points	9 to 10 wickets taken – 4 points

(f) If play starts when less than eight hours playing time remains (in which event a one innings match shall be played as provided for in First Class Playing Condition 20), no first innings points shall be scored. The side winning on the one innings to score 12 points. In a tie, each side to score six points. In a drawn match, each side to score three points. If the scores are equal in a drawn match, the side batting in the second innings to score six points and the opposing side to score three points.

(g) A County which is adjudged to have prepared a pitch which is 'unsuitable for four day First-Class Cricket' shall be liable to have 25 points deducted from its aggregate of points under the procedure agreed by the Board in December 1988 and revised in December 1993. In addition, a penalty of 10 or 15 points may in certain circumstances be imposed on a County in respect of a 'Poor' pitch under the procedure agreed by the Board in March 1995. There shall be no right of appeal against any points penalty provided for in this Clause.

(h) The side which has the highest aggregate of points gained at the end of the season shall be the Champion County. Should any sides in the Championship table be equal on points, the side with most wins will have priority.

COUNTY CHAMPIONS

The English County Championship was not officially constituted until December 1889. Prior to that date there was no generally accepted method of awarding the title; although the 'least matches lost' method existed, it was not consistently applied. Rules governing playing qualifications were not agreed until 1873, and the first unofficial points system was not introduced until 1888.

Research has produced a list of champions dating back to 1826, but at least seven different versions exist for the period from 1864 to 1889 (see *The Wisden Book of Cricket Records*). Only from 1890 can any authorised list of county champions commence.

That first official Championship was contested between eight counties: Gloucestershire, Kent, Lancashire, Middlesex, Nottinghamshire, Surrey, Sussex and Yorkshire. The remaining counties were admitted in the following seasons: 1891 – Somerset, 1895 – Derbyshire, Essex, Hampshire, Leicestershire and Warwickshire, 1899 – Worcestershire, 1905 – Northamptonshire, 1921 – Glamorgan, and 1992 – Durham.

The Championship pennant was introduced by the 1951 champions, Warwickshire, and the Lord's Taverners' Trophy was first presented in 1973. The first sponsors, Schweppes (1977 to 1983), were succeeded by BRITANNIC ASSURANCE in 1984.

1890	Surrey	1928	Lancashire	1966	Yorkshire
1891	Surrey	1929	Nottinghamshire	1967	Yorkshire
1892	Surrey	1930	Lancashire	1968	Yorkshire
1893	Yorkshire	1931	Yorkshire	1969	Glamorgan
1894	Surrey	1932	Yorkshire	1970	Kent
1895	Surrey	1933	Yorkshire	1971	Surrey
1896	Yorkshire	1934	Lancashire	1972	Warwickshire
1897	Lancashire	1935	Yorkshire	1973	Hampshire
1898	Yorkshire	1936	Derbyshire	1974	Worcestershire
1899	Surrey	1937	Yorkshire	1975	Leicestershire
1900	Yorkshire	1938	Yorkshire	1976	Middlesex
1901	Yorkshire	1939	Yorkshire	1977	{ Kent
1902	Yorkshire	1946	Yorkshire		{ Middlesex
1903	Middlesex	1947	Middlesex	1978	Kent
1904	Lancashire	1948	Glamorgan	1979	Essex
1905	Yorkshire	1949	{ Middlesex	1980	Middlesex
1906	Kent		{ Yorkshire	1981	Nottinghamshire
1907	Nottinghamshire	1950	{ Lancashire	1982	Middlesex
1908	Yorkshire		{ Surrey	1983	Essex
1909	Kent	1951	Warwickshire	1984	Essex
1910	Kent	1952	Surrey	1985	Middlesex
1911	Warwickshire	1953	Surrey	1986	Essex
1912	Yorkshire	1954	Surrey	1987	Nottinghamshire
1913	Kent	1955	Surrey	1988	Worcestershire
1914	Surrey	1956	Surrey	1989	Worcestershire
1919	Yorkshire	1957	Surrey	1990	Middlesex
1920	Middlesex	1958	Surrey	1991	Essex
1921	Middlesex	1959	Yorkshire	1992	Essex
1922	Yorkshire	1960	Yorkshire	1993	Middlesex
1923	Yorkshire	1961	Hampshire	1994	Warwickshire
1924	Yorkshire	1962	Yorkshire	1995	Warwickshire
1925	Yorkshire	1963	Yorkshire	1996	Leicestershire
1926	Lancashire	1964	Worcestershire		
1927	Lancashire	1965	Worcestershire		

CHAPPLE DEMOLISHES ESSEX

This match will long be recalled as the freakest of all Lord's finals, except in Essex where its flimsiest reference is likely to bring about painful retribution. The combination of a seaming surface with erratic bounce and the lavish swing of a 'Duke' ball rendered the contest a farce, neither the capacity crowd nor the sponsors being granted value for money. It will be used as evidence for those who want all limited-overs cricket to be honed to the 50-over format governing internationals, thus avoiding the unfortunate 10.30am start for a September match. Another solution would be to move it to a pitch guaranteeing a better balance between bat and ball.

These comments should not detract from Lancashire's remarkable performance in recent limited-overs cricket, a marked contrast to their results in the County Championship. They now stand supreme in this competition with six titles and 68 matches won. They also became the first team since Essex in 1985 to win a NatWest final after being compelled to bat first.

John Crawley's innings of 66, some 45 runs more than any other batsman achieved in these mischievous conditions, was an exceptionally skilful effort. He was, perhaps, a shade fortunate to survive a frenzied lbw appeal when his first ball nipped back down the slope. Lancashire would not have been content with their meagre total of 186 and the stage seemed set for Graham Gooch to make an important contribution to what was likely to be his last major match at Headquarters.

In the event poor Gooch could only watch in dismay as the Essex innings developed into a doleful procession. At one point, when Essex were 33 for six, he looked likely to carry his bat through the innings – for the princely score of 10. When Jason Gallian's first ball removed that bizarre possibility, the entire audience must have felt for England's premier batsman in his moment of total dispair.

Peter Martin and Glen Chapple used the conditions superbly and Essex did well in the circumstances to pass 50. Several of their offerings were quite unplayable, shooters which pitched leg and hit off. Chapple's performance uplifted a modest season, his final analysis of 6 for 18 usurping Joel Garner's 1979 haul of 6 for 29 as the best return in a Lord's county final.

Needless to say, Essex registered the lowest total in any inter-county final and their dismissal at 5.26pm marked the shortest match. It was not, however, the earliest finish. In 1982, the second year of NatWest's sponsorship, Surrey overhauled Warwickshire's tally of 158 at 5.13pm, but that game had begun 30 minutes earlier at 10 o'clock.

GILLETTE CUP WINNERS

1963 Sussex	1969 Yorkshire	1975 Lancashire
1964 Sussex	1970 Lancashire	1976 Northamptonshire
1965 Yorkshire	1971 Lancashire	1977 Middlesex
1966 Warwickshire	1972 Lancashire	1978 Sussex
1967 Kent	1973 Gloucestershire	1979 Somerset
1968 Warwickshire	1974 Kent	1980 Middlesex

NATWEST TROPHY WINNERS

1981 Derbyshire	1987 Nottinghamshire	1993 Warwickshire
1982 Surrey	1988 Middlesex	1994 Worcestershire
1983 Somerset	1989 Warwickshire	1995 Warwickshire
1984 Middlesex	1990 Lancashire	1996 Lancashire
1985 Essex	1991 Hampshire	
1986 Sussex	1992 Northamptonshire	

1996 NATWEST TROPHY FINAL

ESSEX v LANCASHIRE

At Lord's, London on 7 September.
Toss: Essex. Result: LANCASHIRE won by 129 runs.
Award: G.Chapple.

LANCASHIRE		Runs	Balls	4/6	Fall
J.E.R.Gallian	lbw b Irani	21	61	3	2- 48
M.A.Atherton	b Ilott	4	13	–	1- 16
J.P.Crawley	st Rollins b Such	66	129	7	6-139
N.H.Fairbrother	b Irani	9	38	–	3- 86
G.D.Lloyd	c Gooch b Irani	1	4	–	4- 88
*M.Watkinson	b Such	18	31	2	5-122
†W.K.Hegg	b Grayson	15	33	1	7-157
I.D.Austin	c Cowan b Grayson	18	18	1/1	8-168
G.Chapple	c Cowan b Grayson	4	13	–	9-175
G.Yates	run out (Grayson)	9	11	–	10-186
P.J.Martin	not out	5	11	–	
Extras	(B 4, LB 3, W 5, NB 4)	16			
Total	(60 overs)	**186**			

ESSEX		Runs	Balls	4/6	Fall
G.A.Gooch	lbw b Gallian	10	55	1	7-33
A.P.Grayson	c Hegg b Martin	6	16	–	1-13
N.Hussain	c Hegg b Martin	2	8	–	2-17
*P.J.Prichard	c Fairbrother b Martin	6	15	1	3-25
R.C.Irani	b Chapple	5	12	1	4-31
D.D.J.Robinson	c Fairbrother b Chapple	2	12	–	5-33
†R.J.Rollins	b Chapple	0	1	–	6-33
M.C.Ilott	lbw b Chapple	0	4	–	8-34
N.F.Williams	not out	11	19	1	
A.P.Cowan	b Chapple	11	21	2	9-57
P.M.Such	b Chapple	0	1	–	10-57
Extras	(LB 1, W 3)	4			
Total	(27.2 overs)	**57**			

ESSEX	O	M	R	W	LANCASHIRE	O	M	R	W
Ilott	12	2	29	1	Martin	10	2	17	3
Williams	7.4	0	39	0	Austin	7	3	10	0
Irani	12	5	25	3	Chapple	6.2	1	18	6
Cowan	12	2	33	0	Gallian	4	0	11	1
Such	12	1	29	2					
Grayson	4.2	0	24	3					

Umpires: D.R.Shepherd and P.Willey.

THE NATWEST TROPHY 1996 RESULTS CHART

First Round 25, 26 June	Second Round 10 July	Quarter-finals 30, 31 July	Semi-finals 13 August	Final 7 September
LANCASHIRE	LANCASHIRE†	LANCASHIRE†	LANCASHIRE†	LANCASHIRE (£40,000)
Oxfordshire†	Northamptonshire	Derbyshire (£5,000)		
NORTHAMPTONSHIRE†	DERBYSHIRE†			
Cheshire	Kent			
DERBYSHIRE	YORKSHIRE†	YORKSHIRE	Yorkshire (£10,000)	
Staffordshire	Middlesex	Sussex (£5,000)		
KENT	SUSSEX			
Cambridgeshire†	Leicestershire†			
YORKSHIRE†	SOMERSET†	Somerset (£5,000)	Surrey† (£10,000)	Essex (£20,000)
Nottinghamshire	Gloucestershire	SURREY†		
MIDDLESEX	SURREY			
Cumberland†	Warwickshire†			
SUSSEX	Worcestershire†	Hampshire† (£5,000)	ESSEX	
Ireland†	HAMPSHIRE	ESSEX		
LEICESTERSHIRE†	Durham			
Berkshire	ESSEX†			
SOMERSET†				
Suffolk				
GLOUCESTERSHIRE				
Lincolnshire				
SURREY†				
Holland				
WARWICKSHIRE				
Cornwall†				
WORCESTERSHIRE				
Glamorgan†				
HAMPSHIRE†				
Norfolk				
DURHAM†				
Scotland				
ESSEX†				
Devon				

† Home team. Winning teams are in capitals. Prize-money shown in brackets.

Dates to catch 24 hour 'flu.

First Round
Tuesday 24th June

Second Round
Wednesday 9th July

Quarter Finals
Tuesday 29th July

Semi Finals
Tuesday 12th August
Wednesday 13th August

Final
Saturday 6th September

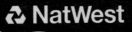

NATWEST TROPHY
PRINCIPAL RECORDS 1963-96
(Including The Gillette Cup)

Highest Total	413-4	Somerset v Devon	Torquay	1990
Highest Total in a Final	322-5	Warwicks v Sussex	Lord's	1993
Highest Total by a Minor County	305-9	Durham v Glam	Darlington	1991
Highest Total Batting Second	350	Surrey v Worcs	The Oval	1994
Highest Total to Win Batting 2nd	322-5	Warwicks v Sussex	Lord's	1993
Lowest Total	39	Ireland v Sussex	Lord's	1985
Lowest Total in a Final	57	Essex v Lancashire	Lord's	1996
Lowest Total to Win Batting First	98	Worcs v Durham	Chester-le-St	1968

Highest Score	206 A.I.Kallicharran	Warwicks v Oxon	Birmingham	1984
HS (Minor County)	132 G.Robinson	Lincs v Northumb	Jesmond	1971
Hundreds	287 (Gillette Cup 93; NatWest Trophy 194)			1963-96
Fastest Hundred	36 balls – G.D.Rose	Somerset v Devon	Torquay	1990
Most Hundreds	7 C.L.Smith	Hampshire		1980-91
Most Runs	2547 (av 48.98)	G.A.Gooch	Essex	1973-96

Highest Partnership for each Wicket

1st	269	J.P.Stephenson/J.S.Laney	Hampshire v Norfolk	Southampton	1996
2nd	286	I.S.Anderson/A.Hill	Derbys v Cornwall	Derby	1986
3rd	309*	T.S.Curtis/T.M.Moody	Worcs v Surrey	The Oval	1994
4th	234*	D.Lloyd/C.H.Lloyd	Lancashire v Glos	Manchester	1978
5th	166	M.A.Lynch/G.R.J.Roope	Surrey v Durham	The Oval	1982
6th	127	S.G.Law/R.J.Rollins	Essex v Hampshire	Southampton	1996
7th	160*	C.J.Richards/I.R.Payne	Surrey v Lincs	Sleaford	1983
8th	112	A.L.Penberthy/J.E.Emburey	Northants v Lancs	Manchester	1996
9th	87	M.A.Nash/A.E.Cordle	Glamorgan v Lincs	Swansea	1974
10th	81	S.Turner/R.E.East	Essex v Yorkshire	Leeds	1982

Best Bowling	8-21	M.A.Holding	Derbys v Sussex	Hove	1988
	8-31	D.L.Underwood	Kent v Scotland	Edinburgh	1987
Most Wickets	81 (av 14.85)	G.G.Arnold	Surrey	1963-80

Hat-Tricks
J.D.F.Larter (Northamptonshire 1963), D.A.D.Sydenham (Surrey 1964), R.N.S.Hobbs (Essex 1968), N.M.McVicker (Warwickshire 1971), G.S.Le Roux (Sussex 1985), M.Jean-Jacques (Derbyshire 1987), J.F.M.O'Brien (Cheshire 1988), R.A.Pick (Nottinghamshire 1995), J.E.Emburey (Northamptonshire 1996), A.R.Caddick (Somerset 1996).

Most Wicket-Keeping Dismissals in an Innings			
7 (7ct)	A.J.Stewart	Surrey v Glamorgan	Swansea	1994

Most Catches in an Innings
4 – A.S.Brown (Gloucestershire 1963), G.Cook (Northamptonshire 1972), C.G.Greenidge (Hampshire 1981), D.C.Jackson (Durham 1984), T.S.Smith (Hertfordshire 1984), H.Morris (Glamorgan 1988), C.C.Lewis (Nottinghamshire 1992).

Most Appearances	61	D.P.Hughes	Lancashire	1969-91
	61	M.W.Gatting	Middlesex	1975-96
Most Match Awards	9	G.A.Gooch	Essex	1973-96

Most Match Wins	68 – Lancashire.	Most Cup/Trophy Wins 6 – Lancashire.

1996 BENSON AND HEDGES CUP FINAL

LANCASHIRE v NORTHAMPTONSHIRE

At Lord's, London on 13 July.
Toss: Lancashire. Result: LANCASHIRE won by 31 runs.
Award: I.D.Austin.

LANCASHIRE		Runs	Balls	4/6	Fall
M.A.Atherton	c Bailey b Emburey	48	93	5	4-131
*M.Watkinson	c Emburey b Taylor	7	15	1	1- 18
J.E.R.Gallian	run out (Penberthy)	17	22	3	2- 52
J.P.Crawley	c Warren b Penberthy	34	40	4	3-105
N.H.Fairbrother	b Capel	63	70	6	7-236
G.D.Lloyd	b Taylor	26	25	3	5-180
†W.K.Hegg	run out (Capel/Emburey)	11	15	–	6-203
I.D.Austin	c and b Ambrose	14	18	1	9-243
G.Yates	c Penberthy b Capel	0	1	–	8-236
G.Chapple	not out	6	4	–	
P.J.Martin	not out	1	1	–	
Extras (W 10, NB 8)		18			
Total (50 overs; 9 wickets)		245			

NORTHAMPTONSHIRE		Runs	Balls	4/6	Fall
D.J.Capel	c Hegg b Austin	0	7	–	1- 1
A.Fordham	b Austin	4	20	–	2- 10
*R.J.Bailey	c Hegg b Chapple	46	89	2	3- 97
R.R.Montgomerie	c Hegg b Yates	42	56	5	4-111
K.M.Curran	c Crawley b Chapple	35	47	2	7-186
†R.J.Warren	c Crawley b Watkinson	11	15	–/1	5-132
T.C.Walton	st Hegg b Watkinson	28	26	2	6-184
A.L.Penberthy	b Austin	8	14	–	10-214
J.E.Emburey	b Austin	6	6	1	8-194
C.E.L.Ambrose	run out (Chapple/Austin)	10	12	1	9-214
J.P.Taylor	not out	0	–	–	
Extras (LB 10, W 12, NB 2)		24			
Total (48.3 overs)		214			

NORTHANTS	O	M	R	W	LANCASHIRE	O	M	R	W
Ambrose	10	2	35	1	Austin	9.3	2	21	4
Taylor	9	0	55	2	Martin	9	2	32	0
Curran	7	0	48	0	Chapple	10	1	51	2
Capel	8	1	37	2	Watkinson	10	0	66	2
Penberthy	6	0	31	1	Yates	10	0	34	1
Emburey	10	1	39	1					

Scores after 15 overs: Lancashire 59-2; Northamptonshire 47-2.

Umpires: M.J.Kitchen and G.Sharp.

Lancashire are the first to win this final four times and the second after
Somerset (1981-82) to win in successive years.

1996 BENSON AND HEDGES CUP

FINAL GROUP TABLES

GROUP A	P	W	L	NR	Pts	Net Run Rate
LANCASHIRE	5	5	–	–	10	11.57
WARWICKSHIRE	5	3	1	1	7	39.57
Leicestershire	5	3	2	–	6	–3.92
Derbyshire	5	2	3	–	4	–4.78
Durham	5	1	3	1	3	–6.83
Minor Counties	5	–	5	–	–	–26.53
GROUP B						
NORTHAMPTONSHIRE	4	4	–	–	8	11.05
YORKSHIRE	4	3	1	–	6	15.25
Nottinghamshire	4	2	2	–	4	4.55
Worcestershire	4	1	3	–	2	2.28
Scotland	4	–	4	–	–	–36.25
GROUP C						
GLAMORGAN	5	4	1	–	8	8.73
KENT	5	4	1	–	8	4.07
Essex	5	3	2	–	6	11.24
Somerset	5	3	2	–	6	4.76
Middlesex	5	1	4	–	2	–11.46
British Universities	5	–	5	–	–	–17.94
GROUP D						
SURREY	4	4	–	–	8	18.97
GLOUCESTERSHIRE	4	3	1	–	6	17.85
Hampshire	4	2	2	–	4	12.38
Sussex	4	1	3	–	2	–1.28
Ireland	4	–	4	–	–	–49.52

FINAL ROUNDS

QUARTER-FINALS	SEMI-FINALS	FINAL
28, 29 May	11, 12 June	13 July

NORTHAMPTONSHIRE†
Kent
(£5,000)
} NORTHAMPTONSHIRE†

WARWICKSHIRE
Glamorgan†
(£5,000)
} Warwickshire
(£10,000)

Northamptonshire
(£20,500)

YORKSHIRE
Surrey†
(£5,000)
} Yorkshire
(£10,000)

Gloucestershire
(£5,000)
LANCASHIRE†
} LANCASHIRE†

LANCASHIRE (£40,000)

† Home team. Winning teams are in capitals. Prize-money in brackets.

BENSON AND HEDGES CUP
PRINCIPAL RECORDS 1972-96

Highest Total	388-7	Essex v Scotland	Chelmsford	1992
Highest Total Batting Second	318-5	Lancashire v Leics	Manchester	1995
Highest Total to Lose Batting 2nd	303-7	Derbys v Somerset	Taunton	1990
Lowest Total	50	Hampshire v Yorks	Leeds	1991
Highest Score	198* G.A.Gooch	Essex v Sussex	Hove	1982
Hundreds	283			1972-96
Fastest Hundred	62 min – M.A.Nash	Glamorgan v Hants	Swansea	1976

Highest Partnership for each Wicket

1st	252	V.P.Terry/C.L.Smith	Hants v Comb Us	Southampton	1990
2nd	285*	C.G.Greenidge/D.R.Turner	Hants v Minor C (S)	Amersham	1973
3rd	269*	P.M.Roebuck/M.D.Crowe	Somerset v Hants	Southampton	1987
4th	184*	D.Lloyd/B.W.Reidy	Lancashire v Derbys	Chesterfield	1980
5th	160	A.J.Lamb/D.J.Capel	Northants v Leics	Northampton	1986
6th	167*	M.G.Bevan/R.J.Blakey	Yorkshire v Lancs	Manchester	1996
7th	149*	J.D.Love/C.M.Old	Yorks v Scotland	Bradford	1981
8th	109	R.E.East/N.Smith	Essex v Northants	Chelmsford	1977
9th	83	P.G.Newman/M.A.Holding	Derbyshire v Notts	Nottingham	1985
10th	80*	D.L.Bairstow/M.Johnson	Yorkshire v Derbys	Derby	1981

Best Bowling	7-12	W.W.Daniel	Middx v Minor C (E)	Ipswich	1978
	7-22	J.R.Thomson	Middx v Hampshire	Lord's	1981
	7-32	R.G.D.Willis	Warwicks v Yorks	Birmingham	1981
Four wickets in Four Balls	S.M.Pollock		Warwicks v Leics	Birmingham	1996
Hat-Tricks	G.D.McKenzie		Leics v Worcs	Worcester	1972
	K.Higgs		Leics v Surrey	Lord's	1974
	A.A.Jones		Middlesex v Essex	Lord's	1977
	M.J.Procter		Glos v Hampshire	Southampton	1977
	W.Larkins		Northants v Comb Us	Northampton	1980
	E.A.Moseley		Glamorgan v Kent	Cardiff	1981
	G.C.Small		Warwickshire v Leics	Leicester	1984
	N.A.Mallender		Somerset v Comb Us	Taunton	1987
	W.K.M.Benjamin		Leics v Notts	Leicester	1987
	A.R.C.Fraser		Middlesex v Sussex	Lord's	1988

Most Wicket-Keeping Dismissals in an Innings				
8 (8ct)	D.J.S.Taylor	Somerset v Comb Us	Taunton	1982
Most Catches in an Innings				
5	V.J.Marks	Comb Us v Kent	Oxford	1976
Most Match Awards	22	G.A.Gooch	Essex	1973-96

BENSON AND HEDGES CUP WINNERS

1972	Leicestershire	1981	Somerset	1990	Lancashire
1973	Kent	1982	Somerset	1991	Worcestershire
1974	Surrey	1983	Middlesex	1992	Hampshire
1975	Leicestershire	1984	Lancashire	1993	Derbyshire
1976	Kent	1985	Leicestershire	1994	Warwickshire
1977	Gloucestershire	1986	Middlesex	1995	Lancashire
1978	Kent	1987	Yorkshire	1996	Lancashire
1979	Essex	1988	Hampshire		
1980	Northamptonshire	1989	Nottinghamshire		

SUNDAY LEAGUE
FINAL TABLE 1996

		P	W	L	T	NR	Pts	NRR
1	SURREY (9)	17	12	4	–	1	50	16.31
2	Nottinghamshire (11)	17	12	4	–	1	50	9.20
3	Yorkshire (12)	17	11	6	–	–	44	11.47
4	Warwickshire (2)	17	10	6	–	1	42	4.88
5	Somerset (14)	17	10	6	–	1	42	1.14
6	Northamptonshire (13)	17	10	6	–	1	42	0.42
7	Middlesex (17)	17	9	7	–	1	38	–0.92
8	Worcestershire (3)	17	8	6	–	3	38	1.88
9	Lancashire (4)	17	9	8	–	–	36	–0.16
10	Kent (1)	17	8	8	1	–	34	–7.65
11	Derbyshire (8)	17	7	7	1	2	34	4.35
12	Leicestershire (7)	17	7	7	–	3	34	–0.10
13	Glamorgan (6)	17	7	8	–	2	32	2.73
14	Sussex (10)	17	6	9	–	2	28	–11.67
15	Hampshire (18)	17	4	10	–	3	22	–6.22
16	Gloucestershire (15)	17	4	10	–	3	22	–8.19
17	Essex (5)	17	4	12	–	1	18	–3.57
18	Durham (16)	17	1	15	–	1	6	–15.37

Win = 4 points. Tie (T)/No Result (NR) = 2 points. Positions of counties finishing equal on points are decided by most wins or, if equal, by higher net run-rate (NRR – overall run-rate in all matches, i.e. total runs scored x 100 divided by balls received, minus the run-rate of its opponents in those same matches).

1995 final positions are shown in brackets.

The Sunday League's sponsors have been John Player & Sons (1969-1986), Refuge Assurance (1987-1991), TCCB (1992) and AXA Equity & Law Insurance (1993 to date). The competition has been limited to 40 overs per innings, apart from 1993 when it was experimentally extended to 50.

WINNERS

1969 Lancashire	1979 Somerset	1989 Lancashire
1970 Lancashire	1980 Warwickshire	1990 Derbyshire
1971 Worcestershire	1981 Essex	1991 Nottinghamshire
1972 Kent	1982 Sussex	1992 Middlesex
1973 Kent	1983 Yorkshire	1993 Glamorgan
1974 Leicestershire	1984 Essex	1994 Warwickshire
1975 Hampshire	1985 Essex	1995 Kent
1976 Kent	1986 Hampshire	1996 Surrey
1977 Leicestershire	1987 Worcestershire	
1978 Hampshire	1988 Worcestershire	

SUNDAY LEAGUE
PRINCIPAL RECORDS 1969-96

Highest Total		375-4	Surrey v Yorkshire	Scarborough	1994
Highest Total Batting Second		317-6	Surrey v Notts	The Oval	1993
Lowest Total		23	Middlesex v Yorks	Leeds	1974
Highest Score	176	G.A.Gooch	Essex v Glamorgan	Southend	1983
Hundreds	552				1969-96
Fastest Hundred	44 balls	M.A.Ealham	Kent v Derbyshire	Maidstone	1995

Highest Partnership for each Wicket

1st	239	G.A.Gooch/B.R.Hardie	Essex v Notts	Nottingham	1985
2nd	273	G.A.Gooch/K.S.McEwan	Essex v Notts	Nottingham	1983
3rd	223	S.J.Cook/G.D.Rose	Somerset v Glam	Neath	1990
4th	219	C.G.Greenidge/C.L.Smith	Hampshire v Surrey	Southampton	1987
5th	190	R.J.Blakey/M.J.Foster	Yorkshire v Leics	Leicester	1993
6th	137	M.P.Speight/I.D.K.Salisbury	Sussex v Surrey	Guildford	1996
7th	132	K.R.Brown/N.F.Williams	Middx v Somerset	Lord's	1988
8th	110*	C.L.Cairns/B.N.French	Notts v Surrey	The Oval	1993
9th	105	D.G.Moir/R.W.Taylor	Derbyshire v Kent	Derby	1984
10th	82	G.Chapple/P.J.Martin	Lancashire v Worcs	Manchester	1996

Best Bowling	8-26	K.D.Boyce	Essex v Lancashire	Manchester	1971
	7-15	R.A.Hutton	Yorkshire v Worcs	Leeds	1969
	7-39	A.Hodgson	Northants v Somerset	Northampton	1976
	7-41	A.N.Jones	Sussex v Notts	Nottingham	1986

Four Wkts in Four Balls	A.Ward		Derbyshire v Sussex	Derby	1970

Hat-Tricks (24): Derbyshire – A.Ward (1970), C.J.Tunnicliffe (1979); Essex – K.D.Boyce (1971); Glamorgan – M.A.Nash (1975), A.E.Cordle (1979), G.C.Holmes (1987), A.Dale (1993); Gloucestershire – K.M.Curran (1989); Hampshire – J.M.Rice (1975), M.D.Marshall (1981); Kent – R.M.Ellison (1983), M.J.McCague (1992); Leicestershire – G.D.McKenzie (1972); Northamptonshire – A.Hodgson (1976); Nottinghamshire – K.Saxelby (1987), K.P.Evans (1994); Somerset – R.Palmer (1970), I.V.A.Richards (1982); Surrey – M.P.Bicknell (1992); Sussex – A.Buss (1974); Warwickshire – R.G.D.Willis (1973), W.Blenkiron (1974); Worcestershire – R.K.Illingworth (1993); Yorkshire – P.W.Jarvis (1982).

Most Wicket-Keeping Dismissals in an Innings

7	(6ct, 1st)	R.W.Taylor	Derbyshire v Lancs	Manchester	1975

Most Catches in an Innings

5	J.M.Rice		Hampshire v Warwicks	Southampton	1978

COUNTY CAPS AWARDED IN 1996

Derbyshire	A.J.Harris, D.M.Jones
Durham	C.L.Campbell, S.L.Campbell, P.D.Collingwood, M.J.Foster, M.J.Saggers
Essex	A.P.Grayson, S.G.Law, N.F.Williams
Glamorgan	–
Gloucestershire	M.C.J.Ball, A.Symonds, R.C.J.Williams
Hampshire	J.S.Laney
Kent	–
Lancashire	–
Leicestershire	D.L.Maddy
Middlesex	–
Northamptonshire	–
Nottinghamshire	–
Somerset	S.Lee
Surrey	M.A.Butcher, B.P.Julian, G.J.Kersey
Sussex	V.C.Drakes, K.Greenfield, D.R.Law, J.D.Lewry
Warwickshire	A.F.Giles, S.M.Pollock
Worcestershire	–
Yorkshire	C.E.W.Silverwood, R.D.Stemp

MINOR COUNTIES CHAMPIONSHIP

FINAL TABLE 1996

		P	W	L	D	NR	Bonus Points Bat	Bonus Points Bowl	Total Points
EASTERN DIVISION									
Norfolk	NW	9	4	1	4	0	23	20	107
Cambridgeshire	NW	9	3	2	4	0	19	30	97
Buckinghamshire	NW	9	3	4	2	0	21	27	96
Staffordshire	NW	9	3	1	5	0	13	29	90
Cumberland	NW	9	3	1	5	0	18	20	86
Bedfordshire	NW	9	2	4	3	0	23	29	84
Lincolnshire	NW	9	2	1	5	1	24	22	83
Suffolk		9	2	1	6	0	20	23	75
Hertfordshire		9	1	3	4	1	12	21	62
Northumberland		9	0	5	4	0	24	14	38
WESTERN DIVISION									
Devon	NW	9	5	3	1	0	26	18	124
Herefordshire	NW	9	5	1	3	0	21	23	124
Shropshire	NW	9	3	1	4	1	26	24	103
Berkshire	NW	9	3	4	1	1	15	24	92
Cornwall		9	2	2	4	1	24	21	82
Cheshire		9	2	3	4	0	27	20	79
Oxfordshire		9	2	0	7	0	17	18	75
Dorset		9	2	2	5	0	16	15	63
Wales		9	1	5	3	0	16	18	50
Wiltshire		9	0	4	4	1	21	14	40

Hertfordshire's and Oxfordshire's records each include eight points for a drawn match in which the scores finished level.

In the Western Division, points and number of wins being identical, Devon took precedence over Herefordshire on the basis of Nett Batting Averages.

NW signifies qualification for the 1997 NatWest Trophy.

1996 CHAMPIONSHIP FINAL
DEVON v NORFOLK

At Exmouth on 8, 9 September.
Toss: Norfolk. Result: DEVON won by 168 runs.

DEVON

Batsman	First innings		Second innings	
N.R.Gaywood	c Newman b Powell	134	st Crowley b Powell	40
H.J.Morgan	c and b D.R.Thomas	19	lbw b Newman	49
N.A.Folland	c M.Thomas b D.Thomas	17	c Boon b Newman	49
G.T.J. Townsend	st Crowley b Powell	38	b Newman	0
*P.M.Roebuck	c Fox b Powell	30	(6) not out	43
A.J.Pugh	not out	2	(5) b Newman	44
†C.M.W.Read	not out	4	c Rogers b Newman	6
K.Donohue			not out	5
M.C.Theedom				
I.A.Bond				
R.Horrell				
Extras	(B 4, LB 4, W 3, NB 4)	15	(B 5, LB 8, NB 2)	15
Total	**(5 wickets; 50 overs)**	**259**	**(6 wickets declared)**	**251**

NORFOLK

Batsman	First innings		Second innings	
T.J.Boon	c Read b Roebuck	18	c Horrell b Roebuck	55
C.J.Rogers	b Roebuck	25	c Read b Theedom	0
S.C.Goldsmith	lbw b Roebuck	8	c Pugh b Donohue	2
C.Amos	run out	14	c Donohue b Theedom	0
M.G.Powell	c Pugh b Horrell	4	(6) c Morgan b Roebuck	20
D.R.Thomas	run out	2	(5) run out	33
*P.G.Newman	not out	41	c Townsend b Horrell	5
N.Fox	b Bond	29	st Folland b Horrell	6
M.W.Thomas	not out	1	b Roebuck	29
P.J.Bradshaw			c Theedom b Horrell	1
†S.C.Crowley			not out	5
Extras	(B 14, LB 8, W 1)	23	(B 14, LB 6, W 1)	21
Total	**(7 wickets; 50 overs)**	**165**		**177**

LINCOLNSHIRE	O	M	R	W	O	M	R	W
Newman	13	0	73	0	23	2	69	5
D.R.Thomas	15	0	62	2	10	1	36	0
Fox	9	0	43	0	3	1	7	0
Powell	11	1	56	3	20	3	83	1
Boon	2	0	17	0				
Goldsmith					3	0	10	0
Bradshaw					2	0	12	0
M.W.Thomas					5	0	21	0
DEVON								
Donohue	4	0	27	0	6	1	23	1
Bond	5	0	27	1				
Roebuck	23	6	49	3	19.3	4	38	3
Horrell	17	4	37	1	17	5	45	3
Pugh	1	0	3	0	5	0	14	0
Theedom					10	3	26	2
Morgan					1	0	11	0

FALL OF WICKETS

	D	N	D	N
Wkt	1st	1st	2nd	2nd
1st	64	35	61	8
2nd	112	49	133	12
3rd	184	65	135	15
4th	253	75	164	96
5th	254	77	217	103
6th	–	101	223	117
7th	–	162	–	139
8th	–	–	–	149
9th	–	–	–	151
10th	–	–	–	177

Umpires: P.Adams and M.K.Reed.

MINOR COUNTIES CHAMPIONS

1895	Norfolk	1928	Berkshire	1966	Lincolnshire
	Durham	1929	Oxfordshire	1967	Cheshire
	Worcestershire	1930	Durham	1968	Yorkshire II
1896	Worcestershire	1931	Leicestershire II	1969	Buckinghamshire
1897	Worcestershire	1932	Buckinghamshire	1970	Bedfordshire
1898	Worcestershire	1933	*Undecided*	1971	Yorkshire II
1899	Northamptonshire	1934	Lancashire II	1972	Bedfordshire
	Buckinghamshire	1935	Middlesex II	1973	Shropshire
	Glamorgan	1936	Hertfordshire	1974	Oxfordshire
1900	Durham	1937	Lancashire II	1975	Hertfordshire
	Northamptonshire	1938	Buckinghamshire	1976	Durham
1901	Durham	1939	Surrey II	1977	Suffolk
1902	Wiltshire	1946	Suffolk	1978	Devon
1903	Northamptonshire	1947	Yorkshire II	1979	Suffolk
1904	Northamptonshire	1948	Lancashire II	1980	Durham
1905	Norfolk	1949	Lancashire II	1981	Durham
1906	Staffordshire	1950	Surrey II	1982	Oxfordshire
1907	Lancashire II	1951	Kent II	1983	Hertfordshire
1908	Staffordshire	1952	Buckinghamshire	1984	Durham
1909	Wiltshire	1953	Berkshire	1985	Cheshire
1910	Norfolk	1954	Surrey II	1986	Cumberland
1911	Staffordshire	1955	Surrey II	1987	Buckinghamshire
1912	*In abeyance*	1956	Kent II	1988	Cheshire
1913	Norfolk	1957	Yorkshire II	1989	Oxfordshire
1920	Staffordshire	1958	Yorkshire II	1990	Hertfordshire
1921	Staffordshire	1959	Warwickshire II	1991	Staffordshire
1922	Buckinghamshire	1960	Lancashire II	1992	Staffordshire
1923	Buckinghamshire	1961	Somerset II	1993	Staffordshire
1924	Berkshire	1962	Warwickshire II	1994	Devon
1925	Buckinghamshire	1963	Cambridgeshire	1995	Devon
1926	Durham	1964	Lancashire II	1996	Devon
1927	Staffordshire	1965	Somerset II		

MINOR COUNTIES CHAMPIONSHIP RECORDS

Highest Total		621		Surrey II v Devon	The Oval	1928
Lowest Total		14		Cheshire v Staffs	Stoke	1909
Highest Score		282	E.Garnett	Berkshire v Wiltshire	Reading	1908
Most Runs – Season		1212	A.F.Brazier	Surrey II		1949
Record Partnership						
2nd	388*		T.H.Clark and A.F.Brazier	Surrey II v Sussex II	The Oval	1949
Best Bowling – Innings		10- 11	S.Turner	Cambs v Cumberland	Penrith	1987
– Match		18-100	N.W.Harding	Kent II v Wiltshire	Swindon	1937
Most Wickets – Season		119	S.F.Barnes	Staffordshire		1906

1996 MINOR COUNTIES CHAMPIONSHIP

LEADING BATTING AVERAGES

(Qualification: 8 completed innings (or 500 runs), average 43.00)

		I	NO	HS	Runs	Avge
N.A.Folland	Devon	18	7	127	1055	95.90
W.Larkins	Bedfordshire	18	4	155*	1024	73.14
J.P.J.Sylvester	Wales	15	3	143*	854	71.16
H.J.Morgan	Devon	10	1	144	629	69.88
Asif Din	Shropshire	15	2	175	890	68.46
T.J.Boon	Norfolk	18	4	116*	902	64.42
M.J.Roberts	Buckinghamshire	14	3	177*	699	63.54
S.A.Kellett	Cambridgeshire	18	5	126*	813	62.53
G.W.Ecclestone	Cambridgeshire	12	3	126*	559	62.11
G.M.Thomas	Cornwall	17	2	148*	832	55.46
D.W.Randall	Suffolk	15	0	121	814	54.26
N.D.Burns	Buckinghamshire	18	5	100*	693	53.30
S.M.Williams	Cornwall	17	2	106*	779	51.93
M.R.Davies	Shropshire	12	4	67	412	51.50
T.W.Adcock	Northumberland	16	2	150*	716	51.14
N.R.Gaywood	Devon	17	1	134	816	51.00
J.D.Bean	Cheshire	17	2	102	756	50.40
G.R.Morris	Northumberland	12	3	69*	433	48.11
S.M.Brogan	Herefordshire	12	1	87	511	46.45
C.S.Knightley	Oxfordshire	10	2	98*	359	44.87
R.Hall	Herefordshire	13	4	93*	398	44.22
R.J.Scott	Dorset	15	4	71*	480	43.63
D.J.M.Mercer	Wiltshire	17	3	147	610	43.57

LEADING BOWLING AVERAGES

(Qualification: 20 wickets, average 30.00)

		O	M	R	W	Avge
R.N.Dalton	Bedfordshire	121.4	33	358	23	15.56
P.M.Roebuck	Devon	329	85	735	47	15.63
K.E.Cooper	Herefordshire	194.2	50	467	27	17.29
N.V.Radford	Herefordshire	207.2	62	545	30	18.16
S.D.Myles	Berkshire	153.5	33	501	27	18.55
S.Oakes	Lincolnshire	135	21	435	23	18.91
P.J.O'Reilly	Hertfordshire	122	29	393	20	19.65
D.F.Ralfs	Cambridgeshire	158.3	26	530	26	20.38
M.J.Bailey	Herefordshire	165	50	455	21	21.66
M.A.Sharp	Cumberland	244.2	67	684	31	22.06
A.Richardson	Staffordshire	279.4	67	903	39	23.15
S.C.Goldsmith	Norfolk	162.1	28	490	21	23.33
M.G.Scothern	Cumberland	152.5	32	551	23	23.95
K.A.Arnold	Oxfordshire	205	40	701	29	24.17
A.W.Thomas	Buckinghamshire	259.2	39	903	35	25.80
A.R.Clarke	Buckinghamshire	300.1	73	908	35	25.94
J.M.Fielding	Cumberland	164.1	25	632	24	26.33
Asif Din	Shropshire	170.4	39	559	21	26.61
B.T.P.Donelan	Cambridgeshire	275	37	966	36	26.83
A.K.Golding	Suffolk	348.4	64	1088	39	27.89
A.D.Greasley	Cheshire	195.1	63	563	20	28.15
A.J.Murphy	Cheshire	196.2	44	658	23	28.60
P.G.Newman	Norfolk	292.3	74	859	29	29.62
J.H.Shackleton	Dorset	221.1	59	653	22	29.68
A.B.Byram	Shropshire	195	42	720	24	30.00

SECOND XI CHAMPIONSHIP 1996
FINAL TABLE

	P	W	L	D	Bonus Points Bat	Bowl	Total Points
1 WARWICKSHIRE (6)	17	10	4	3	47	56	263
2 Northamptonshire (2)	17	6	2	9	58	59	213
3 Middlesex (10)	17	7	2	8	46	43	201
4 Yorkshire (5)	17	6	3	8	45	42	183
5 Lancashire (13)	17	6	1	10	37	48	181
6 Kent (4)	17	4	3	10	55	55	174
7 Leicestershire (12)	17	5	5	7	40	53	173
8 Durham (3)	17	4	5	8	53	48	165
9 Derbyshire (16)	17	3	4	10	49	45	150
10 Worcestershire (8)	17	3	4	10	42	55	145
11 Nottinghamshire (11)	17	3	2	12	53	40	141
12 Gloucestershire (14)	17	2	–	15	45	53	130
13 Glamorgan (18)	17	2	5	10	47	48	127
14 Somerset (15)	17	2	6	9	45	46	123
15 Hampshire (1)	17	2	6	9	40	50	122
16 Sussex (9)	17	2	3	12	41	48	121
17 Surrey (7)	17	1	8	8	47	56	119
18 Essex (17)	17	1	6	10	45	46	107

Win = 16 points. Derbyshire's total includes 8 points from a match drawn with the scores level.

1995 final positions are shown in brackets.

SECOND XI CHAMPIONSHIP – 1996 AWARDS

Player of the Season   K.P.Dutch   Middlesex

Player of the Month
April/May	A.D.Shaw	Glamorgan
June	J.N.Snape	Northamptonshire
July	M.J.Powell	Warwickshire
August/September	B.Parker	Yorkshire

SECOND XI CHAMPIONS

1959 Gloucestershire	1972 Nottinghamshire	1985 Nottinghamshire
1960 Northamptonshire	1973 Essex	1986 Lancashire
1961 Kent	1974 Middlesex	1987 Kent/Yorkshire
1962 Worcestershire	1975 Surrey	1988 Surrey
1963 Worcestershire	1976 Kent	1989 Middlesex
1964 Lancashire	1977 Yorkshire	1990 Sussex
1965 Glamorgan	1978 Sussex	1991 Yorkshire
1966 Surrey	1979 Warwickshire	1992 Surrey
1967 Hampshire	1980 Glamorgan	1993 Middlesex
1968 Surrey	1981 Hampshire	1994 Somerset
1969 Kent	1982 Worcestershire	1995 Hampshire
1970 Kent	1983 Leicestershire	1996 Warwickshire
1971 Hampshire	1984 Yorkshire	

FIRST-CLASS CAREER RECORDS

Compiled by Philip Bailey

The following career records are for all players who appeared in first-class or limited-overs cricket during the 1996 season, and are complete to the end of that season. Some players who did not appear in 1996 but may do so in 1997, are also included.

BATTING AND FIELDING

'1000' denotes instances of scoring 1000 runs in a season. Where these have been achieved outside the UK, they are shown after a plus sign.

	M	I	NO	HS	Runs	Avge	100	1000	Ct/St
Aamer Sohail	156	267	16	205	9486	37.79	18	1+2	131
Ackerman, H.D.	35	55	4	154	1998	39.17	3	–	25
Adams, C.J.	140	228	19	239	7664	36.66	19	3	154
Adams, P.R.	12	11	6	29	96	19.20	–	–	5
Afford, J.A.	169	166	72	22*	385	4.09	–	–	57
Afzaal, U.	13	22	3	67*	398	20.94	–	–	6
Aldred, P.	12	17	2	33	147	9.80	–	–	6
Alleyne, M.W.	200	329	33	256	9180	31.01	12	4	155/2
Allingham, M.J.D.	1	2	2	50*	86	–	–	–	1
Altree, D.A.	3	5	2	0*	0	0.00	–	–	1
Ambrose, C.E.L.	186	238	58	78	2681	14.89	–	–	71
Amjad, M.	1	2	–	7	8	4.00	–	–	–
Andrew, S.J.W.	129	109	42	35	472	7.04	–	–	26
Ankola, S.A.	50	50	11	46	588	15.07	–	–	20
Archer, G.F.	59	104	11	168	3650	39.24	8	1	61
Arthurton, K.L.T.	105	164	23	157*	6483	45.97	18	1	55
Asif Mujtaba	184	287	57	208	11476	49.89	35	1+2	167
Ata-ur-Rehman	59	57	13	34	369	8.38	–	–	18
Atherton, M.A.	223	386	35	199	15416	43.92	41	6	178
Athey, C.W.J.	455	763	69	184	24771	35.69	54	13	420/2
Austin, I.D.	88	121	27	115*	2524	26.85	2	–	20
Aymes, A.N.	127	189	52	113	4329	31.59	3	–	286/24
Azharuddin, M.	184	275	30	226	12857	52.47	44	1+2	171
Bahl, J.	1	1	1	0*	0	–	–	–	1
Bailey, R.J.	300	507	75	224*	18021	41.71	39	12	222
Bailey, T.M.B.	2	2	1	31*	33	33.00	–	–	4
Bainbridge, P.	324	539	73	169	15707	33.70	24	9	149
Ball, M.C.J.	85	131	25	71	1644	15.50	–	–	98
Barnett, K.J.	399	646	59	239*	23272	39.64	49	13	239
Bartle, S.	1	1	–	32	32	32.00	–	–	1
Barwick, S.R.	212	203	74	30	873	6.76	–	–	47
Base, S.J.	133	170	35	58	1526	11.30	–	–	60
Bates, R.T.	22	31	5	34	364	14.00	–	–	12
Batty, J.D.	84	97	25	51	1149	15.95	–	–	32
Batty, J.N.	12	16	4	56	342	28.50	–	–	11/2
Bell, M.A.V.	17	21	10	22*	79	7.18	–	–	7
Benjamin, J.E.	105	119	34	49	943	11.09	–	–	23
Benjamin, W.K.M.	171	213	36	117	3985	22.51	2	–	95
Betts, M.M.	24	38	9	57*	367	12.65	–	–	6
Bevan, M.G.	108	187	30	203*	8432	53.70	28	2+1	63
Bicknell, D.J.	191	337	34	235*	12102	39.94	28	6	74
Bicknell, M.P.	166	195	53	88	2674	18.83	–	–	55
Birbeck, S.D.	7	9	2	75*	120	17.14	–	–	2
Birks, M.J.	3	3	2	23*	43	43.00	–	–	3

157

	M	I	NO	HS	Runs	Avge	100	1000	Ct/St
Bishop, I.E.	1	2	–	2	4	2.00	–	–	1
Blain, J.A.R.	1	–	–	–	–	–	–	–	–
Blakey, R.J.	240	389	59	221	10684	32.37	10	5	468/42
Blenkiron, D.A.	19	33	3	145	774	25.80	3	–	7
Blewett, G.S.	63	111	7	268	4762	45.78	14	0+3	34
Boden, D.J.P.	8	5	–	5	13	2.60	–	–	5
Boiling, J.	71	99	34	69	826	12.70	–	–	57
Boje, N.	47	62	14	102	1438	29.95	1	–	19
Boon, D.C.	267	449	41	227	18811	46.10	59	2+7	224
Boswell, S.A.J.	3	4	2	2*	5	2.50	–	–	2
Botham, L.J.	3	3	–	30	31	10.33	–	–	2
Bovill, J.N.B.	29	40	14	31	259	9.96	–	–	2
Bowen, M.N.	26	32	6	23*	289	11.11	–	–	6
Bowler, P.D.	196	342	32	241*	12772	41.20	28	8	120/1
Brimson, M.T.	26	27	12	25	136	9.06	–	–	3
Brinkley, J.E.	14	16	4	29	89	7.41	–	–	5
Broadhurst, M.	6	3	–	6	7	2.33	–	–	1
Brown, A.D.	79	129	13	187	4780	41.20	11	3	81
Brown, D.R.	47	73	8	85	1639	25.21	–	–	25
Brown, J.F.	1	1	1	0*	0	–	–	–	1
Brown, K.R.	211	319	60	200*	9310	35.94	12	2	378/25
Brown, S.J.E.	107	148	45	69	1369	13.29	–	–	34
Browne, B.S.	42	51	20	29	201	6.48	–	–	9
Bull, J.J.	2	1	–	4	4	4.00	–	–	–
Burns, M.	20	34	2	81	640	20.00	–	–	41/5
Butcher, G.P.	20	33	6	89	750	27.77	–	–	10
Butcher, M.A.	56	100	10	167	3697	41.07	6	2	61
Butler, O.F.X.	1	–	–	–	–	–	–	–	–
Byas, D.	180	304	28	213	9913	35.91	17	4	223
Caddick, A.R.	79	101	18	92	1355	16.32	–	–	29
Cairns, C.L.	133	203	24	120	6318	35.29	7	1	61
Cake, R.Q.	37	67	13	108	2055	38.05	4	–	16
Campbell, C.L.	1	1	–	7	7	7.00	–	–	–
Campbell, S.L.	58	100	4	208	3955	41.19	10	2	60
Capel, D.J.	307	470	66	175	12062	29.85	16	3	155
Carr, J.D.	212	331	51	261*	10895	38.91	24	5	260
Cassar, M.E.	3	4	–	66	134	33.50	–	–	2
Chapman, C.A.	4	7	1	20	72	12.00	–	–	5/2
Chapman, R.J.	14	16	3	25	114	8.76	–	–	3
Chapple, G.	61	86	32	109*	1106	20.48	1	–	21
Childs, J.H.	381	359	173	43	1690	9.08	–	–	116
Church, M.J.	14	25	1	152	471	19.62	1	–	8
Churton, D.R.H.	13	17	–	39	152	8.94	–	–	14/6
Clarke, V.P.	7	13	1	43	144	12.00	–	–	2
Collingwood, P.D.	11	20	–	91	464	23.20	–	–	6
Commins, J.B.	72	129	14	165	4474	38.90	10	–	29
Connor, C.A.	212	201	51	59	1780	11.86	–	–	61
Cooper, K.E.	305	330	83	52	2484	10.05	–	–	93
Cork, D.G.	126	186	27	104	3896	24.50	2	–	78
Cosker, D.A.	5	6	1	24	45	9.00	–	–	3
Cottam, A.C.	13	16	1	36	153	10.20	–	–	1
Cottey, P.A.	167	276	42	203	9132	39.02	19	6	107
Cousins, D.M.	14	23	5	18*	145	8.05	–	–	5
Cowan, A.P.	17	24	7	34	235	13.82	–	–	7
Cowdrey, G.R.	170	269	29	147	8416	35.06	16	3	90
Cox, D.M.	13	22	5	95*	489	28.76	–	–	3
Crawley, J.P.	128	213	22	286	9388	49.15	18	5	102

	M	I	NO	HS	Runs	Avge	100	1000	Ct/St
Croft, R.D.B.	159	233	47	143	4773	25.66	2	–	75
Crookes, D.N.	43	63	6	155*	2348	41.19	5	–	38
Crowe, C.D.	1	2	–	9	10	5.00	–	–	1
Cunliffe, R.J.	20	32	4	190*	1018	36.35	2	–	11
Curran, K.M.	282	441	74	150	13690	37.30	23	6	171
Curtis, T.S.	325	556	66	248	20083	40.98	39	11	180
Dakin, J.M.	11	17	2	101*	360	24.00	1	–	6
Dale, A.	127	213	19	214*	6269	32.31	12	2	51
Daley, J.A.	44	77	8	159*	2178	31.56	1	–	24
Dalton, A.J.	13	23	3	51*	426	21.30	–	–	9
Davies, A.G.	2	3	2	26*	55	55.00	–	–	6/2
Davies, A.P.	3	2	1	11*	19	19.00	–	–	–
Davis, R.P.	160	196	46	67	2317	15.44	–	–	146
Dawood, I.	2	2	1	2*	3	3.00	–	–	3
Dawson, R.I.	47	84	7	127*	2046	26.57	2	1	24
Deakin, P.J.	6	9	4	24*	100	20.00	–	–	–
Dean, K.J.	8	8	1	12	33	4.71	–	–	1
DeFreitas, P.A.J.	254	361	34	113	7140	21.83	6	–	91
Derbyshire, N.A.	5	5	1	17	52	13.00	–	–	2
Dibden, R.R.	5	8	2	1	1	0.16	–	–	–
Dimond, M.	4	4	1	26	67	22.33	–	–	4
Dodemaide, A.I.C.	174	263	65	123	5843	29.51	5	–	86
Donald, A.A.	221	252	99	46*	1872	12.23	–	–	86
Dowman, M.P.	21	37	2	107	996	28.45	3	–	11
Drakes, V.C.	46	74	12	180*	1700	27.41	4	–	8
Dravid, R.S.	61	97	18	200*	4755	60.18	15	0+1	61/1
Dunlop, A.R.	3	5	–	57	166	33.20	–	–	2
Du Preez, S.P.	10	2	1	9	10	10.00	–	–	3
Dutch, K.P.	5	4	–	27	39	9.75	–	–	6
Eagleson, R.L.	1	2	–	50*	91	–	–	–	2
Ealham, M.A.	85	137	18	121	3497	29.38	1	–	32
Ecclestone, S.C.	28	44	7	94	1140	30.81	–	–	6
Edmond, M.D.	1	1	1	8*	8	–	–	–	–
Edwards, A.D.	3	3	–	22	38	12.66	–	–	2
Ellis, S.W.K.	10	11	4	15	63	9.00	–	–	7
Elworthy, S.	71	114	20	88	1910	20.31	–	–	25
Emburey, J.E.	510	641	130	133	11982	23.44	7	–	458
Evans, A.W.	7	13	3	71*	376	37.60	–	–	5
Evans, K.P.	136	189	43	104	3861	26.44	3	–	102
Fairbrother, N.H.	287	459	66	366	16295	41.46	35	10	201
Fay, R.A.	16	25	3	26	164	7.45	–	–	5
Feltham, M.A.	160	197	48	101	3199	21.46	1	–	67
Fisher, I.D.	3	1	1	0*	0	–	–	–	–
Fleming, M.V.	131	213	23	116	5899	31.04	8	–	55
Flintoff, A.	2	3	–	7	9	3.00	–	–	3
Flower, A.	52	86	16	156	3379	48.27	8	–	92/8
Flower, G.W.	52	94	7	201*	3596	41.33	6	–	44
Foley, G.I.	17	30	2	155	835	29.82	1	–	11
Follett, D.	7	8	6	17	27	13.50	–	–	3
Ford, J.A.	1	–	–	–	–	–	–	–	1
Fordham, A.	158	280	22	206*	10266	39.79	25	5	107
Foster, M.J.	8	13	1	63*	232	19.33	–	–	6
Francis, N.B.	15	20	1	26	153	8.05	–	–	6
Franks, P.J.	1	–	–	–	–	–	–	–	–
Fraser, A.R.C.	201	235	57	92	1931	10.84	–	–	38
Fulton, D.P.	43	77	5	134*	2152	29.88	3	–	67
Gallian, J.E.R.	79	138	10	312	5184	40.50	11	2	50

	M	I	NO	HS	Runs	Avge	100	1000	Ct/St
Ganguly, S.C.	60	91	16	200*	3762	50.16	10	–	47
Garaway, M.	1	1	–	44	44	44.00	–	–	–
Gardner, G.E.	1	1	1	2*	2	–	–	–	4/1
Gatting, M.W.	515	803	118	258	34357	50.15	90	17+1	451
Gibbs, H.H.	46	80	4	183	2980	39.21	6	–	29
Gibson, O.D.	79	116	18	101*	2279	23.25	1	–	29
Giddins, E.S.H.	80	96	39	34	321	5.63	–	–	12
Gie, N.A.	4	6	–	34	98	16.33	–	–	–
Gilder, G.M.	8	9	1	23	60	7.50	–	–	1
Giles, A.F.	25	36	10	106*	737	28.34	1	–	11
Gillespie, P.G.	1	2	–	53	53	26.50	–	–	–
Gooch, G.A.	570	971	74	333	44472	49.57	128	20+1	543
Goodchild, D.J.	1	2	–	4	4	2.00	–	–	–
Gough, D.	116	156	29	121	2217	17.45	1	–	31
Gould, I.J.	298	399	63	128	8756	26.05	4	–	536/67
Govan, J.W.	13	15	1	50	142	10.14	–	–	6
Grayson, A.P.	69	110	13	140	2897	29.86	3	1	55
Green, R.J.	8	11	3	25*	92	11.50	–	–	2
Greenfield, K.	67	114	15	154*	3178	32.10	8	–	53
Griffith, F.A.	43	63	9	81	1087	20.12	–	–	28
Griffiths, S.P.	5	9	–	20	75	8.33	–	–	14
Gupte, C.M.	53	80	10	132	2334	33.34	5	–	15
Habib, A.	20	31	5	215	1041	40.03	2	–	10
Hall, J.W.	97	175	10	140*	4997	30.28	6	2	47
Hamilton, G.M.	14	16	5	61	236	21.45	–	–	7
Hancock, T.H.C.	75	134	10	123	3161	25.49	3	–	48
Harden, R.J.	222	363	56	187	12201	39.74	26	7	169
Harmison, S.J.	1	2	–	6	10	5.00	–	–	–
Harris, A.J.	18	25	6	17	160	8.42	–	–	3
Harrison, G.D.	12	20	4	105*	670	41.87	1	–	3
Harrison, J.C.	10	18	3	46*	298	19.86	–	–	12
Hart, J.P.	1	2	2	18*	18	–	–	–	–
Hartley, P.J.	189	231	52	127*	3754	20.97	2	–	59
Harvey, M.E.	3	4	–	23	67	16.75	–	–	1
Haste, N.J.	32	37	9	51*	372	13.28	–	–	9
Hayden, M.L.	77	140	17	234	6971	56.67	21	1+3	64
Hayhurst, A.N.	164	263	34	172*	7819	34.14	14	3	53
Haynes, G.R.	62	95	6	158	2630	29.55	3	1	31
Haynes, J.J.	1	2	–	16	26	13.00	–	–	0/1
Headley, D.W.	83	106	27	91	1418	17.94	–	–	35
Hegg, W.K.	203	298	58	134	6200	25.83	4	–	485/61
Hemp, D.L.	76	133	12	157	3877	32.04	6	1	50
Hewitt, J.P.	10	15	4	72	312	28.36	–	–	5
Hewson, D.R.	6	12	1	87	261	23.72	–	–	2
Hibbert, A.J.E.	3	6	1	85	134	26.80	–	–	–
Hick, G.A.	327	535	53	405*	26895	55.79	90	12+1	396
Hindson, J.E.	25	32	5	53*	330	12.22	–	–	12
Hirwani, N.D.	95	105	41	59	688	10.75	–	–	30
Hoggard, M.J.	1	1	–	10	10	10.00	–	–	–
Hollioake, A.J.	57	93	11	138	3695	45.06	10	2	46
Hollioake, B.C.	3	4	–	46	63	15.75	–	–	3
Holloway, P.C.L.	40	65	14	168	2016	39.52	4	–	42/1
Hooper, C.L.	209	329	32	236*	13330	44.88	33	6	238
House, W.J.	8	15	5	136	526	52.60	2	–	2
How, E.J.	6	6	–	7*	7	3.50	–	–	1
Hughes, J.G.	18	25	1	17	123	5.12	–	–	5
Humphries, S.	2	–	–	–	–	–	–	–	3

160

	M	I	NO	HS	Runs	Avge	100	1000	Ct/St
Hussain, N.	184	287	34	197	11443	45.22	29	4	231
Hutchison, P.M.	3	2	–	0	0	0.00	–	–	1
Hutton, S.	58	105	5	172*	2983	29.83	3	–	33
Hyam, B.J.	3	6	–	49	74	12.33	–	–	5/1
Ijaz Ahmed	124	202	11	201*	7779	40.72	18	0+2	89
Illingworth, R.K.	324	362	105	120*	5633	21.91	3	–	141
Ilott, M.C.	124	148	34	60	1593	13.97	–	–	31
Innes, K.J.	5	7	–	63	108	15.42	–	–	3
Inzamam-ul-Haq	131	210	37	201*	8967	51.83	24	0+3	111
Irani, R.C.	68	111	14	119	3482	35.89	4	2	31
Jadeja, A.	62	97	10	264	4503	51.75	10	0+1	45
James, K.D.	195	292	46	162	7569	30.76	10	2	65
James, S.P.	150	266	21	235	8710	35.55	24	4	119
Janisch, A.N.	10	11	5	25	67	11.16	–	–	2
Jarrett, M.E.D.	31	43	9	51	602	17.70	–	–	17/1
Jarvis, P.W.	190	234	64	80	2815	16.55	–	–	54
Johnson, P.	284	472	43	187	15712	36.62	34	8	176/1
Johnson, R.L.	38	53	7	50*	685	14.89	–	–	17
Jones, D.M.	220	369	40	324*	17313	52.62	50	3+5	171
Jones, R.O.	8	13	1	61	205	17.08	–	–	4
Joshi, S.B.	32	44	9	118	1416	40.45	3	–	22
Julian, B.P.	91	127	21	119	2445	23.06	2	–	55
Kallis, J.H.	28	39	3	186*	1581	43.91	2	–	17
Keech, M.	39	68	7	104	1618	26.52	1	–	26
Keedy, G.	30	32	20	26	147	12.25	–	–	9
Kendall, W.S.	32	49	9	145*	1755	43.87	4	1	26
Kendrick, N.M.	81	106	30	59	1206	15.86	–	–	58
Kenlock, S.G.	7	10	2	12	55	6.87	–	–	4
Kennis, G.J.	3	6	1	29	91	18.20	–	–	3
Kerr, J.I.D.	27	41	8	80	597	18.09	–	–	9
Kersey, G.J.	53	82	14	83	1578	23.20	–	–	169/12
Kettleborough, R.A.	10	14	2	108	424	35.33	1	–	7
Khan, A.A.	4	–	–	–	–	–	–	–	1
Khan, G.A.	13	18	2	101*	608	38.00	1	–	7
Khan, W.G.	28	51	7	181	1585	36.02	4	–	28
Killeen, N.	12	20	4	48	177	11.06	–	–	5
Kirtley, R.J.	10	14	6	7*	25	3.12	–	–	7
Klusener, L.	34	46	14	105	1069	33.40	1	–	19
Knight, N.V.	86	146	17	174	5215	40.42	13	1	123
Knott, J.A.	2	2	1	49*	52	52.00	–	–	3/1
Koenig, S.G.	31	53	3	149*	1688	33.76	2	–	21
Krikken, K.M.	132	194	42	104	3499	23.01	1	–	329/23
Kumble, A.	92	113	26	154*	2331	26.79	4	–	46
Lampitt, S.R.	160	205	41	122	3907	23.82	1	–	100
Laney, J.S.	28	51	1	112	1736	34.72	4	1	22
Lathwell, M.N.	102	184	8	206	6282	35.69	11	5	74
Law, D.R.	28	43	–	115	878	20.41	1	–	13
Law, S.G.	106	180	18	179	7423	45.82	21	1+1	101
Lawrence, D.V.	181	205	35	66	1819	10.70	–	–	44
Lawson, A.G.	36	64	3	117*	1690	27.70	3	–	16
Leatherdale, D.A.	107	166	16	157	4829	32.19	6	–	96
Lee, S.	41	65	14	167*	2461	48.25	8	1	32
Lenham, N.J.	185	320	29	222*	9845	33.83	20	3	71
Lewis, C.C.	148	222	27	247	6050	31.02	7	–	121
Lewis, D.A.	8	15	3	122*	640	53.33	2	–	5
Lewis, J.	13	19	2	22*	122	7.17	–	–	4
Lewis, J.J.B.	58	101	14	136*	2959	34.01	4	–	49

161

	M	I	NO	HS	Runs	Avge	100	1000	Ct/St
Lewry, J.D.	26	40	11	34	302	10.41	–	–	2
Liebenberg, G.F.J.	75	131	7	229	4291	34.60	11	–	68/4
Ligertwood, D.G.C.	28	51	7	56	733	16.65	–	–	71/9
Lightfoot, C.G.R.	4	4	1	9	15	5.00	–	–	–
Llong, N.J.	58	90	10	130	2736	34.20	6	–	48
Lloyd, G.D.	129	212	22	241	7233	38.06	14	3	78
Lockhart, D.R.	1	2	–	36	40	20.00	–	–	1
Lockie, B.G.	1	2	–	32	38	19.00	–	–	1
Longley, J.I.	35	62	3	110	1381	23.40	2	–	18
Loye, M.B.	74	118	12	205	3695	34.85	7	1	46
Lugsden, S.	9	11	4	9	26	3.71	–	–	1
Lynch, M.A.	347	566	63	172*	17860	35.50	39	9	358
McCague, M.J.	95	129	30	63*	1501	15.16	–	–	55
McCallan, W.K.	1	2	–	51	62	31.00	–	–	–
McGrath, A.	31	54	3	137	1552	30.43	3	–	24
McKeown, P.C.	2	2	–	64	73	36.50	–	–	1
Maclay, A.W.	12	10	6	6*	17	4.25	–	–	–
Macmillan, G.I.	43	69	8	122	1749	28.67	3	–	48
Maddy, D.L.	32	53	3	131	1302	26.04	2	–	35
Malcolm, D.E.	213	253	77	51	1432	8.13	–	–	31
Malik, H.S.	33	44	8	64*	748	20.77	–	–	24
Mallender, N.A.	345	396	122	100*	4709	17.18	1	–	111
Manjrekar, S.V.	128	195	29	377	9099	54.81	28	0+1	77/2
Marc, K.	3	3	–	9	17	5.66	–	–	–
March, S.A.	242	352	57	127	8175	27.71	8	–	557/48
Martin, P.J.	117	135	34	133	2035	20.14	1	–	30
Martin-Jenkins, R.S.C.	4	3	1	50	70	35.00	–	–	–
Maru, R.J.	223	225	56	74	2871	16.98	–	–	246
Mascarenhas, A.D.	2	3	–	14	24	8.00	–	–	–
Mason, T.J.	2	1	–	3	3	3.00	–	–	3
Mather, D.P.	16	8	3	8*	21	4.20	–	–	2
May, M.R.	3	4	2	63*	160	80.00	–	–	1
Maynard, M.P.	266	442	44	243	17217	43.25	40	10	251/5
Metcalfe, A.A.	206	355	20	216*	11663	34.81	26	6	78
Metson, C.P.	230	301	71	96	4059	17.64	–	–	557/50
Mhambrey, P.L.	35	40	11	42*	406	14.00	–	–	11
Mike, G.W.	43	66	12	66*	1019	18.87	–	–	13
Milburn, S.M.	16	20	4	54*	202	12.62	–	–	–
Millns, D.J.	125	146	48	103	1813	18.50	1	–	62
Moffat, G.R.	8	8	3	27	45	9.00	–	–	4
Moffat, S.P.	1	1	–	0	0	0.00	–	–	–
Mohammad Akram	21	26	7	24	113	5.94	–	–	11
Moin Khan	105	150	21	129	3643	28.24	7	–	265/30
Moles, A.J.	218	394	37	230*	14670	41.09	28	6	136
Molins, G.L.	1	–	–	–	–	–	–	–	–
Mongia, N.R.	63	99	18	165	3727	46.01	8	–	142/19
Montgomerie, R.R.	78	136	13	192	4171	33.91	9	2	73
Moody, T.M.	235	394	33	272	16961	46.98	50	5+1	230
Moore, D.M.P.	1	2	–	51	68	34.00	–	–	1
Moores, P.	211	311	37	185	6724	24.54	6	–	464/44
Morris, A.C.	9	14	2	60	245	20.41	–	–	8
Morris, H.	297	516	49	202*	18523	39.66	49	9	183
Morris, J.E.	296	497	30	229	17730	37.96	42	10	127
Morris, R.S.M.	37	67	4	174	1830	29.04	3	–	43
Moxon, M.D.	305	523	47	274*	20572	43.21	44	11	215
Mullally, A.D.	124	141	36	75	959	9.13	–	–	24
Munton, T.A.	205	206	85	54*	1339	11.06	–	–	68

	M	I	NO	HS	Runs	Avge	100	1000	Ct/St
Mushtaq Ahmed	130	165	20	90	1972	13.60	–	–	68
Nash, D.J.	67	97	23	67	1341	18.12	–	–	30
Newell, K.	16	30	3	135	798	29.55	2	–	4
Newell, Mark (Sx)	1	2	–	0	0	0.00	–	–	1
Newell, Michael (Nt)	102	178	26	203*	4636	30.50	6	1	93/1
Newport, P.J.	257	299	87	98	5344	25.20	–	–	72
Nixon, P.A.	124	179	39	131	4029	28.77	8	1	324/27
Noon, W.M.	62	102	17	75	1881	22.12	–	–	129/16
Nowell, R.W.	12	22	3	28*	162	8.52	–	–	5
O'Gorman, T.J.G.	117	197	24	148	5372	31.05	10	2	76
Ormond, J.	1	–	–	–	–	–	–	–	1
Ostler, D.P.	132	224	19	208	7240	35.31	9	4	149
Owen, J.E.H.	13	23	–	105	699	30.39	2	–	3
Palframan, S.J.	51	79	7	123	1495	20.76	1	–	143/17
Parker, B.	17	31	3	127	853	30.46	1	–	10
Parkin, O.T.	12	14	9	14	67	13.40	–	–	4
Parsons, G.J.	331	441	98	76	6620	19.30	–	–	145
Parsons, K.A.	33	59	5	105	1402	25.96	1	–	20
Patel, M.M.	79	112	25	56	1193	13.71	–	–	42
Patterson, B.P.	1	2	–	29	45	22.50	–	–	–
Patterson, M.W.	1	2	–	4	6	3.00	–	–	–
Pearson, R.M.	50	55	16	37	474	12.15	–	–	14
Peirce, M.T.E.	7	12	–	60	243	20.25	–	–	5
Penberthy, A.L.	88	132	19	101*	2511	22.22	1	–	50
Pennett, D.B.	31	31	11	50	196	9.80	–	–	7
Penney, T.L.	98	156	29	151	5484	43.18	13	2	56
Peters, S.D.	4	7	1	110	142	23.66	1	–	5
Philip, I.L.	10	17	1	145	748	46.75	4	–	10
Phillips, B.J.	3	3	–	2	5	1.66	–	–	1
Phillips, N.C.	16	24	9	53	443	29.53	–	–	9
Pick, R.A.	190	203	54	65*	2227	14.94	–	–	50
Pierson, A.R.K.	130	162	60	58	1654	16.21	–	–	64
Pigott, A.C.S.	260	317	66	104*	4841	19.28	1	–	121
Piper, K.J.	130	180	26	116*	3086	20.03	2	–	348/23
Pollard, P.R.	142	250	15	180	7667	32.62	12	3	136
Pollock, S.M.	42	56	9	150*	1404	29.87	2	–	16
Pooley, J.C.	63	109	11	138*	3192	32.57	8	1	60
Pothas, N.	32	51	8	147	1505	35.00	1	–	100/8
Powell, M.J.	4	8	–	39	182	22.75	–	–	2
Prasad, B.K.V	46	49	24	28	271	10.84	–	–	25
Preece, B.E.A.	3	4	2	3*	5	2.50	–	–	1
Preston, N.W.	8	11	4	17*	63	9.00	–	–	3
Prichard, P.J.	263	427	44	245	13585	35.46	26	7	168
Pringle, M.W.	83	110	21	105	1639	18.41	1	–	20
Radford, T.A.	12	20	4	69	345	21.56	–	–	10
Ragnauth, R.T.	14	27	2	82	456	18.24	–	–	11
Raju, S.L.V.	95	104	32	54	959	13.31	–	–	32
Ralph, J.T.	1	2	–	0	0	0.00	–	–	1
Ramprakash, M.R.	205	334	43	235	13143	45.16	33	7	111
Rao, R.K.	2	3	1	38	87	43.50	–	–	–
Rashid, U.B.A.	1	2	–	9	15	7.50	–	–	–
Rashid Latif	80	109	21	68*	2115	24.03	–	–	215/39
Ratcliffe, J.D.	96	177	9	127*	4907	29.20	3	–	55
Rathore, V.	70	118	7	250	5310	47.83	14	0+2	81/2
Ratledge, J.	19	36	–	79	674	18.72	–	–	11
Rawnsley, M.J.	4	1	1	4*	4	–	–	–	1
Reeve, D.A.	241	322	77	202*	8541	34.86	7	2	200

163

	M	I	NO	HS	Runs	Avge	100	1000	Ct/St
Remy, C.C.	22	29	3	60	480	18.46	–	–	7
Renshaw, S.J.	8	8	5	9*	10	3.33	–	–	3
Rhodes, S.J.	309	425	120	122*	10185	33.39	9	1	773/104
Ridley, A.C.	20	29	2	155	857	31.74	2	–	5
Ripley, D.	230	299	81	134*	5477	25.12	6	–	496/67
Roberts, A.R.	61	83	18	62	1173	18.04	–	–	23
Roberts, D.J.	4	7	–	73	254	36.28	–	–	–
Roberts, G.M.	1	1	–	52	52	52.00	–	–	1
Robinson, D.D.J.	32	60	2	123	1600	27.58	2	–	34
Robinson, M.A.	155	161	68	23	312	3.35	–	–	31
Robinson, P.E.	159	261	35	189	7617	33.70	7	3	130
Robinson, R.T.	384	668	78	220*	25667	43.50	61	14	234
Rollins, A.S.	59	111	12	200*	3296	33.29	5	2	50/1
Rollins, R.J.	45	76	8	133*	1570	23.08	1	–	115/18
Rose, G.D.	186	258	45	138	6318	29.66	6	1	100
Roseberry, M.A.	192	324	36	185	10106	35.09	19	4	141
Russell, R.C.	347	505	111	129*	11824	30.01	6	–	838/104
Rutherford, A.T.	1	–	–	–	–	–	–	–	3
Saeed Anwar	93	149	5	221	6622	45.98	20	1+1	51
Saggers, M.J.	5	9	1	18	89	11.12	–	–	–
Sales, D.J.G.	4	8	1	210*	280	40.00	1	–	4
Salim Malik	239	369	55	237	14871	47.35	39	2+2	147
Salisbury, I.D.K.	165	217	48	86	3176	18.79	–	–	124
Salmond, G.	5	8	1	181	533	76.14	2	–	2
Saqlain Mushtaq	27	42	11	78	354	11.41	–	–	19
Sargeant, N.F.	52	67	11	49	786	14.03	–	–	120/16
Schofield, C.J.	1	1	–	25	25	25.00	–	–	–
Schultz, B.N.	46	43	12	36*	258	8.32	–	–	9
Scott, C.W.	129	176	31	108	3228	22.26	2	–	283/17
Searle, J.P.	2	4	3	5*	7	7.00	–	–	–
Shadab Kabir	19	31	2	99	752	25.93	–	–	15
Shadford, D.J.	2	2	1	1	1	1.00	–	–	–
Shah, O.A.	5	9	1	75	212	26.50	–	–	2
Shahid, N.	91	143	21	139	3997	32.76	5	1	85
Shahid Anwar	140	238	15	195	8696	38.99	18	0+4	59
Shahid Nazir	7	9	4	60*	149	29.80	–	–	2
Shaw, A.D.	18	25	3	74	319	14.50	–	–	37/7
Sheeraz, K.P.	11	14	7	3*	12	1.71	–	–	4
Sheriyar, A.	28	30	12	19	125	6.94	–	–	7
Shine, K.J.	81	71	30	40	424	10.34	–	–	16
Sidhu, N.S.	111	163	9	286	6859	44.53	20	–	38
Silverwood, C.E.W.	34	50	12	50	439	11.55	–	–	11
Simmons, P.V.	160	274	12	261	9877	37.69	20	2	188
Singh, A.	13	24	2	157	730	33.18	2	–	7
Slater, M.J.	78	136	10	219	6146	48.77	16	–	38
Small, G.C.	312	400	96	70	4396	14.46	–	–	94
Smith, A.M.	74	89	15	55*	879	11.87	–	–	11
Smith, A.W.	38	59	7	202*	1379	26.51	1	–	12
Smith, B.F.	95	146	20	190	4070	32.30	5	1	38
Smith, E.T.	7	12	–	101	576	48.00	2	–	1
Smith, G.J.	27	37	15	68	259	11.77	–	–	6
Smith, N.M.K.	112	160	22	161	3442	24.94	1	–	37
Smith, P.A.	221	351	42	140	8173	26.44	4	2	60
Smith, R.A.	319	545	77	209*	20727	44.28	51	10	188
Snape, J.N.	28	40	8	87	833	26.03	–	–	25
Solanki, V.S.	20	33	4	90	978	33.72	–	–	17
Speak, N.J.	123	214	21	232	7400	38.34	12	3	84

	M	I	NO	HS	Runs	Avge	100	1000	Ct/St
Speight, M.P.	123	206	15	184	6814	35.67	13	3	100
Spiring, K.R.	20	36	6	144	1196	39.86	3	1	12
Srinath, J.	76	98	21	60	1302	16.90	–	–	34
Stanford, E.J.	4	5	4	10*	16	16.00	–	–	2
Stemp, R.D.	107	125	38	65	1138	13.08	–	–	46
Stephenson, J.P.	220	379	38	202*	11733	34.40	19	5	128
Stewart, A.J.	309	511	58	206*	18197	40.16	36	8	387/14
Strang, P.A.	33	50	12	97	1027	27.02	–	–	28
Such, P.M.	218	218	70	54	1143	7.72	–	–	93
Sutcliffe, I.J.	27	40	5	163*	1308	37.37	1	–	12
Swann, A.J.	3	5	1	76*	100	25.00	–	–	1
Symonds, A.	48	81	8	254*	3082	42.21	9	2	22
Taylor, J.P.	116	124	52	86	981	13.62	–	–	38
Taylor, N.R.	303	515	68	204	17771	39.75	42	10	151
Telemachus, R.	22	28	6	59	272	12.36	–	–	4
Tendulkar, S.R.	112	167	18	179	8824	59.22	25	1+1	81
Tennant, A.M.	1	–	–	–	–	–	–	–	–
Tennent, R.W.	2	–	–	–	–	–	–	–	1
Terry, V.P.	292	493	45	190	16427	36.66	38	11	332
Thomas, P.A.	19	22	4	25	103	5.72	–	–	1
Thomas, S.D.	35	50	15	78*	628	17.94	–	–	9
Thompson, J.B.D.	9	13	3	40*	175	17.50	–	–	1
Thomson, R.B.	10	6	6	14*	34	–	–	–	1
Thorpe, G.P.	192	325	44	216	12377	44.04	25	7	142
Thursfield, M.J.	22	24	5	47	277	14.57	–	–	10
Titchard, S.P.	69	122	8	163	3765	33.02	4	–	50
Tolley, C.M.	72	88	23	84	1411	21.70	–	–	29
Trainor, N.J.	8	14	1	67	261	20.87	–	–	5
Trescothick, M.E.	41	74	1	178	2075	28.42	4	–	42
Trump, H.R.J.	107	121	41	48	991	12.38	–	–	76
Tudor, A.J.	5	9	–	56	123	13.66	–	–	1
Tufnell, P.C.R.	196	204	84	67*	1275	10.62	–	–	83
Turner, R.J.	102	158	33	106*	3362	26.89	4	–	221/34
Tweats, T.A.	13	24	3	89*	462	22.00	–	–	12
Udal, S.D.	108	156	27	94	2752	21.33	–	–	57
Vandrau, M.J.	54	86	17	66	1381	20.01	–	–	28
Van Troost, A.P.	60	70	23	35	380	8.08	–	–	9
Vaughan, M.P.	62	114	4	183	3805	34.59	7	3	25
Wagh, M.A.	11	13	3	43	198	19.80	–	–	4
Walker, A.J.	115	120	53	41*	825	12.31	–	–	43
Walker, L.N.P.	8	10	1	36	136	15.11	–	–	18/3
Walker, M.J.	23	36	5	275*	1046	33.74	2	–	12
Walsh, C.A.	339	429	105	66	4020	12.40	–	–	89
Walsh, C.D.	1	1	1	56*	56	–	–	–	–
Walton, T.C.	12	19	2	71	422	24.82	–	–	4
Waqar Younis	132	147	40	55	1368	12.78	–	–	34
Ward, D.M.	155	244	34	294*	8078	38.46	16	2	120/3
Ward, I.J.	2	3	–	15	19	6.33	–	–	1
Ward, T.R.	168	288	17	235*	10223	37.72	22	5	150
Warner, A.E.	200	272	52	95*	3763	17.10	–	–	46
Warren, R.J.	46	75	10	201*	2049	31.52	2	–	63/2
Wasim Akram	193	265	30	123	5043	21.45	4	–	64
Watkin, S.L.	193	216	71	41	1393	9.60	–	–	51
Watkinson, M.	278	415	46	161	9756	26.43	9	1	141
Weekes, P.N.	88	133	15	171*	3986	33.77	7	1	66
Welch, G.	27	36	4	84*	666	20.81	–	–	15
Wellings, P.E.	4	8	1	48	237	33.85	–	–	1

	M	I	NO	HS	Runs	Avge	100	1000	Ct/St
Wells, A.P.	321	537	77	253*	18508	40.23	43	10	204
Wells, C.M.	318	510	78	203	14289	33.07	24	6	111
Wells, V.J.	96	153	14	204	4466	32.12	6	1	65
Weston, R.M.S.	6	11	–	15	44	4.00	–	–	6
Weston, W.P.C.	88	151	15	171*	4832	35.52	9	2	51
Wharf, A.G.	5	6	1	62	167	33.40	–	–	1
Whitaker, J.J.	292	465	49	218	16034	38.54	34	10	165
Whitaker, P.R.	27	46	3	119	1293	30.06	1	–	7
White, C.	110	169	26	181	4670	32.65	6	–	66
White, G.W.	40	69	6	104	1715	27.22	1	–	39
Whittall, A.R.	34	39	7	91*	585	18.28	–	–	15
Whitticase, P.	132	174	40	114*	3113	23.23	1	–	309/14
Wild, R.D.	1	–	–	–	–	–	–	–	–
Wileman, J.R.	12	21	6	109	447	29.80	1	–	9
Williams, N.F.	242	281	56	77	4220	18.75	–	–	62
Williams, R.C.J.	35	44	8	90	640	17.77	–	–	94/14
Williamson, D.	1	–	–	–	–	–	–	–	–
Williamson, J.G.	2	2	–	55	104	52.00	–	–	–
Willis, S.C.	9	11	2	82	294	32.66	–	–	23
Windows, M.G.N.	32	60	4	184	1695	30.26	2	–	28
Wood, J.	45	68	11	63*	707	12.40	–	–	10
Wood, N.T.	1	1	–	1	1	1.00	–	–	–
Wren, T.N.	29	33	12	23	130	6.19	–	–	12
Wright, A.J.	263	462	35	193	12679	29.69	18	6	202
Wright, G.J.	1	–	–	–	–	–	–	–	–
Yates, G.	55	74	31	134*	1302	30.27	3	–	19
Young, S.	60	98	17	175*	3418	42.19	6	–	43

BOWLING

'50wS' denotes instances of taking 50 or more wickets in a season. Where these have been achieved outside the UK, they are shown after a plus sign.

	Runs	Wkts	Avge	Best	5wI	10wM	50wS
Aamer Sohail	4684	131	35.75	7- 53	2	1	–
Ackerman, H.D.	10	0					
Adams, C.J.	1072	18	59.55	4- 29	–	–	–
Adams, P.R.	1455	53	27.45	6-101	3	–	–
Afford, J.A.	15397	465	33.11	6- 51	16	2	5
Afzaal, U.	781	8	97.62	2- 41	–	–	–
Aldred, P.	912	23	39.65	3- 47	–	–	–
Alleyne, M.W.	6859	212	32.35	5- 32	3	–	1
Allingham, M.J.D.	98	4	24.50	3- 53	–	–	–
Altree, D.A.	267	6	44.50	3- 41	–	–	–
Ambrose, C.E.L.	15388	752	20.46	8- 45	40	8	5+1
Amjad, M.	25	0					
Andrew, S.J.W.	10456	313	33.40	7- 47	7	–	–
Ankola, S.A.	4221	170	24.82	6- 47	8	–	–
Archer, G.F.	431	9	47.88	3- 18	–	–	–
Arthurton, K.L.T.	777	22	35.31	3- 14	–	–	–
Asif Mujtaba	4943	208	23.76	6- 19	10	2	0+1
Ata-ur-Rehman	4945	146	33.86	8- 56	3	1	–
Atherton, M.A.	4726	108	43.75	6- 78	3	–	–
Athey, C.W.J.	2652	48	55.25	3- 3	–	–	–
Austin, I.D.	5283	170	31.07	5- 23	5	1	–
Aymes, A.N.	75	1	75.00	1- 75	–	–	–
Azharuddin, M.	673	12	56.08	2- 22	–	–	–

	Runs	Wkts	Avge	Best	5wI	10wM	50wS
Bailey, R.J.	4194	95	44.14	5- 54	2	–	–
Bainbridge, P.	13094	349	37.51	8- 53	10	–	–
Ball, M.C.J.	6066	166	36.54	8- 46	7	1	–
Barnett, K.J.	6717	180	37.31	6- 28	3	–	–
Bartle, S.	42	0					
Barwick, S.R.	16186	456	35.49	8- 42	10	1	2
Base, S.J.	11363	388	29.28	7- 60	16	1	1
Bates, R.T.	1763	39	45.20	5- 88	1	–	–
Batty, J.D.	7441	179	41.56	6- 48	4	–	–
Bell, M.A.V.	1333	46	28.97	7- 48	3	–	–
Benjamin, J.E.	10125	351	28.84	6- 19	16	1	3
Benjamin, W.K.M.	12358	476	25.96	7- 54	23	2	1
Betts, M.M.	2625	62	42.33	5- 68	2	–	–
Bevan, M.G.	1641	22	74.59	3- 6	–	–	–
Bicknell, D.J.	751	22	34.13	3- 7	–	–	–
Bicknell, M.P.	15231	586	25.99	9- 45	26	2	6
Birbeck, S.D.	428	10	42.80	3- 88	–	–	–
Bishop, I.E.	29	0					
Blain, J.A.R.	103	0					
Blakey, R.J.	68	1	68.00	1- 68	–	–	–
Blenkiron, D.A.	187	6	31.16	4- 43	–	–	–
Blewett, G.S.	1796	45	39.91	4- 39	–	–	–
Boden, D.J.P.	611	15	40.73	4- 11	–	–	–
Boiling, J.	5708	119	47.96	6- 84	4	1	–
Boje, N.	4635	134	34.58	6-100	5	–	–
Boon, D.C.	478	9	53.11	1- 0	–	–	–
Boswell, S.A.J.	243	7	34.71	2- 52	–	–	–
Botham, L.J.	268	8	33.50	5- 67	1	–	–
Bovill, J.N.B.	2482	81	30.64	6- 29	4	1	–
Bowen, M.N.	2477	63	39.31	5- 53	2	–	–
Bowler, P.D.	1756	24	73.16	3- 41	–	–	–
Brimson, M.T.	1829	54	33.87	5- 12	2	–	–
Brinkley, J.E.	1115	34	32.79	6- 35	2	–	–
Broadhurst, M.	291	7	41.57	3- 61	–	–	–
Brown, A.D.	139	0					
Brown, D.R.	3244	120	27.03	6- 52	4	2	–
Brown, J.F.	64	0					
Brown, K.R.	276	6	46.00	2- 7	–	–	–
Brown, S.J.E.	10837	341	31.78	7- 70	21	1	4
Browne, B.S.	3328	116	28.68	6- 51	5	–	–
Burns, M.	21	0					
Butcher, G.P.	1093	23	47.52	7- 77	1	–	–
Butcher, M.A.	2389	61	39.16	4- 31	–	–	–
Butler, O.F.X.	31	0					
Byas, D.	719	12	59.91	3- 55	–	–	–
Caddick, A.R.	8564	317	27.01	9- 32	20	8	4
Cairns, C.L.	11438	401	28.52	8- 47	15	3	3
Campbell, C.L.	44	1	44.00	1- 29	–	–	–
Campbell, S.L.	63	1	63.00	1- 38	–	–	–
Capel, D.J.	17327	543	31.90	7- 44	14	–	4
Carr, J.D.	2939	68	43.22	6- 61	3	–	–
Cassar, M.E.	185	8	23.12	4- 54	–	–	–
Chapman, R.J.	1224	23	53.21	4-109	–	–	–
Chapple, G.	5411	180	30.06	6- 48	8	–	2
Childs, J.H.	30600	1028	29.76	9- 56	52	8	9
Church, M.J.	163	9	18.11	4- 50	–	–	–
Clarke, V.P.	441	7	63.00	3- 72	–	–	–

	Runs	Wkts	Avge	Best	5wI	10wM	50wS
Collingwood, P.D.	181	3	60.33	1- 13	–	–	–
Commins, J.B.	170	4	42.50	2- 28	–	–	–
Connor, C.A.	18908	599	31.56	9- 38	17	4	5
Cooper, K.E.	22010	817	26.94	8- 44	26	1	8
Cork, D.G.	10570	404	26.16	9- 43	12	2	3
Cosker, D.A.	622	16	38.87	4- 60	–	–	–
Cottam, A.C.	819	13	63.00	2- 5	–	–	–
Cottey, P.A.	748	13	57.53	4- 49	–	–	–
Cousins, D.M.	1086	26	41.76	6- 35	1	–	–
Cowan, A.P.	1577	41	38.46	5- 68	1	–	–
Cowdrey, G.R.	841	12	70.08	1- 5	–	–	–
Cox, D.M.	1650	38	43.42	5- 97	2	1	–
Crawley, J.P.	108	1	108.00	1- 90	–	–	–
Crookes, D.N.	3065	94	32.60	5- 59	4	–	–
Croft, R.D.B.	15822	407	38.87	8- 66	18	2	4
Crowe, C.D.	4	0					
Curran, K.M.	15519	562	27.61	7- 47	15	4	5
Curtis, T.S.	748	13	57.53	2- 17	–	–	–
Dakin, J.M.	490	11	44.54	4- 45	–	–	–
Dale, A.	5097	132	38.61	6- 18	1	–	–
Daley, J.A.	9	0					
Davies, A.P.	135	1	135.00	1- 25	–	–	–
Davis, R.P.	13936	397	35.10	7- 64	16	2	2
Dawson, R.I.	110	3	36.66	2- 38	–	–	–
Deakin, P.J.	249	9	27.66	2- 17	–	–	–
Dean, K.J.	471	16	29.43	3- 47	–	–	–
DeFreitas, P.A.J.	23806	849	28.04	7- 21	42	3	9
Derbyshire, N.A.	303	5	60.60	1- 18	–	–	–
Dibden, R.R.	592	8	74.00	2- 36	–	–	–
Dimond, M.	286	6	47.66	4- 73	–	–	–
Dodemaide, A.I.C.	16254	514	31.62	6- 58	17	–	3
Donald, A.A.	19369	837	23.14	8- 37	46	7	4+1
Dowman, M.P.	197	2	98.50	2- 43	–	–	–
Drakes, V.C.	4344	144	30.16	7- 47	5	–	1
Dravid, R.S.	64	0					
Dunlop, A.R.	143	2	71.50	1- 8	–	–	–
Du Preez, S.P.	634	5	126.80	2- 44	–	–	–
Dutch, K.P.	127	3	42.33	3- 25	–	–	–
Eagleson, R.L.	149	3	49.66	2- 50	–	–	–
Ealham, M.A.	5696	194	29.36	8- 36	8	1	–
Ecclestone, S.C.	1208	33	36.60	4- 66	–	–	–
Edmond, M.D.	79	1	79.00	1- 6	–	–	–
Edwards, A.D.	310	3	103.33	3- 83	–	–	–
Ellis, S.W.K.	832	19	43.78	5- 59	1	–	–
Elworthy, S.	7092	233	30.43	7- 65	8	1	–
Emburey, J.E.	41699	1604	25.99	8- 40	72	12	17
Evans, K.P.	10015	289	34.65	6- 67	6	–	–
Fairbrother, N.H.	440	5	88.00	2- 91	–	–	–
Fay, R.A.	1146	31	36.96	4- 53	–	–	–
Feltham, M.A.	12279	388	31.64	6- 41	8	–	1
Fisher, I.D.	182	11	16.54	5- 35	1	–	–
Fleming, M.V.	5581	136	41.03	4- 31	–	–	–
Flintoff, A.	39	0					
Flower, A.	163	4	40.75	1- 1	–	–	–
Flower, G.W.	1456	35	41.60	3- 20	–	–	–
Foley, G.I.	852	20	42.60	3- 64	–	–	–
Follett, D.	684	24	28.50	8- 22	3	1	–

	Runs	Wkts	Avge	Best	5wI	10wM	50wS
Ford, J.A.	54	0					
Fordham, A.	289	4	72.25	1- 0	–	–	–
Foster, M.J.	461	14	32.92	4- 21	–	–	–
Francis, N.B.	1195	32	37.34	4- 34	–	–	–
Franks, P.J.	102	3	34.00	2- 65	–	–	–
Fraser, A.R.C.	16748	613	27.31	8- 75	24	3	6
Fulton, D.P.	65	1	65.00	1- 37	–	–	–
Gallian, J.E.R.	2924	74	39.51	6-115	1	–	–
Ganguly, S.C.	1993	51	39.07	4- 67	–	–	–
Gardner, G.E.	74	2	37.00	1- 36	–	–	–
Gatting, M.W.	4648	156	29.79	5- 34	2	–	–
Gibbs, H.H.	74	3	24.66	2- 14	–	–	–
Gibson, O.D.	8160	269	30.33	7- 55	11	3	1
Giddins, E.S.H.	7427	248	29.94	6- 47	13	1	2
Gilder, G.M.	521	32	16.28	8- 22	3	2	–
Giles, A.F.	2097	83	25.26	6- 45	4	–	1
Gillespie, P.G.	136	5	27.20	3- 93	–	–	–
Gooch, G.A.	8454	246	34.36	7- 14	3	–	–
Goodchild, D.J.	26	0					
Gough, D.	10674	376	28.38	7- 28	13	2	4
Gould, I.J.	365	7	52.14	3- 10	–	–	–
Govan, J.W.	1153	42	27.45	6- 70	2	–	–
Grayson, A.P.	1605	31	51.77	4- 82	–	–	–
Green, R.J.	686	25	27.44	6- 41	1	–	–
Greenfield, K.	479	5	95.80	2- 40	–	–	–
Griffith, F.A.	2571	73	35.21	4- 33	–	–	–
Gupte, C.M.	312	4	78.00	2- 41	–	–	–
Hall, J.W.	14	0					
Hamilton, G.M.	1126	32	35.18	5- 65	1	–	–
Hancock, T.H.C.	559	13	43.00	3- 10	–	–	–
Harden, R.J.	1011	20	50.55	2- 7	–	–	–
Harmison, S.J.	77	0					
Harris, A.J.	1899	72	26.37	6- 40	2	1	1
Harrison, G.D.	703	23	30.56	9-113	2	–	–
Hart, J.P.	51	0					
Hartley, P.J.	17121	558	30.68	9- 41	20	2	6
Haste, N.J.	2953	49	60.26	5- 73	1	–	–
Hayden, M.L.	116	1	116.00	1- 24	–	–	–
Hayhurst, A.N.	4961	109	45.51	4- 27	–	–	–
Haynes, G.R.	1643	35	46.94	4- 33	–	–	–
Headley, D.W.	7770	258	30.11	8- 98	15	1	1
Hegg, W.K.	7	0					
Hemp, D.L.	330	10	33.00	3- 23	–	–	–
Hewitt, J.P.	681	24	28.37	3- 27	–	–	–
Hick, G.A.	8513	195	43.65	5- 18	5	1	–
Hindson, J.E.	2758	82	33.63	5- 42	7	2	1
Hirwani, N.D.	11734	425	27.60	8- 52	34	6	0+3
Hoggard, M.J.	41	1	41.00	1- 41	–	–	–
Hollioake, A.J.	2777	64	43.39	4- 22	–	–	–
Hollioake, B.C.	252	10	25.20	4- 74	–	–	–
Holloway, P.C.L.	46	0					
Hooper, C.L.	12063	341	35.37	5- 33	10	–	–
House, W.J.	412	2	206.00	1- 44	–	–	–
How, E.J.	460	1	460.00	1- 24	–	–	–
Hughes, J.G.	1481	33	44.87	5- 69	1	–	–
Hussain, N.	307	2	153.50	1- 38	–	–	–
Hutchison, P.M.	287	12	23.91	4- 23	–	–	–

	Runs	Wkts	Avge	Best	5wI	10wM	50wS
Hutton, S.	18	0					
Ijaz Ahmed	1015	33	30.75	5- 95	1	–	–
Illingworth, R.K.	23290	758	30.72	7- 50	26	5	5
Ilott, M.C.	12062	425	28.38	9- 19	22	3	5
Innes, K.J.	226	8	28.25	4- 61	–	–	–
Inzamam-ul-Haq	1286	37	34.75	5- 80	2	–	–
Irani, R.C.	3785	115	32.91	5- 19	3	–	–
Jadeja, A.	1303	33	39.48	4- 37	–	–	–
James, K.D.	10819	330	32.78	6- 22	9	–	–
James, S.P.	3	0					
Janisch, A.N.	986	14	70.42	3- 38	–	–	–
Jarrett, M.E.D.	5	0					
Jarvis, P.W.	16695	591	28.24	7- 55	20	3	4
Johnson, P.	561	6	93.50	1- 9	–	–	–
Johnson, R.L.	2988	108	27.66	10- 45	4	2	–
Jones, D.M.	1449	26	55.73	5-112	1	–	–
Jones, R.O.	660	9	73.33	2- 45	–	–	–
Joshi, S.B.	2541	105	24.20	7- 60	5	1	0+1
Julian, B.P.	8717	286	30.47	6- 37	17	1	1
Kallis, J.H.	1010	27	37.40	5- 96	1	–	–
Keech, M.	332	7	47.42	2- 28	–	–	–
Keedy, G.	2786	62	44.93	4- 35	–	–	–
Kendall, W.S.	345	10	34.50	3- 37	–	–	–
Kendrick, N.M.	6891	179	38.49	7-115	6	1	1
Kenlock, S.G.	666	11	60.54	3-104	–	–	–
Kennis, G.J.	0	0					
Kerr, J.I.D.	2216	54	41.03	5- 82	1	–	–
Kettleborough, R.A.	79	2	39.50	2- 26	–	–	–
Khan, A.A.	160	8	20.00	4- 51	–	–	–
Khan, G.A.	190	3	63.33	2- 48	–	–	–
Khan, W.G.	24	0					
Killeen, N.	1201	29	41.41	5-118	1	–	–
Kirtley, R.J.	859	29	29.62	5- 51	1	–	–
Klusener, L.	2835	119	23.82	8- 34	4	1	–
Knight, N.V.	105	1	105.00	1- 61	–	–	–
Koenig, S.G.	9	0					
Krikken, K.M.	40	0					
Kumble, A.	9606	416	23.09	8- 41	27	6	1+1
Lampitt, S.R.	11798	395	29.86	5- 32	12	–	5
Laney, J.S.	64	0					
Lathwell, M.N.	624	12	52.00	2- 21	–	–	–
Law, D.R.	1740	53	32.83	5- 33	2	–	–
Law, S.G.	2387	54	44.20	5- 39	1	–	–
Lawrence, D.V.	16162	507	31.87	7- 47	21	1	5
Lawson, A.G.	2	0					
Leatherdale, D.A.	905	21	43.09	4- 75	–	–	–
Lee, S.	3287	72	45.65	4- 20	–	–	–
Lenham, N.J.	1847	42	43.97	4- 13	–	–	–
Lewis, C.C.	13396	448	29.90	6- 22	17	3	2
Lewis, D.A.	276	5	55.20	2- 39	–	–	–
Lewis, J.	1055	30	35.16	4- 34	–	–	–
Lewis, J.J.B.	48	0					
Lewry, J.D.	2504	95	26.35	6- 43	7	1	–
Liebenberg, G.F.J.	11	1	11.00	1- 10	–	–	–
Lightfoot, C.G.R.	129	2	64.50	2- 65	–	–	–
Llong, N.J.	1059	31	34.16	5- 21	2	–	–
Lloyd, G.D.	190	2	95.00	1- 4	–	–	–

170

	Runs	Wkts	Avge	Best	5wI	10wM	50wS
Longley, J.I.	47	0					
Loye, M.B.	1	0					
Lugsden, S.	759	16	47.43	3- 45	–	–	–
Lynch, M.A.	1398	26	53.76	3- 6	–	–	–
McCague, M.J.	9244	344	26.87	9- 86	20	2	4
McCallan, W.K.	64	0					
McGrath, A.	64	0					
Maclay, A.W.	867	11	78.81	3- 30	–	–	–
Macmillan, G.I.	1162	23	50.52	3- 13	–	–	–
Maddy, D.L.	145	4	36.25	2- 21	–	–	–
Malcolm, D.E.	22486	718	31.31	9- 57	26	5	5
Malik, H.S.	2108	30	70.26	3- 10	–	–	–
Mallender, N.A.	24654	937	26.31	7- 27	36	5	6
Manjrekar, S.V.	238	3	79.33	1- 4	–	–	–
Marc, K.	275	6	45.83	3- 91	–	–	–
Marsh, S.A.	240	2	120.00	2- 20	–	–	–
Martin, P.J.	9072	283	32.05	7- 50	4	–	1
Martin-Jenkins, R.S.C.	169	1	169.00	1- 26	–	–	–
Maru, R.J.	17211	522	32.97	8- 41	15	1	4
Mascarenhas, A.D.	297	16	18.56	6- 88	1	–	–
Mason, T.J.	101	1	101.00	1- 22	–	–	–
Mather, D.P.	1246	27	46.14	4- 65	–	–	–
May, M.R.	19	0					
Maynard, M.P.	704	6	117.33	3- 21	–	–	–
Metcalfe, A.A.	362	4	90.50	2- 18	–	–	–
Metson, C.P.	0	0					
Mhambrey, P.L.	2795	106	22.68	6- 47	7	–	0+1
Mike, G.W.	3420	87	39.31	5- 44	2	–	–
Milburn, S.M.	1370	31	44.19	4- 68	–	–	–
Millns, D.J.	11233	406	27.66	9- 37	19	3	4
Moffat, G.R.	788	8	98.50	2- 50	–	–	–
Mohammad Akram	1538	60	25.63	7- 51	3	–	–
Moin Khan	81	2	40.50	2- 78	–	–	–
Moles, A.J.	1882	40	47.05	3- 21	–	–	–
Molins, G.L.	119	4	29.75	3- 62	–	–	–
Mongia, N.R.	4	0					
Montgomerie, R.R.	65	0					
Moody, T.M.	6669	212	31.45	7- 38	5	2	–
Moore, D.M.P.	37	0					
Moores, P.	16	0					
Morris, A.C.	219	5	43.80	1- 11	–	–	–
Morris, H.	380	2	190.00	1- 6	–	–	–
Morris, J.E.	912	7	130.28	1- 6	–	–	–
Morris, R.S.M.	1	0					
Moxon, M.D.	1481	28	52.89	3- 24	–	–	–
Mullally, A.D.	10936	343	31.88	7- 22	9	2	3
Munton, T.A.	15577	594	26.22	8- 89	26	6	5
Mushtaq Ahmed	14692	579	25.37	9- 93	41	11	3+1
Nash, D.J.	4859	168	28.92	6- 30	7	1	1
Newell, K.	211	1	211.00	1- 38	–	–	–
Newell, Michael (Nt)	282	7	40.28	2- 38	–	–	–
Newport, P.J.	21598	791	27.30	8- 52	34	3	8
Noon, W.M.	22	0					
Nowell, R.W.	1397	34	41.08	4- 43	–	–	–
O'Gorman, T.J.G.	215	3	71.66	1- 7	–	–	–
Ormond, J.	65	2	32.50	2- 65	–	–	–
Ostler, D.P.	122	0					

	Runs	Wkts	Avge	Best	5wI	10wM	50wS
Parkin, O.T.	914	21	43.52	3- 22	–	–	–
Parsons, G.J.	23952	796	30.09	9- 72	19	1	3
Parsons, K.A.	647	8	80.87	2- 11	–	–	–
Patel, M.M.	8106	250	32.42	8- 96	15	7	2
Patterson, M.W.	124	7	17.71	6- 80	1	–	–
Pearson, R.M.	5426	98	55.36	5-108	2	–	–
Peirce, M.T.E.	30	0					
Penberthy, A.L.	5126	145	35.35	5- 37	3	–	–
Pennett, D.B.	2697	60	44.95	5- 36	1	–	–
Penney, T.L.	183	6	30.50	3- 18	–	–	–
Philip, I.L.	47	0					
Phillips, B.J.	109	4	27.25	3- 34	–	–	–
Phillips, N.C.	1529	26	58.80	3- 39	–	–	–
Pick, R.A.	16089	489	32.90	7-128	16	3	5
Pierson, A.R.K.	10216	283	36.09	8- 42	12	–	1
Pigott, A.C.S.	20831	672	30.99	7- 74	26	2	5
Piper, K.J.	57	1	57.00	1- 57	–	–	–
Pollard, P.R.	268	4	67.00	2- 79	–	–	–
Pollock, S.M.	3327	146	22.78	7- 33	6	1	–
Pooley, J.C.	68	0					
Pothas, N.	5	0					
Powell, M.J.	18	1	18.00	1- 18	–	–	–
Prasad, B.K.V.	3493	137	25.49	7- 37	6	1	0+1
Preece, B.E.A.	388	8	48.50	4- 79	–	–	–
Preston, N.W.	352	11	32.00	4- 68	–	–	–
Prichard, P.J.	497	2	248.50	1- 28	–	–	–
Pringle, M.W.	7370	299	24.64	7- 60	14	2	–
Radford, T.A.	0	1	0.00	1- 0	–	–	–
Raju, S.L.V.	8719	333	26.18	7- 82	18	4	0+2
Ramprakash, M.R.	1025	16	64.06	3- 91	–	–	–
Rao, R.K.	7	0					
Rashid, U.B.A.	17	0					
Rashid Latif	102	3	34.00	2- 17	–	–	–
Ratcliffe, J.D.	401	9	44.55	2- 26	–	–	–
Rathore, V.	31	0					
Ratledge, J.	108	1	108.00	1- 16	–	–	–
Rawnsley, M.J.	219	5	43.80	1- 4	–	–	–
Reeve, D.A.	12232	456	26.82	7- 37	8	–	2
Remy, C.C.	1051	19	55.31	4- 63	–	–	–
Renshaw, S.J.	934	17	54.94	4- 56	–	–	–
Rhodes, S.J.	30	0					
Ridley, A.C.	19	0					
Ripley, D.	103	2	51.50	2- 89	–	–	–
Roberts, A.R.	4829	107	45.13	6- 72	1	–	–
Roberts, G.M.	73	1	73.00	1- 55	–	–	–
Robinson, D.D.J.	31	0					
Robinson, M.A.	12059	369	32.68	9- 37	7	2	1
Robinson, P.E.	329	3	109.66	1- 10	–	–	–
Robinson, R.T.	289	4	72.25	1- 22	–	–	–
Rollins, A.S.	101	1	101.00	1- 19	–	–	–
Rose, G.D.	13186	440	29.96	7- 47	11	1	3
Roseberry, M.A.	406	4	101.50	1- 1	–	–	–
Russell, R.C.	53	1	53.00	1- 4	–	–	–
Saeed Anwar	393	9	43.66	3- 83	–	–	–
Saggers, M.J.	443	13	34.07	6- 65	1	–	–
Salim Malik	2877	84	34.25	5- 19	3	–	–
Salisbury, I.D.K.	16349	479	34.13	8- 75	24	4	4

	Runs	Wkts	Avge	Best	5wI	10wM	50wS
Saqlain Mushtaq	2415	114	21.18	7- 66	8	1	0+1
Sargeant, N.F.	88	1	88.00	1- 88	–	–	–
Schultz, B.N.	4226	171	24.71	7- 70	8	–	–
Scott, C.W.	40	0					
Searle, J.P.	133	2	66.50	2-126	–	–	–
Shadab Kabir	27	0					
Shadford, D.J.	107	3	35.66	2- 40	–	–	–
Shah, O.A.	24	1	24.00	1- 24	–	–	–
Shahid, N.	1913	41	46.65	3- 91	–	–	–
Shahid Anwar	856	30	28.53	3- 6	–	–	–
Shahid Nazir	552	32	17.25	6- 64	2	–	–
Sheeraz, K.P.	1064	27	39.40	6- 67	2	1	–
Sheriyar, A.	2860	77	37.14	6- 30	3	1	–
Shine, K.J.	7094	190	37.33	8- 47	9	1	–
Sidhu, N.S.	71	0					
Silverwood, C.E.W.	3076	95	32.37	5- 62	3	–	–
Simmons, P.V.	4330	149	29.06	6- 14	4	–	1
Singh, A.	14	0					
Slater, M.J.	24	1	24.00	1- 4	–	–	–
Small, G.C.	24234	849	28.54	7- 15	29	2	6
Smith, A.M.	6452	216	29.87	8- 73	8	2	2
Smith, A.W.	2435	43	56.62	5-103	1	–	–
Smith, B.F.	190	2	95.00	1- 5	–	–	–
Smith, G.J.	2232	83	26.89	5- 24	3	–	–
Smith, N.M.K.	9034	242	37.33	7- 42	15	–	–
Smith, P.A.	10109	283	35.72	6- 91	7	–	–
Smith, R.A.	693	12	57.75	2- 11	–	–	–
Snape, J.N.	2207	50	44.14	5- 65	1	–	–
Solanki, V.S.	1222	30	40.73	5- 69	3	1	–
Speak, N.J.	164	2	82.00	1- 0	–	–	–
Speight, M.P.	32	2	16.00	1- 2	–	–	–
Srinath, J.	6957	265	26.25	9- 76	9	2	1
Stanford, E.J.	378	8	47.25	3- 84	–	–	–
Stemp, R.D.	8488	250	33.95	6- 37	11	1	–
Stephenson, J.P.	7291	217	33.59	7- 51	8	–	–
Stewart, A.J.	417	3	139.00	1- 7	–	–	–
Strang, P.A.	3118	86	36.25	7- 75	6	–	–
Such, P.M.	18061	618	29.22	8- 93	33	6	4
Sutcliffe, I.J.	129	4	32.25	2- 21	–	–	–
Swann, A.J.	15	0					
Symonds, A.	997	22	45.31	3- 77	–	–	–
Taylor, J.P.	10437	350	29.82	7- 23	13	2	4
Taylor, N.R.	891	16	55.68	2- 20	–	–	–
Telemachus, R.	1596	58	27.51	5- 72	2	–	–
Tendulkar, S.R.	1700	25	68.00	3- 60	–	–	–
Tennant, A.M.	122	3	40.66	3- 28	–	–	–
Tennent, R.W.	136	4	34.00	2- 34	–	–	–
Terry, V.P.	58	0					
Thomas, P.A.	2129	45	47.31	5- 70	1	–	–
Thomas, S.D.	3808	96	39.66	5- 76	5	–	–
Thompson, J.B.D.	613	16	38.31	5- 72	1	–	–
Thomson, R.B.	527	9	58.55	2- 24	–	–	–
Thorpe, G.P.	1210	24	50.41	4- 40	–	–	–
Thursfield, M.J.	1431	35	40.88	6-130	1	–	–
Titchard, S.P.	124	1	124.00	1- 51	–	–	–
Tolley, C.M.	4267	110	38.79	5- 55	1	–	–
Trescothick, M.E.	240	5	48.00	4- 36	–	–	–

	Runs	Wkts	Avge	Best	5wI	10wM	50wS
Trainor, N.J.	4	0					
Trump, H.R.J.	9424	243	38.78	7- 52	9	2	1
Tudor, A.J.	320	14	22.85	5- 32	1	–	–
Tufnell, P.C.R.	20275	683	29.68	8- 29	35	4	6
Turner, R.J.	29	0					
Tweats, T.A.	208	4	52.00	1- 23	–	–	–
Udal, S.D.	11124	322	34.54	8- 50	20	4	4
Vandrau, M.J.	4258	128	33.26	6- 34	7	2	–
Van Troost, A.P.	4703	124	37.92	6- 48	4	–	–
Vaughan, M.P.	2446	56	43.67	4- 39	–	–	–
Wagh, M.A.	632	10	63.20	3- 82	–	–	–
Walker, A.	8553	265	32.27	8-118	4	1	1
Walker, M.J.	19	0					
Walsh, C.A.	31022	1404	22.09	9- 72	82	16	9+2
Walsh, C.D.	64	0					
Walton, T.C.	237	4	59.25	1- 26	–	–	–
Waqar Younis	12659	609	20.78	7- 64	51	12	3+3
Ward, D.M.	113	2	56.50	2- 66	–	–	–
Ward, I.J.	84	0					
Ward, T.R.	609	8	76.12	2- 10	–	–	–
Warner, A.E.	13399	426	31.53	6- 21	8	1	–
Wasim Akram	17431	813	21.44	8- 30	62	14	5+1
Watkin, S.L.	19327	665	29.06	8- 59	22	4	8
Watkinson, M.	23135	689	33.57	8- 30	26	3	7
Weekes, P.N.	4473	114	39.23	8- 39	3	–	–
Welch, G.	2124	60	35.40	4- 50	–	–	–
Wells, A.P.	765	10	76.50	3- 67	–	–	–
Wells, C.M.	14748	428	34.45	7- 42	7	–	2
Wells, V.J.	4126	156	26.44	5- 43	2	–	–
Weston, R.M.S.	76	1	76.00	1- 41	–	–	–
Weston, W.P.C.	516	4	129.00	2- 39	–	–	–
Wharf, A.G.	299	7	42.71	4- 29	–	–	–
Whitaker, J.J.	268	2	134.00	1- 29	–	–	–
Whitaker, P.R.	457	11	41.54	3- 36	–	–	–
White, C.	4215	139	30.32	5- 40	3	–	–
White, G.W.	140	1	140.00	1- 30	–	–	–
Whittall, A.R.	4025	69	58.33	6- 46	2	1	–
Whitticase, P.	7	0					
Wild, R.D.	62	1	62.00	1- 62	–	–	–
Wileman, J.R.	217	4	54.25	2- 33	–	–	–
Williams, N.F.	19263	636	30.28	8- 75	21	2	3
Williamson, D.	95	1	95.00	1- 32	–	–	–
Williamson, J.G.	200	2	100.00	2- 51	–	–	–
Windows, M.G.N.	39	2	19.50	1- 6	–	–	–
Wood, J.	4339	118	36.77	6-110	4	–	–
Wren, T.N.	2394	64	37.40	6- 48	3	–	–
Wright, A.J.	68	1	68.00	1- 16	–	–	–
Wright, G.J.	33	0					
Yates, G.	4858	108	44.98	5- 34	2	–	–
Young, S.	5100	147	34.69	5- 36	6	1	–

LEADING CURRENT PLAYERS

The leading career records of players currently registered for first-class county cricket, subject to non-selection for the Australian touring team in the cases of D.M.Jones, T.M.Moody and S.G.Law. All figures are to the end of the 1996 English season.

BATTING
(Qualification: 100 innings)

	Runs	Avge
G.A.Hick	26895	55.79
D.M.Jones	17313	52.62
M.W.Gatting	34357	50.15
G.A.Gooch	44472	49.57
J.P.Crawley	9388	49.15
T.M.Moody	16961	46.98
D.C.Boon	18811	46.10
S.G.Law	7423	45.82
N.Hussain	11443	45.22
M.R.Ramprakash	13143	45.16
C.L.Hooper	13330	44.88
R.A.Smith	20727	44.28
G.P.Thorpe	12377	44.04
M.A.Atherton	15416	43.92
R.T.Robinson	25667	43.50
M.P.Maynard	17217	43.25
M.D.Moxon	20572	43.21
T.L.Penney	5484	43.18
R.J.Bailey	18021	41.71
N.H.Fairbrother	16295	41.46
A.D.Brown	4780	41.206
P.D.Bowler	12772	41.200
M.A.Butcher	3697	41.07
A.J.Moles	14670	41.09
T.S.Curtis	20083	40.98
J.E.R.Gallian	5184	40.50
N.V.Knight	5215	40.42
A.P.Wells	18508	40.23
A.J.Stewart	18197	40.16
D.J.Bicknell	12102	39.94
A.Fordham	10266	39.79
N.R.Taylor	17771	39.75
R.J.Harden	12201	39.74
J.E.Morris	18523	39.66
K.J.Barnett	23272	39.64

BOWLING
(Qualification: 100 wickets)

	Wkts	Avge
Waqar Younis	609	20.78
Wasim Akram	813	21.44
A.A.Donald	837	23.14
Mushtaq Ahmed	579	25.37
M.P.Bicknell	586	25.991
J.E.Emburey	1604	25.996
D.G.Cork	404	26.16
T.A.Munton	594	26.22
V.J.Wells	156	26.44
M.J.McCague	344	26.87
A.R.Caddick	317	27.01
D.R.Brown	120	27.03
P.J.Newport	791	27.30
A.R.C.Fraser	613	27.31
K.M.Curran	562	27.61
R.L.Johnson	108	27.666
D.J.Millns	406	27.667
P.A.J.DeFreitas	849	28.04
P.W.Jarvis	591	28.24
M.C.Ilott	425	28.381
D.Gough	376	28.388
C.L.Cairns	401	28.52
G.C.Small	849	28.54
J.E.Benjamin	351	28.84
P.V.Simmons	149	29.060
S.L.Watkin	665	29.063
P.M.Such	618	29.22
M.A.Ealham	194	29.36
P.C.R.Tufnell	683	29.68
M.W.Gatting	156	29.79
J.P.Taylor	350	29.82
S.R.Lampitt	395	29.86
A.M.Smith	216	29.87
C.C.Lewis	448	29.90
G.D.Rose	440	29.96

FIELDING

	Ct
G.A.Gooch	543
J.E.Emburey	458
M.W.Gatting	451
C.W.J.Athey	420
G.A.Hick	396
M.A.Lynch	358

WICKET-KEEPING

	Total	Ct	St
R.C.Russell	942	838	104
S.J.Rhodes	877	773	104
C.P.Metson	607	557	50
S.A.Marsh	605	557	48
D.Ripley	563	496	67
W.K.Hegg	546	485	61
R.J.Blakey	510	468	42
P.Moores	508	464	44

TEST CAREER RECORDS

These records, complete to the end of the New Zealand v England series (18 February 1997), include all players registered for county cricket in 1997 at the time of going to press, plus those who have appeared in Test matches since August 1995 (No. 1304 onwards).

ENGLAND – BATTING AND FIELDING

	M	I	NO	HS	Runs	Avge	100	50	Ct/St
M.A.Atherton	67	122	4	185*	4986	42.25	11	31	47
C.W.J.Athey	23	41	1	123	919	22.97	1	4	13
R.J.Bailey	4	8	–	43	119	14.87	–	–	–
K.J.Barnett	4	7	–	80	207	29.57	–	2	1
J.E.Benjamin	1	1	–	0	0	0.00	–	–	–
M.P.Bicknell	2	4	–	14	26	6.50	–	–	–
R.J.Blakey	2	4	–	6	7	1.75	–	–	2
S.J.E.Brown	1	2	1	10*	11	11.00	–	–	1
A.R.Caddick	11	18	2	29*	213	13.31	–	–	5
D.J.Capel	15	25	1	98	374	15.58	–	2	6
D.G.Cork	19	27	4	59	482	20.95	–	2	10
J.P.Crawley	17	26	3	112	785	34.13	2	5	18
R.D.B.Croft	5	6	1	31	63	12.60	–	–	5
T.S.Curtis	5	9	–	41	140	15.55	–	–	3
P.A.J.DeFreitas	44	68	5	88	934	14.82	–	4	14
M.A.Ealham	2	3	–	51	81	27.00	–	1	1
J.E.Emburey	64	96	20	75	1713	22.53	–	10	34
N.H.Fairbrother	10	15	1	83	219	15.64	–	1	4
A.R.C.Fraser	32	43	10	29	265	7.36	–	–	7
J.E.R.Gallian	3	6	–	28	74	12.33	–	–	1
M.W.Gatting	79	138	14	207	4409	35.55	10	21	59
G.A.Gooch	118	215	6	333	8900	42.58	20	46	103
D.Gough	17	24	4	65	346	17.30	–	2	8
G.A.Hick	46	80	6	178	2672	36.10	4	15	62
N.Hussain	17	29	3	128	960	36.92	3	3	15
A.P.Igglesden	3	5	3	3*	6	3.00	–	–	1
R.K.Illingworth	9	14	7	28	128	18.28	–	–	5
M.C.Ilott	5	6	2	15	28	7.00	–	–	–
R.C.Irani	2	3	–	41	76	25.33	–	–	–
P.W.Jarvis	9	15	2	29*	132	10.15	–	–	2
N.V.Knight	11	19	–	113	573	30.15	1	4	21
M.N.Lathwell	2	4	–	33	78	19.50	–	–	–
C.C.Lewis	32	51	3	117	1105	23.02	1	4	25
M.J.McCague	3	5	–	11	21	4.20	–	–	1
D.E.Malcolm	36	53	18	29	224	6.40	–	–	5
P.J.Martin	7	11	–	29	92	8.36	–	–	5
M.P.Maynard	4	8	–	35	87	10.87	–	–	3
H.Morris	3	6	–	44	115	19.16	–	–	3
J.E.Morris	3	5	2	32	71	23.66	–	–	3
M.D.Moxon	10	17	1	99	455	28.43	–	3	10
A.D.Mullally	9	12	4	24	79	9.87	–	–	1
T.A.Munton	2	2	1	25*	25	25.00	–	–	–
P.J.Newport	3	5	1	40*	110	27.50	–	–	1
M.M.Patel	2	2	–	27	45	22.50	–	–	2
M.R.Ramprakash	19	33	1	72	533	16.65	–	2	13
S.J.Rhodes	11	17	5	65*	294	24.50	–	1	46/3

ENGLAND – BATTING AND FIELDING (continued)

	M	I	NO	HS	Runs	Avge	100	50	Ct/St
R.T.Robinson	29	49	5	175	1601	36.38	4	6	8
R.C.Russell	49	77	15	128*	1807	29.14	2	6	141/11
I.D.K.Salisbury	9	17	2	50	255	17.00	–	1	3
C.E.W.Silverwood	1	1	–	0	0	0.00	–	–	1
G.C.Small	17	24	7	59	263	15.47	–	1	9
R.A.Smith	62	112	15	175	4236	43.67	9	28	39
J.P.Stephenson	1	2	–	25	36	18.00	–	–	–
A.J.Stewart	63	111	7	190	4433	42.62	10	22	89/7
P.M.Such	8	11	4	14*	65	9.28	–	–	2
J.P.Taylor	2	4	2	17*	34	17.00	–	–	–
G.P.Thorpe	37	67	6	123	2511	41.16	4	19	31
P.C.R.Tufnell	27	37	20	22*	111	6.52	–	–	11
S.L.Watkin	3	5	–	13	25	5.00	–	–	1
M.Watkinson	4	6	1	82*	167	33.40	–	1	1
A.P.Wells	1	2	1	3*	3	3.00	–	–	–
J.J.Whitaker	1	1	–	11	11	11.00	–	–	1
C.White	8	12	–	51	166	13.83	–	1	3
N.F.Williams	1	1	–	38	38	38.00	–	–	–

ENGLAND – BOWLING

	O	R	W	Avge	Best	5wI	10wM
M.A.Atherton	68	302	2	151.00	1- 20	–	–
K.J.Barnett	6	32	0				
J.E.Benjamin	28	80	4	20.00	4- 42	–	–
M.P.Bicknell	87	263	4	65.75	3- 99	–	–
S.J.E.Brown	33	138	2	69.00	1- 60	–	–
A.R.Caddick	468.3	1372	37	37.08	6- 65	2	–
D.J.Capel	333.2	1064	21	50.66	3- 88	–	–
D.G.Cork	724.1	2249	74	30.39	7- 43	3	–
R.D.B.Croft	229.5	465	20	23.25	5- 95	1	–
T.S.Curtis	3	7	0				
P.A.J.DeFreitas	1639.4	4700	140	33.57	7- 70	4	–
M.A.Ealham	80	192	7	27.42	4- 21	–	–
J.E.Emburey	2565.1	5646	147	38.40	7- 78	6	–
N.H.Fairbrother	2	9	0				
A.R.C.Fraser	1327.5	3509	119	29.48	8- 75	8	–
J.E.R.Gallian	14	62	0				
M.W.Gatting	125.2	317	4	79.25	1- 14	–	–
G.A.Gooch	442.3	1069	23	46.47	3- 39	–	–
D.Gough	611.4	1890	69	27.39	6- 49	2	–
G.A.Hick	495.3	1247	22	56.68	4-126	–	–
A.P.Igglesden	92.3	329	6	54.83	2- 91	–	–
R.K.Illingworth	247.3	615	19	32.36	4- 96	–	–
M.C.Ilott	173.4	542	12	45.16	3- 48	–	–
R.C.Irani	21	74	2	37.00	1- 22	–	–
P.W.Jarvis	318.4	965	21	45.95	4-107	–	–
C.C.Lewis	1142	3490	93	37.52	6-111	3	–
M.J.McCague	98.5	390	6	65.00	4-121	–	–
D.E.Malcolm	1320.2	4441	122	36.40	9- 57	5	2
P.J.Martin	223	529	17	31.11	4- 60	–	–
M.D.Moxon	8	30	0				
A.D.Mullally	396.3	927	28	33.10	3- 44	–	–
T.A.Munton	67.3	200	4	50.00	2- 22	–	–
P.J.Newport	111.3	417	10	41.70	4- 87	–	–

ENGLAND – BOWLING (continued)

	O	R	W	Avge	Best	5wI	10wM
M.M.Patel	46	180	1	180.00	1-101	–	–
M.R.Ramprakash	44.1	149	0				
R.T.Robinson	1	0	0				
I.D.K.Salisbury	295.3	1154	18	64.11	4-163	–	–
C.E.W.Silverwood	25	71	4	17.75	3- 63	–	–
G.C.Small	654.3	1871	55	34.01	5- 48	2	–
R.A.Smith	4	6	0				
A.J.Stewart	3.2	13	0				
P.M.Such	362.5	805	22	36.59	6- 67	1	–
J.P.Taylor	48	156	3	52.00	1- 18	–	–
G.P.Thorpe	23	37	0				
P.C.R.Tufnell	1277.5	3105	82	37.86	7- 47	4	1
S.L.Watkin	89	305	11	27.72	4- 65	–	–
M.Watkinson	112	348	10	34.80	3- 64	–	–
C.White	135.1	452	11	41.09	3- 18	–	–
N.F.Williams	41	148	2	74.00	2-148	–	–

AUSTRALIA – BATTING AND FIELDING

	M	I	NO	HS	Runs	Avge	100	50	Ct/St
M.G.Bevan	11	19	2	91	658	38.70	–	6	7
A.J.Bichel	2	3	–	18	40	13.33	–	–	–
G.S.Blewett	13	22	2	115	769	38.45	2	5	15
D.C.Boon	107	190	20	200	7422	43.65	21	32	99
M.T.G.Elliott	2	4	1	78*	128	42.66	–	1	1
J.N.Gillespie	2	3	2	16*	22	22.00	–	–	–
M.L.Hayden	4	7	–	125	197	28.14	1	–	4
I.A.Healy	85	128	17	161*	3188	28.72	3	17	271/20
G.B.Hogg	1	2	–	4	5	2.50	–	–	–
B.P.Julian	7	9	1	56*	128	16.00	–	1	4
M.S.Kasprowicz	2	2	–	21	27	13.50	–	–	–
J.L.Langer	8	12	–	69	272	22.66	–	3	2
S.G.Law	1	1	1	54*	54	–	–	1	1
C.J.McDermott	71	90	13	42*	940	12.20	–	–	19
G.D.McGrath	25	29	7	24	70	3.18	–	–	4
P.E.McIntyre	2	4	1	16	22	7.33	–	–	–
R.T.Ponting	6	10	–	96	330	33.00	–	3	9
P.R.Reiffel	25	35	9	56	469	18.03	–	2	13
M.J.Slater	34	59	3	219	2655	47.41	7	10	11
M.A.Taylor	78	140	9	219	5719	43.65	14	33	114
S.K.Warne	49	65	9	74*	797	14.23	–	1	36
M.E.Waugh	60	97	4	140	4046	43.50	10	26	78
S.R.Waugh	86	133	27	200	5257	49.59	11	31	63

AUSTRALIA – BOWLING

	O	R	W	Avge	Best	5wI	10wM
M.G.Bevan	91.3	332	16	20.75	6- 82	1	1
A.J.Bichel	37.2	143	1	143.00	1- 31	–	–
G.S.Blewett	63.5	186	3	62.00	2- 25	–	–
D.C.Boon	6	14	0				
J.N.Gillespie	33	94	2	47.00	2- 62	–	–
G.B.Hogg	17	69	1	69.00	1- 69	–	–
B.P.Julian	183	599	15	39.93	4- 36	–	–
M.S.Kasprowicz	48	126	0				

TESTS

AUSTRALIA – BOWLING (continued)

	O	R	W	Avge	Best	5wI	10wM
S.G.Law	3	9	0				
C.J.McDermott	2764.2	8332	291	28.63	8- 97	14	2
G.D.McGrath	994	2646	106	24.96	6- 47	5	–
P.E.McIntyre	65.3	194	5	38.80	3-103	–	–
R.T.Ponting	5.5	8	2	4.00	1- 0	–	–
P.R.Reiffel	770	2108	80	26.35	6- 71	4	–
M.J.Slater	1.1	4	1	4.00	1- 4	–	–
M.A.Taylor	7	26	1	26.00	1- 11	–	–
S.K.Warne	2403.3	5464	229	23.86	8- 71	10	3
M.E.Waugh	514	1435	39	36.79	5- 40	1	–
S.R.Waugh	1057.2	2798	79	35.41	5- 28	3	–

SOUTH AFRICA – BATTING AND FIELDING

	M	I	NO	HS	Runs	Avge	100	50	Ct/St
P.R.Adams	7	9	1	29	45	5.62	–	–	5
A.M.Bacher	3	6	–	55	141	23.50	–	1	3
W.J.Cronje	33	58	6	135	1808	34.76	5	5	11
D.J.Cullinan	25	43	4	153*	1656	42.46	3	11	18
P.S.de Villiers	16	23	6	67*	305	17.94	–	2	10
A.A.Donald	30	39	18	33	289	13.76	–	–	7
C.E.Eksteen	6	10	2	22	87	10.87	–	–	4
H.H.Gibbs	3	6	–	31	87	14.50	–	–	1
A.C.Hudson	31	56	3	163	1889	35.64	4	13	33
J.H.Kallis	2	2	–	7	8	4.00	–	–	2
G.Kirsten	26	47	2	133	1724	38.31	4	9	21
L.Klusener	5	9	3	102*	243	40.50	1	–	6
B.M.McMillan	29	47	10	113	1583	42.78	3	9	41
C.R.Matthews	18	25	6	62*	348	18.31	–	1	4
S.M.Pollock	8	12	3	79	278	30.88	–	1	3
M.W.Pringle	4	6	2	33	67	16.75	–	–	–
J.N.Rhodes	28	45	5	101*	1237	30.92	1	7	16
D.J.Richardson	34	51	5	109	1149	24.97	1	7	122/1
B.N.Schultz	7	6	2	6	6	1.50	–	–	1
P.L.Symcox	9	12	1	50	243	22.09	–	1	–

SOUTH AFRICA – BOWLING

	O	R	W	Avge	Best	5wI	10wM
P.R.Adams	265	777	31	25.06	6-55	1	–
A.M.Bacher	1	4	0				
W.J.Cronje	356.4	674	13	51.84	2-11	–	–
P.S.de Villiers	742.1	1909	75	25.45	6-43	4	2
A.A.Donald	1146.1	3296	144	22.88	8-71	7	2
C.E.Eksteen	243	447	8	55.87	3-12	–	–
J.H.Kallis	4	2	0				
G.Kirsten	54.1	135	2	67.50	1- 0	–	–
L.Klusener	154.4	499	17	29.35	8-64	1	–
B.M.McMillan	855	2160	70	30.85	4-65	–	–
C.R.Matthews	663.2	1502	52	28.88	5-42	2	–
S.M.Pollock	245.5	608	26	23.38	5-32	1	–
M.W.Pringle	108.4	270	5	54.00	2-62	–	–
J.N.Rhodes	2	5	9				
B.N.Schultz	236.5	600	30	20.00	5-48	2	–
P.L.Symcox	271.5	750	15	50.00	3-75	–	–

TESTS　　**WEST INDIES – BATTING AND FIELDING**

	M	I	NO	HS	Runs	Avge	100	50	Ct/St
J.C.Adams	29	46	11	208*	1991	56.88	5	9	30
C.E.L.Ambrose	65	93	19	53	889	12.01	–	1	14
K.C.G.Benjamin	24	32	7	43*	215	8.60	–	–	2
I.R.Bishop	31	47	9	48	442	11.63	–	–	5
C.O.Browne	8	13	4	34	186	20.66	–	–	38/1
S.L.Campbell	16	28	2	208	1176	45.23	2	7	16
S.Chanderpaul	16	25	4	82	1011	48.14	–	11	8
C.E.Cuffy	3	5	2	3*	6	2.00	–	–	1
R.Dhanraj	4	4	–	9	17	4.25	–	–	1
A.F.G.Griffith	1	2	–	13	14	7.00	–	–	–
C.L.Hooper	57	96	8	178*	2910	33.06	6	14	66
B.C.Lara	38	64	2	375	3493	56.33	8	18	53
J.R.Murray	26	34	3	101*	824	26.58	1	3	90/3
R.G.Samuels	6	12	2	125	372	37.20	1	1	8
P.V.Simmons	25	45	2	110	1000	23.25	1	4	26
P.I.C.Thompson	2	3	1	10*	17	8.50	–	–	–
C.A.Walsh	87	116	36	30*	743	9.28	–	–	14

WEST INDIES – BOWLING

	O	R	W	Avge	Best	5wI	10wM
J.C.Adams	199.3	654	15	43.60	5-17	1	–
C.E.L.Ambrose	2547.2	6102	285	21.41	8-45	16	3
K.C.G.Benjamin	792.2	2619	89	29.42	6-66	4	1
I.R.Bishop	1128.3	3075	137	22.44	6-40	6	–
S.Chanderpaul	106	334	3	111.33	1- 2	–	–
C.E.Cuffy	85.2	306	7	43.71	3-80	–	–
R.Dhanraj	181.1	595	8	74.37	2-49	–	–
C.L.Hooper	1126	2989	54	55.35	5-40	2	–
B.C.Lara	7	12	0				
P.V.Simmons	102	248	4	62.00	2-34	–	–
P.I.C.Thompson	38	215	5	43.00	2-58	–	–
C.A.Walsh	3122.1	8330	328	25.39	7-37	13	2

NEW ZEALAND – BATTING AND FIELDING

	M	I	NO	HS	Runs	Avge	100	50	Ct/St
G.I.Allott	4	6	2	8*	12	3.00	–	–	1
N.J.Astle	9	18	1	125	554	32.58	3	1	7
C.L.Cairns	21	36	–	120	1000	27.77	1	8	9
M.D.Crowe	77	131	11	299	5444	45.36	17	18	71
H.T.Davis	2	4	2	8	9	4.50	–	–	2
S.B.Doull	16	28	5	31*	293	12.73	–	–	10
S.P.Fleming	25	44	2	129	1537	36.59	1	11	30
L.K.Germon	12	21	3	55	382	21.22	–	1	27/2
M.J.Greatbatch	41	71	5	146*	2021	30.62	3	10	27
C.Z.Harris	9	18	1	56	191	11.23	–	1	4
M.N.Hart	14	24	4	45	353	17.65	–	–	9
M.J.Haslam	4	2	1	3	4	4.00	–	–	2
M.J.Horne	1	2	–	42	55	27.50	–	–	–
R.J.Kennedy	4	5	1	22	28	7.00	–	–	2
G.R.Larsen	8	13	4	26*	127	14.11	–	–	5
G.B.Loveridge	1	1	1	4*	4	–	–	–	–
D.K.Morrison	48	71	26	42	379	8.42	–	–	14
D.J.Nash	14	21	6	56	236	15.73	–	1	7

	M	I	NO	HS	Runs	Avge	100	50	Ct/St
A.C.Parore	32	56	6	100*	1258	25.16	1	7	63/2
D.N.Patel	35	63	7	99	1153	20.58	–	5	13
B.A.Pocock	9	18	–	70	317	17.61	–	2	2
C.Pringle	14	21	4	30	175	10.29	–	–	3
C.J.Spearman	5	10	–	112	352	35.20	1	1	4
S.A.Thomson	19	35	4	120*	958	30.90	1	5	7
R.G.Twose	7	11	1	94	314	31.40	–	3	1
J.T.C.Vaughan	6	12	1	44	201	18.27	–	–	4
D.L.Vettori	2	4	3	29*	59	59.00	–	–	1
B.A.Young	23	46	1	120	1367	30.37	1	10	35

NEW ZEALAND – BOWLING

	O	R	W	Avge	Best	5wI	10wM
G.I.Allott	127.4	406	9	45.11	4-74	–	–
N.J.Astle	85	185	6	30.83	2-26	–	–
C.L.Cairns	655.5	2206	60	36.76	6-52	3	–
M.D.Crowe	229.3	676	14	48.28	2-25	–	–
H.T.Davis	57	186	2	93.00	1-50	–	–
S.B.Doull	504	1547	52	29.75	5-46	4	–
M.J.Greatbatch	1	0	0				
C.Z.Harris	126	375	7	53.57	2-57	–	–
M.N.Hart	514.2	1438	29	49.58	5-77	1	–
M.J.Haslam	82.1	245	2	122.50	1-33	–	–
R.J.Kennedy	106	380	6	63.33	3-28	–	–
G.R.Larsen	327.5	689	24	28.70	3-57	–	–
D.K.Morrison	1677.2	5549	160	34.68	7-89	10	–
D.J.Nash	462	1308	44	29.72	6-76	2	1
D.N.Patel	1047	2992	72	41.55	6-50	3	–
B.A.Pocock	4	20	0				
C.Pringle	497.3	1389	30	46.30	7-52	1	1
S.A.Thomson	331.4	953	19	50.15	3-63	–	–
R.G.Twose	26	80	3	26.66	2-36	–	–
J.T.C.Vaughan	173.2	450	11	40.90	4-27	–	–
D.L.Vettori	103.3	208	7	29.71	4-97	–	–

INDIA – BATTING AND FIELDING

	M	I	NO	HS	Runs	Avge	100	50	Ct/St
M.Azharuddin	78	115	6	199	4948	45.39	17	16	79
R.K.Chauhan	15	11	3	15*	65	8.12	–	–	8
R.Dravid	9	16	1	148	679	45.26	1	4	11
D.Ganesh	2	4	2	2*	4	2.00	–	–	–
S.C.Ganguly	8	15	1	136	690	49.28	2	3	–
N.D.Hirwani	17	22	12	17	54	5.40	–	–	5
A.Jadeja	8	12	1	73	295	26.81	–	2	3
D.Johnson	2	3	1	5	8	4.00	–	–	–
S.B.Joshi	5	9	–	23	97	10.77	–	–	2
V.G.Kambli	17	21	1	227	1084	54.20	4	3	7
A.R.Kapoor	4	6	1	42	97	19.40	–	–	1
A.Kumble	33	41	7	88	560	16.47	–	2	13
V.V.S.Laxman	4	7	2	51	117	23.40	–	1	1
S.V.Manjrekar	37	61	6	218	2043	37.14	4	9	25/1
P.L.Mhambrey	2	3	1	28	58	29.00	–	–	1
N.R.Mongia	20	32	2	152	849	28.30	1	2	48/4

INDIA – BATTING AND FIELDING (continued)

	M	I	NO	HS	Runs	Avge	100	50	Ct/St
M.Prabhakar	39	58	9	120	1600	32.65	1	9	20
B.K.V.Prasad	10	17	7	15	57	5.70	–	–	–
S.L.V.Raju	24	30	10	31	229	11.45	–	–	5
W.V.Raman	11	19	1	96	448	24.88	–	4	6
V.Rathore	6	10	–	44	131	13.10	–	–	12
N.S.Sidhu	36	54	2	124	2087	40.13	6	10	8
J.Srinath	27	38	12	60	432	16.61	–	3	11
S.R.Tendulkar	48	74	7	179	3328	49.67	11	15	37

INDIA – BOWLING

	O	R	W	Avge	Best	5wI	10wM
M.Azharuddin	1.1	12	0				
R.K.Chauhan	542.5	1189	34	34.97	3- 8	–	–
D.Ganesh	42.5	165	1	165.00	1- 38	–	–
S.C.Ganguly	76.5	220	9	24.44	3- 71	–	–
N.D.Hirwani	716.2	1987	66	30.10	8- 61	4	1
D.Johnson	40	143	3	47.66	2- 52	–	–
S.B.Joshi	134.3	342	10	34.20	4- 43	–	–
A.R.Kapoor	107	255	6	42.50	2- 19	–	–
A.Kumble	1681.2	3897	144	27.06	7- 59	7	1
S.V.Manjrekar	2.5	15	0				
P.L.Mhambrey	43	148	2	74.00	1- 43	–	–
M.Prabhakar	1245.5	3581	96	37.30	6-132	3	–
B.K.V.Prasad	381	1111	44	25.25	6-104	4	1
S.L.V.Raju	1100	2439	85	28.69	6- 12	5	1
W.V.Raman	58	129	2	64.50	1- 7	–	–
N.S.Sidhu	1	9	0				
J.Srinath	1051.3	2932	92	31.86	6- 21	2	–
S.R.Tendulkar	85.4	238	4	59.50	2- 10	–	–

PAKISTAN – BATTING AND FIELDING

	M	I	NO	HS	Runs	Avge	100	50	Ct/St
Aamir Nazir	6	11	6	11	31	6.20	–	–	2
Aamir Sohail	34	62	3	205	2103	35.64	2	13	31
Aqib Javed	21	25	6	28*	100	5.26	–	–	2
Asif Mujtaba	23	38	3	65*	852	24.34	–	8	18
Ata-ur-Rehman	13	15	6	19	76	8.44	–	–	2
Azam Khan	1	1	–	14	14	14.00	–	–	–
Basit Ali	19	33	1	103	858	26.81	1	5	6
Hasan Raza	1	1	–	27	27	27.00	–	–	–
Ijaz Ahmed	34	51	2	141	1870	38.16	6	9	22
Ijaz Ahmed II	2	3	–	16	29	9.66	–	–	3
Inzamam-ul-Haq	35	60	7	148	2382	44.94	5	16	35
Mohammad Akram	6	9	3	5	8	1.33	–	–	4
Mohammad Hussain	1	1	–	0	0	0.00	–	–	1
Mohammad Wasim	2	3	1	109*	114	57.00	1	–	3
Mohammad Zahid	1	1	–	0	0	0.00	–	–	–
Moin Khan	24	36	5	117*	957	30.87	3	4	53/5
Mushtaq Ahmed	26	40	7	42	328	9.93	–	–	9
Ramiz Raja	55	91	5	122	2747	31.94	2	21	32
Rashid Latif	19	29	4	68*	623	24.92	–	3	58/8
Saeed Anwar	21	37	1	176	1739	48.30	4	13	12
Salim Elahi	2	4	–	17	43	10.75	–	–	1

TESTS   PAKISTAN – BATTING AND FIELDING (continued)

	M	I	NO	HS	Runs	Avge	100	50	Ct/St
Salim Malik	94	139	21	237	5291	44.83	14	27	62
Saqlain Mushtaq	7	11	3	79	170	21.25	–	1	3
Shadab Kabir	3	5	–	35	89	17.80	–	–	4
Shahid Nazir	4	5	1	13*	25	6.25	–	–	–
Shoaib Mohammad	45	68	7	203*	2705	44.34	7	13	22
Waqar Younis	44	57	11	34	429	9.32	–	–	6
Wasim Akram	72	100	13	257*	1944	22.34	2	4	27
Zahid Fazal	9	16	–	78	288	18.00	–	1	5
Zahoor Elahi	2	3	–	22	30	10.00	–	–	1

PAKISTAN – BOWLING

	O	R	W	Avge	Best	5wI	10wM
Aamir Nazir	176.1	597	20	29.85	5- 46	1	–
Aamir Sohail	268.5	710	17	41.76	4- 54	–	–
Aqib Javed	625.4	1786	54	33.07	5- 84	1	–
Asif Mujtaba	51	158	2	79.00	1- 0	–	–
Ata-ur-Rehman	328.5	1071	31	34.54	4- 50	–	–
Basit Ali	1	6	0				
Ijaz Ahmed	9	18	1	18.00	1- 9	–	–
Ijaz Ahmed II	4	6	0				
Mohammad Akram	172.1	522	10	52.20	3- 39	–	–
Mohammad Hussain	10	21	1	21.00	1- 7	–	–
Mohammad Zahid	41	130	11	11.81	7- 66	1	1
Mushtaq Ahmed	1057.1	2889	107	27.00	7- 56	7	2
Rashid Latif	2	10	0				
Saeed Anwar	3	4	0				
Salim Malik	82.2	289	5	57.80	1- 3	–	–
Saqlain Mushtaq	312.2	874	24	36.41	4- 75	–	–
Shadab Kabir	1	9	0				
Shahid Nazir	98.3	287	13	22.07	5- 53	1	–
Shoaib Mohammad	66	170	5	34.00	2- 8	–	–
Waqar Younis	1511.5	4844	227	21.33	7- 76	19	4
Wasim Akram	2744	7054	311	22.68	7-119	21	4

SRI LANKA – BATTING AND FIELDING

	M	I	NO	HS	Runs	Avge	100	50	Ct/St
P.A.de Silva	55	95	4	267	3227	35.46	8	13	24
H.D.P.K.Dharmasena	11	19	2	62*	349	20.52	–	2	5
C.I.Dunusinghe	5	10	–	91	160	16.00	–	1	13/2
A.P.Gurusinha	41	70	7	143	2452	38.92	7	8	33
U.C.Hathurusinghe	24	42	1	83	1260	30.73	–	8	6
S.T.Jayasuriya	19	30	6	112	830	34.58	1	4	18
R.S.Kaluwitharana	8	12	1	132*	448	40.72	1	3	17/1
R.S.Mahanama	39	66	3	153	1857	28.56	3	9	34
M.Muralitharan	25	34	18	20*	206	12.87	–	–	13
K.R.Pushpakumara	8	13	6	23	68	9.71	–	–	4
A.Ranatunga	63	106	6	135*	3552	35.52	4	24	26
S.Ranatunga	8	15	1	118	522	37.28	2	2	2
K.J.Silva	3	3	1	6*	6	3.00	–	–	1
H.P.Tillekeratne	38	63	9	126*	2312	42.81	5	12	70
W.P.U.C.J.Vaas	14	23	2	51	362	17.23	–	1	5
G.P.Wickremasinghe	23	37	4	28	280	8.48	–	–	8

TESTS   **SRI LANKA – BOWLING**

	O	R	W	Avge	Best	5wI	10wM
P.A.de Silva	200.3	623	17	36.64	3- 39	–	–
H.D.P.K.Dharmasena	455.2	1088	25	43.52	6- 99	1	–
A.P.Gurusinha	234.4	681	20	34.05	2- 7	–	–
U.C.Hathurusinghe	284	668	16	41.75	4- 66	–	–
S.T.Jayasuriya	119	403	6	67.16	2- 16	–	–
R.S.Mahanama	6	30	0				
M.Muralitharan	1122	2940	95	30.94	5- 33	6	–
K.R.Pushpakumara	198.4	749	20	37.45	7-116	1	–
A.Ranatunga	360.2	942	14	67.28	2- 17	–	–
K.J.Silva	104.4	220	14	15.71	4- 16	–	–
H.P.Tillekeratne	3.4	11	0				
W.P.U.C.J.Vaas	537.2	1289	54	23.87	6- 87	4	1
G.P.Wickremasinghe	725.5	2220	46	48.26	5- 73	1	–

ZIMBABWE – BATTING AND FIELDING

	M	I	NO	HS	Runs	Avge	100	50	Ct/St
E.A.Brandes	9	13	2	39	111	10.09	–	–	4
A.D.R.Campbell	22	38	1	99	1115	30.13	–	9	17
S.V.Carlisle	6	10	1	58	175	19.44	–	1	10
M.H.Dekker	14	22	1	68*	333	15.85	–	2	12
C.N.Evans	1	2	–	9	10	5.00	–	–	1
A.Flower	22	37	5	156	1330	41.56	3	9	50/4
G.W.Flower	22	38	1	201*	1175	31.75	2	6	11
D.L.Houghton	20	32	2	266	1396	46.53	4	4	15
A.C.I.Lock	1	2	1	8*	8	8.00	–	–	–
E.Matambanadzo	1	2	1	7	7	7.00	–	–	–
M.Mbangwa	1	2	–	2	2	1.00	–	–	–
H.K.Olonga	7	9	1	7	14	1.75	–	–	4
A.H.Shah	3	5	–	62	122	24.40	–	1	–
B.C.Strang	9	15	5	42	117	11.70	–	–	6
P.A.Strang	13	21	5	106*	505	31.56	1	1	6
H.H.Streak	15	22	5	53	225	13.23	–	1	5
A.C.Waller	2	3	–	50	69	23.00	–	1	1
A.R.Whittall	3	6	1	12	27	5.40	–	–	2
G.J.Whittall	18	30	2	113*	642	22.92	1	3	7
C.B.Wishart	6	12	1	51	154	14.00	–	1	3

ZIMBABWE – BOWLING

	O	R	W	Avge	Best	5wI	10wM
E.A.Brandes	311.4	886	22	40.27	3- 45	–	–
A.D.R.Campbell	5	7	0				
M.H.Dekker	10	15	0				
C.N.Evans	6	27	0				
A.Flower	0.1	0	0				
G.W.Flower	112	322	3	107.33	1- 4	–	–
D.L.Houghton	0.5	0	0				
A.C.I.Lock	30	105	5	21.00	3- 68	–	–
E.Matambanadzo	16	89	2	44.50	2- 62	–	–
M.Mbangwa	24	81	2	40.50	2- 67	–	–
H.K.Olonga	133.4	487	10	48.70	3- 90	–	–
A.H.Shah	31	125	1	125.00	1- 46	–	–
B.C.Strang	296	661	24	27.54	5-101	1	–
P.A.Strang	482.2	1278	32	39.93	5-106	3	–
H.H.Streak	606.5	1551	69	22.47	6- 90	3	–
A.R.Whittall	89.2	261	2	130.50	2-146	–	–
G.J.Whittall	369	919	27	34.03	4- 18	–	–

LIMITED-OVERS INTERNATIONALS CAREER RECORDS

These records, complete to the end of the New Zealand v England series (4 March 1997) include all players registered for county cricket in 1997 at the time of going to press, plus those who have appeared in international cricket since 31 August 1995.

ENGLAND – BATTING AND FIELDING

	M	I	NO	HS	Runs	Avge	100	50	Ct/St
M.A.Atherton	50	50	2	127	1609	33.52	1	11	14
C.W.J.Athey	31	30	3	142*	848	31.40	2	4	1
R.J.Bailey	4	4	2	43*	137	68.50	–	–	1
K.J.Barnett	1	1	–	84	84	84.00	–	1	–
J.E.Benjamin	2	1	–	0	0	0.00	–	–	–
M.P.Bicknell	7	6	2	31*	96	24.00	–	–	2
R.J.Blakey	3	2	–	25	25	12.50	–	–	2/1
A.D.Brown	3	3	–	118	155	51.66	1	–	1
A.R.Caddick	9	5	4	20*	35	35.00	–	–	2
D.J.Capel	23	19	2	50*	327	19.23	–	1	6
D.G.Cork	25	15	2	31*	132	10.15	–	–	6
J.P.Crawley	9	8	–	73	128	16.00	–	1	1
R.D.B.Croft	11	9	3	30*	89	14.83	–	–	4
P.A.J.DeFreitas	101	66	23	67	690	16.04	–	1	26
M.A.Ealham	2	1	–	40	40	40.00	–	–	–
N.H.Fairbrother	56	54	13	113	1539	37.53	1	11	24
A.R.C.Fraser	33	14	6	38*	80	10.00	–	–	1
M.W.Gatting	92	88	17	115*	2095	29.50	1	9	22
G.A.Gooch	125	122	6	142	4290	36.98	8	23	45
D.Gough	35	24	7	45	203	11.94	–	–	4
D.W.Headley	2	1	1	3*	3	–	–	–	–
G.A.Hick	62	61	7	105*	2105	38.98	2	16	32
A.J.Hollioake	2	2	–	15	28	14.00	–	–	1
N.Hussain	12	12	4	49*	155	19.37	–	–	5
A.P.Igglesden	4	3	1	18	20	10.00	–	–	1
R.K.Illingworth	25	11	5	14	68	11.33	–	–	8
R.C.Irani	10	10	2	45*	78	9.75	–	–	2
P.W.Jarvis	16	8	2	16*	31	5.16	–	–	1
N.V.Knight	10	10	3	125*	412	58.85	2	1	3
C.C.Lewis	51	38	13	33	348	13.92	–	–	20
G.D.Lloyd	2	2	1	15	17	17.00	–	–	1
M.A.Lynch	3	3	–	6	8	2.66	–	–	1
D.E.Malcolm	10	5	2	4	9	3.00	–	–	1
P.J.Martin	16	10	6	6	33	8.25	–	–	1
M.P.Maynard	10	10	–	41	153	17.00	–	–	3
J.E.Morris	8	8	1	63*	167	23.85	–	1	2
M.D.Moxon	8	8	–	70	174	21.75	–	1	5
A.D.Mullally	8	3	–	20	22	7.33	–	–	3
M.R.Ramprakash	10	10	3	32	184	26.28	–	–	5
D.A.Reeve	29	21	9	35	291	24.25	–	–	12
S.J.Rhodes	9	8	2	56	107	17.83	–	1	9/2
R.T.Robinson	26	26	–	83	597	22.96	–	3	6
R.C.Russell	38	29	7	50	383	17.40	–	1	41/6
I.D.K.Salisbury	4	2	1	5	7	7.00	–	–	1
C.E.W.Silverwood	5	4	–	12	17	4.25	–	–	–

ENGLAND – BATTING AND FIELDING (continued)

	M	I	NO	HS	Runs	Avge	100	50	Ct/St
G.C.Small	53	24	9	18*	98	6.53	–	–	7
N.M.K.Smith	7	6	1	31	100	20.00	–	–	1
R.A.Smith	71	70	8	167*	2419	39.01	4	15	26
A.J.Stewart	87	82	7	103	2326	31.01	1	13	75/7
J.P.Taylor	1	1	–	1	1	1.00	–	–	–
G.P.Thorpe	36	36	4	89	1222	38.18	–	11	18
P.C.R.Tufnell	20	10	9	5*	15	15.00	–	–	4
S.D.Udal	10	6	4	11*	35	17.50	–	–	1
S.L.Watkin	4	2	–	4	4	2.00	–	–	–
M.Watkinson	1	–	–	–	–	–	–	–	–
A.P.Wells	1	1	–	15	15	15.00	–	–	–
C.M.Wells	2	2	–	17	22	11.00	–	–	–
J.J.Whitaker	2	2	1	44*	48	48.00	–	–	1
C.White	15	13	–	38	187	14.38	–	–	2

ENGLAND – BOWLING

	O	R	W	Avge	Best	4w
C.W.J.Athey	1	10	0			
R.J.Bailey	6	25	0			
J.E.Benjamin	12	47	1	47.00	1-22	–
M.P.Bicknell	68.5	347	13	26.69	3-55	–
A.R.Caddick	87	398	15	26.53	3-35	–
D.J.Capel	173	805	17	47.35	3-38	–
D.G.Cork	240	1071	35	30.60	3-27	–
R.D.B.Croft	100	410	13	31.53	2-26	–
P.A.J.DeFreitas	935	3693	115	32.11	4-35	1
M.A.Ealham	6	23	0			
N.H.Fairbrother	1	9	0			
A.R.C.Fraser	312.4	1132	38	29.78	4-22	1
M.W.Gatting	65.2	336	10	33.60	3-32	–
G.A.Gooch	344.2	1516	36	42.11	3-19	–
D.Gough	323.2	1319	51	25.86	5-44	3
D.W.Headley	17	84	0			
G.A.Hick	140	696	18	38.66	3-41	–
A.J.Hollioake	15.3	68	8	8.50	4-23	2
A.P.Igglesden	28	122	2	61.00	2-12	–
R.K.Illingworth	250.1	1059	30	35.30	3-33	–
R.C.Irani	54.5	246	4	61.50	1-23	–
P.W.Jarvis	146.3	672	24	28.00	5-35	2
C.C.Lewis	418.5	1854	65	28.52	4-30	4
D.E.Malcolm	87.4	404	16	25.25	3-40	–
P.J.Martin	139.4	610	25	24.40	4-44	1
A.D.Mullally	66	276	10	27.60	3-29	–
M.R.Ramprakash	2	14	0			
D.A.Reeve	191.1	820	20	41.00	3-20	–
I.D.K.Salisbury	31	177	5	35.40	3-41	–
C.E.W.Silverwood	36	157	3	52.33	2-27	–
G.C.Small	465.3	1942	58	33.48	4-31	1
N.M.K.Smith	43.3	190	6	31.66	3-29	–
J.P.Taylor	3	20	0			
G.P.Thorpe	20	97	2	48.50	2-15	–
P.C.R.Tufnell	170	699	19	36.78	4-22	1
S.D.Udal	95	371	8	46.37	2-37	–
S.L.Watkin	36.5	193	7	27.57	4-49	1
M.Watkinson	9	43	0			
C.White	101.2	445	15	29.66	4-37	1

AUSTRALIA – BATTING AND FIELDING

	M	I	NO	HS	Runs	Avge	100	50	Ct/St
M.G.Bevan	49	44	17	79*	1469	54.40	–	9	19
A.J.Bichel	4	2	1	16*	18	18.00	–	–	1
G.S.Blewett	16	16	3	57*	282	21.69	–	1	5
D.W.Fleming	27	9	6	5*	19	6.33	–	–	5
A.C.Gilchrist	2	2	–	18	18	9.00	–	–	2
J.N.Gillespie	5	2	–	6	8	4.00	–	–	–
M.L.Hayden	13	12	1	67	286	26.00	–	2	4
I.A.Healy	161	113	34	56	1657	20.97	–	4	192/38
G.B.Hogg	7	7	4	11*	38	12.66	–	–	2
B.P.Julian	2	1	–	11	11	11.00	–	–	–
M.S.Kasprowicz	2	–	–	–	–	–	–	–	–
J.L.Langer	7	6	2	36	131	32.75	–	–	1/1
S.G.Law	37	35	3	110	1000	31.25	1	6	8
S.Lee	8	6	1	39	61	12.20	–	–	5
D.S.Lehmann	3	3	–	15	27	9.00	–	–	2
C.J.McDermott	138	78	17	37	432	7.08	–	–	27
G.D.McGrath	66	22	12	10	44	4.40	–	–	8
T.M.Moody	40	36	4	89	766	23.93	–	7	11
R.T.Ponting	33	33	3	123	929	30.96	2	5	4
P.R.Reiffel	71	45	19	58	427	16.42	–	1	22
M.J.Slater	40	40	1	73	969	24.84	–	9	8
A.M.Stuart	3	1	–	1	1	1.00	–	–	2
M.A.Taylor	109	106	1	105	3472	33.06	1	28	56
S.K.Warne	67	35	11	55	310	12.91	–	1	21
M.E.Waugh	128	124	10	130	4293	37.65	9	27	50
S.R.Waugh	211	191	42	102*	4731	31.75	1	26	75

AUSTRALIA – BOWLING

	O	R	W	Avge	Best	4w
M.G.Bevan	118.3	537	16	33.56	3-36	–
A.J.Bichel	35.2	157	4	39.25	3-17	–
G.S.Blewett	75.4	372	9	41.33	2-34	–
D.W.Fleming	226	995	40	24.87	5-36	3
J.N.Gillespie	45	224	4	56.00	2-39	–
G.B.Hogg	49.1	218	3	72.66	1-23	–
B.P.Julian	21	116	3	38.66	3-50	–
M.S.Kasprowicz	16	83	2	41.50	1-32	–
S.G.Law	116	520	11	47.27	2-22	–
S.Lee	54	207	4	51.75	1-20	–
D.S.Lehmann	13	65	1	65.00	1-29	–
C.J.McDermott	1243.3	5018	203	24.71	5-44	5
G.D.McGrath	590.3	2317	82	28.25	5-52	4
T.M.Moody	193.5	854	21	40.66	3-56	–
P.R.Reiffel	610.4	2356	89	26.47	4-13	5
M.J.Slater	2	11	0			
A.M.Stuart	30	109	8	13.62	5-26	1
S.K.Warne	626.5	2458	118	20.83	5-33	10
M.E.Waugh	429	2063	70	29.47	5-24	2
S.R.Waugh	1298	5810	172	33.77	4-33	2

LOIs   **SOUTH AFRICA – BATTING AND FIELDING**

	M	I	NO	HS	Runs	Avge	100	50	Ct/St
P.R.Adams	9	4	1	10	10	3.33	–	–	1
A.M.Bacher	2	2	–	14	27	13.50	–	–	1
N.Boje	7	5	2	13*	27	9.00	–	–	2
R.E.Bryson	3	1	1	2*	2	–	–	–	1
W.J.Cronje	107	101	19	112	3222	39.29	2	20	45
D.N.Crookes	13	10	1	54	151	16.77	–	1	7
D.J.Cullinan	69	68	9	124	2195	37.20	3	13	30
P.S.de Villiers	79	34	15	20*	163	8.57	–	–	13
A.A.Donald	79	20	10	7*	34	3.40	–	–	12
H.H.Gibbs	3	3	–	35	83	27.66	–	–	1
A.C.Hudson	84	83	1	161	2523	30.76	2	18	15
J.H.Kallis	17	16	5	79	455	41.36	–	3	2
G.Kirsten	65	65	7	188*	2703	46.60	7	14	20/1
L.Klusener	11	8	1	88*	151	21.57	–	1	–
A.P.Kuiper	25	23	7	63*	539	33.68	–	3	3
G.F.J.Liebenberg	1	1	–	12	12	12.00	–	–	–
B.M.McMillan	68	46	16	127	787	26.23	1	–	38
C.R.Matthews	56	22	9	26	141	10.84	–	–	10
S.J.Palframan	7	4	–	28	55	13.75	–	–	9
S.M.Pollock	25	15	8	75	281	40.14	–	2	6
J.N.Rhodes	102	95	17	121	2454	31.46	1	9	38
D.J.Richardson	100	64	27	53	780	21.08	–	1	125/15
R.P.Snell	42	28	8	63	322	16.10	–	2	7
P.J.R.Steyn	1	1	–	4	4	4.00	–	–	–
P.L.Symcox	43	28	3	61	356	14.24	–	1	10

SOUTH AFRICA – BOWLING

	O	R	W	Avge	Best	4w
P.R.Adams	70	296	13	22.76	3-26	–
N.Boje	63	263	9	29.22	2-38	–
R.E.Bryson	25	132	1	132.00	1-41	–
W.J.Cronje	549.2	2342	64	36.59	5-32	2
D.N.Crookes	76.1	371	9	41.22	3-30	–
D.J.Cullinan	4	22	1	22.00	1- 7	–
P.S.de Villiers	700	2480	90	27.55	4-27	2
A.A.Donald	711.1	2904	136	21.35	6-23	7
J.H.Kallis	54	237	6	39.50	3-21	–
G.Kirsten	5	23	0			
L.Klusener	84.4	439	13	33.76	5-42	1
A.P.Kuiper	98	518	18	28.77	3-33	–
B.M.McMillan	529.5	2269	62	36.59	4-32	1
C.R.Matthews	500.3	1975	79	25.00	4-10	3
S.M.Pollock	228.1	921	34	27.08	4-34	1
R.P.Snell	349.1	1574	44	35.77	5-40	3
P.L.Symcox	365	1408	41	34.34	3-20	–

WEST INDIES – BATTING AND FIELDING

	M	I	NO	HS	Runs	Avge	100	50	Ct/St
J.C.Adams	70	55	19	81*	994	27.61	–	7	47/5
C.E.L.Ambrose	141	74	31	31*	487	11.32	–	–	34
H.A.G.Anthony	3	3	–	21	23	7.66	–	–	–
K.L.T.Arthurton	86	76	15	84	1652	27.08	–	9	21
K.C.G.Benjamin	26	13	7	17	65	10.83	–	–	4
I.R.Bishop	81	42	18	33*	359	14.95	–	–	12
C.O.Browne	20	16	3	26	155	11.92	–	–	27/5
S.L.Campbell	36	36	–	86	835	23.19	–	3	10
S.Chanderpaul	38	35	1	80	1001	29.44	–	8	9
C.E.Cuffy	11	7	3	17*	25	6.25	–	–	3
A.C.Cummins	63	41	11	44*	459	15.30	–	–	11
V.C.Drakes	5	2	–	16	25	12.50	–	–	1
O.D.Gibson	13	10	1	52	138	15.33	–	1	3
A.F.G.Griffith	5	4	1	47	50	16.66	–	–	4
R.A.Harper	105	73	20	45*	855	16.13	–	–	55
R.I.C.Holder	30	26	5	65	540	25.71	–	2	8
C.L.Hooper	150	135	32	113*	3504	34.01	3	20	71
R.D.Jacobs	4	3	–	10	13	4.33	–	–	1/1
B.C.Lara	113	112	11	169	4756	47.08	11	30	57
N.A.M.McLean	6	3	–	7	8	2.66	–	–	2
J.R.Murray	48	29	6	86	555	24.13	–	4	44/7
R.B.Richardson	224	217	30	122	6248	33.41	5	44	74
R.G.Samuels	8	5	2	36*	54	18.00	–	–	5
P.V.Simmons	119	117	7	122	3242	29.47	5	17	51
P.I.C.Thompson	2	1	–	2	2	2.00	–	–	–
P.A.Wallace	12	12	–	52	217	18.08	–	1	3
C.A.Walsh	171	64	27	30	288	7.78	–	–	26
L.R.Williams	4	2	–	5	6	3.00	–	–	2
S.C.Williams	28	28	2	73*	738	28.38	–	5	5

WEST INDIES – BOWLING

	O	R	W	Avge	Best	4w
J.C.Adams	131	639	21	30.42	5-37	1
C.E.L.Ambrose	1259.2	4375	193	22.66	5-17	9
H.A.G.Anthony	26	143	3	47.66	2-47	–
K.L.T.Arthurton	132.5	666	22	30.27	3-31	–
K.C.G.Benjamin	219.5	923	33	27.96	3-34	–
I.R.Bishop	706	3013	116	25.97	5-25	9
S.Chanderpaul	69.4	378	7	54.00	2-16	–
C.E.Cuffy	91.1	352	9	39.11	2-19	–
A.C.Cummins	523.5	2246	78	28.79	5-31	3
V.C.Drakes	39.5	204	3	68.00	1-36	–
O.D.Gibson	105.1	512	29	17.65	5-40	3
R.A.Harper	862.3	3431	100	34.31	4-40	3
C.L.Hooper	1010.4	4400	133	33.08	4-34	1
B.C.Lara	4	22	2	11.00	2- 5	–
N.A.M.McLean	34	145	3	48.33	2-33	–
R.B.Richardson	9.4	46	1	46.00	1- 4	–
P.V.Simmons	505.4	2185	62	35.24	4- 3	2
P.I.C.Thompson	19	110	2	55.00	1-46	–
C.A.Walsh	1507.4	5806	192	30.23	5- 1	6
L.R.Williams	17.5	85	5	17.00	3-16	–

LOIs

NEW ZEALAND – BATTING AND FIELDING

	M	I	NO	HS	Runs	Avge	100	50	Ct/St
G.I.Allott	3	2	1	3	4	4.00	–	–	2
N.J.Astle	41	41	1	120	1207	30.17	3	7	13
C.L.Cairns	62	58	5	103	1412	26.64	1	6	21
M.D.Crowe	143	141	19	107*	4704	38.55	4	34	66
H.T.Davis	5	3	1	7*	8	4.00	–	–	–
S.B.Doull	20	16	8	22	117	14.62	–	–	4
S.P.Fleming	60	59	5	106*	1712	31.70	1	11	26
L.K.Germon	37	31	9	89	519	19.96	–	3	21/9
M.J.Greatbatch	84	83	5	111	2206	28.28	2	13	35
C.Z.Harris	80	71	17	130	1326	24.55	1	3	23
M.N.Hart	11	6	–	16	49	8.16	–	–	7
R.J.Kennedy	7	4	3	8*	17	17.00	–	–	1
G.R.Larsen	89	53	21	37	488	15.25	–	–	14
D.K.Morrison	96	43	24	20*	171	9.00	–	–	19
D.J.Nash	28	18	5	40*	128	9.84	–	–	6
A.C.Parore	67	63	9	108	1821	33.72	1	10	35/8
D.N.Patel	72	60	10	71	604	12.08	–	1	23
C.M.Spearman	24	24	–	78	485	20.20	–	2	6
S.A.Thomson	56	52	10	83	964	22.95	–	5	18
R.G.Twose	21	20	–	92	612	30.60	–	4	5
J.T.C.Vaughan	18	16	7	33	162	18.00	–	–	4
B.A.Young	57	56	4	74	1239	23.82	–	5	25

NEW ZEALAND – BOWLING

	O	R	W	Avge	Best	4w
G.I.Allott	22	110	5	22.00	2-21	–
N.J.Astle	219.5	993	26	38.19	3-42	–
C.L.Cairns	410	1871	58	32.25	4-55	1
M.D.Crowe	216	954	29	32.89	2- 9	–
H.T.Davis	38.4	199	7	28.42	3-44	–
S.B.Doull	150	806	18	44.77	3-42	–
S.P.Fleming	4.5	28	1	28.00	1- 8	–
M.J.Greatbatch	1	5	0			
C.Z.Harris	590.2	2579	82	31.45	5-42	1
M.N.Hart	91.2	347	13	26.69	5-22	1
R.J.Kennedy	52	283	5	56.60	2-36	–
G.R.Larsen	797.1	2949	81	36.40	4-24	1
D.K.Morrison	764.2	3470	126	27.53	5-34	3
D.J.Nash	214	1024	26	39.38	3-26	–
D.N.Patel	514.5	2144	44	48.72	3-22	–
C.M.Spearman	0.3	6	0			
S.A.Thomson	353.3	1602	42	38.14	3-14	–
R.G.Twose	45.2	237	4	59.25	2-31	–
J.T.C.Vaughan	116	524	15	34.93	4-33	1

INDIA – BATTING AND FIELDING

	M	I	NO	HS	Runs	Avge	100	50	Ct/St
S.A.Ankola	20	13	4	9	34	3.77	–	–	2
M.Azharuddin	239	223	42	108*	6574	36.32	3	38	106
U.Chatterjee	3	2	1	3*	6	6.00	–	–	1
P.Dharmani	1	1	–	8	8	8.00	–	–	–
R.Dravid	27	26	2	90	722	30.08	–	6	17
D.Ganesh	1	1	–	4	4	4.00	–	–	–
S.C.Ganguly	19	18	1	83	483	28.41	–	3	3

190

LOIs

INDIA – BATTING AND FIELDING (continued)

	M	I	NO	HS	Runs	Avge	100	50	Ct/St
A.Jadeja	82	76	11	104	2132	32.80	1	12	23
S.B.Joshi	17	10	2	48	114	14.25	–	–	9
V.G.Kambli	75	70	18	106	2003	38.51	2	11	12
A.R.Kapoor	15	6	–	19	43	7.16	–	–	1
S.S.Karim	6	6	1	55	121	24.20	–	1	2/1
A.Kumble	111	55	17	24	373	9.81	–	–	40
S.V.Manjrekar	74	70	10	105	1994	33.23	1	15	23
P.L.Mhambrey	2	1	1	7*	7	–	–	–	–
N.R.Mongia	68	44	14	69	581	19.36	–	1	60/23
M.Prabhakar	129	97	20	106	1855	24.09	2	11	27
B.K.V.Prasad	59	24	15	19	63	7.00	–	–	20
S.L.V.Raju	53	16	8	8	32	4.00	–	–	8
W.V.Raman	27	27	1	114	617	23.73	1	3	2
V.Rathore	7	7	–	54	193	27.57	–	2	4
N.S.Sidhu	108	105	8	134*	3949	40.71	6	31	15
R.R.Singh	13	13	3	48	240	24.00	–	–	3
S.Somasunder	2	2	–	10	17	8.50	–	–	–
J.Srinath	121	63	19	53	500	11.36	–	1	17
S.R.Tendulkar	141	138	12	137	5036	39.96	11	31	44
P.S.Vaidya	4	2	–	12	15	7.50	–	–	2

INDIA – BOWLING

	O	R	W	Avge	Best	4w
S.A.Ankola	134.3	615	13	47.30	3-33	–
M.Azharuddin	92	479	12	39.91	3-19	–
U.Chatterjee	26.5	117	3	39.00	2-35	–
D.Ganesh	5	20	1	20.00	1-20	–
S.C.Ganguly	13	80	0			
A.Jadeja	182.2	968	14	69.14	2-16	–
S.B.Joshi	151.5	654	19	34.42	3-40	–
V.G.Kambli	0.4	7	1	7.00	1- 7	–
A.R.Kapoor	136	547	8	68.37	2-33	–
A.Kumble	1019.2	4131	159	25.98	6-12	7
S.V.Manjrekar	1.2	10	1	10.00	1- 2	–
P.L.Mhambrey	15	98	2	49.00	2-69	–
M.Prabhakar	1060	4534	157	28.87	5-33	6
B.K.V.Prasad	503.5	2387	74	32.25	4-27	1
S.L.V.Raju	461.4	2014	63	31.96	4-46	2
W.V.Raman	27	170	2	85.00	1-23	–
N.S.Sidhu	0.4	3	0			
R.R.Singh	81.2	402	11	36.54	2-18	–
J.Srinath	1057.3	4564	157	29.07	5-24	4
S.R.Tendulkar	529.4	2564	44	58.27	4-34	1
P.S.Vaidya	30.4	174	4	43.50	2-41	–

PAKISTAN – BATTING AND FIELDING

	M	I	NO	HS	Runs	Avge	100	50	Ct/St
Aamir Hanif	5	4	2	36*	89	44.50	–	–	–
Aamir Sohail	121	120	2	134	3897	33.02	5	26	40
Abdul Razak	2	1	1	0*	0	–	–	–	–
Aqib Javed	133	42	24	45*	237	13.16	–	–	19
Arshad Khan	5	4	3	9*	15	15.00	–	–	3
Asif Mujtaba	66	55	14	113*	1068	26.04	1	6	18
Ata-ur-Rehman	30	13	6	11*	34	4.85	–	–	–

	M	I	NO	HS	Runs	Avge	100	50	Ct/St
Azam Khan	5	4	–	72	113	28.25	–	1	1
Azhar Mahmood	7	7	1	15	41	6.83	–	–	1
Basit Ali	49	43	6	127*	1265	34.18	1	9	15
Hasan Raja	5	4	–	12	29	7.25	–	–	–
Ijaz Ahmed	166	150	22	124*	4029	31.47	5	23	58
Ijaz Ahmed II	2	1	1	3*	3	–	–	–	–
Inzamam-ul-Haq	127	122	16	137*	3929	37.06	4	27	31
Javed Miandad	233	218	41	119*	7381	41.70	8	50	71/2
Mohammad Akram	7	5	3	7*	11	5.50	–	–	2
Mohammad Wasim	10	10	1	54	290	32.22	–	2	4
Mohammad Zahid	4	2	1	1	1	1.00	–	–	–
Moin Khan	72	55	13	50*	825	19.64	–	1	76/28
Mujahid Jamshed	4	3	1	23	27	13.50	–	–	–
Mushtaq Ahmed	119	59	24	26	309	8.82	–	–	25
Ramiz Raja	180	179	14	119*	5396	32.70	9	29	28
Rashid Latif	84	57	16	50	664	16.19	–	1	81/22
Saeed Anwar	117	116	11	131	4132	39.35	11	17	25
Saeed Azad	4	4	–	31	65	16.25	–	–	2
Salim Elahi	14	14	1	102*	437	33.61	1	3	4
Salim Malik	248	223	36	102	6340	33.90	5	41	76
Saqlain Mushtaq	45	29	8	30*	202	9.61	–	–	13
Shadab Kabir	3	3	–	0	0	0.00	–	–	1
Shahid Afridi	23	20	–	102	438	21.90	1	2	11
Shahid Anwar	1	1	–	37	37	37.00	–	–	–
Shahid Nazir	12	6	5	8	25	25.00	–	–	2
Waqar Younis	150	73	27	37	432	9.39	–	–	15
Wasim Akram	227	176	33	86	2144	14.99	–	4	53
Zafar Iqbal	8	6	–	18	48	8.00	–	–	1
Zahoor Elahi	14	14	1	86	297	22.84	–	3	2

PAKISTAN – BOWLING

	O	R	W	Avge	Best	4w
Aamir Hanif	21.4	122	4	30.50	3-36	–
Aamir Sohail	671.4	3010	70	43.00	4-22	1
Abdul Razak	12.3	53	3	17.66	2-29	–
Aqib Javed	1112.1	4637	146	31.76	7-37	3
Arshad Khan	38.5	159	2	79.50	1-29	–
Asif Mujtaba	126	658	7	94.00	2-38	–
Ata-ur-Rehman	248.4	1186	27	43.92	3-27	–
Azhar Mahmood	42	245	2	122.50	2-38	–
Basit Ali	5	21	1	21.00	1-17	–
Ijaz Ahmed	83.5	362	4	90.50	2-31	–
Ijaz Ahmed II	5	25	1	25.00	1- 9	–
Inzamam-ul-Haq	6.4	52	2	26.00	1- 4	–
Javed Miandad	72.4	297	7	42.42	2-22	–
Mohammad Akram	57	307	9	34.11	2-36	–
Mohammad Zahid	36	164	3	54.66	2-53	–
Mujahid Jamshed	4	6	1	6.00	1- 6	–
Mushtaq Ahmed	1028.5	4469	134	33.35	5-36	2
Ramiz Raja	1	10	0			
Saeed Anwar	29	154	3	51.33	1- 9	–
Salim Malik	476.3	2356	70	33.65	5-35	1
Saqlain Mushtaq	403	1674	85	19.69	5-29	6
Shahid Afridi	183.5	800	24	33.33	3-33	–

LOIs

	O	R	W	Avge	Best	5wI	10wM
Shahid Nazir	89	394	12	32.83	3-14	–	
Waqar Younis	1250.2	5597	257	21.77	6-26	20	
Wasim Akram	1951.2	7365	329	22.38	5-15	18	
Zafar Iqbal	33	137	3	45.66	2-37	–	

SRI LANKA – BATTING AND FIELDING

	M	I	NO	HS	Runs	Avge	100	50	Ct/St
M.S.Atapattu	11	10	3	58	127	18.14	–	1	2
U.U.Chandana	14	9	1	26	96	12.00	–	–	10
P.A.de Silva	195	191	20	145	5893	34.46	7	39	57
S.C.de Silva	7	6	4	4*	8	4.00	–	–	3
H.D.P.K.Dharmasena	43	27	11	51	386	24.12	–	2	9
A.P.Gurusinha	146	143	5	117*	3902	28.27	2	22	49
U.C.Hathurusinghe	32	30	1	66	648	22.34	–	4	5
S.T.Jayasuriya	119	113	3	140	2610	23.72	3	13	50
R.S.Kalpage	74	61	27	51	750	22.05	–	1	24
R.S.Kaluwitharana	61	58	4	100*	978	18.11	1	5	40/24
R.S.Mahanama	153	145	17	119*	3894	30.42	4	26	80
A.M.N.Munasinghe	5	4	1	8	13	4.33	–	–	–
M.Muralitharan	56	24	11	8	57	4.38	–	–	28
K.R.Pushpakumara	22	6	4	14*	34	17.00	–	–	4
A.Ranatunga	198	189	36	102*	5425	35.45	2	34	44
S.Ranatunga	12	11	–	70	253	23.00	–	2	2
H.P.Tillekeratne	143	124	30	104	2753	29.28	2	9	61/5
K.E.A.Upashanta	3	2	1	8*	11	11.00	–	–	1
W.P.U.C.J.Vaas	60	35	15	33	310	15.50	–	–	10
G.P.Wickremasinghe	83	31	12	21*	140	7.36	–	–	15

SRI LANKA – BOWLING

	O	R	W	Avge	Best	4w
M.S.Atapattu	0.3	4	0			
U.U.Chandana	72	330	9	36.66	4-35	1
P.A.de Silva	472.2	2324	58	40.06	3-36	–
S.C.de Silva	57	241	12	20.08	3-18	–
H.D.P.K.Dharmasena	351	1599	46	34.76	4-37	1
A.P.Gurusinha	264.1	1354	26	52.07	2-25	–
U.C.Hathurusinghe	140	614	14	43.85	4-57	1
S.T.Jayasuriya	678.3	3272	93	35.18	6-29	3
R.S.Kalpage	576	2548	67	38.02	4-36	1
R.S.Mahanama	0.2	7	0			
A.M.N.Munasinghe	36.1	146	4	36.50	3-30	–
M.Muralitharan	507.1	2105	71	29.64	4-18	3
K.R.Pushpakumara	172.2	837	17	49.23	3-25	–
A.Ranatunga	772	3691	78	47.32	4-14	1
H.P.Tillekeratne	20.4	92	4	23.00	1- 3	–
K.E.A.Upashanta	19	91	3	30.33	2-24	–
W.P.U.C.J.Vaas	489.4	1901	72	26.40	4-20	2
G.P.Wickremasinghe	600.2	2648	60	44.13	3-28	–

ZIMBABWE – BATTING AND FIELDING

	M	I	NO	HS	Runs	Avge	100	50	Ct/St
D.H.Brain	23	18	4	27	117	8.35	–	–	5
E.A.Brandes	40	27	6	55	231	11.00	–	–	5
G.B.Brent	1	1	–	1	1	1.00	–	1	7
A.D.R.Campbell	52	49	4	131*	1165	25.88	1	7	24
S.V.Carlisle	6	6	1	28	69	13.80	–	–	3
S.G.Davies	4	4	–	45	67	16.75	–	–	–
M.H.Dekker	23	22	2	79	379	18.95	–	2	5
C.N.Evans	23	22	4	96*	406	22.55	–	1	3
A.Flower	60	58	2	115*	1582	28.25	1	12	49/10
G.W.Flower	50	48	2	91	1446	31.43	–	11	25
D.L.Houghton	60	57	2	142	1485	27.00	1	12	29/2
W.R.James	11	8	1	29	101	14.42	–	–	6
A.C.I.Lock	7	3	2	5	8	8.00	–	–	1
E.Matambanadzo	2	1	1	2*	2	–	–	–	–
M.Mbangwa	1	1	–	11	11	11.00	–	–	–
H.K.Olonga	3	1	–	6	6	6.00	–	–	1
S.G.Peall	20	15	1	21	91	6.50	–	–	1
G.J.Rennie	2	2	–	6	6	3.00	–	–	2
J.A.Rennie	21	11	6	27	81	16.20	–	–	6
A.H.Shah	28	28	2	60*	437	16.80	–	1	6
B.C.Strang	11	8	4	17	17	4.25	–	–	7
P.A.Strang	33	30	10	47	520	26.00	–	–	9
H.H.Streak	39	31	10	43*	377	17.95	–	–	6
A.C.Waller	38	37	3	83*	815	23.97	–	4	10
A.R.Whittall	4	3	2	4*	5	5.00	–	–	–
G.J.Whittall	41	41	5	70	637	17.69	–	2	11
C.B.Wishart	6	6	–	53	94	15.66	–	1	1

ZIMBABWE – BOWLING

	O	R	W	Avge	Best	4w
D.H.Brain	181.5	849	21	40.42	3-51	–
E.A.Brandes	334	1635	55	29.72	5-28	3
G.B.Brent	5	29	0			
A.D.R.Campbell	27.3	116	3	38.66	2-22	–
M.H.Dekker	57.5	290	9	32.22	2-16	–
C.N.Evans	41	171	5	34.20	1- 6	–
A.Flower	5	23	0			
G.W.Flower	139.1	704	15	46.93	3-15	–
D.L.Houghton	2	19	1	19.00	1-19	–
A.C.I.Lock	48.1	4	8	27.37	5-44	1
E.Matambanadzo	16.3	85	5	17.00	4-32	1
M.Mbangwa	5.4	48	0			
H.K.Olonga	20	138	3	46.00	2-47	–
S.G.Peall	150	678	8	84.75	3-54	–
J.A.Rennie	148.4	732	18	40.66	3-27	–
A.H.Shah	179.3	812	18	45.11	3-33	–
B.C.Strang	81.2	347	10	34.70	4-36	1
P.A.Strang	264.5	1195	33	36.21	5-21	2
H.H.Streak	356	1557	49	31.77	5-32	3
A.R.Whittall	33	154	4	38.50	3-36	–
G.J.Whittall	233.3	1189	31	38.35	3-46	–

FIRST-CLASS CRICKET RECORDS

To the end of the 1996 season

TEAM RECORDS

HIGHEST INNINGS TOTALS

1107	Victoria v New South Wales	Melbourne	1926-27
1059	Victoria v Tasmania	Melbourne	1922-23
951-7d	Sind v Baluchistan	Karachi	1973-74
944-6d	Hyderabad v Andhra	Secunderabad	1993-94
918	New South Wales v South Australia	Sydney	1900-01
912-8d	Holkar v Mysore	Indore	1945-46
910-6d	Railways v Dera Ismail Khan	Lahore	1964-65
903-7d	England v Australia	The Oval	1938
887	Yorkshire v Warwickshire	Birmingham	1896
863	Lancashire v Surrey	The Oval	1990
860-6d	Tamil Nadu v Goa	Panjim	1988-89

Excluding penalty runs in India, there have been 29 innings totals of 800 runs or more in first-class cricket, the most recent being 802-8d by Karachi Blues v Lahore at Peshawar in 1994-95. Tamil Nadu's total of 860-6d was boosted to 912 by 52 penalty runs.

HIGHEST SECOND INNINGS TOTAL

770	New South Wales v South Australia	Adelaide	1920-21

HIGHEST FOURTH INNINGS TOTAL

654-5	England v South Africa	Durban	1938-39

HIGHEST MATCH AGGREGATE

2376	Maharashtra v Bombay	Poona	1948-49

RECORD MARGIN OF VICTORY

Innings and 851 runs: Railways v Dera Ismail Khan	Lahore	1964-65

MOST RUNS IN A DAY

721	Australians v Essex	Southend	1948

MOST HUNDREDS IN AN INNINGS

6	Holkar v Mysore	Indore	1945-46

LOWEST INNINGS TOTALS

12	†Oxford University v MCC and Ground	Oxford	1877
12	Northamptonshire v Gloucestershire	Gloucester	1907
13	Auckland v Canterbury	Auckland	1877-78
13	Nottinghamshire v Yorkshire	Nottingham	1901
14	Surrey v Essex	Chelmsford	1983
15	MCC v Surrey	Lord's	1839
15	†Victoria v MCC	Melbourne	1903-04
15	†Northamptonshire v Yorkshire	Northampton	1908
15	Hampshire v Warwickshire	Birmingham	1922

† Batted one man short

There have been 26 instances of a team being dismissed for under 20, the most recent being by Surrey in 1983 (above).

LOWEST MATCH AGGREGATE BY ONE TEAM

34 (16 and 18) Border v Natal   East London   1959-60

LOWEST COMPLETED MATCH AGGREGATE BY BOTH TEAMS

105   MCC v Australians   Lord's   1878

FEWEST RUNS IN AN UNINTERRUPTED DAY'S PLAY

95   Australia (80) v Pakistan (15-2)   Karachi   1956-57

TIED MATCHES

Before 1948 a match was considered to be tied if the scores were level after the fourth innings, even if the side batting last had wickets in hand when play ended. Law 22 was amended in 1948 and since then a match has been tied only when the scores are level after the fourth innings has been completed. There have been 53 tied first-class matches, five of which would not have qualified under the current law. The most recent is:
Worcestershire (203/325-8d) v Nottinghamshire (233/295)   Nottingham   1993

BATTING RECORDS

HIGHEST INDIVIDUAL INNINGS

501*	B.C.Lara	Warwickshire v Durham	Birmingham	1994
499	Hanif Mohammad	Karachi v Bahawalpur	Karachi	1958-59
452*	D.G.Bradman	New South Wales v Queensland	Sydney	1929-30
443*	B.B.Nimbalkar	Maharashtra v Kathiawar	Poona	1948-49
437	W.H.Ponsford	Victoria v Queensland	Melbourne	1927-28
429	W.H.Ponsford	Victoria v Tasmania	Melbourne	1922-23
428	Aftab Baloch	Sind v Baluchistan	Karachi	1973-74
424	A.C.MacLaren	Lancashire v Somerset	Taunton	1895
405*	G.A.Hick	Worcestershire v Somerset	Taunton	1988
385	B.Sutcliffe	Otago v Canterbury	Christchurch	1952-53
383	C.W.Gregory	New South Wales v Queensland	Brisbane	1906-07
377	S.V.Manjrekar	Bombay v Hyderabad	Bombay	1990-91
375	B.C.Lara	West Indies v England	St John's	1993-94
369	D.G.Bradman	South Australia v Tasmania	Adelaide	1935-36
366	N.H.Fairbrother	Lancashire v Surrey	The Oval	1990
366	M.V.Sridhar	Hyderabad v Andhra	Secunderabad	1993-94
365*	C.Hill	South Australia v NSW	Adelaide	1900-01
365*	G.St A.Sobers	West Indies v Pakistan	Kingston	1957-58
364	L.Hutton	England v Australia	The Oval	1938
359*	V.M.Merchant	Bombay v Maharashtra	Bombay	1943-44
359	R.B.Simpson	New South Wales v Queensland	Brisbane	1963-64
357*	R.Abel	Surrey v Somerset	The Oval	1899
357	D.G.Bradman	South Australia v Victoria	Melbourne	1935-36
356	B.A.Richards	South Australia v W Australia	Perth	1970-71
355*	G.R.Marsh	W Australia v S Australia	Perth	1989-90
355	B.Sutcliffe	Otago v Auckland	Dunedin	1949-50
352	W.H.Ponsford	Victoria v New South Wales	Melbourne	1926-27
350	Rashid Israr	Habib Bank v National Bank	Lahore	1976-77

There have been 116 triple hundreds in first-class cricket, W.V.Raman (313) and Arjan Kripal Singh (302*) for Tamil Nadu v Goa at Panjim in 1988-89 providing the only instance of two batsmen scoring 300 in the same innings.

MOST HUNDREDS IN SUCCESSIVE INNINGS

6	C.B.Fry	Sussex and Rest of England		1901
6	D.G.Bradman	South Australia and D.G.Bradman's XI		1938-39
6	M.J.Procter	Rhodesia		1970-71

TWO DOUBLE HUNDREDS IN A MATCH

244	202*	A.E.Fagg	Kent v Essex	Colchester	1938

TRIPLE HUNDRED AND HUNDRED IN A MATCH

333	123	G.A.Gooch	England v India	Lord's	1990

DOUBLE HUNDRED AND HUNDRED IN A MATCH MOST TIMES

4	Zaheer Abbas	Gloucestershire	1976-81

TWO HUNDREDS IN A MATCH MOST TIMES

8	Zaheer Abbas	Gloucestershire and PIA	1976-82
7	W.R.Hammond	Gloucestershire, England and MCC	1927-45

MOST HUNDREDS IN A SEASON

18	D.C.S.Compton	1947	16	J.B.Hobbs	1925

100 HUNDREDS IN A CAREER

	Total		100th Hundred	
	Hundreds	Inns	Season	Inns
J.B.Hobbs	197	1315	1923	821
E.H.Hendren	170	1300	1928-29	740
W.R.Hammond	167	1005	1935	679
C.P.Mead	153	1340	1927	892
G.Boycott	151	1014	1977	645
H.Sutcliffe	149	1088	1932	700
F.E.Woolley	145	1532	1929	1031
L.Hutton	129	814	1951	619
G.A.Gooch	128	971	1992-93	820
W.G Grace	126	1493	1895	1113
D.C.S.Compton	123	839	1952	552
T.W.Graveney	122	1223	1964	940
D.G.Bradman	117	338	1947-48	295
I.V.A.Richards	114	796	1988-89	658
Zaheer Abbas	108	768	1982-83	658
A.Sandham	107	1000	1935	871
M.C.Cowdrey	107	1130	1973	1035
T.W.Hayward	104	1138	1913	1076
J.H.Edrich	103	979	1977	945
G.M.Turner	103	792	1982	779
G.E.Tyldesley	102	961	1934	919
L.E.G.Ames	102	951	1950	915
D.L.Amiss	102	1139	1986	1081

MOST 400s: 2 – W.H.Ponsford
MOST 300s or more: 6 – D.G.Bradman
MOST 200s or more: 37 – D.G.Bradman; 36 – W.R.Hammond

MOST RUNS IN A MONTH

1294 (avge 92.42)	L.Hutton	Yorkshire	June 1949

MOST RUNS IN A SEASON

Runs			I	NO	HS	Avge	100	Season
3816	D.C.S.Compton	Middlesex	50	8	246	90.85	18	1947
3539	W.J.Edrich	Middlesex	52	8	267*	80.43	12	1947
3518	T.W.Hayward	Surrey	61	8	219	66.37	13	1906

The feat of scoring 3000 runs in a season has been achieved on 28 occasions, the most recent instance being by W.E.Alley (3019) in 1961. The highest aggregate in a season since 1969, when the number of County Championship matches was substantially reduced, is 2755 by S.J.Cook in 1991.

1000 RUNS IN A SEASON MOST TIMES

28	W.G.Grace (Gloucestershire), F.E.Woolley (Kent)

HIGHEST BATTING AVERAGE IN A SEASON
(Qualification: 12 innings)

Avge			I	NO	HS	Runs	100	Season
115.66	D.G.Bradman	Australians	26	5	278	2429	13	1938
102.53	G.Boycott	Yorkshire	20	5	175*	1538	6	1979
102.00	W.A.Johnston	Australians	17	16	28*	102	–	1953
101.70	G.A.Gooch	Essex	30	3	333	2746	12	1990
100.12	G.Boycott	Yorkshire	30	5	233	2503	13	1971

FASTEST HUNDRED AGAINST AUTHENTIC BOWLING

35 min	P.G.H.Fender	Surrey v Northamptonshire	Northampton	1920

FASTEST DOUBLE HUNDRED

113 min	R.J.Shastri	Bombay v Baroda	Bombay	1984-85

FASTEST TRIPLE HUNDRED

181 min	D.C.S.Compton	MCC v NE Transvaal	Benoni	1948-49

MOST SIXES IN AN INNINGS

16	A.Symonds	Gloucestershire v Glamorgan	Abergavenny	1995

MOST SIXES IN A MATCH

20	A.Symonds	Gloucestershire v Glamorgan	Abergavenny	1995

MOST SIXES IN A SEASON

80	I.T.Botham	Somerset and England	1985

MOST BOUNDARIES IN AN INNINGS

72	B.C.Lara	Warwickshire v Durham	Birmingham	1994

MOST RUNS OFF ONE OVER

36	G.St A.Sobers	Nottinghamshire v Glamorgan	Swansea	1968
36	R.J.Shastri	Bombay v Baroda	Bombay	1984-85

Both batsmen hit for six all six balls of overs bowled by M.A.Nash and Tilak Raj respectively.

MOST RUNS IN A DAY

390*	B.C.Lara	Warwickshire v Durham	Birmingham	1994

There have been 19 instances of a batsman scoring 300 or more runs in a day.

HIGHEST PARTNERSHIPS FOR EACH WICKET

First Wicket

561	Waheed Mirza/Mansoor Akhtar	Karachi W v Quetta	Karachi	1976-77
555	P.Holmes/H.Sutcliffe	Yorkshire v Essex	Leyton	1932
554	J.T.Brown/J.Tunnicliffe	Yorkshire v Derbys	Chesterfield	1898

Second Wicket

475	Zahir Alam/L.S.Rajput	Assam v Tripura	Gauhati	1991-92
465*	J.A.Jameson/R.B.Kanhai	Warwickshire v Glos	Birmingham	1974
455	K.V.Bhandarkar/B.B.Nimbalkar	Maha'tra v Kathiawar	Poona	1948-49

Third Wicket

467	A.H.Jones/M.D.Crowe	N Zealand v Sri Lanka	Wellington	1990-91
456	Khalid Irtiza/Aslam Ali	United Bank v Multan	Karachi	1975-76
451	Mudassar Nazar/Javed Miandad	Pakistan v India	Hyderabad	1982-83
445	P.E.Whitelaw/W.N.Carson	Auckland v Otago	Dunedin	1936-37
434	J.B.Stollmeyer/G.E.Gomez	Trinidad v Br Guiana	Port-of-Spain	1946-47
424*	W.J.Edrich/D.C.S.Compton	Middlesex v Somerset	Lord's	1948

Fourth Wicket

577	V.S.Hazare/Gul Mohamed	Baroda v Holkar	Baroda	1946-47
574*	C.L.Walcott/F.M.M.Worrell	Barbados v Trinidad	Port-of-Spain	1945-46
502*	F.M.M.Worrell/J.D.C.Goddard	Barbados v Trinidad	Bridgetown	1943-44
470	A.I.Kallicharran/G.W.Humpage	Warwickshire v Lancs	Southport	1982

Fifth Wicket

464*	†M.E.Waugh/S.R.Waugh	NSW v W Australia	Perth	1990-91
405	S.G.Barnes/D.G.Bradman	Australia v England	Sydney	1946-47
397	W.Bardsley/C.Kelleway	NSW v S Australia	Sydney	1920-21
393	E.G.Arnold/W.B.Burns	Worcs v Warwickshire	Birmingham	1909

† Includes 20 runs credited under ACB playing conditions for 10 no-balls which, under the Laws of cricket, would have produced 7 runs.

Sixth Wicket

487*	G.A.Headley/C.C.Passailaigue	Jamaica v Tennyson's	Kingston	1931-32
428	W.W.Armstrong/M.A.Noble	Australians v Sussex	Hove	1902
411	R.M.Poore/E.G.Wynyard	Hampshire v Somerset	Taunton	1899

Seventh Wicket

460	Bhupinder Singh jr/P.Dharmani	Punjab v Delhi	Delhi	1994-95
347	D.St E.Atkinson/C.C.Depeiza	W Indies v Australia	Bridgetown	1954-55
344	K.S.Ranjitsinhji/W.Newham	Sussex v Essex	Leyton	1902

Eighth Wicket

433	V.T.Trumper/A.Sims	Australians v C'bury	Christchurch	1913-14
292	R.Peel/Lord Hawke	Yorkshire v Warwicks	Birmingham	1896
270	V.T.Trumper/E.P.Barbour	NSW v Victoria	Sydney	1912-13

Ninth Wicket

283	J.Chapman/A.Warren	Derbys v Warwicks	Blackwell	1910
268	J.B.Commins/N.Boje	SA 'A' v Mashonaland	Harare	1994-95
251	J.W.H.T.Douglas/S.N.Hare	Essex v Derbyshire	Leyton	1921

Tenth Wicket

307	A.F.Kippax/J.E.H.Hooker	NSW v Victoria	Melbourne	1928-29
249	C.T.Sarwate/S.N.Banerjee	Indians v Surrey	The Oval	1946
235	F.E.Woolley/A.Fielder	Kent v Worcs	Stourbridge	1909

35000 RUNS IN A CAREER

	Career	*I*	*NO*	*HS*	**Runs**	*Avge*	*100*
J.B.Hobbs	1905-34	1315	106	316*	**61237**	50.65	197
F.E.Woolley	1906-38	1532	85	305*	**58969**	40.75	145
E.H.Hendren	1907-38	1300	166	301*	**57611**	50.80	170
C.P.Mead	1905-36	1340	185	280*	**55061**	47.67	153
W.G.Grace	1865-1908	1493	105	344	**54896**	39.55	126
W.R.Hammond	1920-51	1005	104	336*	**50551**	56.10	167
H.Sutcliffe	1919-45	1088	123	313	**50138**	51.95	149
G.Boycott	1962-86	1014	162	261*	**48426**	56.83	151
T.W.Graveney	1948-71/72	1223	159	258	**47793**	44.91	122
G.A.Gooch	1973-96	971	74	333	**44472**	49.57	128
T.W.Hayward	1893-1914	1138	96	315*	**43551**	41.79	104
D.L.Amiss	1960-87	1139	126	262*	**43423**	42.86	102
M.C.Cowdrey	1950-76	1130	134	307	**42719**	42.89	107
A.Sandham	1911-37/38	1000	79	325	**41284**	44.82	107
L.Hutton	1934-60	814	91	364	**40140**	55.51	129
M.J.K.Smith	1951-75	1091	139	204	**39832**	41.84	69
W.Rhodes	1898-1930	1528	237	267*	**39802**	30.83	58
J.H.Edrich	1956-78	979	104	310*	**39790**	45.47	103
R.E.S.Wyatt	1923-57	1141	157	232	**39405**	40.04	85
D.C.S.Compton	1936-64	839	88	300	**38942**	51.85	123
G.E.Tyldesley	1909-36	961	106	256*	**38874**	45.46	102
J.T.Tyldesley	1895-1923	994	62	295*	**37897**	40.60	86
K.W.R.Fletcher	1962-88	1167	170	228*	**37665**	37.77	63
C.G.Greenidge	1970-92	889	75	273*	**37354**	45.88	92
J.W.Hearne	1909-36	1025	116	285*	**37252**	40.98	96
L.E.G.Ames	1926-51	951	95	295	**37248**	43.51	102
D.Kenyon	1946-67	1159	59	259	**37002**	33.63	74
W.J.Edrich	1934-58	964	92	267*	**36965**	42.39	86
J.M.Parks	1949-76	1227	172	205*	**36673**	34.76	51
D.Denton	1894-1920	1163	70	221	**36479**	33.37	69
G.H.Hirst	1891-1929	1215	151	341	**36323**	34.13	60
I.V.A.Richards	1971/72-93	796	63	322	**36212**	49.40	114
A.Jones	1957-83	1168	72	204*	**36049**	32.89	56
W.G.Quaife	1894-1928	1203	185	255*	**36012**	35.37	72
R.E.Marshall	1945/46-72	1053	59	228*	**35725**	35.94	68
G.Gunn	1902-32	1061	82	220	**35208**	35.96	62

BOWLING RECORDS

ALL TEN WICKETS IN AN INNINGS

This feat has been achieved on 74 occasions at first-class level.
Three Times: A.P.Freeman (1929, 1930, 1931)
Twice: V.E.Walker (1859, 1865); H.Verity (1931, 1932); J.C.Laker (1956)

Instances since 1945:

W.E.Hollies	Warwickshire v Notts	Birmingham	1946
J.M.Sims	East v West	Kingston on Thames	1948
J.K.R.Graveney	Gloucestershire v Derbyshire	Chesterfield	1949
T.E.Bailey	Essex v Lancashire	Clacton	1949
R.Berry	Lancashire v Worcestershire	Blackpool	1953
S.P.Gupte	President's XI v Combined XI	Bombay	1954-55
J.C.Laker	Surrey v Australians	The Oval	1956
K.Smales	Nottinghamshire v Glos	Stroud	1956
G.A.R.Lock	Surrey v Kent	Blackheath	1956

J.C.Laker	England v Australia	Manchester	1956
P.M.Chatterjee	Bengal v Assam	Jorhat	1956-57
J.D.Bannister	Warwicks v Combined Services	Birmingham (M & B)	1959
A.J.G.Pearson	Cambridge U v Leicestershire	Loughborough	1961
N.I.Thomson	Sussex v Warwickshire	Worthing	1964
P.J.Allan	Queensland v Victoria	Melbourne	1965-66
I.J.Brayshaw	Western Australia v Victoria	Perth	1967-68
Shahid Mahmood	Karachi Whites v Khairpur	Karachi	1969-70
E.E.Hemmings	International XI v W Indians	Kingston	1982-83
P.Sunderam	Rajasthan v Vidarbha	Jodhpur	1985-86
S.T.Jefferies	Western Province v OFS	Cape Town	1987-88
Imran Adil	Bahawalpur v Faisalabad	Faisalabad	1989-90
G.P.Wickremasinghe	Sinhalese v Kalutara	Colombo	1991-92
R.L.Johnson	Middlesex v Derbyshire	Derby	1994
Naeem Akhtar	Rawalpindi B v Peshawar	Peshawar	1995-96

MOST WICKETS IN A MATCH

| 19 | J.C.Laker | England v Australia | Manchester | 1956 |

MOST WICKETS IN A SEASON

Wkts		Career	Matches	Overs	Mdns	Runs	Avge
304	A.P.Freeman	1928	37	1976.1	423	5489	18.05
298	A.P.Freeman	1933	33	2039	651	4549	15.26

The feat of taking 250 wickets in a season has been achieved on 12 occasions, the last instance been by A.P.Freeman in 1933. 200 or more wickets in a season have been taken on 59 occasions, the last being by G.A.R.Lock (212 wickets, average 12.02) in 1957.

The highest aggregates of wickets taken in a season since the reduction of County Championship matches in 1969 are as follows:

Wkts		Season	Matches	Overs	Mdns	Runs	Avge
134	M.D.Marshall	1982	22	822	225	2108	15.73
131	L.R.Gibbs	1971	23	1024.1	295	2475	18.89
125	F.D.Stephenson	1988	22	819.1	196	2289	18.31
121	R.D.Jackman	1980	23	746.2	220	1864	15.40

Since 1969 there have been 47 instances of bowlers taking 100 wickets in a season.

MOST HAT-TRICKS IN A CAREER

7	D.V.P.Wright
6	T.W.J.Goddard, C.W.L.Parker
5	S.Haigh, V.W.C.Jupp, A.E.G.Rhodes, F.A.Tarrant

2000 WICKETS IN A CAREER

	Career	Runs	Wkts	Avge	100w
W.Rhodes	1898-1930	69993	**4187**	16.71	23
A.P.Freeman	1914-36	69577	**3776**	18.42	17
C.W.L.Parker	1903-35	63817	**3278**	19.46	16
J.T.Hearne	1888-1923	54352	**3061**	17.75	15
T.W.J.Goddard	1922-52	59116	**2979**	19.84	16
W.G.Grace	1865-1908	51545	**2876**	17.92	10
A.S.Kennedy	1907-36	61034	**2874**	21.23	15
D.Shackleton	1948-69	53303	**2857**	18.65	20
G.A.R.Lock	1946-70/71	54709	**2844**	19.23	14
F.J.Titmus	1949-82	63313	**2830**	22.37	16
M.W.Tate	1912-37	50571	**2784**	18.16	13+1
G.H.Hirst	1891-1929	51282	**2739**	18.72	15

	Career	Runs	Wkts	Avge	100w
C.Blythe	1899-1914	42136	**2506**	16.81	14
D.L.Underwood	1963-87	49993	**2465**	20.28	10
W.E.Astill	1906-39	57783	**2431**	23.76	9
J.C.White	1909-37	43759	**2356**	18.57	14
W.E.Hollies	1932-57	48656	**2323**	20.94	14
F.S.Trueman	1949-69	42154	**2304**	18.29	12
J.B.Statham	1950-68	36999	**2260**	16.37	13
R.T.D.Perks	1930-55	53770	**2233**	24.07	16
J.Briggs	1879-1900	35431	**2221**	15.95	12
D.J.Shepherd	1950-72	47302	**2218**	21.32	12
E.G.Dennett	1903-26	42571	**2147**	19.82	12
T.Richardson	1892-1905	38794	**2104**	18.43	10
T.E.Bailey	1945-67	48170	**2082**	23.13	9
R.Illingworth	1951-83	42023	**2072**	20.28	10
F.E.Woolley	1906-38	41066	**2068**	19.85	8
N.Gifford	1960-88	48731	**2068**	23.56	4
G.Geary	1912-38	41339	**2063**	20.03	11
D.V.P.Wright	1932-57	49307	**2056**	23.98	10
J.A.Newman	1906-30	51111	**2032**	25.15	9
A.Shaw	1864-97	24580	**2027**+1	12.12	9
S.Haigh	1895-1913	32091	**2012**	15.94	11

ALL-ROUND RECORDS

THE 'DOUBLE'

3000 runs and 100 wickets: J.H.Parks (1937)
2000 runs and 200 wickets: G.H.Hirst (1906)
2000 runs and 100 wickets: F.E.Woolley (4), J.W.Hearne (3), W.G.Grace (2), G.H.Hirst (2), W.Rhodes (2), T.E.Bailey, D.E.Davies, G.L.Jessop, V.W.C.Jupp, J.Langridge, F.A.Tarrant, C.L.Townsend, L.F.Townsend
1000 runs and 200 wickets: M.W.Tate (3), A.E.Trott (2), A.S.Kennedy

Most Doubles: 16 – W.Rhodes; 14 – G.H.Hirst; 10 – V.W.C.Jupp

Double in Debut Season: D.B.Close (1949) – the youngest (18) to achieve this feat.
   The feat of scoring 1000 runs and taking 100 wickets in a season has been achieved on 305 occasions, R.J.Hadlee (1984) and F.D.Stephenson (1988) being the only players to complete the 'double' since the reduction of County Championship matches in 1969.

WICKET-KEEPING RECORDS

MOST DISMISSALS IN AN INNINGS

9	(8ct, 1st)	Tahir Rashid	Habib Bank v PACO	Gujranwala	1992-93
9	(7ct, 2st)	W.R.James	Matabeleland v Mashonaland CD	Bulawayo	1995-96
8	(8ct)	A.T.W.Grout	Queensland v W Australia	Brisbane	1959-60
8	(8ct)	D.E.East	Essex v Somerset	Taunton	1985
8	(8ct)	S.A.Marsh	Kent v Middlesex	Lord's	1991
8	(6ct, 2st)	T.J.Zoehrer	Australians v Surrey	The Oval	1993

MOST DISMISSALS IN A MATCH

13	(11ct, 2st)	W.R.James	Matabeleland v Mashonaland CD Bulawayo	1995-96
12	(8ct, 4st)	E.Pooley	Surrey v Sussex	The Oval	1868
12	(9ct, 3st)	D.Tallon	Queensland v NSW	Sydney	1938-39
12	(9ct, 3st)	H.B.Taber	NSW v South Australia	Adelaide	1968-69

MOST DISMISSALS IN A SEASON

128 (79ct, 49st) L.E.G.Ames   1929

1000 DISMISSALS IN A CAREER

	Career	Dismissals	Ct	St
R.W.Taylor	1960-88	**1649**	1473	176
J.T.Murray	1952-75	**1527**	1270	257
H.Strudwick	1902-27	**1497**	1242	255
A.P.E.Knott	1964-85	**1344**	1211	133
F.H.Huish	1895-1914	**1310**	933	377
B.Taylor	1949-73	**1294**	1083	211
D.Hunter	1889-1909	**1253**	906	347
H.R.Butt	1890-1912	**1228**	953	275
J.H.Board	1891-1914/15	**1207**	852	355
H.Elliott	1920-47	**1206**	904	302
J.M.Parks	1949-76	**1181**	1088	93
R.Booth	1951-70	**1126**	948	178
L.E.G.Ames	1926-51	**1121**	703	418
D.L.Bairstow	1970-90	**1099**	961	138
G.Duckworth	1923-47	**1096**	753	343
H.W.Stephenson	1948-64	**1082**	748	334
J.G.Binks	1955-75	**1071**	895	176
T.G.Evans	1939-69	**1066**	816	250
A.Long	1960-80	**1046**	922	124
G.O.Dawkes	1937-61	**1043**	895	148
R.W.Tolchard	1965-83	**1037**	912	125
W.L.Cornford	1921-47	**1017**	675	342

FIELDING RECORDS

MOST CATCHES IN AN INNINGS

7	M.J.Stewart	Surrey v Northamptonshire	Northampton	1957
7	A.S.Brown	Gloucestershire v Nottinghamshire	Nottingham	1966

MOST CATCHES IN A MATCH

10   W.R.Hammond   Gloucestershire v Surrey   Cheltenham   1928

MOST CATCHES IN A SEASON

78   W.R.Hammond   1928   77   M.J.Stewart   1957

750 CATCHES IN A CAREER

1018	F.E.Woolley	1906-38	784	J.G.Langridge	1928-55
887	W.G.Grace	1865-1908	764	W.Rhodes	1898-1930
830	G.A.R.Lock	1946-70/71	758	C.A.Milton	1948-74
819	W.R.Hammond	1920-51	754	E.H.Hendren	1907-38
813	D.B.Close	1949-86			

LIMITED-OVERS INTERNATIONALS
RESULTS SUMMARY

1970-71 to 23 September 1996

	Opponents	Matches	E	A	SA	WI	NZ	I	P	SL	Z	B	C	EA	H	K	UAE	Tied	NR
England	Australia	57	26	29	–	–	–	–	–	–	–	–	–	–	–	–	–	1	1
	South Africa	12	5	–	7	–	–	–	–	–	–	–	–	–	–	–	–	–	–
	West Indies	51	22	–	–	27	–	–	–	–	–	–	–	–	–	–	–	–	2
	New Zealand	42	21	–	–	–	18	–	–	–	–	–	–	–	–	–	–	–	3
	India	32	18	–	–	–	–	13	–	–	–	–	–	–	–	–	–	–	1
	Pakistan	40	25	–	–	–	–	–	14	–	–	–	–	–	–	–	–	–	1
	Sri Lanka	12	8	–	–	–	–	–	–	4	–	–	–	–	–	–	–	–	–
	Zimbabwe	3	1	–	–	–	–	–	–	–	2	–	–	–	–	–	–	–	–
	Canada	1	1	–	–	–	–	–	–	–	–	–	0	–	–	–	–	–	–
	East Africa	1	1	–	–	–	–	–	–	–	–	–	–	0	–	–	–	–	–
	Holland	1	1	–	–	–	–	–	–	–	–	–	–	–	0	–	–	–	–
	U A Emirates	1	1	–	–	–	–	–	–	–	–	–	–	–	–	–	0	–	–
Australia	South Africa	20	–	12	8	–	–	–	–	–	–	–	–	–	–	–	–	–	–
	West Indies	80	–	31	–	47	–	–	–	–	–	–	–	–	–	–	–	1	1
	New Zealand	63	–	44	–	–	17	–	–	–	–	–	–	–	–	–	–	–	2
	India	45	–	26	–	–	–	16	–	–	–	–	–	–	–	–	–	–	3
	Pakistan	42	–	21	–	–	–	–	18	–	–	–	–	–	–	–	–	1	2
	Sri Lanka	35	–	22	–	–	–	–	–	11	–	–	–	–	–	–	–	–	2
	Zimbabwe	9	–	8	–	–	–	–	–	–	1	–	–	–	–	–	–	–	–
	Bangladesh	1	–	1	–	–	–	–	–	–	–	0	–	–	–	–	–	–	–
	Canada	1	–	1	–	–	–	–	–	–	–	–	0	–	–	–	–	–	–
	Kenya	1	–	1	–	–	–	–	–	–	–	–	–	–	–	0	–	–	–
S Africa	West Indies	9	–	–	4	5	–	–	–	–	–	–	–	–	–	–	–	–	–
	New Zealand	8	–	–	4	–	4	–	–	–	–	–	–	–	–	–	–	–	–
	India	17	–	–	11	–	–	6	–	–	–	–	–	–	–	–	–	–	–
	Pakistan	14	–	–	7	–	–	–	7	–	–	–	–	–	–	–	–	–	–
	Sri Lanka	7	–	–	3	–	–	–	–	3	–	–	–	–	–	–	–	–	1
	Zimbabwe	4	–	–	3	–	–	–	–	–	0	–	–	–	–	–	–	–	1
	Holland	1	–	–	1	–	–	–	–	–	–	–	–	–	0	–	–	–	–
	U A Emirates	1	–	–	1	–	–	–	–	–	–	–	–	–	–	–	0	–	–
W Indies	New Zealand	24	–	–	–	18	4	–	–	–	–	–	–	–	–	–	–	–	2
	India	51	–	–	–	32	–	18	–	–	–	–	–	–	–	–	–	1	–
	Pakistan	75	–	–	–	51	–	–	22	–	–	–	–	–	–	–	–	2	–
	Sri Lanka	27	–	–	–	19	–	–	–	7	–	–	–	–	–	–	–	–	1
	Zimbabwe	5	–	–	–	5	–	–	–	–	0	–	–	–	–	–	–	–	–
	Kenya	1	–	–	–	0	–	–	–	–	–	–	–	–	–	1	–	–	–
N Zealand	India	41	–	–	–	–	18	23	–	–	–	–	–	–	–	–	–	–	–
	Pakistan	41	–	–	–	–	16	–	23	–	–	–	–	–	–	–	–	1	1
	Sri Lanka	32	–	–	–	–	22	–	–	8	–	–	–	–	–	–	–	–	2
	Zimbabwe	8	–	–	–	–	7	–	–	–	1	–	–	–	–	–	–	–	–
	Bangladesh	1	–	–	–	–	1	–	–	–	–	0	–	–	–	–	–	–	–
	East Africa	1	–	–	–	–	1	–	–	–	–	–	–	0	–	–	–	–	–
	Holland	1	–	–	–	–	1	–	–	–	–	–	–	–	0	–	–	–	–
	U A Emirates	1	–	–	–	–	1	–	–	–	–	–	–	–	–	–	0	–	–
India	Pakistan	50	–	–	–	–	–	16	32	–	–	–	–	–	–	–	–	–	2
	Sri Lanka	41	–	–	–	–	–	25	–	14	–	–	–	–	–	–	–	–	2
	Zimbabwe	12	–	–	–	–	–	11	–	–	0	–	–	–	–	–	–	1	–
	Bangladesh	3	–	–	–	–	–	3	–	–	–	0	–	–	–	–	–	–	–
	East Africa	1	–	–	–	–	–	1	–	–	–	–	–	0	–	–	–	–	–
	Kenya	1	–	–	–	–	–	1	–	–	–	–	–	–	–	0	–	–	–
	U A Emirates	1	–	–	–	–	–	1	–	–	–	–	–	–	–	–	0	–	–

	Opponents	Matches	E	A	SA	WI	NZ	I	P	SL	Z	B	C	EA	H	K	UAE	Tied	NR
										Won by								Tied	NR
Pakistan	Sri Lanka	56	–	–	–	–	–	–	41	14	–	–	–	–	–	–	–	–	1
	Zimbabwe	9	–	–	–	–	–	–	7	1	–	–	–	–	–	–	–	–	1
	Bangladesh	3	–	–	–	–	–	–	3	–	–	0	–	–	–	–	–	–	–
	Canada	1	–	–	–	–	–	–	1	–	–	–	0	–	–	–	–	–	–
	Holland	1	–	–	–	–	–	–	1	–	–	–	–	–	0	–	–	–	–
	U A Emirates	2	–	–	–	–	–	–	2	–	–	–	–	–	–	–	0	–	–
Sri Lanka	Zimbabwe	8	–	–	–	–	–	–	–	7	1	–	–	–	–	–	–	–	–
	Bangladesh	4	–	–	–	–	–	–	–	4	–	0	–	–	–	–	–	–	–
	Kenya	1	–	–	–	–	–	–	–	1	–	–	–	–	–	0	–	–	–
Zimbabwe	Kenya	1	–	–	–	–	–	–	–	–	1	–	–	–	–	0	–	–	–
Holland	U A Emirates	1	–	–	–	–	–	–	–	–	–	–	–	–	0	–	1	–	–
		1116	130	196	49	204	110	134	171	73	7	0	0	0	0	1	1	9	31

MERIT TABLE OF ALL L-O INTERNATIONALS

1970-71 to 23 September 1996 (1116 matches)

	Matches	Won	Lost	Tied	No Result	% Won (exc NR)
West Indies	323	204	109	4	6	64.35
Australia	354	196	144	3	11	57.14
South Africa	93	49	42	–	2	53.84
England	253	130	114	1	8	53.06
Pakistan	334	171	151	5	7	52.29
India	295	134	151	2	8	46.68
New Zealand	263	110	142	1	10	43.47
Sri Lanka	223	73	141	–	9	34.11
Kenya	5	1	4	–	–	20.00
United Arab Emirates	7	1	6	–	–	14.28
Zimbabwe	59	7	49	2	1	12.06
Canada	3	–	3	–	–	–
East Africa	3	–	3	–	–	–
Holland	5	–	5	–	–	–
Bangladesh	12	–	12	–	–	–

RECORDS

To 23 September 1996

TEAM RECORDS

HIGHEST TOTALS

398-5	(50 overs)	Sri Lanka v Kenya	Kandy	1995-96
363-7	(55 overs)	England v Pakistan	Nottingham	1992
360-4	(50 overs)	West Indies v Sri Lanka	Karachi	1987-88
349-9	(50 overs)	Sri Lanka v Pakistan	Singapore	1995-96
348-8	(50 overs)	New Zealand v India	Nagpur	1995-96
338-4	(50 overs)	New Zealand v Bangladesh	Sharjah	1989-90
338-5	(60 overs)	Pakistan v Sri Lanka	Swansea	1983
334-4	(60 overs)	England v India	Lord's	1975
333-7	(50 overs)	West Indies v Sri Lanka	Sharjah	1995-96
333-8	(45 overs)	West Indies v India	Jamshedpur	1983-84
333-9	(60 overs)	England v Sri Lanka	Taunton	1983
332-3	(50 overs)	Australia v Sri Lanka	Sharjah	1989-90
330-6	(60 overs)	Pakistan v Sri Lanka	Nottingham	1975

The highest totals by other ICC Full Members are:

328-3	(50 overs)	South Africa v Holland	Rawalpindi	1995-96
312-4	(50 overs)	Zimbabwe v Sri Lanka	New Plymouth	1991-92
305-5	(50 overs)	India v Pakistan	Sharjah	1995-96

HIGHEST TOTALS BATTING SECOND

WINNING:

313-7	(49.2 overs)	Sri Lanka v Zimbabwe	New Plymouth	1991-92

LOSING:

329	(49.3 overs)	Sri Lanka v West Indies	Sharjah	1995-96

HIGHEST MATCH AGGREGATES

664-19	(99.4 overs)	Pakistan v Sri Lanka	Singapore	1995-96
662-17	(99.3 overs)	West Indies v Sri Lanka	Sharjah	1995-96
652-12	(100 overs)	Sri Lanka v Kenya	Kandy	1995-96

LARGEST MARGINS OF VICTORY

232 runs	Australia beat Sri Lanka	Adelaide	1984-85
206 runs	New Zealand beat Australia	Adelaide	1985-86
202 runs	England beat India	Lord's	1975
10 wickets	Nine instances		

LOWEST TOTALS†

43	(19.5 overs)	Pakistan v West Indies	Cape Town	1992-93
45	(40.3 overs)	Canada v England	Manchester	1979
55	(28.3 overs)	Sri Lanka v West Indies	Sharjah	1986-87
63	(25.5 overs)	India v Australia	Sydney	1980-81
64	(35.5 overs)	New Zealand v Pakistan	Sharjah	1985-86
69	(28 overs)	South Africa v Australia	Sydney	1993-94
70	(25.2 overs)	Australia v England	Birmingham	1977
70	(26.3 overs)	Australia v New Zealand	Adelaide	1985-86

The lowest totals by other ICC Full Members are:

87	(29.3 overs)	West Indies v Australia	Sydney	1992-93
93	(36.2 overs)	England v Australia	Leeds	1975
99	(36.3 overs)	Zimbabwe v West Indies	Hyderabad (Ind)	1993-94

† *Excluding instances when the number of overs was reduced after play began.*

LOWEST MATCH AGGREGATE

88-13	(32.2 overs)	West Indies v Pakistan	Cape Town	1992-93

TIED MATCHES

Australia	222-9	(50)	West Indies	222-5	(50)	Melbourne	1983-84
England	226-5	(55)	Australia	226-8	(55)	Nottingham	1989
West Indies	186-5	(39)	Pakistan	186-9	(39)	Lahore	1991-92
India	126	(47.4)	Pakistan	126	(41)	Perth	1991-92
Australia	228-7	(50)	Pakistan	228-9	(50)	Hobart	1992-93
Pakistan	244-6	(50)	West Indies	244-5	(50)	Georgetown	1992-93
India	248-5	(50)	Zimbabwe	248	(50)	Indore	1993-94
Pakistan	161-9	(50)	New Zealand	161	(49.4)	Auckland	1993-94
Zimbabwe	219-9	(50)	Pakistan	219	(49.5)	Harare	1994-95

200 APPEARANCES

	LOI	E	A	SA	WI	NZ	I	P	SL	Z	Ass
A.R.Border (A)	273	43	–	15	61	52	38	34	23	5	2
D.L.Haynes (WI)	238	35	64	8	–	13	36	65	14	3	–
Salim Malik (P)	234	24	24	14	45	36	37	–	42	8	4
Javed Miandad (P)	233	27	35	3	64	24	35	–	35	6	4
M.Azharuddin (I)	224	21	33	16	37	29	–	37	36	10	5
Kapil Dev (I)	224	23	41	13	42	29	–	32	33	9	2
R.B.Richardson (WI)	224	35	51	9	–	11	32	61	21	3	1
Wasim Akram (P)	206	24	25	10	46	21	33	–	32	9	6
S.R.Waugh (A)	200	23	–	18	37	40	31	24	20	5	2

Most Appearances for other ICC Full Members

	LOI	E	A	SA	WI	NZ	I	P	SL	Z	Ass
A.Ranatunga (SL)	191	10	28	7	20	27	37	50	–	8	4
J.G.Wright (NZ)	149	30	42	–	11	–	21	18	24	2	1
G.A.Gooch (E)	125	–	32	1	32	16	18	16	6	3	1
W.J.Cronje (SA)	88	12	20	–	8	8	15	13	6	4	2
A.Flower (Z)	47	3	5	4	3	6	8	9	8	–	1
D.L.Houghton (Z)	47	2	7	4	4	5	10	9	6	–	–

BATTING RECORDS
HIGHEST INDIVIDUAL INNINGS

189*	I.V.A.Richards	West Indies v England	Manchester	1984
188*	G.Kirsten	South Africa v UAE	Rawalpindi	1995-96
181	I.V.A.Richards	West Indies v Sri Lanka	Karachi	1987-88
175*	Kapil Dev	India v Zimbabwe	Tunbridge Wells	1983
171*	G.M.Turner	New Zealand v East Africa	Birmingham	1975
169*	D.J.Callaghan	South Africa v New Zealand	Verwoerdburg	1994-95
169	B.C.Lara	West Indies v Sri Lanka	Sharjah	1995-96
167*	R.A.Smith	England v Australia	Birmingham	1993
161	A.C.Hudson	South Africa v Holland	Rawalpindi	1995-96
158	D.I.Gower	England v New Zealand	Brisbane	1982-83
153*	I.V.A.Richards	West Indies v Australia	Melbourne	1979-80
153	B.C.Lara	West Indies v Pakistan	Sharjah	1993-94
152*	D.L.Haynes	West Indies v India	Georgetown	1988-89

The highest individual innings for other ICC Full Members are:

145	D.M.Jones	Australia v England	Brisbane	1990-91
145	P.A.de Silva	Sri Lanka v Kenya	Kandy	1995-96
142	D.L.Houghton	Zimbabwe v New Zealand	Hyderabad, India	1987-88
137*	Inzamam-ul-Haq	Pakistan v New Zealand	Sharjah	1993-94

HIGHEST PARTNERSHIP FOR EACH WICKET

1st	212	G.R.Marsh/D.C.Boon	Australia v India	Jaipur	1986-87
2nd	263	Aamir Sohail/Inzamam-ul-Haq	Pakistan v New Zealand	Sharjah	1993-94
3rd	224*	D.M.Jones/A.R.Border	Australia v Sri Lanka	Adelaide	1984-85
4th	173	D.M.Jones/S.R.Waugh	Australia v Pakistan	Perth	1986-87
5th	159	R.T.Ponting/M.G.Bevan	Australia v Sri Lanka	Melbourne	1995-96
6th	154	R.B.Richardson/P.J.L.Dujon	West Indies v Pakistan	Sharjah	1991-92
7th	115	P.J.L.Dujon/M.D.Marshall	West Indies v Pakistan	Gujranwala	1986-87
8th	119	P.R.Reiffel/S.K.Warne	Australia v South Africa	Pt Elizabeth	1993-94
9th	126*	Kapil Dev/S.M.H.Kirmani	India v Zimbabwe	Tunbridge Wells	1983
10th	106*	I.V.A.Richards/M.A.Holding	West Indies v England	Manchester	1984

4000 RUNS IN A CAREER

		LOI	I	NO	HS	Runs	Avge	100	50
D.L.Haynes	WI	238	237	28	152*	**8648**	41.37	17	57
Javed Miandad	P	233	218	41	119*	**7381**	41.70	8	50
I.V.A.Richards	WI	187	167	24	189*	**6721**	47.00	11	45
A.R.Border	A	273	252	39	127*	**6524**	30.62	3	39
R.B.Richardson	WI	224	217	30	122	**6248**	33.41	5	45
M.Azharuddin	I	224	208	41	108*	**6091**	36.47	3	34
D.M.Jones	A	164	161	25	145	**6068**	44.61	7	46
Salim Malik	P	234	211	33	102	**6006**	33.74	5	39
D.C.Boon	A	181	177	16	122	**5964**	37.04	5	37
P.A.de Silva	SL	188	184	20	145	**5661**	34.51	6	38
Ramiz Raja	P	177	176	14	119*	**5386**	33.24	9	29
A.Ranatunga	SL	191	182	35	102*	**5250**	35.71	2	33
C.G.Greenidge	WI	128	127	13	133*	**5134**	45.03	11	31

		LOI	I	NO	HS	Runs	Avge	100	50
M.D.Crowe	NZ	143	141	19	107*	**4704**	38.55	4	34
S.R.Waugh	A	200	180	42	102*	**4420**	32.02	1	25
S.R.Tendulkar	I	126	123	12	137	**4378**	39.44	9	27
G.R.Marsh	A	117	115	6	126*	**4357**	39.97	9	22
B.C.Lara	WI	104	103	9	169	**4332**	46.08	9	29
G.A.Gooch	E	125	122	6	142	**4290**	36.98	8	23
K.Srikkanth	I	146	145	4	123	**4092**	29.02	4	27
A.J.Lamb	E	122	118	16	118	**4010**	39.31	4	26

The highest aggregates for other ICC Full Members are:

		LOI	I	NO	HS	Runs	Avge	100	50
W.J.Cronje	SA	88	84	12	112	**2681**	37.23	2	15
D.L.Houghton	Z	47	45	1	142	**1279**	29.06	1	10

EIGHT HUNDREDS IN A CAREER

		E	A	SA	WI	NZ	I	P	SL	Z	Ass
17	D.L.Haynes (WI)	2	6	–	–	2	2	4	1	–	–
11	C.G.Greenidge (WI)	–	1	–	–	3	3	2	1	1	–
11	I.V.A.Richards (WI)	3	3	–	–	1	3	–	1	–	–
9	B.C.Lara (WI)	–	1	2	–	2	–	3	1	–	–
9	G.R.Marsh (A)	1	–	–	2	2	3	1	–	–	–
9	Ramiz Raja (P)	1	–	–	2	3	–	–	3	–	–
9	S.R.Tendulkar (I)	–	1	–	1	1	–	2	3	–	1
9	G.A.Gooch (E)	–	4	–	1	1	1	1	–	–	–
9	Javed Miandad (P)	1	–	1	1	–	3	–	2	–	–
8	Saeed Anwar (P)	–	1	–	1	1	–	–	4	1	–
8	M.E.Waugh (A)	1	–	1	–	2	1	1	1	–	1

BOWLING RECORDS
BEST ANALYSES

7-37	Aqib Javed	Pakistan v India	Sharjah	1991-92
7-51	W.W.Davis	West Indies v Australia	Leeds	1983
6-12	A.Kumble	India v West Indies	Calcutta	1993-94
6-14	G.J.Gilmour	Australia v England	Leeds	1975
6-14	Imran Khan	Pakistan v India	Sharjah	1984-85
6-15	C.E.H.Croft	West Indies v England	Arnos Vale	1980-81
6-26	Waqar Younis	Pakistan v Sri Lanka	Sharjah	1989-90
6-29	B.P.Patterson	West Indies v India	Nagpur	1987-88
6-29	S.T.Jayasuriya	Sri Lanka v England	Moratuwa	1992-93
6-30	Waqar Younis	Pakistan v New Zealand	Auckland	1993-94
6-39	K.H.MacLeay	Australia v India	Nottingham	1983
6-41	I.V.A.Richards	West Indies v India	Delhi	1989-90
6-50	A.H.Gray	West Indies v Australia	Port-of-Spain	1990-91

The best analyses for other ICC Full Members are:

5-20	V.J.Marks	England v New Zealand	Wellington	1983-84
5-21	P.A.Strang	Zimbabwe v Kenya	Patna	1995-96
5-22	M.N.Hart	New Zealand v West Indies	Margao	1994-95
5-29	A.A.Donald	South Africa v India	Calcutta	1991-92

HAT-TRICKS

Jalaluddin	Pakistan v Australia	Hyderabad	1982-83
B.A.Reid	Australia v New Zealand	Sydney	1985-86
C.Sharma	India v New Zealand	Nagpur	1987-88
Wasim Akram	Pakistan v West Indies	Sharjah	1989-90
Wasim Akram	Pakistan v Australia	Sharjah	1989-90
Kapil Dev	India v Sri Lanka	Calcutta	1990-91
Aqib Javed	Pakistan v India	Sharjah	1991-92
D.K.Morrison	New Zealand v India	Napier	1993-94
Waqar Younis	Pakistan v New Zealand	East London	1994-95

100 WICKETS IN A CAREER

		LOI	O	R	W	Avge	Best	4w
Wasim Akram	P	206	1772.3	6707	297	22.58	5-15	16
Kapil Dev	I	224	1867	6945	253	27.45	5-43	4
Waqar Younis	P	133	1103	4992	220	22.69	6-26	17
C.J.McDermott	A	138	1243.3	5018	203	24.71	5-44	5
C.E.L.Ambrose	WI	133	1184.1	4129	184	22.44	5-17	9
Imran Khan	P	175	1243.3	4845	182	26.62	6-14	4
C.A.Walsh	WI	162	1425.4	5484	182	30.13	5- 1	6
S.R.Waugh	A	200	1282	5710	170	33.58	4-33	2
R.J.Hadlee	NZ	115	1030.2	3407	158	21.56	5-25	6
M.D.Marshall	WI	136	1195.5	4233	157	26.96	4-18	6
M.Prabhakar	I	129	1060	4534	157	28.88	5-33	6
J.Srinath	I	107	926.2	3991	148	26.96	5-24	4
J.Garner	WI	98	888.2	2752	146	18.84	5-31	5
Aqib Javed	P	133	1112.1	4667	146	31.96	7-37	3
I.T.Botham	E	116	1045.1	4139	145	28.54	4-31	3
M.A.Holding	WI	102	912.1	3034	142	21.36	5-26	6
E.J.Chatfield	NZ	114	1010.5	3618	140	25.84	5-34	4
A.Kumble	I	96	881.2	3544	133	26.64	6-12	6
Abdul Qadir	P	104	850	3453	132	26.15	5-44	6
C.L.Hooper	WI	141	937.4	4107	129	31.83	4-34	1
R.J.Shastri	I	150	1102.1	4650	129	36.04	5-15	3
Mushtaq Ahmed	P	106	904.5	3981	124	32.10	5-36	2
I.V.A.Richards	WI	187	940.4	4228	118	35.83	6-41	3
D.K.Morrison	NZ	92	730.2	3318	117	28.34	5-46	2
P.A.J.DeFreitas	E	101	935	3693	115	32.11	4-35	1
M.C.Snedden	NZ	93	754.1	3237	114	28.39	4-34	1
Mudassar Nazar	P	122	809.1	3432	111	30.91	5-28	2
I.R.Bishop	WI	75	653.1	2777	110	25.24	5-25	8
S.P.O'Donnell	A	87	725	3102	108	28.72	5-13	6
D.K.Lillee	A	63	598.5	2145	103	20.82	5-34	6
C.Pringle	NZ	64	552.2	2455	103	23.83	5-45	3
W.K.M.Benjamin	WI	85	740.2	3079	100	30.79	5-22	1
R.A.Harper	WI	105	862.3	3431	100	34.31	4-40	3

The highest aggregates for other ICC Full Members are:

A.A.Donald	SA	61	544.2	2195	89	24.66	5-29	3
S.T.Jayasuriya	SL	112	626.3	3004	85	35.34	6-29	3
J.R.Ratnayeke	SL	78	595.3	2866	85	33.71	4-23	1
E.A.Brandes	Z	30	249.1	1258	34	37.00	4-21	1
H.H.Streak	Z	29	254.1	1077	34	31.67	4-25	2

WICKET-KEEPING RECORDS

FIVE DISMISSALS IN AN INNINGS

5 (5 ct)	R.W.Marsh	Australia v England	Leeds	1981
5 (5 ct)	R.G.de Alwis	Sri Lanka v Australia	Colombo (PSS)	1982-83
5 (5 ct)	S.M.H.Kirmani	India v Zimbabwe	Leicester	1983
5 (3ct, 2st)	S.Viswanath	India v England	Sydney	1984-85
5 (3ct, 2st)	K.S.More	India v New Zealand	Sharjah	1987-88
5 (5 ct)	H.P.Tillekeratne	Sri Lanka v Pakistan	Sharjah	1990-91
5 (3ct, 2st)	N.R.Mongia	India v New Zealand	Auckland	1993-94
5 (3ct, 2st)	A.C.Parore	New Zealand v West Indies	Margao	1994-95
5 (5 ct)	D.J.Richardson	South Africa v Pakistan	Johannesburg	1994-95
5 (5 ct)	Moin Khan	Pakistan v Zimbabwe	Harare	1994-95
5 (4ct, 1st)	R.S.Kaluwitharana	Sri Lanka v Pakistan	Sharjah	1994-95

5 (5 ct)	D.J.Richardson	South Africa v Zimbabwe	Harare	1995-96
5 (5 ct)	A.Flower	Zimbabwe v South Africa	Harare	1995-96
5 (5 ct)	C.O.Browne	West Indies v Sri Lanka	Brisbane	1995-96
5 (4ct, 1st)	J.C.Adams	West Indies v Kenya	Poona	1995-96
5 (4ct, 1st)	Rashid Latif	Pakistan v New Zealand	Lahore	1995-96
5 (3ct, 2st)	N.R.Mongia	India v Pakistan	Toronto	1996

100 DISMISSALS IN A CAREER

		LOI	Ct	St	Dis
I.A.Healy	Australia	150	181	32	**213**
P.J.L.Dujon	West Indies	169	183	21	**204**
R.W.Marsh	Australia	92	120	4	**124**
D.J.Richardson	South Africa	82	108	13	**121**
Rashid Latif	Pakistan	84	81	22	**103**
Salim Yousuf	Pakistan	86	80	22	**102**

FIELDING RECORDS

FIVE CATCHES IN AN INNINGS

5	J.N.Rhodes	South Africa v West Indies	Bombay	1993-94

70 CATCHES IN A CAREER

		LOI	Ct
A.R.Border	Australia	273	**127**
I.V.A.Richards	West Indies	187	**101**
M.Azharuddin	India	224	**94**
R.S.Mahanama	Sri Lanka	148	**75**
R.B.Richardson	West Indies	224	**75**
Kapil Dev	India	224	**71**
S.R.Waugh	Australia	200	**70**

ALL-ROUND RECORDS

1000 RUNS AND 100 WICKETS

		LOI	Runs	Wkts
I.T.Botham	England	116	2113	145
R.J.Hadlee	New Zealand	115	1751	158
C.L.Hooper	West Indies	141	3270	129
Imran Khan	Pakistan	175	3709	182
Kapil Dev	India	224	3783	253
Mudassar Nazar	Pakistan	122	2653	111
S.P.O'Donnell	Australia	87	1242	108
M.Prabhakar	India	129	1855	157
I.V.A.Richards	West Indies	187	6721	118
R.J.Shastri	India	150	3108	129
Wasim Akram	Pakistan	206	1894	297
S.R.Waugh	Australia	200	4420	170

1000 RUNS AND 100 DISMISSALS

		LOI	Runs	Dis
P.J.L.Dujon	West Indies	169	1945	204
I.A.Healy	Australia	150	1592	213
R.W.Marsh	Australia	92	1225	124

TEST CRICKET RECORDS

To the end of the 1995-96 season (excluding West Indies v New Zealand)

TEAM RECORDS
HIGHEST INNINGS TOTALS

903-7d	England v Australia	The Oval	1938
849	England v West Indies	Kingston	1929-30
790-3d	West Indies v Pakistan	Kingston	1957-58
758-8d	Australia v West Indies	Kingston	1954-55
729-6d	Australia v England	Lord's	1930
708	Pakistan v England	The Oval	1987
701	Australia v England	The Oval	1934
699-5	Pakistan v India	Lahore	1989-90
695	Australia v England	The Oval	1930
692-8d	West Indies v England	The Oval	1995
687-8d	West Indies v England	The Oval	1976
681-8d	West Indies v England	Port-of-Spain	1953-54
676-7	India v Sri Lanka	Kanpur	1986-87
674-6	Pakistan v India	Faisalabad	1984-85
674	Australia v India	Adelaide	1947-48
671-4	New Zealand v Sri Lanka	Wellington	1990-91
668	Australia v West Indies	Bridgetown	1954-55
660-5d	West Indies v New Zealand	Wellington	1994-95
659-8d	Australia v England	Sydney	1946-47
658-8d	England v Australia	Nottingham	1938
657-8d	Pakistan v West Indies	Bridgetown	1957-58
656-8d	Australia v England	Manchester	1964
654-5	England v South Africa	Durban	1938-39
653-4d	England v India	Lord's	1990
653-4d	Australia v England	Leeds	1993
652-7d	England v India	Madras	1984-85
652-8d	West Indies v England	Lord's	1973
652	Pakistan v India	Faisalabad	1982-83
650-6d	Australia v West Indies	Bridgetown	1964-65

The highest innings for other countries are:

622-9d	South Africa v Australia	Durban	1969-70
547-8d	Sri Lanka v Australia	Colombo (SSC)	1992-93
544-4d	Zimbabwe v Pakistan	Harare	1994-95

LOWEST INNINGS TOTALS

26	New Zealand v England	Auckland	1954-55
30	South Africa v England	Port Elizabeth	1895-96
30	South Africa v England	Birmingham	1924
35	South Africa v England	Cape Town	1898-99
36	Australia v England	Birmingham	1902
36	South Africa v Australia	Melbourne	1931-32
42	Australia v England	Sydney	1887-88
42	New Zealand v Australia	Wellington	1945-46
42	India v England	Lord's	1974
43	South Africa v England	Cape Town	1888-89
44	Australia v England	The Oval	1896
45	England v Australia	Sydney	1886-87
45	South Africa v Australia	Melbourne	1931-32

46	England v West Indies	Port-of-Spain	1993-94
47	South Africa v England	Cape Town	1888-89
47	New Zealand v England	Lord's	1958

The lowest innings for other countries are:

53	West Indies v Pakistan	Faisalabad	1986-87
62	Pakistan v Australia	Perth	1981-82
71	Sri Lanka v Pakistan	Kandy	1994-95
134	Zimbabwe v Pakistan	Karachi	1993-94

BATTING RECORDS
HIGHEST INDIVIDUAL INNINGS

375	B.C.Lara	WI v E	St John's	1993-94
365*	G.St A.Sobers	WI v P	Kingston	1957-58
364	L.Hutton	E v A	The Oval	1938
337	Hanif Mohammad	P v WI	Bridgetown	1957-58
336*	W.R.Hammond	E v NZ	Auckland	1932-33
334	D.G.Bradman	A v E	Leeds	1930
333	G.A.Gooch	E v I	Lord's	1990
325	A.Sandham	E v WI	Kingston	1929-30
311	R.B.Simpson	A v E	Manchester	1964
310*	J.H.Edrich	E v NZ	Leeds	1965
307	R.M.Cowper	A v E	Melbourne	1965-66
304	D.G.Bradman	A v E	Leeds	1934
302	L.G.Rowe	WI v E	Bridgetown	1973-74
299*	D.G.Bradman	A v SA	Adelaide	1931-32
299	M.D.Crowe	NZ v SL	Wellington	1990-91
291	I.V.A.Richards	WI v E	The Oval	1976
287	R.E.Foster	E v A	Sydney	1903-04
285*	P.B.H.May	E v WI	Birmingham	1957
280*	Javed Miandad	P v I	Hyderabad	1982-83
278	D.C.S.Compton	E v P	Nottingham	1954
277	B.C.Lara	WI v A	Sydney	1992-93
274	R.G.Pollock	SA v A	Durban	1969-70
274	Zaheer Abbas	P v E	Birmingham	1971
271	Javed Miandad	P v NZ	Auckland	1988-89
270*	G.A.Headley	WI v E	Kingston	1934-35
270	D.G.Bradman	A v E	Melbourne	1936-37
268	G.N.Yallop	A v P	Melbourne	1983-84
267	P.A.de Silva	SL v NZ	Wellington	1990-91
266	W.H.Ponsford	A v E	The Oval	1934
266	D.L.Houghton	Z v SL	Bulawayo	1994-95
262*	D.L.Amiss	E v WI	Kingston	1973-74
261	F.M.M.Worrell	WI v E	Nottingham	1950
260	C.C.Hunte	WI v P	Kingston	1957-58
260	Javed Miandad	P v E	The Oval	1987
259	G.M.Turner	NZ v WI	Georgetown	1971-72
258	T.W.Graveney	E v WI	Nottingham	1957
258	S.M.Nurse	WI v NZ	Christchurch	1968-69
256	R.B.Kanhai	WI v I	Calcutta	1958-59
256	K.F.Barrington	E v A	Manchester	1964
255*	D.J.McGlew	SA v NZ	Wellington	1952-53
254	D.G.Bradman	A v E	Lord's	1930
251	W.R.Hammond	E v A	Sydney	1928-29
250	K.D.Walters	A v NZ	Christchurch	1976-77
250	S.F.A.F.Bacchus	WI v I	Kanpur	1978-79

The highest individual innings for India is:

| 236* | S.M.Gavaskar | I v WI | Madras | 1983-84 |

750 RUNS IN A SERIES

Runs			Series	M	I	NO	HS	Avge	100	50
974	D.G.Bradman	A v E	1930	5	7	–	334	139.14	4	–
905	W.R.Hammond	E v A	1928-29	5	9	1	251	113.12	4	–
839	M.A.Taylor	A v E	1989	6	11	1	219	83.90	2	5
834	R.N.Harvey	A v SA	1952-53	5	9	–	205	92.66	4	3
829	I.V.A.Richards	WI v E	1976	4	7	–	291	118.42	3	2
827	C.L.Walcott	WI v A	1954-55	5	10	–	155	82.70	5	2
824	G.St A.Sobers	WI v P	1957-58	5	8	2	365*	137.33	3	3
810	D.G.Bradman	A v E	1936-37	5	9	–	270	90.00	3	1
806	D.G.Bradman	A v SA	1931-32	5	5	1	299*	201.50	4	–
798	B.C.Lara	WI v E	1993-94	5	8	–	375	99.75	2	2
779	E.de C.Weekes	WI v I	1948-49	5	7	–	194	111.28	4	2
774	S.M.Gavaskar	I v WI	1970-71	4	8	3	220	154.80	4	3
765	B.C.Lara	WI v E	1995	6	10	1	179	85.00	3	3
761	Mudassar Nazar	P v I	1982-83	6	8	2	231	126.83	4	1
758	D.G.Bradman	A v E	1934	5	8	–	304	94.75	2	1
753	D.C.S.Compton	E v SA	1947	5	8	–	208	94.12	4	2
752	G.A.Gooch	E v I	1990	3	6	–	333	125.33	3	2

HIGHEST PARTNERSHIP FOR EACH WICKET

1st	413	V.Mankad/Pankaj Roy	I v NZ	Madras	1955-56
2nd	451	W.H.Ponsford/D.G.Bradman	A v E	The Oval	1934
3rd	467	A.H.Jones/M.D.Crowe	NZ v SL	Wellington	1990-91
4th	411	P.B.H.May/M.C.Cowdrey	E v WI	Birmingham	1957
5th	405	S.G.Barnes/D.G.Bradman	A v E	Sydney	1946-47
6th	346	J.H.W.Fingleton/D.G.Bradman	A v E	Melbourne	1936-37
7th	347	D.St E.Atkinson/C.C.Depeiza	WI v A	Bridgetown	1954-55
8th	246	L.E.G.Ames/G.O.B.Allen	E v NZ	Lord's	1931
9th	190	Asif Iqbal/Intikhab Alam	P v E	The Oval	1967
10th	151	B.F.Hastings/R.O.Collinge	NZ v P	Auckland	1972-73

WICKET PARTNERSHIPS OF OVER 350

467	3rd	A.H.Jones/M.D.Crowe	NZ v SL	Wellington	1990-91
451	2nd	W.H.Ponsford/D.G.Bradman	A v E	The Oval	1934
451	3rd	Mudassar Nazar/Javed Miandad	P v I	Hyderabad	1982-83
446	2nd	C.C.Hunte/G.St A.Sobers	WI v P	Kingston	1957-58
413	1st	V.Mankad/Pankaj Roy	I v NZ	Madras	1955-56
411	4th	P.B.H.May/M.C.Cowdrey	E v WI	Birmingham	1957
405	5th	S.G.Barnes/D.G.Bradman	A v E	Sydney	1946-47
399	4th	G.St A.Sobers/F.M.M.Worrell	WI v E	Bridgetown	1959-60
397	3rd	Qasim Omar/Javed Miandad	P v SL	Faisalabad	1985-86
388	4th	W.H.Ponsford/D.G.Bradman	A v E	Leeds	1934
387	1st	G.M.Turner/T.W.Jarvis	NZ v WI	Georgetown	1971-72
382	2nd	L.Hutton/M.Leyland	E v A	The Oval	1938
382	1st	W.M.Lawry/R.B.Simpson	A v WI	Bridgetown	1964-65
370	3rd	W.J.Edrich/D.C.S.Compton	E v SA	Lord's	1947
369	2nd	J.H.Edrich/K.F.Barrington	E v NZ	Leeds	1965
359	1st	L.Hutton/C.Washbrook	E v SA	Johannesburg	1948-49
351	2nd	G.A.Gooch/D.I.Gower	E v A	The Oval	1985
350	4th	Mushtaq Mohammad/Asif Iqbal	P v NZ	Dunedin	1972-73

4000 RUNS IN TESTS

Runs			M	I	NO	HS	Avge	100	50
11174	A.R.Border	A	156	265	44	205	50.56	27	63
10122	S.M.Gavaskar	I	125	214	16	236*	51.12	34	45
8900	G.A.Gooch	E	118	215	6	333	42.58	20	46
8832	Javed Miandad	P	124	189	21	280*	52.57	23	43
8540	I.V.A.Richards	WI	121	182	12	291	50.23	24	45
8231	D.I.Gower	E	117	204	18	215	44.25	18	39
8114	G.Boycott	E	108	193	23	246*	47.72	22	42
8032	G.St A.Sobers	WI	93	160	21	365*	57.78	26	30
7624	M.C.Cowdrey	E	114	188	15	182	44.06	22	38
7558	C.G.Greenidge	WI	108	185	16	226	44.72	19	34
7515	C.H.Lloyd	WI	110	175	14	242*	46.67	19	39
7487	D.L.Haynes	WI	116	202	25	184	42.49	18	39
7422	D.C.Boon	A	107	190	20	200	43.65	21	32
7249	W.R.Hammond	E	85	140	16	336*	58.45	22	24
7110	G.S.Chappell	A	87	151	19	247*	53.86	24	31
6996	D.G.Bradman	A	52	80	10	334	99.94	29	13
6971	L.Hutton	E	79	138	15	364	56.67	19	33
6868	D.B.Vengsarkar	I	116	185	22	166	42.13	17	35
6806	K.F.Barrington	E	82	131	15	256	58.67	20	35
6227	R.B.Kanhai	WI	79	137	6	256	47.53	15	28
6149	R.N.Harvey	A	79	137	10	205	48.41	21	24
6080	G.R.Viswanath	I	91	155	10	222	41.93	14	35
5949	R.B.Richardson	WI	86	146	12	194	44.39	16	27
5807	D.C.S.Compton	E	78	131	15	278	50.06	17	28
5502	M.A.Taylor	A	72	129	9	219	45.85	14	33
5444	M.D.Crowe	NZ	77	131	11	299	45.36	17	18
5410	J.B.Hobbs	E	61	102	7	211	56.94	15	28
5357	K.D.Walters	A	74	125	14	250	48.26	15	33
5345	I.M.Chappell	A	75	136	10	196	42.42	14	26
5334	J.G.Wright	NZ	82	148	7	185	37.82	12	23
5248	Kapil Dev	I	131	184	15	163	31.05	8	27
5234	W.M.Lawry	A	67	123	12	210	47.15	13	27
5200	I.T.Botham	E	102	161	6	208	33.54	14	22
5138	J.H.Edrich	E	77	127	9	310*	43.54	12	24
5101	Salim Malik	P	90	134	21	237	45.14	14	25
5062	Zaheer Abbas	P	78	124	11	274	44.79	12	20
5002	S.R.Waugh	A	81	125	26	200	50.52	11	28
4882	T.W.Graveney	E	79	123	13	258	44.38	11	20
4869	R.B.Simpson	A	62	111	7	311	46.81	10	27
4737	I.R.Redpath	A	66	120	11	171	43.45	8	31
4656	A.J.Lamb	E	79	139	10	142	36.09	14	18
4627	M.A.Atherton	E	62	114	3	185*	41.68	10	29
4555	H.Sutcliffe	E	54	84	9	194	60.73	16	23
4537	P.B.H.May	E	66	106	9	285*	46.77	13	22
4502	E.R.Dexter	E	62	102	8	205	47.89	9	27
4455	E.de C.Weekes	WI	48	81	5	207	58.61	15	19
4415	K.J.Hughes	A	70	124	6	213	37.41	9	22
4409	M.W.Gatting	E	79	138	14	207	35.55	10	21
4399	A.I.Kallicharran	WI	66	109	10	187	44.43	12	21
4389	A.P.E.Knott	E	95	149	15	135	32.75	5	30
4378	M.Amarnath	I	69	113	10	138	42.50	11	24
4362	M.Azharuddin	I	71	101	4	199	44.96	14	15
4334	R.C.Fredericks	WI	59	109	7	169	42.49	8	26
4236	R.A.Smith	E	62	112	15	175	43.67	9	28
4114	Mudassar Nazar	P	76	116	8	231	38.09	10	17

The highest aggregates for other countries are:

Runs			M	I	NO	HS	Avge	100	50
3471	B.Mitchell	SA	42	80	9	189*	48.88	8	21
3471	A.Ranatunga	SL	61	104	6	135*	35.41	4	23
1113	D.L.Houghton	Z	16	25	2	266	48.39	4	2

20 HUNDREDS IN A CAREER

			200s	Inns	E	A	SA	Opponents WI	NZ	I	P	SL	Z
34	S.M.Gavaskar	I	4	214	4	8	–	13	2	–	5	2	–
29	D.G.Bradman	A	12	80	19	–	4	2	–	4	–	–	–
27	A.R.Border	A	2	265	8	–	3	5	4	6	1	–	–
26	G.St A.Sobers	WI	2	160	10	4	–	–	1	8	3	–	–
24	G.S.Chappell	A	4	151	9	–	5	3	1	6	–	–	–
24	I.V.A.Richards	WI	3	182	8	5	–	–	1	8	2	–	–
23	Javed Miandad	P	6	189	2	6	–	2	7	5	–	1	–
22	W.R.Hammond	E	7	140	–	9	6	1	4	2	–	–	–
22	M.C.Cowdrey	E	–	188	–	5	3	6	2	3	3	–	–
22	G.Boycott	E	1	193	–	7	1	5	2	4	3	–	–
21	R.N.Harvey	A	2	137	6	–	8	3	–	4	–	–	–
21	D.C.Boon	A	1	190	7	–	3	3	6	1	1	–	–
20	K.F.Barrington	E	1	131	–	5	2	3	3	3	4	–	–
20	G.A.Gooch	E	2	215	–	4	5	4	5	4	5	1	1

The most hundreds for countries not included above is: South Africa – 9 in 62 innings by A.D.Nourse; New Zealand – 17 in 131 innings by M.D.Crowe; Sri Lanka – 8 in 93 innings by P.A.de Silva; Zimbabwe – 4 in 25 innings by D.L.Houghton. The most double hundreds by batsmen not qualifying for the above list is four by Zaheer Abbas (12 hundreds for Pakistan) and three by R.B.Simpson (12 hundreds for Australia).

BOWLING RECORDS

MOST WICKETS IN AN INNINGS

10- 53	J.C.Laker	E v A	Manchester	1956
9- 28	G.A.Lohmann	E v SA	Johannesburg	1895-96
9- 37	J.C.Laker	E v A	Manchester	1956
9- 52	R.J.Hadlee	NZ v A	Brisbane	1985-86
9- 56	Abdul Qadir	P v E	Lahore	1987-88
9- 57	D.E.Malcolm	E v SA	The Oval	1994
9- 69	J.M.Patel	I v A	Kanpur	1959-60
9- 83	Kapil Dev	I v WI	Ahmedabad	1983-84
9- 86	Sarfraz Nawaz	P v A	Melbourne	1978-79
9- 95	J.M.Noreiga	WI v I	Port-of-Spain	1970-71
9-102	S.P.Gupte	I v WI	Kanpur	1958-59
9-103	S.F.Barnes	E v SA	Johannesburg	1913-14
9-113	H.J.Tayfield	SA v E	Johannesburg	1956-57
9-121	A.A.Mailey	A v E	Melbourne	1920-21

The best innings analyses for other countries are:

8- 83	J.R.Ratnayeke	SL v P	Sialkot	1985-86
6- 90	H.H.Streak	Z v P	Harare	1994-95

15 WICKETS IN A TEST († *On debut*)

19- 90	J.C.Laker	E v A	Manchester	1956
17-159	S.F.Barnes	E v SA	Johannesburg	1913-14
16-136†	N.D.Hirwani	I v WI	Madras	1987-88
16-137†	R.A.L.Massie	A v E	Lord's	1972
15- 28	J.Briggs	E v SA	Cape Town	1888-89
15- 45	G.A.Lohmann	E v SA	Port Elizabeth	1895-96
15- 99	C.Blythe	E v SA	Leeds	1907
15-104	H.Verity	E v A	Lord's	1934
15-123	R.J.Hadlee	NZ v A	Brisbane	1985-86
15-124	W.Rhodes	E v A	Melbourne	1903-04

35 WICKETS IN A SERIES

Wkts			Series	M	Balls	Runs	Avge	5 wI	10 wM
49	S.F.Barnes	E v SA	1913-14	4	1356	536	10.93	7	3
46	J.C.Laker	E v A	1956	5	1703	442	9.60	4	2
44	C.V.Grimmett	A v SA	1935-36	5	2077	642	14.59	5	3
42	T.M.Alderman	A v E	1981	6	1950	893	21.26	4	—
41	R.M.Hogg	A v E	1978-79	5	1740	527	12.85	5	2
41	T.M.Alderman	A v E	1989	6	1616	712	17.36	6	1
40	Imran Khan	P v I	1982-83	6	1339	558	13.95	4	2
39	A.V.Bedser	E v A	1953	5	1591	682	17.48	5	1
39	D.K.Lillee	A v E	1981	6	1870	870	22.30	2	1
38	M.W.Tate	E v A	1924-25	5	2528	881	23.18	5	1
37	W.J.Whitty	A v SA	1910-11	5	1395	632	17.08	2	—
37	H.J.Tayfield	SA v E	1956-57	5	2280	636	17.18	4	1
36	A.E.E.Vogler	SA v E	1909-10	5	1349	783	21.75	4	1
36	A.A.Mailey	A v E	1920-21	5	1465	946	26.27	4	2
35	G.A.Lohmann	E v SA	1895-96	3	520	203	5.80	4	2
35	B.S.Chandrasekhar	I v E	1972-73	5	1747	662	18.91	4	—
35	M.D.Marshall	WI v E	1988	5	1219	443	12.65	3	1

200 WICKETS IN TESTS

Wkts			M	Balls	Runs	Avge	5 wI	10 wM
434	Kapil Dev	I	131	27740	12867	29.64	23	2
431	R.J.Hadlee	NZ	86	21918	9611	22.29	36	9
383	I.T.Botham	E	102	21815	10878	28.40	27	4
376	M.D.Marshall	WI	81	17584	7876	20.94	22	4
362	Imran Khan	P	88	19458	8258	22.81	23	6
355	D.K.Lillee	A	70	18467	8493	23.92	23	7
325	R.G.D.Willis	E	90	17357	8190	25.20	16	—
309	C.A.Walsh	WI	82	17578	7738	25.04	11	2
309	L.R.Gibbs	WI	79	27115	8989	29.09	18	2
307	F.S.Trueman	E	67	15178	6625	21.57	17	3
300	Wasim Akram	P	70	16034	6874	22.91	20	3
297	D.L.Underwood	E	86	21862	7674	25.83	17	6
291	C.J.McDermott	A	71	16586	8332	28.63	14	2
266	C.E.L.Ambrose	WI	61	14319	5658	21.27	14	3
266	B.S.Bedi	I	67	21364	7637	28.71	14	1
259	J.Garner	WI	58	13169	5433	20.97	7	—
252	J.B.Statham	E	70	16056	6261	24.84	9	1
249	M.A.Holding	WI	60	12680	5898	23.68	13	2
248	R.Benaud	A	63	19108	6704	27.03	16	1

Wkts			M	Balls	Runs	Avge	5 wI	10 wM
246	G.D.McKenzie	A	60	17681	7328	29.78	16	3
242	B.S.Chandrasekhar	I	58	15963	7199	29.74	16	2
236	A.V.Bedser	E	51	15918	5876	24.89	15	5
236	Abdul Qadir	P	67	17126	7742	32.80	15	5
235	G.St A.Sobers	WI	93	21599	7999	34.03	6	–
228	R.R.Lindwall	A	61	13650	5251	23.03	12	–
216	Waqar Younis	P	41	8483	4553	21.07	19	4
216	C.V.Grimmett	A	37	14513	5231	24.21	21	7
212	M.G.Hughes	A	53	12285	6017	28.38	7	1
207	S.K.Warne	A	44	13118	4870	23.52	10	3
202	A.M.E.Roberts	WI	47	11136	5174	25.61	11	2
202	J.A.Snow	E	49	12021	5387	26.66	8	1
200	J.R.Thomson	A	51	10535	5601	28.00	8	–

The highest aggregates for other countries are:

170	H.J.Tayfield	SA	37	13568	4405	25.91	14	2
81	M.Muralitharan	SL	23	6099	2745	33.88	5	–
58	H.H.Streak	Z	12	2986	1257	21.67	3	–

HAT-TRICKS

F.R.Spofforth	Australia v England	Melbourne	1878-79
W.Bates	England v Australia	Melbourne	1882-83
J.Briggs	England v Australia	Sydney	1891-92
G.A.Lohmann	England v South Africa	Port Elizabeth	1895-96
J.T.Hearne	England v Australia	Leeds	1899
H.Trumble	Australia v England	Melbourne	1901-02
H.Trumble	Australia v England	Melbourne	1903-04
T.J.Matthews (2)**	Australia v South Africa	Manchester	1912
M.J.C.Allom*†	England v New Zealand	Christchurch	1929-30
T.W.J.Goddard	England v South Africa	Johannesburg	1938-39
P.J.Loader	England v West Indies	Leeds	1957
L.F.Kline	Australia v South Africa	Cape Town	1957-58
W.W.Hall	West Indies v Pakistan	Lahore	1958-59
G.M.Griffin	South Africa v England	Lord's	1960
L.R.Gibbs	West Indies v Australia	Adelaide	1960-61
P.J.Petherick*	New Zealand v Pakistan	Lahore	1976-77
C.A.Walsh‡	West Indies v Australia	Brisbane	1988-89
M.G.Hughes‡	Australia v West Indies	Perth	1988-89
D.W.Fleming*	Australia v Pakistan	Rawalpindi	1994-95
S.K.Warne	Australia v England	Melbourne	1994-95
D.G.Cork	England v West Indies	Manchester	1995

*On debut. ** Hat-trick in each innings. † Four wickets in five balls. ‡ Involving both innings.*

WICKET-KEEPING RECORDS

SIX DISMISSALS IN AN INNINGS

7	Wasim Bari	Pakistan v New Zealand	Auckland	1978-79
7	R.W.Taylor	England v India	Bombay	1979-80
7	I.D.S.Smith	New Zealand v Sri Lanka	Hamilton	1990-91
6	A.T.W.Grout	Australia v South Africa	Johannesburg	1957-58
6	D.T.Lindsay	South Africa v Australia	Johannesburg	1966-67
6	J.T.Murray	England v India	Lord's	1967
6†	S.M.H.Kirmani	India v New Zealand	Christchurch	1975-76
6	R.W.Marsh	Australia v England	Brisbane	1982-83
6	S.A.R.Silva	Sri Lanka v India	Colombo (SSC)	1985-86
6	R.C.Russell	England v Australia	Melbourne	1990-91
6	R.C.Russell	England v South Africa	Johannesburg	1995-96

†Including one stumping.

FIVE STUMPINGS IN AN INNINGS

5	K.S.More	India v West Indies	Madras	1987-88

NINE DISMISSALS IN A TEST

11	R.C.Russell	England v South Africa	Johannesburg	1995-96
10	R.W.Taylor	England v India	Bombay	1979-80
9†	G.R.A.Langley	Australia v England	Lord's	1956
9	D.A.Murray	West Indies v Australia	Melbourne	1981-82
9	R.W.Marsh	Australia v England	Brisbane	1982-83
9	S.A.R.Silva	Sri Lanka v India	Colombo (SSC)	1985-86
9†	S.A.R.Silva	Sri Lanka v India	Colombo (PSS)	1985-86
9	D.J.Richardson	South Africa v India	Port Elizabeth	1992-93
9	Rashid Latif	Pakistan v New Zealand	Auckland	1993-94
9	I.A.Healy	Australia v England	Brisbane	1994-85
9	C.O.Browne	West Indies v England	Nottingham	1995
9††R.C.Russell		England v South Africa	Port Elizabeth	1995-96

† Including one stumping. †† Including two stumpings.

25 DISMISSALS IN A SERIES

28	R.W.Marsh	Australia v England	1982-83
27 (inc 2st)	R.C.Russell	England v South Africa	1995-96
26 (inc 3st)	J.H.B.Waite	South Africa v New Zealand	1961-62
26	R.W.Marsh	Australia v West Indies (6 Tests)	1975-76
26 (inc 5st)	I.A.Healy	Australia v England (6 Tests)	1993
25 (inc 2st)	I.A.Healy	Australia v England	1994-95

100 DISMISSALS IN TESTS

Dis			Tests	Ct	St
355	R.W.Marsh	Australia	96	343	12
275	I.A.Healy	Australia	79	255	20
272†	P.J.L.Dujon	West Indies	81	267	5
269	A.P.E.Knott	England	95	250	19
228	Wasim Bari	Pakistan	81	201	27
219	T.G.Evans	England	91	173	46
198	S.M.H.Kirmani	India	88	160	38
189	D.L.Murray	West Indies	62	181	8
187	A.T.W.Grout	Australia	51	163	24
176	I.D.S.Smith	New Zealand	63	168	8
174	R.W.Taylor	England	57	167	7
152	R.C.Russell	England	49	141	11
141	J.H.B.Waite	South Africa	50	124	17
130	K.S.More	India	49	110	20
130	W.A.S.Oldfield	Australia	54	78	52
114†	J.M.Parks	England	46	103	11
107	D.J.Richardson	South Africa	28	107	–
104	Salim Yousuf	Pakistan	32	91	13

The most dismissals for other countries are:

41††	A.Flower	Zimbabwe	16	39	2
34	S.A.R.Silva	Sri Lanka	9	33	1

† Including two catches taken in the field.   †† Including five catches taken in the field.

FIELDING RECORDS
FIVE CATCHES IN AN INNINGS

5	V.Y.Richardson	Australia v South Africa	Durban	1935-36
5	Yajurvindra Singh	India v England	Bangalore	1976-77
5	M.Azharuddin	India v Pakistan	Karachi	1989-90
5	K.Srikkanth	India v Australia	Perth	1991-92

SEVEN CATCHES IN A TEST

7	G.S.Chappell	Australia v England	Perth	1974-75
7	Yajurvindra Singh	India v England	Bangalore	1976-77
7	H.P.Tillekeratne	Sri Lanka v New Zealand	Colombo (SSC)	1992-93

15 CATCHES IN A SERIES

15	J.M.Gregory	Australia v England	1920-21

100 CATCHES IN TESTS

Total			Tests
156	A.R.Border	Australia	156
122	G.S.Chappell	Australia	87
122	I.V.A.Richards	West Indies	121
120	I.T.Botham	England	102
120	M.C.Cowdrey	England	114
110	R.B.Simpson	Australia	62
110	W.R.Hammond	England	85
109	G.St A.Sobers	West Indies	93
108	S.M.Gavaskar	India	125
105	M.A.Taylor	Australia	72
105	I.M.Chappell	Australia	75
103	G.A.Gooch	England	118

APPEARANCE RECORDS

MOST TEST APPEARANCES FOR EACH COUNTRY

			Opponents								
			E	A	SA	WI	NZ	I	P	SL	Z
England	118	G.A.Gooch	–	42	3	26	15	19	10	3	–
Australia	156	A.R.Border	47	–	6	31	23	20	22	7	–
South Africa	50	J.H.B.Waite	21	14	–	–	15	–	–	–	–
West Indies	121	I.V.A.Richards	36	34	–	–	7	28	16	–	–
New Zealand	86	R.J.Hadlee	21	23	–	10	–	14	12	6	–
India	131	Kapil Dev	27	20	4	25	10	–	29	14	2
Pakistan	124	Javed Miandad	22	25	–	16	18	28	–	12	3
Sri Lanka	61	A.Ranatunga	4	9	3	1	11	14	16	–	3

The **most appearances for Zimbabwe** is 16 by A.D.R.Campbell, A.Flower, G.W.Flower and D.L.Houghton.

100 CONSECUTIVE TEST APPEARANCES

153	A.R.Border	Australia	March 1979 to March 1994
106	S.M.Gavaskar	India	January 1975 to February 1987

100 MATCHES BETWEEN APPEARANCES

104	Younis Ahmed	Pakistan	November 1969 to February 1987
103	D.Shackleton	England	November 1951 to June 1963

The longest interval between appearances is 22 years 222 days (March 1970 to October 1992) by A.J.Traicos of South Africa and Zimbabwe.

75 TESTS AS CAPTAIN

93	A.R.Border	Australia	December 1984 to March 1994

50 UMPIRING APPEARANCES

66	H.D.Bird	July 1973 to June 1996

SUMMARY OF ALL TEST MATCHES

To 26 August 1996

	Opponents	Tests	E	A	SA	WI	NZ	I	P	SL	Z	Tied	Drawn
						Won by							
England	Australia	285	90	111	–	–	–	–	–	–	–	–	84
	South Africa	110	47	–	20	–	–	–	–	–	–	–	43
	West Indies	115	27	–	–	48	–	–	–	–	–	–	40
	New Zealand	75	34	–	–	–	4	–	–	–	–	–	37
	India	84	32	–	–	–	–	14	–	–	–	–	38
	Pakistan	55	14	–	–	–	–	–	9	–	–	–	32
	Sri Lanka	5	3	–	–	–	–	–	–	1	–	–	1
Australia	South Africa	59	–	31	13	–	–	–	–	–	–	–	15
	West Indies	81	–	32	–	27	–	–	–	–	–	1	21
	New Zealand	32	–	13	–	–	7	–	–	–	–	–	12
	India	50	–	24	–	–	–	8	–	–	–	1	17
	Pakistan	40	–	14	–	–	–	–	11	–	–	–	15
	Sri Lanka	10	–	7	–	–	–	–	–	0	–	–	3
South Africa	West Indies	1	–	–	0	1	–	–	–	–	–	–	–
	New Zealand	21	–	–	12	–	3	–	–	–	–	–	6
	India	4	–	–	1	–	–	0	–	–	–	–	3
	Pakistan	1	–	–	1	–	–	–	0	–	–	–	–
	Sri Lanka	3	–	–	1	–	–	–	–	0	–	–	2
	Zimbabwe	1	–	–	1	–	–	–	–	–	0	–	–
West Indies	New Zealand	28	–	–	–	10	4	–	–	–	–	–	14
	India	65	–	–	–	27	–	7	–	–	–	–	31
	Pakistan	31	–	–	–	12	–	–	7	–	–	–	12
	Sri Lanka	1	–	–	–	0	–	–	–	0	–	–	1
New Zealand	India	35	–	–	–	–	6	13	–	–	–	–	16
	Pakistan	37	–	–	–	–	4	–	17	–	–	–	16
	Sri Lanka	13	–	–	–	–	4	–	–	2	–	–	7
	Zimbabwe	4	–	–	–	–	1	–	–	–	0	–	3
India	Pakistan	44	–	–	–	–	–	4	7	–	–	–	33
	Sri Lanka	14	–	–	–	–	–	7	–	1	–	–	6
	Zimbabwe	2	–	–	–	–	–	1	–	–	0	–	1
Pakistan	Sri Lanka	17	–	–	–	–	–	–	9	3	–	–	5
	Zimbabwe	6	–	–	–	–	–	–	4	–	1	–	1
Sri Lanka	Zimbabwe	3	–	–	–	–	–	–	–	0	0	–	3
		1332	247	232	49	125	33	54	64	7	1	2	518

	Tests	Won	Lost	Drawn	Tied	Toss Won
England	729	247	207	275	–	359
Australia	557	232	156	167	2	277
South Africa	200	49	82	69	–	96
West Indies	322	125	77	119	1	168
New Zealand	245	33	101	111	–	125
India	298	54	98	145	1	151
Pakistan	231	64	53	114	–	115
Sri Lanka	66	7	31	28	–	33
Zimbabwe	16	1	7	8	–	8

AUSTRALIA v SRI LANKA (1st Test)

At W.A.C.A.Ground, Perth on 8, 9, 10, 11 December 1995.
Toss: Sri Lanka. Result: AUSTRALIA won by an innings and 36 runs.
Debuts: Australia – S.G.Law, R.T.Ponting.

SRI LANKA

R.S.Mahanama	c Warne b McDermott	15	b McGrath	48
U.C.Hathurusinghe	c Law b McGrath	14	c Healy b McGrath	11
A.P.Gurusinha	b McGrath	46	c Healy b McDermott	7
P.A.de Silva	c and b Warne	10	c Ponting b Warne	20
*A.Ranatunga	c Healy b McGrath	32	b McGrath	46
H.P.Tillekeratne	lbw b McDermott	6	c Ponting b Warne	119
†R.S.Kaluwitharana	c Taylor b Warne	50	c Ponting b Julian	40
H.D.P.K.Dharmasena	b McDermott	30	lbw b McDermott	18
W.P.U.C.J.Vaas	c Healy b Warne	4	c Healy b Warne	4
G.P.Wickremasinghe	c Julian b McGrath	28	c Warne b McDermott	0
M.Muralitharan	not out	0	not out	3
Extras	(B 4, LB 9, NB 3)	16	(LB 4, NB 10)	14
Total		**251**		**330**

AUSTRALIA

M.J.Slater	c and b Muralitharan	219
*M.A.Taylor	lbw b De Silva	96
D.C.Boon	c Hathurusinghe b Muralitharan	13
M.E.Waugh	c Kaluwitharana b Vaas	111
R.T.Ponting	lbw b Vaas	96
S.G.Law	not out	54
†I.A.Healy		
B.P.Julian		
S.K.Warne		
C.J.McDermott		
G.D.McGrath		
Extras	(B 4, LB 6, NB 18)	28
Total (5 wickets declared)		**617**

AUSTRALIA	O	M	R	W	O	M	R	W	FALL OF WICKETS			
McDermott	18.4	5	44	3	(2) 20	3	73	3		SL	A	SL
McGrath	24	3	81	4	(1) 24	7	86	3	Wkt	1st	1st	2nd
Julian	17	8	32	0	(4) 13	4	40	1	1st	25	228	35
Warne	27	7	75	3	(3) 29.4	6	96	3	2nd	38	266	56
Waugh	3	1	6	0	4	0	22	0	3rd	54	422	87
Law					3	1	9	0	4th	129	496	105
									5th	132	617	193
SRI LANKA									6th	172	–	258
Wickremasinghe	31	3	123	0					7th	193	–	310
Vaas	31	5	103	2					8th	205	–	318
Muralitharan	54	3	224	2					9th	251	–	319
Hathurusinghe	9	3	31	0					10th	251	–	330
Dharmasena	31	5	84	0								
De Silva	18	1	42	1								

Umpires: Khizer Hayat (*Pakistan*) (33) and P.D.Parker (3).
Referee: G.T.Dowling (*New Zealand*) (1). Test No. 1320/8 (A 555/SL 64)

AUSTRALIA v SRI LANKA (2nd Test)

At Melbourne Cricket Ground on 26, 27, 28, 29, 30 December 1995.
Toss: Sri Lanka. Result: AUSTRALIA won by 10 wickets.
Debuts: Sri Lanka – K.J.Silva.

AUSTRALIA

M.J.Slater c Wickremasinghe b Vaas		62	(2) not out	13
*M.A.Taylor b Wickremasinghe		7	(1) not out	25
D.C.Boon c Muralitharan b Wickremasinghe		110		
M.E.Waugh b Muralitharan		61		
S.R.Waugh not out		131		
R.T.Ponting c Gurusinha b De Silva		71		
†I.A.Healy c Muralitharan b De Silva		41		
P.R.Reiffel not out		4		
S.K.Warne				
C.J.McDermott				
G.D.McGrath				
Extras (LB 8, W 2, NB 3)		13	(LB 1, NB 2)	3
Total (6 wickets declared)		**500**	(0 wickets)	**41**

SRI LANKA

R.S.Mahanama c Taylor b McGrath	3	c Warne b Reiffel	3
U.C.Hathurusinghe lbw b McGrath	23	lbw b Warne	39
A.P.Gurusinha c Healy b Ponting	27	lbw b Reiffel	143
P.A.de Silva c Reiffel b McGrath	18	c Healy b McDermott	28
*A.Ranatunga c Warne b McDermott	51	(7) not out	11
H.P.Tillekeratne c Taylor b Warne	14	c Ponting b M.E.Waugh	38
†R.S.Kaluwitharana c Boon b McDermott	50	(5) st Healy b Warne	2
W.P.U.C.J.Vaas c Healy b Reiffel	0	c Boon b McGrath	6
G.P.Wickremasinghe c Healy b McGrath	10	st Healy b Warne	17
M.Muralitharan c Slater b McGrath	11	c Taylor b Warne	0
K.J.Silva not out	6	b McGrath	0
Extras (B 6, LB 7, NB 7)	20	(B 7, LB 5, NB 8)	20
Total	**233**		**307**

SRI LANKA	O	M	R	W		O	M	R	W		FALL OF WICKETS			
											A	SL	SL	A
Wickremasinghe	30.2	9	77	2							*Wkt*	*1st*	*1st*	*2nd*	*2nd*
Vaas	40.4	11	93	1	(1)	3	0	25	0		1st	14	3	11	–
Hathurusinghe	9	0	23	0							2nd	116	64	97	–
Gurusinha	2	0	8	0	(2)	3	1	6	0		3rd	219	68	193	–
Muralitharan	38	7	124	1							4th	280	128	172	–
Silva	35	5	120	1							5th	395	140	255	–
De Silva	10	0	47	1	(3)	1	0	4	0		6th	488	182	273	–
Tillekeratne					(4)	0.4	0	5	0		7th	–	183	285	–
											8th	–	213	306	–
AUSTRALIA											9th	–	221	306	–
McDermott	23	8	63	2	(2)	17	1	54	1		10th	–	233	307	–
McGrath	23.4	9	40	5	(1)	33.5	6	92	2						
Reiffel	20	5	60	1		20	7	59	2						
Ponting	4	2	8	1											
Warne	18	5	49	1	(4)	37	10	71	4						
M.E.Waugh					(5)	9	1	19	1						

Umpires: R.S.Dunne (*New Zealand*) (19) and D.B.Hair (14).
Referee: G.T.Dowling (*New Zealand*) (2).   Test No. 1321/9 (A 556/SL 65)

AUSTRALIA v SRI LANKA (3rd Test)

At Adelaide Oval on 25, 26, 27, 28, 29 January 1996.
Toss: Australia. Result: AUSTRALIA won by 148 runs.
Debuts: None.

AUSTRALIA

*M.A.Taylor	c Kaluwitharana b Vaas	21	(2) b Pushpakumara	10
M.J.Slater	c Kaluwitharana b Vaas	0	(1) b Wickremasinghe	15
D.C.Boon	b Pushpakumara	43	c Kaluwitharana b Vaas	35
M.E.Waugh	c Pushpakumara b Wickremasinghe	71	c Tillekeratne b Vaas	12
S.R.Waugh	b Pushpakumara	170	not out	61
R.T.Ponting	c Kaluwitharana b Vaas	6	c Kaluwitharana b Vaas	20
†I.A.Healy	c Pushpakumara b Dharmasena	70	c Hathurusinghe b Pushpakumara	43
P.R.Reiffel	c Gurusinha b Wickremasinghe	56	not out	14
S.K.Warne	c Pushpakumara b Wickremasinghe	33		
C.J.McDermott	not out	15		
G.D.McGrath				
Extras	(B 5, LB 9, W 1, NB 2)	17	(B 1, LB 1, NB 3)	5
Total	(9 wickets declared)	**502**	(6 wickets declared)	**215**

SRI LANKA

U.C.Hathurusinghe	c M.E.Waugh b Reiffel	28	(2) c Healy b McGrath	14
S.T.Jayasuriya	b Reiffel	48	(1) c Healy b S.R.Waugh	112
A.P.Gurusinha	c Reiffel b McGrath	17	b Reiffel	2
S.Ranatunga	c S.R.Waugh b McDermott	60	c Healy b S.R.Waugh	65
†R.S.Kaluwitharana	lbw b Reiffel	31	b S.R.Waugh	0
H.P.Tillekeratne	c Healy b McGrath	65	c Healy b McGrath	3
*P.A.de Silva	c Taylor b McGrath	19	c Taylor b M.E.Waugh	3
H.D.P.K.Dharmasena	c Healy b McGrath	0	c Taylor b S.R.Waugh	2
W.P.U.C.J.Vaas	c M.E.Waugh b Reiffel	8	c Healy b McGrath	26
G.P.Wickremasinghe	b Reiffel	10	b Warne	6
K.R.Pushpakumara	not out	2	not out	3
Extras	(B 8, LB 13, W 1, NB 7)	29	(B 1, LB 6, NB 9)	16
Total		**317**		**252**

SRI LANKA	O	M	R	W		O	M	R	W	FALL OF WICKETS				
Vaas	42	11	106	3		21	6	44	2		A	SL	A	SL
Pushpakumara	34	4	126	2		17	2	63	2	*Wkt*	*1st*	*1st*	*2nd*	*2nd*
Wickremasinghe	39.3	7	120	3		13	1	39	1	1st	1	86	22	51
Hathurusinghe	4	0	15	0						2nd	36	89	36	70
Dharmasena	25	3	80	1	(4)	22	1	67	0	3rd	96	129	70	195
Jayasuriya	13	2	41	0						4th	181	171	75	195
AUSTRALIA										5th	196	237	122	199
McDermott	20	5	81	1	(5)	9	3	20	0	6th	326	290	186	208
McGrath	27	4	91	4	(1)	22.2	6	48	3	7th	443	290	—	216
Warne	26	4	74	0	(4)	27	11	68	1	8th	467	299	—	225
Reiffel	19.1	4	39	5	(2)	15	0	60	1	9th	502	309	—	232
M.E.Waugh	5	2	11	0	(6)	4	1	15	1	10th	—	317	—	252
S.R.Waugh					(3)	19	8	34	4					

Umpires: L.H.Barker (*West Indies*) (22) and S.G.Randell (25).
Referee: G.T.Dowling (*New Zealand*) (3).   Test No. 1322/10 (A 557/SL 66)

AUSTRALIA v SRI LANKA 1995-96

AUSTRALIA – BATTING AND FIELDING

	M	I	NO	HS	Runs	Avge	100	50	Ct/St
S.R.Waugh	2	3	2	170	362	362.00	2	1	1
M.J.Slater	3	5	1	219	309	77.25	1	1	1
P.R.Reiffel	2	3	2	56	74	74.00	–	1	2
M.E.Waugh	3	4	–	111	255	63.75	1	2	2
I.A.Healy	3	3	–	70	154	51.33	–	1	17/2
D.C.Boon	3	4	–	110	201	50.25	1	–	2
R.T.Ponting	3	4	–	96	193	48.25	–	2	4
M.A.Taylor	3	5	1	96	159	39.75	–	1	7
S.K.Warne	3	1	–	33	33	33.00	–	–	5
C.J.McDermott	3	1	1	15*	15	–	–	–	–
G.D.McGrath	3	–							

Played in one Test: B.P.Julian (1 ct) did not bat; S.G.Law 54* (1 ct).

AUSTRALIA – BOWLING

	O	M	R	W	Avge	Best	5wI	10wM
S.R.Waugh	19	8	34	4	8.50	4-34	–	–
G.D.McGrath	154.5	35	438	21	20.85	5-40	1	–
P.R.Reiffel	74.1	16	218	9	24.22	5-39	1	–
C.J.McDermott	107.4	25	335	10	33.50	3-44	–	–
S.K.Warne	164.4	43	433	12	36.08	4-71	–	–

Also bowled: B.P.Julian 30-12-72-1; S.G.Law 3-1-9-0; R.T.Ponting 4-2-8-1; M.E.Waugh 25-5-73-2.

SRI LANKA – BATTING AND FIELDING

	M	I	NO	HS	Runs	Avge	100	50	Ct/St
A.Ranatunga	2	4	1	51	140	46.66	–	1	–
H.P.Tillekeratne	3	6	–	119	245	40.83	1	1	1
A.P.Gurusinha	3	6	–	143	242	40.33	1	–	2
R.S.Kaluwitharana	3	6	–	50	173	28.83	–	2	6
U.C.Hathurusinghe	3	6	–	39	129	21.50	–	–	2
R.S.Mahanama	2	4	–	48	69	17.25	–	–	–
P.A.de Silva	3	6	–	28	98	16.33	–	–	–
H.D.P.K.Dharmasena	2	4	–	30	50	12.50	–	–	–
G.P.Wickremasinghe	3	6	–	28	71	11.83	–	–	1
W.P.U.C.J.Vaas	3	6	–	26	48	8.00	–	–	–
M.Muralitharan	2	4	2	11	14	7.00	–	–	3

Played in one Test: S.T.Jayasuriya 48, 112; K.R.Pushpakumara 2*, 3* (3 ct); S.Ranatunga 60, 65; K.J.Silva 6*, 0.

SRI LANKA – BOWLING

	O	M	R	W	Avge	Best	5wI	10wM
W.P.U.C.J.Vaas	137.4	33	371	9	41.22	3- 44	–	–
K.R.Pushpakumara	51	6	189	4	47.25	2- 63	–	–
G.P.Wickremasinghe	113.5	20	359	6	59.83	3-120	–	–
M.Muralitharan	92	10	348	3	116.00	2-224	–	–

Also bowled: P.A.de Silva 29-1-93-2; H.D.P.K.Dharmasena 78-9-231-1; A.P.Gurusinha 5-1-14-0; U.C.Hathurusinghe 22-3-69-0; S.T.Jayasuriya 13-2-41-0; K.J.Silva 35-5-120-1; H.P.Tillekeratne 0.4-0-5-0.

NEW ZEALAND v ZIMBABWE (1st Test)

At Trust Bank Park, Hamilton on 13, 14, 15, 16, 17 January 1996.
Toss: Zimbabwe. Result: MATCH DRAWN.
Debuts: New Zealand – N.J.Astle, G.I.Allott, R.G.Kennedy, G.R.Loveridge.

NEW ZEALAND

C.M.Spearman c A.Flower b Streak	0	lbw b Streak		27
R.G.Twose b Brandes	42	run out		8
S.P.Fleming run out	49	c A.Flower b P.A.Strang		21
A.C.Parore c A.Flower b Streak	16	not out		84
N.J.Astle lbw b Streak	18	c Olonga b B.C.Strang		32
C.L.Cairns c A.Flower b Streak	7	c Olonga b Brandes		7
*†L.K.Germon c Carlisle b Olonga	24	not out		22
D.N.Patel c Olonga b P.A.Strang	31			
G.R.Loveridge retired hurt	4			
R.J.Kennedy not out	2			
G.I.Allott not out	0			
Extras (B 4, LB 11, W 1, NB 21)	37	(B 4, LB 7, W 4, NB 6)		21
Total (8 wickets declared)	**230**	(5 wickets declared)		**222**

ZIMBABWE

G.W.Flower b Cairns	5	c Germon b Cairns		59
S.V.Carlisle c Germon b Cairns	4	c Fleming b Patel		19
A.D.R.Campbell c Astle b Allott	5	(6) c Germon b Patel		3
D.L.Houghton b Cairns	31	lbw b Twose		31
*†A.Flower c Spearman b Kennedy	6	not out		58
G.J.Whittall c Germon b Kennedy	54	(3) c Kennedy b Twose		20
H.H.Streak c Spearman b Cairns	24	lbw b Cairns		6
P.A.Strang b Patel	49	not out		0
H.K.Olonga c Germon b Kennedy	0			
E.A.Brandes not out	3			
B.C.Strang c Astle b Patel	4			
Extras (LB 3, W 2, NB 6)	11	(LB 4, W 1, NB 7)		12
Total	**196**	(6 wickets)		**208**

ZIMBABWE	O	M	R	W		O	M	R	W	FALL OF WICKETS			
										NZ	Z	NZ	Z
Streak	25	7	52	4		22	4	56	1	*1st*	*1st*	*2nd*	*2nd*
B.C.Strang	24	11	51	0	(3)	5	1	19	1	*Wkt*			
Olonga	14	2	65	1	(6)	3	1	20	0	1st	0	8	36	56
Brandes	15	3	46	1	(2)	18	4	52	1	2nd	67	13	63	99
P.A.Strang	2	1	1	1	(4)	24	4	57	1	3rd	115	21	64	125
G.W.Flower					(5)	3	1	9	0	4th	143	41	121	143
										5th	160	56	140	151
NEW ZEALAND										6th	164	98	–	177
Cairns	24	7	56	4		15	4	43	2	7th	216	189		
Allott	17	5	51	1		7	0	49	0	8th	226	189	–	–
Kennedy	12	4	28	3		5	0	19	0	9th	–	191	–	–
Twose	5	1	14	0	(5)	13	0	36	2	10th	–	196	–	–
Patel	16.5	4	44	2	(4)	21	6	57	2					

Umpires: L.H.Barker (*West Indies*) (23) and D.M.Quested (2).
Referee: Nasim-ul-Ghani (*Pakistan*) (1).   Test No. 1323/3 (NZ 242/Z 15)

NEW ZEALAND v ZIMBABWE (2nd Test)

At Eden Park, Auckland on 20, 21, 22, 23, 24 January 1996.
Toss: New Zealand. Result: MATCH DRAWN.
Debuts: None.

NEW ZEALAND

C.M.Spearman c G.W.Flower b B.C.Strang	42	c Carlisle b Streak	112
R.G.Twose c A.Flower b Brandes	18	c and b Streak	94
S.P.Fleming c Carlisle b Whittall	84	c Wishart b Streak	3
A.C.Parore c A.Flower b B.C.Strang	0	not out	76
N.J.Astle c and b Brandes	14	c A.Flower b Brandes	13
C.L.Cairns c and b P.A.Strang	57	b Streak	120
*†L.K.Germon c A.Flower b Streak	25	not out	1
D.N.Patel not out	7		
G.R.Larsen lbw b Streak	0		
R.J.Kennedy c Campbell b Streak	0		
G.I.Allott c and b B.C.Strang	0		
Extras (LB 3, NB 1)	4	(B 6, LB 15, NB 1)	22
Total	**251**	(5 wickets declared)	**441**

ZIMBABWE

G.W.Flower lbw b Allott	5	c Kennedy b Patel	71
S.V.Carlisle c Astle b Kennedy	12	c Fleming b Kennedy	58
G.J.Whittall c Germon b Cairns	27	c Germon b Patel	10
D.L.Houghton retired hurt	104		
*†A.Flower lbw b Allott	35	(4) not out	45
A.D.R.Campbell lbw b Allott	17	(5) c Germon b Twose	34
C.B.Wishart b Larsen	7	(6) not out	12
H.H.Streak b Cairns	2		
P.A.Strang c Parore b Patel	44		
E.A.Brandes c Astle b Patel	39		
B.C.Strang not out	14		
Extras (B 1, LB 11, W 2, NB 6)	20	(LB 6, W 2, NB 8)	16
Total	**326**	(4 wickets)	**246**

ZIMBABWE	O	M	R	W		O	M	R	W		FALL OF WICKETS			
												NZ	Z	NZ	Z
Streak	22	9	50	3		30	7	110	4	*Wkt*	*1st*	*1st*	*2nd*	*2nd*
Brandes	18	3	69	2		13	3	41	1	1st	5	214	120	
B.C.Strang	31.3	8	64	3		27	8	64	0	2nd	78	38	217	144
P.A.Strang	12	2	29	1	(5)	43	7	142	0	3rd	86	50	221	145
Whittall	12	4	36	1	(4)	13	4	40	0	4th	117	138	261	225
Campbell						2	0	3	0	5th	216	196	427	–
G.W.Flower						5	0	20	0	6th	232	217		
										7th	244	222		
NEW ZEALAND										8th	246	310		
Cairns	31	12	92	2	(2)	23	6	49	0	9th	246	326		
Allott	23	7	56	3	(1)	19	3	53	0	10th	251			
Kennedy	20	3	73	1		22	3	61	1					
Larsen	21	8	30	1	(5)	5	3	8	0					
Patel	12	0	60	2	(4)	27	6	60	2					
Astle	3	1	3	0	(7)	1	0	4	0					
Twose					(6)	3	1	5	1					

Umpires: D.B.Cowie (2) and Mahboob Shah (*Pakistan*). (26).
Referee: Nasim-ul-Ghani (*Pakistan*) (2).   Test No. 1324/4 (NZ 243/Z 16)

NEW ZEALAND v ZIMBABWE 1995-96

NEW ZEALAND – BATTING AND FIELDING

	M	I	NO	HS	Runs	Avge	100	50	Ct/St
A.C.Parore	2	4	2	84*	176	88.00	–	2	1
C.L.Cairns	2	4	–	120	191	47.75	1	1	–
C.J.Spearman	2	4	–	112	181	45.25	1	–	2
R.G.Twose	2	4	–	94	162	40.50	–	1	–
S.P.Fleming	2	4	–	84	157	39.25	–	1	2
D.N.Patel	2	2	1	31	38	38.00	–	–	–
L.K.Germon	2	4	2	25	72	36.00	–	–	8
N.J.Astle	2	4	–	32	77	19.25	–	–	4
R.J.Kennedy	2	2	1	2*	2	2.00	–	–	2
G.I.Allott	2	2	1	0*	0	0.00	–	–	–

Played in one Test: G.R.Larsen 0; G.B.Loveridge 4*.

NEW ZEALAND – BOWLING

	O	M	R	W	Avge	Best	5wI	10wM
R.G.Twose	21	2	55	3	18.33	2-36	–	–
D.N.Patel	76.5	16	221	8	27.62	2-44	–	–
C.L.Cairns	93	29	240	8	30.00	4-56	–	–
R.J.Kennedy	59	10	181	5	36.20	3-28	–	–
G.I.Allott	66	15	209	4	52.25	3-56	–	–

Also bowled: N.J.Astle 4-1-7-0; G.R.Larsen 26-11-38-1.

ZIMBABWE – BATTING AND FIELDING

	M	I	NO	HS	Runs	Avge	100	50	Ct/St
D.L.Houghton	2	3	1	104*	166	83.00	1	–	–
A.Flower	2	4	2	58*	144	72.00	–	1	8
P.A.Strang	2	3	1	49	93	46.50	–	–	1
E.A.Brandes	2	2	1	39	42	42.00	–	–	1
G.W.Flower	2	4	–	71	140	35.00	–	2	1
G.J.Whittall	2	4	–	54	111	27.75	–	1	–
S.V.Carlisle	2	4	–	58	93	23.25	–	1	3
B.C.Strang	2	2	1	14*	18	18.00	–	–	1
A.D.R.Campbell	2	4	–	34	59	14.75	–	–	1
H.H.Streak	2	3	–	24	32	10.66	–	–	1

Played in one Test: H.K.Olonga 0 (3 ct); C.B.Wishart 7, 12* (1 ct).

ZIMBABWE – BOWLING

	O	M	R	W	Avge	Best	5wI	10wM
H.H.Streak	99	27	268	12	22.33	4-52	–	–
E.A.Brandes	64	12	208	5	41.60	2-69	–	–
B.C.Strang	87.3	28	198	4	49.50	3-64	–	–
P.A.Strang	81	17	229	3	76.33	1- 1	–	–

Also bowled: A.D.R.Campbell 2-0-3-0; G.W.Flower 8-1-27-0; H.K.Olonga 17-3-85-1;
G.J.Whittall 25-8-76-1.

WEST INDIES v NEW ZEALAND (1st Test)

At Kensington Oval, Bridgetown, Barbados on 19, 20, 21, 23 April 1996.
Toss: West Indies. Result: WEST INDIES won by 10 wickets.
Debuts: West Indies – R.G.Samuels, P.I.C.Thompson.

NEW ZEALAND

C.M.Spearman	c Browne b Ambrose	0	c Lara b Thompson		20
R.G.Twose	c Samuels b Walsh	2	c Lara b Walsh		0
S.P.Fleming	c Chanderpaul b Walsh	1	c Samuels b Bishop		22
A.C.Parore	c Simmons b Adams	59	(7) c Campbell b Bishop		1
N.J.Astle	c Browne b Thompson	54	(4) c Campbell b Thompson		125
C.Z.Harris	c Lara b Thompson	0	(5) c Samuels b Bishop		0
J.T.C.Vaughan	c Bishop b Adams	44	(6) lbw b Bishop		24
*†L.K.Germon	c Chanderpaul b Adams	0	lbw b Walsh		23
G.R.Larsen	st Browne b Adams	12	lbw b Walsh		6
D.K.Morrison	not out	4	not out		26
R.J.Kennedy	c Browne b Adams	0	c Adams b Walsh		22
Extras	(LB 1, W 1, NB 17)	19	(LB 7, NB 29)		36
Total		**195**			**305**

WEST INDIES

S.L.Campbell	b Harris	208	not out	29
R.G.Samuels	lbw b Larsen	12	not out	0
B.C.Lara	c Spearman b Larsen	35		
P.V.Simmons	lbw b Larsen	22		
J.C.Adams	c Germon b Vaughan	21		
S.Chanderpaul	c Harris b Morrison	82		
†C.O.Browne	c Astle b Kennedy	20		
I.R.Bishop	c Germon b Harris	31		
C.E.L.Ambrose	c Germon b Vaughan	8		
*C.A.Walsh	not out	12		
P.I.C.Thompson	lbw b Morrison	1		
Extras	(LB 8, NB 12)	20		
Total		**472**	(0 wickets)	**29**

WEST INDIES	O	M	R	W		O	M	R	W		FALL OF WICKETS			
											NZ	WI	NZ	WI
Ambrose	13	4	33	1		18	6	41	0	*Wkt*	*1st*	*1st*	*2nd*	*2nd*
Walsh	17	6	30	2		22	3	72	4	1st	2	46	14	–
Bishop	10	3	36	0	(4)	19	1	67	4	2nd	2	103	28	–
Thompson	8	0	58	2	(3)	14	1	77	2	3rd	6	129	48	–
Simmons	3	0	11	0						4th	86	182	57	–
Adams	9	4	17	5	(5)	6	1	32	0	5th	87	337	201	–
Chanderpaul	2	0	9	0	(6)	3	1	9	0	6th	154	386	215	–
										7th	157	445	219	–
NEW ZEALAND										8th	186	458	254	–
Morrison	29.3	4	120	2		2	0	8	0	9th	193	466	260	–
Kennedy	22	3	89	1		2	0	21	0	10th	195	472	305	–
Larsen	40	15	76	3										
Vaughan	34	10	81	2										
Harris	34	11	75	2										
Twose	4	0	20	0										
Astle	3	0	3	0										

Umpires: S.A.Bucknor (21) and P.Willey (*England*) (1).
Referee: M.H.Denness (*England*) (1).   Test No. 1325/27 (WI 321/NZ 244)

WEST INDIES v NEW ZEALAND (2nd Test)

At Recreation Ground, St John's, Antigua on 27, 28, 29 April, 1, 2 May 1996.
Toss: New Zealand. Result: MATCH DRAWN.
Debuts: None.

WEST INDIES

S.L.Campbell	run out	13	c Fleming b Vaughan	36
R.G.Samuels	b Harris	125	lbw b Morrison	4
B.C.Lara	c Germon b Patel	40	c Fleming b Morrison	74
P.V.Simmons	b Harris	59	c Vaughan b Harris	0
J.C.Adams	not out	208	c and b Vaughan	6
S.Chanderpaul	c Astle b Patel	41	b Morrison	8
†C.O.Browne	run out	18	lbw b Larsen	5
I.R.Bishop	c Fleming b Larsen	14	c Germon b Morrison	9
C.E.L.Ambrose	not out	21	lbw b Morrison	6
*C.A.Walsh			not out	17
R.Dhanraj			b Vaughan	9
Extras	(LB 3, NB 6)	9	(LB 2, NB 8)	10
Total	**(7 wickets declared)**	**548**		**184**

NEW ZEALAND

C.M.Spearman	c Browne b Walsh	54	c Browne b Ambrose	24
R.G.Twose	b Ambrose	2	c Samuels b Ambrose	2
D.K.Morrison	lbw b Ambrose	0		
S.P.Fleming	c Browne b Bishop	39	(3) not out	56
N.J.Astle	c Simmons b Ambrose	103	(4) c Adams b Simmons	8
J.T.C.Vaughan	b Dhanraj	26	(5) lbw b Walsh	32
C.Z.Harris	c Adams b Ambrose	40	(6) c and b Dhanraj	4
*†L.K.Germon	c Browne b Ambrose	49	(7) not out	0
D.N.Patel	c Browne b Bishop	78		
G.R.Larsen	not out	17		
R.J.Kennedy	c Browne b Bishop	4		
Extras	(LB 7, NB 18)	25	(LB 1, W 2, NB 1)	4
Total		**437**	**(5 wickets)**	**130**

NEW ZEALAND	O	M	R	W		O	M	R	W
Morrison	26	6	124	0		20	2	61	5
Larsen	25	9	69	1		11	3	27	1
Vaughan	29	8	79	0	(4)	16.3	5	30	3
Patel	38	6	131	2					
Kennedy	13	2	59	0	(3)	10	2	30	0
Harris	35	11	83	2	(5)	4	0	34	1

WEST INDIES	O	M	R	W		O	M	R	W
Ambrose	32	12	68	5		12	3	22	2
Walsh	27	5	70	1		16	5	32	1
Dhanraj	38	9	132	1	(4)	18	6	33	1
Bishop	26.3	6	90	3	(5)	7	1	25	0
Adams	13	1	60	0	(6)	2	1	5	0
Chanderpaul	2	0	10	0					
Simmons					(3)	10	6	12	1

FALL OF WICKETS

Wkt	WI 1st	NZ 1st	WI 2nd	NZ 2nd
1st	35	9	5	19
2nd	96	9	89	30
3rd	193	98	94	39
4th	280	108	119	96
5th	405	202	128	127
6th	448	276	133	–
7th	495	281	147	–
8th	–	391	155	–
9th	–	425	158	–
10th	–	437	184	–

Umpires: L.H.Barker (24) and C.J.Mitchley (*South Africa*) (12).
Referee: M.H.Denness (*England*) (2).   Test No. 1326/28 (WI 322/NZ 245)

WEST INDIES v NEW ZEALAND 1995-96

WEST INDIES – BATTING AND FIELDING

	M	I	NO	HS	Runs	Avge	100	50	Ct/St
J.C.Adams	2	3	1	208*	235	117.50	1	–	3
S.L.Campbell	2	4	1	208	286	95.33	1	–	4
B.C.Lara	2	3	–	74	149	49.66	–	1	3
R.G.Samuels	2	4	1	125	141	47.00	1	–	4
S.Chanderpaul	2	3	–	82	131	43.66	–	1	2
P.V.Simmons	2	3	–	59	81	27.00	–	1	2
I.R.Bishop	2	3	–	31	54	18.00	–	–	1
C.E.L.Ambrose	2	3	1	21*	35	17.50	–	–	–
C.O.Browne	2	3	–	20	43	14.33	–	–	9/1
C.A.Walsh	2	2	2	17*	29	–	–	–	–

Played in one Test: R.Dhanraj 9 (1 ct); P.I.C.Thompson 1.

WEST INDIES – BOWLING

	O	M	R	W	Avge	Best	5wI	10wM
C.E.L.Ambrose	75	25	164	8	20.50	5-68	1	–
J.C.Adams	30	7	114	5	22.80	5-17	1	–
C.A.Walsh	82	19	204	8	25.50	4-72	–	–
I.R.Bishop	62.3	11	218	7	31.14	4-67	–	–
P.I.C.Thompson	22	1	135	4	33.75	2-58	–	–

Also bowled: S.Chanderpaul 7-1-28-0; R.Dhanraj 56-15-165-2; P.V.Simmons 13-6-23-1.

NEW ZEALND – BATTING AND FIELDING

	M	I	NO	HS	Runs	Avge	100	50	Ct/St
N.J.Astle	2	4	–	125	290	72.50	2	1	2
S.P.Fleming	2	4	1	56*	118	39.33	–	1	3
J.T.C.Vaughan	2	4	–	44	126	31.50	–	–	2
D.K.Morrison	2	3	2	26*	30	30.00	–	–	–
C.J.Spearman	2	4	–	54	98	24.50	–	1	1
L.K.Germon	2	4	1	49	72	24.00	–	–	5
G.R.Larsen	2	3	1	17*	35	17.50	–	–	–
C.Z.Harris	2	4	–	40	44	11.00	–	–	1
R.J.Kennedy	2	3	–	22	26	8.66	–	–	–
R.G.Twose	2	4	–	2	6	1.50	–	–	–

Played in one Test: A.C.Parore 59, 1; D.N.Patel 78.

NEW ZEALAND – BOWLING

	O	M	R	W	Avge	Best	5wI	10wM
G.R.Larsen	76	27	172	5	34.40	3-76	–	–
J.T.C.Vaughan	79.3	23	190	5	38.00	3-30	–	–
C.Z.Harris	73	22	192	5	38.40	2-75	–	–
D.K.Morrison	77.3	12	313	7	44.71	5-61	1	–

Also bowled: N.J.Astle 1-0-3-0; R.J.Kennedy 47-7-199-1; D.N.Patel 38-6-131-2; R.G.Twose 4-0-20-0.

ENGLAND v INDIA (1st Test)

At Edgbaston, Birmingham on 6, 7, 8, 9 June 1996.
Toss: India. Result: ENGLAND won by 8 wickets.
Debuts: England – R.C.Irani, A.D.Mullally, M.M.Patel; India – S.B.Joshi, P.L.Mhambrey, B.K.V.Prasad, V.Rathore.

INDIA

V.L.Rathore c Knight b Cork	20	c Hick b Cork	7
A.Jadeja c Atherton b Lewis	0	c Russell b Lewis	6
S.V.Manjrekar c Atherton b Lewis	23	(7) c Knight b Lewis	18
S.R.Tendulkar b Cork	24	c Thorpe b Lewis	122
*M.Azharuddin c Knight b Irani	13	b Mullally	0
†N R.Mongia b Mullally	20	(3) c Hussain b Cork	9
S.B.Joshi c Thorpe b Mullally	12	(6) c Russell b Mullally	12
A.Kumble c Knight b Cork	5	run out	15
J.Srinath c Russell b Mullally	52	lbw b Lewis	1
P.L.Mhambrey c Thorpe b Cork	28	b Lewis	15
B.K.V.Prasad not out	0	not out	0
Extras (B 3, LB 10, NB 4)	17	(B 4, LB 9, NB 1)	14
Total	**214**		**219**

ENGLAND

N.V.Knight c Mongia b Srinath	27	lbw b Prasad	14
*M.A.Atherton c Rathore b Mhambrey	33	not out	53
N.Hussain c sub (R.Dravid) b Srinath	128	c Srinath b Prasad	19
G.P.Thorpe b Srinath	21	not out	17
G.A.Hick c Mhambrey b Prasad	8		
R.C.Irani c Mongia b Srinath	34		
†R.C.Russell b Prasad	0		
C.C.Lewis c Rathore b Prasad	0		
D.G.Cork c Jadeja b Prasad	4		
M.M.Patel lbw b Kumble	18		
A.D.Mullally not out	14		
Extras (B 16, LB 3, NB 7)	26	(B 8, LB 7, W 1, NB 2)	18
Total	**313**	**(2 wickets)**	**121**

ENGLAND	O	M	R	W	O	M	R	W
Lewis	18	2	44	2	22.4	6	72	5
Cork	20.1	5	61	4	19	5	40	2
Mullally	22	7	60	3	15	4	43	2
Irani	7	4	22	1	2	0	21	0
Patel	2	0	14	0	8	3	18	0
Hick					4	1	12	0
INDIA								
Srinath	28.2	5	103	4	14.5	3	47	0
Prasad	28	9	71	4	14	0	50	2
Kumble	24	4	77	1	5	3	9	0
Mhambrey	10	0	43	1				

FALL OF WICKETS

Wkt	1st I	1st E	2nd I	2nd E
1st	8	60	15	37
2nd	41	72	17	77
3rd	64	109	35	–
4th	93	149	36	–
5th	103	195	68	–
6th	118	205	127	–
7th	127	205	185	–
8th	150	215	193	–
9th	203	264	208	–
10th	214	313	219	–

Umpires: D.B.Hair (*Australia*) (15) and D.R.Shepherd (29).
Referee: C.W.Smith (*West Indies*) (7).   Test No. 1327/82 (E 724/I 296)

ENGLAND v INDIA (2nd Test)

At Lord's, London on 20, 21, 22, 23, 24 June 1996.
Toss: India. Result: MATCH DRAWN.
Debuts: India – R.Dravid, S.C.Ganguly.

ENGLAND

*M.A.Atherton lbw b Srinath	0		b Kumble	17
A.J.Stewart b Srinath	20		b Srinath	66
N.Hussain c Rathore b Ganguly	36		c Dravid b Srinath	28
G.P.Thorpe b Srinath	89	(5)	c Rathore b Kumble	21
G.A.Hick c Srinath b Ganguly	1	(6)	c Mongia b Prasad	6
R.C.Irani b Prasad	1	(7)	b Mhambrey	41
†R.C.Russell c Tendulkar b Prasad	124	(8)	lbw b Ganguly	38
C.C.Lewis c Mongia b Prasad	31	(9)	not out	26
D.G.Cork c Mongia b Prasad	0	(10)	c Azharuddin b Kumble	1
P.J.Martin c Tendulkar b Prasad	4	(4)	c Rathore b Prasad	23
A.D.Mullally not out	0		not out	0
Extras (B 13, LB 11, NB 14)	38		(B 1, LB 5, NB 5)	11
Total	**344**		**(9 wickets declared)**	**278**

INDIA

V.Rathore c Hussain b Cork	15
†N.R.Mongia lbw b Lewis	24
S.C.Ganguly b Mullally	131
S.R.Tendulkar b Lewis	31
*M.Azharuddin c Russell b Mullally	16
A.Jadeja b Irani	10
R.Dravid c Russell b Lewis	95
A.Kumble lbw b Martin	14
J.Srinath b Mullally	19
P.L.Mhambrey not out	15
B.K.V.Prasad c Stewart b Cork	4
Extras (B 11, LB 25, W 10, NB 9)	55
Total	**429**

INDIA	O	M	R	W		O	M	R	W	FALL OF WICKETS			
Srinath	33	9	76	3		29	8	76	2		E	I	E
Prasad	33.3	10	76	5		24	6	54	2	*Wkt*	*1st*	*1st*	*2nd*
Mhambrey	19	3	58	0	(5)	14	3	47	1	1st	0	25	49
Kumble	28	9	60	0	(3)	51	14	90	3	2nd	67	59	109
Ganguly	15	2	49	2	(4)	3	0	5	1	3rd	98	123	114
Tendulkar	2	1	1	0						4th	102	154	154
										5th	107	202	167
ENGLAND										6th	243	296	168
Lewis	40	11	101	3						7th	326	351	228
Cork	42.3	10	112	2						8th	337	388	274
Mullally	39	14	71	3						9th	343	419	275
Martin	34	10	70	1						10th	344	429	–
Irani	12	3	31	1									
Hick	2	0	8	0									

Umpires: H.D.Bird (66) and D.B.Hair (*Australia*) (16).
Referee: C.W.Smith (*West Indies*) (8).   Test No. 1328/83 (E 725/I 297)

ENGLAND v INDIA (3rd Test)

At Trent Bridge, Nottingham on 4, 5, 6, 8, 9 July 1996.
Toss: India. Result: MATCH DRAWN.
Debuts: England – M.A.Ealham.

INDIA

V.Rathore	c Russell b Cork	4		absent hurt	
†N.R.Mongia	c Russell b Lewis	9	(1)	c Lewis b Mullally	45
S.C.Ganguly	c Hussain b Mullally	136		b Cork	48
S.R.Tendulkar	c Patel b Ealham	177		c Stewart b Lewis	74
S.V.Manjrekar	c Hick b Patel	53	(2)	c Stewart b Lewis	11
*M.Azharuddin	c Patel b Lewis	5		c Cork b Ealham	8
R.Dravid	c Russell b Ealham	84	(5)	c Thorpe b Mullally	8
A.Kumble	lbw b Mullally	0	(7)	lbw b Ealham	2
J.Srinath	c Cork b Lewis	1	(8)	c Thorpe b Ealham	3
B.K.V.Prasad	run out	13	(9)	not out	0
S.L.V.Raju	not out	1	(10)	c sub (N.A.Gie) b Ealham	0
Extras	(B 6, LB 12, W 7, NB 13)	38		(B 1, LB 1, W 1, NB 9)	12
Total		**521**			**211**

ENGLAND

*M.A.Atherton	c Manjrekar b Prasad	160
A.J.Stewart	c Mongia b Srinath	50
N.Hussain	retired hurt	107
G.P.Thorpe	lbw b Ganguly	45
G.A.Hick	c Srinath b Raju	20
M.A.Ealham	c sub (A.Jadeja) b Srinath	51
†R.C.Russell	c Mongia b Prasad	0
C.C.Lewis	lbw b Kumble	21
D.G.Cork	not out	32
M.M.Patel	c Manjrekar b Ganguly	27
A.D.Mullally	c Mongia b Ganguly	1
Extras	(B 18, LB 18, NB 14)	50
Total		**564**

ENGLAND	O	M	R	W	O	M	R	W		FALL OF WICKETS		
Lewis	37	10	89	3	14	4	50	2			I	E	I
Cork	32	6	124	1	7	0	32	1	*Wkt*	*1st*	*1st*	*2nd*
Mullally	40	12	88	2	13	3	36	2	1st	7	130	17
Ealham	29	9	90	2	14	5	21	4	2nd	33	360	103
Patel	24	2	101	1	12	3	47	0	3rd	288	396	140
Hick	4	1	8	0	9	4	23	0	4th	377	444	160
Thorpe	1	0	3	0					5th	385	444	204
									6th	446	491	208
INDIA									7th	447	497	208
Srinath	47	12	131	2					8th	453	558	211
Prasad	43	12	124	2					9th	513	564	211
Kumble	39	6	98	1					10th	521	–	–
Raju	43	12	76	1								
Ganguly	19.5	2	71	3								
Tendulkar	7	0	28	0								

Umpires: K.T.Francis (*Sri Lanka*) (16) and G.Sharp (1).
Referee: C.W.Smith (*West Indies*) (9).   Test No. 1329/84 (E 726/I 298)

ENGLAND v INDIA 1996

ENGLAND – BATTING AND FIELDING

	M	I	NO	HS	Runs	Avge	100	50	Ct/St
N.Hussain	3	5	1	128	318	79.50	2	–	3
M.A.Atherton	3	5	1	160	263	65.75	1	1	2
G.P.Thorpe	3	5	1	89	193	48.25	–	1	5
A.J.Stewart	2	3	–	66	136	45.33	–	2	3
R.C.Russell	3	4	–	124	162	40.50	1	–	8
C.C.Lewis	3	4	1	31	78	26.00	–	–	1
R.C.Irani	2	3	–	41	76	25.33	–	–	–
M.M.Patel	2	2	–	27	45	22.50	–	–	2
A.D.Mullally	3	4	3	14*	15	15.00	–	–	–
D.G.Cork	3	4	1	32*	37	12.33	–	–	2
G.A.Hick	3	4	–	20	35	8.75	–	–	2

Played in one Test: M.A.Ealham 51; N.V.Knight 27, 14 (4 ct); P.J.Martin 4, 23.

ENGLAND – BOWLING

	O	M	R	W	Avge	Best	5wI	10wM
M.A.Ealham	43	14	111	6	18.50	4-21	–	–
C.C.Lewis	131.4	33	356	15	23.73	5-72	1	–
A.D.Mullally	129	40	298	12	24.83	3-60	–	–
D.G.Cork	120.4	26	369	10	36.90	4-61	–	–

Also bowled: G.A.Hick 19-6-51-0; R.C.Irani 21-7-74-2; P.J.Martin 34-10-70-1; M.M.Patel 46-8-180-1; G.P.Thorpe 1-0-3-0.

INDIA – BATTING AND FIELDING

	M	I	NO	HS	Runs	Avge	100	50	Ct/St
S.C.Ganguly	2	3	–	136	315	105.00	2	–	–
S.R.Tendulkar	3	5	–	177	428	85.60	2	1	2
R.Dravid	2	3	–	95	187	62.33	–	2	1
P.L.Mhambrey	2	3	1	28	58	29.00	–	–	1
S.V.Manjrekar	2	3	–	53	105	26.25	–	1	2
N.R.Mongia	3	5	–	45	107	21.40	–	–	8
J.Srinath	3	5	–	52	76	15.20	–	1	3
V.Rathore	3	4	–	20	46	11.50	–	–	5
B.K.V.Prasad	3	5	3	13	17	8.50	–	–	–
M.Azharuddin	3	5	–	16	42	8.40	–	–	1
A.Kumble	3	5	–	16	36	7.20	–	–	–
A.Jadeja	2	3	–	10	16	5.33	–	–	1

Played in one Test: S.B.Joshi 12, 12; S.L.V.Raju 1*, 0.

INDIA – BOWLING

	O	M	R	W	Avge	Best	5wI	10wM
S.C.Ganguly	37.5	4	125	6	20.83	3- 71	–	–
B.K.V.Prasad	142.3	39	375	15	25.00	5- 76	1	–
J.Srinath	152.1	37	433	11	39.36	4-103	–	–
A.Kumble	147	36	334	5	66.80	3- 90	–	–

Also bowled: P.L.Mhambrey 43-6-148-2; S.L.V.Raju 43-12-76-1; S.R.Tendulkar 9-1-29-0.

ENGLAND v PAKISTAN (1st Test)

At Lord's, London on 25, 26, 27, 28, 29 July 1996.
Toss: Pakistan. Result: PAKISTAN won by 164 runs.
Debuts: England – S.J.E.Brown; Pakistan – Shadab Kabir.

PAKISTAN

Aamir Sohail	lbw b Brown	2		
Saeed Anwar	c Russell b Hick	74	(1) c Russell b Mullally	88
Ijaz Ahmed	b Cork	1	lbw b Cork	76
Inzamam-ul-Haq	b Mullally	148	(5) c Ealham b Cork	70
Salim Malik	run out	7	(6) not out	27
Shadab Kabir	lbw b Cork	17	(2) c Russell b Cork	33
*Wasim Akram	lbw b Ealham	10	not out	34
†Rashid Latif	c Hick b Salisbury	45		
Mushtaq Ahmed	c Russell b Mullally	11	(4) c Thorpe b Brown	5
Waqar Younis	c Brown b Mullally	4		
Ata-ur-Rehman	not out	10		
Extras	(B 3, LB 5, NB 3)	11	(B 4, LB 14, NB 1)	19
Total		**340**	(5 wickets declared)	**352**

ENGLAND

N.V.Knight	lbw b Waqar	51	lbw b Waqar	1
*M.A.Atherton	lbw b Wasim	12	c sub (Asif Mujtaba) b Mushtaq	64
A.J.Stewart	lbw b Mushtaq	39	c sub (Moin Khan) b Mushtaq	89
G.P.Thorpe	b Rehman	77	lbw b Mushtaq	3
G.A.Hick	b Waqar	4	b Waqar	4
M.A.Ealham	c Rashid b Rehman	25	b Mushtaq	5
†R.C.Russell	not out	41	c Rashid b Waqar	1
D.G.Cork	c Saeed b Rehman	3	b Waqar	3
I.D.K.Salisbury	lbw b Waqar	5	c Rashid b Wasim	40
A.D.Mullally	b Waqar	0	c sub (Moin Khan) b Mushtaq	6
S.J.E.Brown	b Rehman	1	not out	10
Extras	(B 9, LB 13, W 1, NB 4)	27	(B 6, LB 7, NB 4)	17
Total		**285**		**243**

ENGLAND	O	M	R	W	O	M	R	W
Cork	28	6	100	2	24	4	86	3
Brown	17	2	78	1	16	2	60	1
Mullally	24	8	44	3	(4) 30.2	9	70	1
Salisbury	12.2	1	42	1	(3) 20	4	63	0
Ealham	21	4	42	1	(6) 16	4	39	0
Hick	6	0	26	1	(5) 7	2	16	0

PAKISTAN	O	M	R	W	O	M	R	W
Wasim Akram	22	4	49	1	21.1	5	45	1
Waqar Younis	24	6	69	4	25	3	85	4
Mushtaq Ahmed	38	5	92	1	38	15	57	5
Ata-ur-Rehman	15.4	3	50	4	11	2	33	0
Aamir Sohail	3	1	3	0				
Salim Malik					(5) 1	0	1	0
Shadab Kabir					(6) 1	0	9	0

FALL OF WICKETS				
	P	E	P	E
Wkt	1st	1st	2nd	2nd
1st	7	27	136	14
2nd	12	107	136	168
3rd	142	107	161	171
4th	153	116	279	176
5th	209	180	308	181
6th	257	260	–	182
7th	267	264	–	186
8th	290	269	–	186
9th	290	269	–	208
10th	340	285	–	243

Umpires: S.A.Bucknor (*West Indies*) (22) and P.Willey (2).
Referee: P.L.van der Merwe (*South Africa*) (9).   Test No. 1330/53 (E 727/P 229)

ENGLAND v PAKISTAN (2nd Test)

At Headingley, Leeds on 8, 9, 10, 11, 12 August 1996.
Toss: England. Result: MATCH DRAWN.
Debuts: None.

PAKISTAN

Saeed Anwar c Atherton b Mullally	1	c Russell b Cork	22
Shadab Kabir lbw b Caddick	35	c and b Lewis	2
Ijaz Ahmed c Russell b Cork	141	c Russell b Caddick	52
Inzamam-ul-Haq c Atherton b Mullally	2	c Stewart b Caddick	65
Salim Malik b Cork	55	c Cork b Caddick	6
Asif Mujtaba c Thorpe b Cork	51	run out	26
*Wasim Akram c Russell b Caddick	7	lbw b Atherton	7
†Moin Khan c Russell b Cork	105	not out	30
Mushtaq Ahmed c Atherton b Caddick	20	not out	6
Waqar Younis c and b Cork	7		
Ata-ur-Rehman not out	0		
Extras (B 4, LB 10, NB 10)	24	(B 4, LB 12, NB 10)	26
Total	**448**	(7 wickets declared)	**242**

ENGLAND

*M.A.Atherton c Moin b Wasim	12
A.J.Stewart c and b Mushtaq	170
N.Hussain c and b Waqar	48
G.P.Thorpe c Shadab b Mushtaq	16
J.P.Crawley c Moin b Rehman	53
N.V.Knight c Mushtaq b Waqar	113
†R.C.Russell b Wasim	9
C.C.Lewis b Mushtaq	9
D.G.Cork c Shadab b Wasim	26
A.R.Caddick b Waqar	4
A.D.Mullally not out	9
Extras (B 7, LB 23, NB 2)	32
Total	**501**

ENGLAND	O	M	R	W	O	M	R	W	FALL OF WICKETS			
										P	E	P
Caddick	40.2	6	113	3	(3)	17	4	52	3	*Wkt*	*1st*	*1st*	*2nd*
Mullally	41	10	99	2	(1)	15	2	43	0	1st	1	14	16
Lewis	32	4	100	0	(2)	16	3	52	1	2nd	98	121	34
Cork	37	6	113	5		16	2	49	1	3rd	103	168	132
Thorpe	3	1	9	0		10	3	10	0	4th	233	257	142
Atherton						7	1	20	1	5th	252	365	188
										6th	266	402	201
PAKISTAN										7th	378	441	221
Wasim Akram	39.5	10	106	3						8th	434	465	–
Waqar Younis	33	7	127	3						9th	444	471	–
Ata-ur-Rehman	22	1	90	1						10th	448	501	–
Mushtaq Ahmed	55	17	142	3									
Asif Mujtaba	7	5	6	0									

Umpires: S.A.Bucknor (*West Indies*) (23) and D.R.Shepherd (30).
Referee: P.L.van der Merwe (*South Africa*) (10).   Test No. 1331/54 (E 728/P 230)

ENGLAND v PAKISTAN (3rd Test)

At Kennington Oval, London on 22, 23, 24, 25, 26 August 1996.
Toss: England. Result: PAKISTAN won by 9 wickets.
Debuts: England – R.D.B.Croft.

ENGLAND

*M.A.Atherton b Waqar	31	c Inzamam b Mushtaq	43
†A.J.Stewart b Mushtaq	44	c Asif b Mushtaq	54
N.Hussain c Saeed b Waqar	12	lbw b Mushtaq	51
G.P.Thorpe lbw b Mohammad Akram	54	c Wasim b Mushtaq	9
J.P.Crawley b Waqar	106	c Aamir b Wasim	19
N.V.Knight b Mushtaq	17	c and b Mushtaq	8
C.C.Lewis b Wasim	5	lbw b Waqar	4
I.D.K.Salisbury c Inzamam b Wasim	5	(10) not out	0
D.G.Cork c Moin b Waqar	0	(8) b Mushtaq	26
R.D.B.Croft not out	5	(9) c Ijaz b Wasim	6
A.D.Mullally b Wasim	24	b Wasim	0
Extras (LB 12, W 1, NB 10)	23	(B 6, LB 2, W 1, NB 13)	22
Total	**326**		**242**

PAKISTAN

Saeed Anwar c Croft b Cork	176	c Knight b Mullally	1
Aamir Sohail c Cork b Croft	46	not out	29
Ijaz Ahmed c Stewart b Mullally	61	not out	13
Inzamam-ul-Haq c Hussain b Mullally	35		
Salim Malik not out	100		
Asif Mujtaba run out	13		
*Wasim Akram st Stewart b Croft	40		
†Moin Khan b Salisbury	23		
Mushtaq Ahmed c Crawley b Mullally	2		
Waqar Younis not out	0		
Mohammad Akram			
Extras (B 4, LB 5, NB 16)	25	(NB 5)	5
Total (8 wickets declared)	**521**	(1 wicket)	**48**

PAKISTAN	O	M	R	W	O	M	R	W
Wasim Akram	29.2	9	83	3	15.4	1	67	3
Waqar Younis	25	6	95	4	18	3	55	1
Mohammad Akram	12	1	41	1	(5) 10	3	30	2
Mushtaq Ahmed	27	5	78	2	(3) 37	10	78	6
Aamir Sohail	6	1	17	0	(4) 2	1	4	0
ENGLAND								
Lewis	23	3	112	0				
Mullally	37.1	7	97	3	3	0	24	1
Croft	47	10	116	2	0.4	0	9	0
Cork	23	5	71	1	(1) 3	0	15	0
Salisbury	29	3	116	1				

FALL OF WICKETS

Wkt	E 1st	P 1st	E 2nd	P 2nd
1st	64	106	96	7
2nd	85	239	136	–
3rd	116	334	166	–
4th	205	334	179	–
5th	248	365	187	–
6th	273	440	205	–
7th	283	502	220	–
8th	284	519	238	–
9th	295	–	242	–
10th	326	–	242	–

Umpires: B.C.Cooray (*Sri Lanka*) (7) and M.J.Kitchen (12).
Referee: P.L.van der Merwe (*South Africa*) (11).   Test No. 1332/55 (E 729/P 231)

ENGLAND v PAKISTAN 1996

ENGLAND – BATTING AND FIELDING

	M	I	NO	HS	Runs	Avge	100	50	Ct/St
A.J.Stewart	3	5	–	170	396	79.20	1	2	2/1
J.P.Crawley	2	3	–	106	178	59.33	1	1	1
N.V.Knight	3	5	–	113	190	38.00	1	1	1
N.Hussain	2	3	–	51	111	37.00	–	1	1
M.A.Atherton	3	5	–	64	162	32.40	–	1	3
G.P.Thorpe	3	5	–	77	159	31.80	–	2	2
R.C.Russell	2	3	1	41*	51	25.50	–	–	9
I.D.K.Salisbury	2	4	1	40	50	16.66	–	–	–
D.G.Cork	3	5	–	26	58	11.60	–	–	3
A.D.Mullally	3	5	1	24	39	9.75	–	–	–
C.C.Lewis	2	3	–	9	18	6.00	–	–	1

Played in one Test: S.J.E.Brown 1, 10* (1 ct); A.R.Caddick 4; R.D.B.Croft 5*, 6 (1 ct);
M.A.Ealham 25, 5 (1 ct); G.A.Hick 4, 4 (1 ct).

ENGLAND – BOWLING

	O	M	R	W	Avge	Best	5wI	10wM
A.R.Caddick	57.2	10	165	6	27.50	3- 52	–	–
D.G.Cork	131	23	434	12	36.16	5-113	1	–
A.D.Mullally	150.3	36	377	10	37.70	3- 44	–	–

Also bowled: M.A.Atherton 7-1-20-1; S.J.E.Brown 33-4-138-2; R.D.B.Croft
47.4-10-125-2; M.A.Ealham 37-8-81-1; G.A.Hick 13-2-42-1; C.C.Lewis 71-10-264-1;
I.D.K.Salisbury 61.2-8-221-2; G.P.Thorpe 13-4-19-0.

PAKISTAN – BATTING AND FIELDING

	M	I	NO	HS	Runs	Avge	100	50	Ct/St
Moin Khan	2	3	1	105	158	79.00	1	–	3
Ijaz Ahmed	3	6	1	141	344	68.80	1	3	1
Salim Malik	3	5	2	100*	195	65.00	1	1	–
Inzamam-ul-Haq	3	5	–	148	320	64.00	1	2	2
Saeed Anwar	3	6	–	176	362	60.33	1	2	2
Aamir Sohail	2	3	1	46	77	38.50	–	–	1
Asif Mujtaba	2	3	–	51	90	30.00	–	1	1
Wasim Akram	3	5	1	40	98	24.50	–	–	1
Shadab Kabir	2	4	–	35	87	21.75	–	–	2
Mushtaq Ahmed	3	5	1	20	44	11.00	–	–	3
Waqar Younis	3	3	1	7	11	5.50	–	–	1
Ata-ur-Rehman	2	2	2	10*	10	–	–	–	–

Played in one Test: Mohammad Akram did not bat; Rashid Latif 45 (3 ct).

PAKISTAN – BOWLING

	O	M	R	W	Avge	Best	5wI	10wM
Mushtaq Ahmed	195	52	447	17	26.29	6-78	2	–
Waqar Younis	125	25	431	16	26.93	4-69	–	–
Wasim Akram	128	29	350	11	31.81	3-67	–	–
Ata-ur-Rehman	48.4	6	173	5	34.60	4-50	–	–

Also bowled: Aamir Sohail 11-3-24-0; Asif Mujtaba 7-5-6-0; Mohammad Akram
22-4-71-1; Salim Malik 1-0-1-0; Shadab Kabir 1-0-9-0.

SRI LANKA v ZIMBABWE (1st Test)

At R.Premadasa Stadium, Colombo on 11, 12, 13, 14 September 1996.
Toss: Sri Lanka. Result: SRI LANKA won by an innings and 77 runs.
Debuts: Zimbabwe – C.N.Evans, A.R.Whittall.

SRI LANKA

R.S.Mahanama	lbw b Streak	4
S.T.Jayasuriya	c Evans b Olonga	0
A.P.Gurusinha	c Olonga b Strang	52
P.A.de Silva	b Strang	35
H.P.Tillekeratne	c A.Flower b Olonga	20
*A.Ranatunga	lbw b Streak	75
†R.S.Kaluwitharana	c and b Streak	71
H.D.P.K.Dharmasena	not out	42
W.P.U.C.J.Vaas	b Strang	34
M.Muralitharan	b Strang	0
K.J.Silva	c and b Strang	0
Extras	(LB 6, W 1, NB 9)	16
Total		**349**

ZIMBABWE

G.W.Flower	c Kaluwitharana b Vaas	0		b Muralitharan	27
M.H.Dekker	lbw b Vaas	10		c Jayasuriya b Dharmasena	20
*A.D.R.Campbell	c Mahanama b Vaas	12	(4)	c Mahanama b Muralitharan	26
†A.Flower	c Ranatunga b Dharmasena	2	(5)	c Mahanama b Muralitharan	0
G.J.Whittall	lbw b Silva	39	(6)	c Mahanama b Silva	13
C.B.Wishart	c Vaas b Silva	51	(3)	b Silva	3
H.K.Olonga	c Tillekeratne b Muralitharan	1	(9)	c Mahanama b Silva	0
C.N.Evans	c Kaluwitharana b Vaas	9	(7)	lbw b Silva	1
P.A.Strang	b Muralitharan	0	(8)	c Vaas b Muralitharan	8
A.R.Whittall	c Dharmasena b Silva	1		b Muralitharan	11
H.H.Streak	not out	0		not out	3
Extras	(B 4, LB 4, W 2, NB 4)	14		(B 6, LB 4, W 1, NB 4)	15
Total		**145**			**127**

ZIMBABWE	O	M	R	W		O	M	R	W
Streak	20	6	54	3					
Olonga	17	3	57	2					
G.J.Whittall	12	1	43	0					
Strang	34.3	3	106	5					
A.R.Whittall	13	3	40	0					
Evans	6	0	27	0					
G.W.Flower	4	1	16	0					

SRI LANKA	O	M	R	W		O	M	R	W
Vaas	22	3	73	4		12	1	34	0
Gurusinha	3	1	3	0		2	0	4	0
Dharmasena	9	3	23	1	(4)	14	7	19	1
Muralitharan	24	9	28	2	(5)	20.3	4	33	5
Silva	14.4	9	10	3	(6)	19	12	25	4
De Silva					(3)	2	1	1	0
Jayasuriya						4	3	1	0

FALL OF WICKETS

Wkt	SL 1st	Z 1st	Z 2nd
1st	4	0	35
2nd	4	15	42
3rd	53	21	65
4th	105	45	65
5th	128	103	98
6th	271	105	99
7th	272	123	102
8th	345	138	102
9th	349	145	113
10th	349	145	127

Umpires: S.A.Bucknor (*West Indies*) (24) and B.C.Cooray (8).
Referee: J.R.Reid (*New Zealand*) (22).   Test No. 1333/4 (SL 67/Z 17)

SRI LANKA v ZIMBABWE (2nd Test)

At Sinhalese Sports Club, Colombo on 18, 19, 20, 21 September 1996.
Toss: Zimbabwe. Result: SRI LANKA won by 10 wickets.
Debuts: None.

ZIMBABWE

G.W.Flower	c Mahanama b Muralitharan	52	lbw b Silva	13
M.H.Dekker	c Mahanama b Muralitharan	18	lbw b Vaas	4
A.H.Shah	c Kaluwitharana b Pushpakumara	1	c Vaas b Pushpakumara	62
*A.D.R.Campbell	st Kaluwitharana b Silva	36	c sub (M.S.Atapattu) b Silva	4
†A.Flower	run out	3	c Gurusinha b Muralitharan	31
C.B.Wishart	c Kaluwitharana b Silva	2	c Kaluwitharana b Jayasuriya	25
G.J.Whittall	c Silva b Muralitharan	0	c Gurusinha b Jayasuriya	3
P.A.Strang	not out	2	(9) c and b Vaas	50
A.R.Whittall	c Gurusinha b Muralitharan	3	(8) b Muralitharan	12
B.C.Strang	c De Silva b Silva	3	b Muralitharan	2
H.K.Olonga	c Mahanama b Silva	3	not out	3
Extras	(B 3, LB 10, NB 5)	18	(B 2, LB 6, W 1, NB 17)	26
Total		**141**		**235**

SRI LANKA

R.S.Mahanama	c A.Flower b B.C.Strang	3	(2) not out	12
S.T.Jayasuriya	c A.R.Whittall b P.A.Strang	41	(1) not out	18
A.P.Gurusinha	c Wishart b B.C.Strang	88		
P.A.de Silva	c and b P.A.Strang	16		
*A.Ranatunga	c Wishart b B.C.Strang	6		
H.P.Tillekeratne	not out	126		
†R.S.Kaluwitharana	c A.Flower b G.J.Whittall	27		
W.P.U.C.J.Vaas	st A.Flower b P.A.Strang	8		
K.R.Pushpakumara	c B.C.Strang b P.A.Strang	23		
M.Muralitharan	not out	1		
K.J.Silva				
Extras	(LB 4, W 3, NB 4)	11		
Total (8 wickets declared)		**350**	(0 wickets)	**30**

SRI LANKA	O	M	R	W	O	M	R	W	FALL OF WICKETS			
										Z	SL	Z	SL
Vaas	10	1	31	0	26.3	11	34	2		Z	SL	Z	SL
Pushpakumara	11	3	34	1	8	0	24	1	*Wkt*	*1st*	*1st*	*2nd*	*2nd*
Muralitharan	20	5	40	4	41	9	94	3	1st	44	19	9	
Silva	10	4	16	4	26	7	49	2	2nd	54	58	30	
De Silva	2	0	7	0	5	1	10	0	3rd	119	86	34	
Jayasuriya					7	3	16	2	4th	121	102	91	
									5th	123	216	135	
ZIMBABWE									6th	125	267	144	
Olonga	26	6	81	0	3.4	0	17	0	7th	126	276	167	
B.C.Strang	20	6	63	3					8th	133	340	193	
A.R.Whittall	31	7	75	0					9th	136	–	201	
P.A.Strang	38	11	66	4	(2) 3	0	13	0	10th	141	–	235	
G.J.Whittall	17	4	48	1									
G.W.Flower	2	0	13	0									

Umpires: K.T.Francis (17) and C.J.Mitchley (*South Africa*) (13).
Referee: J.R.Reid (*New Zealand*) (23).   Test No. 1334/5 (SL 68/Z 18)

SRI LANKA v ZIMBABWE 1996-97

SRI LANKA – BATTING AND FIELDING

	M	I	NO	HS	Runs	Avge	100	50	Ct/St
H.P.Tillekeratne	2	2	1	126*	146	146.00	1	–	1
A.P.Gurusinha	2	2	–	88	140	70.00	–	2	3
R.S.Kaluwitharana	2	2	–	71	98	49.00	–	1	5/1
A.Ranatunga	2	2	–	75	81	40.50	–	1	1
S.T.Jayasuriya	2	3	1	41	59	29.50	–	–	1
P.A.de Silva	2	2	–	35	51	25.50	–	–	1
W.P.U.C.J.Vaas	2	2	–	34	42	21.00	–	–	4
R.S.Mahanama	2	3	1	12*	19	9.50	–	–	8
M.Muralitharan	2	2	1	1*	1	1.00	–	–	–
K.J.Silva	2	1	–	0	0	0.00	–	–	1

Played in one Test: H.D.P.K.Dharmasena 42* (1 ct); K.R.Pushpakumara 23.

SRI LANKA – BOWLING

	O	M	R	W	Avge	Best	5wI	10wM
K.J.Silva	69.4	32	100	13	7.69	4-16	–	–
M.Muralitharan	105.3	27	195	14	13.92	5-33	1	–
W.P.U.C.J.Vaas	70.3	16	172	6	28.66	4-73	–	–

Also bowled: P.A.de Silva 9-2-18-0; H.D.P.K.Dharmasena 23-10-42-2; A.P.Gurusinha 5-1-7-0; S.T.Jayasuriya 11-6-17-2; K.R.Pushpakumara 19-3-58-2.

ZIMBABWE – BATTING AND FIELDING

	M	I	NO	HS	Runs	Avge	100	50	Ct/St
G.W.Flower	2	4	–	52	92	23.00	–	1	–
P.A.Strang	2	4	1	50	66	22.00	–	1	2
C.B.Wishart	2	4	–	51	81	20.25	–	1	2
A.D.R.Campbell	2	4	–	36	78	19.50	–	–	1
G.J.Whittall	2	4	–	39	55	13.75	–	–	1
M.H.Dekker	2	4	–	20	52	13.00	–	–	1
A.Flower	2	4	–	31	36	9.00	–	–	3/1
A.R.Whittall	2	4	–	12	27	6.75	–	–	1
H.K.Olonga	2	4	1	3*	7	2.33	–	–	1

Played in one Test: C.N.Evans 9, 1 (1 ct); A.H.Shah 1, 62; B.C.Strang 3, 2 (1 ct); H.H.Streak 0*, 3* (1 ct).

ZIMBABWE – BOWLING

	O	M	R	W	Avge	Best	5wI	10wM
H.H.Streak	20	6	54	3	18.00	3- 54	–	–
P.A.Strang	75.3	14	185	9	20.55	5-106	1	–
B.C.Strang	20	6	63	3	21.00	3- 63	–	–

Also bowled: C.N.Evans 6-0-27-0; G.W.Flower 6-1-29-0; H.K.Olonga 46.4-9-155-2; A.R.Whittall 44-10-115-0; G.J.Whittall 29-5-91-1.

INDIA v AUSTRALIA (Only Test)

At Feroz Shah Kotla, Delhi on 10, 11, 12, 13 October 1996.
Toss: Australia. Result: INDIA won by seven wickets.
Debuts: India – D.Johnson; Australia – G.B.Hogg.

AUSTRALIA

Batsman	1st		2nd	
M.J.Slater c and b Kumble	44	(2) c Azharuddin b Johnson	0
*M.A.Taylor lbw b Prasad	27	(1) c Rathore b Kapoor	37
R.T.Ponting b Kapoor	14	b Prasad	13
M.E.Waugh c Dravid b Joshi	26	c Mongia b Kumble	23
S.R.Waugh c Mongia b Kapoor	0	(6) not out	67
M.G.Bevan lbw b Joshi	26	(5) c Azharuddin b Kumble	33
†I.A.Healy b Kumble	17	st Mongia b Kumble	12
G.B.Hogg c Rathore b Kumble	1	c Rathore b Kumble	4
P.R.Reiffel c Dravid b Kumble	7	lbw b Kumble	6
P.E.McIntyre not out	6	lbw b Prasad	16
G.D.McGrath run out	6	c Mongia b Prasad	0
Extras (B 4, LB 3, NB 1)	8	(B 9, LB 6, W 1, NB 7)	23
Total	**182**		**234**

INDIA

Batsman	1st		2nd	
V.Rathore c Ponting b Reiffel	5	b Reiffel	14
†N.R.Mongia b Reiffel	152	lbw b Reiffel	0
S.C.Ganguly c M.E.Waugh b Hogg	66	not out	21
*S.R.Tendulkar c M.E.Waugh b McIntyre	10	b McGrath	0
M.Azharuddin b McGrath	17	not out	21
R.Dravid c Healy b S.R.Waugh	40		
S.B.Joshi c Ponting b McIntyre	23		
A.R.Kapoor c Ponting b M.E.Waugh	22		
A.Kumble lbw b Reiffel	2		
D.Johnson not out	0		
B.K.V.Prasad b McIntyre	3		
Extras (B 10, LB 1, NB 10)	21	(W 1, NB 1)	2
Total	**361**	**(3 wickets)**	**58**

INDIA	O	M	R	W		O	M	R	W
Prasad	12	4	34	1		13.3	7	18	3
Johnson	4	1	12	0		12	2	40	1
Joshi	23	7	36	2	(4)	20	7	52	0
Kumble	24	7	63	4	(3)	41	12	67	5
Kapoor	10	3	30	2		22	5	42	1
AUSTRALIA									
McGrath	29	10	56	1		7	2	30	1
Reiffel	17	7	35	3		6	2	24	2
S.R.Waugh	13	5	25	1					
McIntyre	37.4	7	103	3		0.2	0	4	0
Hogg	17	3	69	1					
M.E.Waugh	18	0	62	1					

FALL OF WICKETS

Wkt	1st A	1st I	2nd A	2nd I
1st	47	13	4	1
2nd	81	144	25	25
3rd	93	169	72	26
4th	94	199	78	—
5th	143	260	145	—
6th	144	303	159	—
7th	147	341	171	—
8th	169	353	191	—
9th	170	354	232	—
10th	182	361	234	—

Umpires: S.Venkataraghavan (14) and P.Willey (*England*) (3).
Referee: J.R.Reid (*New Zealand*) (24).   Test No. 1335/51 (I 299/A 558)

PAKISTAN v ZIMBABWE (1st Test)

At Sheikhupura Stadium on 17, 18, 19, 20, 21 October 1996.
Toss: Zimbabwe. Result: MATCH DRAWN.
Debuts: Pakistan – Azam Khan, Shahid Nazir.

ZIMBABWE

G.W.Flower	c sub (Shahid Afridi) b Saqlain	110	(2)	c Shadab b Saqlain	46
M.H.Dekker	b Wasim	14	(1)	c Wasim b Saqlain	13
*A.D.R.Campbell	lbw b Nazir	8		lbw b Waqar	15
D.L.Houghton	run out	43		b Saqlain	65
†A.Flower	lbw b Nazir	11		b Nazir	18
C.B.Wishart	lbw b Nazir	0		b Nazir	10
G.J.Whittall	c Shadab b Saqlain	0		c sub (Shahid Afridi) b Saqlain	32
P.A.Strang	not out	106		not out	13
A.R.Whittall	lbw b Nazir	0		not out	0
B.C.Strang	b Saqlain	42			
H.K.Olonga	b Nazir	7			
Extras	(B 9, LB 16, W 1, NB 8)	34		(B 11, LB 10, NB 8)	29
Total		**375**		**(7 wickets)**	**241**

PAKISTAN

Saeed Anwar	st A.Flower b P.A.Strang	51
Aamir Sohail	c A.Flower b P.A.Strang	46
Shadab Kabir	c Houghton b A.R.Whittall	2
Ijaz Ahmed	lbw b Olonga	9
Salim Malik	b P.A.Strang	52
Azam Khan	lbw b P.A.Strang	14
†Moin Khan	c A.R.Whittall b P.A.Strang	18
*Wasim Akram	not out	257
Saqlain Mushtaq	b G.J.Whittall	79
Waqar Younis	b G.J.Whittall	0
Shahid Nazir	c Dekker b A.R.Whittall	0
Extras	(B 10, LB 8, W 2, NB 5)	25
Total		**553**

PAKISTAN	O	M	R	W		O	M	R	W	FALL OF WICKETS		
											Z	P	Z
Wasim Akram	28	9	58	1	(4)	5	0	16	0	*Wkt*	*1st*	*1st*	*2nd*
Waqar Younis	22	3	90	0	(1)	20	3	60	1	1st	33	64	13
Saqlain Mushtaq	37	3	127	3	(3)	40	16	75	4	2nd	41	77	40
Shahid Nazir	22.4	3	53	5	(2)	19	6	45	2	3rd	119	91	124
Aamir Sohail	6	0	22	0		11	6	12	0	4th	141	142	159
Salim Malik						5	1	12	0	5th	141	176	177
ZIMBABWE										6th	142	183	221
Olonga	19	6	60	1						7th	273	237	232
B.C.Strang	20	2	34	0						8th	274	550	–
A.R.Whittall	45.2	7	146	2						9th	361	550	–
P.A.Strang	69	12	212	5						10th	375	553	–
G.J.Whittall	25	5	73	2									
G.W.Flower	10	4	10	0									

Umpires: Khizer Hayat (34) and D.L.Orchard (*South Africa*) (3).
Referee: J.L.Hendriks (*West Indies*) (7).   Test No. 1336/7 (P 232/Z 19)

PAKISTAN v ZIMBABWE (2nd Test)

At Iqbal Stadium, Faisalabad on 24, 25, 26 October 1996.
Toss: Zimbabwe. Result: PAKISTAN won by 10 wickets.
Debuts: Pakistan – Hasan Raza, Mohammad Hussain; Zimbabwe – E.Matambanadzo, M.Mbangwa.

ZIMBABWE

G.W.Flower b Wasim	15	(2)	lbw b Wasim	0
M.H.Dekker c Moin b Wasim	19	(1)	lbw b Waqar	0
C.B.Wishart lbw b Waqar	0		c Salim b Waqar	7
D.L.Houghton b Wasim	1		lbw b Wasim	74
*A.D.R.Campbell c Moin b Saqlain	9		c Moin b Nazir	51
†A.Flower c Hussain b Nazir	61		c Saeed b Waqar	23
G.J.Whittall b Wasim	9		lbw b Nazir	0
P.A.Strang c Salim b Hussain	3		b Waqar	9
B.C.Strang b Wasim	1		not out	13
M.Mbangwa b Wasim	0	(11)	lbw b Wasim	2
E.Matambanadzo not out	0	(10)	b Wasim	7
Extras (B 4, LB 10, NB 1)	15		(LB 8, NB 6)	14
Total	**133**			**200**

PAKISTAN

Saeed Anwar c A.Flower b Matambanadzo	81	not out	50
Aamir Sohail lbw b Matambanadzo	2	not out	18
Ijaz Ahmed c A.Flower b Mbangwa	2		
Salim Malik c A.Flower b B.C.Strang	18		
Hasan Raza c Houghton b B.C.Strang	27		
*Wasim Akram b Mbangwa	35		
†Moin Khan c A.Flower b B.C.Strang	58		
Mohammad Hussain run out	0		
Saqlain Mushtaq not out	15		
Waqar Younis b G.W.Flower	23		
Shahid Nazir lbw b P.A.Strang	1		
Extras (LB 4, NB 1)	5	(W 1)	1
Total	**267**	**(0 wickets)**	**69**

PAKISTAN	O	M	R	W	O	M	R	W
Wasim Akram	20	8	48	6	18.4	4	58	4
Waqar Younis	11	6	13	1	15	3	54	4
Saqlain Mushtaq	15	5	28	1	7	1	33	0
Shahid Nazir	5.5	0	23	1	11	5	25	2
Mohammad Hussain	6	3	7	1	4	1	14	0
Salim Malik					2	0	8	0
ZIMBABWE								
Matambanadzo	11	0	62	2	5	0	27	0
Mbangwa	17	1	67	2	7	3	14	0
B.C.Strang	18	8	53	3	4.5	0	20	0
G.J.Whittall	7	4	11	0				
P.A.Strang	24.1	8	66	1	(4) 2	0	8	0
G.W.Flower	2	0	4	1				

FALL OF WICKETS

Wkt	Z 1st	P 1st	Z 2nd	P 2nd
1st	22	7	0	
2nd	33	10	0	
3rd	34	67	23	
4th	49	127	136	
5th	55	141	136	
6th	102	194	140	
7th	111	200	169	
8th	118	235	174	
9th	129	264	198	
10th	133	267	200	

Umpires: D.B.Cowie (*New Zealand*) (3) and Mahboob Shah (27).
Referee: J.L.Hendriks (*West Indies*) (8).   Test No. 1337/8 (P 233/Z 20)

PAKISTAN v ZIMBABWE 1996-97

PAKISTAN – BATTING AND FIELDING

	M	I	NO	HS	Runs	Avge	100	50	Ct/St
Wasim Akram	2	2	1	257*	292	292.00	1	–	1
Saqlain Mushtaq	2	2	1	79	94	94.00	–	1	–
Saeed Anwar	2	3	1	81	182	91.00	–	3	1
Moin Khan	2	2	–	58	76	38.00	–	1	3
Salim Malik	2	2	–	52	70	35.00	–	1	2
Aamir Sohail	2	3	1	46	66	33.00	–	–	–
Waqar Younis	2	2	–	23	23	11.50	–	–	–
Ijaz Ahmed	2	2	–	9	11	5.50	–	–	–
Shahid Nazir	2	2	–	1	1	0.50	–	–	–

Played in one Test: Azam Khan 14; Hasan Raza 27; Mohammad Hussain 0 (1 ct); Shadab Kabir 2 (2 ct).

PAKISTAN – BOWLING

	O	M	R	W	Avge	Best	5wI	10wM
Shahid Nazir	58.3	14	146	10	14.60	5-53	1	–
Wasim Akram	71.4	21	180	11	16.36	6-48	1	1
Saqlain Mushtaq	99	25	263	8	32.87	4-75	–	–
Waqar Younis	68	15	217	6	36.16	4-54	–	–

Also bowled: Aamir Sohail 17-6-34-0; Mohammad Hussain 10-4-21-1; Salim Malik 7-1-20-0.

ZIMBABWE – BATTING AND FIELDING

	M	I	NO	HS	Runs	Avge	100	50	Ct/St
P.A.Strang	2	4	2	106*	131	65.50	1	–	–
D.L.Houghton	2	4	–	74	183	45.75	–	2	2
G.W.Flower	2	4	–	110	171	42.75	1	–	–
A.Flower	2	4	–	61	113	28.25	–	1	5/1
B.C.Strang	2	3	1	42	56	28.00	–	–	–
A.D.R.Campbell	2	4	–	51	83	20.75	–	1	–
M.H.Dekker	2	4	–	19	46	11.50	–	–	1
G.J.Whittall	2	4	–	32	41	10.25	–	–	–
C.B.Wishart	2	4	–	10	17	4.25	–	–	–

Played in one Test: E.Matambanadzo 0*, 7; M.Mbangwa 0, 2; H.K.Olonga 7; A.R.Whittall 0, 0* (1 ct).

ZIMBABWE – BOWLING

	O	M	R	W	Avge	Best	5wI	10wM
B.C.Strang	42.5	10	107	3	35.66	3- 53	–	–
P.A.Strang	95.1	20	286	6	47.66	5-212	1	–

Also bowled: G.W.Flower 12-4-14-1; E:Matambanadzo 16-0-89-2; M.Mbangwa 24-4-81-2; H.K.Olonga 19-6-60-1; A.R.Whittall 45.2-7-146-2; G.J.Whittall 32-9-84-2.

INDIA v SOUTH AFRICA (1st Test)

At Gujarat Stadium, Ahmedabad on 20, 21, 22, 23 November 1996.
Toss: India. Result: INDIA won by 64 runs.
Debuts: India – V.V.S.Laxman.

INDIA

S.V.Manjrekar	b Adams	34	c Hudson b Donald	5
†N.R.Mongia	lbw b De Villiers	9	c Richardson b Donald	5
R.Dravid	lbw b Symcox	24	lbw b Symcox	34
*S.R.Tendulkar	c Rhodes b Symcox	42	c Rhodes b McMillan	7
M.Azharuddin	run out	35	c McMillan b Donald	24
V.V.S.Laxman	lbw b Donald	11	lbw b Adams	51
S.B.Joshi	c Hudson b Donald	16	c McMillan b Symcox	13
J.Srinath	c Cullinan b Donald	14	lbw b De Villiers	1
A.Kumble	c Kirsten b Donald	17	not out	30
B.K.V.Prasad	c Donald b De Villiers	9	c McMillan b Adams	0
N.D.Hirwani	not out	0	c sub (D.N.Crookes) b Adams	9
Extras	(LB 9, NB 3)	12	(B 4, LB 4, NB 3)	11
Total		**223**		**190**

SOUTH AFRICA

G.Kirsten	st Mongia b Kumble	17 (2)	lbw b Joshi	20
A.C.Hudson	b Kumble	23 (1)	lbw b Srinath	0
D.J.Cullinan	lbw b Joshi	43	c Mongia b Srinath	0
*W.J.Cronje	lbw b Hirwani	1	not out	48
J.N.Rhodes	c Manjrekar b Joshi	14 (7)	lbw b Srinath	0
B.M.McMillan	b Joshi	8 (5)	c Joshi b Kumble	17
†D.J.Richardson	b Hirwani	4 (6)	c Mongia b Srinath	7
P.L.Symcox	lbw b Joshi	32	b Kumble	0
P.S.de Villiers	not out	67	c Azharuddin b Kumble	0
A.A.Donald	b Srinath	17	b Srinath	4
P.R.Adams	c Azharuddin b Srinath	1	b Srinath	0
Extras	(B 7, LB 9, NB 1)	17	(B 1, LB 3, W 5)	9
Total		**244**		**105**

SOUTH AFRICA	O	M	R	W		O	M	R	W
Donald	27	14	37	4		15	3	32	3
De Villiers	18	5	55	2		17	4	45	1
McMillan	11	4	20	0		9	4	18	1
Cronje	5	3	8	0	(5)	7	1	10	0
Adams	17	2	46	1	(6)	9.2	4	30	3
Symcox	21	5	48	2	(4)	22	8	47	2
INDIA									
Srinath	19.1	7	47	2		11.5	4	21	6
Prasad	9	2	24	0		7	0	18	0
Kumble	31	6	76	2		12	2	34	3
Joshi	24	4	43	4		8	1	28	1
Hirwani	15	3	38	2					

FALL OF WICKETS

	I	SA	I	SA
Wkt	1st	1st	2nd	2nd
1st	22	29	10	0
2nd	63	46	15	0
3rd	98	49	38	40
4th	129	95	82	65
5th	159	102	91	96
6th	165	113	123	96
7th	193	119	124	100
8th	196	182	180	100
9th	221	242	180	105
10th	223	244	190	105

Umpires: S.K.Bansal (5) and G.Sharp (*England*) (2).
Referee: J.R.Reid (*New Zealand*) (25).

Test No. 1338/5 (I 300/SA 201)

INDIA v SOUTH AFRICA (2nd Test)

At Eden Gardens, Calcutta on 27, 28, 29, 30 November, 1 December 1996.
Toss: South Africa. Result: SOUTH AFRICA won by 329 runs.
Debuts: South Africa – H.H.Gibbs, L.Klusener.

SOUTH AFRICA

A.C.Hudson b Prasad	146	retired hurt	6
G.Kirsten b Srinath	102	run out	133
H.H.Gibbs lbw b Prasad	31	c Dravid b Srinath	9
D.J.Cullinan lbw b Prasad	43	not out	153
*W.J.Cronje c Mongia b Srinath	4	c and b Kumble	34
B.M.McMillan lbw b Prasad	0	not out	17
†D.J.Richardson not out	36		
L.Klusener b Prasad	10		
P.L.Symcox b Prasad	13		
A.A.Donald c Laxman b Kumble	0		
P.R.Adams b Kumble	4		
Extras (B 6, LB 24, NB 9)	39	(LB 10, W 1, NB 4)	15
Total	**428**	(3 wickets declared)	**367**

INDIA

†N.R.Mongia run out	35	c Cullinan b Klusener	8
R.Dravid c Hudson b McMillan	31	b McMillan	23
S.C.Ganguly b McMillan	6	c Richardson b Klusener	0
*S.R.Tendulkar b Donald	18	c Kirsten b Symcox	2
M.Azharuddin c and b Adams	109	(6) c McMillan b Klusener	52
V.V.S.Laxman b Donald	14	(5) b Klusener	1
S.B.Joshi run out	4	c McMillan b Klusener	1
J.Srinath b Donald	11	(9) c McMillan b Klusener	19
A.Kumble run out	88	(8) b Klusener	17
B.K.V.Prasad c Richardson b Adams	1	not out	3
N.D.Hirwani not out	0	b Klusener	0
Extras (LB 5, NB 7)	12	(LB 2, NB 9)	11
Total	**329**		**137**

INDIA	O	M	R	W	O	M	R	W
Srinath	37	7	107	2	24	2	97	1
Prasad	35	6	104	6	15	0	63	0
Joshi	12	1	48	0	(5) 11	0	56	0
Ganguly	3	1	10	0				
Kumble	20.1	1	78	2	(3) 33	5	101	2
Hirwani	14	2	51	0	(4) 11	1	40	0

SOUTH AFRICA	O	M	R	W	O	M	R	W
Donald	21.2	4	72	3				
Klusener	14	1	75	0	21.3	4	64	8
Adams	13	1	69	2				
McMillan	16	4	52	2	(1) 19	8	33	1
Cronje	6	3	13	0	(3) 7	4	10	0
Symcox	11	1	43	0	(4) 6	1	28	1

FALL OF WICKETS

Wkt	1st SA	1st I	2nd SA	2nd I
1st	236	68	39	17
2nd	296	71	251	18
3rd	346	77	306	27
4th	361	114	–	28
5th	362	119	–	88
6th	363	119	–	92
7th	379	161	–	97
8th	421	322	–	132
9th	422	324	–	137
10th	428	329	–	137

Umpires: B.C.Cooray (*Sri Lanka*) (9) and V.K.Ramaswamy (20).
Referee: J.R.Reid (*New Zealand*) (26). Test No. 1339/6 (I 301/SA 202)

INDIA v SOUTH AFRICA (3rd Test)

At Green Park, Kanpur on 8, 9, 10, 11, 12 December 1996.
Toss: India. Result: INDIA won by 280 runs.
Debuts: None.

INDIA

†N.R.Mongia b McMillan	41	(2)	lbw b Klusener	18
W.V.Raman c Klusener b McMillan	57	(1)	lbw b De Villiers	2
S.C.Ganguly lbw b Cronje	39	(4)	c McMillan b Symcox	41
*S.R.Tendulkar c De Villiers b Adams	61	(5)	c Richardson b Klusener	36
R.Dravid lbw b Adams	7	(7)	c McMillan b Adams	56
M.Azharuddin c and b Adams	5		not out	163
S.B.Joshi c Klusener b Adams	0	(8)	b Adams	16
A.Kumble b Cronje	5	(3)	c Gibbs b De Villiers	42
A.R.Kapoor c De Villiers b Adams	11		not out	6
J.Srinath c and b Adams	0			
B.K.V.Prasad not out	1			
Extras (B 3, LB 6, NB 1)	10		(B 4, LB 14, NB 2)	20
Total	**237**		(7 wickets declared)	**400**

SOUTH AFRICA

A.C.Hudson lbw b Kumble	15	c sub (V.V.S.Laxman) b Kumble	31
G.Kirsten c Raman b Kapoor	43	lbw b Srinath	7
H.H.Gibbs b Kapoor	17	b Prasad	5
D.J.Cullinan c Azharuddin b Kumble	29	run out	2
*W.J.Cronje c sub (V.V.S.Laxman) b Kumble	15	c Tendulkar b Joshi	50
B.M.McMillan b Srinath	1	c sub (V.V.S.Laxman) b Joshi	18
†D.J.Richardson b Srinath	4	lbw b Srinath	5
L.Klusener c Dravid b Srinath	9	not out	34
P.L.Symcox not out	23	c and b Joshi	11
P.S.de Villiers lbw b Kumble	6	b Prasad	2
P.R.Adams run out	8	c Azharuddin b Srinath	1
Extras (B 4, LB 3)	7	(LB 14)	14
Total	**177**		**180**

SOUTH AFRICA	O	M	R	W	O	M	R	W	FALL OF WICKETS			
									I	SA	I	SA
De Villiers	15	7	18	0	24	10	58	2				
Klusener	17	4	47	0	25	7	72	2	*Wkt*	*1st*	*1st*	*2nd*	*2nd*
Symcox	21	5	57	0	(6) 26	2	101	1	1st	76	34	2	21
McMillan	18	7	40	2	(3) 16	6	36	0	2nd	111	73	41	26
Adams	19.1	6	55	6	20	1	84	2	3rd	160	94	91	39
Cronje	10	5	11	2	(4) 15	5	31	0	4th	185	121	121	97
INDIA									5th	193	126	192	109
Srinath	16	7	42	3	19.1	6	38	3	6th	193	130	357	127
Prasad	14	5	25	0	11	5	25	2	7th	214	131	385	138
Kumble	27	2	71	4	24	11	27	1	8th	224	144	–	167
Kapoor	8	2	19	2	13	8	10	0	9th	224	163	–	179
Joshi	7.3	2	13	0	29	9	66	3	10th	237	177	–	180

Umpires: D.R.Shepherd (*England*) (31) and S.Venkataraghavan (15).
Referee: J.R.Reid (*New Zealand*) (27).   Test No. 1340/7 (I 302/SA 203)

INDIA v SOUTH AFRICA 1996-97

INDIA – BATTING AND FIELDING

	M	I	NO	HS	Runs	Avge	100	50	Ct/St
M.Azharuddin	3	6	1	163*	388	77.60	2	1	4
A.Kumble	3	6	1	88	199	39.80	–	1	1
R.Dravid	3	6	–	56	175	29.16	–	1	2
S.R.Tendulkar	3	6	–	61	166	27.66	–	1	1
S.C.Ganguly	2	4	–	41	86	21.50	–	–	–
N.R.Mongia	3	6	–	41	116	19.33	–	–	3/1
V.V.S.Laxman	2	4	–	51	77	19.25	–	1	1
J.Srinath	3	5	–	19	45	9.00	–	–	–
S.B.Joshi	3	6	–	16	50	8.33	–	–	2
B.K.V.Prasad	3	5	2	9	14	4.66	–	–	–
N.D.Hirwani	2	4	2	9	9	4.50	–	–	–

Played in one Test: A.R.Kapoor 11, 6*; S.V.Manjrekar 34, 5 (1 ct); W.V.Raman 57, 2 (1 ct).

INDIA – BOWLING

	O	M	R	W	Avge	Best	5wI	10wM
J.Srinath	127.1	33	352	17	20.70	6- 21	1	–
A.Kumble	147.1	27	387	13	29.76	4- 71	–	–
S.B.Joshi	91.3	17	254	8	31.75	4- 43	–	–
B.K.V.Prasad	91	18	259	8	32.37	6-104	1	–

Also bowled: S.C.Ganguly 3-1-10-0; N.D.Hirwani 40-6-129-2; A.R.Kapoor 21-18-29-2.

SOUTH AFRICA – BATTING AND FIELDING

	M	I	NO	HS	Runs	Avge	100	50	Ct/St
D.J.Cullinan	3	6	1	153*	270	54.00	1	–	2
G.Kirsten	3	6	–	133	322	53.66	2	–	2
A.C.Hudson	3	6	1	146	221	44.20	1	–	3
W.J.Cronje	3	6	1	50	152	30.40	–	1	–
L.Klusener	2	3	1	34*	53	26.50	–	–	2
P.S.de Villiers	2	4	1	67*	75	25.00	–	1	2
P.L.Symcox	3	5	1	32	79	19.75	–	–	–
H.H.Gibbs	2	4	–	31	62	15.50	–	–	1
D.J.Richardson	3	5	1	36*	56	14.00	–	–	4
B.M.McMillan	3	6	1	18	61	12.20	–	–	8
A.A.Donald	2	3	–	17	21	7.00	–	–	1
P.R.Adams	3	5	–	8	14	2.80	–	–	3

Played in one Test: J.N.Rhodes 14, 0 (2 ct).

SOUTH AFRICA – BOWLING

	O	M	R	W	Avge	Best	5wI	10wM
A.A.Donald	63.2	21	141	10	14.10	4-37	–	–
P.R.Adams	78.3	14	284	14	20.28	6-55	1	–
L.Klusener	77.3	16	258	10	25.80	8-64	1	–
B.M.McMillan	89	33	199	6	33.16	2-40	–	–
P.S.de Villiers	74	26	176	5	35.20	2-55	–	–
P.L.Symcox	107	22	324	6	54.00	2-47	–	–

Also bowled: W.J.Cronje 50-21-83-2.

PAKISTAN v NEW ZEALAND (1st Test)

At Gaddafi Stadium, Lahore on 21, 22, 23, 24 November 1996.
Toss: New Zealand. Result: NEW ZEALAND won by 44 runs.
Debuts: Pakistan – Mohammad Wasim, Zahoor Elahi.

NEW ZEALAND

B.A.Young lbw b Waqar	8	c Wasim b Mushtaq Ahmed	36
J.T.C.Vaughan lbw b Nazir	3	b Mushtaq Ahmed	11
A.C.Parore c Salim b Saqlain	37	lbw b Saqlain	15
S.P.Fleming c Salim b Mushtaq Ahmed	19	not out	92
N.J.Astle lbw b Mushtaq Ahmed	0	lbw b Mushtaq Ahmed	3
M.J.Greatbatch c Wasim b Waqar	18	b Waqar	1
C.L.Cairns c Inzamam b Mushtaq Ahmed	4	lbw b Mushtaq Ahmed	93
C.Z.Harris b Waqar	16	c Salim b Mushtaq Ahmed	0
*†L.K.Germon lbw b Waqar	0	lbw b Mushtaq Ahmed	11
D.N.Patel lbw b Mushtaq Ahmed	26	lbw b Nazir	0
S.B.Doull not out	15	st Moin b Saqlain	26
Extras (B 4, LB 5)	9	(B 6, LB 16, NB 1)	23
Total	**155**		**311**

PAKISTAN

*Saeed Anwar b Doull	8	lbw b Doull	0
Zahoor Elahi c Fleming b Doull	22	c Young b Patel	6
Ijaz Ahmed lbw b Cairns	3	b Doull	8
Inzamam-ul-Haq c Astle b Doull	0	c Young b Cairns	14
Salim Malik c Young b Doull	21 (6)	c Germon b Doull	21
Mohammad Wasim b Doull	0 (7)	not out	109
†Moin Khan b Vaughan	59 (8)	c Germon b Astle	38
Saqlain Mushtaq lbw b Vaughan	23 (5)	c Fleming b Vaughan	0
Waqar Younis lbw b Vaughan	2 (10)	b Patel	1
Mushtaq Ahmed c Germon b Vaughan	25 (9)	c Fleming b Patel	15
Shahid Nazir not out	13	c Harris b Patel	1
Extras (B 5, LB 7, NB 3)	15	(B 8, LB 8, NB 2)	18
Total	**191**		**231**

PAKISTAN	O	M	R	W	O	M	R	W
Waqar Younis	15	3	48	4	15	6	26	1
Shahid Nazir	8	3	15	1	16	1	84	1
Mushtaq Ahmed	22.1	4	59	4	32	8	84	6
Saqlain Mushtaq	12	3	24	1	22.2	4	95	2

NEW ZEALAND	O	M	R	W	O	M	R	W
Cairns	19	5	79	1	(2)16	5	62	1
Doull	16	3	46	5	(1)16	4	39	3
Harris	1	0	3	0	(5)6	2	20	0
Vaughan	12.5	2	27	4	(3)14	5	48	1
Patel	7	2	24	0	(4)15.1	6	36	4
Astle					4	1	10	1

FALL OF WICKETS

	NZ	P	NZ	P
Wkt	*1st*	*1st*	*2nd*	*2nd*
1st	6	21	46	0
2nd	16	29	59	8
3rd	67	34	85	25
4th	70	37	88	26
5th	73	37	101	42
6th	83	85	242	60
7th	102	141	242	135
8th	102	143	262	211
9th	117	164	263	219
10th	155	191	311	231

Umpires: Shakoor Rana (18) and R.B.Tiffin (*Zimbabwe*) (2).
Referee: C.W.Smith (*West Indies*) (10).   Test No. 1341/38 (P 234/NZ 246)

PAKISTAN v NEW ZEALAND (2nd Test)

At Rawalpindi Cricket Stadium on 28, 29, 30 November, 1 December 1996.
Toss: Pakistan. Result: PAKISTAN won by an innings and 13 runs.
Debuts: Pakistan – Mohammad Zahid.

NEW ZEALAND

B.A.Young lbw b Mushtaq	39		c Zahoor b Zahid		61
J.T.C.Vaughan lbw b Zahid	12		lbw b Zahid		27
A.C.Parore lbw b Zahid	3		lbw b Zahid		6
S.P.Fleming c Moin b Mushtaq	67	(7)	c Moin b Nazir		4
N.J.Astle c Moin b Mushtaq	11	(6)	lbw b Zahid		1
M.J.Greatbatch c Saeed b Mushtaq	2	(5)	c Saeed b Mushtaq		19
C.L.Cairns c Mohammad Wasim b Mushtaq	9	(8)	b Mushtaq		11
C.Z.Harris lbw b Zahid	1	(9)	lbw b Zahid		14
*†L.K.Germon c Moin b Zahid	55	(4)	b Zahid		0
D.N.Patel c Ijaz b Mushtaq	21		lbw b Zahid		0
S.B.Doull not out	1		not out		4
Extras (B 4, LB 14, NB 10)	28		(LB 7, W 1, NB 13)		21
Total	**249**				**168**

PAKISTAN

*Saeed Anwar c Doull b Cairns	149
Zahoor Elahi c Fleming b Cairns	2
Ijaz Ahmed lbw b Cairns	125
Mushtaq Ahmed lbw b Harris	42
Inzamam-ul-Haq c Vaughan b Harris	1
Salim Malik b Cairns	78
Mohammad Wasim c Cairns b Doull	5
†Moin Khan lbw b Doull	2
Shahid Nazir c and b Cairns	10
Mohammad Zahid lbw b Astle	0
Mohammad Akram not out	0
Extras (LB 14, NB 2)	16
Total	**430**

PAKISTAN	O	M	R	W		O	M	R	W
Mohammad Zahid	21	5	64	4		20	3	66	7
Shahid Nazir	9	3	23	0	(4)	7	1	19	1
Mohammad Akram	12	1	48	0	(2)	7	2	11	0
Mushtaq Ahmed	30	3	87	6	(3)	22	7	52	2
Salim Malik	2	0	9	0		2	0	13	0
NEW ZEALAND									
Doull	31	7	86	2					
Cairns	30.4	2	137	5					
Vaughan	17	1	72	0					
Astle	9	1	31	1					
Patel	15	4	33	0					
Harris	24	7	57	2					

FALL OF WICKETS			
	NZ	P	NZ
Wkt	*1st*	*1st*	*2nd*
1st	33	6	82
2nd	43	268	105
3rd	69	290	109
4th	77	291	112
5th	87	375	119
6th	110	394	137
7th	111	398	137
8th	192	419	163
9th	241	420	163
10th	249	430	168

Umpires: L.H.Barker (*West Indies*) (25) and Javed Akhtar (13).
Referee: C.W.Smith (*West Indies*) (11).   Test No. 1342/39 (P 235/NZ 247)

PAKISTAN v NEW ZEALAND 1996-97

PAKISTAN – BATTING AND FIELDING

	M	I	NO	HS	Runs	Avge	100	50	Ct/St
Mohammad Wasim	2	3	1	109*	114	57.00	1	–	3
Saeed Anwar	2	3	–	149	157	52.33	1	–	2
Ijaz Ahmed	2	3	–	125	136	45.33	1	–	1
Salim Malik	2	3	–	78	120	40.00	–	1	3
Moin Khan	2	3	–	59	99	33.00	–	1	4/1
Mushtaq Ahmed	2	3	–	42	82	27.33	–	–	–
Shahid Nazir	2	3	1	13*	24	12.00	–	–	–
Zahoor Elahi	2	3	–	22	30	10.00	–	–	1
Inzamam-ul-Haq	2	3	–	14	15	5.00	–	–	1

Played in one Test: Mohammad Akram 0*; Mohammad Zahid 0; Saqlain Mushtaq 23, 0; Waqar Younis 2, 1.

PAKISTAN – BOWLING

	O	M	R	W	Avge	Best	5wI	10wM
Mohammad Zahid	41	8	130	11	11.81	7-66	1	1
Waqar Younis	30	9	74	5	14.80	4-48	–	–
Mushtaq Ahmed	106.1	22	282	18	15.66	6-84	2	1
Saqlain Mushtaq	34.2	7	119	3	39.66	2-95	–	–
Shahid Nazir	40	8	141	3	47.00	1-15	–	–

Also bowled: Salim Malik 4-0-22-0; Mohammad Akram 19-3-59-0.

NEW ZEALAND – BATTING AND FIELDING

	M	I	NO	HS	Runs	Avge	100	50	Ct/St
S.P.Fleming	2	4	1	92*	182	60.66	–	2	4
S.B.Doull	2	4	3	26	46	46.00	–	–	1
B.A.Young	2	4	–	61	144	36.00	–	1	3
C.L.Cairns	2	4	–	93	117	29.25	–	1	2
L.K.Germon	2	4	–	55	66	16.50	–	1	3
A.C.Parore	2	4	–	37	61	15.25	–	–	1
J.T.C.Vaughan	2	4	–	27	53	13.25	–	–	–
D.N.Patel	2	4	–	26	47	11.75	–	–	–
M.J.Greatbatch	2	4	–	19	40	10.00	–	–	–
C.Z.Harris	2	4	–	16	31	7.75	–	–	1
N.J.Astle	2	4	–	11	15	3.75	–	–	1

NEW ZEALAND – BOWLING

	O	M	R	W	Avge	Best	5wI	10wM
S.B.Doull	63	14	171	10	17.10	5- 46	1	–
D.N.Patel	37.1	12	93	4	23.25	4- 36	–	–
J.T.C.Vaughan	43.5	8	147	5	29.40	4- 27	–	–
C.L.Cairns	65.4	12	278	7	39.71	5-137	1	–

Also bowled: N.J.Astle 13-2-41-2; C.Z.Harris 31-9-80-2.

AUSTRALIA v WEST INDIES (1st Test)

At Woolloongabba Ground, Brisbane on 22, 23, 24, 25, 26 November 1996.
Toss: West Indies. Result: AUSTRALIA won by 123 runs.
Debuts: Australia – M.T.G.Elliott, M.S.Kasprowicz. ‡ (J.N.Gillespie)

AUSTRALIA

*M.A.Taylor b Walsh	43	(2)	c Browne b Benjamin	36
M.T.G.Elliott c Browne b Ambrose	0	(1)	b Bishop	21
R.T.Ponting c Walsh b Benjamin	88		c Browne b Bishop	9
M.E.Waugh c Browne b Walsh	38		c Browne b Bishop	57
S.R.Waugh c Lara b Bishop	66			
M.G.Bevan c Samuels b Walsh	0	(5)	c sub (A.F.G.Griffith) b Ambrose	20
†I.A.Healy not out	161	(6)	not out	45
P.R.Reiffel c and b Walsh	20	(7)	run out	11
S.K.Warne c and b Bishop	24			
M.S.Kasprowicz c Benjamin b Bishop	6			
G.D.McGrath b Benjamin	0			
Extras (LB 8, W 3, NB 22)	33		(B 1, LB 3, NB 14)	18
Total	**479**		(6 wickets declared)	**217**

WEST INDIES

S.L.Campbell c Warne b Reiffel	18	lbw b Bevan	113
R.G.Samuels c Healy b McGrath	10	c Taylor b Warne	29
B.C.Lara c M.E.Waugh b McGrath	26	c M.E.Waugh b Reiffel	44
C.L.Hooper c Ponting b S.R.Waugh	102	c Healy b Bevan	23
S.Chanderpaul c M.E.Waugh b Reiffel	82	b McGrath	14
J.C.Adams lbw b Ponting	0	lbw b Warne	2
†C.O.Browne c M.E.Waugh b Reiffel	4	c Healy b McGrath	20
I.R.Bishop lbw b Warne	0	c Ponting b Bevan	24
C.E.L.Ambrose c sub ‡ b Reiffel	0	c Warne b McGrath	7
K.C.G.Benjamin lbw b Warne	9	lbw b McGrath	1
*C.A.Walsh not out	0	not out	1
Extras (LB 8, W 1, NB 17)	26	(B 8, LB 3, NB 7)	18
Total	**277**		**296**

WEST INDIES	O	M	R	W	O	M	R	W	FALL OF WICKETS				
										A	WI	A	WI
Ambrose	34	4	93	1	18	2	47	1	Wkt	1st	1st	2nd	2nd
Walsh	35	6	112	4	17	1	58	0	1st	4	30	55	54
Benjamin	33	6	97	2	(4) 15	1	52	1	2nd	130	43	74	118
Bishop	30	2	105	3	(3) 13	2	49	3	3rd	146	77	82	154
Hooper	19	3	64	0	2	0	7	0	4th	196	249	137	187
AUSTRALIA									5th	196	255	189	202
McGrath	21	7	32	2	29.5	12	60	4	6th	338	267	217	241
Reiffel	24.1	6	58	4	(4) 9	0	58	1	7th	407	268	–	281
Kasprowicz	22	5	60	0	(2) 13	2	39	0	8th	468	268	–	293
Warne	27	3	88	2	(3) 41	16	92	2	9th	477	277	–	293
S.R.Waugh	8.1	1	15	1					10th	479	277	–	296
M.E.Waugh	4	1	16	0									
Ponting	1.5	1	0	1									
Bevan					(5) 14	3	46	3					

Umpires: C.J.Mitchley (*South Africa*) (14) and S.G.Randell (26).
Referee: P.L.van der Merwe (*South Africa*) (12).   Test No. 1343/82 (A 559/WI 323)

AUSTRALIA v WEST INDIES (2nd Test)

At Sydney Cricket Ground on 29, 30 November, 1, 2, 3 December 1996.
Toss: Australia. Result: AUSTRALIA won by 124 runs.
Debuts: Australia – J.N.Gillespie.

AUSTRALIA

*M.A.Taylor	c Chanderpaul b Bishop	27	(2) c Lara b Bishop	16
M.T.G.Elliott	c Lara b Bishop	29	(1) retired hurt	78
R.T.Ponting	c Samuels b Walsh	9	c Browne b Bishop	4
M.E.Waugh	c Lara b Walsh	19	c Browne b Ambrose	67
M.G.Bevan	c Hooper b Benjamin	16	c Browne b Benjamin	52
G.S.Blewett	c Adams b Walsh	69	not out	47
†I.A.Healy	c Lara b Walsh	44	not out	22
S.K.Warne	c Browne b Bishop	28		
M.S.Kasprowicz	c Campbell b Walsh	21		
J.N.Gillespie	not out	16		
G.D.McGrath	lbw b Adams	24		
Extras	(LB 10, W 1, NB 18)	29	(B 4, LB 10, W 3, NB 9)	26
Total		**331**	(4 wickets declared)	**312**

WEST INDIES

S.L.Campbell	b Blewett	77	lbw b McGrath	15
R.G.Samuels	lbw b McGrath	35	b Warne	16
B.C.Lara	c Healy b McGrath	2	c Healy b McGrath	1
C.L.Hooper	lbw b Warne	27	c Taylor b Bevan	57
S.Chanderpaul	c and b Warne	48	b Warne	71
J.C.Adams	c Bevan b Warne	30	c Blewett b McGrath	5
†C.O.Browne	c Blewett b McGrath	0	not out	25
I.R.Bishop	c Elliott b Warne	48	run out	0
C.E.L.Ambrose	b Gillespie	9	b Bevan	0
K.C.G.Benjamin	b Gillespie	6	c Taylor b Warne	4
*C.A.Walsh	not out	2	c McGrath b Warne	18
Extras	(B 4, LB 6, NB 10)	20	(LB 2, NB 1)	3
Total		**304**		**215**

WEST INDIES	O	M	R	W		O	M	R	W
Ambrose	25	5	73	0		20	2	66	1
Walsh	30	6	98	5		19	6	36	0
Benjamin	22	4	69	1	(4)	16	4	46	1
Hooper	14	6	15	0	(6)	27	7	75	0
Bishop	23	5	55	3	(3)	20	6	54	2
Adams	5.5	1	11	1	(5)	4	0	21	0
AUSTRALIA									
McGrath	31	9	82	4		17	7	36	3
Kasprowicz	13	2	37	0					
Warne	35.2	13	65	3	(4)	27.4	6	95	4
Gillespie	23	5	62	2	(3)	7	2	27	0
Bevan	11	0	35	0		14	2	40	2
Blewett	4	0	13	1					
Waugh					(2)	4	0	15	0

FALL OF WICKETS

	A	WI	A	WI
Wkt	1st	1st	2nd	2nd
1st	54	92	51	33
2nd	68	108	67	33
3rd	73	136	209	35
4th	94	166	274	152
5th	131	229	–	157
6th	224	229	–	176
7th	245	244	–	176
8th	283	286	–	176
9th	288	298	–	183
10th	331	304	–	215

Umpires: D.B.Hair (17) and D.R.Shepherd (*England*) (32).
Referee: P.L.van der Merwe (*South Africa*) (13).   Test No. 1344/83 (A 560/WI 324)

AUSTRALIA v WEST INDIES (3rd Test)

At Melbourne Cricket Ground on 26, 27, 28 December 1996.
Toss: Australia. Result: WEST INDIES won by 6 wickets.
Debuts: None.

AUSTRALIA

*M.A.Taylor	b Ambrose	7	(2)	c Hooper b Walsh	10
M.L.Hayden	c Hooper b Ambose	5	(1)	b Ambrose	0
J.L.Langer	run out	12		c Hooper b Ambrose	0
M.E.Waugh	lbw b Ambrose	0		lbw b Walsh	19
S.R.Waugh	c Murray b Bishop	58		b Benjamin	37
G.S.Blewett	run out	62		c Murray b Walsh	7
†I.A.Healy	c Hooper b Ambrose	36		b Benjamin	0
P.R.Reiffel	c Samuels b Benjamin	0		lbw b Benjamin	8
S.K.Warne	c Campbell b Bishop	10		c Adams b Ambrose	18
J.N.Gillespie	not out	4		lbw b Ambrose	2
G.D.McGrath	c Hooper b Ambrose	0		not out	5
Extras	(LB 8, NB 17)	25		(LB 4, W 1, NB 11)	16
Total		**219**			**122**

WEST INDIES

S.L.Campbell	lbw b McGrath	7		c Hayden b McGrath	0
R.G.Samuels	c Taylor b Warne	17		lbw b McGrath	13
S.Chanderpaul	c and b McGrath	58		b Reiffel	40
B.C.Lara	c Warne b McGrath	2		c Hayden b McGrath	2
C.L.Hooper	run out	7		not out	27
J.C.Adams	not out	74		not out	1
†J.R.Murray	c Reiffel b McGrath	53			
I.R.Bishop	lbw b McGrath	0			
C.E.L.Ambrose	b Warne	8			
K.C.G.Benjamin	b Reiffel	11			
*C.A.Walsh	c M.E.Waugh b Warne	4			
Extras	(B 4, LB 7, NB 3)	14		(NB 4)	4
Total		**255**		(4 wickets)	**87**

WEST INDIES	O	M	R	W	O	M	R	W	FALL OF WICKETS			
Ambrose	24.5	7	55	5	12	4	17	4		A	WI	A	WI
Bishop	11	1	31	2	10	2	26	0	Wkt	1st	1st	2nd	2nd
Benjamin	19	2	64	1	12.5	5	34	3	1st	5	12	0	0
Walsh	14	0	43	0	11	4	41	3	2nd	26	62	3	25
Adams	1	0	4	0					3rd	26	71	28	32
Hooper	5	1	14	0					4th	27	86	47	82
AUSTRALIA									5th	129	107	64	
McGrath	30	11	50	5	9	1	41	3	6th	195	197	65	
Reiffel	29	8	76	1	9	2	16	1	7th	200	197	76	
Warne	28.1	3	72	3	3	0	17	0	8th	203	215	107	
Gillespie	3	2	5	0					9th	217	230	113	
Blewett	9	3	19	0	(4) 2.5	0	13	0	10th	219	255	122	
S.R.Waugh	10	5	22	0									

Umpires: P.D.Parker (4) and S.Venkataraghavan (*India*) (16).
Referee: P.L.van der Merwe (*South Africa*) (14).   Test No. 1345/84 (A 561/WI 325)

AUSTRALIA v WEST INDIES (4th Test)

At Adelaide Oval on 25, 26, 27, 28 January 1997.
Toss: West Indies. Result: AUSTRALIA won by an innings and 183 runs.
Debuts: Australia – A.J.Bichel; West Indies – A.F.G.Griffith.

WEST INDIES

S.L.Campbell c Healy b McGrath	0		c Taylor b Bevan	24
A.F.G.Griffith lbw b Bichel	13		c S.R.Waugh b McGrath	1
S.Chanderpaul c Taylor b Warne	20		c Taylor b Bevan	8
B.C.Lara c Blewett b Warne	9		c Healy b Warne	78
C.L.Hooper c M.E.Waugh b McGrath	17		lbw b Warne	45
J.C.Adams c and b Warne	10		c M.E.Waugh b Bevan	0
†J.R.Murray c Blewett b Bevan	34	(8)	c Taylor b Bevan	25
I.R.Bishop c Healy b Bevan	1	(7)	c Bevan b Warne	0
*C.A.Walsh c Healy b Bevan	0		c S.R.Waugh b Bevan	1
C.E.Cuffy c Healy b Bevan	2		not out	3
P.I.C.Thompson not out	10		c Hayden b Bevan	6
Extras (B 4, LB 1, NB 9)	14		(B 2, LB 5, NB 6)	13
Total	**130**			**204**

AUSTRALIA

*M.A.Taylor lbw b Bishop	11
M.L.Hayden st Murray b Hooper	125
J.L.Langer c Murray b Cuffy	19
M.E.Waugh c Murray b Hooper	82
S.R.Waugh c Hooper b Chanderpaul	26
G.S.Blewett b Cuffy	99
M.G.Bevan not out	85
†I.A.Healy c Lara b Thompson	12
S.K.Warne c Hooper b Bishop	9
A.J.Bichel c Lara b Walsh	7
G.D.McGrath b Walsh	1
Extras (B 2, LB 15, W 4, NB 20)	41
Total	**517**

AUSTRALIA	O	M	R	W	O	M	R	W
McGrath	12	4	21	2	17	4	31	1
Bichel	10	1	31	1	8	4	16	0
Bevan	9.5	2	31	4	22.4	3	82	6
Warne	16	4	42	3	20	4	68	3
Blewett					2	2	0	0

WEST INDIES	O	M	R	W
Walsh	37.3	6	101	2
Bishop	34	6	92	2
Cuffy	33	4	116	2
Thompson	16	0	80	1
Hooper	31	7	86	2
Adams	8	0	23	0
Chanderpaul	3	1	2	1

FALL OF WICKETS

Wkt	WI 1st	A 1st	WI 2nd
1st	11	35	6
2nd	22	78	22
3rd	45	242	42
4th	58	288	138
5th	72	288	145
6th	113	453	154
7th	117	475	181
8th	117	494	192
9th	119	507	196
10th	130	517	204

Umpires: D.R.Shepherd (*England*) (33) and S.G.Randell (27).
Referee: R.Subba Row (*England*) (17).   Test No. 1346/85 (A 562/WI 326)

AUSTRALIA v WEST INDIES (5th Test)

At W.A.C.A.Ground, Perth on 1, 2, 3, February 1997.
Toss: Australia. Result: WEST INDIES won by 10 wickets.
Debuts: None.

AUSTRALIA

M.L.Hayden	c Lara b Ambrose	0	(2) lbw b Hooper	47
*M.A.Taylor	run out	2	(1) c Browne b Ambrose	1
G.S.Blewett	c Browne b Simmons	17	b Ambrose	0
M.E.Waugh	c Campbell b Ambrose	79	c Browne b Walsh	9
S.R.Waugh	c Browne b Ambrose	1	c Hooper b Walsh	0
M.G.Bevan	not out	87	c Simmons b Walsh	15
†I.A.Healy	b Ambrose	7	c Chanderpaul b Walsh	29
P.R.Reiffel	c Simmons b Ambrose	0	c Adams b Walsh	5
S.K.Warne	c Browne b Bishop	9	c Simmons b Bishop	30
A.J.Bichel	c Browne b Bishop	15	c Samuels b Bishop	18
G.D.McGrath	c Ambrose b Bishop	0	not out	2
Extras	(LB 10, W 2, NB 14)	26	(B 2, LB 8, W 6, NB 22)	38
Total		**243**		**194**

WEST INDIES

S.L.Campbell	c Healy b Reiffel	21	not out	16
R.G.Samuels	c M.E.Waugh b Warne	76	not out	35
S.Chanderpaul	c Reiffel b McGrath	3		
B.C.Lara	c Healy b Warne	132		
C.L.Hooper	c Healy b Reiffel	57		
J.C.Adams	c Healy b McGrath	18		
P.V.Simmons	c M.E.Waugh b Reiffel	0		
†C.O.Browne	c Warne b Reiffel	0		
I.R.Bishop	c Taylor b Reiffel	13		
C.E.L.Ambrose	run out	15		
*C.A.Walsh	not out	5		
Extras	(B 5, LB 10, W 1, NB 28)	44	(LB 2, W 1, NB 3)	6
Total		**384**	(0 wickets)	**57**

WEST INDIES	O	M	R	W	O	M	R	W		FALL OF WICKETS			
Ambrose	18	5	43	5	9	2	50	2		A	WI	A	WI
Bishop	18	5	54	3	12.3	1	44	2	*Wkt*	*1st*	*1st*	*2nd*	*2nd*
Walsh	9	0	29	0	20	4	74	5	1st	0	30	7	–
Simmons	20	5	58	1	3	0	9	0	2nd	7	43	17	–
Hooper	15	1	49	0	3	0	7	1	3rd	45	251	43	–
									4th	49	275	48	–
AUSTRALIA									5th	169	331	84	–
McGrath	30	5	86	2	4	1	14	0	6th	186	332	105	–
Bichel	18	1	79	0	(3) 1.2	0	17	0	7th	186	332	110	–
Reiffel	26	6	73	5	(2) 5	0	24	0	8th	216	359	133	–
Warne	19	8	55	2					9th	243	367	189	–
Blewett	6	2	19	0					10th	243	384	194	–
Bevan	5	0	31	0									
S.R.Waugh	7	1	26	0									

Umpires: D.B.Hair (18) and P.Willey (*England*) (5).
Referee: R.Subba Row (*England*) (18).   Test No. 1347/86 (A 563/WI 327)

AUSTRALIA v WEST INDIES 1996-97

AUSTRALIA – BATTING AND FIELDING

	M	I	NO	HS	Runs	Avge	100	50	Ct/St
I.A.Healy	5	9	3	161*	356	59.33	1	–	15
M.G.Bevan	4	7	2	87*	275	55.00	–	3	2
G.S.Blewett	4	7	1	99	301	50.16	–	3	4
M.T.G.Elliott	2	4	1	78*	128	42.66	–	1	1
M.E.Waugh	5	9	–	82	370	41.11	–	4	8
M.L.Hayden	3	5	–	125	177	35.40	1	–	3
S.R.Waugh	4	6	–	66	188	31.33	–	2	2
R.T.Ponting	2	4	–	88	110	27.50	–	1	2
J.N.Gillespie	2	3	2	16*	22	22.00	–	–	–
S.K.Warne	5	7	–	30	128	18.28	–	–	6
M.A.Taylor	5	9	–	43	153	17.00	–	–	9
M.S.Kasprowicz	2	2	–	21	27	13.50	–	–	–
A.J.Bichel	2	3	–	18	40	13.33	–	–	–
J.L.Langer	2	3	–	19	31	10.33	–	–	–
P.R.Reiffel	3	6	–	20	44	7.33	–	–	2
G.D.McGrath	5	7	2	24	32	6.40	–	–	2

AUSTRALIA – BOWLING

	O	M	R	W	Avge	Best	5wI	10wM
G.D.McGrath	200.5	61	453	26	17.42	5-50	1	–
M.G.Bevan	76.3	10	265	15	17.66	6-82	1	1
P.R.Reiffel	102.1	22	305	12	25.41	5-73	1	–
S.K.Warne	217.1	57	594	22	27.00	4-95	–	–

Also bowled: G.S.Blewett 23.5-7-64-1; A.J.Bichel 37.2-6-143-1; J.N.Gillespie 33-9-94-2; M.S.Kasprowicz 48-9-126-0; R.T.Ponting 1.5-1-0-1; M.E.Waugh 8-1-31-0; S.R.Waugh 25.1-7-63-1.

WEST INDIES – BATTING AND FIELDING

	M	I	NO	HS	Runs	Avge	100	50	Ct/St
C.L.Hooper	5	9	1	102	362	45.25	1	2	9
S.Chanderpaul	5	9	–	82	344	38.22	–	3	2
J.R.Murray	2	3	–	53	112	37.33	–	1	4/1
R.G.Samuels	4	8	1	76	231	33.00	–	1	4
B.C.Lara	5	9	–	132	296	32.88	1	1	8
S.L.Campbell	5	10	1	113	291	32.33	1	1	3
J.C.Adams	5	9	2	74*	140	20.00	–	1	3
C.O.Browne	3	5	1	25*	49	12.25	–	–	15
I.R.Bishop	5	8	–	48	86	10.75	–	1	–
C.A.Walsh	5	8	4	18	31	7.75	–	–	2
C.E.L.Ambrose	4	6	–	15	39	6.50	–	–	1
K.C.G.Benjamin	3	5	–	11	31	6.20	–	–	1

Played in one Test: C.E.Cuffy 2, 3*; A.F.G.Griffith 13, 1; P.V.Simmons 0 (3 ct); P.I.C.Thompson 10*, 6.

WEST INDIES – BOWLING

	O	M	R	W	Avge	Best	5wI	10wM
C.E.L.Ambrose	160.5	31	444	19	23.36	5-43	2	–
I.R.Bishop	171.3	30	510	20	25.50	3-49	–	–
C.A.Walsh	192.3	33	592	19	31.15	5-74	2	–
K.C.G.Benjamin	117.5	22	362	9	40.22	3-34	–	–

Also bowled: J.C.Adams 18.5-1-59-1; S.Chanderpaul 3-1-2-1; C.E.Cuffy 33-4-116-2; C.L.Hooper 116-25-317-3; P.V.Simmons 23-5-67-1; P.I.C.Thompson 16-0-80-1.

ZIMBABWE v ENGLAND (1st Test)

At Queens Sports Club, Bulawayo on 18, 19, 20, 21, 22 December 1996.
Toss: Zimbabwe. Result: MATCH DRAWN (SCORES LEVEL).
Debuts: Zimbabwe – A.C.Waller; England – C.E.W.Silverwood.

ZIMBABWE

G.W.Flower c Hussain b Silverwood	43		lbw b Gough	0
S.V.Carlisle c Crawley b Gough	0		c Atherton b Mullally	4
*A.D.R.Campbell c Silverwood b Croft	84		b Croft	29
D.L.Houghton c Stewart b Croft	34		c Croft b Tufnell	37
†A.Flower c Stewart b Tufnell	112		c Crawley b Tufnell	14
A.C.Waller c Crawley b Croft	15		c Knight b Gough	50
G.J.Whittall c Atherton b Silverwood	7	(8)	c Croft b Tufnell	56
P.A.Strang c Tufnell b Silverwood	38	(9)	c Crawley b Croft	19
H.H.Streak b Mullally	19	(10)	not out	8
B.C.Strang not out	4	(7)	c Mullally b Tufnell	3
H.K.Olonga c Knight b Tufnell	0		c Stewart b Silverwood	0
Extras (LB 4, W 3, NB 13)	20		(B 4, LB 6, W 2, NB 2)	14
Total	**376**			**234**

ENGLAND

N.V.Knight lbw b Olonga	56		run out	96
*M.A.Atherton lbw b P.A.Strang	16		b Olonga	4
†A.J.Stewart lbw b P.A.Strang	48		c Campbell b P.A.Strang	73
N.Hussain c B.C.Strang b Streak	113		c Carlisle b P.A.Strang	0
G.P.Thorpe c Campbell b P.A.Strang	13	(6)	c Campbell b Streak	2
J.P.Crawley c A.Flower b P.A.Strang	112	(5)	c Carlisle b Whittall	7
R.D.B.Croft lbw b Olonga	7			
D.Gough c G.W.Flower b Olonga	2	(7)	not out	3
C.E.W.Silverwood c Houghton b P.A.Strang	0			
A.D.Mullally c Waller b Streak	4			
P.C.R.Tufnell not out	2			
Extras (B 4, LB 4, W 1, NB 24)	33		(B 2, LB 13, W 3, NB 1)	19
Total	**406**		**(6 wickets)**	**204**

ENGLAND	O	M	R	W		O	M	R	W		FALL OF WICKETS			
Mullally	23	4	69	1	(2)	18	5	49	1			Z	E	Z	E
Gough	26	4	87	1	(1)	12	2	44	2	*Wkt*	*1st*	*1st*	*2nd*	*2nd*
Silverwood	18	5	63	3	(4)	7	3	8	1	1st	3	48	6	17
Croft	44	15	77	3	(3)	33	9	62	2	2nd	130	92	6	154
Tufnell	26.5	4	76	2		31	12	61	4	3rd	136	160	57	156
										4th	206	180	82	178
ZIMBABWE										5th	235	328	103	182
Streak	36	8	86	2		11	0	64	1	6th	252	340	111	204
B.C.Strang	17	5	54	0						7th	331	344	178	–
P.A.Strang	58.4	14	123	5		14	0	63	2	8th	372	353	209	–
Olonga	23	2	90	3	(2)	2	0	16	1	9th	376	378	233	–
Whittall	10	2	25	0		2	0	10	1	10th	376	406	234	–
G.W.Flower	7	3	20	0	(4)	8	0	36	0					

Umpires: R.S.Dunne (*New Zealand*) (20) and I.D.Robinson (14).
Referee: Hanumant Singh (*India*) (1).   Test No. 1348/1 (E 730/Z 21)

ZIMBABWE v ENGLAND (2nd Test)

At Harare Sports Club on 26, 27, 28, 29, 30 (*no play*) **December 1996.**
Toss: Zimbabwe. Result: MATCH DRAWN.
Debuts: None.

ENGLAND

N.V.Knight	c A.Flower b Olonga	15	c Campbell b Strang	30
*M.A.Atherton	c Campbell b Whittall	13	c Campbell b Streak	1
†A.J.Stewart	c G.W.Flower b Streak	19	not out	101
N.Hussain	c A.Flower b Streak	11	c Houghton b Strang	6
G.P.Thorpe	c Dekker b Streak	5	not out	50
J.P.Crawley	not out	47		
C.White	c Campbell b Whittall	9		
R.D.B.Croft	c G.W.Flower b Whittall	14		
D.Gough	b Strang	2		
A.D.Mullally	c and b Whittall	0		
P.C.R.Tufnell	b Streak	9		
Extras	(B 1, LB 5, W 1, NB 5)	12	(LB 5, W 1, NB 1)	7
Total		**156**	(3 wickets)	**195**

ZIMBABWE

G.W.Flower	c Crawley b Gough	73
M.H.Dekker	c Stewart b Mullally	2
*A.D.R.Campbell	c Thorpe b White	22
D.L.Houghton	c Stewart b Gough	29
†A.Flower	lbw b Gough	6
A.C.Waller	lbw b Tufnell	4
G.J.Whittall	b Gough	1
P.A.Strang	not out	47
H.H.Streak	c Crawley b Croft	7
E.A.Brandes	c Gough b Croft	9
H.K.Olonga	c Hussain b Croft	0
Extras	(LB 8, W 1, NB 6)	15
Total		**215**

ZIMBABWE	O	M	R	W	O	M	R	W	FALL OF WICKETS			
										E	Z	E
Streak	24.1	7	43	4	18	5	47	1	*Wkt*	*1st*	*1st*	*2nd*
Brandes	16	6	35	0	21	6	45	0	1st	24	5	7
Olonga	9	1	23	1	7	0	31	0	2nd	50	46	75
Whittall	16	5	18	4	14	6	16	0	3rd	50	110	89
Strang	18	7	31	1	26	6	42	2	4th	65	131	–
G.W.Flower					7	2	9	0	5th	73	136	–
									6th	94	138	–
ENGLAND									7th	128	159	–
Mullally	23	7	32	1					8th	133	197	–
Gough	26	10	40	4					9th	134	211	–
Croft	15	2	39	3					10th	156	215	–
White	16	4	41	1								
Tufnell	25	3	55	1								

Umpires: K.T.Francis (*Sri Lanka*) **(18) and R.B.Tiffin (3).**
Referee: Hanumant Singh (*India*) **(2).**   Test No. 1349/2 (E 731/Z 22)

ZIMBABWE v ENGLAND 1996-97

ZIMBABWE – BATTING AND FIELDING

	M	I	NO	HS	Runs	Avge	100	50	Ct/St
P.A.Strang	2	3	1	47*	104	52.00	–	–	–
A.D.R.Campbell	2	3	–	84	135	45.00	–	1	7
A.Flower	2	3	–	112	132	44.00	1	–	3
G.W.Flower	2	3	–	73	116	38.66	–	1	3
D.L.Houghton	2	3	–	37	100	33.33	–	–	2
A.C.Waller	2	3	–	50	69	23.00	–	1	1
G.J.Whittall	2	3	–	56	64	21.33	–	1	1
H.H.Streak	2	3	1	19	34	17.00	–	–	–
H.K.Olonga	2	3	–	0	0	0.00	–	–	–

Played in one Test: E.A.Brandes 9; S.V.Carlisle 0, 4 (2 ct); M.H.Dekker 2 (1 ct); B.C.Strang 4*, 3 (1 ct).

ZIMBABWE – BOWLING

	O	M	R	W	Avge	Best	5wI	10wM
G.J.Whittall	42	13	69	5	13.80	4- 18	–	–
P.A.Strang	116.4	27	259	10	25.90	5-123	1	–
H.H.Streak	89.1	20	240	8	30.00	4- 43	–	–
H.K.Olonga	41	3	160	5	32.00	3- 90	–	–

Also bowled: E.A.Brandes 37-12-80-0; G.W.Flower 22-5-65-0; B.C.Strang.17-5-54-0.

ENGLAND – BATTING AND FIELDING

	M	I	NO	HS	Runs	Avge	100	50	Ct/St
J.P.Crawley	2	3	1	112	166	83.00	1	–	6
A.J.Stewart	2	4	1	101*	241	80.33	1	1	5
N.V.Knight	2	4	–	96	197	49.25	–	2	2
N.Hussain	2	4	–	113	130	32.50	1	–	2
G.P.Thorpe	2	4	–	50*	70	23.33	–	1	1
P.C.R.Tufnell	2	2	1	9	11	11.00	–	–	1
R.D.B.Croft	2	2	–	14	21	10.50	–	–	2
M.A.Atherton	2	4	–	16	34	8.50	–	–	2
D.Gough	2	3	1	3*	7	3.50	–	–	1
A.D.Mullally	2	2	–	4	4	2.00	–	–	1

Played in one Test: C.E.W.Silverwood 0 (1 ct); C.White 9.

ENGLAND – BOWLING

	O	M	R	W	Avge	Best	5wI	10wM
C.E.W.Silverwood	25	8	71	4	17.75	3-63	–	–
R.D.B.Croft	92	26	178	8	22.25	3-39	–	–
D.Gough	64	16	171	7	24.42	4-40	–	–
P.C.R.Tufnell	82.5	19	192	7	27.42	4-61	–	–
A.D.Mullally	64	16	150	3	50.00	1-32	–	–

Also bowled: C.White 16-4-41-1.

SOUTH AFRICA v INDIA (1st Test)

At Kingsmead, Durban on 26, 27, 28 December 1996.
Toss: India. Result: SOUTH AFRICA won by 328 runs.
Debuts: South Africa – A.M.Bacher.

SOUTH AFRICA

A.C.Hudson	c Mongia b Ganguly	80	c Tendulkar b Kumble	52
G.Kirsten b Prasad		2	c Dravid b Prasad	2
A.M.Bacher lbw b Srinath		25	c Tendulkar b Kumble	55
D.J.Cullinan	c Mongia b Prasad	1	c Mongia b Prasad	3
*W.J.Cronje	c Mongia b Prasad	15	c Mongia b Prasad	17
H.H.Gibbs	c Mongia b Johnson	0	lbw b Srinath	25
B.M.McMillan lbw b Johnson		34	not out	51
S.M.Pollock not out		23	c Rathore b Prasad	2
†D.J.Richardson b Prasad			b Srinath	4
L.Klusener	c Mongia b Srinath	1	c Mongia b Srinath	4
A.A.Donald	c Rathore b Prasad	5	c Rathore b Prasad	26
Extras	(B 4, LB 10, NB 11)	25	(B 7, LB 6, NB 5)	18
Total		**235**		**259**

INDIA

V.Rathore	c Hudson b Donald	7	c Richardson b Donald	2
W.V.Raman b Pollock		0	b Donald	1
S.C.Ganguly	c Klusener b Pollock	16	b Donald	0
*S.R.Tendulkar b Donald		15	c Kirsten b Donald	4
M.Azharuddin	c Bacher b McMillan	15	c Klusener b Pollock	8
R.Dravid lbw b McMillan		7	not out	27
†N.R.Mongia	c Richardson b Donald	4	c Cronje b Klusener	4
A.Kumble not out		13	c Hudson b Klusener	2
J.Srinath	c Cullinan b Donald	0	run out	7
D.Johnson	c Bacher b Donald	3	c Klusener b Pollock	5
B.K.V.Prasad	c Richardson b Klusener	4	c Hudson b Donald	1
Extras	(B 4, LB 3, W 2, NB 7)	16	(LB 2, NB 3)	5
Total		**100**		**66**

INDIA	O	M	R	W	O	M	R	W		FALL OF WICKETS			
Srinath	20	7	36	2	23	5	80	3		SA	I	SA	I
Prasad	19	6	60	5	25	4	93	5	Wkt	1st	1st	2nd	2nd
Johnson	15	2	52	2	9	1	39	0	1st	8	2	4	2
Tendulkar	2.4	2	0	0					2nd	70	22	115	2
Kumble	20.2	3	61	0	(4) 11	3	26	2	3rd	71	36	120	7
Ganguly	9	4	12	1	(5) 2	0	8	0	4th	99	52	120	15
									5th	113	68	164	20
SOUTH AFRICA									6th	162	74	164	25
Donald	16	5	40	5	11.1	4	14	4	7th	190	74	171	40
Pollock	8	2	18	2	12	4	25	3	8th	229	74	181	51
Klusener	7.1	2	8	1	9	2	16	2	9th	230	89	185	59
McMillan	8	2	27	2	2	0	9	0	10th	235	100	259	66

Umpires: R.S.Dunne (*New Zealand*) (21) and D.L.Orchard (4).
Referee: B.N.Jarman (*Australia*) (6).   Test No. 1350/8 (SA 204/I 303)

SOUTH AFRICA v INDIA (2nd Test)

At Newlands, Cape Town on 2, 3, 4, 5, 6 January 1997.
Toss: South Africa. Result: SOUTH AFRICA won by 282 runs.
Debuts: India – D.Ganesh.

SOUTH AFRICA

A.C.Hudson	c Mongia b Prasad	16	b Srinath	55
G.Kirsten	run out	103	lbw b Ganesh	0
A.M.Bacher	c Mongia b Srinath	25	lbw b Srinath	0
D.J.Cullinan	c Mongia b Prasad	77	(5) b Kumble	55
*W.J.Cronje	c Mongia b Srinath	41	(6) c Dravid b Kumble	18
B.M.McMillan	not out	103	(7) not out	59
S.M.Pollock	c Tendulkar b Prasad	1	(8) not out	40
†D.J.Richardson	c Dravid b Srinath	39		
L.Klusener	not out	102	(4) c Dravid b Srinath	12
A.A.Donald				
P.R.Adams				
Extras	(B 5, LB 9, NB 8)	22	(B 4, LB 12, W 1)	17
Total	(7 wickets declared)	529	(6 wickets declared)	256

INDIA

W.V.Raman	run out	5	c Richardson b Pollock	16
R.Dravid	b Klusener	2	(3) c Richardson b Adams	12
S.C.Ganguly	c McMillan b Donald	23	(4) c McMillan b Pollock	30
B.K.V.Prasad	b Adams	0	(10) st Richardson b Adams	15
*S.R.Tendulkar	c Bacher b McMillan	169	c Klusener b McMillan	9
V.V.S.Laxman	c Richardson b Pollock	5	(7) not out	35
M.Azharuddin	run out	115	(6) c Hudson b Donald	2
†N.R.Mongia	lbw b Adams	5	(2) b Donald	2
A.Kumble	c Richardson b Donald	2	(8) c Richardson b Adams	14
J.Srinath	b Pollock	11	absent hurt	
D.Ganesh	not out	2	(9) b Donald	1
Extras	(LB 9, NB 11)	20	(LB 1, W 2, NB 5)	8
Total		359		144

INDIA	O	M	R	W	O	M	R	W
Srinath	38	8	130	3	18	5	78	3
Prasad	36	1	114	3	(4) 7	1	16	0
Ganesh	23.5	6	93	0	(2) 10	3	38	1
Kumble	51	7	136	0	(3) 25	5	58	2
Ganguly	9	1	24	0	2	0	5	0
Raman	5	1	18	0	10	0	45	0
SOUTH AFRICA								
Donald	24	4	99	2	18	5	40	3
Pollock	23	2	76	2	12	2	29	2
Adams	18	5	49	2	(5) 16.2	4	45	3
Klusener	12	1	88	1	3	0	13	0
McMillan	6.2	0	22	1	(4) 11	4	16	1
Cronje	9	5	16	0				

FALL OF WICKETS

Wkt	SA 1st	I 1st	SA 2nd	I 2nd
1st	37	7	6	7
2nd	89	24	7	26
3rd	203	25	33	44
4th	251	33	127	59
5th	291	58	133	61
6th	299	280	155	87
7th	382	298	–	115
8th	–	315	–	121
9th	–	340	–	144
10th	–	359	–	–

Umpires: D.B.Hair (*Australia*) (19) and R.E.Koertzen (1).
Referee: B.N.Jarman (*Australia*) (7).   Test No. 1351/9 (SA 205/I 304)

SOUTH AFRICA v INDIA (3rd Test)

At The Wanderers, Johannesburg on 16, 17, 18, 19, 20 January 1997.
Toss: India. Result: MATCH DRAWN.
Debuts: None.

INDIA

V.Rathore c Richardson b Adams	13		lbw b Donald	44
†N.R.Mongia b Donald	21		c McMillan b Donald	50
R.Dravid c Pollock b Cronje	148		c Cullinan b Adams	81
*S.R.Tendulkar c McMillan b Cronje	35		c Richardson b Cronje	9
S.C.Ganguly c McMillan b Klusener	73		b Adams	60
M.Azharuddin c Hudson b Klusener	18		lbw b Pollock	2
V.V.S.Laxman retired hurt	0			
A.Kumble c Richardson b Klusener	29	(7)	b Adams	6
J.Srinath c Hudson b Donald	41	(8)	lbw b Donald	4
D.Ganesh c Cullinan b Donald	1	(9)	not out	0
B.K.V.Prasad not out	2	(10)	not out	1
Extras (LB 15, W 5, NB 9)	29		(LB 3; W 4, NB 2)	9
Total	**410**		**(8 wickets declared)**	**266**

SOUTH AFRICA

A.C.Hudson c Azharuddin b Kumble	18		b Kumble	3
G.Kirsten b Prasad	29		c Rathore b Prasad	1
A.M.Bacher lbw b Srinath	13		b Prasad	23
D.J.Cullinan c sub (P.Dharmani) b Srinath	33		not out	122
*W.J.Cronje c Mongia b Srinath	43		run out	6
B.M.McMillan lbw b Ganguly	47		c sub (P.Dharmani) b Srinath	2
S.M.Pollock c Mongia b Srinath	79		b Srinath	0
†D.J.Richardson c Azharuddin b Ganguly	13		c Azharuddin b Kumble	7
L.Klusener not out	22		c Dravid b Kumble	49
A.A.Donald b Prasad	4		not out	0
P.R.Adams c Dravid b Srinath	2			
Extras (B 2, LB 7, W 1, NB 8)	18		(B 1, LB 13, NB 1)	15
Total	**321**		**(8 wickets)**	**228**

SOUTH AFRICA	O	M	R	W		O	M	R	W	FALL OF WICKETS				
											I	SA	I	SA
Donald	32.1	9	88	3		18	6	38	3	Wkt	1st	1st	2nd	2nd
Pollock	30	11	55	0	(3)	11	0	28	1	1st	25	36	90	4
McMillan	20.5	4	50	0	(4)	11	0	48	0	2nd	46	64	109	4
Klusener	27	6	75	3	(2)	13	1	41	0	3rd	100	73	124	49
Adams	24	6	88	1		21	1	80	3	4th	245	139	232	71
Cronje	16.3	5	39	2	(7)	8	3	24	1	5th	266	147	235	76
Bacher					(6)	1	0	4	0	6th	327	259	256	78
INDIA										7th	403	285	265	95
Srinath	25.1	3	104	5		24	6	89	2	8th	408	303	265	222
Prasad	20	2	83	2		15	1	59	2	9th	410	318	–	–
Kumble	25	5	63	1		23	7	40	3	10th	410	321	–	–
Ganesh	7	1	26	0		2	0	8	0					
Ganguly	12	1	36	2	(6)	2	2	0	0					
Tendulkar					(5)	2	0	18	0					

Umpires: C.J.Mitchley (15) and P.Willey (*England*) (4).
Referee: B.N.Jarman (*Australia*) (8).   Test No. 1352/10 (SA 206/I 305)

SOUTH AFRICA v INDIA 1996-97

SOUTH AFRICA – BATTING AND FIELDING

	M	I	NO	HS	Runs	Avge	100	50	Ct/St
B.M.McMillan	3	6	3	103*	296	98.66	1	2	5
D.J.Cullinan	3	6	1	122*	291	58.20	1	2	3
L.Klusener	3	6	2	102*	190	47.50	1	–	4
A.C.Hudson	3	6	–	80	224	37.33	–	3	6
S.M.Pollock	3	6	2	79	145	36.25	–	1	1
A.M.Bacher	3	6	–	55	141	23.50	–	1	3
W.J.Cronje	3	6	–	43	140	23.33	–	–	1
G.Kirsten	3	6	–	103	137	22.83	1	–	1
D.J.Richardson	3	5	–	39	87	17.40	–	–	11/1
A.A.Donald	3	4	1	26	35	11.66	–	–	–
P.R.Adams	2	1	–	2	2	2.00	–	–	–

Played in one Test: H.H.Gibbs 0, 25.

SOUTH AFRICA – BOWLING

	O	M	R	W	Avge	Best	5wI	10wM
A.A.Donald	119.2	33	319	20	15.95	5-40	1	–
S.M.Pollock	96	21	231	10	23.10	3-25	–	–
P.R.Adams	79.2	16	262	9	29.11	3-45	–	–
L.Klusener	77.1	15	241	7	34.42	3-75	–	–
B.M.McMillan	59.1	10	172	4	43.00	2-27	–	–

Also bowled: A.M.Bacher 1-0-4-0; W.J.Cronje 33.3-13-79-3.

INDIA – BATTING AND FIELDING

	M	I	NO	HS	Runs	Avge	100	50	Ct/St
R.Dravid	3	6	1	148	277	55.40	1	1	6
S.R.Tendulkar	3	6	–	169	241	40.16	1	–	3
V.V.S.Laxman	2	3	2	35*	40	40.00	–	–	–
S.C.Ganguly	3	6	–	73	202	33.66	–	2	–
M.Azharuddin	3	6	–	115	160	26.66	1	–	3
V.Rathore	2	4	–	44	66	16.50	–	–	4
N.R.Mongia	3	6	–	50	86	14.33	–	1	14
A.Kumble	3	6	1	29	66	13.20	–	–	–
J.Srinath	3	5	–	41	63	12.60	–	–	–
B.K.V.Prasad	3	6	2	15	23	5.75	–	–	–
W.V.Raman	2	4	–	16	22	5.50	–	–	–
D.Ganesh	2	4	2	2*	4	2.00	–	–	–

Played in one Test: D.Johnson 3, 5.

INDIA – BOWLING

	O	M	R	W	Avge	Best	5wI	10wM
B.K.V.Prasad	122	15	425	17	25.00	5- 60	2	1
J.Srinath	148.1	34	517	18	28.72	5-104	1	–
A.Kumble	155.2	30	384	8	48.00	3- 40	–	–

Also bowled: D.Ganesh 42.5-10-165-1; S.C.Ganguly 36-8-85-3; D.Johnson 24-3-91-2; W.V.Raman 15-1-63-0; S.R.Tendulkar 4.4-2-18-0.

NEW ZEALAND v ENGLAND (1st Test)

At Eden Park, Auckland on 24, 25, 26, 27, 28 January 1997.
Toss: England. Result: MATCH DRAWN.
Debuts: None.

NEW ZEALAND

B.A.Young lbw b Mullally	44	(2)	c Hussain b Cork	3
B.A.Pocock lbw b Gough	70	(1)	lbw b Gough	20
A.C.Parore c Stewart b Cork	6		st Stewart b Tufnell	33
S.P.Fleming c and b Cork	129		c Crawley b Tufnell	9
N.J.Astle c Stewart b White	10	(6)	not out	102
J.T.C.Vaughan lbw b Cork	3	(7)	lbw b Tufnell	2
C.L.Cairns c Stewart b White	67	(8)	b Mullally	7
*†L.K.Germon c Stewart b Gough	14	(5)	run out	13
D.N.Patel lbw b Gough	0		lbw b Mullally	0
S.B.Doull c Knight b Gough	5		b Gough	26
D.K.Morrison not out	6		not out	14
Extras (B 5, LB 12, W 2, NB 17)	36		(LB 11, NB 8)	19
Total	**390**		**(9 wickets declared)**	**248**

ENGLAND

N.V.Knight lbw b Doull	5
*M.A.Atherton c and b Patel	83
†A.J.Stewart c and b Doull	173
N.Hussain c Fleming b Patel	8
G.P.Thorpe hit wkt b Cairns	119
J.P.Crawley run out	14
C.White lbw b Vaughan	0
D.G.Cork c Young b Morrison	59
D.Gough c Germon b Morrison	2
A.D.Mullally c Germon b Morrison	21
P.C.R.Tufnell not out	19
Extras (B 2, LB 12, W 2, NB 2)	18
Total	**521**

ENGLAND	O	M	R	W		O	M	R	W
Cork	32.5	8	96	3		16	3	45	1
Mullally	27	11	55	1		26	11	47	2
Gough	32	5	91	4	(4)	22	3	66	2
Tufnell	25	5	80	0	(5)	40	18	53	3
White	15	3	51	2	(3)	10	2	26	0

NEW ZEALAND	O	M	R	W
Morrison	24.4	4	104	3
Doull	39	10	118	2
Cairns	30	3	103	1
Astle	14	3	33	0
Vaughan	36	10	57	1
Patel	44	10	92	2

FALL OF WICKETS

Wkt	NZ 1st	E 1st	NZ 2nd
1st	85	18	17
2nd	114	200	28
3rd	193	222	47
4th	210	304	88
5th	215	339	90
6th	333	339	92
7th	362	453	101
8th	362	471	105
9th	380	478	142
10th	390	521	–

Umpires: S.A.Bucknor (*West Indies*) (25) and R.S.Dunne (22).
Referee: P.J.P.Burge (*Australia*) (18).   Test No. 1353/76 (E 732/NZ 248)

NEW ZEALAND v ENGLAND (2nd Test)

At Basin Reserve, Wellington on 6, 7, 8, 9, 10 February 1997.
Toss: New Zealand. Result: ENGLAND won by an innings and 68 runs.
Debuts: New Zealand – D.L.Vettori.

NEW ZEALAND

B.A.Young	c Stewart b Gough	8	(2)	c Stewart b Tufnell	56
B.A.Pocock	c Cork b Caddick	6	(1)	c Knight b Gough	64
A.C.Parore	c Stewart b Gough	4		lbw b Croft	15
S.P.Fleming	c and b Caddick	1		c and b Croft	0
N.J.Astle	c Croft b Gough	36	(7)	c Stewart b Gough	4
C.L.Cairns	c Hussain b Gough	3	(8)	c Knight b Caddick	22
*†L.K.Germon	c Stewart b Caddick	10	(6)	b Gough	11
D.N.Patel	c Cork b Caddick	45	(5)	lbw b Croft	0
S.B.Doull	c Stewart b Gough	0		c Knight b Gough	0
G.I.Allott	c Knight b Cork	1		b Caddick	2
D.L.Vettori	not out	3		not out	2
Extras	(LB 5, NB 2)	7		(B 5, LB 4, NB 6)	15
Total		**124**			**191**

ENGLAND

N.V.Knight	c Patel b Doull	8
*M.A.Atherton	lbw b Doull	30
†A.J.Stewart	c Fleming b Allott	52
N.Hussain	c Young b Vettori	64
G.P.Thorpe	st Germon b Patel	108
J.P.Crawley	c Germon b Doull	56
D.G.Cork	lbw b Astle	7
R.D.B.Croft	c Fleming b Doull	0
D.Gough	c Fleming b Doull	18
A.R.Caddick	c Allott b Vettori	20
P.C.R.Tufnell	not out	6
Extras	(B 3, LB 9, NB 2)	14
Total		**383**

ENGLAND	O	M	R	W	O	M	R	W	FALL OF WICKETS			
										NZ	E	NZ
Cork	14	4	34	1	10	1	42	0	*Wkt*	*1st*	*1st*	*2nd*
Caddick	18.3	5	45	4	27.2	11	40	2	1st	14	10	89
Gough	16	6	40	5	(4) 23	9	52	4	2nd	18	80	125
Croft					(3) 20	9	19	3	3rd	19	106	125
Tufnell					23	9	29	1	4th	19	213	125
									5th	23	331	161
NEW ZEALAND									6th	48	331	164
Doull	28	10	75	5					7th	85	331	175
Allott	31	6	91	1					8th	85	357	175
Vettori	34.3	10	98	2					9th	106	357	182
Cairns	4	2	8	0					10th	124	383	191
Astle	14	5	30	1								
Patel	24	6	59	1								
Pocock	2	0	10	0								

Umpires: S.A.Bucknor (*West Indies*) (26) and D.B.Cowie (4).
Referee: P.J.P.Burge (*Australia*) (19).　　　　Test No. 1354/77 (NZ 249/E 733)

NEW ZEALAND v ENGLAND (3rd Test)

At Lancaster Park, Christchurch on 14, 15, 16, 17, 18 February 1997.
Toss: England. Result: ENGLAND won by 4 wickets.
Debuts: New Zealand – M.J.Horne.

NEW ZEALAND

B.A.Young c Cork	11	(2)	c Knight b Tufnell	49
B.A.Pocock c Atherton b Croft	22	(1)	b Cork	0
M.J.Horne c Thorpe b Gough	42	(8)	c Stewart b Caddick	13
*S.P.Fleming st Stewart b Croft	62		c Knight b Tufnell	11
N.J.Astle c Hussain b Croft	15		c Hussain b Croft	5
†A.C.Parore c Hussain b Croft	59	(3)	c Stewart b Gough	8
C.L.Cairns c Stewart b Caddick	57	(6)	c Knight b Tufnell	52
S.B.Doull run out	1	(7)	c Knight b Croft	5
D.L.Vettori run out	25		not out	29
H.T.Davis c Hussain b Croft	8		b Gough	1
G.I.Allott not out	8		c Stewart b Gough	1
Extras (B 1, LB 16, NB 19)	36		(LB 8, NB 4)	12
Total	**346**			**186**

ENGLAND

N.V.Knight c Fleming b Allott	14		c Davis b Vettori	29
*M.A.Atherton not out	94		c Parore b Astle	118
†A.J.Stewart c sub (C.Z.Harris) b Allott	15		c Pocock b Vettori	17
N.Hussain c Parore b Cairns	12	(5)	c Fleming b Vettori	33
G.P.Thorpe b Astle	18	(6)	c and b Vettori	2
J.P.Crawley c Parore b Allott	1	(7)	not out	40
D.G.Cork c Parore b Davis	16	(8)	not out	39
R.D.B.Croft c Davis b Astle	31			
D.Gough b Vettori	0			
A.R.Caddick c sub (C.Z.Harris) b Allott	4	(4)	c Fleming b Doull	15
P.C.R.Tufnell c Young b Doull	13			
Extras (LB 4, W 1, NB 5)	10		(B 2, LB 8, W 1, NB 3)	14
Total	**228**		(6 wickets)	**307**

ENGLAND	O	M	R	W	O	M	R	W
Cork	20	3	78	1	6	2	5	1
Caddick	32	8	64	1	10	1	25	1
Gough	21	3	70	1 (4)	13.3	5	42	3
Croft	39.1	5	95	5 (3)	31	13	48	2
Tufnell	16	6	22	0	28	9	58	3
Thorpe	1	1	0	0				

NEW ZEALAND	O	M	R	W	O	M	R	W
Allott	18	3	74	4	12.4	2	32	0
Doull	17.4	3	49	1 (3)	21	8	57	1
Davis	18	2	50	1 (2)	18	6	43	0
Vettori	12	4	13	1	57	18	97	4
Cairns	8	5	12	1	10	1	23	0
Astle	11	2	26	2	28	10	45	1

FALL OF WICKETS

	NZ	E	NZ	E
Wkt	1st	1st	2nd	2nd
1st	14	20	0	64
2nd	78	40	42	116
3rd	106	70	61	146
4th	137	103	76	226
5th	201	104	80	226
6th	283	145	89	231
7th	288	198	107	–
8th	310	199	178	–
9th	337	210	184	–
10th	346	228	186	–

Umpires: R.S.Dunne (23) and D.B.Hair (*Australia*) (20).
Referee: P.J.P.Burge (*Australia*) (20).   Test No. 1355/78 (NZ 250/E 734)

NEW ZEALAND v ENGLAND 1996-97

NEW ZEALAND – BATTING AND FIELDING

	M	I	NO	HS	Runs	Avge	100	50	Ct/St
D.L.Vettori	2	4	3	29*	59	59.00	–	–	1
S.P.Fleming	3	6	–	129	212	35.33	1	1	7
C.L.Cairns	3	6	–	67	208	34.66	–	3	–
N.J.Astle	3	6	1	102*	172	34.40	1	–	–
B.A.Pocock	3	6	–	70	182	30.33	–	2	1
B.A.Young	3	6	–	56	171	28.50	–	1	3
A.C.Parore	3	6	–	59	125	20.83	–	1	4
L.K.Germon	2	4	–	14	48	12.00	–	–	3/1
D.N.Patel	2	4	–	45	45	11.25	–	–	2
S.B.Doull	3	6	–	26	37	6.16	–	–	1
G.I.Allott	2	4	1	8*	12	4.00	–	–	1

Played in one Test: H.T.Davis 8, 1 (2 ct); M.J.Horne 42, 13; D.K.Morrison 6*, 14*;
J.T.C.Vaughan 3, 2.

NEW ZEALAND – BOWLING

	O	M	R	W	Avge	Best	5wI	10wM
D.L.Vettori	103.3	32	208	7	29.71	4- 97	–	–
S.B.Doull	105.4	31	299	9	33.22	5- 75	1	–
N.J.Astle	67	20	134	4	33.50	2- 26	–	–
D.K.Morrison	24.4	4	104	3	34.66	3-104	–	–
G.I.Allott	61.4	11	197	5	39.40	4- 74	–	–
D.N.Patel	68	16	151	3	50.33	2- 92	–	–

Also bowled: C.L.Cairns 52-11-146-2; H.T.Davis 36-8-93-1; B.A.Pocock 2-0-10-0;
J.T.C.Vaughan 36-10-57-1.

ENGLAND – BATTING AND FIELDING

	M	I	NO	HS	Runs	Avge	100	50	Ct/St
M.A.Atherton	3	4	1	118	325	108.33	1	2	1
A.J.Stewart	3	4	–	173	257	64.25	1	1	14/2
G.P.Thorpe	3	4	–	119	247	61.75	2	–	1
P.C.R.Tufnell	3	3	2	19*	38	38.00	–	–	–
J.P.Crawley	3	4	1	56	111	37.00	–	1	1
R.D.B.Croft	2	3	1	39*	70	35.00	–	–	2
N.Hussain	3	4	–	64	117	29.25	–	1	6
D.G.Cork	3	3	–	59	82	27.33	–	1	3
N.V.Knight	3	4	–	29	56	14.00	–	–	9
A.R.Caddick	2	3	–	20	39	13.00	–	–	1
D.Gough	3	3	–	18	20	6.66	–	–	–

Played in one Test: A.D.Mullally 21; C.White 0.

ENGLAND – BOWLING

	O	M	R	W	Avge	Best	5wI	10wM
R.D.B.Croft	90.1	27	162	10	16.20	5-95	1	–
D.Gough	127.3	31	361	19	19.00	5-40	1	–
A.R.Caddick	87.5	25	174	8	21.75	4-45	–	–
A.D.Mullally	53	22	102	3	34.00	2-47	–	–
P.C.R.Tufnell	132	47	242	7	34.57	3-53	–	–
D.G.Cork	98.5	21	300	7	42.85	3-96	–	–

Also bowled: G.P.Thorpe 1-1-0-0; C.White 25-5-77-2.

SECOND XI FIXTURES 1997

Abbreviations: (SEC) Second Eleven Championship Matches (Three days unless
                      otherwise stated)
              (BHT) Bain Hogg Trophy (One day)

APRIL

Wed 23	(SEC)	Middx v Notts	Uxbridge CC	01895 237571
	(SEC)	Somerset v Sussex	Taunton	01823 272946
	(SEC)	Worcs v Leics	Worcester	01905 748474
Mon 28	(BHT)	Yorks v Lancs	Bradford (Park Ave)	01274 391564
Tue 29	(BHT)	Durham v Lancs	Boldon CC	0191 536 4180
Wed 30	(SEC)	Essex v Glam	Chelmsford	01245 252420
	(SEC)	Kent v Yorks	Eltham	0181 859 1579
	(SEC)	Leics v Notts	Hinckley Town CC	01455 615336
	(SEC)	Surrey v Middx	Cheam	0181 642 1817

MAY

Tue 6	(BHT)	Notts v Lancs	Mansfield	
	(BHT)	Somerset v Hants	Taunton	01823 272946
	(BHT)	Surrey v MCC YCs	The Oval	0171 582 6660
	(BHT)	Warwicks v Middx	Leamington	01926 423853
Wed 7	(SEC)	Essex v Durham	Chelmsford	01245 252420
	(SEC)	Glam v Yorks	Pontypridd	01443 486542
	(SEC)	Hants v Worcs	Southampton	01703 333788
	(SEC)	Leics v Kent	Leicester	0116 283 2128
	(SEC)	Notts v Lancs	Trent Bridge	0115 982 1525
	(SEC)	Somerset v Glos	Taunton	01823 272946
	(SEC)	Surrey v Derbys	The Oval	0171 582 6660
	(SEC)	Sussex v Northants	Eastbourne	01323 724328
Mon 12	(BHT)	Hants v Somerset	Portsmouth	01705 830125
	(BHT)	Lancs v Durham	Urmston	0161 748 4660
	(BHT)	Leics v Middx	Leicester	0116 283 2128
	(BHT)	Worcs v Glos	Worcester	01905 748474
Tue 13	(BHT)	Glos v Glam	Old Bristolians/Westbury	01275 392137
	(SEC)	Notts v Derbys (Four days)	Trent Bridge	0115 982 1525
	(SEC)	Sussex v Surrey (Four days)	Hove	01273 732161
	(BHT)	Kent v Essex	Maidstone	01622 754545
Wed 14	(SEC)	Durham v Hants	Felling CC	0191 469 3645
	(SEC)	Kent v Essex	Maidstone	01622 754545
	(SEC)	Lancs v Glam	Fleetwood	01253 771807
	(SEC)	Somerset v Leics	North Perrott	01460 77953
	(SEC)	Yorks v Warwicks	Bingley	01274 775441
Mon 19	(BHT)	Hants v Glam	Southampton	01703 333788
	(BHT)	Kent v MCC YCs	Canterbury	01227 456886
	(BHT)	Minor Cos v Warwicks	Leek	01538 383693
	(BHT)	Yorks v Derbys	Bradford (Park Ave)	01274 391564
Tue 20	(BHT)	Essex v Sussex	Saffron Walden	01799 522683
	(BHT)	Minor Cos v Leics	Leek	01538 383693
Wed 21	(SEC)	Essex v Sussex	Saffron Walden	01799 522683
	(SEC)	Glam v Kent	Pontarddulais	01792 882556
	(SEC)	Glos v Derbys	Bristol	0117 924 5216
	(SEC)	Hants v Notts	Southampton	01703 333788
	(SEC)	Middx v Leics	Uxbridge CC	01895 237571
	(SEC)	Northants v Somerset	Northampton	01604 32917
	(SEC)	Surrey v Yorks	Oxted	01883 712792
	(SEC)	Warwicks v Lancs	Stratford-upon-Avon	01789 297968
	(SEC)	Worcs v Durham	Worcester	01905 748474

Tue 27	(BHT)	Derbys v Lancs	Glossop	01457 869755
Wed 28	(SEC)	Derbys v Lancs	Cheadle CC (Stoke-on Trent)	01538 752728
	(SEC)	Durham v Glam	Stockton CC	01642 672835
	(SEC)	Kent v Somerset	Ashford	01233 611700
	(SEC)	Leics v Glos	Hinckley Town CC	01455 615336
	(SEC)	Northants v Worcs	Milton Keynes (Campbell Pk)	01908 233600
	(SEC)	Warwicks v Hants	Knowle & Dorridge CC	01564 774338
	(SEC)	Yorks v Essex	Elland	01422 372682

JUNE

Mon 2	(BHT)	Glam v Hants	Brecon (Christ Coll)	01874 622786
	(BHT)	MCC YCs v Surrey	Shenley	01923 859022
	(BHT)	Minor Cos v Northants	North Runcton	
	(BHT)	Yorks v Notts	Bradford (Park Ave)	01274 391564
Tue 3	(BHT)	Derbys v Notts	Duffield CC (Eyes Meadow)	01332 852610
	(BHT)	Essex v Kent	Chelmsford	01245 252420
	(BHT)	Leics v Minor Cos	Egerton Park CC (Melton Mowbray)	01664 62277
	(SEC)	Worcs v Somerset (Four days)	Kidderminster	01562 824175
Wed 4	(SEC)	Derbys v Sussex	Rocester (Abbotsholme S)	01889 590217
	(SEC)	Essex v Warwicks	Ilford	0181 554 8381
	(SEC)	Glam v Northants	Swansea	01792 424242
	(SEC)	Glos v Yorks	Gloucester (Tuffley Park)	01452 524621
	(SEC)	Hants v Surrey	Southampton	01703 333788
	(SEC)	Middx v Durham	Lensbury CC	0181 977 8821
Thu 5	(BHT)	Lancs v Notts	Old Trafford	0161 282 4000
Mon 9	(BHT)	Lancs v Yorks	Old Trafford	0161 282 4000
	(BHT)	Sussex v Kent	Eastbourne	01323 724328
	(BHT)	Warwicks v Leics	Aston U	0121 308 5857
Tue 10	(BHT)	Glam v Somerset	Ebbw Vale	01495 305368
	(BHT)	MCC YCs v Essex	Shenley	01923 859022
	(BHT)	Minor Cos v Middx	Sleaford	01529 303368
	(BHT)	Notts v Durham	Worksop College	01909 472286
Wed 11	(SEC)	Derbys v Middx	Rocester (Abbotsholme S)	01889 590217
	(SEC)	Essex v Leics	Wickford	01268 763023
	(SEC)	Glam v Notts	Ammanford	01269 594988
	(SEC)	Hants v Northants	Finchampstead	01734 732890
	(SEC)	Lancs v Glos	Southport	01704 569951
	(SEC)	Surrey v Worcs	Cheam	0181 642 1817
	(SEC)	Warwicks v Durham	Griff & Coton	01203 386798
	(SEC)	Yorks v Sussex	York	01904 623602
Mon 16	(BHT)	Hants v Worcs	Southampton	01703 333788
	(BHT)	Kent v Surrey	Canterbury	01227 456886
	(BHT)	MCC YCs v Sussex	Shenley	01923 859022
Tue 17	(SEC)	Essex v Middx (Four days)	Coggeshall	01376 562988
	(BHT)	Lancs v Derbys	Wigan	01942 241581
Wed 18	(SEC)	Glam v Glos	Swansea	01792 424242
	(SEC)	Kent v Derbys	Canterbury	01227 456886
	(SEC)	Lancs v Northants	Middleton	0161 643 3595
	(SEC)	Leics v Surrey	Hinckley Town CC	01455 615336
	(SEC)	Somerset v Durham	Taunton	01823 272946
	(SEC)	Sussex v Warwicks	Horsham	01403 254628
	(SEC)	Yorks v Worcs	Middlesbrough	01642 818567
Mon 23	(BHT)	Durham v Derbys	Bishop Auckland	01388 603371
	(BHT)	Essex v Surrey	Chelmsford	01245 252420
	(BHT)	Hants v Glos	Southampton	01703 333788
	(BHT)	Middx v Northants	Southgate CC	0181 886 8381
Tue 24	(BHT)	Notts v Yorks	Farnsfield CC	01623 882986

	(BHT)	Sussex v MCC YCs	Haywards Heath	01444 451384
Wed 25	(SEC)	Derbys v Glam	Belper Meadows	01773 824900
	(SEC)	Durham v Surrey	Boldon CC	0191 536 4180
	(SEC)	Glos v Northants	Shirehampton CC	0117 982 3309
	(SEC)	Kent v Worcs	Sittingbourne	01795 423813
	(SEC)	Leics v Hants	Kibworth CC	0116 279 3328
	(SEC)	Notts v Yorks	Collingham CC	01636 892921
	(SEC)	Somerset v Lancs	North Perrott	01460 77953
	(SEC)	Warwicks v Middx	Moseley	0121 744 5694
Mon 30	(BHT)	Middx v Warwicks	Harrow CC	0181 422 0932
	(BHT)	Somerset v Worcs	Taunton (King's Coll)	01823 334222

JULY

Tue 1	(SEC)	Derbys v Leics (Four days)	Chesterfield	01246 273090
	(BHT)	Glos v Somerset	Bristol	0117 924 5216
	(BHT)	Surrey v Kent	The Oval	0171 582 6660
	(BHT)	Yorks v Durham	Bradford (Park Ave)	01274 391564
Wed 2	(SEC)	Glos v Surrey	Bristol	0117 924 5216
	(SEC)	Middx v Sussex	Harrow CC	0181 422 0932
	(SEC)	Northants v Kent	Luton (Wardown Park)	01582 27855
	(SEC)	Notts v Essex	Worksop CC	01909 472681
	(SEC)	Somerset v Glam	Taunton	01823 272946
	(SEC)	Worcs v Warwicks	Worcester	01905 748474
	(SEC)	Yorks v Durham	Todmorden	01706 813140
Mon 7	(BHT)	MCC YCs v Kent	Shenley	01923 859022
	(BHT)	Middx v Leics	Harrow CC	0181 422 0932
	(BHT)	Northants v Warwicks	Northampton	01604 32917
	(BHT)	Somerset v Glam	Taunton	01823 272946
Tue 8	(283)	Derbys v Durham	Dunstall	01283 712346
	(BHT)	Glos v Hants	Bristol	0117 924 5216
	(BHT)	Worcs v Glam	Worcester	01905 748474
	(SEC)	Northants v Essex (Four days)	Northampton	01604 32917
Wed 9	(SEC)	Derbys v Durham	Chesterfield	01246 273090
	(SEC)	Lancs v Kent	Haslingden	01706 215365
	(SEC)	Notts v Surrey	Trent Bridge	0115 982 1525
	(SEC)	Somerset v Hants	Clevedon	01275 877583
	(SEC)	Sussex v Glos	Horsham	01403 254628
	(SEC)	Yorks v Middx	Harrogate	01423 561301
Thu 10	(BHT)	Warwicks v Minor Cos	West Brom (Dartmouth)	0121 553 0168
Mon 14	(BHT)	Durham v Yorks	Benwell Hill CC	0191 274 1222
	(BHT)	Glam v Worcs	Llanarth	01873 840410
	(BHT)	Somerset v Glos	Taunton	01823 272946
Tue 15	(BHT)	Essex v MCC YCs	Chelmsford	01245 252420
	(BHT)	Glos v Worcs	Bristol	0117 924 5216
	(BHT)	Notts v Derbys	Welbeck CC	
	(SEC)	Somerset v Warwicks (Four days)	Taunton	01823 272946
	(SEC)	Surrey v Kent (Four days)	The Oval	0171 582 6660
Wed 16	(SEC)	Durham v Leics	South Shields	0191 456 1506
	(SEC)	Essex v Lancs	Chelmsford	01245 252420
	(SEC)	Hants v Yorks	Southampton	01703 333788
	(SEC)	Middx v Glos	Southgate CC	0181 886 8381
	(SEC)	Northants v Notts	Wellingborough S	01933 222427
	(SEC)	Sussex v Glam	Hove	01273 732161
	(SEC)	Worcs v Derbys	Halesowen	0121 550 2744
Mon 21	(BHT)	Derbys v Yorks	Belper Meadows	01773 824900
	(BHT)	Durham v Notts	Chester-le-Street (Riverside)	0191 387 1717
	(BHT)	Leics v Warwicks	Leicester	0116 283 2128
	(BHT)	Northants v Minor Cos	Milton Keynes (Campbell Pk)	01908 233600

	(BHT)	Surrey v Sussex	The Oval	0171 582 6660
	(BHT)	Worcs v Somerset	Bromsgrove CC	01527 78252
Tue 22	(SEC)	Durham v Notts (Four days)	Chester-le-Street (Riverside)	0191 387 1717
	(SEC)	Glam v Hants (Four days)	Pontypridd	01443 486542
	(BHT)	Kent v Sussex	Canterbury	01227 456886
	(BHT)	Middx v Minor Cos	Uxbridge CC	01895 237571
	(BHT)	Northants v Leics	Bedford S	01234 353493
Wed 23	(SEC)	Kent v Middx	Canterbury	01227 456886
	(SEC)	Northants v Derbys	Dunstable	01582 663735
	(SEC)	Surrey v Somerset	The Oval	0171 582 6660
	(SEC)	Warwicks v Glos	Solihull	0121 705 5271
	(SEC)	Worcs v Essex	Worcester	01905 748474
Mon 28	(BHT)	Glam v Glos	Newport	01633 281236
	(BHT)	Sussex v Surrey	East Grinstead	01342 321210
	(BHT)	Warwicks v Northants	Leamington	01926 423854
	(BHT)	Worcs v Hants	Kidderminster	01562 824175
Tue 29	(SEC)	Glam v Surrey	Usk	01291 673754
	(SEC)	Lancs v Durham (Four days)	Ramsbottom	01706 822799
	(BHT)	Sussex v Essex	Hastings	01424 422991
Wed 30	(SEC)	Kent v Warwicks	Folkestone	01303 253366
	(SEC)	Middx v Hants	Harrow CC	0181 422 0932
	(SEC)	Notts v Worcs	Nottingham HS	0115 960 5605
	(SEC)	Sussex v Leics	Hastings	01424 422991
	(SEC)	Yorks v Somerset	Marske	0642 484361

AUGUST

Fri 1	(BHT)	Surrey v Essex	The Oval	0171 582 6660
Mon 4	(BHT)	Northants v Middx	Tring	01422 823080
Tue 5	(SEC)	Hants v Glos (Four days)	Southampton	01703 333788
	(SEC)	Warwicks v Glam (Four days)	Studley	01527 853668
	(BHT)	Leics v Northants	Leicester	0116 283 2128
Wed 6	(SEC)	Durham v Kent	Seaton Carew	01429 260945
	(SEC)	Leics v Northants	Lutterworth CC	
	(SEC)	Middx v Lancs	Southgate CC	0181 886 8381
	(SEC)	Notts v Somerset	Worksop Coll	01909 472286
	(SEC)	Surrey v Essex	Oxted	01883 712792
	(SEC)	Worcs v Sussex	Barnt Green	0121 445 1684
Tue 12	(SEC)	Leics v Yorks (Four days)	Oakham S	01572 722487
Wed 13	(SEC)	Derbys v Hants	Chesterfield	01246 273090
	(SEC)	Durham v Northants	Chester-le-Street CC	0191 388 3684
	(SEC)	Glos v Notts	Hatherly & Reddings CC (Cheltenham)	01242 862608
	(SEC)	Surrey v Warwicks	Guildford	01483 572181
	(SEC)	Sussex v Lancs	Middleton-on-Sea	01243 583157
	(SEC)	Worcs v Middx	Ombersley	
Mon 18 or Tue 19	(BHT)	*Bain Hogg Trophy Semi-Finals (One day)*		
Wed 20	(SEC)	Derbys v Somerset	Derby	01332 383211
	(SEC)	Glos v Essex	Bristol	0117 924 5216
	(SEC)	Lancs v Hants	Old Trafford	0161 282 4000
	(SEC)	Middx v Glam	Lensbury CC	0181 977 8821
	(SEC)	Northants v Yorks	Milton Keynes (Campbell Pk)	01908 233600
	(SEC)	Notts v Kent	Trent Bridge	0115 982 1525
	(SEC)	Sussex v Durham	Hove	01273 732161
	(SEC)	Warwicks v Leics	Walmley	0121 351 1349
Tue 26	(SEC)	Kent v Sussex (Four days)	Tunbridge Wells	01892 520846
	(SEC)	Middx v Northants (Four days)	Uxbridge (RAF Vine Lane)	01895 237144
	(SEC)	Yorks v Lancs (Four days)	Bradford (Park Ave)	01274 391564

Wed 27	(SEC)	Derbys v Warwicks	Chesterfield	01246 273090
	(SEC)	Durham v Glos	Sunderland	0191 528 4536
	(SEC)	Glam v Worcs	Panteg	01495 763605
	(SEC)	Hants v Essex	Southampton	01703 333788

SEPTEMBER

Tue 2	(SEC)	Warwicks v Notts	Edgbaston	0121 446 4422
	(SEC)	Yorks v Derbys	Castleford	01977 553627
Wed 3	(SEC)	Essex v Somerset	Colchester	01206 574028
	(SEC)	Glos v Kent	Bristol	0117 924 5216
	(SEC)	Leics v Glam	Hinckley Town CC	01455 615336
	(SEC)	Northants v Surrey	Northampton	01604 32917
	(SEC)	Sussex v Hants	Hove	01273 732161
	(SEC)	Worcs v Lancs	Worcester	01905 748474
Mon 8	(BHT)	*Bain Hogg Trophy Final (Reserve day Tuesday 9th)*		
Tue 9	(SEC)	Glos v Worcs (Four days)	Bristol	0117 924 5216
Wed 10	(SEC)	Essex v Derbys	Chelmsford	01245 252420
	(SEC)	Hants v Kent	Bournemouth Sports Club	01202 581933
	(SEC)	Lancs v Surrey	Old Trafford	0161 282 4000
	(SEC)	Notts v Sussex	Trent Bridge	0115 982 1525
	(SEC)	Somerset v Middx	Taunton	01823 272946
	(SEC)	Warwicks v Northants	Kenilworth Wardens	01926 852476
Mon 15	(SEC)	Lancs v Leics	Liverpool	0151 4272930

MINOR COUNTIES FIXTURES 1997

APRIL
Benson and Hedges Cup

Mon 28	Lakenham	Minor Counties v Derbyshire
Wed 30	Edgbaston	Warwickshire v Minor Counties

MAY

Fri 2	Worcester	Worcestershire v Minor Counties
Mon 5	Walsall	Minor Counties v Lancashire
Mon 12	Headingley	Yorkshire v Minor Counties

MCC Trophy, Preliminary Round

Sun 18	Shenley Park	Hertfordshire v Lincolnshire
	Copdock CC	Suffolk v Staffordshire
	Finchampstead	Berkshire v Shropshire
	Brockhampton	Herefordshire v Cornwall

Bain Hogg Trophy

Mon 19	Leek	Minor Counties v Warwickshire II
Tue 20	Leek	Minor Counties v Leicestershire II

Championship

Sun 25	Askam	(E) Cumberland v Bedfordshire
	Sidmouth	(W) Devon v Wales
	Sherborne	(W) Dorset v Herefordshire
	Sleaford	(E) Lincolnshire v Hertfordshire
	Challow and Childrey	(W) Oxfordshire v Berkshire

JUNE
MCC Trophy, First Round

Sun 1	Shenley Park or	Hertfordshire or Lincolnshire v Suffolk or
	Grantham	Staffordshire
	Finchampstead or	Berkshire or Shropshire v Herefordshire or
	Wellington	Cornwall
	Exmouth	Devon v Wales
	Thame	Oxfordshire v Bedfordshire
	Penrith	Cumberland v Dorset

	March	Cambridgeshire v Cheshire
	Jesmond	Northumberland v Buckinghamshire
	Corsham	Wiltshire v Norfolk
		Bain Hogg Trophy
Mon 2	North Runcton	Minor Counties v Northamptonshire II
Tue 3	Melton Mowbray	Leicestershire II v Minor Counties
		Championship
Wed 4	Beaconsfield	(E) Buckinghamshire v Staffordshire
Sun 8	Dunstable	(E) Bedfordshire v Suffolk
	Neston	(W) Cheshire v Wiltshire
	Dean Park	(W) Dorset v Wales
	Bourne	(E) Lincolnshire v Buckinghamshire
	Jesmond	(E) Northumberland v Norfolk
	Challow and Childrey	(W) Oxfordshire v Shropshire
Tue 10	Hurst CC	(W) Berkshire v Shropshire
		Bain Hogg Trophy
	Sleaford	Minor Counties v Middlesex II
		Championship
Sun 15	Bedford Town	(E) Bedfordshire v Staffordshire
	High Wycombe	(E) Buckinghamshire v Northumberland
	Swansea	(W) Wales v Oxfordshire
	Westbury	(W) Wiltshire v Herefordshire
Mon 16	New Brighton	(W) Cheshire v Cornwall
	Netherfield	(E) Cumberland v Lincolnshire
Tue 17	St Albans	(E) Hertfordshire v Northumberland
Wed 18	Saffron Walden	(E) Cambridgeshire v Norfolk
	Newport	(W) Shropshire v Cornwall
		MCC Trophy, Quarter-Finals
		Championship
Sun 29	Leominster (Dales)	(W) Herefordshire v Berkshire
	Cleethorpes	(E) Lincolnshire v Suffolk
	Banbury CC	(W) Oxfordshire v Dorset
	Bridgnorth	(W) Shropshire v Devon
	Panteg (Newport)	(W) Wales v Wiltshire
JULY		
Tue 1	Toft	(W) Cheshire v Devon
	Jesmond	(E) Northumberland v Suffolk
Wed 2	Cannock	(E) Staffordshire v Cambridgeshire
Sun 6	Reading CC	(W) Berkshire v Dorset
	Aylesbury	(E) Buckinghamshire v Cumberland
	South Wilts CC	(W) Wiltshire v Devon
Mon 7	Stone	(E) Staffordshire v Northumberland
Tue 8	Fenner's	(E) Cambridgeshire v Bedfordshire
	Hertford	(E) Hertfordshire v Cumberland
		Tourist Match
	Jesmond	Minor Counties v Australians
		Bain Hogg Trophy
Thu 10	W Brom Dartmouth	Warwickshire II v Minor Counties
		Championship
Sun 13	Southill Park	(E) Bedfordshire v Lincolnshire
	Radlett	(E) Hertfordshire v Norfolk
	Tynemouth	(E) Northumberland v Cambridgeshire
	Oswestry	(W) Shropshire v Wales
	Marlborough CC	(W) Wiltshire v Cornwall
Tue 15	Carlisle	(E) Cumberland v Cambridgeshire
	Weymouth	(W) Dorset v Cornwall
Sun 20		*MCC Trophy, Semi-Finals*

| Mon 21 | Milton Keynes | Northamptonshire II v Minor Counties |
| Tue 22 | Uxbridge | Middlesex II v Minor Counties |

Championship

Tue 22	Brockhampton	(W) Herefordshire v Cheshire
Thu 24	Bishop's Stortford	(E) Hertfordshire v Staffordshire
Sun 27	Torquay	(W) Devon v Berkshire
	Colwall	(W) Herefordshire v Shropshire
	Shenley Park	(E) Hertfordshire v Bedfordshire
	Lakenham	(E) Norfolk v Cumberland
	Thame	(W) Oxfordshire v Wiltshire
	Ransome's CC	(E) Suffolk v Buckinghamshire
	Pontypridd	(W) Wales v Cheshire
Tue 29	Falmouth	(W) Cornwall v Berkshire
	Lakenham	(E) Norfolk v Buckinghamshire
	Mildenhall	(E) Suffolk v Cumberland
Wed 30	Fenner's	(E) Cambridgeshire v Lincolnshire

AUGUST

Sun 3	Rover Cowley	(W) Oxfordshire v Cheshire
	Pontarddulais	(W) Wales v Herefordshire
Mon 4	Lakenham	(E) Norfolk v Staffordshire
Tue 5	Finchampstead	(W) Berkshire v Cheshire
Wed 6	March	(E) Cambridgeshire v Hertfordshire
	Lakenham	(E) Norfolk v Bedfordshire
	Bury St Edmunds	(E) Suffolk v Staffordshire
Sun 10	Falkland CC	(W) Berkshire v Wiltshire
	Slough	(E) Buckinghamshire v Cambridgeshire
	St Austell	(W) Cornwall v Oxfordshire
	Lakenham	(E) Norfolk v Suffolk
	Jesmond	(E) Northumberland v Lincolnshire
	Wellington	(W) Shropshire v Dorset
Tue 12	Bowdon	(W) Cheshire v Dorset
	Bovey Tracey	(W) Devon v Oxfordshire
Sun 17	Camborne	(W) Cornwall v Wales
	Barrow	(E) Cumberland v Northumberland
	Exmouth	(W) Devon v Herefordshire
Mon 18	Ipswich School	(E) Suffolk v Hertfordshire
Tue 19	Truro	(W) Cornwall v Herefordshire
	Brewood	(E) Staffordshire v Lincolnshire
Sun 24	Wardown Park	(E) Bedfordshire v Buckinghamshire
	Dean Park	(W) Dorset v Devon
	Trowbridge	(W) Wiltshire v Shropshire
Wed 27	Lord's	*MCC Trophy Final*

Championship

Sun 31	Marlow	(E) Buckinghamshire v Hertfordshire
	Instow	(W) Devon v Cornwall
	Dean Park	(W) Dorset v Wiltshire
	Kington	(W) Herefordshire v Oxfordshire
	Lincoln Lindum	(E) Lincolnshire v Norfolk
	Jesmond	(E) Northumberland v Bedfordshire
	Shifnal	(W) Shropshire v Cheshire
	Longton	(E) Staffordshire v Cumberland
	Ransome's CC	(E) Suffolk v Cambridgeshire
	Colwyn Bay	(W) Wales v Berkshire

SEPTEMBER

| Sun 14 | tba | *Championship Final (Two days)* |

PRINCIPAL FIXTURES 1997

* Includes Sunday play

Tuesday 15 April

Fenner's: Cambridge U v Derbys
The Parks: Oxford U v Durham

Wednesday 16 April

Headingley: Yorks v Lancs (Four days)

Friday 18 April

Tetley's Shield
*Edgbaston: England 'A' v The Rest (Four days)
Other Matches
*Fenner's: Cambridge U v Leics
The Parks: Oxford U v Hants

Wednesday 23 April

Britannic Assurance Championship
Chelmsford: Essex v Hants
Cardiff: Glam v Warwicks
Canterbury: Kent v Derbys
Old Trafford: Lancs v Durham
Leicester: Leics v Glos
Trent Bridge: Notts v Worcs
The Oval: Surrey v Somerset
Hove: Sussex v Northants
Other Matches
Fenner's: Cambridge U v Middx
The Parks: Oxford U v Yorks

Saturday 26 April

The Parks: British Us v Yorks (One day)

Sunday 27 April

AXA Life League
Chelmsford: Essex v Hants
Cardiff: Glam v Warwicks
Canterbury: Kent v Derbys
Old Trafford: Lancs v Durham
Leicester: Leics v Glos
Trent Bridge: Notts v Worcs
The Oval: Surrey v Somerset
Hove: Sussex v Northants

Monday 28 April

Benson and Hedges Cup
Chelmsford: Essex v Glam
Bristol: Glos v British Us
Dublin (Castle Ave): Ireland v Middx
Old Trafford: Lancs v Yorks
Leicester: Leics v Scotland
Lakenham: Minor Cos v Derbys
Trent Bridge: Notts v Durham
The Oval: Surrey v Kent
Hove: Sussex v Hants
Worcester: Worcs v Warwicks

Wednesday 30 April

Benson and Hedges Cup
Fenner's: British Us v Sussex
Chester-le-Street (Riverside): Durham v Northants
Bristol: Glos v Surrey
Canterbury: Kent v Hants
Old Trafford: Lancs v Derbys
Leicester: Leics v Notts
Lord's: Middx v Essex
Taunton: Somerset v Glam
Edgbaston: Warwicks v Minor Cos
Headingley: Yorks v Worcs

Friday 2 May

Benson and Hedges Cup
Derby: Derbys v Yorks
Cardiff: Glam v Middx
Southampton: Hants v Glos
Canterbury: Kent v Sussex
Trent Bridge: Notts v Northants
Forfar: Scotland v Durham
Taunton: Somerset v Ireland
The Oval: Surrey v British Us
Edgbaston: Warwicks v Lancs
Worcester: Worcs v Minor Cos

Sunday 4 May

AXA Life League
Derby: Derbys v Lancs
Chelmsford: Essex v Middx
Southampton: Hants v Yorks
Canterbury: Kent v Surrey
Taunton: Somerset v Glam

Hove: Sussex v Notts
Edgbaston: Warwicks v Northants

Monday 5 May

Benson and Hedges Cup
Derby: Derbys v Worcs
Chester-le-Street (Riverside): Durham v
    Leics
Chelmsford: Essex v Somerset
Cardiff: Glam v Ireland
Southampton: Hants v Surrey
Canterbury: Kent v British Us
Walsall: Minor Cos v Lancs
Northampton: Northants v Scotland
Hove: Sussex v Glos
Edgbaston: Warwicks v Yorks

Wednesday 7 May

Britannic Assurance Championship
Derby: Derbys v Surrey
Hartlepool: Durham v Notts
Bristol: Glos v Hants
Lord's: Middx v Sussex
Northampton: Northants v Somerset
Worcester: Worcs v Leics
Headingley: Yorks v Glam
Other Matches
Fenner's: Cambridge U v Essex
The Parks: Oxford U v Warwicks

Sunday 11 May

AXA Life League
Derby: Derbys v Surrey
Hartlepool: Durham v Notts
Bristol: Glos v Hants
Lord's: Middx v Sussex
Northampton: Northants v Somerset
Worcester: Worcs v Leics
Headingley: Yorks v Glam

Monday 12 May

Benson and Hedges Cup
The Parks: British Us v Hants
Derby: Derbys v Warwicks
Bristol: Glos v Kent
Downpatrick: Ireland v Essex
Old Trafford: Lancs v Worcs
Lord's: Middx v Somerset
Northampton: Northants v Leics
Glasgow (Titwood): Scotland v Notts
The Oval: Surrey v Sussex
Headingley: Yorks v Minor Cos

Wednesday 14 May

Britannic Assurance Championship
Chelmsford: Essex v Durham
Southampton: Hants v Leics
Canterbury: Kent v Glam
Old Trafford: Lancs v Notts
Lord's: Middx v Derbys
Taunton: Somerset v Sussex
The Oval: Surrey v Glos
Edgbaston: Warwicks v Yorks
Other Matches
Fenner's: Cambridge U v Northants
The Parks: Oxford U v Worcs

Thursday 15 May

Tourist Match
Arundel: Duke of Norfolk's XI v
    Australians (One day)

Saturday 17 May

Tourist Match
Northampton: Northants v Australians
    (One day)
Other Match
Fenner's: Cambridge U v Oxford U (One
    day)

Sunday 18 May

AXA Life League
Chelmsford: Essex v Durham
Southampton: Hants v Leics
Canterbury: Kent v Glam
Old Trafford: Lancs v Notts
Lord's: Middx v Derbys
Taunton: Somerset v Sussex
The Oval: Surrey v Glos
Edgbaston: Warwicks v Yorks
Tourist Match
Worcester: Worcs v Australians (One
    day)

Tuesday 20 May

Tourist Match
Chester-le-Street (Riverside): Durham v
    Australians (One day)

Wednesday 21 May

Britannic Assurance Championship
Chester-le-Street (Riverside): Durham v
    Worcs
Cardiff: Glam v Hants

Gloucester: Glos v Essex
Old Trafford: Lancs v Northants
Leicester: Leics v Surrey
Trent Bridge: Notts v Derbys
Taunton: Somerset v Yorks
Horsham: Sussex v Kent
Edgbaston: Warwicks v Middx

Thursday 22 May

TEXACO TROPHY
Headingley: ENGLAND v AUSTRALIA
(First Limited-overs International)

Saturday 24 May

TEXACO TROPHY
The Oval: ENGLAND v AUSTRALIA
(Second Limited-overs International)

Sunday 25 May

TEXACO TROPHY
Lord's: ENGLAND v AUSTRALIA
(Third Limited-overs International)
AXA Life League
Chester-le-Street (Riverside): Durham v
    Worcs
Cardiff: Glam v Hants
Gloucester: Glos v Essex
Old Trafford: Lancs v Northants
Leicester: Leics v Surrey
Trent Bridge: Notts v Derbys
Taunton: Somerset v Yorks
Horsham: Sussex v Kent
Edgbaston: Warwicks v Middx

Tuesday 27 May

Benson and Hedges Cup
Quarter-Finals
Tetley's Challenge Series
†Bristol or Hove: Glos or Sussex v
    Australians
†Surrey to play the Australians at The Oval
    if both Gloucestershire and Sussex
    involved in B&H Quarter-Finals

Thursday 29 May

Britannic Assurance Championship
Ilford: Essex v Yorks
Cardiff: Glam v Durham
Southampton: Hants v Warwicks
Leicester: Leics v Lancs
Lord's: Middx v Northants
Trent Bridge: Notts v Kent

Worcester: Worcs v Somerset

Friday 30 May

The Parks: Oxford U v Sussex

Saturday 31 May

Tetley's Challenge Series
*Derby: Derbys v Australians

Sunday 1 June

AXA Life League
Ilford: Essex v Yorks
Pontypridd: Glam v Durham
Southampton: Hants v Warwicks
Leicester: Leics v Lancs
Lord's: Middx v Northants
Trent Bridge: Notts v Kent
Worcester: Worcs v Somerset

Wednesday 4 June

Britannic Assurance Championship
Chesterfield: Derbys v Hants
Chester-le-Street (Riverside): Durham v
    Sussex
Tunbridge Wells: Kent v Warwicks
Lord's: Middx v Leics
Northampton: Northants v Notts
Taunton: Somerset v Lancs
The Oval: Surrey v Essex
Headingley: Yorks v Glos

Thursday 5 June

FIRST CORNHILL INSURANCE
TEST MATCH
*Edgbaston: ENGLAND v AUSTRALIA
Other Match
The Parks: Oxford U v Glam

Sunday 8 June

AXA Life League
Chesterfield: Derbys v Hants
Chester-le-Street (Riverside): Durham v
    Sussex
Tunbridge Wells: Kent v Warwicks
Lord's: Middx v Leics
Milton Keynes (Campbell Park):
    Northants v Notts
Taunton: Somerset v Lancs
The Oval: Surrey v Essex
Headingley: Yorks v Glos

Monday 9 June

Harrogate: Costcutter Cup (Three days)

Tuesday 10 June

Benson and Hedges Cup
Semi-Finals

Wednesday 11 June

Tetley's Challenge Series
†Northampton or Trent Bridge: Northants
  or Notts v Australians
†Durham to play Australians if both
  Northamptonshire and
  Nottinghamshire involved in B&H
  Semi-Finals

Thursday 12 June

Britannic Assurance Championship
Cardiff: Glam v Middx
Bristol: Glos v Worcs
Basingstoke: Hants v Somerset
Old Trafford: Lancs v Kent
The Oval: Surrey v Yorks
Hove: Sussex v Essex
Edgbaston: Warwicks v Derbys

Saturday 14 June

Tetley's Challenge Series
*Leicester: Leics v Australians
Other Matches
*Fenner's: Cambridge U v Durham
The Parks: Oxford U v Notts

Sunday 15 June

AXA Life League
Cardiff: Glam v Middx
Bristol: Glos v Worcs
Basingstoke: Hants v Somerset
Old Trafford: Lancs v Kent
The Oval: Surrey v Yorks
Hove: Sussex v Essex
Edgbaston: Warwicks v Derbys

Wednesday 18 June

Britannic Assurance Championship
Derby: Derbys v Sussex
Darlington: Durham v Kent
Bristol: Glos v Middx
Liverpool: Lancs v Glam
Northampton: Northants v Hants

Trent Bridge: Notts v Yorks
Bath: Somerset v Leics
Worcester: Worcs v Surrey

Thursday 19 June

**SECOND CORNHILL INSURANCE
TEST MATCH
*Lord's: ENGLAND v AUSTRALIA**

Friday 20 June

*Chelmsford: Essex v Oxford U

Sunday 22 June

AXA Life League
Derby: Derbys v Sussex
Darlington: Durham v Kent
Bristol: Glos v Middx
Old Trafford: Lancs v Glam
Northampton: Northants v Hants
Trent Bridge: Notts v Yorks
Bath: Somerset v Leics
Worcester: Worcs v Surrey

Tuesday 24 June

NatWest Trophy
First Round
Beaconsfield: Bucks v Essex
Wisbech: Cambs v Hants
Barrow: Cumberland v Northants
Exmouth: Devon v Leics
Cardiff: Glam v Beds
Bristol: Glos v Scotland
Old Trafford: Lancs v Berks
Lincoln Lindum: Lincs v Derbys
Lord's: Middx v Kent
Trent Bridge: Notts v Staffs
Taunton: Somerset v Herefords
The Oval: Surrey v Durham
Hove: Sussex v Shrops
Edgbaston: Warwicks v Norfolk
Worcester: Worcs v Holland
Headingley: Yorks v Ireland

Wednesday 25 June

Tourist Match
The Parks: British Us v Australians
  (Three days)

Thursday 26 June

Britannic Assurance Championship
Southend: Essex v Derbys

Swansea: Glam v Sussex
Leicester: Leics v Warwicks
Luton: Northants v Glos
The Oval: Surrey v Notts
Worcester: Worcs v Lancs
Headingley: Yorks v Middx
AXA Life League
The Oval: Surrey v Notts (floodlit)

Friday 27 June

Britannic Assurance Championship
*The Oval: Surrey v Notts

Saturday 28 June

Tetley's Challenge Series
*Southampton: Hants v Australians
Other Matches
*Canterbury: Kent v Cambridge U
*Taunton: Somerset v Oxford U

Sunday 29 June

AXA Life League
Southend: Essex v Derbys
Swansea: Glam v Sussex
Leicester: Leics v Middx
Luton: Northants v Glos
Worcester: Worcs v Lancs
Headingley: Yorks v Middx

Wednesday 2 July

Britannic Assurance Championship
Chester-le-Street (Riverside): Durham v
    Hants
Chelmsford: Essex v Somerset
Swansea: Glam v Glos
Maidstone: Kent v Northants
Leicester: Leics v Yorks
Uxbridge: Middx v Lancs
Arundel: Sussex v Worcs
Edgbaston: Warwicks v Surrey
Tourist Match
Trent Bridge: Notts v Pakistan 'A' (Three
    days)
Other Match
Lord's: Oxford U v Cambridge U
    (Varsity Match) (Three days)

Thursday 3 July

**THIRD CORNHILL INSURANCE
TEST MATCH**
*Old Trafford: ENGLAND v
    AUSTRALIA

Saturday 5 July

Tourist Match
*Derby: Derbys v Pakistan 'A' (Three
    days)

Sunday 6 July

AXA Life League
Chester-le-Street (Riverside): Durham v
    Hants
Chelmsford: Essex v Somerset
Swansea: Glam v Glos
Maidstone: Kent v Northants
Leicester: Leics v Yorks
Uxbridge: Middx v Lancs
Arundel: Sussex v Worcs
Edgbaston: Warwicks v Surrey

Tuesday 8 July

Tourist Match
Jesmond: Minor Cos v Australians (One
    day)

Wednesday 9 July

NatWest Trophy
Second Round
Marlow or Chelmsford: Bucks or Essex v
    Worcs or Holland
Wisbech or Southampton: Cambs or
    Hants v Glam or Beds
Exmouth or Leicester: Devon or Leics v
    Yorks or Ireland
Lincoln Lindum or Derby: Lincs or
    Derbys v Cumberland or Northants
Uxbridge or Canterbury: Middx or Kent
    v Glos or Scotland
The Oval or Chester-le-Street (Riverside):
    Surrey or Durham v Notts or Staffs
Hove or St Georges (Telford): Sussex or
    Shrops v Lancs or Berks
Edgbaston or Lakenham: Warwicks or
    Norfolk v Somerset or Herefords
Tourist Match
Shenley: MCC v Pakistan 'A' (Three
    days)

Saturday 12 July

Lord's: *Benson and Hedges Cup Final*
Reserve days Sun 13 and Mon 14 July
Edinburgh (Grange CC): Scotland v
    Australians (One day)

282

Sunday 13 July

#AXA Life League
Derby: Derbys v Yorks
Chester-le-Street (Riverside): Durham v
    Warwicks
Southampton: Hants v Worcs
Trent Bridge: Notts v Somerset
Hove: Sussex v Glos
Tourist Match
Walsall: Non-First-Class Team (TBC) v
    Pakistan 'A' (One day)
#Matches involving B&H Cup Finalists to
    be played on Tue 15 July

Wednesday 16 July

Britannic Assurance Championship
Cheltenham: Glos v Derbys
Canterbury: Kent v Leics
Old Trafford: Lancs v Sussex
Northampton: Northants v Essex
Trent Bridge: Notts v Warwicks
Guildford: Surrey v Hants
Scarborough: Yorks v Durham
Tetley's Challenge Series
Cardiff: Glam v Australians
Tourist Match
Worcester: Worcs v Pakistan 'A' (Three days)

Saturday 19 July

Tetley's Challenge Series
*Lord's: Middx v Australians
Tourist Match
*Taunton: Somerset v Pakistan 'A' (Three
    days)

Sunday 20 July

AXA Life League
Cheltenham: Glos v Derbys
Canterbury: Kent v Leics
Old Trafford: Lancs v Sussex
Northampton: Northants v Essex
Trent Bridge: Notts v Warwicks
Guildford: Surrey v Hants
Worcester: Worcs v Glam
Scarborough: Yorks v Durham

Tuesday 22 July

Tourist Match
Cheltenham: Glos v Pakistan 'A' (One day)

Wednesday 23 July

Britannic Assurance Championship
Derby: Derbys v Glam
Chelmsford: Essex v Worcs
Cheltenham: Glos v Durham
Southampton: Hants v Lancs
Leicester: Leics v Notts
Lord's: Middx v Kent
Northampton: Northants v Surrey
Edgbaston: Warwicks v Somerset

Thursday 24 July

**FOURTH CORNHILL INSURANCE
TEST MATCH**
*Headingley: ENGLAND v AUSTRALIA
Tourist Match
*Hove: Sussex v Pakistan 'A' (Four days)

Sunday 27 July

AXA Life League
Derby: Derbys v Glam
Chelmsford: Essex v Worcs
Cheltenham: Glos v Durham
Southampton: Hants v Lancs
Leicester: Leics v Notts
Lord's: Middx v Kent
Northampton: Northants v Surrey
Edgbaston: Warwicks v Somerset

Tuesday 29 July

NatWest Trophy
Quarter-Finals
Tourist Match
†Cardiff or Southampton: Glam or Hants v
    Pakistan 'A' (One day)
†Depending on outcome of NWT Second
    Round

Thursday 31 July

Britannic Assurance Championship
Chester-le-Street (Riverside): Durham v
    Derbys
Colchester: Essex v Leics
Colwyn Bay: Glam v Notts
Edgbaston: Warwicks v Sussex
Worcester: Worcs v Kent
Headingley: Yorks v Northants
Tourist Match
Swansea: Wales v Pakistan 'A' (One day)

Friday 1 August

Tetley's Challenge Series
*Taunton: Somerset v Australians (Four days)
Tourist Match
*Bristol: Glos v Pakistan 'A' (Four days)

Saturday 2 August

NatWest U-19 International Match
Southampton: England U-19 v Zimbabwe U-19 (First Limited-overs International)

Sunday 3 August

AXA Life League
Chester-le-Street (Riverside): Durham v Derbys
Colchester: Essex v Leics
Colwyn Bay: Glam v Notts
Lord's: Middx v Surrey
Edgbaston: Warwicks v Sussex
Worcester: Worcs v Kent
Headingley: Yorks v Northants

Monday 4 August

NatWest U-19 International Match
Hove (TBC): England U-19 v Zimbabwe U-19 (Second Limited-overs International)

Wednesday 6 August

Britannic Assurance Championship
Canterbury: Kent v Essex
Blackpool: Lancs v Warwicks
Lord's: Middx v Hants
Northampton: Northants v Worcs
Taunton: Somerset v Glos
The Oval: Surrey v Durham
Eastbourne: Sussex v Leics

Thursday 7 August

FIFTH CORNHILL INSURANCE TEST MATCH
*Trent Bridge: ENGLAND v AUSTRALIA
Tourist Match
*Headingley: Yorks v Pakistan 'A' (Four days)
NatWest U-19 International Match
*Edgbaston: England U-19 v Zimbabwe U-19 (First Test Match) (Four days)

Saturday 9 August

*Dublin (Malahide): Ireland v Scotland (Three days)

Sunday 10 August

AXA Life League
Canterbury: Kent v Essex
Old Trafford: Lancs v Warwicks
Lord's: Middx v Hants
Northampton: Northants v Worcs
Taunton: Somerset v Glos
The Oval: Surrey v Durham
Eastbourne: Sussex v Leics

Tuesday 12 and Wednesday 13 August

NatWest Trophy
Semi-Finals

Tuesday 12 August

Tourist Match
†Derby or Northampton: Derbys or Northants v Pakistan 'A' (One day)
†Depending on outcome of NWT Second Round

Friday 15 August

Britannic Assurance Championship
*Derby: Derbys v Lancs
*Portsmouth: Hants v Yorks
*Lord's: Middx v Surrey
*Trent Bridge: Notts v Somerset
*Hove: Sussex v Glos
*Worcester: Worcs v Glam
Tourist Match
*Chelmsford: ECB XI v Pakistan 'A' (Four days)

Saturday 16 August

Tetley's Challenge Series
*Canterbury: Kent v Australians

Monday 18 or Tuesday 19 August

Bain Hogg Trophy
Semi-Finals

Wednesday 20 August

Britannic Assurance Championship
Chester-le-Street (Riverside): Durham v Middx

Abergavenny: Glam v Northants
Leicester: Leics v Derbys
Worksop: Notts v Essex
Taunton: Somerset v Kent
Edgbaston: Warwicks v Worcs
Scarborough: Yorks v Sussex

Thursday 21 August

SIXTH CORNHILL INSURANCE TEST MATCH
*The Oval: ENGLAND v AUSTRALIA
NatWest U-19 International Match
*Headingley: England U-19 v Zimbabwe
U-19 (Second Test Match) (Four days)

Sunday 24 August

AXA Life League
Chester-le-Street (Riverside): Durham v
Middx
Cardiff: Glam v Northants
Bristol: Glos v Lancs
Leicester: Leics v Derbys
Trent Bridge: Notts v Essex
Taunton: Somerset v Kent
Worcester: Worcs v Warwicks
Scarborough: Yorks v Sussex

Wednesday 27 August

Britannic Assurance Championship
Derby: Derbys v Somerset
Chelmsford: Essex v Warwicks
Bristol: Glos v Notts
Portsmouth: Hants v Kent
Old Trafford: Lancs v Yorks
Leicester: Leics v Glam
Northampton: Northants v Durham
Hove: Sussex v Surrey
Kidderminster: Worcs v Middx

Thursday 28 August

NatWest U-19 International Match
*Canterbury: England U-19 v Zimbabwe
U-19 (Third Test Match) (Four days)

Sunday 31 August

AXA Life League
Derby: Derbys v Somerset
Chelmsford: Essex v Warwicks
Bristol: Glos v Notts
Portsmouth: Hants v Kent
Old Trafford: Lancs v Yorks
Leicester: Leics v Glam

Northampton: Northants v Durham
Hove: Sussex v Surrey
Worcester: Worcs v Middx

Tuesday 2 September

Britannic Assurance Championship
Derby: Derbys v Northants
Chester-le-Street (Riverside): Durham v
Warwicks
Canterbury: Kent v Glos
Old Trafford: Lancs v Hants
Trent Bridge: Notts v Hants
Taunton: Somerset v Middx
The Oval: Surrey v Glam
Headingley: Yorks v Worcs

Saturday 6 September

†Lord's: *NatWest Trophy Final*
†Reserve days Sun 7 and Mon 8
September

Sunday 7 September

#*AXA Life League*
Derby: Derbys v Northants
Canterbury: Kent v Glos
Old Trafford: Lancs v Essex
Leicester: Leics v Durham
Trent Bridge: Notts v Hants
Taunton: Somerset v Middx
The Oval: Surrey v Glam
Headingley: Yorks v Worcs
#Matches involving NWT Finalists to be
played on Tue 9 September

Monday 8 September

TBC: *Bain Hogg Trophy Final*

Wednesday 10 September

Britannic Assurance Championship
Chester-le-Street (Riverside): Durham v
Somerset
Cardiff: Glam v Essex
Southampton: Hants v Sussex
Lord's: Middx v Notts
Northampton: Northants v Leics
The Oval: Surrey v Lancs
Edgbaston: Warwicks v Glos
Worcester: Worcs v Derbys
Headingley: Yorks v Kent

Sunday 14 September

AXA Life League
Chester-le-Street (Riverside): Durham v Somerset
Cardiff: Glam v Essex
Southampton: Hants v Sussex
Lord's: Middx v Notts
Northampton: Northants v Leics
The Oval: Surrey v Lancs
Edgbaston: Warwicks v Glos
Worcester: Worcs v Derbys
Headingley: Yorks v Kent

Thursday 18 September

Britannic Assurance Championship
*Derby: Derbys v Yorks
*Chelmsford: Essex v Middx
*Bristol: Glos v Lancs
*Southampton: Hants v Worcs
*Canterbury: Kent v Surrey
*Leicester: Leics v Durham
*Taunton: Somerset v Glam
*Hove: Sussex v Notts
*Edgbaston: Warwicks v Northants

WOMEN'S CRICKET

In August, South Africa's women cricketers will be touring England for the first time. Their five-match series of limited-overs internationals, the first they will have played against any country, includes a match at Lord's.

August

Fri	15	Bristol (County Ground)	First International
Sun	17	Taunton (County Ground)	Second International
Wed	20	Lord's	Third International
Wed	27	Hinckley (Hinckley Town CC)	Fourth International
Sat	30	Milton Keynes (Campbell Park)	Fifth International

ICC TOURS PROGRAMME

Confirmed tours only – as at 24 February 1997.

1997
Apr   Pakistan to Sri Lanka
May   NZ/SL to India
May/Aug Australia to England
May/Jun Sri Lanka to West Indies

1997-98
Oct/Nov SA/WI/SL to Pakistan
Nov/Dec Sri Lanka to India
Nov/Jan New Zealand to Australia
Dec/Jan South Africa to Australia
Jan/Apr England to West Indies
Jan/Feb Zimbabwe to Sri Lanka
Feb   Australia to New Zealand
Feb/Mar Sri Lanka to New Zealand
Feb/Apr Pakistan to South Africa
Mar/Apr Australia to India
Mar/Apr Pakistan to Zimbabwe
Mar/Apr Sri Lanka to South Africa

1998
May/Jun New Zealand to Sri Lanka
May/Aug South Africa to England

1998-99
Sep/Nov Australia to Pakistan
Oct   West Indies to Zimbabwe
Nov/Feb England to Australia
Nov/Dec India/Zimbabwe to Pakistan
Nov/Jan West Indies to South Africa
Dec/Jan Sri Lanka to Australia
Dec/Jan India to New Zealand

**1999   New Zealand to England
          World Cup in England**

FIELDING CHART

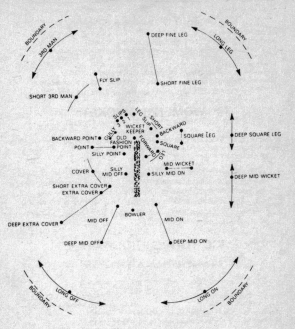

287

First published in 1997
by HEADLINE BOOK PUBLISHING

Cover photographs: (*left*) Shane Warne (Australia) and
(*right*) Graham Thorpe (Surrey and England)
by Patrick Eagar

10 9 8 7 6 5 4 3 2 1

ISBN 0 7472 5382 X

Typeset by
Letterpart Limited, Reigate, Surrey

Printed and bound in Great Britain by
Clays Ltd, St Ives plc.

HEADLINE BOOK PUBLISHING
A division of Hodder Headline PLC
338 Euston Road
London NW1 3BH